Official Rules of Sports & Games 1992-93

Official Rules of Sports & Games 1992-93

Edited by Tony Pocock

The Kingswood Press

First published in 1949 by Nicholas Kaye Ltd
Eighteenth edition 1992
Copyright © 1992 The Kingswood Press

The Kingswood Press
An imprint of Methuen London Ltd
Michelin House
81 Fulham Road
London SW3 6RB

A CIP catalogue record for this book
is available from the British Library
ISBN 0 413 64880 X

Phototypeset by Wilmaset Ltd, Birkenhead, Wirral
Printed in Great Britain
by Mackays of Chatham PLC, Chatham, Kent

Contents

Introduction

Now in its eighteenth edition, the *Official Rules of Sports and Games* has grown into an essential reference book for all engaged in sport and in sports administration in schools, universities and colleges of further education. Moreover, since 1949, when the first edition appeared, sport has enlarged its frontiers on a massive scale and space must be found for some of the minority sports that are now played competitively in Great Britain and abroad. Curling, handball, korfball and softball are four that have won a place in *Official Rules* for the first time. Others are boxing and baseball.

The frequency with which many sports and games change their rules is a hazard for any editor. But this eighteenth edition is now as up to date as possible and will continue to claim its place in institutional, public and private libraries.

I must acknowledge with gratitude the generous help given me by Christine Forrest throughout the compilation of this new edition. For reasons of space a number of Rules have had to be shortened. Decisions as to which sections or paragraphs should be omitted from a compilation of this size, without reducing its authority, are never easy. Without Christine's dogged determination to reach logical answers to these problems and to find a way through a mass of detail in order to achieve some reasonable consistency of style and expression, the publication of this book in 1992 would not have been possible. And warm thanks are due also to Michael Page for his help and advice as the book was made ready for press.

I must also acknowledge with thanks the helpful co-operation of the following associations. Without the advice of many of their officials, always patiently given, and of course their permission to reproduce their copyright Rules and Laws, the publication of this new edition would not have been possible at all.

London, 1992   Tony Pocock

British American Football Association, 92 Palace Gardens Terrace, London W8 4RS; British American Football Referees' Association, c/o Dr J. Briggs, Department of Computer Science, University of York,

York YO1 5DD; Grand National Archery Society, 7th Street, National Agricultural Centre, Stoneleigh, Kenilworth CV8 2LG; Amateur Athletic Association, Edgbaston House, 3 Duchess Place, Hagley Road, Edgbaston, Birmingham B16 8NM; Women's Amateur Athletic Association, Francis House, Francis Street, London SW1P 1DE; Badminton Association of England, National Badminton Centre, Bradwell Road, Loughton Lodge, Milton Keynes MK8 9LA; British Baseball Federation, 20 Teesdale Road, Long Eaton, Nottingham NG10 3PG; English Basket Ball Association, Calomax House, Lupton Avenue, Leeds LS9 6EE; International Bowling Board, Lyndhurst Road, Worthing, West Sussex BN11 2AZ; British Crown Green Bowling Association, 14 Leighton Avenue, Maghull, Liverpool L31 0AH; Amateur Boxing Association of England, Francis House, Francis Street, London SW1R 1DE; Marylebone Cricket Club, Lord's Cricket Ground, London NW8 8QN; English Curling Association, 66 Preston Old Road, Freckleton, Preston PR4 1PD; Football Association, 16 Lancaster Gate, London W2 3LW; Royal and Ancient Golf Club of St Andrews, Fife KY16 9JD; Commonwealth Handball Association, 60 Church Street, Radcliffe, Manchester M26 8SQ; Hockey Rules Board, 26 Stompond Lane, Walton-on-Thames, Surrey KT12 1HB; British Ice Hockey Association, 2 Downham Gardens, Ravenshead, Nottinghamshire NG15 9DF; British Korfball Association, PO Box 179, Maidstone, Kent ME14 1LU; English Lacrosse Union, 8 Dickens Close, Cheadle Hulme, Cheshire SK8 7PP; All England Women's Lacrosse Association, 4 Western Court, Bromley Street, Digbeth, Birmingham B9 4AN; All England Netball Association, Francis House, Francis Street, London SW1P 1DE; Tennis and Rackets Association, c/o The Queen's Club, Palliser Road, West Kensington, London W14 9EQ; National Rounders Association, 110 Broadmead Road, Woodford Green, Essex 1G8 7EH; Rugby Football League, 180 Chapeltown Road, Leeds LS7 4HT; Rugby Football Union, Twickenham TW1 1DZ; Great Britain Softball Association, PO Box 1303, London NW3 5TU; Squash Rackets Association, The Salons, 33/34 Warple Way, Acton, London W3 0RQ; International Table Tennis Federation, 53 London Road, St Leonards-on-Sea, East Sussex TN37 6AY; International Tennis Federation, Palliser Road, Barons Court, London W14 9EN; British Volleyball Federation and the English Volleyball Association, 27 South Road, West Bridgford, Nottingham NG2 7AG; Amateur Swimming Association, Harold Fern House, Derby Square, Loughborough LE11 0AL.

American Football

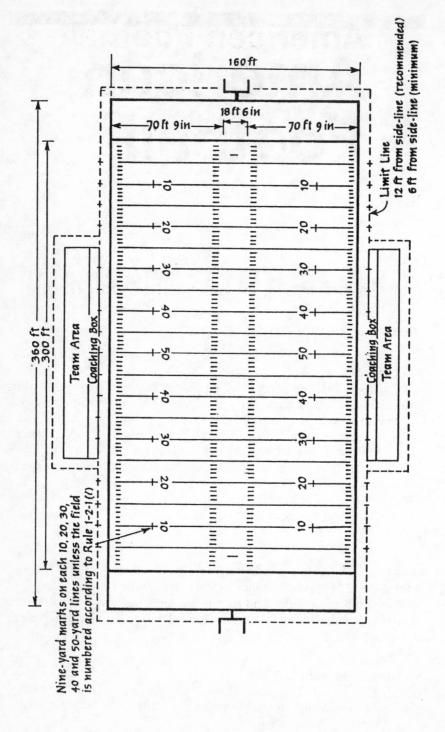

160 ft

70 ft 9 in — 18 ft 6 in — 70 ft 9 in

360 ft
300 ft

Team Area — Coaching Box

Coaching Box — Team Area

Limit Line
12 ft from side-line (recommended)
6 ft from side-line (minimum)

10 10
20 20
30 30
40 40
50 50
40 40
30 30
20 20
10 10

Nine-yard marks on each 10, 20, 30,
40 and 50-yard lines unless the field
is numbered according to Rule 1-2-1(f)

American Football

RULE 1

The Game, Field, Players and Equipment

SECTION 1. GENERAL PROVISIONS

The Game

ARTICLE 1. (*a*) The game shall be played between two teams of no more than 11 players each, on a rectangular field and with an inflated ball having the shape of a prolate spheroid.

(*b*) A team legally may play with fewer than 11 players but is penalised if the following requirements are not met:

1. At least 5 men are within 5 yards of the restraining line when receiving a free kick (Rule 6-1-2).

2. At the snap, at least 7 men are on the offensive scrimmage line, with not less than 5 numbered 50-79 (Rules 2-21-2, 7-1-3-b-1; *Exception*: Rule 1-4-2-b).

Goal-lines

ARTICLE 2. Goal-lines, one for each team, shall be established at opposite ends of the field, and each team shall be allowed opportunities to advance the ball across the other team's goal-line by running, passing or kicking it.

Winning Team and Final Score

ARTICLE 3. (*a*) The teams shall be awarded points for scoring according to rule and, unless the game is forfeited, the team having the larger score at the end of the game, including extra periods, shall be the winning team.

(*b*) The game is ended and the score is final when the Referee so declares.

(*c*) The score of a terminated-suspended game shall be the final score at the time of the suspension.

Supervision
ARTICLE 4. (*a*) The game shall be played under the supervision of either 3, 4, 5, 6 or 7 officials: A Referee, an Umpire, a Linesman, a Field Judge, a Back Judge, a Line Judge and a Side Judge. The use of a Line Judge, Back Judge, Side Judge and Field Judge is optional.

(*b*) The officials' jurisdiction begins with the scheduled coin toss at midfield and ends when the Referee declares the score final.

Team Captains
ARTICLE 5. (*a*) Each team shall designate to the Referee one or more players as its field captain(s) and one player at a time shall speak for his team in all dealings with the officials. A field captain's first announced choice of any options offered his team shall be irrevocable.

(*b*) Any player may request a team charged time-out.

Persons Subject to the Rules
ARTICLE 6. All players, substitutes, replaced players, coaches, trainers, cheerleaders in uniform, band members in uniform, mascots in uniform, public address announcers and other persons affiliated with the teams are subject to the Rules and shall be governed by the decisions of the officials. Affiliated persons are those authorised to be in the team area.

SECTION 2. THE FIELD

Dimensions
ARTICLE 1. The field shall be a rectangular area with dimensions, lines, zones, goals and pylons as indicated and titled in the field diagram.

(*a*) All field dimension lines shown must be marked 4in in width with a white non-toxic material that is not injurious to the eyes or skin. (*Exception*: side-lines and end-lines may exceed 4in in width.)

(*b*) Short yard-line extensions 4in inside the side-lines and at the in-bounds lines are mandatory and all yard-lines shall be 4in from the side-lines.

(*c*) A solid white area between the side-line and the coaching line is mandatory.

(*d*) White field markings or contrasting decorative markings (i.e. logos, team names, emblems, event name etc.) are permissible in the end-zones but shall not be closer than 4ft to any line.

(*e*) Contrasting colouring on playing surfaces in the end-zones may abut, but shall not obliterate, any line.

(*f*) Contrasting decorative material is permissible within the side-lines and between the goal-lines, but shall not obliterate yard-lines, goal-lines or side-lines.

(*g*) Goal-lines may be of contrasting colours.

(*h*) Field yard-line numbers measuring 6ft in height and 4ft in width 9yd from the in-bounds line are recommended.

(*i*) Directional arrows next to the field numbers (except the 50) indicating the direction towards the opponents' goal are permitted. The arrow shall be white with the top of the base 4in from the top of the number. The arrow is a triangle with an 18in base and two sides that are 36in each.

Marking Boundary Areas

ARTICLE 2. Measurements shall be from the inside edges of the boundary markings. The entire width of each goal-line shall be in the end-zone.

Limit Lines and Coaching Lines

ARTICLE 3. (*a*) Limit lines shall be marked with 12in lines and at 24in intervals 12ft outside the side-lines and the end-lines, except in stadiums where total field surface does not permit. In these stadiums, the limit lines shall not be less than 6ft from the side-lines and end-lines. Limit lines shall be 4in in width and may be yellow. No person outside the team area shall be within the limit lines (See Rules 9-1-5-a, 9-2-1-b-1 and field diagram).

(*b*) The limit lines shall continue 6ft from the team area around the side and back of the team area where the stadium permits.

(*c*) A coaching line shall be marked with a solid line 6ft outside the side-line between the 25-yard lines.

(*d*) A 4in by 4in mark at each 5-yard line extended between the goal-lines as an extension of the coaching line for yardage chain and down indicator 6ft reference points is mandatory.

Team Area

ARTICLE 4. (*a*) On each side of the field, a team area outside the limit line and between the 25-yard lines shall be marked for the exclusive use of substitutes, trainers and other persons affiliated with the team. The area between the coaching line and the limit line between the 25-yard line shall contain white diagonal lines or be marked distinctly for use of coaches.

(b) The team area shall be limited to players in uniform and a maximum of 40 other individuals directly involved in the game. The 40 individuals not in uniform shall wear special identification.

(c) Coaches are permitted in the area between the limit line and coaching line between the 25-yard lines. This area is the coaching box.

(d) Marking the team areas from the 25-yard lines is a game management requirement.

(e) No media personnel, including journalists, radio and television personnel or their equipment, shall be in the team area or coaching box, and no media personnel shall communicate in any way with persons in the team area or coaching box.

(f) Game management shall remove all persons not authorised by rule.

(g) Practice kicking nets are not permitted outside the team area.

Goals
ARTICLE 5. (a) Each goal shall consist of two uprights extending at least 30ft above the ground with a connecting white or yellow horizontal cross-bar, the top of which is 10ft above the ground. The inside of the uprights and cross-bar shall be in the same vertical plane as the inside edge of the end-line.

(b) Above the cross-bar the uprights shall be white or yellow and 18ft 6in apart inside to inside.

(c) The designated white or yellow posts and cross-bar shall be free of decorative material. (*Exception*: 4in by 42in orange wind directional streamers at the top of the uprights are permitted.)

(d) The height of the cross-bar shall be measured from the top of each end of the cross-bar to the ground directly below.

(e) Goal post(s) shall be padded with resilient material from the ground to a height of at least 6ft. 'Offset uprights' may be used.

(f) The following procedure is recommended when one or both goals have been taken down and the original goals are not available for a try or field goal attempt:

> A team is entitled to a kicking try and is not required to attempt a two-point play if the goals are not in position or complying with the dimensions required by Rule 1-2-5. A team is also entitled to a field goal attempt under the same conditions. Kicking tries and field goal attempts must be made in the direction of the goal the team was attacking when they elected to make the kick. The

home team is responsible for the availability of a portable goal if original goals are removed during the game for any reason. The portable goal shall be erected or held in place for the kicks.

Pylons
ARTICLE 6. Soft flexible four-sided pylons 4in by 4in with an overall height of 18in, which may include a 2in space between the bottom of the pylon and the ground, are required. They shall be red or orange in colour and placed at the inside corners of the eight intersections of the end-lines and in-bounds lines extended.

Yardage Chain, Down Indicator
ARTICLE 7. The official yardage chain and down indicator shall be operated approximately 6ft outside the side-line opposite the press box except in stadiums where the total playing enclosure does not permit.

(*a*) The chain shall join two rods not less than 5ft high, the rods' inside edges being exactly 10yd apart when the chain is fully extended.

(*b*) The down indicator shall be mounted on a rod not less than 5ft high.

(*c*) An unofficial auxiliary line to gain indicator and an unofficial down indicator may be used 6ft outside the other side-line.

(*d*) Unofficial red or orange non-slip line-to-gain ground markers may be positioned off the side-lines on both sides of the field. Markers are rectangular, weighted material 10in by 32in. A triangle with altitude of 5in is attached to the rectangle at the end towards the side-line.

(*e*) All yardage chains and down indicator rods shall have flat ends.

Markers or Obstructions
ARTICLE 8. All markers and obstructions within the playing enclosure shall be placed or constructed in such a manner as to avoid any possible hazard to players. This includes anything dangerous to anyone at the limit lines. The Referee shall order removed any markers or obstructions constituting such a hazard.

Field Surface
ARTICLE 9. (*a*) No material or device shall be used to improve the playing surface or other conditions and give one player or team an advantage. (*Exception*: Rule 2-15-4-b.)
Penalty: Penalise under Rule 9-2-3-a-3 (S.27)

(*b*) The Referee may effect any improvement deemed necessary for proper game administration.

SECTION 3. THE BALL

Specifications
ARTICLE 1. The ball shall meet
the following specifications:

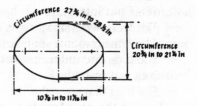

    (*a*) New or nearly new. (A
nearly new ball is a ball that has not
been altered and retains the properties and qualities of a new ball.)

    (*b*) Cover consisting of four
panels of pebble-grained leather
without corrugations other than
seams.

    (*c*) One set of eight equally
spaced lacings.

    (*d*) Natural tan colour.

    (*e*) Two 1in-wide white stripes that are 3in to 3.25in from the end of
the ball and located only on the two panels adjacent to the laces are
optional.

    (*f*) Conforms to maximum and minimum dimensions and shape
indicated in the diagram.

    (*g*) Inflated to the pressure of 12.5–13.5 psi.

    (*h*) Weight 14 to 15 ounces.

    (*i*) The ball may not be altered.

Administration and Enforcement
ARTICLE 2. (*a*) The Referee shall test and be sole judge of no more
than 6 balls offered for play by each team prior to and during the game.
The Referee may approve additional balls if warranted by the conditions.

    (*b*) Home management shall provide a pressure pump and measuring
device.

    (*c*) The home team is responsible for providing legal balls and should
notify the opponent of the type to be used.

    (*d*) During the entire game, either team may use new or nearly new
balls of its choice when it is in possession providing the ball meets the
required specifications and has been measured and tested according to
rule.

    (*e*) The visiting team is responsible for providing the legal balls it
wishes to use while it is in possession if the balls provided by the home
team are not acceptable.

    (*f*) All balls to be used must be presented to the Referee for testing
60 minutes prior to the start of the game.

(*g*) When the ball becomes dead nearer the side-lines than the hash mark, is unfit for play, is subject to measurement in a side-zone or is inaccessible, a replacement ball shall be obtained from the ball-person.

(*h*) The Referee or Umpire shall determine the legality of each ball before it is put into play.

(*i*) The following procedures shall be used when measuring a ball.

1. All measurements shall be made after the ball is inflated to 13 psi.

2. The long circumference shall be measured around the ends of the ball but not over the laces.

3. The long diameter shall be measured with calipers from end to end but not in the nose indentation.

4. The short circumference shall be measured around the ball, over the valve, over the lace, but not over the cross lace.

Marking Balls
ARTICLE 3. Marking a ball indicating a preference for any player or any situation is prohibited.
Penalty: Live-ball foul. Fifteen yards from previous spot (S27).

SECTION 4. PLAYERS AND PLAYING EQUIPMENT

Recommended Numbering
ARTICLE 1. It is strongly recommended that offensive players be numbered according to the following diagram that shows one of many offensive formations.

80-99	70-79	60-69	50-59	60-69	70-79	80-99
End	Tackle	Guard	Centre	Guard	Tackle	End

1-49
Backs

Players' Numbering
ARTICLE 2. (*a*) All players shall be numbered 1 to 99.

(*b*) On the scrimmage down, at least 5 offensive players on the scrimmage line shall be numbered 50 to 79. (*Exception*: During a scrimmage kick formation, a player who initially is an exception to the 50-79 mandatory numbering in a scrimmage kick formation remains an ineligible receiver continuously during the down, and he must be positioned on the line of scrimmage and between the end players on the line of scrimmage.) A player remains an ineligible receiver and is an exception to the 50-79 mandatory numbering until the down is over, a time-out is charged to a team or the Referee, or a period ends.

(*c*) No 2 players of the same team shall participate in the same down wearing identical numbers.

(*d*) Numbers shall not be changed during a game to deceive opponents.

(*e*) Markings in the vicinity of the numbers are not permitted.
Penalty: Live-ball foul. Five yards from previous spot.

Contrasting Colours
ARTICLE 3. (*a*) Players of opposing teams shall wear jerseys of contrasting colours. In the event of a clash, the visiting team shall wear white jerseys. Players of a team shall wear the same colour jerseys.

(*b*) A white jersey is one with only contrasting playing numbers, player's name, team, league, game or memorial insignia attached. Jersey number colours should be in sharp contrast to jersey colours.

Mandatory Equipment
ARTICLE 4. All players shall wear the following mandatory equipment, which shall be professionally manufactured and not altered to decrease protection:

(*a*) Soft knee pads at least ½in thick worn over the knees and covered by pants. No pads or protective equipment may be worn outside the pants.

(*b*) Head protectors with a secured four-point chin strap. If a chin strap is not secured it is a violation. Officials should inform players when less than four snaps are secured without charging a time-out unless the player ignores the warning.

(*c*) Shoulder pads, hip pads and tailbone protector, thigh guards.

(*d*) An intra-oral yellow or any other readily visible coloured mouthpiece with FDA approved base materials (FDCS) that covers all upper teeth.

(*e*) One jersey with sleeves that completely cover the shoulder pads, that is not altered or designed to tear and conforms with Rule 1-4-4-f. Vests and/or a second jersey worn concurrently during the game are prohibited.

(*f*) Clearly visible permanent Arabic block or Gothic numerals on one jersey at least 8in and 10in in height front and back respectively, of a colour in direct contrast with the jersey, and each player shall have the same colour numbers. A solid colour border is permitted. The individual bars must be approximately 1.5 in wide. Identical numbers shall be worn on front and back of each player's jersey.

(g) Numbers on any part of the uniform shall correspond with the mandatory front and back numbers.

Note: If a player is not wearing mandatory equipment in compliance in all respects with Rule 1-4-4, the team shall be charged with a time-out.

Violation: See Rules 3-3-6 and 3-4-2-b-2 (S23, S3 or S21).

NOCSAE: All players shall wear head protectors that carry a warning label regarding the risk of injury and a manufacturer's or reconditioners certification indicating satisfaction of NOCSAE test standards. All such reconditioned helmets shall show recertification to indicate satisfaction with NOCSAE standard.

Illegal Equipment

ARTICLE 5. No player wearing illegal equipment shall be permitted to play. Any question as to the legality of a player's equipment shall be decided by the Umpire. Illegal equipment includes:

(a) Equipment worn by a player which, in the opinion of the Umpire, would confuse his opponents, or any equipment including artificial limbs that would endanger other players.

(b) Hard, abrasive or unyielding substances on the hand, wrist, forearm or elbow of any player unless covered on all sides with closed-cell, slow recovery foam padding no less than $\frac{1}{2}$in thick or an alternate material of the same minimum thickness and similar physical properties. Hard or unyielding substances are permitted only to protect an injury, and hand and arm protectors (casts or splints) are not permitted.

(c) Thigh guards of any hard substances, unless all surfaces are covered with material such as closed-cell vinyl foam that is at least $\frac{1}{4}$in thick on the outside surface and at least $\frac{3}{8}$in thick on the inside surface and the overlaps of the edges. Shin guards not covered on both sides and all of their edges with closed-cell, slow-recovery foam padding at least $\frac{1}{2}$in thick, or an alternative material of the same minimum thickness having similar physical properties. Therapeutic or preventive knee braces worn under the pants unless entirely covered from direct external exposure.

(d) Projection of metal or other hard substance from a player's person or clothing.

(e) Shoe cleats – detachable:

1. More than $\frac{1}{2}$in in length (measured from tip of cleat to the shoe). (*Exception*: If attached to a $\frac{5}{32}$in or less raised platform wider than the base of the cleat and extended across the width of the shoe to within $\frac{1}{4}$in or less of the outer edges of the sole. A single toe cleat does not require a raised platform that extends across the width of the sole. The raised platform of the toe cleat is limited to $\frac{5}{32}$in or less. The $\frac{5}{32}$in or less is measured from the lowest point of the platform to the sole of the shoe.)

2. Made of any material liable to chip or fracture. Aluminium cleats are not permitted.

3. Without an effective locking device.

4. With concave sides.

5. Conical cleats with flat ends not parallel with their bases or less than $\frac{3}{8}$in in diameter or with rounded free ends having arcs greater than $\frac{7}{16}$in in diameter.

6. Oblong cleats with free ends not parallel with bases or that measure less than $\frac{1}{4}$in by $\frac{3}{4}$in.

7. Circular or ring cleats without rounded edges and a wall less than $\frac{3}{16}$ in thick.

8. Steel-tipped cleats without steel equivalent to SAE 1070 hardener and drawn to Rockwell C scale 42–45.

(*f*) Shoe cleats – non-detachable:

1. More than $\frac{1}{2}$in in length (measured from tip of cleat to sole of shoe).

2. Made of any material that burrs, chips or fractures.

3. With abrasive surfaces or cutting edges.

4. Made of any metallic material.

(*g*) Tape or any bandage on a hand, wrist, forearm or elbow unless used to protect an injury and specifically sanctioned by the Umpire.

(*h*) Head protectors, jerseys or attachments that tend to conceal the ball by closely resembling it in colour.

(*i*) Adhesive material, grease or any other slippery substance applied on an attachment, a player's person or clothing that affects the ball or an opponent.

(*j*) Any face protector except those constructed of non-breakable material with rounded edges covered with resilient material designed to prevent chipping, burrs or an abrasiveness that would endanger players.

(*k*) Shoulder pads with the leading edge of the epaulet rounded with a radius more than half the thickness of the material used.

(*l*) Uniform attachments designating anything except a player's numbers, a player's name, team, game or memorial insignia or authorized advertising material. (This applies to towels or any other item attached to the uniform.)

(*m*) Gloves worn intentionally to closely resemble the opponent's jersey colour or not in conformance with Rule 1-4-5-b.

(*n*) Jerseys that have been taped or tied in any manner.

(*o*) Uniform attachments. (*Exceptions*: (1) One white towel exposed 4in by 12in without any markings worn on the front of the uniform. (2) Hand warmers worn during inclement weather.

Note: No player wearing illegal equipment shall be permitted to play. If illegal equipment is discovered by an official, the team shall be charged a team time-out.

Violation: See Rules 3-3-6 and 3-4-2-b-2 (S23, S3 or S21).

Exceptions: If equipment in Rule 1-4-5 becomes illegal through play, the player must leave the game but will not be charged a team time-out.

Mandatory and Illegal Equipment Enforcement

ARTICLE 6. Failure to wear mandatory equipment or the use of illegal equipment is enforced as follows:

(*a*) Each of the first three infractions for failure to wear mandatory equipment or wearing illegal equipment requires a charged time-out. The fourth infraction in a half requires a 5-yard penalty. The delay for the fourth time-out could be for not wearing mandatory equipment or wearing illegal equipment. The first three time-outs could have been taken by the team as charged team time-outs.

1. The time-outs are granted.

2. There is no offset for the first three violations when an opponent has fouled.

3. When time-outs are exhausted, the next violation is a dead-ball delay penalty at the succeeding spot.

4. A time-out is called, the offending team is indicated by the Referee and the captain and coaches are notified through the officials nearest the side-lines.

(*b*) Officials should ascertain before the ready-for-play signal if players are not wearing mandatory equipment or wearing illegal equipment. Only in an emergency should the 25-second clock be interrupted.

(*c*) No jersey may be changed on the field of play and such changes must be made in the team area of the player making the change. When it is determined that a jersey does not comply with Rule 1-4-4-e, a team time-out will be charged to that team at the succeeding spot. If the team has expended its three time-outs, a delay will be charged under Rule 3-4-2-b-2. Players may change torn jerseys during team time-outs and return to play. A player may change a jersey and return during a delay penalty only if the game is not further delayed by that action.

(*d*) Tape may not cover or partially cover a glove. Tape may be used to secure glove fasteners.

Coaches' Certification

ARTICLE 7. The Head Coach or his designated representative shall certify to the Umpire prior to the game that all players:

(*a*) Have been informed what equipment is mandatory by rule and what constitutes illegal equipment.

(*b*) Have been provided the equipment mandated by rule.

(*c*) Have been instructed to wear and how to wear mandatory equipment during the game.

(*d*) Have been instructed to notify the coaching staff when equipment becomes illegal through play during the game.

Prohibited Signal Devices
ARTICLE 8. Players are prohibited from being equipped with any electronic, mechanical or other signal devices for the purpose of communicating with any source. (*Exception*: A medically prescribed hearing aid of the sound amplifier type for hard-of-hearing players.)
Penalty: 15 yards and disqualification of the player. Penalise as dead-ball foul at succeeding spot (S27 and S47).

Prohibited Field Equipment
ARTICLE 9. (*a*) Television replay or monitor equipment is prohibited at the side-lines, pressbox or other locations adjacent to the playing field for coaching purposes during the game.

(*b*) Motion pictures or any type of film for coaching purposes are prohibited any time during the game or between the periods.

(*c*) Media communicating equipment, including cameras, sound devices and microphones, is prohibited on the field or in the team area.

(*d*) Microphones may be used only on Referees for penalty or other game announcements, if controlled by the Referee, and may not be open at other times. Microphones on other officials are prohibited.

(*e*) Microphones attached to coaches for media transmission are prohibited during the game.

Coaches' Phones
ARTICLE 10. Coaches' phones and headsets are not subject to the rules before or during the game.

RULE 2
Definitions

SECTION 1. APPROVED RULINGS AND OFFICIALS' SIGNALS

ARTICLE 1. (*a*) An Approved Ruling (AR) is an official decision on a given statement of facts. It serves to illustrate the spirit and application of the rules. The relationship between the rules and the Approved Ruling is analogous to that between statutory law and a decision of the Supreme Court. If there is a conflict between the Official Rules and the Approved Rulings, the Rules take precedence.

(*b*) An official's signal (S) refers to the Official Football Signals 1 to 47.

SECTION 2. THE BALL: LIVE, DEAD, LOOSE

Live Ball
ARTICLE 1. A live ball is a ball in play. A pass, kick or fumble that has not yet touched the ground is a live ball in flight.

Dead Ball
ARTICLE 2. A dead ball is a ball not in play.

Loose Ball
ARTICLE 3. A loose ball is a live ball not in player possession during:
  (*a*) A running play
  (*b*) A scrimmage or free kick before possession is gained, regained or the ball is dead by rule.
  (*c*) The interval after a legal forward pass is touched and before it becomes complete, incomplete or intercepted. (*Note*: This interval is during a forward pass play and the ball may be batted in any direction by a player eligible to touch it.)
  (*d*) All players are eligible to touch or recover a ball that is loose from a fumble or a backward pass, but eligibility to touch a ball loose from a kick is governed by Kick Rules (Rule 6) and eligibility to touch a forward pass is governed by Pass Rules (Rule 7).

When Ball is Ready for Play
ARTICLE 4. A dead ball is ready for play when the Referee:
  (*a*) If time is in, sounds his whistle and signals ready for play.
  (*b*) If time is out, sounds his whistle and signals either 'start the clock' or 'ball ready for play'. (*Exception*: Rules 3-3-f-4-c and 3-3-f-4-f.)

In Possession
ARTICLE 5. 'In possession' is an abbreviation meaning the holding or controlling of a live ball or a ball to be free kicked.
  (*a*) A player is 'in possession' when he is holding or controlling the ball.
  (*b*) A team is 'in possession' when one of its players is 'in possession' or attempting a punt, drop kick or place kick, while a forward pass thrown by one of its players is in flight or was last in possession during a loose ball.

Belongs To
ARTICLE 6. 'Belongs to' as contrasted with 'in possession' denotes temporary custody of a dead ball. Legality of such custody is immaterial

because the ball must next be put in play in accordance with Rules governing the existing situation.

Catch, Interception, Recovery

ARTICLE 7. A catch is an act of establishing player possession of a live ball in flight.

(*a*) A catch of an opponent's fumble or pass is an interception.

(*b*) Securing player possession of a live ball after it strikes the ground is 'recovering it'.

(*c*) To catch, intercept or recover a ball, a player who jumps to make a catch, interception or recovery must have the ball in his possession when he first returns to ground in-bounds or is so held that the dead ball provisions of Rule 4-1-3-a apply.

1. If one foot first lands in-bounds and the receiver has possession and control of the ball, it is a catch or interception even though a subsequent step or fall takes the receiver out of bounds.

2. A catch by any kneeling or prone in-bounds player is a completion or interception (Rules 7-3-1, 7-3-2, 7-3-6 and 7-3-7).

3. Loss of ball simultaneous with returning to the ground is not a catch, interception or recovery.

4. When in question, the catch, recovery or interception is not completed.

Simultaneous Catch or Recovery

ARTICLE 8. A simultaneous catch or recovery is a catch or recovery in which there is joint possession of a live ball by opposing players in-bounds.

SECTION 3. BLOCKING

Legal Block

ARTICLE 1. (*a*) Blocking is obstructing an opponent by contacting him with any part of the blocker's body.

(*b*) Pushing is blocking an opponent with open hands.

Below Waist

ARTICLE 2. (*a*) Blocking below the waist is the initial contact below the waist with any part of the blocker's body against an opponent other than the runner (Rule 9-1-2-3).

(*b*) Blocking below the waist applies to the original contact by the blocker against an opponent who has one or both feet on the ground. A blocker who makes contact above the waist and then slides below the waist has not fouled. If the blocker first contacts the opposing player's hands at the waist or above, it is a legal 'above the waist' block (Rule 9-1-2-e).

(c) The position of the ball at the snap refers (see Rule 9-1-2-e) to an imaginary line through the ball parallel to the side-lines from end-line to end-line and is in effect until the ball crosses the neutral-zone.

Chop Block

ARTICLE 3. A chop block is an illegal delayed block at the knee or below against an opponent who is in contact with a team-mate of the blocker. A chop block is delayed if it occurs more than one second after a team-mate contacts the opponent.

Frame (of the body)

ARTICLE 4. The frame of the opponent's body is at the shoulders or below other than the back (See exception to Rule 9-3-3-a-1-c).

SECTION 4. CLIPPING

ARTICLE 1. (a) Clipping is an illegal block against an opponent occurring when the force of the initial contact, except against the runner, is from behind. This includes running or diving into the back, or throwing or dropping the body across the back of the leg or legs of an opponent other than the runner, or pushing an opponent in the back. (*Exceptions*: Rule 9-1-2-d Exceptions 1-5.)

(b) Position of blocker's head or feet does not necessarily indicate the point of initial contact.

SECTION 5. CRAWLING

ARTICLE 1. Crawling is an attempt by the runner to advance the ball after any part of his person, other than a hand or foot, has touched the ground. (*Exception*: Rule 4-1-3-b.)

SECTION 6. DOWN AND BETWEEN DOWNS

ARTICLE 1. A down is unit of the game that starts with a legal snap or legal free kick after the ball is ready for play and ends when the ball next becomes dead. Between downs is the interval during which the ball is dead.

SECTION 7. FAIR CATCH

Fair Catch

ARTICLE 1. (a) A fair catch of a scrimmage kick is a catch beyond the neutral zone by a player of Team B who has made a valid signal during a scrimmage kick that is untouched beyond the neutral zone.

(*b*) A fair catch of a free kick is a catch by a player of Team B who has made a valid signal during an untouched free kick.

(*c*) A valid, invalid or illegal fair catch signal deprives the receiving team of the opportunity to advance the ball and the ball is declared dead at the spot of the catch or recovery or at the spot of the foul if the catch precedes the signal.

(*d*) If the receiver shades his eyes from the sun, the ball is live and may be advanced.

Valid Signal
ARTICLE 2. A valid signal is a signal given by a player of Team B who has obviously signalled his intention by extending one hand only clearly above his head and waving the hand from side to side of the body more than once.

Illegal Signal
ARTICLE 3. (*a*) An illegal signal is a valid or invalid signal by a player of Team B beyond the neutral-zone when a scrimmage kick is made and a fair catch is not permissible by rule.

(*b*) An illegal signal is a valid or invalid signal by a player of Team B when a free kick is made and a fair catch is not permissible by rule.

Invalid Signal
ARTICLE 4. An invalid signal is any signal by a player of Team B that does not meet the requirements of a valid signal.

SECTION 8. FORWARD, BEYOND AND FORWARD PROGRESS

Forward, Beyond
ARTICLE 1. Forward, beyond or in advance of, as related to either team, denotes direction toward the opponent's end-line. Converse terms are backward or behind.

Forward Progress
ARTICLE 2. Forward progress is a term indicating the end of advancement by the runner and applies to the position of the ball when it became dead by Rule (Rules 4-1-3-a and b, 4-2-1 and 4).

SECTION 9. FOUL AND VIOLATION

ARTICLE 1. A foul is a Rule infraction for which a distance penalty is prescribed. A violation is a Rule infraction for which no distance penalty is prescribed and that does not offset the penalty for a foul. (*Exception*: Rule 7-3-4.)

SECTION 10. FUMBLING, MUFFING, TOUCHING, BATTING OR BLOCKING A KICK

Fumble
ARTICLE 1. A fumble is any act other than a passing, kicking or successful handing that results in loss of player possession.

Muff
ARTICLE 2. A muff is an unsuccessful attempt to catch or recover a ball that is touched in the attempt.

Batting
ARTICLE 3. Batting the ball is intentionally striking it or intentionally changing its direction with a hand or arm.

Touching
ARTICLE 4. Touching of a ball not in player possession denotes any contact with the ball. It may be intentional or unintentional and it always precedes possession and control. (*Exception*: Rules 6-1-4-a and b, 6-3-4-a and b.)

Blocking a Scrimmage Kick
ARTICLE 5. Blocking a scrimmage kick is touching the ball in or behind the neutral zone by an opponent of the kicker.

SECTION 11. LINES

Goal Lines
ARTICLE 1. Each goal-line is a vertical plane separating an end-zone from the field of play when a ball is touched or is in player possession. A team's goal-line is that which it is defending.

Restraining Lines
ARTICLE 2. A restraining line is a vertical plane when a ball is touched or is in possession.

Yard Lines
ARTICLE 3. A yard-line is any line in the field of play parallel to the end-lines. A team's own yard-lines, marked or unmarked, are numbered consecutively from its own goal-line to the 50-yard line.

In-bounds Lines (Hash Marks)
ARTICLE 4. The two in-bounds lines are 70ft 9in in-bounds from the side-lines and divide the field of play into three. Short yard-line extensions at the in-bounds lines shall measure 24in in length.

Out-of-Bounds Lines
ARTICLE 5. The area enclosed by the side-lines and end-lines is 'in-bounds' and the area surrounding and including the side-lines and end-lines is 'out-of-bounds'.

Nine-Yard Marks
ARTICLE 6. Nine-yard marks, 12in in length, every 10 yards, shall be located 9 yards from the side-line towards the in-bounds lines. These marks are required if the field is numbered according to Rule 1-2-1.

SECTION 12. HANDING THE BALL

ARTICLE 1. (*a*) Handing the ball is transfering player possession from one team-mate to another without throwing, fumbling, or kicking it.

(*b*) Except when permitted by Rule, handing the ball forward to a team-mate is illegal.

(*c*) Loss of player possession by unsuccessful execution of attempted handing is a fumble.

(*d*) A backward handoff occurs when the runner releases the ball before it is beyond the yard-line where the runner is positioned.

SECTION 13. HUDDLE

ARTICLE 1. A huddle is two or more players grouped together before the snap or a free kick.

SECTION 14. HURDLING

ARTICLE 1. (*a*) Hurdling is an attempt by a player to jump with one or both feet or knees foremost over an opponent who is still on his feet.

(*b*) 'On his feet' means that no part of the opponent's body other than one or both feet is in contact with the ground.

(*c*) Hurdling an offensive player prior to the snap is a dead-ball foul. This includes offensive players in a three- or four-point stance.

SECTION 15. KICKS

Legal and Illegal Kicks
ARTICLE 1. Kicking the ball is intentionally striking the ball with the knee, lower leg or foot.

(*a*) A legal kick is a punt, drop kick or place kick, made according to the Rules by a player of Team A before a change of team possession. Kicking the ball in any other manner is illegal.

(*b*) Any free kick or scrimmage kick continues to be a kick until it is caught or recovered by a player or becomes dead.

(*c*) A return kick is an illegal kick.

Punt
ARTICLE 2. A punt is a kick by a player who drops the ball and kicks it before it strikes the ground.

Drop Kick
ARTICLE 3. A drop kick is a kick by a player who drops the ball and kicks it as it touches the ground.

Place Kick
ARTICLE 4. (*a*) A field goal place kick is a kick by a player of the team in possession while the ball is controlled on the ground by a team-mate.

(*b*) A free kick place kick by a player of the team in possession while the ball is positioned on a tee or the ground. It may be controlled by a team-mate. If a tee is used, it may not elevate the ball's lowest point more than 2in above the ground.

Free Kick
ARTICLE 5. A free kick is a kick by a player of the team in possession made under restrictions that prohibit either team from advancing beyond established restraining lines until the ball is kicked. Team B may not move behind its rear restraining line until the ball is kicked. A ball that falls from a tee and touches the ground may not be kicked.

Kick-off
ARTICLE 6. A kick-off is a free kick that starts each half and follows each try or field goal. It must be a place kick or drop kick.

Scrimmage Kick
ARTICLE 7. A scrimmage kick made in or behind the neutral zone is a legal kick by Team A during a scrimmage down before team possession changes. A scrimmage kick has crossed the neutral-zone when it touches the ground, a player, an official or anything beyond the neutral-zone.

Return Kick
ARTICLE 8. A return kick is a kick by a player of the team in

possession after change of team possession during a down and is an illegal kick. It is a live-ball foul, and the ball becomes dead.

Field Goal Attempt
ARTICLE 9. A field goal attempt is any place kick or drop kick from scrimmage.

Scrimmage Kick Formation
ARTICLE 10. A scrimmage kick formation is a formation with at least one player 7yd or more behind the neutral-zone and no player in position to receive a hand to hand snap from between the snapper's legs.

SECTION 16. LOSS OF A DOWN

ARTICLE 1. 'Loss of a down' is an abbreviation meaning 'loss of the right to repeat a down'.

SECTION 17. THE NEUTRAL-ZONE

ARTICLE 1. The neutral-zone is the space between the two lines of scrimmage extended to the side-lines and is the length of the ball. The neutral-zone is established when the ball is ready for play and is resting on the ground with its long axis at right angles to the scrimmage line and parallel to the side-lines.

SECTION 18. ENCROACHMENT AND OFFSIDE

Encroachment
ARTICLE 1. (*a*) Encroachment occurs when an offensive player is in or beyond the neutral-zone after the snapper touches, or simulates touching the ball and prior to the snap.

(*b*) Encroachment occurs when players of the kicking team are not behind the restraining line when the ball is free kicked. (*Exception*: When the ball is put in play, the snapper is not encroaching when he is beyond his scrimmage line and the kicker and holder are not encroaching when they are beyond their restraining line).

Offside
ARTICLE 2. Offside occurs when a defensive player is in or beyond the neutral-zone when the ball is snapped, illegally contacts an opponent beyond the neutral zone, contacts the ball before it is snapped, or is not within the restraining lines when the ball is free kicked.

SECTION 19. PASSES

Passing
ARTICLE 1. Passing the ball is throwing it. A pass continues to be a pass until it is caught, intercepted by a player or the ball becomes dead.

Forward and Backward Pass
ARTICLE 2. (*a*) An attempted backward pass is a live ball thrown toward or parallel to the passer's end-line; an attempted forward pass is a live ball thrown toward the opponents' end-line. A forward or backward pass is determined by the point where the ball first strikes the ground, a player, an official or anything beyond or behind the spot of the pass.

(*b*) When a Team A player is holding the ball to pass it forward toward the neutral-zone, any intentional forward movement of his arm starts the forward pass. If a Team B player contacts the passer or ball after forward movement begins and the ball leaves the passer's hand, a forward pass is ruled regardless of where the ball strikes the ground or a player.

(*c*) When in question, the ball is a pass and not a fumble during an attempted forward pass.

Crosses Neutral-Zone
ARTICLE 3. (*a*) A legal forward pass has crossed the neutral-zone when it first strikes the ground, a player, an official or anything beyond the neutral-zone in-bounds. It has not crossed the neutral zone when it first strikes the ground, a player, an official or anything in or behind the neutral-zone in-bounds.

(*b*) A passer has crossed the neutral-zone when any part of his body is beyond the neutral-zone when the ball is released.

(*c*) A legal forward pass is beyond or behind the neutral-zone where it crosses the side-line.

Catchable Forward Pass
ARTICLE 4. A catchable forward pass is an untouched legal forward pass beyond the neutral-zone to an eligible Team A player who has a reasonable opportunity to catch the ball. When in question, a legal forward pass is catchable.

SECTION 20. PENALTY

ARTICLE 1. A penalty is a yardage loss imposed by Rule against a team that has committed a foul and may include a loss of down. (*Exception*: Rule 7-3-4 no yardage exception.)

SECTION 21. SCRIMMAGE

Scrimmage
ARTICLE 1. A scrimmage is the interplay of the two teams during a down in which play begins with a snap.

Scrimmage-line
ARTICLE 2. (*a*) The scrimmage-line for each team is the yard-line and its vertical plane that passes through the point of the ball nearest its own goal-line and extends to the side-lines.

(*b*) A player of Team A is 'on his scrimmage-line' at the snap when he faces his opponents' goal-line with the line of his shoulders approximately parallel thereto and his head breaks the plane of the line drawn through the waistline of the snapper.

Backfield Line
ARTICLE 3. To be legally in the backfield, a Team A player's head must not break the plane of the line drawn through the rearmost part, other than the legs or feet, of the nearest Team A player (except the snapper) on the line of scrimmage.

SECTION 22. SHIFT

ARTICLE 1. A shift is a simultaneous change of position by 2 or more offensive players after the ball is ready for play for a scrimmage and before the next snap.

SECTION 23. SNAPPING THE BALL

ARTICLE 1. (*a*) Legally snapping the ball (a snap) is handing or passing it backward from its position on the ground with a quick and continuous motion of the hand or hands, the ball actually leaving the hand or hands in this motion.

(*b*) The snap starts when the ball is moved legally or illegally and ends when the ball leaves the snapper's hand.

(*c*) If, during any backward motion of a legal snap, the ball slips from the snapper's hand, it is a snap and in play, provided the ball had been declared 'ready' (Rule 4-1-1).

(*d*) While resting on the ground and before the snap, the long axis of the ball must be at right angles to the scrimmage line.

(*e*) Unless moved in a backward direction, the movement of the ball does not start a legal snap. It is not a legal snap if the ball is first moved forward or lifted.

(*f*) If a legal snap is touched by Team B, the ball remains dead and

Team B is penalised. If an illegal snap is touched by Team B, the ball is dead and Team A is penalised.

(g) The snap need not be between the snapper's legs; but to be legal, it must be a quick and continuous backward motion.

(h) The ball must be snapped on or between the inbounds-lines.

SECTION 24. SPEARING

ARTICLE 1. Spearing is the intentional use of the helmet in an attempt to punish an opponent.

SECTION 25. SPOTS

Enforcement Spot
ARTICLE 1. An enforcement spot is the point from which the penalty for a foul or violation is enforced.

Previous Spot
ARTICLE 2. The previous spot is the point from which the ball was last put in play.

Succeeding Spot
ARTICLE 3. (a) The succeeding spot is the point at which the ball is next put in play. (*Exception*: 10-2-2-g-3.)

(b) The succeeding spot may be one of the most advantageous spots.

Dead-Ball Spot
ARTICLE 4. The dead-ball spot is the point at which the ball became dead.

Spot of the Foul
ARTICLE 5. The spot of the foul is the point at which that foul occurs. If out-of-bounds between the goal-lines, it shall be the intersection of the nearer in-bounds line and the yard-line extended through the spot of the foul.

Out-of-Bounds Spot
ARTICLE 6. The out-of-bounds spot is the point at which, according to the Rule, the ball becomes dead because of going or being declared out-of-bounds.

In-Bounds Spot
ARTICLE 7. The in-bounds spot is the intersection of the nearer in-

bounds line and the yard-line passing through the dead-ball spot, or the spot where the ball is left in a side-zone by a penalty.

Spot Where Run Ends
ARTICLE 8. The spot where the run ends is where the ball is declared dead or where player possession is lost during a running play. The spot where the run ends is at that point:
(*a*) Where the ball is declared dead in player possession.
(*b*) Where a player possession is lost on a fumble.
(*c*) Where a legal (or illegal) handing of the ball occurs.
(*d*) From where an illegal forward pass is thrown.
(*e*) From where a backward pass is thrown.

Spot Where Kick Ends
ARTICLE 9. A scrimmage kick that crosses the neutral-zone ends at the spot where possession is gained or regained or the ball is declared dead by Rule.
Exceptions:
1. When a kick ends in Team B's end zone, the basic enforcement spot is Team B's 20-yard line.
2. An unsuccessful field goal attempt untouched by Team B beyond the neutral-zone – Basic enforcement spot: previous spot. If the previous spot is between Team B's 20yd-line and the goal-line, and the unsuccessful field goal attempt is untouched by Team B beyond the neutral-zone, the spot where the kick ends is the 20yd-line.

Basic Spot
ARTICLE 10. The basic spot is the application of the '3 and 1' principle with enforcement of the penalty either from the spot where the related run ends, the spot where the kick ends or the previous spot. Fouls by the team 'in possession' behind the basic spot are spot fouls.
The following are the basic spots for enforcement on running plays, forward pass plays and legal kick plays utilising the '3 and 1' principle:
(*a*) The basic spot on running plays when the run ends beyond the neutral zone is the spot where the related run ends, and fouls by the team 'in possession' behind the basic spot are spot fouls (Rule 10-2-2-c-1). (*Exception*: Rules 9-1-2-d and 9-3-3-a and b.)
(*b*) The basic spot on running plays when the run ends behind the neutral-zone is the previous spot and fouls by the team 'in possession' behind the basic spot are spot fouls (Rule 10-2-2-c-2). (*Exception*: Rules 9-1-2-d and 9-3-3-a and b.)
(*c*) The basic spot on running plays that occur when there is no neutral-zone (interception run-backs, kick run-backs, fumble advances

etc.) is the spot where the related run ends and fouls by the team 'in possession' behind the basic spot are spot fouls (Rule 10-2-2-c-3).

(*d*) The basic spot on legal forward pass plays is the previous spot, and fouls by the team 'in possession' behind the basic spot are spot fouls (Rule 10-2-2-d).

Exceptions:

1. Defensive pass interference may be a spot foul.

2. Illegal use of hands, holding, or clipping by the offence behind the neutral-zone during a legal forward pass play is not a spot foul and is penalised from the previous spot (Rules 9-1-2-d and 9-3-3-a and b).

3. Enforce roughing the passer on a completed forward pass from the end of the last run when it ends beyond the neutral-zone and there is no change of team possession.

4. Illegal touching.

(*e*) The basic spot on legal kick plays before a change of possession is the previous spot, and fouls by the team in possession behind the basic spot are spot fouls (Rule 10-2-2-e, Exceptions). (*Exceptions*: Rules 9-1-2-d and 9-3-3-a and b on scrimmage kicks.)

Post-scrimmage Kick Spot

ARTICLE 11. The post-scrimmage kick spot is the spot where the kick ends if the penalty is accepted. Team B retains the ball after penalty enforcement from the post-scrimmage kick spot. Fouls behind the basic spot are spot fouls (Rule 10-2-2-e-5).

Most Advantageous Spot

ARTICLE 12. The most advantageous spot is any enforcement spot the offended team chooses for the enforcement of a live-ball foul, (Rules 9-1-4-a and b, 9-2-2 and 10-2-1).

SECTION 26. TACKLING

ARTICLE 1. Tackling is grasping or encircling an opponent with a hand(s) or arm(s).

SECTION 27. TEAM AND PLAYER DESIGNATIONS

Teams A and B

ARTICLE 1. Team A is the team that is designated to put the ball in play and it retains that designation until the ball is next declared ready for play; Team B designates the opponents.

Offensive and Defensive Teams

ARTICLE 2. The offensive team is the team in possession, or the team to which the ball belongs; the defensive team is the opposing team.

Kicker
ARTICLE 3. The kicker is any player who punts, drop kicks or place kicks according to Rule. He remains the kicker until he has had a reasonable time to regain his balance.

Lineman and Back
ARTICLE 4. A lineman is any Team A player legally on his scrimmage line when the ball is snapped; a back is any Team A player whose head does not break the plane of the line drawn through the rearmost part, other than the legs or feet, of the nearest Team A player (except the snapper) on the line of scrimmage when the ball is snapped. (*Exception*: Rule 7-1-3-b-1.)

Passer
ARTICLE 5. The passer is the player who throws a legal forward pass. He is a passer from the time he releases the ball until it is complete, incomplete, intercepted, or moves to participate in the play.

Player
ARTICLE 6. (*a*) A player is any one of the participants in the game who is not a substitute or a replaced player and is subject to the Rules when in-bounds or out-of-bounds.
  (*b*) An airborne player is a player not in contact with the ground.

Runner
ARTICLE 7. The runner is a player in possession of a live ball or simulating possession of a live ball.

Snapper
ARTICLE 8. The snapper is the player who snaps the ball.

Substitute
ARTICLE 9 (*a*) A legal substitute is a replacement for a player or a player vacancy during the interval between downs.
  (*b*) A legal incoming substitute becomes a player when he enters the field and communicates with a team-mate or an official, enters the huddle, is positioned in an offensive formation or participates in a play.
  (*c*) The player he replaces becomes a replaced player when he leaves the field of play.

Replaced Player
ARTICLE 10. A replaced player is one who participated during the previous down and has been replaced by a substitute.

Player Vacancy
ARTICLE 11. A player vacancy occurs when a team has fewer than 11 players in the game.

Disqualified Player
ARTICLE 12. A disqualified player is one who is declared ineligible for further particpation in the game.

SECTION 28. TRIPPING

ARTICLE 1. Tripping is using the lower leg or foot to obstruct an opponent (except the runner) below the knees.

SECTION 29. TIMING DEVICES

Game Clock
ARTICLE 1. Any device under the direction of the appropriate judge used to time the 60 or 48 minutes of the game.

25-Second Clock
ARTICLE 2. Any device under the direction of the appropriate official to time the 25 seconds between the ready for play and the ball being put in play. The type of device is determined by the game management.

SECTION 30. PLAY CLASSIFICATION

Forward Pass Play
ARTICLE 1. A legal forward pass play is the interval between the snap and when a legal forward pass is complete, incomplete or intercepted.

Free Kick Play
ARTICLE 2. A free kick play is the interval from the time the ball is legally kicked until it comes into player possession or the ball is declared dead by Rule.

Scrimmage Kick Play and Field Goal Play
ARTICLE 3. A scrimmage kick play or field goal play is the interval between the snap and when a scrimmage kick comes into player possession or the ball is declared dead by Rule.

Running Play
ARTICLE 4. A running play is any live ball action other than that which occurs before player possession is re-established during a free kick play, a scrimmage kick play, or a legal forward pass play.

(*a*) A running play includes the spot where the run ends and the interval of any subsequent fumble or backward or illegal pass from the time the run ends until possession is gained, regained or the ball is declared dead by Rule.

1. There may be more than one running play during a down if player possession is gained or regained beyond the neutral-zone.

2. There may not be more than one running play behind the neutral-zone if no change of team possession occurs, and the basic spot is the previous spot (Rule 10-2-2-c-2).

(*b*) A run is that segment of a running play before player possession is lost.

SECTION 31. FIELD AREAS

The Field
ARTICLE 1. The field is the area within the limit-lines and includes the limit-lines and team areas and the space above it. (*Exception*: Enclosures over the field.)

Field-of-Play
ARTICLE 2. The field-of-play is the area within the boundary lines other than the end-zones.

End-Zones
ARTICLE 3. The end-zones are the 10-yard areas at both ends of the field between the end-lines and the goal-lines. The goal-lines and goal-line pylons are in the end-zone and a team's end-zone is the one they are defending.

Playing Surface
ARTICLE 4. The playing surface is the material or substance within the field.

Playing Enclosure
ARTICLE 5. The playing enclosure is that area bounded by the stadium, dome, stands, fences or other structures. (*Exception*: Scoreboards are not considered to be within the playing enclosure.)

RULE 3

Periods, Time Factors and Substitutions

SECTION 1. START OF EACH PERIOD

First and Third Periods
ARTICLE 1. Each half shall start with a kick-off. Three minutes before the scheduled starting time the Referee shall toss a coin at midfield in the presence of no more than 4 field captains from each team and other game officials, first designating which field captain shall call the fall of the coin. During the coin toss, each team shall remain in the area between the side-line and 9-yard marks nearest its team area or in the team area.

(*a*) The winner of the toss shall choose one of the following options for the first or second half at the beginning of the half selected.

1. To designate which team shall kick off.

2. To designate which goal-line his team shall defend.

(*b*) The loser shall choose one of the above options for the half the winner of the toss did not select.

(*c*) The team not having the choice of options for a half shall exercise the option not chosen by the opponent.

(*d*) If the winner of the toss selects the second half option, the Referee shall use (S10).

Second and Fourth Periods
ARTICLE 2. Between the first and second periods and also between the third and fourth periods, the teams shall defend opposite goal-lines.

(*a*) The ball shall be relocated at a spot corresponding exactly, in relation to goal-lines and side-lines, to its location at the end of the preceding period.

(*b*) Possession of the ball, the number of the down and the distance to be gained shall remain unchanged.

Extra Periods
ARTICLE 3. (*a*) When it is necessary to decide a tied game, extra time shall be played. This shall be by way of extra periods of 15 or 12 minutes each. The first team to score shall be declared the winner. If the first score is a touch-down no extra point attempt shall be allowed.

(*b*) Prior to the start of the extra time, the Referee shall toss a coin in the presence of the field captains of both teams. The winner of the toss shall choose to designate which team shall kick-off *or* which goal-line his team will defend.

(*c*) At the end of each extra period the teams shall defend opposite goal-lines in accordance with Rule 3.1.2.

(*d*) Each team shall be entitled to one charged time-out during each extra period.

SECTION 2. PLAYING TIME AND INTERMISSIONS

Length of Periods and Intermissions
ARTICLE 1. The total playing time in a game shall be 60 or 48 minutes divided into four periods of 15 or 12 minutes each, with 1-minute intermissions between the first and second periods (first half) and between the third and fourth periods (second half).

(*a*) No period shall end until the ball is dead.

(*b*) The intermission between halves, which begins when the field is clear of all players and coaches, shall be 20 minutes.

Time Adjustments
ARTICLE 2. Before the game starts playing time may be shortened by the Referee if he is of the opinion that darkness may interfere with the game. The four periods must be of equal length if the game is shortened before its start.

(*a*) Any time during the game, the playing time of any remaining period or periods may be shortened by mutual agreement of the opposing Head Coaches and the Referee.

(*b*) Timing errors on the game clock, the 25-second clock, or by an official, may be corrected by the Referee.

(*c*) The 25-second clock is not started when the game clock is running with less than 25 seconds in a period.

Extension of Periods
ARTICLE 3. A period shall be extended until a down, other than a try, free from live-ball fouls not penalised as dead-ball fouls has been played when:

(*a*) A penalty is accepted for a live-ball foul(s) not penalised as a dead-ball foul that occurs during a down in which time expires.

(*b*) An inadvertent whistle is sounded during a down in which time expires.

(*c*) A touch-down is scored during a down in which time expires. (*Exception*: If the winner of the game has been decided and both head coaches agree to forgo the try, the period is not extended.)

(*d*) Offsetting fouls occur during a down in which time expires.

Timing Devices
ARTICLE 4. (*a*) Playing time shall be kept with a game clock that may

be either a stop watch operated by the Field Judge, Line Judge or Back Judge, or a game clock operated by an assistant under the direction of the appropriate Judge. The use of a game clock shall be determined by the game management.

(*b*) The 25 seconds between the ready for play and the ball being put in play shall be timed with a watch operated by the appropriate official or 25-second clocks at each end of the playing enclosure operated by an assistant under the direction of the appropriate official. The use of a visual 25-second clock shall be determined by the game management. *Note*: If visual timing devices become inoperative, both coaches shall be notified by the Referee immediately and both 25-second clocks shall be turned off.

When Clock Starts
ARTICLE 5. Following a free kick, the game clock shall be started when the ball is legally touched in the field of play or crosses the goal-line after being legally touched by Team B in its end-zone. On a scrimmage down, the game clock shall be started when the ball is snapped or on prior signal by the Referee. The clock shall not run during a try or during an extension of a period.

(*a*) When the clock has been stopped, the Referee shall declare the ball ready for play (Rule 11-2-1-c), and the clock shall start on the snap, unless it was stopped because of one of the following situations:

1. When Team A is awarded a first down. (*Exception*: After a kick.)
2. For a Referee's time-out for an injured player or official.
3. At the Referee's discretion (Rule 3-4-3).
4. To complete a penalty.
5. For an inadvertent whistle. (*Exception*: During a kick.)
6. For a Head Coach's conference.
7. For a side-line warning.
8. For an illegal pass to conserve time.

(*b*) If the clock was stopped for incidents 1 to 8, it shall be started on the ready for play.

(*c*) If incidents in (*a*) above, occur in conjunction with a charged team time-out or any other incident following which the clock would not start until the ball is put in play, it shall be started when the ball is put in play.

(*d*) The clock stops at the end of a legal scrimmage kick-down and starts on the snap. (*Exception*: When the next play is a free kick.)

When Clock Stops
ARTICLE 6. The game clock shall be stopped when each periods ends. Any official may signal time-out when the rules provide for stopping the

clock or when a time-out is charged to a team or to the Referee. (*Exception*: Rule 3-3-4-e.) Other officials should repeat time-out signals.

SECTION 3. TIME-OUTS

How Charged
ARTICLE 1. (*a*) The Referee shall declare a time-out when he suspends play for any reason. Each time-out shall be charged to one of the teams or designated as Referee's time-out.

(*b*) When a team's time-outs are exhausted and it requests a time-out with the 25-second clock running, the official should not acknowledge the request, interrupt the 25-second count or stop the game clock.

(*c*) During a time-out, players shall not practise with a ball on the field of play. (*Exception*: During the half-time intermission.)

Time-out
ARTICLE 2. (*a*) The Referee shall declare a Referee's time-out:
1. When a touch-down, field goal, touch-back or safety is scored.
2. When an injury time-out is allowed for one or more players.
3. When the clock is stopped to complete a penalty.
4. When a live ball goes out-of-bounds or is declared out-of-bounds.
5. When a forward pass becomes incomplete.
6. When Team A or B is awarded a first down.
7. When an inadvertent whistle is sounded.
8. When there is a possible first-down measurement.
9. When a delay is caused by both teams.
10. When a charged time-out is granted.
11. When there is a side-line warning.
12. When the ball becomes illegal.
13. When the ball is in the possession of an official.
14. When there is a mandatory equipment (Rule 1-4-4) or illegal equipment (Rule 1-4-5) violation.

(*b*) The Referee only shall declare a time-out:
1. When a Head Coach's conference is requested.
2. When an unfair noise time-out is required.
3. When a radio or TV time-out is allowed.
4. When a discretionary time-out is declared.

Referee's Discretionary Time-out
ARTICLE 3. (*a*) The Referee may temporarily suspend the game when conditions warrant such action. The Referee may declare and charge

himself with a time-out for any contingency not elsewhere covered by the Rules.

(*b*) When the game is stopped by actions of a person(s) not subject to the Rules or for any other reasons not in the Rules and cannot continue, the Referee shall:

1. Suspend play and direct the players to their team areas.

2. Refer the problem to those responsible for the game's management.

3. Resume the game when he determines conditions are satisfactory.

(*c*) If a game may not be resumed immediately after Rule 3-3-3-a and b suspensions, it shall be terminated or resumed at a later time only by mutual consent of both teams.

(*d*) A suspended game, if resumed, will begin with the same time remaining and under the identical conditions of down, distance and field position.

(*e*) The game is a non-contest unless there is mutual consent of both teams to resume or terminate the game. (*Exception*: Conference or league regulations).

(*f*) The Referee's discretionary time-out also applies to the following play situations:

1. When there is undue delay by officials in placing the ball for the next snap.

2. When there is a consultation with team captains.

3. When conditions warrant temporary suspension.

4. When the offensive team believes it is unable to communicate its signals to team-mates other than players positioned more than 7 yards from the middle lineman of the offensive formation because of crowd noise.

Administrative procedures for unfair noise:

(*a*) When the signal caller believes he is unable to communicate signals to team-mates because of crowd noise, he may raise his hands and look to the Referee to request a legal delay.

(*b*) The Referee may deny the request by pointing toward the defensive team's goal-line or may charge himself with a time-out and the offensive team may huddle.

(*c*) When the offensive team returns to the line of scrimmage, the game clock will start on the snap. The Referee shall declare the ball ready for play by sounding his whistle with no hand signal. The 25-second clock is not in operation.

(*d*) Should the signal caller then, or later in the game, request a second legal delay by raising his hands and looking to the Referee, the Referee will again charge himself with a time-out if, in his opinion, the crowd noise makes it impossible to hear offensive signals.

(*e*) The Referee will then request the defensive captain to ask the crowd for quiet. This signals the public address announcer to request co-operation and courtesy to the offensive team. The announcer will state that the defensive team will be charged a time-out, or penalised 5 yards if time-outs are exhausted, for the next crowd noise infraction.

(*f*) When the offensive team returns to the line of scrimmage, the game clock will start on the snap. The Referee shall declare the ball ready for play by sounding his whistle with no hand signal. The 25-second clock is not in operation.

(*g*) If the signal caller again, during the game, indicates by raising his hands and looking to the Referee to request a legal crowd noise delay and the Referee agrees, a team time-out will be charged to the defensive team. If the defensive team has exhausted its allotment of time-outs, a 5-yard penalty is assessed.

(*h*) After this time-out or the penalty, the defensive team will be penalised 5 yards for each subsequent unsuccessful attempt to start a play.

Violation: Rules 3-3-6 and 3-4-2b (S3 or S21)

Step 1 – Referees' time-out.

Step 2 – Referees' time-out plus captain's notification and public address announcement.

Step 3 – Time-out or 5yd penalty if time-outs are exhausted.

Step 4 – 5-yard penalty for each additional infraction.

Charged Team Time-outs

ARTICLE 4. When time-outs are not exhausted an official shall allow a charged team time-out when requested by any player when the ball is dead.

(*a*) Each team is entitled to three charged team time-outs during each half.

(*b*) After the ball is declared dead and before the snap, a legal substitute may request a time-out if he is within 15yd of the ball.

(*c*) A player who participated during the previous down may request a time-out between the time the ball is declared dead and the snap without being within 15yd of the ball.

(*d*) A player or incoming substitute may request a coach's conference with the Referee if the coach believes a Rule has been improperly enforced. If the Rule enforcement is not changed, the coach's team will be charged a time-out, or a delay penalty if all time-outs have been used.

1. Only the Referee may stop the clock for a coach's conference.

2. A request for a conference must be requested before the ball is snapped or free kicked for the next play and before the end of the second and fourth period.

3. After a coach's conference, the full team time-out is granted if charged by the Referee.

Injury Time-out

ARTICLE 5. (*a*) In the event of an injured player:

1. The Referee may charge himself with a time-out, provided the player for whom the time-out is taken is removed from the game for at least one down.

2. The player may remain in the game if his team is charged a time-out in the interval between downs or the period ends.

3. After a team's charged time-outs have been exhausted, the injured player must leave for one down.

(*b*) Any official may stop the clock for an injured player.

(*c*) To curtail a possible time-gaining advantage by feigning injuries, attention is directed to the strongly worded statement in 'The Football Code' concerning the feigning of any injury.

(*d*) An injury time-out may follow a charged team time-out (Rule 3-3-5).

(*e*) The Referee may charge himself with a time-out for an injured official.

Violation Time-outs

ARTICLE 6. For non-compliance with Rules 1-4-4, 1-4-5, 3-3-4-e or 3-3-f-4-g during a down, a time-out shall be charged to a team at the succeeding spot (Rule 3-4-2-b).

Length of Time-outs

ARTICLE 7. (*a*) A charged team time-out requested by any player shall not exceed 1 minute 30 seconds. Other time-outs shall be no longer than the Referee deems necessary to fulfil the purpose for which they are declared, including a radio or TV time-out, but any time-out may be extended by the Referee for the benefit of an injured player.

(*b*) If the team charged with a 1 minute 30 second team time-out wishes to resume play before the expiration of 1 minute and its opponent indicates readiness, the Referee will declare the ball ready for play.

(*c*) The length of a Referee's time-outs depend on the circumstances of each time-out.

(*d*) The field captain must exercise his penalty option before he or a team-mate consults with his coach on a side-line during a time-out.

Referee's Notification

ARTICLE 8. The Referee shall notify both teams 30 seconds before a charged team time-out expires and 5 seconds later shall declare the ball ready for play.

(*a*) When a third time-out is charged to a team in either half, the Referee shall notify the field captain and Head Coach of that team.

(*b*) Unless a game clock is the official timepiece, the Referee also shall inform each field captain and Head Coach when approximately 2 minutes of playing time remain in each half. He may order the clock stopped for that purpose.

(*c*) If a visible game clock is not the official timing device during the last 2 minutes of each half, the Referee or his representative shall notify each captain and Head Coach of the time remaining each time the clock is stopped by rule. Also, a representative may leave the team area along the limit line to relay timing information under these conditions.

SECTION 4. DELAYS

Delaying the Start of a Half
ARTICLE 1. (*a*) Each team shall have its players on the field for the opening play at the scheduled time for the beginning of each half.
Penalty: 15 yards (S7 and S21).

(*b*) The home management is responsible for clearing the field of play and end-zones at the beginning of each half so the periods may start at the scheduled time. Bands, speeches, presentations, homecoming and similar activities are under the jurisdiction of home management and a prompt start of each half is mandatory.
Penalty: 10 yards (S7 and S21). (*Exception*: The Referee may waive the penalty for circumstances beyond the control of the home management.)

Illegal Delay of the Game
ARTICLE 2. (*a*) The ball shall be declared ready for play consistently throughout the game by the Referee when the officials are in position. Consuming more than 25 seconds to put the ball in play after it is declared ready for play is an illegal delay. (*Exceptions*: When the 25-second count is interrupted by circumstances beyond the control of either team, a new 25-second count shall be started and the game clock shall start on the snap.)

(*b*) Illegal delay also includes:
1. Crawling or deliberately advancing the ball after it is dead.
2. When a team has expended its three timeouts and commits a 1-4-4, 1-4-5, 3-3-4-e or 3-3-f-4-g Rules infraction.
3. When a team is not ready to play after an intermission between

periods other than the half, after a try or successful field goal or after a radio/television time-out, or at any time the Referee orders the ball put in play.

4. Taking the ball off the field of play or end-zone.
Penalty: 5 yards (S7 and S21).

Unfair Game Clock Tactics
ARTICLE 3. The Referee shall order the game clock started or stopped whenever, in his opinion, either team is trying to conserve or consume playing time by tactics obviously unfair. This includes starting the clock on the snap if the foul is by the team ahead in the score. The clock will start on the ready for play following an illegal forward or backward pass that conserves time for Team A.
Penalty: 5 yards (S7 and S21).

SECTION 5. SUBSTITUTIONS

Substitution Procedures
ARTICLE 1. Any number of legal substitutes for either team may enter the game between periods, after a score or try, or during the interval between downs only for the purpose of replacing a player(s).
Penalty: 5 yards (S22).

Legal Substitutions
ARTICLE 2. A legal substitute may replace a player or fill a player vacancy provided none of the following restrictions is violated:

(*a*) No incoming substitute or replaced player shall enter or leave the field of play or end-zone while the ball is in play.

(*b*) An incoming legal substitute must enter the field directly from his team area and a substitute or player leaving must depart at the side-line nearest his team area. A replaced player must also leave at the side-line nearest his team area.

(*c*) Substitutes who become players must remain in the game for one play and replaced players must remain out of the game for one play except during the interval between periods, after a score, or when a time-out has been charged to a team or to the Referee.

(*d*) Substitutes of the scrimmage-kicking team shall not delay for the purposes of confusing the receiving team (Live-ball foul S22).
Penalty: If a ball is dead: 5 yards from succeeding spot; otherwise, 5 yards from previous spot (S7 and S22).

RULE 4

Ball in Play, Dead ball, Out of Bounds

SECTION 1. BALL IN PLAY – DEAD BALL

Dead Ball Becomes Alive
ARTICLE 1. After a dead ball has been declared ready for play, it becomes a live ball when it is legally snapped, or free kicked legally. A ball snapped or free kicked before the ready for play remains dead.

Live Ball Becomes Dead
ARTICLE 2. (*a*) A live ball becomes a dead ball as provided in the Rules or when an official sounds his whistle (even though inadvertently), or otherwise declares the ball dead.
(*b*) An official sounds his whistle inadvertently during a down when:
1. The ball is in player possession – the team in possession may elect to put the ball in play where declared dead or replay the down.
2. The ball is loose from a fumble, backward pass or illegal pass – the team in possession may elect to put the ball in play where possession was lost or replay the down.
3. During a legal forward pass or a free or scrimmage kick – the ball is returned to the previous spot and the down replayed.
4. Team B gets possession on a try, the try is over.
Note: If a foul occurs during any of the above downs, the penalty shall be administered as in any other play situations if not in conflict with other rules.

Ball Declared Dead
ARTICLE 3. A live ball becomes dead and an official shall sound his whistle or declare it dead:
(*a*) When it goes out-of-bounds other than a kick that scores a goal after touching the goal-posts, when a runner is out-of-bounds or when a runner is so held that his forward progress is stopped. When in question the ball is dead.
(*b*) When any part of the runner's body, except his hand or foot, touches the ground or when the runner is tackled or otherwise falls and loses possession of the ball as he contacts the ground with any part of his body, except his hand or foot. When in question, the ball is dead. (*Exception*: The ball remains alive when an offensive player has simulated a kick or is in position to kick the ball held for a place kick by a team-mate. The ball may be kicked, passed or advanced by Rule.)
(*c*) When a touch-down, touch-back, safety, field goal, or successful

try occurs, or when Team A completes an illegal forward pass in Team B's end-zone, or Team A completes a forward pass to an ineligible player in Team B's end-zone.

(*d*) When during a try, a Dead-ball Rule applies.

(*e*) When a player of the kicking team catches or recovers any free kick or a scrimmage kick that has crossed the neutral-zone.

(*f*) When a free kick or scrimmage kick comes to rest and no player attempts to secure it.

(*g*) When a free kick or scrimmage kick (beyond the neutral-zone) is caught or recovered by any play following a valid, invalid or illegal fair catch signal.

(*h*) When a return kick or scrimmage kick beyond the neutral-zone is made.

(*i*) When a forward pass strikes the ground.

(*j*) When a live ball not in player possession touches anything in-bounds other than a player, official or the ground.

(*k*) When a simultaneous catch or recovery of a live ball is made in-bounds by opposing players.

(*l*) When the ball becomes illegal while in play, inadvertent whistle provisions apply.

(*m*) When the ball is in possession of an official.

(*n*) When a runner simulates placing his knee on the ground.

(*o*) When a loose ball comes to rest and no player attempts to secure it.

Ball Ready For Play
ARTICLE 4. No player shall put the ball in play until it is declared ready for play.
Penalty: Dead-ball foul. 5 yards from the spot succeeding spot (S7 and S19).

25-Second Count
ARTICLE 5. The ball shall be put in play within 25 seconds after it is declared ready for play, unless, during that interval, play is suspended. If play is suspended, the 25-second count will start again. (*Exception*: Unfair crowd noise situations.)
Penalty: 5 yards (S7 and S21).

SECTION 2. OUT-OF-BOUNDS

Player Out-of-Bounds
ARTICLE 1. (*a*) A player or an airborne player is out-of-bounds when any part of his person touches anything, other than another player or game official, on or outside a boundary line.

(*b*) A player or an airborne player who touches a pylon is out-of-bounds behind the goal-line.

Held Ball Out-of-Bounds

ARTICLE 2. A ball in player possession is out-of-bounds when either the ball or any part of the runner touches the ground or anything else that is on or outside a boundary line except another player or game official.

Ball Out-of-Bounds

ARTICLE 3. (*a*) A ball not in player possession, other than a kick that scores a goal, is out-of-bounds when it touches the ground, a player or anything else that is on or outside a boundary line.

(*b*) A ball that touches a pylon is out-of-bounds behind the goal-line.

(*c*) If a live ball not in player possession crosses a boundary line and is then declared out-of-bounds, it is out-of-bounds at the crossing point.

Out-of-Bounds at Forward Point

ARTICLE 4. (*a*) If a live ball is declared out-of-bounds and the ball does not cross a boundary line, it is out-of-bounds at the ball's most forward point when it was declared dead.

(*b*) A touch-down may be scored if the ball is in-bounds and has broken the plane of the goal-line before or simultaneously with the runner's going out-of-bounds.

(*c*) An eligible receiver who is in the opponent's end-zone and contacting the ground is credited with a completion if he reaches over the side-line or end-line and catches a legal pass.

(*d*) The most forward point of the ball when declared out-of-bounds between the goal-lines is the point of forward progress.

(*e*) When a runner dives or jumps toward the side-line and is airborne as he crosses the side-line, forward progress is determined by the position of the ball as it crosses the side-line.

RULE 5

Series of Downs, Line to Gain

SECTION 1. A SERIES: STARTED, BROKEN, RENEWED

When to Award Series

ARTICLE 1. (*a*) A series of 4 consecutive scrimmage downs shall be awarded to the team that is next to put the ball in play by a snap following a free kick, touch-back, fair catch or change in team possession.

(*b*) A new series shall be awarded to Team A if it is in legal possession of the ball on or beyond its line to gain when it is declared dead.

(*c*) A new series shall be awarded to Team B if, after fourth down, Team A has failed to earn a first down.

(*d*) A new series shall be awarded to Team B if A's scrimmage kick goes out-of-bounds or comes to rest and no player attempts to secure it.

(*e*) A new series shall be awarded to the team in legal possession:

1. If a change of team possession occurs during the down.

2. If a player of Team B first touches a scrimmage kick that has crossed the neutral zone. (*Exception*: When a penalty for a foul by either team is accepted and the down is replayed, or offsetting fouls are enforced and the down is replayed.)

3. If an accepted penalty awards the ball to the offended team.

4. If an accepted penalty mandates a first down.

(*f*) A new series shall be awarded to Team B whenever Team B, after a scrimmage kick, elects to take the ball at a spot of illegal touching. (*Exception*: When a penalty for a foul by either team is accepted and the down is replayed or offsetting fouls are enforced and the down is replayed.)

Line to Gain
ARTICLE 2. The line to gain for a series shall be established 10 yards in advance of the most forward point of the ball; but if this line is in the opponents' end-zone, the goal-line becomes the line to gain.

Forward Progress
ARTICLE 3. (*a*) The most forward point of the ball when declared dead between the goal-lines shall be the determining point in measuring distance gained or lost by either team during any down. The ball shall always be placed with its length axis parallel to the side-line before measuring. (*Exception*: When an airborne receiver completes a catch in-bounds after an opponent has driven him backward and the ball is declared dead at the spot of the catch, the forward progress is where the player received the ball.)

(*b*) Unnecessary measurements to determine first downs shall not be granted, but any doubtful distance should be measured without request.

(*c*) No request for a measurement shall be granted after the ball is declared ready for play.

Continuity of Downs Broken
ARTICLE 4. The continuity of a series of downs is broken when:

(*a*) Team possession of the ball changes during a down.

(*b*) A player of Team B first touches a scrimmage kick that has crossed the neutral-zone.

(*c*) A kick goes out-of-bounds.

(*d*) A kick comes to rest and no player attempts to secure it.

(*e*) At the end of a down, Team A has earned a first down. Any down may be repeated if so provided by the Rules.

(*f*) After fourth down, Team A has failed to earn a first down.

(*g*) An accepted penalty mandates a first down.

(*h*) There is a score.

(*i*) The first half ends.

SECTION 2. DOWN AND POSSESSION AFTER A PENALTY

Foul During Free Kick
ARTICLE 1. When a scrimmage follows the penalty for a foul committed during a free kick, the down and distance established by that penalty shall be first down with a new line or goal to gain. (*Exception*: Live-ball penalised as dead-ball foul.)

Penalty Resulting in First Down
ARTICLE 2. It is a first down with a new line or goal to gain:

(*a*) After a penalty that leaves the ball in possession of Team A beyond its line to gain.

(*b*) After a pass interference penalty has awarded the ball to Team A.

(*c*) When a penalty stipulates a first down.

Foul Before Change of Team Possession
ARTICLE 3. After a distance penalty between the goal-lines, incurred during a scrimmage down and before any change of team possession during that down, the ball belongs to Team A and the down shall be repeated unless the penalty also involves loss of a down, stipulates a first down, or leaves the ball on or beyond the line to gain. (*Exception*: Rules 10-2-2-e-5 and 10-2-2-g.) If the penalty involves loss of a down, the down shall count as one of the 4 in that series.

Foul After of Change of Team Possession
ARTICLE 4. If a distance penalty is accepted for a foul incurred during a down after change of team possession, the ball belongs to the team in possession when the foul occurred. The down and distance established by any distance penalty incurred after change of team possession during that down shall be first down with a new line or goal to gain. (*Exception*: Live-ball fouls penalised as dead-ball fouls.)

Penalty Declined

ARTICLE 5. If a penalty is declined, the number of the next down shall be whatever it would have been if that foul had not occurred.

Foul Between Downs

ARTICLE 6. After a distance penalty incurred between downs, the number of the next down shall be the same as that established before the foul occurred, unless enforcement for a foul by Team B leaves the ball on or beyond the line to gain or a penalty mandates a first down (Rules 9-1-1, 9-1-2).

Foul Between Series

ARTICLE 7. A scrimmage following a penalty incurred after a series ends and before the next series begins shall be first down, but the line to gain shall be established before the penalty is enforced.

Fouls by Both Teams

ARTICLE 8. If offsetting fouls occur during a down, that down shall be repeated (Rule 10-1-4 Exceptions).

Fouls During a Loose Ball

ARTICLE 9. Live-ball fouls not penalised as dead-ball fouls when the ball is loose shall be penalised from the basic or previous spot (Rules 10-2-2-c, d, e and f).

Rule Decisions Final

ARTICLE 10. No Rule decision may be changed after the ball is next legally snapped or legally free kicked.

RULE 6

Kicks

SECTION 1. FREE KICKS

Restraining Lines

ARTICLE 1. For any free-kick formation, the kicking team's restraining line shall be the yard-line through the most forward point from which the ball shall be kicked, and the receiving team's restraining line shall be the yard-line 10 yards beyond that point. Unless relocated by a penalty, the kicking team's restraining line on a kick-off shall be its 35-yard line and for a free kick after a safety, its 20-yard line.

Free-Kick Formation
ARTICLE 2. A ball from a free-kick formation must be kicked legally and from some point on Team A's restraining line and on or between the in-bound lines. After the ball is ready for play and for any reason it falls from the tee, Team A shall not kick the ball and the official shall sound his whistle immediately. When the ball is kicked:

(*a*) All players of each team must be in-bounds.

(*b*) Each Team A player except the holder and kicker of a place kick must be behind the ball. After a safety, when a punt or drop kick is used, the ball shall be kicked within 1 yard behind the kicking team's restraining line.

(*c*) All Team B players must be behind their restraining line.

(*d*) At least five Team B players must be within 5 yards of their restraining line.

(*e*) Team A substitutes may not touch a kick if they enter the field after the ball is declared ready for play.

(*f*) A Team A player who goes out-of-bounds during a free-kick down may not return in-bounds during the down. (*Exception*: This does not apply to a Team A player who is blocked out-of-bounds and attempts to return in-bounds immediately.)

(*g*) No Team A player may block an opponent until Team A is eligible to touch a free-kicked ball.
Penalty: 5 yards from previous spot live-ball foul (S18 or S19).

Free-kick Recovery
ARTICLE 3. A Team A player may touch a free-kicked ball:

(*a*) After it touches a Team B player.

(*b*) After it breaks the plane of and remains beyond Team B's restraining line.

(*c*) After it touches any player, the ground or an official beyond Team B's restraining line. Thereafter, all players of Team A become eligible to touch, recover or catch the kick. (*Exception*: Rules 6-1-2-e and f.) Illegal touching of a free kick is a violation that, when the ball becomes dead, gives the receiving team the privilege of taking the ball at the spot of the violation. However, if there are offsetting fouls or a penalty incurred by either team before the ball becomes dead is accepted, this privilege is cancelled.

Forced Touching Disregarded
ARTICLE 4. (*a*) An in-bounds player pushed or blocked by an opponent into a free kick is not, while in-bounds, deemed to have touched the kick.

(*b*) An in-bounds player touched by a ball batted by an opponent is not deemed to have touched the ball.

Free Kick at Rest
ARTICLE 5. If a free kick comes to rest in-bounds and no player attempts to secure it, the ball becomes dead and belongs to the receiving team at the dead-ball spot.

Free Kick Caught or Recovered
ARTICLE 6. (*a*) If a free kick is caught or recovered by a player of the receiving team, the ball continues in play. (*Exceptions*: Rules 6-1-7, 6-5-1 and 2, and 4-1-3-g.) If caught or recovered by a player of the kicking team the ball becomes dead.
   (*b*) When opposing players, each eligible to touch the ball, simultaneously recover a rolling kick or catch a free kick, the simultaneous possession makes the ball dead. A kick declared dead in joint possession is awarded to the receiving team.

Touching Ground on or Beyond Goal-Lines
ARTICLE 7. The ball becomes dead and belongs to the team defending its goal-line when a free kick is untouched by Team B prior to touching the ground on or behind Team B's goal-line.

SECTION 2. FREE KICK OUT OF BOUNDS

Kicking Team
ARTICLE 1. A free kick out-of-bounds between the goal-lines untouched in-bounds by a player of Team B is a foul.
Penalty: Live-ball foul. 5 yards from previous spot (S19).

Receiving team
ARTICLE 2. When a free kick goes out-of-bounds between the goal-lines, the ball belongs to the receiving team at the in-bounds spot. When a free kick goes out-of-bounds behind the goal-line, the ball belongs to the team defending that goal-line.

SECTION 3. SCRIMMAGE KICKS

Behind the Neutral Zone
ARTICLE 1. (*a*) A scrimmage kick that fails to cross the neutral-zone continues in play. All players may catch or recover the ball behind the neutral-zone and advance it.
   (*b*) Blocking of a kick that occurs in the vicinity of the neutral-zone is ruled as having occurred within or behind that zone.

Beyond the Neutral-Zone

ARTICLE 2. No in-bounds player of the kicking team shall touch a scrimmage kick that has crossed the neutral-zone before it touches an opponent. Such illegal touching is a violation which, when the ball becomes dead, gives the receiving team the privilege of taking the ball at the spot of the violation. Illegal touching in Team A's end-zone is ignored. However, if a penalty incurred by either team before the ball becomes dead is enforced, or there are offsetting fouls, the privilege is cancelled. (Exceptions: See Rule 8-4-2-b.)

All Become Eligible

ARTICLE 3. When a scrimmage kick that has crossed the neutral-zone touches a player of the receiving team who is in-bounds, any player may catch or recover the ball.

Forced Touching Disregarded

ARTICLE 4. (*a*) A player pushed or blocked by an opponent into a scrimmage kick that has crossed the neutral-zone, shall not, while in-bounds, be deemed to have touched the kick.

(*b*) An in-bounds player touched by a ball batted by an opponent is not deemed to have touched the ball.

Catch or Recovery by Receiving Team

ARTICLE 5. If a scrimmage kick is caught or recovered by a player of the receiving team, the ball continues in play. (*Exception*: Rules 4-1-3-g, 6-3-9, 6-5-1 and 6-5-2.)

Catch or Recovery by Kicking Team

ARTICLE 6. (*a*) If a player of the kicking team catches or recovers a scrimmage kick that crossed the neutral-zone, the ball becomes dead.

(*b*) When opposing players, each eligible to touch the ball, simultaneously recover a rolling kick or catch a scrimmage kick, this simultaneous possession makes the ball dead. A kick declared dead in joint possession of opposing players is awarded to the receiving team (Rules 2-2-8 and 4-1-3-k).

Out-of-Bounds Between Goal-Lines or at Rest

ARTICLE 7. If a scrimmage kick goes out-of-bounds between the goal-lines, or comes to rest in-bounds and no player attempts to secure it, the ball becomes dead and belongs to the receiving team at the dead-ball spot. (*Exception*: Rule 8-4-2-b.)

Out-of-Bounds Behind Goal-Line

ARTICLE 8. If a scrimmage kick (other than the one that scores a field goal) goes out-of-bounds behind a goal-line, the ball becomes dead and belongs to the team defending that goal-line. (*Exception*: See Rule 8-4-2-b.)

Touching Ground on or Behind Goal-line
ARTICLE 9. (*a*) The ball becomes dead and belongs to the team defending its goal-line when a scrimmage kick is untouched by Team B beyond the neutral-zone prior to touching the ground on or behind Team B's goal-line (See Rule 8-4-2-b).

(*b*) A foul after an untouched scrimmage kick strikes the ground in Team B's end-zone is a dead-ball foul.

(*a*) A foul after a scrimmage kick strikes the ground in Team B's end-zone after touching a Team B player beyond the neutral-zone and before it is declared dead is a live-ball foul.

Legal Kick
ARTICLE 10. (*a*) A legal scrimmage kick is a punt, drop kick or place kick made according to the Rules.

(*b*) A return kick is an illegal kick and live-ball foul that causes the ball to become dead.
Penalty: For a return kick, 5 yards from the spot of the foul (S31).

(*c*) A scrimmage kick beyond the neutral-zone is a live-ball foul that causes the ball to become dead.
Penalty: For an illegal kick beyond the neutral-zone, 5 yards from the previous spot and loss of down (S31 and S9).

(*d*) Any device or material used to mark the spot of a scrimmage place kick or elevate the ball makes the kick illegal.
Penalty: For an illegal kick (live-ball foul) – 5 yards from the previous spot (S31).

Loose Behind the Goal-Line
ARTICLE 11. If a Team A player bats a scrimmage kick, untouched beyond the neutral-zone by Team B, in Team B's end zone, it is a violation and Team B may elect a touch-back when the ball is declared dead.
Violation: Touch-back (S7 and S16). (*Exception*: Rule 8-4-2-b.)

Out-of-Bounds Player
ARTICLE 12. No Team A player who goes out-of bounds during a scrimmage kick down may return in-bounds during the down. (*Exception*: This does not apply to a Team A player who is blocked out-of-bounds and attempts to return in-bounds immediately.)
Penalty: Live-ball foul. 5 yards from previous spot (S19).

SECTION 4. OPPORTUNITY TO CATCH A KICK

Interference with Opportunity
ARTICLE 1. A player of the receiving team within the boundary lines attempting to catch a kick, and so located that he could have caught a free kick or a scrimmage kick that is beyond the neutral-zone, must be given an unmolested opportunity to catch the kick.

(*a*) No player of the kicking team may be within 2 yd of a player of the receiving team positioned to catch a free or scrimmage kick.

(*b*) This protection terminates when the kick touches the ground or is touched by any player of Team B beyond the neutral-zone.

(*c*) If contact with a potential receiver is the result of a player being blocked or pushed by an opponent, it is not a foul.

(*d*) It is not a foul if a member of the kicking team is blocked by an opponent to within 2 yd of the receiver.

(*e*) It is a contact foul if the kicking team contacts the potential receiver prior to, or simultaneous with, his first touching of the ball.
Penalty: For foul between goal-lines – receiving team's ball, first down, 15 yards beyond spot of foul for contact foul and 5 yards for non-contact foul. For foul behind goal-line – award touch-back and penalise from succeeding spot (S33). Flagrant offenders shall be disqualified.

SECTION 5. FAIR CATCH

Dead Where Caught
ARTICLE 1. (*a*) When a Team B player makes a fair catch, the ball becomes dead where caught and belongs to Team B at that spot.

(*b*) Rules pertaining to a fair catch apply only when a scrimmage kick crosses the neutral-zone or during free kicks.

(*c*) The purpose of the fair catch provision is to protect the receiver who, by his fair catch signal, agrees he or a team-mate will not advance after the catch.

(*d*) The ball shall be put in play by a snap by the receiving team at the spot of the catch, if the ball is caught.

No Advance
ARTICLE 2. No Team B player shall carry a caught or recovered ball more than 2 steps in any direction following a valid, invalid or illegal fair catch signal by any Team B player.
Penalty: Dead-ball foul. 5 yards from succeeding spot (S7 and S21).

Illegal Signals
ARTICLE 3. (*a*) During a down in which a kick is made, no player of

Team B shall make any illegal fair catch signal during a free kick or beyond the neutral-zone during a scrimmage kick. Any signal is illegal after a scrimmage kick is caught beyond the neutral-zone or after it strikes the ground, or after it touches another player beyond the neutral-zone. A signal is illegal after a free kick is caught, strikes the ground or touches another player.

(*b*) A catch following an illegal signal is a not a fair catch and the ball is dead where caught. When the signal follows the catch, the ball is dead where the signal is first given.

(*c*) Fouls for illegal signals beyond the neutral-zone apply only to Team B.

(*d*) An illegal signal beyond the neutral-zone is possible only when the ball has crossed the neutral-zone (Rule 2-15-7).

Penalty: Free kick – receiving team's ball 15 yards from spot of foul (Rule 10-2-2-e) (S32). Scrimmage kick – receiving team's ball 15 yards from basic spot (Rule 10-2-2-e-5) (S32).

Illegal Block
ARTICLE 4. A player of Team B who has made a valid, invalid or illegal signal for a fair catch and does not touch the ball shall not block or foul an opponent during that down.

Penalty: Free kick – receiving team's ball 15 yards from spot of foul (Rule 10-2-2-e) (S38, S39 or S40). Scrimmage kick – receiving team's ball 15 yards from basic spot (Rule 10-2-2-e-5) (S38, S39 or S40).

No Tackling
ARTICLE 5. No player of the kicking team shall tackle or block an opponent who has completed a fair catch. Only the player making a fair catch signal has this protection.

Penalty: Dead-ball foul. Receiving team's ball 15 yards from succeeding spot (S7 and S38).

RULE 7

Snapping and Passing the Ball

SECTION 1. THE SCRIMMAGE

Starting with a Snap
ARTICLE 1. The ball shall be put in play by a legal snap unless the Rules provide for a legal free kick.

Penalty: Dead-ball foul. 5 yards – Penalise from succeeding spot (S7 and S19).

Not in a Side-Zone
ARTICLE 2. The ball may not be snapped in a side-zone. If the starting point for any scrimmage down is in a side-zone, it shall be transferred to the in-bounds spot.

Offensive Team Requirements
ARTICLE 3. The offensive requirements for scrimmage are as follows.
(*a*) *Before the ball is snapped*:
1. The snapper, after assuming his position for the succeeding snap and adjusting or simulating touching the ball, may neither move to a different position nor change the position of the ball in a manner simulating the beginning of a play. An infraction of this provision may be penalised whether or not the ball is snapped and the penalty for any resultant offsides or contact foul by an opponent shall be cancelled (S7 and S19).
2. After the ball is ready for play and before the snap, each player or entering substitute of Team A must have been between the 9-yard marks (S19).
3. No player of the offensive team shall be in or beyond the neutral-zone after the snapper touches or simulates touching the ball and before the snap. *Exceptions*: (1) Substitutes and replaced players.(2) Offensive players in a scrimmage kick formation who, after the snapper touches the ball, point at opponents and break the neutral-zone with their hand(s).
4. After the ball is ready for play, no offensive player shall contact an opponent or make a false start, which includes (S7 and S19):
    a. Feigning a charge.
    b. A shift or movement that simulates the beginning of a play. This includes the snapper, who after assuming a position for the succeeding snap and touching or simulating touching the ball, moves to another position.
    c. A lineman between the snapper and the player on the end of the line or a lineman other than the snapper wearing a number 50-79, after having placed a hand(s) on or near the ground, moves his hand(s), or makes any quick movement.
    d. An offensive player between the snapper and the player on the end of the line, neither legally in the backfield nor legally on the line of scrimmage after having placed a hand(s) on or near the ground (below the knees), moves his hand(s) or makes any quick movement.

(*Exception*: (1) It is not a false start if any player on the line of scrimmage moves when threatened by a Team B player in the neutral-zone. The threatened Team A player may not enter the neutral-zone. (2) The snapper may take his hands off the ball if he does not simulate the start of play.

5. An official shall sound his whistle when:

    a. There is a false start.

    b. An offensive player is in or beyond the neutral-zone after the snapper touches the ball.

    c. A Team A player moves when threatened by a Team B player in the neutral-zone.

Note: An infraction of this rule may be penalised whether or not the ball is snapped and the penalty for any resultant off-side or contact foul other than unsportmanlike or personal fouls by an opponent shall be cancelled (S19 and S7).

(*b*) *When the snap starts*:

The offensive team must be in a formation that meets these requirements:

1. At least 7 players on their scrimmage line, not less than 5 of whom shall be numbered 50 to 79. The remaining players must be either on their scrimmage line or behind their backfield line.

Exceptions: (1) Rule 1-4-2-b. (2) One player may be between his scrimmage line and his backfield line if in a position to receive a hand-to-hand snap from between the snapper's legs. When in such position, that player may receive the snap himself or it may go directly to any player legally in the backfield (S19).

Additional Requirements:

(*a*) The player on each side of and next to the snapper may lock legs with the snapper, but any other line-man of the team on offence must have both feet outside the outside foot of the player next to him when the ball is snapped (S19).

(*b*) All players must be in-bounds and only the snapper may be encroaching on the neutral-zone, but no part of his person may be beyond the neutral-zone and his feet must be stationary behind the ball (S19).

(*c*) One offensive player may be in motion, but not in motion toward his opponents' goal-line. If such player starts from his scrimmage line, he must be at least 5 yards behind that line when the ball is snapped. Other offensive players must be stationary in their positions without movement of the feet, body, head or arms (S20).

Penalty: For foul before ball is snapped – 5 yards from succeeding spot. For foul when the ball is snapped – 5 yards from previous spot (S7 and S19).

Defensive Team Requirements
ARTICLE 4. The defensive team requirements are as follows:

(*a*) After the ball is ready for play and until it is snapped, no player on defence may touch the ball except when moved illegally as in Rule 7-1-3-a-1 nor may any player contact an opponent or in any other way interefere with him (S7, S18). An official shall sound his whistle immediately.

(*b*) No defensive player may be in or beyond the neutral-zone at the snap (S18).

(*c*) No player of the team on defence shall use words or signals that disconcert opponents when they are preparing to put the ball in play. No player may call defensive signals that simulate the sound or cadence of (or otherwise interfere with) offensive starting signals. An official shall sound his whistle immediately (S7 and S19).

(*d*) At the snap, all defensive players must be in-bounds (S18).
Penalty: For foul before ball is snapped – 5 yards from succeeding spot. For fouls when the ball is snapped – 5 yards from previous spot (S7 and S18).

Shift Plays
ARTICLE 5. (*a*) If a snap is preceded by a huddle or shift, all players of the offensive team must come to an absolute stop and remain stationary in their positions, without movement of the feet, body, head or arms, for at least one full second before the ball is snapped.

(*b*) It is not intended that Rule 7-1-3-a should prohibit smooth, rhythmical shifts if properly executed. A smooth, cadence shift or unhurried motion is not an infraction. However, it is the responsibility of an offensive player who moves before the snap to do so in a manner that in no way simulates the beginning of a play. After the ball is ready for play and all players are in scrimmage formation, no offensive player shall make a quick, jerky movement before the snap. Any such motion is an infraction of the Rule. Although not intended to be all-inclusive, the following examples illustrate the type of movement prohibited before the snap:

1. A lineman moving his foot, shoulder, arm, body or head in a quick, jerky motion in any direction.

2. A centre shifting or moving the ball, or moving his thumb or fingers, or flexing elbows, jerking head or dipping shoulders or buttocks.

3. The quarterback 'chucking' hands at centre, flexing elbows under centre or dropping shoulders quickly just before the snap.

4. A player starting in motion before the snap simulating receiving the ball by 'chucking' his hands towards the centre or quarterback, or

making any quick, jerky movement that simulates the beginning of a play.

Penalty: 5 yards from previous spot, 5 yards from succeeding spot for foul before the ball is snapped (S7 and S20).

Handing the Ball Forward

ARTICLE 6. No player may hand the ball forward except during a scrimmage down as follows:

(*a*) A Team A player who is behind his scrimmage line may hand the ball forward to a backfield team-mate who is also behind that line.

(*b*) A Team A player who is behind his scrimmage line may hand the ball forward to a team-mate who was on his scrimmage line when the ball was snapped, provided that team-mate left his line position by a movement of both feet that faced him toward his own end-line and was at least 2yd behind his scrimmage line when he received the ball.

Penalty: 5 yards from spot of foul, also loss of a down if by Team A before team possession changes during a scrimmage down (S35 and S9).

SECTION 2. BACKWARD PASS AND FUMBLE

During Live Ball

ARTICLE 1. A runner may hand or pass the ball backward at any time, except to throw the ball intentionally out-of-bounds to conserve time.

Penalty: 5 yards from spot of foul, also loss of down if by Team A before team possession changes during a scrimmage down (S35 and S9). (*Exception*: Penalise from the previous spot if the foul, to conserve time, occurs beyond the neutral-zone before a change of team possession.)

Caught or Recovered

ARTICLE 2. A backward pass or fumble may be caught or recovered by any in-bounds player. (*Exception*: Rule 7-2-3.)

(*a*) If caught in flight in-bounds, the ball continues in play unless the catch is made on or behind the opponents' goal-line.

(*b*) If recovered by either team, the ball continues in play.

(*c*) If a backward pass or fumble is caught or recovered simultaneously by opposing players, the ball becomes dead and belongs to the team last in possession.

After the Ball is Snapped

ARTICLE 3. No offensive lineman may receive a snap although it is a backward pass.

Penalty: Live-ball foul. 5 yards from previous spot (S19).

Out-of-Bounds

ARTICLE 4. (*a*) When a backward pass goes out-of-bounds between the goal-lines, the ball belongs to the passing team at the out-of-bounds spot; if out-of-bounds behind a goal-line, it is touch-back or a safety.

(*b*) When a fumble is out-of-bounds in advance of the spot of the fumble, the ball is returned to the fumbling team at the spot of the fumble. Fumbles out-of-bounds behind the spot of the fumble belong to the fumbling team at the out-of-bounds spot. (*Exception*: The ball belongs to the defending team at the spot of the fumble when the offensive team fumbles and the ball goes out-of-bounds in the opponent's end-zone.)

At Rest

ARTICLE 5. When a backward pass or fumble comes to rest in-bounds and no player attempts to secure it, the ball becomes dead and belongs to the passing or fumbling team at the dead-ball spot.

SECTION 3. FORWARD PASS

Legal Forward Pass

ARTICLE 1. Team A may make one forward pass during each scrimmage down before team possession changes, provided the pass is thrown from a point in or behind the neutral-zone.

Illegal Forward Pass

ARTICLE 2. A forward pass is illegal:

(*a*) If thrown by Team A when the passer is beyond the neutral-zone.

(*b*) If thrown by Team B, or if thrown by Team A after team possessions has changed during the down.

(*c*) If it is the second forward pass by Team A during the same down.

(*d*) If intentionally thrown into an area not occupied by an eligible Team A player to save loss of yardage.

(*e*) If to conserve time, the pass is not thrown immediately after receiving the snap.

(*f*) If thrown from behind the neutral-zone after the runner has crossed the neutral-zone.

Penalty: 5 yards from spot of foul, also loss of a down if by Team A before team possession changes during a scrimmage down (S35 or S36 and S9). (*Exception*: Penalise 5 yards from the previous spot and loss of down if the foul, to conserve time, occurs beyond the neutral-zone before a change of team possession.)

Eligibility to Touch Legal Pass

ARTICLE 3. Eligibility rules apply during a down when a legal forward pass is thrown. All Team B players are eligible to touch or catch a pass. When the ball is snapped, the following Team A players are eligible:

(a) Each player who is in an end position on his scrimmage line and who is wearing a number other than 50 to 79.

(b) Each player who is legally in his backfield wearing a number other than 50 to 79.

(c) A player wearing a number other than 50 to 79, in position to receive a hand-to-hand snap from between the snapper's legs.

Eligibility Lost by Going Out of Bounds

ARTICLE 4. No eligible offensive player who goes out-of-bounds during a down shall touch a legal forward pass in the field of play or end-zone until it has been touched by an opponent.

Exception: This does not apply to an eligible offensive player who attempts to return in-bounds immediately after being blocked or pushed out-of-bounds by an opponent.

Penalty: Loss of down at previous spot [S16 and S9].

Eligibility Regained

ARTICLE 5. When a Team B player touches a legal forward pass all players become eligible.

Completed Pass

ARTICLE 6. Any forward pass is completed when caught by a player of the passing team who is in-bounds, and the ball continues in play unless the completion results in a touch-down, or the pass has been caught simultaneously by opposing players. If a forward pass is caught simultaneously by opposing players in-bounds, the ball becomes dead and belongs to the passing team.

Incompleted Pass

ARTICLE 7. (a) Any forward pass is incomplete when the pass touches the ground or goes out-of-bounds. It is also incomplete when a player jumps and receives the pass but first lands on or outside a boundary line unless his forward progress has been stopped in the field of play (Rule 2-2-7-c).

(b) When a legal forward pass is incomplete, the ball belongs to the passing team at the previous spot.

(c) When an illegal forward pass is incomplete, the ball belongs to the passing team at the spot of the pass. (*Exception*: If any illegal pass is thrown from the end-zone, the offended team may accept a safety or decline the penalty and accept the result of the play.)

Illegal Contact and Pass Interference

ARTICLE 8. (*a*) During a down in which a legal forward pass crosses the neutral-zone, illegal contact by Team A and Team B players is prohibited from the time the ball is snapped until it is touched by any player.

(*b*) Offensive pass interference by a Team A player beyond the neutral-zone during a legal forward pass play in which a forward pass crosses the neutral-zone is contact that interferes with a Team B eligible player. It is the responsibility of the offensive player to avoid the opponents. It is not offensive pass interference if it is the type that occurs:

1. When, immediately following the snap, a Team A player charges and contacts an opponent at a point not more than 1 yard beyond the neutral-zone and does not continue the contact more than 3 yards beyond the neutral-zone.

2. When 2 or more eligible players are making a simultaneous and bona fide attempt to reach, catch or bat the pass. Eligible players of either team have equal rights to the ball.

(*c*) Defensive pass interference is contact beyond the neutral-zone by a Team B player whose intent to impede an eligible opponent is obvious and it could prevent the opponent the opportunity of receiving a catchable forward pass. When in question, a legal forward pass is catchable. Defensive pass interference occurs only after a forward pass is thrown. It is not defensive pass interference if it is the type that occurs:

1. When, immediately following the snap, opposing players charge and establish contact with opponents at a point that is within 1 yard beyond the neutral-zone.

2. When 2 or more eligible players are making a simultaneous and bona fide attempt to reach, catch or bat the pass, eligible players of either team have equal rights to the ball.

3. When a Team B player legally contacts an opponent before the pass is thrown.

Penalty: Pass interference by Team A: 15 yards from previous spot plus loss of down (S33 and S9). Pass interference by Team B: Team A's ball at spot of foul, first down, if the foul occurs less than 15 yards beyond the previous spot. If the foul occurs 15 or more yards beyond the previous spot, Team A's ball, first down, 15-yard penalty from previous spot. When the ball is snapped between the Team B 17-yard-line and the Team B 2-yard line and the spot of the foul is beyond the 2-yard line, the penalty shall place the ball at the 2-yard line, first down. No penalty enforced from outside the 2-yard line may place the ball inside the 2-

yard line. (*Exception*: Rule 10-2-2-g-2.) If the previous spot was on or inside the 2-yard line, first down halfway between the previous spot and the goal-line (S33) (Rule 10-2-3 Exception).

Contact Interference
ARTICLE 9 (*a*) Either Team A or Team B may legally interfere with opponents behind the neutral-zone.

(*b*) Players of either team may legally interfere beyond the neutral-zone after the pass has been touched.

(*c*) Defensive players may legally contact opponents who have crossed the neutral-zone if the opponents are not in a position to receive a catchable forward pass.

1. Those infractions that occur during a down when a forward pass crosses the neutral-zone are pass interference infractions only if the receiver had the opportunity to receive a catchable forward pass.

2. Those infractions that occur during a down when a forward pass does not cross the neutral-zone are Rule 9-3-4 infractions and are penalised from the previous spot.

(*d*) Pass interference rules apply only during a down in which a legal forward pass crosses the neutral-zone (Rules 2-19-3, 7-3-8-a and c).

(*e*) Contact by Team B with an eligible receiver that involves unnecessary roughness that interferes with a catchable pass is penalised as pass interference, but fouls occurring less than 15 yards beyond the neutral-zone may be penalised 15 yards as personal fouls from the previous spot. Rule 7-3-8 is specific about contact during a pass. However, if the interference involves an act that would ordinarily result in disqualification, the fouling player must leave the game.

(*f*) Physical contact is required to establish interference.

(*g*) Each player has territorial rights and incidental contact is ruled under 'attempting to reach . . . the pass' in Rule 7-3-8. If opponents who are beyond the line collide while moving toward the pass, a foul by one or both players is indicated only if intent to impede the opponent is obvious. It is pass interference by Team B only if a catchable forward pass is involved.

(*h*) Pass interference rules do not apply after the pass has been touched anywhere in-bounds by an in-bounds player. If an opponent is fouled, the penalty is for the foul not the pass interference.

(*i*) After the pass has been touched, any player may execute a legal block during the remaining flight of the pass.

(*j*) Tackling or grasping a receiver or any other intentional contact before he touches the pass is evidence that the tackler is disregarding the ball and is therefore illegal.

(*k*) Tackling or running into a receiver when a forward pass is obviously underthrown or overthrown is disregarding the ball and is illegal. This is not pass interference but a violation of Rule 9-1-2-f and is penalised 15 yards from the previous spot, plus a first down.

Ineligibles Downfield
ARTICLE 10. No eligible player shall be or have been beyond the neutral-zone until a legal forward pass that crosses the neutral-zone has been thrown.
Exceptions:
1. Immediately after the snap, a Team A player charges and contacts an opponent at a point not more than 1 yard beyond the neutral-zone and does not continue the contact more than 3 yards beyond the neutral-zone.
2. When contact that has driven an opponent no more than 3 yards from the neutral-zone is lost by a player who was ineligible at the snap, he must remain stationary at that spot until the pass is thrown.
Penalty: 5 yards from previous spot (S37).

Illegal Touching
ARTICLE 11. No originally ineligible player while in-bounds shall touch a legal forward pass until it has touched an opponent.
Penalty: 5 yards from previous spot plus loss of a down (S16 and S9).

RULE 8

Scoring

SECTION 1. VALUE OF SCORES

Scoring Plays
ARTICLE 1. The point-value of scoring plays shall be:

Touch-down	6 points
Field goal	3 points
Safety (points awarded to opponents)	2 points
Successful try touch-down	2 points
Successful try field goal or safety	1 point

Forfeited Games
ARTICLE 2. The score of a forfeited game shall be: Offended Team – 1 Opponent – 0. If the offended team is ahead at the time of forfeit, the score stands.

SECTION 2. TOUCH-DOWN

How Scored
ARTICLE 1. A touch-down shall be scored when:

(*a*) A runner advancing from the field of play is legally in possession of a live ball when it penetrates the opponents' goal-line (plane).

(*b*) An eligible receiver catches a legal forward pass in the opponent's end-zone.

(*c*) A fumble or backward pass is recovered, caught, intercepted, or awarded in the opponent's end-zone.

(*d*) A free kick is legally caught or recovered in the opponent's end-zone.

(*e*) A scrimmage kick is legally caught or recovered in the opponent's end-zone.

(*f*) The Referee awards a touch-down under the provisions of Rule 9-1-4 penalty and Rule 9-2-3.

SECTION 3. TRY

How Scored
ARTICLE 1. The point or points shall be scored according to the point-values in Rule 8-1-1 if the try results in what would be a touch-down, safety or field goal under Rules governing play at other times.

Opportunity to Score
ARTICLE 2. A try is an opportunity for either team to score 1 or 2 additional points while the game clock is stopped and is a special interval in a game which, for purposes of penalty enforcement only, includes both a down and the 'ready' period that precedes it.

(*a*) The ball shall be put in play by the team that scored a 6-point touch-down. (*Exception*: Rule 3-2-3-c.)

(*b*) The try, which is a scrimmage down, begins when the ball is ready for play.

(*c*) The snap may be from any point on or between the in-bounds lines on or behind the opponents' 3-yard line if the position of the ball is selected prior to the ready for play. The ball may be relocated following a charged time-out to either team unless preceded by a Team A foul or offsetting penalties (Rules 8-3-3-a and 8-3-3-c-1).

(*d*) The try ends when:
1. Either team scores.
2. Neither team scores and the ball is dead by Rule.
3. If an accepted penalty results in a score.
4. A Team A loss of down penalty is accepted (See Rule 8-3-3-c-2).

Foul During Try for Point Before Team B Possession

ARTICLE 3 (*a*) Offsetting fouls: The down shall be replayed if offsetting fouls occur. Any replay after offsetting penalities must be from the previous spot.

(*b*) Fouls by B on successful try:

1. Team A shall have the option of declining the score and repeating the try after enforcement, or accepting the score with enforcement of the penalty from the spot of the next kick-off.

2. A replay after a penalty against Team B may be from any point between the in-bounds lines on the yard-line where the penalty leaves the ball.

(*c*) Fouls by A on successful or unsuccessful try:

1. After a foul by Team A, on a successful try, the ball shall be put in play at the spot where the penalty leaves it.

2. Penalties against Team A on a try, which include loss of down and yardage, nullify the score and yardage is not penalised on the succeeding kick-off. (*Note*: If Team B scores, the penalty is assessed on the succeeding kick-off.)

(*d*) Roughing or running into kicker or holder:

1. Roughing or running into the kicker or holder is a live-ball foul.

(*e*) Kick catch interference:

1. The penalty for interference with a kick catch is penalised on the succeeding kick-off.

Fouls during a Try After Team B Possession

ARTICLE 4. (*a*) Distance penalties by either team are enforced on the succeeding kick-off.

(*b*) Scores by fouling teams are cancelled.

(*c*) Offsetting fouls, whether one or both occur after Team B possession, the down is not replayed.

Fouls After a Try

ARTICLE 5. Fouls after a try down and before the next kick-off are penalised on the succeeding kick-off.

Next Play

ARTICLE 6. After a try the ball shall be put in play by a kick-off. The field captain of the team against which the 6-point touch-down was scored shall designate which team shall kick off.

SECTION 4. FIELD GOAL

How Scored

ARTICLE 1. (*a*) A field goal shall be scored for the kicking team if a drop kick or place kick passes over the cross-bar between the uprights of the receiving team's goal before it touches a player of the kicking team or the ground. The kick shall be a scrimmage kick but may not be a free kick.

(b) If a legal field goal attempt passes over the cross-bar between the uprights and is grounded beyond the end-lines or is blown back but does not return over the cross-bar and is grounded anywhere, it shall score a field goal. The entire goal, cross-bar, and uprights are treated as a line not a plane in determining forward progress of the ball.

Next Play

ARTICLE 2. (a) After a field goal is scored the ball shall be put in play by a kick-off. The field captain of the team scored against shall designate which team shall kick off.

(b) Following an unsuccessful field goal attempt that crosses the neutral-zone, the ball, untouched by Team B beyond the neutral-zone, will next be put in play at the previous spot. If the previous spot was between Team B's 20-yard line and goal-line, the ball shall next be put in play at the 20-yard line. Otherwise, all rules pertaining to scrimmage kicks apply.

SECTION 5. SAFETY

How Scored

ARTICLE 1. It is a safety when:

(a) The ball becomes dead out-of-bounds behind a goal-line (except from an incompleted forward pass), or becomes dead in the possession of a player on, above, or behind his own goal-line, and the defending team is responsible for the ball being there.

(b) An accepted penalty for a foul leaves the ball on or behind the offending team's goal-line.

Exception: When a Team B player intercepts a forward pass or catches a scrimmage or free kick between his 5-yard line and the goal-line and his original momentum carries him into the end-zone where the ball is declared dead in his team's possession or it goes out-of-bounds in the end-zone, the ball belongs to Team B at the spot where the pass was intercepted or the kick was caught.

Kick After Safety

ARTICLE 2. After a safety is scored, the ball belongs to the defending team at its own 20-yard line, and that team shall put the ball in play between the in-bounds lines by a free kick that may be a punt, drop kick or place kick.

SECTION 6. TOUCH-BACK

When Declared
ARTICLE 1. It is a touch-back when:

(*a*) The ball becomes dead out-of-bounds behind a goal-line (except from an incomplete forward pass) or becomes dead in the possession of a player on, above, or behind his own goal-line, and the attacking team is responsible for the ball being there. (*Exception*: Rule 7-2-4-b exception.)

(*b*) A kick becomes dead by Rule behind the defending team's goal-line, and the attacking team is responsible for the ball being there. (*Exception*: Rule 8-4-2-b.)

(*c*) A violation by the kicking team occurs in the receiving team's end-zone.

Snap After a Touch-back
ARTICLE 2. After a touch-back is declared, the ball belongs to the defending team at its own 20-yard line, and that team shall put the ball in play between the in-bound lines by snap.

SECTION 7. RESPONSIBILITY AND IMPETUS

Responsibility
ARTICLE 1. The team responsible for the ball being out-of-bounds behind a goal-line or being dead in the possession of a player on or above or behind a goal-line is the team whose player carries the ball or imparts an impetus to it that forces it on, above or across the goal-line, or is responsible for a loose ball being on, above or behind the goal-line.

Initial Impetus
ARTICLE 2. (*a*) The impetus imparted by a player who kicks, passes, snaps or fumbles the ball shall be considered responsible for the ball's progress in any direction even though its course is deflected or reversed after striking the ground or after touching a player of either team.

(*b*) Initial impetus is considered expended and responsibility for the ball's progress is charged to a player:

1. If he kicks a ball not in player possession or bats a loose ball after it strikes the ground. (*Exception*: The original impetus is not changed when a loose ball is batted or kicked in the end-zone.)

2. If the ball comes to rest and he gives it new impetus by any contact with it. (*Exceptions*: (1) Rules 6-1-4-a and 6-3-4-a. (2) The original impetus is not changed when a ball at rest in the end-zone is moved when touched by a player.)

(*c*) For the purpose of penalty enforcement, a kick remains a kick when there is new impetus.

RULE 9

Conduct of Players and Others Subject to Rules

SECTION 1. PERSONAL AND INTERFERENCE FOULS

Flagrant Fouls
ARTICLE 1. During the game and between periods, all flagrant fouls require disqualification. Team B disqualification fouls may require first downs if not in conflict with other Rules.

Persons Subject to the Rules Restrictions
ARTICLE 2. No person subject to the Rules shall commit a personal foul during the game or between the periods. Any act prohibited hereunder or any other act of unnecessary roughness is a personal foul.

(*a*) No person subject to the Rules shall strike an opponent with the knee, or strike an opponent's head, neck or face or any part of the body with an extended forearm, elbow, locked hands, palm, fist or the heel, back or side of the open hand or gouge an opponent during the game or between the periods.

(*b*) No person subject to the Rules shall strike an opponent with his foot or any part of his leg that is below the knee.

(*c*) There shall be no tripping. (*Exception*: The runner.)

(*d*) There shall be no clipping.

Exceptions: (1) When offensive players are on the line of scrimmage at the snap within a rectangular area centered on the middle lineman of the offensive formation and extending 5 yards laterally, and 3 yards longitudinally in each direction, they may legally clip in the rectangular area.

    a. A player on the line of scrimmage within the legal clipping zone may not leave the zone and return and legally clip.

    b. The legal clipping zone exists until the ball is fumbled, muffed or is in player possession outside the legal clipping zone or the ball is outside the legal clipping zone after a fumble from inside the clipping zone.

(2) When a player turns his back on a potential blocker who has committed himself in intent and direction or movement.

(3) When a player attempts to reach a runner or legally attempts to recover or catch a fumble, a muff, a backward pass, a kick or a touched forward pass, he may use his hands or arms on the back of an opponent to push him out of the way.

(4) When the opponent turns his back to the blocker under Rule 9-3-3-1-c.

(5) When a player behind the neutral zone pushes an opponent in the back to get to a forward pass.

Penalty: 15 yards and first down if Team B fouls and first down is not in conflict with other rules. Previous spot enforcement if by Team A behind the neutral zone (S39).

(*e*) Blocking below the waist is permitted except as follows:

1. Offensive players at the snap positioned more than 7 yards in any direction from the middle lineman of the offensive formation or in motion toward the ball at the snap are prohibited from blocking below the waist towards the ball until the ball has advanced beyond the neutral zone. The following formation sets are legal and the players are not restricted by Rule 9-1-2-e when blocking toward the ball:

   a. An offensive end position less than 2 yards from the legal clipping zone.

   b. A wingback positioned 1 yard to the outside of an end who is flexed no more than 1 yard from the legal clipping zone.

   c. A wingback positioned no more than 1 yard outside the legal clipping zone and inside an end who is 1 yard outside the wingback.

2. During a scrimmage down, defensive players are prohibited from blocking an eligible Team A receiver below the waist beyond the neutral zone unless attempting to get at the ball or runner. A Team A receiver remains eligible until a legal forward pass is no longer possible by rule.

3. During a down in which there is a free kick or scrimmage kick from a scrimmage kick formation, all players are prohibited from blocking below the waist except against the runner.

4. After any change of team possession all players are prohibited from blocking below the waist except against the runner.

5. A Team A player behind the neutral-zone and in position to receive a backward pass shall not be blocked below the waist.

(*f*) No player shall tackle or run into a receiver when a forward pass to him is obviously not catchable. This is a personal foul and is not pass interference.

(*g*) There shall be no piling on, falling on, or throwing the body on an opponent after the ball becomes dead.

(*h*) No opponent shall tackle or block the runner when he is clearly out of bounds or throw him to the ground after the ball becomes dead.

(*i*) There shall be no hurdling.

(*j*) No player shall run into or throw himself against an opponent obviously out of the play either before or after the ball is dead.

(*k*) No player shall grasp the face mask or any helmet opening of an opponent. The open hand may be legally used on the mask.

Penalty: Defensive team 5 yards incidental grasping, 15 yards for twisting, turning or pulling and first down for Team B foul if not in conflict with other rules. Offensive team 15 yards. All dead-ball fouls 15 yards and a first down for a Team B foul if not in conflict with other Rules. Flagrant offenders shall be disqualified (S45).

(*l*) No player shall intentionally use his helmet to butt or ram an opponent.

(*m*) There shall be no spearing.

(*n*) No player shall intentionally strike a runner with the crown or the top of his helmet.

(*o*) No defensive player shall charge into a passer or throw him to the ground when it is obvious the ball has been thrown. This is roughing the passer, and the penalty is added to the end of the last run when it ends beyond the neutral zone and there is no change of team possession.

(*p*) There shall be no chop blocking.

(*q*) No defensive player, in an attempt to gain an advantage, may step, jump or stand on an opponent.

(*r*) No player may swing an arm or hand and miss an opponent, or kick at and miss an opponent.

(*s*) No player shall continuously contact the head of an opponent (*Exception*: The runner.)

Penalty: 15 yards and a first down for Team B fouls and the first down is not in conflict with the other rules (S24, S34, S38, S39, S40, S41, S45 or S46). Flagrant offenders shall be disqualified (S47).

Roughing or Running into Kicker or Holder

ARTICLE 3. (*a*) When it is obvious that a scrimmage kick will be made, no opponent shall run into or rough the kicker or the holder of a place kick.

1. Roughing is a personal foul that endangers the kicker or holder.

2. Running into the kicker or holder is a foul that occurs when the kicker or holder are displaced from their kicking or holding positions but are not roughed.

3. Incidental contact with a kicker or holder is not a foul.

4. The kicker and holder must be protected from injury but contact that occurs when or after a scrimmage kick has been touched is not roughing or running into the kicker.

5. The kicker of a scrimmage kick loses protection as a kicker when he has had a reasonable time to regain his balance.

6. A defensive player blocked into the kicker or holder by a member

of the kicking team is not exempt from running into or roughing the kicker fouls.

7. When a player, other than one who blocks a scrimmage kick, runs into or roughs the kicker or holder after the kick is blocked, it is a foul.

8. When in question whether the foul is 'running into' or 'roughing' the foul is 'roughing'.

Penalty: 5 yards previous spot for running into kicker or holder (S30). 15 yards previous spot and also first down for roughing kicker or holder (S30 and S38). Flagrant offenders shall be disqualified (S47).

(*b*) A kicker or holder simulating being roughed or run into by a defensive player commits an unfair act.

Penalty: 15 yards previous spot (S27).

(*c*) The kicker of a free kick may not be blocked until he has advanced 5 yards beyond his restraining line or the kick has touched a player, an official or the ground.

Penalty: 15 yards previous spot (S40).

Illegal Interference

ARTICLE 4. (*a*) No substitute, coach, authorized attendant or any person subject to the rules other than a player or official, may interfere in any way with the ball or a player while the ball is in play.

Penalty: 15 yards from the enforcement spot most advantageous to the offended team. The Referee may enforce any penalty he considers equitable, including awarding a score (S27).

(*b*) Participation by 12 or more players is illegal participation.

Penalty: 15 yards from the enforcement spot most advantageous to the offended team (S28).

(*c*) No person, not subject to the Rules, may interfere in any way with the ball or a player while the ball is in play.

(*d*) Anything, other than persons subject to the Rules and those not subject to the Rules, interferes in any way with a player or the ball in play.

Penalty: The Referee may replay the down or take any action he deems equitable, including awarding a score (S27).

Game Administration Interference

ARTICLE 5. (*a*) While the ball is in play, coaches, substitutes and authorised attendants in the team area may not be between the side-lines and coaching line.

(*b*) The procedure for enforcement of Rule 9-1-5-a is as follows:

1. The Head Coach is informed by a game official that he is receiving a first or second warning because the area between the side-line and coaching line has been violated by coaches, players or persons authorised in the team area.

2. The official will record the time and period of each warning.

3. After a second warning, the official will notify the Head Coach that he has had two warnings and that the next infraction will result in a 5-yard penalty.

4. After a 5-yard penalty, the official will notify the Head Coach that he has had two warnings and a 5-yard penalty and will receive a 15-yard penalty for the next infraction.

5. The Referee shall stop the clock to give a side-line warning (S15).

Penalty: 5 yards after two official warnings from a game official and 15 yards for each additional foul. Penalise as a dead-ball foul (S27 and S29).

SECTION 2. NON-CONTACT FOULS

Unsportsmanlike Acts

ARTICLE 1. There shall be no unsportmanlike conduct or any act that interferes with orderly game administration on the part of players, substitutes, coaches, authorized attendants or any other persons subject to the Rules, either during the game or between periods.

(*a*) Specifically prohibited acts and conduct include:

1. No player, substitute, coach, authorized attendant or other persons subject to the Rules shall use abusive or insulting language to players or officials or indulge in any conduct that might incite players or spectators against officials.

2. If a player is injured, attendants may come in-bounds to attend him but they must obtain recognition from an official.

3. No person subject to the Rules, except players, officials and eligible substitutes, shall be on the field of play or end-zones during any period without permission from the Referee. (*Exception*: Rule 3-3-5.)

4. After a score or any other play the player in possession should return the ball to an official or leave it near the dead-ball spot. This prohibits:

   a. Kicking or throwing the ball any distance that requires an official to retrieve it.

   b. Spiking the ball to the ground. (*Exception*: A forward pass to conserve time – Rule 7-3-2-e.)

   c. Throwing the ball high into the air.

   d. Any other unsportsmanlike act or action that delays the game.

5. No player or substitutes shall use language, gestures or engage in acts that provoke ill will including:

   a. Pointing the finger(s), hand(s), arm(s) or ball at an opponent.

   b. Baiting an opponent verbally.

   c. Inciting an opponent in any other way.

6. No substitute may enter the field of play or end-zone for purposes other than replacing a player. This includes demonstrations after any play.

7. Any noise from persons subject to the Rules, including bands, that prohibits a team from hearing its signals.

Penalty: 15 yards (S7 and S27). Succeeding spot. Penalise as a dead-ball foul. Flagrant offenders, if players or substitutes, shall be disqualified (S47).

(*b*) Other prohibited acts include:

1. During the game, coaches, substitutes and authorized attendants in the team area shall not be on the field of play or outside the 25-yard lines without permission from the Referee unless legally entering or leaving the field. (*Exception*: Rule 3-3-8-c.)

2. No disqualified player shall enter the field.

Penalty: 15 yards (S7, S27). Succeeding spot. Penalise as a dead-ball foul. Flagrant offenders, if players or substitutes, shall be disqualified (S47).

Unfair Tactics

ARTICLE 2. (*a*) No player shall conceal the ball beneath his clothing or equipment or substitute any other article for the ball.

(*b*) No stimulated replacements or substitutions may be used to confuse opponents.

Penalty: 15 yards from the most advantageous spot to the offended team (S27). Flagrant offenders shall be disqualified (S47).

Unfair Acts

ARTICLE 3. (*a*) The Referee may enforce any penalty he considers equitable, including awarding a score:

1. If a team refuses to play within 2 minutes after ordered to do so by the Referee.

2. If a team repeatedly commits fouls that can be penalised only by halving the distance to its goal-line. The Referee shall, after one warning, forfeit the game to the opponents for Rules 9-2-3-a-1 and 2 infractions.

3. If an obviously unfair act not specifically covered by the Rules occurs during the game.

(*b*) Intentionally contacting a game official physically during the game by persons subject to the Rules is a foul.

SECTION 3. BLOCKING, USE OF HAND AND ARM

Who May Block

ARTICLE 1. Players of either team may block opponents provided it is not forward-pass interference, interference with opportunity to catch a kick, or a personal foul.

Interfering for or Helping the Runner
ARTICLE 2. (*a*) The runner or passer may use his hand or arm to ward off or push opponents.

(*b*) The runner shall not grasp a team-mate, and no other player of his team shall grasp, push, lift or charge into him to assist him in forward progress.

(*c*) Team-mates of the runner or passer may interfere for him by blocking but shall not use interlocked interference by grasping or encircling one another in any manner while contacting an opponent.
Penalty: 5 yards (S44).

Use of Hand or Arm by Offence
ARTICLE 3. (*a*) A team-mate of a runner or a passer may legally block with his shoulders, hands, outer surface of his arms or any other part of his body under the following provisions:
1. The hand(s) shall be:
   a. In advance of the elbow.
   b. Inside the frame of the opponent's body. (*Exception*: When the opponent turns his back to the blocker.)
   c. At or below the shoulder(s) of the blocker and the opponent. (*Exception*: when the opponent squats, ducks or submarines.)
2. The hand(s) shall be open with the palm(s) facing the frame of the opponent or closed or cupped with the palms not facing the opponent.
Penalty: 10 yards basic spot. 10 yards previous spot when the foul is behind the neutral-zone (S43).

(*b*) Holding or illegal obstruction by a team-mate of the runner or passer applies to Rule 9-3-3-a:
1. The hand(s) and arm(s) shall not be used to grasp, pull or encircle in any way that illegally impedes or illegally obstructs an opponent.
2. The hand(s) and arm(s) shall not be used to hook, lock, clamp or otherwise illegally impede or illegally obstruct an opponent.
Penalty: 10 yards basic spot. 10 yards previous spot when the foul is behind the neutral-zone (S42).

(*c*) The following acts by team-mate of the runner or passer are illegal:
1. The hand(s) and arm(s) shall not be used to deliver a blow.
2. During no block shall the hands be locked.
3. Continuous contact to the head of an opponent (Rule 9-1-2-s).
Penalty: 15 yards basic spot (S38). Disqualification if flagrant (S47).

(*d*) A crab or cross-body block is legal if there is no illegal contact with the hand(s) or arm(s).

Penalty: 10 yards (S43).

(*e*) A player on the kicing team may:

1. During a scrimmage kick play, use his hand(s) and/or arm(s) to ward off an opponent attempting to block him when he is beyond the neutral-zone.

2. During a free kick play, use his hand(s) and/or arm(s) to ward off an opponent who is attempting to block him.

3. During a scrimmage kick play when he is eligible to touch the ball, legally use his hand(s) and/or arm(s) to push an opponent in an attempt to reach a loose ball.

4. During a free kick play when he is eligible to touch the ball, legally use his hand(s) and/or arm(s) to push an opponent obstructing his attempt to reach a loose ball.

(*f*) A player of the passing team may legally use his hand(s) and/or arm(s) to ward off or push an opponent in an attempt to reach a loose ball after a legal forward pass has been touched by any player (See Rules 7-3-5, 7-3-8 and 7-3-11).

Use of Hands or Arms by Defence

ARTICLE 4. (*a*) Defensive players may use hands and arms to push, pull, ward off or lift offensive players when attempting to reach the runner.

(*b*) Defensive players may not use the hands and arms to tackle, hold or otherwise illegally obstruct an opponent other than a runner.

Penalty: 10 yards basic spot (S42).

(*c*) Defensive players may use hands and arms to push, grasp, ward off or lift offensive players obviously attempting to block them. Defensive players may ward off, legally block or push an eligible pass receiver until that player occupies the same yard-line as the defender or until the opponent could not possibly block him. Continuous contact is illegal (Rule 7-3-8-c).

Penalty: 5 yards incidental face-mask or 10 yards basic spot (S43).

(*d*) When no attempt is being made to get at the ball or the runner, defensive players must comply with Rules 9-3-3-a, b and c.

Penalty: 5 yards incidental face mask or 10 or 15 yards basic spot (S43, S42, or S38).

(*e*) When a legal forward pass crosses the neutral-zone during a forward pass play, and a contact foul that is not pass interference is committed, the enforcement spot is the previous spot. This includes Rule 9-3-4-c.

Penalty: 5 yards incidental face-mask, 10 or 15 yards plus first down if foul occurred against an eligible receiver (S43, S42, S45 or S38).

(*f*) A defensive player may legally use his hand or arm to ward off or push an opponent in an attempt to reach a loose ball (See Rule 9-1-2-4-d Exception 3).

1. During a backward pass, fumble or kick that he is eligible to touch.

2. During any forward pass that crossed the neutral-zone and has been touched by any player.

(g) A defensive player may not continuously contact an opponent's head with hand(s) or arm(s).

Penalty: First down and 15 yards from basic spot (S38).

Player Restrictions

ARTICLE 5. (a) No player may position himself with his feet on the back or shoulders of a team-mate prior to the snap.

Penalty: Dead-ball foul 15 yards (S27).

(b) No defensive player, in an attempt to block, bat or catch a kick, may:

1. Step, jump or stand on a team-mate.

2. Place a hand(s) on a team-mate to get leverage for additional height.

3. Be picked up by a team-mate.

Penalty: 15 yards basic spot (S27).

When Ball is Loose

ARTICLE 6. When the ball is loose, no player shall grasp, pull or tackle an opponent or commit a personal foul.

Penalty: 10 or 15 yards from the basic or previous spot (Rules 10-2-2-c, d, e and f) (S38 or S42).

SECTION 4. BATTING AND KICKING

Batting a Loose Ball

ARTICLE 1. (a) While a pass is in flight, any player eligible to touch the ball may bat it in any direction.

(b) Any player may block a scrimmage kick in the field of play or the end-zone.

(c) No player shall bat other loose balls forward in the field of play or in any direction if the ball is in the end-zone. (*Exception*: 6-3-11.)

Penalty: 15 yards from the basic spot and loss of down if not in conflict with other Rules (S9 and S31). (*Exception*: No loss of down if the foul occurs when a scrimmage kick is beyond the neutral-zone.) (Rules 10-2-2-c, d, e and f.) (S31).

Batting a Backward Pass
ARTICLE 2. A backward pass in flight shall not be batted forward by the passing team in an attempt to gain yardage.
Penalty: 15 yards from the basic spot (Rule 10-2-2-c) (S31).

Batting Ball in Possession
ARTICLE 3. A ball in player possession may not be batted forward by a player of that team.
Penalty: 15 yards from the basic spot (10-2-2-c) (S31).

Illegally Kicking Ball
ARTICLE 4. A player shall not kick a loose ball, a forward pass or a ball being held for a place kick by an opponent. These illegal acts do not change the status of the loose ball or forward pass; but if the player holding the ball for a place kick loses possession during a scrimmage down, it is a fumble and a loose ball; if during a free kick, the ball remains dead.
Penalty: 15 yards from the basic spot, also loss of down if not in conflict with other Rules (Rules 10-2-2-c, d, e, f) (S9 and S31). (*Exception*: No loss of down if the foul occurs when a scrimmage kick is beyond the neutral-zone.

RULE 10

Penalty Enforcement

SECTION 1. PENALTIES COMPLETED

How and When Completed
ARTICLE 1. (*a*) A penalty is completed when it is accepted, declined, cancelled according to Rule, or when the most advantageous choice is obvious to the Referee.

(*b*) Any penalty may be declined, but a disqualified player must leave the game.

(*c*) When a foul is committed at a time other than following a touchdown and before the ball is ready for play on a try, the penalty shall be completed before the ball is declared ready for play for any ensuing down. (*Exception*: Rule 10-2-2-g Touch-down.)

(*d*) Penalties as stated are not enforced if in conflict with other Rules.

Simultaneous with Snap
ARTICLE 2. A foul that occurs simultaneously with a snap or free kick is considered as occurring during that down.

Live-Ball Fouls by the Same Team
ARTICLE 3. When 2 or more live-ball fouls by the same team are reported to the Referee, the Referee shall explain the alternative penalties to the field captain of the offended team who may then elect only one of these penalties. (*Exception*: When a foul(s) for unsportsmanlike conduct (non-contact fouls) occurs, the penalty(ies) is administered from the succeeding spot as established by the acceptance or declination of the penalty for any other foul.

Offsetting Fouls
ARTICLE 4. If live-ball fouls by both teams are reported to the Referee, each such foul is an off-setting foul and the penalties cancel each other and the down is replayed.
Exceptions: 1. When there is a change of team possession during a down or at the end of a down by Rule, the team last gaining possession may decline off-setting fouls and thereby retain possession after completion of the penalty for its infraction if it had not fouled prior to its last gaining possession. (*Exception*: During a try.)
2. When Team B's foul is post-scrimmage kick enforcement, Team B may decline off-setting fouls and accept post-scrimmage kick enforcement.
3. When a live-ball foul is administered as a dead-ball foul, it does not offset and is enforced in order of occurrence.
4. Rule 8-3-4-c (during a try after Team B possession).

Dead-Ball Fouls
ARTICLE 5. Penalties for dead-ball fouls are administered separately and in order of occurrence.
Exception: When dead-ball fouls by both teams are reported and the order of occurrence cannot be determined, the fouls cancel, the number or type of down established before the fouls occurred is unaffected, and the penalties are disregarded, except that any disqualified player must leave the game (Rules 10-2-2-a and 5-2-6).

Live-Ball – Dead Ball Fouls
ARTICLE 6. When a live-ball foul by one team is followed by one or more dead-ball fouls (including live-ball fouls penalised as dead-ball fouls) by an opponent or by the same team, the penalties are administered separately and in the order of occurrence.

Interval Fouls
ARTICLE 7. Fouls that occur between the end of the fourth period and the start of the extra period for overtime are enforced from the kick-off. (*Exception*: Rule 10-2-2-g.)

SECTION 2. ENFORCEMENT PROCEDURES

Spots
ARTICLE 1. The enforcement spots are the previous spot, the spot of the foul, the succeeding spot, the post-scrimmage spot and the spot where the run ends.

Procedures
ARTICLE 2. When no enforcement spot is specified in a rule penalty, the following procedures apply:

(*a*) Dead Ball: The enforcement spot for a foul committed when the ball is dead is the succeeding spot.

(*b*) Snap or free kick: The enforcement spot for fouls occurring simultaneously with a snap or free kick is the previous spot.

(*c*) Running Plays: The basic enforcement spot for fouls that occur during running plays in the field of play or end-zones are as follows:

1. When the run ends beyond the neutral-zone, the basic enforcement spot is the end of the related run (Rule 2-25-10-a). (*Exceptions*: Rules 9-1-2-d and 9-3-3-a and b.)

2. When the run ends behind the neutral-zone before a change of team possession, the basic enforcement spot is the previous spot (Rule 2-25-10-b). (*Exceptions*: Rules 9-1-2-d and 9-3-3-a and b.)

3. When there is no neutral-zone, the basic enforcement spot is the end of the related run (Rule 2-25-10-c).

(*d*) Pass plays: The basic enforcement spot for fouls during a legal forward pass play is the previous spot.

Exceptions:

1. Team B pass interference spot fouls.

2. Rules 9-1-2-d and 9-3-3-a and b fouls.

3. Roughing the passer enforcement on a completed forward pass from the end of the last run when that run ends beyond the neutral-zone and there is no change of team possession.

4. Illegal Touching.

(*e*) Kick plays: The basic enforcement spot for fouls that occur during a legal free or scrimmage kick play before possession is gained or regained or the ball is declared dead by Rule is the previous spot. (*Exceptions*: Rules 9-1-3-d and 9-3-3-a and b.)

Note – Other kick-play enforcements:

1. Interference with the opportunity to make a catch – spot foul (Rule 6-4-1).

2. Team A, during a scrimmage kick untouched by Team B beyond

the neutral zone, bats a loose ball behind Team B's goal line – a violation and a touch-back.

3. A block or foul after a valid, invalid or illegal signal for a pair catch by a Team B player who signalled for a fair catch during a free kick and had not touched the ball – spot foul (Rule 6-5-4).

4. Illegal fair catch signal during a free kick – spot foul (Rule 6-5-3).

5. Post-scrimmage kick enforcement. The basic enforcement spot is the spot where the kick ends when Team B fouls occur:

   a. During scrimmage kick plays other than a try.
   b. During a kick that crosses the neutral-zone.
   c. Three yards beyond the neutral-zone.
   d. Prior to the end of the kick.
   e. When Team B has possession of the ball when the down ends.

6. The enforcement spot for illegal participation during a free kick or scrimmage kick play is the spot most advantageous to the offended team (Rule 9-1-4-b).

(f) Behind the goal-line:

1. The enforcement spot is the goal-line for fouls by the opponents of the team in possession after a change of team possession (not on a try) in the field of play when the run ends behind the goal-line. Safety if no foul occurred. (*Exception*: Rule 8-5-1.)

2. The basic enforcement spot is the 20-yard line for fouls that occur after a change of team possession in the end-zone and the ball remains in the end-zone where it is declared dead. These are live-ball fouls. Touch-back if no foul occurred.

3. The enforcement spot is the goal-line for fouls by the opponents of the team in possession after change of possession in the end-zone (not on a try) when the run ends behind the goal-line and subsequent loose ball is recovered in the field of play.

(g) Fouls during and after touch-downs, field goals and tries.

1. Distance penalties for fouls by opponent of the scoring team during a down that ends in a touch-down may be penalised on the try or at the succeeding kick-off. The scoring team captain will select the enforcement spot.

2. Defensive pass interference fouls on a touch-down play are penalised one half the distance to the goal on the try or 15 yards on the succeeding kick-off. The scoring team captain will select the enforcement spot.

3. When a foul(s) occur(s) after a touch-down and before the ball is ready for play for the try, the enforcement is on the try or at the succeeding kick-off. The offended team captain will select the enforcement spot.

4. Distance penalties for fouls by the opponents of the scoring team on a successful field goal are penalised on the succeeding kick-off or

the field goal may be cancelled and the penalty enforced by rule. (*Exception*: 10-2-2-e-5.)

5. Fouls during a try down are penalised under Rule 8-3-3.

6. Fouls, following a try down and before the next kick-off will be enforced on the kick-off.

(*h*) Distance penalties for fouls by the receiving team may not extend the receiving team's restraining line behind its 5-yard line. Fouls that place the restraining line of the receiving team behind its 5-yard line are enforced from the next succeeding spot.

Half-Distance Enforcement Procedure
ARTICLE 3. No distance penalty shall exceed half the distance from the enforcement spot to the offending team's goal-line. (*Exception*: Defensive pass interference penalties.)

THE FOOTBALL CODE
The British American Football League (BAFL) Code of Ethics states:

(*a*) The Football Code shall be an integral part of this Code of Ethics and should be carefully read and observed.

(*b*) To gain an advantage by circumvention or disregard for the Rules brands a coach or player as unfit to be associated with football.

Football is and should be an aggressive, rugged, contact sport. However, there is no place in the game for unfair tactics, unsportsmanlike conduct or manoeuvres deliberately designed to inflict injury.

Through the years the Rules Committees have endeavoured by rule and appropriate penalty to prohibit all forms of unnecessary roughness, unfair tactics and unsportsmanlike conduct. But rules alone cannot accomplish this end. Only the continued best efforts of coachs, players, officials and all friends of the game can preserve the high ethical standards that the public has a right to expect. Therefore, as a guide to players, coaches, officials and others responsible for the welfare of the game, the committee publishes the following code:

Coaching Ethics
Deliberately teaching players to violate the Rules is indefensible. The coaching of intentional holding, beating the ball, illegal shifting, feigning injury, interference or illegal forward passing, such as the 'forward fumble', will break down rather than aid in the building of the character of players. Teaching or condoning intentional 'roughing', including the blind side blocking of an opponent below the waist anywhere on the field, is indefensible. Such instruction is not only unfair to one's opponents but is demoralising to the boys entrusted to a coach's care. It has no place in a game that is an essential part of an educational

programme. Changing numbers during the game to deceive opponents is an unethical act.

The football helmet is for the protection of the player and is not to be used as a weapon.

(*a*) The helmet shall not be used as the brunt of the contact in the teaching of blocking and tackling.

(*b*) Self-propelled mechanical apparatus shall not be used in the teaching of blocking and tackling.

(*c*) Greater emphasis by players, coaches and officials should be placed on eliminating spearing.

The use of non-therapeutic drugs in the game of football is not in keeping with the aims and purposes of amateur athletics and is prohibited.

Illegal Use of Hand or Arm

Indiscriminate use of hand or arm is unfair play, eliminates skill and does not belong in the game. The object of the game is to advance the ball by strategy, skill and speed without using illegal tactics.

Perhaps a good game could be invented, the object of which would be to advance the ball as far as possible with the assistance of holding, but it would not be football. It would probably become a team wrestling match of some kind.

'Beating the Ball'

'Beating the ball' by an unfair use of a starting signal is nothing less than deliberately stealing an advantage from the opponents. An honest starting signal is good football; but a signal that has for its purpose starting the team a fraction of a second before the ball is put in play, in the hope that it will not be detected by the officials, is nothing short of crookedness. It is the same as if a sprinter in a 100-yard dash had a secret arrangement with the starter to give him a tenth of a second warning before he fired the pistol.

Illegal Shifting

An honest shift is good football, but shaving the one-second pause, shifting in such manner as to simulate the start of a play or employing any other unfair tactic for the purpose of drawing one's opponents offside can be construed only as a deliberate attempt to gain an unmerited advantage. Such tactics cannot be tolerated in football.

Feigning injuries

An injured player must be given full protection under the rules. However, the feigning of an injury by an uninjured player for the purpose of gaining additional, undeserved time for his team is dishonest, unsportsmanlike and contrary to the spirit of the rules. Such tactics cannot be tolerated among sportsmen of integrity.

Talking to Your Opponents
Talking to opponents, if it falls short of being abusive or insulting, is not prohibited by the rules, but no good sportsman is ever guilty of cheap talk to his opponents.

Talking to Officials
When an official imposes a penalty or makes a decision, he is simply doing his duty as he sees it. He is on the field to uphold the integrity of the game of football, and his decisions are final and conclusive and should be accepted by players and coaches.

(*a*) On- and off-the-record criticism of officials to players or to the public shall be considered unethical.

(*b*) For a coach to address, or permit anyone on his bench to address, uncomplimentary remarks to any official during the progress of a game, or to indulge in conduct that might incite players or spectators against the officials, is a violation of the rules of the game and must likewise be considered conduct unworthy of a member of the coaching profession.

Sportsmanship
The football player who intentionally violates a rule is guilty of unfair play and unsportsmanlike conduct, and whether or not he escapes being penalised he brings discredit to the good name of the game, which it is his duty as a player to uphold.

Reprinted by permission of the British American Football Association, and with special thanks to the British American Football Referees' Association. For reasons of space, Rule 11 (The Officials: Jurisdiction and Duties, including Official Football Signals) and Rules and Interpretations have been omitted. Copies of the complete Rules and Interpretations may be obtained from the British American Football Association.

Archery

Archery

Grand National Archery Society (GNAS) Laws

3. The shooting regulations as prescribed in its Rules of Shooting shall be accepted as governing the relevant branches of the sport of archery throughout the area under the Society's jurisdiction. The Rules of Shooting are the responsibility of the National Council.

4. No Regional Society, County Association, archery club or similar organisation recognised by the Society shall include in its Constitution or Shooting Regulations any provisions which conflict with those of the Society. A copy of each County Association's and Regional Society's Constitution shall be deposited with the National Council.

12. All members, affiliated clubs, associated organisations, associations, county associations and regional societies shall accept the jurisdiction of the Society and shall conform to such conditions, shooting rules and regulations as may be determined from time to time.

14. (*a*) No archer other than a member of the Society or one whose national society is affiliated to the Federation Internationale de Tir a l'Arc may compete or officiate at any of the Society's meetings or at any meeting of a Regional Society or a County Association or at a Club or Association affiliated to a Regional Society. This clause does not apply to Ladies Paramount.

(*b*) No archer other than a British National of the United Kingdom may be the holder of a British National Championship or of any of the challenge trophies offered at the British National Target Championship meetings and the Grand National Archery meeting.

(*c*) A professional archer may not hold a Championship title or challenge trophy nor may he receive any prize in connection with any tournament organised by or held under the auspices of the Grand National Archery Society or any affiliated body unless specifically offered for competition for professional archers only, not shooting in competition with amateurs.

A professional archer is one who uses his skill in shooting with the bow and arrow as a means of making his living.

Declaration of professionalism or reinstatement of amateur status shall be dealt with by the National Council at its discretion. (NB For purposes of international competition the attention of members is drawn to the Rules of Amateur Status laid down from time to time by the Federation Internationale de Tir a l'Arc.)

Amateur Status

An amateur in archery practises the sport in any one or more of the various disciplines as a leisure pursuit.

1. He shall observe the rules of the IOC, his International Federation and his National Federation.

2. Direct financial assistance other than that approved by NOC and NAA to individual archers is not permitted.

3. Full details of amateur status and the IOC Eligibility Code, etc. are to be found in FITA Constitution and Rules.

Juniors – All Disciplines

1. A junior is under 18 years of age.

2. When junior archers are shooting individually or in groups they must be supervised by a GNAS affiliated adult member.

1. TARGET ARCHERY
A. OUTDOOR

100. Target Faces

(*a*) The diameters of the standard faces are 122cm and 80cm.

(*b*) (i) The 122cm face is composed of a circle in the centre of 24.4cm diameter ringed by four concentric bands the breadth of each, measured radially, being 12.2cm.

(ii) The 80cm face is composed of a circle in the centre of 16cm diameter ringed by four concentric bands the breadth of each, measured radially, being 8cm.

(*c*) The colours of both target faces are, from centre outwards, gold, red, blue, black and white.

(*d*) The 122cm face when used for 10 zone scoring and the 80cm face have each colour zone divided into two zones of equal width by a line not exceeding 2mm in width. Such dividing lines shall be entirely within the higher scoring zone.

(*e*) (i) Except between black/white and black/blue dividing lines between colours may be used. Such dividing lines shall not exceed 2mm in width and shall be entirely within the higher scoring zone.

(ii) The line marking the outermost edge of the white shall not exceed 2mm in width and shall be entirely within the scoring zone.

(*f*) The centre of the gold is termed the 'pinhole' and shall be marked with a small cross (x) the lines of which shall not exceed 2mm in width.

(*g*) Tolerances (plus/minus) on target faces are permitted as follows:–

122cm – 3mm on the diameter of each scoring zone.

80cm – 2mm on the diameter of each scoring zone.

(Reference FITA Constitution and Rules.)

101. Range Layout

(*a*) The targets shall be set up at one end of the ground. They shall be inclined at an angle of about 15 degrees, with the pinholes 130cm (4ft 3in) ± 5cm above the ground. The height of the pinhole on a line of faces shall at all times look straight.

(*b*) Minimum spacing of target centres shall be:

Archers shooting singly or in pairs	2.5m (8ft 2in)
Archers shooting in threes	3.66m (12ft)

(*c*) Each target boss shall be securely anchored so that it cannot blow off its stand. Likewise stands shall be anchored to prevent them from blowing over.

(*d*) All targets shall be clearly numbered. At tournaments where FITA rules do not apply, flags to indicate wind direction may, at the tournament organiser's discretion, be placed above the centre of each target. Such flags shall be of a colour easily visible and shall be placed above the centre of each target in such a manner that no part of the flag can obscure any part of the target or boss. Flags shall not be more than 30cm and not less than 25cm in any direction. Alternatively, a wind indicator flag may be placed at each end of the target line.

(*e*) The shooting line (over which the archers shall take up their shooting positions) shall be measured from points vertically below the pinholes. Tolerances on such measurements shall be as follows:–

METRIC   – up to and including 50m – ± 15cm
                  – above 50m   – ± 30cm
IMPERIAL – up to and including 50 yd– ± 6in
                  – above 50 yd   – ± 12in

(*f*) Shooting marks, consisting of discs or other flat markers, shall be positioned opposite the targets at the appropriate distances. The shooting marks are to bear the numbers of the target opposite which they are placed.

(*g*) Lines at right angles to the shooting line and extending from the shooting line to the target line making lanes containing one, two or three bosses may be laid down.

(*h*) A waiting line shall be placed at least five yards behind the shooting line.

(*j*) On grounds where the public have right of access an area shall be roped off to indicate that no one can pass behind the targets within 50 yards of them. Where an efficient backstop netting, a bank or other similar device (not a hedge or penetrable fence) high enough for the top of the stop as seen from the shooting line to be at least as far above the top of the target as the gold is below the top of the target, then this distance may be reduced to 25 yards. The area to be roped shall extend from the ends of the 'safety line' so that no one can pass within 20 yards of the ends of the target line, 10 yards of the shooting line and 15 yards behind the shooting line.

102. Equipment
Four types of bow are recognised.

(*a*) Bows and their accessories which conform in all respects to the following:

(i) A bow of any type may be used provided it subscribes to the accepted principle and meaning of the word bow as used in Target Archery; e.g. an article consisting of a handle (grip), riser and two flexible limbs each ending in a tip with a string nock.

The bow is braced for use by a single bowstring attached directly between the two string nocks only and, in operation, is held in one hand by its handle (grip) while the fingers of the other hand draw, hold back and release the string.

(ii) A bowstring may be made up of any number of strands of the material chosen for the purpose, with a centre serving to accommodate the drawing fingers, a nocking point to which may be added serving(s) to fit the arrow nock as necessary, and to locate this point one or two nock locators may be positioned and in each of the two ends of the bowstring a loop to be placed in the string nocks of the bow when braced.

In addition, one attachment is permitted on the string to serve as nose or lip mark.

The serving on the string must not end within the archer's vision at full draw. A bowstring must not in any way offer aid in aiming through 'peephole', marking or any other means.

(iii) (1) An arrowrest, which can be adjustable, any movable pressure button, pressure point or arrowplate and draw check indicator (audible and/or visual) may all be used on the bow provided they are not electric or electronic and do not offer an additional aid in aiming.

(2) The pressure point shall be placed no further than 4cm back (inside) from the throat of the handle (pivot point) of the bow.

(iv) A bowsight, bowmark or a point of aim on the ground for aiming is permitted, but at no time may more than one such device be used.

(1) A bowsight as attached to the bow for the purpose of aiming may allow for windage adjustment as well as elevation setting but shall not incorporate a prism or lens or other magnifying device, levelling or electric devices nor shall it provide for more than one sighting point. An attachment to which the bowsight is fixed is permitted.

(2) A bowmark is a single mark made on the bow for the purpose of aiming. Such mark may be made in pencil, tape or any other suitable marking material.

A plate or tape with distance markings may be mounted on the bow as a guide but must not in any way offer any additional aid.

(3) A point of aim on the ground is a marker placed in the shooting lane between the shooting line and the target. Such marker may not exceed a diameter of 7.5cm and must not protrude above the ground more than 15cm.

(v) Stabilisers and torque flight compensators on the bow are permitted provided they do not:

(1) Serve as a string guide.

(2) Touch anything but the bow.

(3) Represent any obstacle to other archers as far as place on the shooting line is concerned.

(vi) Arrows of any type may be used provided they subscribe to the accepted principle and meaning of the word arrow as used in Target Archery, and that such arrows do not cause undue damage to target faces and buttresses.

An arrow consists of a shaft with head (point), nock, fletching and, if desired, cresting and/or numbers. The arrows of each archer shall be marked with the archer's name, initials or insignia and all arrows used for the same end of 3 or 6 arrows shall carry the same pattern and colour(s) of fletching, nocks and cresting, if any.

Any captive arrow device is to be treated as though the arrow was non-captive.

(vii) Finger protection in the form of finger stalls or tips, gloves, shooting tab or tape (plaster) to draw, hold back and release the string is permitted, provided they are smooth and with no device to help to hold and/or release the string.

A separator between the fingers to prevent pinching the arrow may be used.

On the bow hand an ordinary glove, mitten or similar may be worn.

(viii) Field glasses, telescopes and other visual aids may be used for spotting arrows.

Ordinary spectacles as necessary or shooting spectacles provided they are fitted with the same lenses normally worn by the archer, and sun glasses, may be worn.

None may be fitted with microhole lenses, glasses or similar nor marked in any way which can assist in aiming.

(ix) Accessories are permitted such as bracers, dress shield, bowsling, belt or ground quiver, tassel and foot markers not protruding above the ground more than one centimetre.

(*b*) Crossbows which conform to the Rules and Conditions stated in Part V.

(*c*) Compound and other bows and their accessories which do not meet the requirements of para. 102a above.

(*d*) Traditional Longbow which conform to conditions specified in Part VI.

103. Separate Styles and Conditions

(*a*) Bows conforming to 102a.

(i) Free Style: As 102a.

(ii) Barebow:

(1) As 102a(i) and the bow must be free from any protrusions, marks or blemishes or laminated pieces which could be used in aiming. The inside of the upper limb shall be without trade marks.

(2) As 102a(ii) except that there shall be no attachments to the string to act as a nose or lip mark or other marks to aid finger position selection.

(3) As 102(a)(iii) except that no draw check indicator may be used nor overdraw facility as defined in 102(a)(iii)(2).

(4) The bow must be bare; therefore sights and mounted stabilisers as defined in 102(a)(iv) and 102(a)(v) cannot be used.

(iii) Traditional: As 203(*c*)

For target archery record purposes this style will be treated as Barebow style.

(*b*) Crossbows (see Part V).

(*c*) Bows conforming to 102(*c*).

(i) Unlimited – No restrictions as to accessories, but the bow must be free and held in the hand.

(ii) Limited – The bow must be held in the hand and the string must be drawn, held back and released by the fingers of the other hand. A level, peepsight and pressure button are permitted but a scope is not allowed. A cable guard may be fitted. A multipin sight is permitted.

(iii) Bowhunter: As 203(*g*).

For target archery record and classification purposes this style will be treated as Limited style.

(*d*) Bows which are recognised in 102(*b*) and 102(*c*) *may not be used in direct competition* with bows recognised in 102(*a*) except that archers using bows as recognised in 102(*c*) may compete for the GNAS Handicap Improvement Medal under the conditions defined in 801(*e*)(iii). The allocation of any separate prize, medal, trophy or other award shall be a matter for each individual tournament organiser. Classification, handicap or other distinction shall remain the sole prerogative of the Grand National Archery Society.

104. Shooting

(*a*) Shooting, except in the case of permanently or semi-permanently disabled archers, shall be from an unsupported standing position, placing one foot on each side of the shooting line.

(*b*) (i) The order in which archers shall shoot at their respective targets shall be the order in which they appear on the target list and the drawing up of the target list shall be a matter for arrangement by the tournament organisers. Unless otherwise directed, No. 3 on each target shall be the Target Captain, and No. 4 the Lieutenant. The Captain shall be responsible for the orderly conduct of shooting in accordance with the Rules of Shooting.

(ii) The order of shooting in all Tournaments of Record Status shall rotate. For other tournaments, including Club Target Days, rotation shall be optional.

(*c*) (i) For all GNAS rounds, the two longest distances of the Metric rounds and the long Metric Rounds, six arrows shall be shot at an end. Each archer shall shoot three arrows and immediately retire and, when all on a target have shot, shall shoot three more. If an archer persists in shooting more than three arrows consecutively he may be disqualified by the Judge.

(ii) For the two shortest distances of the Metric rounds and the Short Metric Rounds, three arrows shall be shot at an end. If an archer persists in shooting more than three arrows consecutively he may be disqualified by the Judge.

(*d*) In the event of an archer shooting more than the specified number of arrows at an end the archer shall be penalised by losing the value of his best arrow(s) in the target, and such arrow(s) shall not be measured for a Gold prize.

(*e*) An arrow shall be deemed not to have been shot, if the archer can touch it with his bow without moving his feet from their normal position in relation to the shooting line. In which case another arrow may be shot in its place. If another arrow is not available he may only retrieve his misnocked arrow with the Judge's permission.

(*f*) If for any cause an archer is not prepared to shoot before all have shot, such archer shall lose the benefit of that end.

(*g*) Archers arriving late shall not be allowed to make up any ends that they have missed.

(*h*) Archers shall retire from the shooting line as soon as their last arrow has been shot except that an archer may remain on the shooting line to keep company with another archer still shooting.

(*j*) Two and a half minutes shall be the maximum time for an archer to shoot three arrows, the time to start from when the archer steps on to the shooting line.

(*k*) Whilst an archer is on the shooting line, he shall receive no information by word or otherwise from anyone except the Judge or Field Captain(s).

(*l*) At any meeting no practice is allowed on the ground the same day, except that six arrows may be shot as sighters before the beginning of each day's shooting, but only after competitors have come under the Judge's orders at the Assembly. Such sighters shall not be recorded.

(*m*) If for any reason an archer is alone on a target he must notify the Judge who shall arrange for him to be transferred to another target or another archer to be transferred to join him.

(*n*) The maximum number of archers on a target shall be six.

105. Control of Shooting

(*a*) The Lady Paramount shall be the supreme arbitrator on all matters connected with the tournament at which she officiates.

(*b*) At all times, whenever shooting takes place, it must be under the control of a Field Captain.

At larger meetings a Judge shall be appointed to take charge of the shooting. Field Captains, to whom the Judge may delegate his authority, may be appointed as necessary. If a Field Captain has not been appointed previously, the Judge may appoint any experienced archer to act in this capacity.

At tournaments the Judge and Field Captains shall be non-shooting.

(*c*) The Judge shall be in sole control of the shooting and shall resolve all disputes (subject to the supreme authority of the Lady Paramount) in accordance with the Rules of Shooting.

106. Scoring

(*a*) The scoring points for hits on the target face for GNAS Rounds are: Gold 9, Red 7, Blue 5, Black 3, White 1.

The scoring points for hits on the target face for Metric Rounds are: Inner Gold 10, Outer Gold 9, Inner Red 8, Outer Red 7, Inner Blue 6, Outer Blue 5, Inner Black 4, Outer Black 3, Inner White 2, Outer White 1.

The value shall be determined by the position of the arrow shaft.

(*b*) Archers shall identify their arrows by pointing at the nocks.

Neither the arrow nor the target face shall be touched until the final decision as to the score has been given and any such interference with the target or arrow shall disqualify the archer from scoring the higher value.

The Lieutenant will identify the arrows with the score called and will assist the Captain in any way that may be required. No. 1 on the target shall identify the Lieutenant's score.

The duty of entering the scores on the score sheet may be shared by the archers on each target, but the Target Captain shall remain responsible for ensuring that scores are correctly recorded. The Target Captain and Lieutenant will check the score sheet and the Target Captain and the archer shall sign it as correct. The Lieutenant shall sign the Target Captain's score sheet. The attention of archers is drawn to their responsibility for ensuring that when signing score sheets the score, etc., that they sign for is correct.

(c) If an arrow touches two colours or any dividing line it shall be scored as being of that of the higher value.

(d) If any doubt or dispute shall arise it shall be decided by the Target Captain subject to appeal to the Judge.

(e) No alteration shall be made in the value of any arrow as entered on the score sheet, to the advantage of its owner, after such arrow has been drawn from the target.

Any alteration to the recorded score must be initialled by the Judge in a different coloured ink prior to the withdrawal of the arrow from the target. No arrows shall be withdrawn from the target (without the express direction of the Captain) until all the archers' scores have been entered on the score sheet and the Captain is satisfied that they are correctly entered.

(f) If an arrow is observed to rebound from a target, the archer concerned shall draw the attention of the Judge to the fact after having shot his sixth arrow (or third if shooting in ends of 3 only) by retiring two paces from the shooting line and holding his bow above his head.

Upon the Judge satisfying himself that the claim is justified, the archer shall be permitted to shoot another arrow separately in the same end after all archers on that target have completed their normal shooting, such arrow to be numbered or preferably marked by the Judge.

To prevent frivolous rebound claims, the archer is to be warned individually that if six original arrows were shot not including a rebound, then his highest scoring arrow may, at the discretion of the Judge on repetition of a false claim, be deducted from that end's score. The Judge shall take part in that competitor's scoring to ensure that only the correct number of arrows are scored, and that the rebound was not caused by striking another arrow already in the target. An arrow passing through a boss cannot be scored.

(g) An arrow passing through the target face but remaining in the boss shall be withdrawn by the Captain or Lieutenant and shall be inserted from the back in the same place and at the assumed angle of original penetration until the pile is visible in the target face, when the score shall be determined.

(*h*) An arrow hitting and remaining embedded in another arrow shall be scored the same as the arrow struck.

(*j*) An arrow in the target, which has or may have been deflected by another arrow already in the target, shall be scored according to the position of its shaft in the target face.

(*k*) An arrow on the ground believed to have hit and rebounded from another arrow shall be scored the value of the struck arrow, if the latter is found in the target with its nock damaged in a compatible manner.

(*l*) If an arrow fails to enter the boss and is hanging in the target face, it shall be pushed in by the Judge or shall be removed and the Judge will ensure that the appropriate score is recorded when scoring takes place.

(*m*) The FITA Rule that rebounds shall only be scored if arrow holes on the target face are marked applies to all FITA/Metric Rounds shot including those shot at Club Target Days, intercounty matches, etc. (see 108(*e*)).

(*n*) An archer may delegate another archer on the same target to record his score and pick up his arrows.

(*p*) An incapacitated archer may nominate an assistant, who shall be under the control and discipline of the Judge, to record his score and pick up his arrows.

(*q*) In the event of a tie for a score prize the winner shall be the one of those who tie who has the greatest number of hits. Should this result in a tie the prize shall be awarded to the archer among those who tie who has the greatest number of Golds. Should this number also be the same the archers shall be declared joint winners. Where the prize is for (i) most hits, or (ii) most Golds, ties shall be resolved on the above principle in the following order (i) highest score, most Golds, (ii) highest score, most hits.

(*r*) When a shoot (other than the annual Grand National Archery Meeting and the UK National Target Championship) is abandoned due to adverse weather conditions, the placings and prizes shall be awarded on the cumulative score at the conclusion of the last full end shot by the competitors, by instruction of the Judge.

107. Dress Regulation

(*a*) At all tournaments with National Record Status (including FITA Star tournaments) members of the Society shooting and officiating are required to wear the accepted dress of the Society.

(*b*) (i) Ladies are required to wear a dress or skirt or trousers or shorts with suitable top (not strapless or beachwear).

(ii) Gentlemen are required to wear trousers or shorts with long or short sleeved shirts.

(iii) Sweaters/cardigans/blazers may be worn.

(iv) Each garment shall be plain dark green or white. There is no objection to wearing green and white garments together.

(v) Waterproof clothing worn only during inclement weather is not subject to these regulations, but both white and green waterproofs are available and are recommended.

(c) Footwear must be worn at all times during the tournament.

(d) Advertising material must not be carried or worn except in conformity with FITA rules. The name/emblem of an archer's Country, Regional or County Association or Club may be worn on the uniform or shooting clothes.

(e) Any archer not conforming to the above regulations shall be requested by the Judge and Organiser to leave the shooting line and will not be permitted to shoot.

108. Recognised Rounds for Record, Handicap and Classification Purposes.

(a) The following rounds are recognised by the Society:

(i) Dozens of arrows at each distance

Outdoor – GNAS ROUNDS (5 Zone Scoring)

See 108 (b) (i)	See 108 (b) (iii)	Round	122cm Face						
			100Y	80Y	60Y	50Y	40Y	30Y	20Y
A	★	York	6	4	2				
A	★	Hereford		6	4	2			
C	★	Bristol I		6	4	2			
D	★	Bristol II			6	4	2		
E	★	Bristol III				6	4	2	
F	★	Bristol IV					6	4	2
A		St. George	3	3	3				
A		Albion		3	3	3			
A		Windsor			3	3	3		
D		Short Windsor				3	3	3	
E		Junior Windsor					3	3	3
A		New Western	4	4					
A		Long Western		4	4				
A		Western			4	4			
D		Short Western				4	4		
E		Junior Western					4	4	
F		Short Junior Western						4	4
A	★	American			$2\frac{1}{2}$	$2\frac{1}{2}$	$2\frac{1}{2}$		
E		St. Nicholas					4	3	
A		New National	4	2					
A		Long National		4	2				
A		National			4	2			
D		Short National				4	2		
E		Junior National					4	2	
F		Short Junior National						4	2

Table 108(a)(ii) Dozens of arrows at each distance

Outdoor – METRIC ROUNDS (10 Zone Scoring)

See 108(b)(i)	See 108(b)(iii)	Round	122cm Face						80cm Face				
			90M	70M	60M	50M	40M	30M	50M	40M	30M	20M	10M
A	★	FITA (Gentlemen)	3	3	3				3		3		
B	★	FITA (Ladies)		3	3				3		3		
C	★	Metric I		3	3				3		3		
D	★	Metric II			3	3				3	3		
E	★	Metric III				3	3				3	3	
F	★	Metric IV					3	3				3	3
A		Long Metric (Gentlemen)	3	3									
B		Long Metric (Ladies)		3	3								
A		Short Metric							3		3		
C		Long Metric I		3	3								
D		Long Metric II			3	3							
E		Long Metric III				3	3						
F		Long Metric IV					3	3					
C		Short Metric I							3		3		
D		Short Metric II								3	3		
E		Short Metric III									3	3	
F		Short Metric IV										3	3

(b) Rounds for National Records Purposes:

(i) The following table allows archers to establish which of the rounds in Tables 108(a)(i) and (ii) may be shot for record purposes.

	Group Letters as shown in Tables 108(a)(i) and (ii)					
	A	B	C	D	E	F
Gentlemen	•					
Ladies	•	•				
Junior Gentlemen U-18	•	•	•			
Junior Gentlemen U-16	•	•	•	•		
Junior Gentlemen U-14	•	•	•	•	•	
Junior Gentlemen U-12	•	•	•	•	•	•
Junior Ladies U-18	•	•	•	•		
Junior Ladies U-16	•	•	•	•	•	
Junior Ladies U-13	•	•	•	•	•	•

(ii) Single round records may be claimed for all rounds specified in Tables 108(a)(i) and (ii) subject to restrictions given in 108(b)(i).

(iii) Double round records may be claimed for rounds marked ★ in Tables 108(a)(i) and (ii) subject to restrictions given in 108(b)(i).

(iv) Distance records may be claimed when shot during the following complete rounds subject to restrictions given in 108(b)(i): FITA (Gentlemen), FITA (Ladies), Metrics I, II, III and IV.

(v) See Part VII for regulations governing record claims.

(c) Rounds for Handicap and Classification Purposes:

(i) All rounds in Tables 108(a)(i) and (ii) may be shot by any archer irrespective of age.

(ii) See GNAS Handicap and Classification Tables for regulations governing the Handicap and Classification schemes.

(iii) See Part VIII for regulations governing the GNAS Handicap Improvement Medal.

(d) In every round the longer or longest distance is shot first and the shorter or shortest distance last.

(e) (i) When FITA/Metric rounds as stated in Table 108(a)(ii) are shot, FITA Rules apply subject to minimum standards give in 108(e)(ii).

(ii) Minimum standards (at the organiser's discretion a higher standard of control may be adopted):

(1) Club Target Days and Non-Record Status Tournaments: Arrow

holes need not be marked in which case rebounds will not score. FITA Time Control need not be applied.

(2) Tournaments with UK Record Status: Arrow holes shall be marked. If Visual Time Control is not available then Time Control must be applied in the following manner:

Two audible signals for archers in the first detail to take their positions on the shooting line.

After 20 seconds one audible signal for shooting to commence.

After $2\frac{1}{2}$ minutes (or earlier if shooting line is clear) 2 audible signals indicate that the archers remaining on the shooting line shall retire and the next detail take their place.

After 20 seconds one audible signal for the second detail to commence shooting.

And so continue until both details have shot their two ends (or one depending on the distances being shot) when 3 audible signals shall indicate that archers are to move forward to score and collect arrows.

If at any time a competitor indicates a rebound then shooting is interrupted strictly in accordance with the procedure set out in FITA Constitution and Rules.

(3) FITA Star Tournaments Visual Time Control shall be adopted as set out in FITA Constitution and Rules. Automatic timing devices need not be incorporated into any adequately designed light system. Rebounds shall be scored (FITA Constitution and Rules).

(4) FITA Star Tournaments with World Record Status: FITA requires conditions as near to World Championships standards as can reasonably be attained. Visual Time Control shall be used.

(f) (i) A FITA Round may be shot in one day or over two consecutive days under FITA Rules.

(ii) All other Rounds to be shot in one day. (Except in accordance with Rule for Championship of more than one day's duration.)

109. Local Rounds

In addition to rounds specified in 108(a(i) and (ii) any 'local' round made up of other numbers of arrows at specified distances may be used in Clubs and Tournaments provided the Rules of Shooting are adhered to in all respects and subject to their non-recognition by the GNAS for Record, Classification or Handicap purposes.

110. Club Events

(a) Target Day

(i) A Target Day is any day and time appointed under the Rules of the Club and previously announced to the members.

(ii) There is no statutory limit to the number of officially appointed Target Days in any one week.

(iii) All scores made must be entered in the Club Record Book.

(iv) Target Days should commence punctually at the announced time.

(v) All shooting shall be in accordance with GNAS Rules of Shooting.

(vi) On any Club Target Day there shall be a minimum of two archers shooting, not necessarily on the same target, each recording the other's scores in order that these scores may be recognised. An archer shooting alone may claim his score provided that it has been recorded throughout by a non-shooting archer.

(b) Open Meeting

An Open Meeting is an event run as a competition open to all members of GNAS and FITA affiliated members, with all the necessary organisation, advertising of the event, judging, etc., run under GNAS Rules of Shooting.

111. Six Gold Badge

(a) There are four types of badge; a senior and junior badge for archers shooting bows as recognised in 102(a) and a senior and junior badge for archers shooting bows as recognised in 102(c).

(b) The award, which is for six consecutive arrows shot during the competition at one end into the gold zone, is open to members of the Society.

(c) The shortest distances at which the badge may be gained are:
Gentlemen – 80yd (70m)   Ladies – 60yd (60m)

(d) The six gold end must be made at a meeting organised by the Society or any of its associated bodies or in competition at an associated club Target Day, under GNAS Rules of Shooting.

(e) (i) Claims for the award must be sumbitted to the GNAS Secretary on the appropriate claim form.

(ii) If the six gold end is made at a tournament the tournament organiser must sign.

(iii) If the six gold end is made at an associated club Target Day the Club Secretary must sign.

(f) An archer is entitled to only one senior six gold badge for each type of bow, but holders of the junior badge(s) are also entitled to claim and hold a senior badge for each type of bow.

112. FITA Star Badge

The award is open to Members of the Society according to qualifications and applications as laid down in FITA Rules. Claims for the award must be submitted to the GNAS Secretary on the appropriate form.

113. GNAS Arrow Award for Juniors

GNAS has instituted the 'GNAS Arrow Awards' scheme for Juniors. The scheme, which commenced on 1.1.89, and details on how the awards can be claimed, are given below.

(*a*) The Arrow Awards are open to juniors of the Society under 16 years of age and are in the form of Red, Blue and Black badges.

(*b*) The Award may be claimed only once in each age group and archers may shoot for an Award in age groups above, but not below, their own. Archers submitting valid claims for Awards higher than their age group may also claim the lower awards down to their age group, providing they have not been gained previously.

(*c*) (i) The table opposite indicates the qualifying rounds and scores for separate bows/styles in each age group, for the relevant colour badge.

(ii) Number of Rounds: Four in a calendar year, including at least one FITA/Metric round. One round must be shot at an open tournament; the remainder may be shot at any associated club target day when a minimum of two archers are shooting together including, or under the supervision of a senior member.

(*d*) Claims for the Award shall be made on the appropriate claim form obtainable from GNAS office by sending a s.a.e. (club secretaries may hold stocks of these forms). The form must be returned to the office fully completed by providing the information requested on the form, and signed by the archer and his/her Club Records Officer or Secretary.

114. GNAS 'Compound Wheel' Awards

Archers shooting Compound Bows at FITA Star Tournaments and National Compound Championships when a FITA round is shot can claim GNAS Compound Wheel awards.

(*a*) The colour of the awards are:–
1000–White, 1100–Black,
1200–Blue, 1300–Red

(*b*) Claims for the award shall be made on the appropriate claim form obtainable from GNAS office.

B. INDOOR

120. GNAS Rules of Shooting for Target Archery – Outdoor shall apply except as enumerated in the following paragraphs.

121. Target Faces

(*a*) The diameters of the standard faces are 40cm, 60cm and 80cm.

(*b*) (i) The 40cm face is composed of a circle in the centre of 8cm

Qualifying rounds and scores for GNAS Arrow Awards for Juniors

	Gentlemen FITA	Ladies FITA / Metric I	Metric II	Metric III	Metric IV	York	Hereford / Bristol I	Bristol II	Bristol III	Bristol IV
RED AWARD Junior Gentlemen U/16:										
H/C 43 Recurve	998	1077	1152	–	–	819	988	1110	–	–
41 Compound Limited	1033	1107	1177	–	–	859	1019	1133	–	–
37 Compound Unlimited	1097	1162	1223	–	–	934	1075	1174	–	–
RED AWARD Junior Ladies U/16:										
H/C 53 Recurve	797	892	996	1130	–	603	802	968	1069	–
51 Compound Limited	840	933	1031	1156	–	647	843	1001	1095	–
47 Compound Unlimited	923	1009	1096	1205	–	735	919	1059	1141	–
BLUE AWARD Junior Gentlemen U/14:										
H/C 55 Recurve	753	849	957	1101	–	560	760	934	1042	–
53 Compound Limited	797	892	996	1130	–	603	802	968	1069	–
49 Compound Unlimited	882	972	1065	1181	–	691	882	1031	1119	–
BLACK AWARD Junior Ladies U/13 and Junior Gentlemen U/12:										
H/C 69 Recurve	451	526	638	840	1051	292	456	640	792	950
H/C 67 Compound Limited	491	571	687	883	1084	325	498	685	883	983
63 Compound Unlimited	576	664	783	965	1141	396	584	774	911	1044

diameter ringed by four concentric bands the breadth of each, measured radially, being 4cm.

(ii) The 60cm face is composed of a circle in the centre of 12cm diameter ringed by four concentric bands the breadth of each, measured radially, being 6cm.

(iii) The 80cm face is as defined in Rule 100.

(c) Colours: 100(c).

(d) The 40cm and 60cm faces have each colour zone divided into two zones of equal width by a line not exceeding 2mm in width. Such dividing lines shall be entirely within the higher scoring zone.

(e) Dividing lines: See 100(e)(i) and (ii).

(f) Pinhole: See 100(f).

(g) Tolerance (plus/minus) on the 40cm and 60cm faces is 1mm on the diameter of each scoring zone.

122. Range Layout

(a) The targets may be set up at any angle between vertical and 15° but a line of targets shall be set up at the same angle.

(b) The height of the pinholes shall be 130cm (4ft 3in) above the ground except if the 40cm target faces are in two lines, one above the other, when the height of the pinholes shall be 100cm and 160cm above the ground. The tolerance on heights shall not exceed ±2cm. The height of the pinholes on a line of faces shall at all times look straight.

(c) Target centres shall be placed so as to allow archers to stand at a minimum of 0.91m (3ft) intervals while shooting.

(d) The shooting line (over which archers shall take up their shooting positions) shall be measured from points vertically below the 'pinholes'. If targets are in two lines, one above the other and at an angle, the measurement shall be taken from points vertically below halfway between the two pinholes. The tolerance on measurements shall be as follows: Metric ±10cm, Imperial ±4in.

(e) A waiting line shall be placed five yards behind the shooting line. If space does not permit, a waiting line may be omitted.

123. Recognised Rounds for Record, Handicap and Classification For bows as defined 102(*a*) and 102(*c*)

(*a*) The following rounds are recognised by the Society:

(i)

INDOOR ROUNDS (10 ZONE SCORING)	
FITA 18m	5 dozen at 18m – 40cm face
FITA 25m	5 dozen at 25m – 60cm face
COMBINED FITA	5 dozen at 25m – 60cm face and 5 dozen at 18m – 40cm face
BRAY I	2½ dozen at 18m – 40cm face
BRAY II	2½ dozen at 25m – 60cm face
★ PORTSMOUTH	5 dozen at 20yd – 60cm face
STAFFORD	6 dozen at 30m – 80cm face

(ii)

INDOOR ROUNDS – SPECIALS	
★ WORCESTER	5 dozen at 20yd – 40-64cm (16in) special face scoring 5, 4, 3, 2, 1 outwards from centre white
VEGAS	5 dozen at 18m – special face scoring 10, 9, 8, 7, 6 outwards from inner gold

(*b*) Rounds for National Record Purposes

(i) Single round records may be claimed for any round stated in Tables 123(*a*)(i) and (ii).

(ii) Double round records may be claimed for rounds marked ★ in Tables 123(*a*)(i) and (ii).

(iii) See part VII for regulations governing record claims.

(*c*) Rounds for Handicap and Classification Purposes

(i) All rounds in Tables 123(*a*)(i) and (ii) may be shot.

(ii) See GNAS Handicap and Classification Tables for regulations governing the Handicap and Classification schemes.

124. Local Rounds
In addition to rounds specified in 123(*a*)(i) and (ii), any 'local' round made up of other numbers of arrows at specified distances may be used in clubs and tournaments provided the Rules of Shooting are adhered to in all respects and subject to their non-recognition by the GNAS for Record, Classification or Handicap purposes.

125. Regulations for the Stafford and Portsmouth Rounds
(*a*) The general Rules of Target Archery – Indoor shall apply.
(*b*) An end shall consist of three arrows.
(*c*) One end of sighter arrows shall be shot.
(*d*) The scoring points on the target, reading from inner gold to outer white, are 10, 9, 8, 7, 6, 5, 4, 3, 2, 1.

126. Regulations for the Bray I and Bray II Rounds
(*a*) The general Rules of Target Archery – Indoor shall apply.
(*b*) An end shall consist of three arrows.
(*c*) Two ends of sighter arrows shall be shot.
(*d*) The scoring points on the target, reading from inner gold to outer white, are 10, 9, 8, 7, 6, 5, 4, 3, 2, 1.

127. Regulations for the FITA 18m, FITA 25m and Combined FITA Rounds
(*a*) When these rounds are shot FITA Rules apply subject to minimum standards given in 127(*a*)(i).
   (i) Minimum standards (at the organiser's discretion a higher standard of control may be adopted).
   (1) Club Target Days and Non-Record Status Tournaments: arrow holes need not be marked, in which case rebounds will not score. FITA Time Control need not be applied.
   (2) Tournaments with UK Record Status: arrow holes shall be marked. If Visual Time Control is not available then Time Control must be applied in the following manner:
   Two audible signals for archers in the first detail detail to take their positions on the shooting line.
   After 20 seconds one audible signal for shooting to commence.
   After 2½ minutes (or earlier if shooting line is clear) 2 audible signals indicate that the archers remaining on the shooting line shall retire and the next detail take their place.
   After 20 seconds one audible signal for the second detail to commence shooting.
   And so continue until both details have shot their two ends (or one depending on the distances being shot) when 3 audible signals shall indicate that archers are to move forward to score and collect arrows.

If at any time a competitor indicates a rebound then shooting is interrupted strictly in accordance with the procedure set out in FITA Constitution and Rules.

(3) Tournaments with World Record Status: FITA requires conditions as near to World Championships standards as can reasonably be attained. Visual Time Control shall be used.

128. Regulations for the Worcester Round

(a) The general Rules of Target Archery – Indoor shall apply except as enumerated in the following paragraphs.

(b) **Target Faces**

(i) The target face used shall be circular 40.64cm (16in) in diameter. This target face is composed as follows:
A circle in the centre 8.13cm (3in) diameter ringed by four concentric bands, the breadth of each measured radially being 4.064cm (1.6in). The centre circle shall be coloured white and the four concentric bands black. The concentric bands shall be divided by white lines. Each of the white dividing lines shall be of no greater width than 1mm (0.04in). Such dividing lines shall be entirely within the higher scoring zone.

(ii) Tolerances on target faces are permitted as follows: 2mm (0.08in) on each zone and 2mm (0.08in) on full 40.64cm (16in) diameter.

(c) **Shooting**

(i) 104(b)(ii) (rotation) will not apply to this round.

(ii) Five arrows shall be shot at an end. Each archer will shoot his five arrows before retiring from the shooting line.

(iii) One end of sighter arrows shall be shot.

(iv) In the event of an archer shooting more than five arrows at an end the archer shall be penalised by losing the value of his arrow(s) in the target.

(v) The maximum number of archers on a target boss shall be four.

(vi) Five minutes shall be the maximum time for an archer to shoot an end, the time to start from when the archer steps on to the shooting line.

(d) **Scoring**
The scoring points for hits on the target face are: 5, 4, 3, 2, 1, reading from the centre white circle.

(e) **Recognised Round**

(i) The Round shall consist of 12 ends (60 arrows).

(ii) The distance to be shot is 20 yards.

(iii) Each boss shall hold four target faces.

(iv) Target faces shall be arranged thus:

1	2
3	4

(v) Two archers of a group shall shoot five arrows when the second group shall then shoot their five arrows.

(vi) The first group of two archers shall shoot at the higher targets; the second group at the lower targets.

(vii) When all archers have shot 30 arrows those who have been shooting at the lower targets shall change to the higher targets and those who have been shooting at the higher targets shall shoot at the lower targets, thus:

those who have been shooting on targets 1 and 2 shall shoot the remaining 30 arrows on targets 3 and 4 retaining their same shooting positions.

129. Regulations for the Vegas Round

(*a*) The general Rules of Target Archery – Indoor shall apply except as enumerated in the following paragraphs.

(*b*) **Target Faces**

The target face is composed as follows:

Three separate 5-zone centres equal in size and colour to the innermost scoring zones of the 40cm FITA Indoor target face as defined in 121. The gold of each centre shall be arranged in triangular form and each shall be numbered. Centre number 1 shall be in the lower left corner, centre number 2 at the apex of the triangle and centre number 3 shall be in the lower right corner. The 'pinholes' of the golds shall be 21.3cm apart.

(*c*) **Range Layout**

Each boss shall hold four faces.

(*d*) **Shooting**

(i) 104(*b*)(ii) (rotation) shall not apply.

(ii) The first groups of two archers shall shoot at the higher targets and the second group at the lower targets. When all archers have shot 30 arrows those who have been shooting at the lower targets shall change to the higher targets and those who have been shooting at the higher targets shall shoot at the lower targets.

(iii) Each archer shall shoot in ends of three arrows.

(iv) Two ends of sighter arrows shall be shot.

(v) Arrows shall be numbered and shall be shot in ascending numerical sequence, one arrow at each target centre in the order 1, 2 and 3.

(*e*) **Scoring**

(i) The scoring points for hits on the target, reading from the inner Gold to the Blue, are 10, 9, 8, 7, 6.

(ii) An arrow not shot in the order prescribed in Rule 129(*d*)(v) or an arrow striking a target centre other than that at which it should have been shot in the order so prescribed shall be scored a miss.

II. FIELD ARCHERY

200. Regulations

(*a*) GNAS Rules of Shooting 102, 103, 201–206 shall apply to GNAS recognised rounds and any other traditional or local rounds run under the GNAS Rules of Shooting.

(*b*) FITA Constitution & Rules, Part V(*c*), shall apply generally to the FITA recognised rounds, i.e. the Hunter and the Field (with exceptions as listed) and to the FITA Combination Round. (See under 201, 206(*b*).

(*c*) There shall be an initial tackle inspection at the All-British & Open Field Archery Championships. At other events, tackle is liable to inspection at any time during the shoot, but judges will inspect any equipment offered to them before the shoot begins. Any tackle found at any time thereafter in contravention of the rules will entail disqualification.

(*d*) There shall be separate classes and styles for Ladies, Gentlemen and Juniors (See 203, 204).

201. Exceptions to FITA Field Archery Rules

Even when FITA Rounds are shot, GNAS permits certain minor variations, as follows:

(*a*) The inclusion of special regulations for Juniors under 15 and under 12, for the participation of archers shooting the Traditional style, and for those shooting in the three GNAS classes of Compound.

(*b*) The GNAS Rebound/Pass-Through Rule. See under 202(*k*).

202. General Field Archery Rules

(*a*) Judges shall be appointed, one of whom shall be the Chairman in charge of the event.

(*b*) The duties of the Chairman and other Judges shall be:

(i) to ensure that adequate safety precautions have been observed in the layout of the course and practice area.

(ii) to address the assembled competitors before the shoot commences on safety precautions and any other appropriate matter, including method of starting the event, the starting points of each group, etc.

(iii) to ensure that all competitors are conversant with the rules of the competition and the method of scoring.

(iv) to resolve disputes or queries that may arise in interpretation of the rules or other matters.

(*c*) Each shooting group shall consist of not more than six and not less than three archers, one of whom shall be designated Target Captain and two others as scorers.

(*d*) The Target Captain shall be responsible for the orderly conduct of shooting within the group, and have the ultimate responsibility for scoring the arrows.

(*e*) Each scorer shall be supplied with and complete a separate set of score cards for the shooting group and the duties of scorers shall be as follows:

  (i) to write down the score of each competitor in the group.

  (ii) to complete the score card at the end of the shooting.

  (iii) to be responsible for deciding the value of each arrow, in the case of a dispute a Judge shall make the final decision.

(*f*) The score cards shall be signed by the scorer at the end of shooting, and by the archer as an acceptance of the final score.

(*g*) Should the two cards not agree, then the lower score shall be taken as the result.

(*h*) The use of binoculars and other visual aids is not permitted in GNAS Field Archery and FITA Unmarked Rounds.

(*j*) The archer's more forward foot must be in contact and behind the shooting post while shooting, except in the FITA Hunter, the FITA Field and the FITA Combination Rounds when the archer shall stand with both feet behind the relevant shooting line, which is an imaginary line parallel to the target through the shooting post.

(*k*) If, in competitions where the arrow holes have not been marked, an arrow is observed to rebound from, or is believed to have passed through, the target butt, a Judge shall check it, and if it appears that the arrow has rebounded or passed through, then another arrow may be shot at that target from the same position from which the rebounding or passing-through arrow was shot.

(*l*) An arrow shall be deemed not to have been shot, if the archer can touch it with his bow without moving his feet from his shooting position, in which case another arrow may be shot in its place.

203. Shooting Styles

  (*a*) **Freestyle** – Archers using equipment that conforms to 102(*a*).

  (*b*) **Barebow** – Archers using equipment that conforms to 103(*a*)(ii).

  (*c*) (i) *Traditional* – Archers using equipment as for Barebow above, but the arrow shafts shall be made of wood and may comprise a metallic pile and a plastic nock. Furthermore, they must adhere to one anchor point and to one finger-position on the string throughout a tournament. An arrowrest is permitted, but may not be adjustable; a pressure button is not permitted.

  (ii) *Traditional Longbow* – Archers using equipment as defined in 601 except that the bow must be bare; therefore marks on bow limb or rubber bands are not allowed, neither is a 'kisser' allowed on the string. Archers must adhere to one anchor point and to one finger-position on the string throughout a tournament.

(*d*) **Crossbow** – Archers using equipment as defined in 501.

(*e*) **Compound Unlimited** – Archers using equipment as defined in 103(*c*)(i).

(*f*) **Compound Limited** – Archers using equipment as defined in 103(*c*)(ii). Multipin sights are permitted.

(*g*) **Compound Bowhunter** – Archers using equipment generally as in Barebow above. No marking or attachment may appear on the bow or the string which might be used as an aid to aiming. A cable-guard, pressure button and an adjustable arrow rest and plate are permitted. Only one stabiliser no longer than 30.5cm (12in) overall may be fitted. No release aid may be used.

Note: In all the above styles, the following exceptions to Target Archery practices apply:

(i) No artificial points of aim are permitted.

(ii) Arrows must be numbered by means of distinctive bands at least 3mm in width and approximately 3mm apart.

(iii) Field glasses and other visual aids shall not be used in shooting unmarked distances in Field Archery Rounds.

(iv) No notes or memoranda may be used which might assist in improving scores.

(v) No aids for estimating distances are allowed.

204. Juniors (General)

(*a*) Junior archers are those under 18 years of age. They are placed in three categories of age-groups. The date of birth must fall before the (first) day of the tournament.

Juniors (15/17)
Juniors (12/14)
Juniors (under 12)

(*b*) There is nothing to prevent a Junior choosing to shoot in a higher age-group than his age would warrant provided that he complies with the regulations appertaining to that group.

(*c*) Where Juniors under 15 years of age shoot in a group containing archers above this age, the Juniors shall shoot last.

205. Target Faces

There are 4 types of face in use:

(*a*) **FITA Round Faces**

There are four FITA Field Archery faces: 60cm, 45cm, 30cm and 15cm diameters.

All four faces consist of an outer ring, an inner ring, and a centre spot. The lines between the scoring zones to be invisible from the post, but an exception may be made for the 30cm and the 15cm faces as the distances are so short.

The dimensions of the faces are:

Diameters of	Outer Ring Face	Inner Ring Face	Centre Spot
	60cm	30cm	10cm
	45cm	22.5cm	7.5cm
	30cm	15cm	5cm
	15cm	7.5cm	2.5cm

Scoring values		
The centre spot	5 points	
The inner ring	4 points	
The outer ring	3 points	

Hunters Round Faces
The outer ring and the inner ring shall be black, and the centre spot shall be white.
The background on which the face is printed shall be the same colour as the outer ring.

Field Round Faces
The outer ring and the centre spot shall be black, and the inner ring shall be white.

Animal Picture Faces Animal pictures bearing the Hunters Round faces and the Field Round faces respectively, may also be used, but the inner ring shall be inside the animal's contour. The lines of the face need only be outlined but the centre spot shall be in a contrasting colour to be plainly visible.

(*b*) **Forester Round Faces**
The target faces shall be of animal or bird design, and shall have inscribed on them an outer circle of fixed diameter, an inner circle of half that diameter, and a spot of one sixth that diameter.

Thus:	24in Face	12in Inner Circle	4in Spot
	18in Face	9in Inner Circle	3in Spot
	12in Face	6in Inner Circle	2in Spot
	6in Face	3in Inner Circle	1in Spot

(*c*) **Big Game Round Faces**
The target faces shall be of animal or bird design, with the scoring area divided into two parts. The high-scoring area is the smaller area,

situated in the 'heart/lung' region of the animal, and is known as the 'kill' zone. The low-scoring area is the remainder of the animal within the marked perimeter, and is known as the 'wound' zone.

Targets are classed into groups one, two, three and four, according to size.

Group 1. 40in × 28in – Bear, deer, moose, elk, caribou.

Group 2. 28in × 22in – Antelope, small deer, wolf, mountain lion.

Group 3. 22in × 14in – Coyote, javelina, turkey, fox, goose, wildcat, pheasant.

Group 4. 14in × 11in – Turtle, duck, grouse, crow, skunk, jackrabbit, wood-chuck.

Any animal or bird consistent in size with a particular group may be used.

(d) National Animal Round Faces

The target faces shall be of an animal or bird design, and shall have described upon them a circle of either 30, 22.5, 15, or 7.5cm diameter according to the size of the animal picture and in the heart/lung region. The higher scoring area (the kill zone) shall be within the circle and the remainder of the animal shall be the lower scoring area (the wound zone).

Swedish Big Game Round faces fulfil the requirements set out above and shall be used at National Record Status events.

206. Field Rounds in GNAS

For Target Faces refer to 205.

Courses should be laid out in such a way as to provide safety, maximum interest and variety, and to make best use of available terrain. Direction indicators should be placed as necessary to ensure safety.

(a) FITA Rounds

For full details, including rules of shooting, refer to FITA Constitution & Rules Part V(C), but in particular the following apply:

 (i) Two posts are to be placed side by side at every position where two archers are expected to shoot together, which is the standard procedure.

 (ii) Arrows shall be shot in ascending numerical order.

(iii) *30cm Faces*   Four faces shall be placed in the form of a square. Every shooting position shall have two posts placed side by side.

Archers shooting from the left post shall shoot their first two arrows at the top left face, and the remaining two arrows at the lower left face; archers shooting for the right post shall shoot similarly at the top and lower right faces.

15cm Faces   Sixteen faces shall be placed in four vertical columns (1, 2, 3 and 4 from the left) of four faces (A, B, C and D from the top). Every shooting position to have two posts placed side by side. Archers shooting in the first detail shall shoot one arrow at each of the faces in column 1 starting at face A and then B, C and D from the appropriate posts; archers shooting from the right post in the first detail shall shoot their arrows in a similar manner at the faces in column 3.

The archers in the second detail shall shoot their arrows in a similar manner from the left post at faces in column 2, and from the right post at faces in column 4.

When more than four archers are in the shooting group then the fifth archer shall shoot from the left-hand post and the sixth from the right-hand post, in a similar manner, after the first four archers have scored and drawn their arrows.

(iv) No archer shall relate to another archer the target distances on unmarked distances during the tournament.

 (v) A time limit of 1½ minutes per arrow shall be allowed from the time the archer takes his position at the post, which he shall do as soon as it becomes available.

A Judge, having observed an archer exceed the time limit, shall caution him by a signed note on the score card, indicating the time of the warning. At the second warning, and any subsequent warnings, during that tournament, the highest scoring arrow at the target where the warning is given, shall be annulled.

FITA Hunter Round   Shot on FITA Hunter faces.
The FITA Hunter Round consists of 28 targets with one arrow from each of four different posts for each target. The Round may be shot Marked or Unmarked.
Four targets with 15cm faces placed between 5 and 15 metres.
Eight targets with 30cm faces placed between 10 and 30 metres.
Ten targets with a 45cm face placed between 20 and 40 metres.
Six targets with a 60cm face placed between 30 and 50 metres.
Tolerance on distances shall not exceed ±0.5%
Total number of arrows, 112.
Scoring 5, 4, 3 for spot, inner and outer respectively.
Maximum possible score, 560.

Juniors
Juniors (15/17) shoot from the same posts as adults in all cases.
Juniors (12/14) shoot two arrows from each of the two nearest shooting posts at single-faced targets, which will be either 45cm or 60cm faces.
Juniors (under 12) shoot all four shots from the front post on *all targets*.
Organisers *may* provide suitably placed extra forward posts for under 12s at their discretion. In this case no under 12 records can be claimed and a statement to this effect must appear on entry forms for Record Status Tournaments.

FITA Field Round   Shot on FITA Field faces.

The FITA Field Round consists of 28 Targets with four arrows at each Target. Distances are marked.

Twice at each of 15, 20, 25 and 30 metres at 30cm faces	32 arrows
Twice at each of 35, 40 and 45 metres at a 45cm face	24 arrows
Twice at each of 50, 55 and 60 metres at a 60cm face	24 arrows
Twice 6, 8, 10 and 12 metres at 15cm faces	8 arrows
Twice 15, 20, 25 and 30 metres at 30cm faces	8 arrows
Twice 30, 35, 40 and 45 metres at a 45cm face	8 arrows
Twice 45, 50, 55 and 60 metres at a 60cm face	8 arrows

Tolerance on distances shall not exceed ±0.5%.

Total number of arrows, 112.

Scoring 5, 4, 3 for spot, inner and outer respectively.

Maximum possible score, 560.

Juniors

Juniors (15/17) shoot from the same posts as adults in all cases.

Juniors (12/14) shoot all four shots from the front post on 60cm walk-up target; and have a forward post provided 15 metres in advance of the Adult posts on the fixed position targets at 60, 55, 50 and 45 metres (Note that this latter target is a 45cm face.)

Juniors (under 12) shoot the same privilege shots as Juniors (12/14), and in addition, shoot from the front post at ALL walk-up targets.

Organisers *may* provide suitably placed extra forward posts for under 12s at their discretion. In this case no under-12 records can be claimed and a statement to this effect must appear on entry forms for Record Status Tournaments.

FITA Combination Round

The FITA Combination Round shall consist of one unit (14 targets representing a correct half of those shot in the full round) of Unmarked Hunter Targets and one unit of Marked FITA Field Targets laid out consecutively. Where both units are shot over the same course, the Hunter unit shall be shot first. The use of binoculars or the carrying of them is not permitted during the shooting of the Hunter unit.

This Combination Round is a GNAS Round and is not recognised as such by FITA.

Total number of arrows, 112.

Scoring 5, 4, 3 for spot, inner and outer respectively.

Maximum possible score, 560.

Juniors

The rules regarding shooting posts for Juniors in the Hunter and Field Rounds apply to the appropriate unit in this Round.

(b) Foresters Round

Shot on Foresters faces. Distances may be marked or unmarked.

The Round consists of 28 targets (or two units)

The standard unit shall consist of the following 14 shots:

Three 24in faces at a distance of up to 70 yards.

Four 18in faces at a distance of up to 50 yards.

Four 12in faces at a distance of up to 40 yards.

Three 6in faces at a distance of up to 20 yards.

Shooting Rules: At a 24in target, four arrows are shot, one from each of four posts. At an 18in target, three arrows are shot, one from each of three posts. At a 12in target, two arrows are shot, one from each of two posts. At a 6in target, only one arrow is shot from one post. Multi-post shots may be equidistant from the target or 'walk-away' or 'walk-up'.

Scoring   Aiming spot   – 15 points

Inner Circle   – 10 points

Outer Circle   – 5 points

Total number of arrows – 70 arrows

Maximum possible score – 1050 points

Juniors

Juniors (15/17) shoot from the same posts as Adults in all cases.

Juniors (12/14) shoot from the same posts as Adults at the 6in and 12in faces. They shoot two arrows from the middle distance post and one arrow from the front post at 18in faces. They shoot two arrows from each of the two nearest posts at the 24in faces.

Juniors (under 12) shoot all arrows from the front post at all targets.

(c) Four-Shot Foresters Round

Shot on Foresters faces. Distances shall not be marked.

The Round consists of 28 targets (or two units), with four walk-up shots on each target.

Distribution of faces, as in Foresters Round.

Scoring as in Foresters Round.

Total number of arrows, 112.

Maximum possible score, 1680 points.

Juniors

Juniors (15/17) shoot from the same posts as Adults in all cases.

Juniors (12/14) shoot two arrows from each of the two nearest shooting posts at the targets showing 18in and 24in faces.

Juniors (under 12) shoot all arrows from the front post at all targets.

(d) The Big Game Round

Shot on Big Game faces, the Big Game Round consists of 28 targets (or two units) marked or unmarked.

The standard unit is made up of the following 14 targets at the suggested ranges:

Three group 1 targets at a distance of 70 to 40 yards.
Three group 2 targets at a distance of 50 to 30 yards.
Four group 3 targets at a distance of 40 to 20 yards
Four group 4 targets at a distance of 30 to 10 yards.
Shooting Rules: Three shots are permitted at each target, one from each
of the three posts, each successive post being closer to the target than the
previous one.
Arrows shall be identifiable as to order of shooting. The archer shall
stop shooting as soon as a hit is considered to have been made.
Scoring: The score is decided by the position of the arrow in the target
(i.e. in the 'kill' or 'wound' zone) and the number of arrows shot.

	kill	wound
1st arrow score	20	16
2nd arrow score	14	10
3rd arrow score	8	4

Only the score of the first 'scoring' arrow counts.
Maximum possibe score, 560.

Juniors
Juniors (15/17) shoot from the same posts as Adults in all cases.
Juniors (12/14) shoot two arrows from the middle distance post and one
from the front post until a hit is scored.
Juniors (under 12) shoot up to three arrows from the front post until a
hit is scored.

(e) The National Animal Round
Shot on Animal faces conforming to the specifications given in 205.
The National Animal Round is shot over 32 targets (or two units) not
marked. When two units are shot, the targets shall be mixed so that the
units are not consecutive.
The course shall be laid out so that each unit shall consist of the
following targets set within the prescribed range. Organisers are
required to provide a good variety of shots.

Number of faces	Kill zone diameter	Distance Range
4	30cm	55–30 metres
4	22.5cm	45–20 metres
4	15cm	35–10 metres
4	7.5cm	20–5 metres

Shooting: Two arrows shall be shot at each target, one from each of two
posts set within the prescribed range.

Scoring: Kill zone   – 10 points
               Wound zone –   5 points
Total number of arrows in a Round, 64
Maximum possible score, 640.

Juniors

Juniors (15/17) shoot from the same posts as Adults in all cases.
Juniors (12/14) shoot both arrows from the nearest shooting post at the
30cm kill zone faces.
Juniors (under 12) shoot both arrows at the 30cm kill zone and the 22.5
kill zone diameter faces from a single privilege post set at an appropriate
distance.

III. FLIGHT SHOOTING

300. Basis

(*a*) The three classes for which competitions may take place are:
   A. Target Bows
   B. Flight Bows
   C. Free-style.
Ladies, Gentlemen and Juniors may compete equally in each class.

(*b*) The classes may be subdivided into bow weights, as follows:
   1 – 16kg (35lb)
   2 – 23kg (50lb)
   3 – Unlimited.
Except for the target bow and unlimited classes flight bows shall be
weighed as follows:

(i) Bows shall be weighed just prior to commencement of shooting.
Weight of bow, length of arrow, and the class for which this
combination is eligible, shall be recorded on a label affixed to the face
of the bow.

(ii) The weight of the bow shall be taken at two inches less than the
length of the longest arrow, and again at one inch less than the length
of this arrow. The difference in these weights shall be added to the last
weight of the bow at full draw.

Weighing bows at full draw is optional with the competitor. When
an overdraw device is used and permits a draw in excess of one inch
from the back of the bow, this excess shall be considered a portion of
the arrow length for bow weighing purposes.

(*c*) For classes A and B only hand bows may be used and the bow
must be held in the unsupported hand.

(*d*) If competitions for both Target and Flight Bows are being held on the same occasion, all shooting with Target Bows must be completed first.

301. Range Layout
(*a*) The Range Line, at right angles to the shooting line shall be clearly marked at 150 yards then at 50 yard intervals to at least 50 yards beyond the existing longest distance shot in the UK.

(*b*) Red warning flags shall be placed at each side of the range at 75 yards from the line of distance markers at a distance of 150 yards from the shooting line.

302. Equipment
(*a*) A Target Bow is any bow with which the user has shot at least two standard Target or Field Rounds. In the event of a breakage, a similar bow may be used as replacement.

(*b*) Any type of bow, other than a crossbow, may be entered for Classes B and C.

(*c*) In the Target Bow class competitors must use their own length standard target arrows and normal tab or shooting glove.

(*d*) In Classes B and C any type of arrow may be used.

(*e*) Sipurs are not permitted in Class A.

(*f*) Mechanical releases, inter-moving drawing and/or release aides are prohibited.

The following may be used in Classes B and C:

Six-gold ring, flipper or strap (single or double), block sipur, and angle measuring device.

(*g*) In the event of a breakage a substitute bow or limb may be used providing it is checked for conforming to its class. In the event of this not being done the archer will automatically be transferred to the unlimited class.

303. Shooting
(*a*) Competitors should be at least six feet apart, and must not advance their leading foot over the shooting line.

(*b*) Each competitor may have one assistant or adviser, who must keep at least one yard behind the shooting line.

(*c*) (i) At least four ends, each of three arrows, will be shot.

(ii) After all classes have shot the first end competitors and officials will go forward. Competitors will stand by their furthest arrow. A marker with a label attached bearing the name of the competitor and class will then be placed at the pile end of the furthest arrow in each class.

(iii) Arrows will then be withdrawn.

(iv) Succeeding ends will then be shot and markers adjusted where necessary.

304. Control of Shooting
There shall be a Range Captain in charge who will act as Referee and Judge. His decision shall be final. He will also be responsible for the safety of the spectators, who must at all times, when shooting is in progress, be not less than 10 yards behind the shooting line.

305. Measurements
Measurement of distances shall be made with a steel tape along the range line. The distances shot shall be measured to that point on the range line at which a line at right angles to the range line passes the point where the arrow enters the ground. If the arrow is lying on the ground the line should pass through the pile end of the arrow.

IV. CLOUT SHOOTING

400. Regulations
GNAS Rules of Shooting for Target Archery – Outdoor shall apply except as enumerated in the following paragraphs.

The organisers shall take all reasonable steps to ensure that there be no risk occasioned to people, animals or property from arrows that miss the target area by overshot or to either side (NB a distance of 75 yards from the Clout centre to the boundary of any land to which the public has access is deemed reasonable).

401. Targets
The centre of the target shall be marked by a brightly coloured distinctive flag 12in square, set as close as practicable to ground level on a smooth vertical stick. The stick should not project above the flag.

402. Shooting
(*a*) Shooting may be either 'two way' or 'one way'.

(*b*) Six sighter arrows shall be shot in each direction when shooting two ways.

(*c*) The organiser, after considering general safety, archers' comfort and the duties of scorers, shall use his discretion as to the number of archers allocated to each target.

403. Scoring
(*a*) Scores shall be determined according to the distance of arrows at point of entry in ground from centre of flag stick.

Within a radius of 18 inches – 5 points

       3 feet – 4 points

       6 feet – 3 points

       9 feet – 2 points

       12 feet – 1 point

Arrows which have hit and remain embedded in the Clout shall score 5 provided they are not embedded in a lower scoring ring whereupon they shall score according to the ring in which they are embedded.

(b) Rings of the above radii may be marked on the ground, the lines drawn being wholly within each circle.

(c) Where it is not practical to draw lines on the ground, scores shall be determined with a non-stretch cord or tape looped round the centre stick and clearly marked to measure the various radii.

Where this method of measuring is used an area should be marked on the ground (conveniently a square or circle) which will contain the whole of the Clout scoring zone and which for all purposes included in (d) be termed the Target Area. The scorer should allow adequate time for all archers shooting to determine the position of the arrows in the said area before carrying out the following procedure. The scorer shall carry the taut cord round at ground level and one assistant scorer following the cord at each 'colour' shall withdraw and carry all arrows from the 'colour' for which he is responsible. An arrow lying loose on the ground shall be scored in accordance with the position of its point. The arrows shall then be placed in distinct groups on or stuck into the ground at the appropriate section of the scoring cord and competitors will call their scores in the usual manner, picking up their arrows as they do so.

(d) No person other than the appointed scorers shall enter the target area until all arrows have been withdrawn and placed in their respective scoring groups. An arrow withdrawn by any other than an appointed scorer shall not be scored.

404. Round

(a) A Clout Round consists of 36 arrows.

(b) At Record Status Tournaments the distances given below must be shot. There is nothing to prevent a junior holding a record in a round of a higher age group.

At other meetings the distance to be shot shall be determined by the organisers but would normally be as given.

   Gentlemen – 9 score yards

   Ladies   – 7 score yards

Junior Gentlemen:
Under 18 years – 7 score yards
Under 16 years – 6 score yards
Under 14 years – 5 score yards
Under 12 years – 4 score yards
Junior Ladies:
Under 18 years – 6 score yards
Under 16 years – 5 score yards
Under 13 years – 4 score yards

405. National Championship Round
The National Championship shall be decided over a Double Clout Round.

V. CROSSBOW ARCHERY

500. Regulations
GNAS Rules of Shooting for Target Archery – Outdoors shall apply except as enumerated in the following paragraphs.

(*a*) Crossbowmen shall shoot on separate targets from other archers and not compete with them.

(*b*) No person less than 12 years of age may shoot or manipulate a crossbow.

501. Equipment
(*a*) A crossbow stock and mechanism may be made from any material. No mechanical aids or rests are permitted. Prods may be made of any other material except metal. The length measured along the curves shall not exceed 36 inches.

(*b*) The draw-length shall be measured from the back of the prod to the string latch. Draw-weight shall not exceed 1280lb/in with a maximum draw of 18 inches. (To determine the lb/in multiply the draw-length by the draw-weight.) The draw-weight shall be marked on the prod, e.g. 70lb @ 18in.

(*c*) A string may be made of any non-metallic material.

(*d*) Bolts may be made of any material and of such design as not to cause unreasonable damage to the target. Bolt length is minimum 12 inches, maximum 15 inches. Three fletchings, feather or plastic, shall be fitted.

(*e*) Telescopic or magnifying sights are not allowed.

(*f*) Stirrups attached to the stock or ground are permitted, provided that Rule 501(*b*) is complied with.

(*g*) Pistol crossbows are not permitted.

502. Recognised Rounds

(a) Windsor Round shot on a 60cm FITA face scoring 9, 7, 5, 3, 1. The Championship Round shall be a Double Windsor.

(b) American Round shot on a 60cm FITA face scoring 10, 9, 8, 7, 6, 5, 4, 3, 2, 1.

(c) Western Round shot on an 80cm FITA face scoring 10, 9, 8, 7, 6, 5, 4, 3, 2, 1.

(d) Any recognised GNAS or FITA Round.

503. Field Archery

(a) Current Field Archery Rules shall apply with those exceptions detailed in 500(a) and (b).

(b) Targets shall be fixed below skyline.

(c) Field Rounds as recognised by GNAS or FITA shall be shot.

504. The Crossbow and the Law

When travelling on public transport or walking in a public thoroughfare it is essential that the prod be removed and the stock and prod be carried in a case or cover.

505. Safety Rules

If shooting is interrupted for any reason, crossbows shall be lowered immediately so that they are directed at the ground immediately in front of the shooting line and the bolt removed. A crossbow may *not* be drawn or cocked except on the shooting line and in the direction of the targets.

PART VI. TRADITIONAL LONGBOW

600. Regulations

GNAS Rules of Shooting for Target Archery – Outdoor shall apply except as enumerated in the following paragraphs.

601. Equipment

(a) The bow shall be the traditional longbow made from wood, with stacked belly, and nocks. For a 24in–26in arrow, not less than 5ft in length; and for a 27in or longer arrow, not less than 5ft 6in in length, this being measured between the string nocks. At no point shall the depth of the bow – measured from back to belly – be less than $\frac{5}{8}$ (five eighths) of the width of the bow at the same section.

Bows of bamboo, constructed in conformity with the above, shall be permitted. Strings may be of either natural or manmade substance, and may, if desired, embody a 'kisser' at any point as required, to facilitate a consistent draw position. The use of extended 'platform' tabs for this purpose is not encouraged.

(*b*) Marks on the bow limb, or rubber bands of no more than ⅛in in depth and thickness, are permitted; but sights as such shall not be allowed. The bow shall carry no support for the arrow.

(*c*) Arrows shall have wooden steles (shafts), shall be fitted with feather fletchings, and may have either horn-reinforced, self or applied nocks. Piles shall be flush fitting. Shouldered Field piles, whilst permitted, should be avoided because of excess damage to targets. Broadhead, edged, bodkin, silver-spoon and other large diameter piles shall not be permitted.

Every archer is expected to have and to shoot arrows properly marked, so that there shall be no dificulty in claiming them.

(*d*) Artificial points of aim on the ground are permitted, but such shall not exceed a height of 6in from the ground, or 3in in diameter; nor shall they impede any other archer. Binoculars and telescopes shall not be used.

VII. RECORDS

700. National Record
A National Record may be established and submitted to National Council for ratification at:

(*a*) Any tournament organised by FITA, FITA Members or GNAS.

(*b*) Any tournament which has been granted Record Status by National Council. Applications (all disciplines) to hold a Record Status Tournament must be received by the GNAS Office at least six calendar months prior to the date of the tournament. It shall be a condition that such tournaments, except for Inter-Regional and Inter-County tournaments, shall be open to all GNAS members shooting bows as recognised in rules 102(*a*) and 102(*c*).

701. Submission of Claims
Claims for National Records shall be submitted to the GNAS Secretary on the appropriate form except for National Championships and UK Masters Tournament when the Secretary will submit claims to National Council.

The claim forms must be completed prior to the dispersal of the Meeting at which the record has been made. One copy shall be handed to the archer and one copy retained by the Tournament Organiser. Both copies must be sent to the Secretary within 28 days of the date on which the record was made.

The claim form sent by the tournament organiser shall be accompanied by the original score sheet (or a photocopy), signed as in 106(*b*), and the results sheet as circulated.

702. Target Archery

(*a*) World Records may be established for the FITA Round and each distance of the FITA Round according to qualifications laid down in FITA Rules.

Claims for World Records shall be submitted to the GNAS Secretary supported by the necessary documents for onward transmissions to FITA for ratification.

(*b*) National Records may be claimed for rounds, either single, double or distance, as defined in rules 108 and 123, when shot at recognised Record Status tournaments. Where a double round is shot on the one day the second round will not be accepted for a single round record.

(*c*) Initial National Records in compund classes will only be ratified if the scores submitted exceed 75% of the existing freestyle record for the round.

703. Field Archery

(*a*) Record Rounds are restricted to National Animal, Unmarked Hunter, Marked Field and FITA Combination Rounds.

(*b*) National Records are to be maintained for all classes and styles in Field Archery. But initial claims for records in Compound classes will only be entertained if the scores submitted exceed 75% of the corresponding record scores for the conventional recurve bow class or style.

(*c*) National Records may be claimed by and granted to Junior Field archers (both under 12 and under 15 years of age) if the round shot was that appropriate to the age of the claimant, or if the claimant has shot a more difficult round than his age demanded. No Junior may hold a National Record for a round for a higher age group unless he has shot to the conditions appropriate to that age-group, and has stated his intentions to the organiser in advance.

(*d*) Records will not be kept for Juniors (under 12) class in respect of the National Animal Round.

704. Flight Shooting

(*a*) National Records may be claimed in all classes at a recognised Record Status tournament. The measurements must be checked and witnessed by the Range Captain and one other responsible person. In addition the Range Captain must certify that the ground over which the shot was made was reasonably flat and level.

(*b*) A new record may be established when the measurement is at least one yard longer than the existing record.

705. Clout Shooting

(*a*) National Records may be claimed for both single and double rounds shot 'one way' and 'two way' at distances stated in 404(*b*). Where a double round is shot on a single day the second round will not be accepted for a single round record.

(*b*) Initial National Records in Compound classes will only be ratified if the scores submitted exceed 75% of the existing freestyle record.

VIII. HANDICAP AND CLASSIFICATION SCHEMES
This section is given in GNAS Rules of Shooting.

IX. OTHER FORMS OF ARCHERY

900. Popinjay Shooting

Set-up for Popinjay

(*a*) The full complement of a Popinjay 'roost' shall consist of:
One Cock Bird
Four Hens
Minimum of twenty-four Chicks.

(*b*) Body size of all birds shall be 1½in long ¾in diameter – only the plumage shall differ:

– that of the Cock Bird being most resplendent and 10in–12in high.

– that of the Hen Birds being shorter 6in–8in high and less colourful.

– that of the Chicks being shortest 3in–4in high.

(*c*) The Chicks shall be perched on spikes 6in long, not less than 4in apart, in three rows, the vertical height between rows being not less than 3 feet. The Hen Birds shall be perched on spikes 18in above the top row and shall be spaced not less than 8in apart.

The Cock Bird shall be perched on a central spike not less than 30in above the top row.

(*d*) The perches may be attached to, or hauled up a mast or wall to a height of 90 feet (measured to the Cock Bird).

Arrangements must be made to ensure that when in position the perches are firmly held against movement by wind.

(*e*) All obstructions on and within the framework of perches must be softened with rubber or sponge rubber (or similar resilient material) to lessen the risk of arrow breakage.

(*f*) No hard and fast shooting position is dictated, although it should be pointed out to all competitors that a near vertical, close to mast attitude will offer a better target to the archer, inasmuch as a greater number of birds will be in line of the arrow flight path.

(*g*) Each and every part of the Popinjay Mast and Framework of Perches must be made to be safe from breakage and/or dislodgement by arrow or the elements.

(*h*) Whenever possible a shelter should be provided for competitors, a temporary structure approx. 7ft 6in high covered on top with ½in wire mesh is sufficient for this purpose. If no shelter is available competitors waiting to shoot must be made to wait outside the arrow fall-out area.

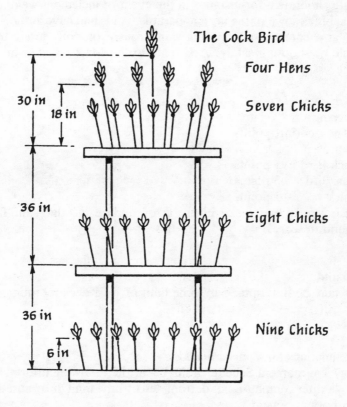

Typical Popinjay 'roost' showing minimum complement.

901. Arrows
Only arrows with blunts ¾in to 1in diameter shall be used.

902. Shooting
(a) Archers will draw for order of shooting.
(b) Only one archer shall shoot at a time.
(c) Archers must shoot in rotation – only one arrow being shot per end.
(d) Disabled archers may shoot with the aid of a prop.

903. Mast Captain
A Mast Captain shall be appointed to ensure that shooting is conducted in a safe and proper manner. This person shall have the authority to terminate shooting – for instance in the event of inclement weather or technical breakdown of the mast apparatus – and shall have authority to dismiss any competitor shooting dangerously or considered to be incapable of shooting safely. Assistants to the Mast Captain may be found necessary.

904. Scoring
(a) The scoring points for hits are:

Cock Bird – 5 points
Hen Bird – 3 points
Chick – 1 point

(b) Birds must be struck with the arrow and be dislodged and fall to the ground to score.

905. Round
Results may be determined by time limit or by a declared number of arrows.

906. Regulations for Tournaments
Popinjay Tournament Schedules shall bear the following information:
(a) Whether competition is determined by time limit or by number of arrows shot per person.
(b) Maximum number of archers that will be accepted.
Note: The GNAS Insurance Scheme does not cover for risks attendant on the erection and dismantling of Popinjay Masts.

920. Archery Golf
Regulations

(*a*) Only one bow shall be used throughout a round. In case of breakage it may be replaced.

(*b*) Any arrows may be used.

(*c*) The archer shall 'hole out' by hitting a white cardboard disc 4in in diameter, placed on the ground at least one yard within the edge of the green level with the hole.

(*d*) An arrow landing off the fairway or in a bunker shall incur one extra stroke.

(*e*) The archer must stand immediately behind where his arrow lands to shoot the next arrow.

(*f*) A lost arrow incurs the normal penalty (as in golf) for stroke play but loses the hole in match play.

(*g*) The winner of the previous 'hole' takes the first shot for the next hole.

(*h*) The current Golf Rules and local Course Regulations shall apply in all cases not covered by the foregoing rules.

940. Archery Darts
Regulations

GNAS Rules of Shooting for Target Archery shall apply except as enumerated in the following paragraphs:

Target Faces

Archery Darts Faces 76.2cm (2ft 6in) in diameter shall be used.

General Rules

(*a*) The targets shall be set up so that the centre of the Bull is at the centre of a 122cm minimum diameter boss 130cm from the ground.

(*b*) The minimum shooting distance shall be 13.7m (15yd).

(*c*) An End shall consist of three arrows unless a game is finished in less.

(*d*) The order of starting shall be determined by the toss of a coin.

(*e*) Each match must start and finish on a Double (the narrow outer ring). The inner ring counts treble; the inner Bull counts 50; and the outer Bull 25.

(*f*) A practice end of three arrows must be shot at the Bull.

(*g*) The value of an arrow shall be determined by the position of the greater part of the shaft.

(*h*) Scoring shall be by the subtraction method, so that the score required for the completion of each game is always shown.

(*j*) If the score required to complete the game is exceeded in the course of an End, then that End ceases, and no account is taken of the score obtained during that End.

Note: Local variations may be used.

APPENDIX A

Etiquette
A Good Archer:
 Does not talk in a loud voice whilst others are shooting.
 Does not talk to another competitor who obviously prefers to be silent.
 Does not make any exclamation on the shooting line which might disconcert a neighbour in the act of shooting.
 Does not go behind the target to retrieve his arrows before his score has been recorded.
 Does not walk up and down the shooting line comparing scores.
 Does not touch anyone else's equipment without permission.
 Does not leave litter.
 When calling scores does so in groups of three, for example '7-7-5' pause '5-5-3'.
 If he breaks another's arrow through his own carelessness, pays for it in cash on the spot.
 Thanks the Target Captain at the end of each round for work on his behalf.

APPENDIX B
Public Liability Insurance
APPENDIX C
Minimum Standard of the Judge for Tournaments
APPENDIX D
Metric Conversion Table
APPENDIX E
Rules of Shooting for Visually-Handicapped Archers

Reprinted by permission of the Grand National Archery Society. A number of the Rules have here been abbreviated for reasons of space. Copies of the complete senior and junior Rules and Regulations and of the FITA Constitution and Rules can be obtained from the Society.

Association Football

The Field of Play

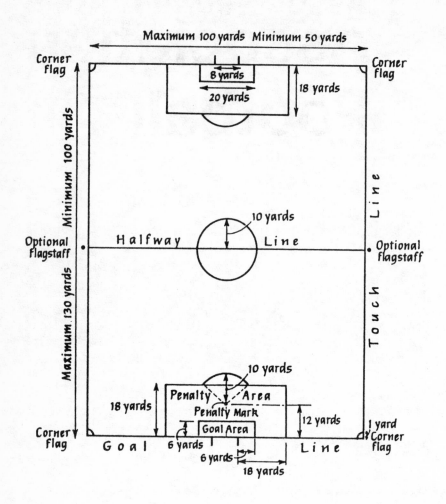

Association Football

1. THE FIELD OF PLAY

The Field of Play and appurtenances are shown in the plan on the opposite page.

(1) Dimensions

The field of play shall be rectangular, its length being not more than 130yd nor less than 100yd and its breadth not more than 100yd nor less than 50yd. (In International Matches the length shall be not more than 120yd nor less than 110yd and the breadth not more than 80yd nor less than 70yd.) The length shall in all cases exceed the breadth.

(2) Marking

The field of play shall be marked with distinctive lines, not more than 5in in width, not by a V-shaped rut, in accordance with the plan, the longer boundary lines being called the touch-lines and the shorter the goal-lines. A flag on a post not less than 5ft high and having a non-pointed top, shall be placed at each corner; a similar flag-post may be placed opposite the halfway-line on each side of the field of play, not less than 1yd outside the touch-line. A half-way line shall be marked out across the field of play. The centre of the field of play shall be indicated by a suitable mark and a circle with a 10yd radius shall be marked round it.

(3) The Goal-Area

At each end of the field of play two lines shall be drawn at right angles to the goal-line, 6yd from each goal-post. These shall extend into the field of play for a distance of 6yd and shall be joined by a line drawn parallel with the goal-line. Each of the spaces enclosed by these lines and the goal-line shall be called the goal-area.

(4) The Penalty-Area

At each end of the field of play two lines shall be drawn at right angles to the goal-line, 18yd from each goal-post. These shall extend into the field of play for a distance of 18yd and shall be joined by a line drawn parallel with the goal-line. Each of the spaces enclosed by these lines and the goal-line shall be called a penalty-area. A suitable mark shall be made within each penalty-area, 12yd from the mid-point of the goal-line, measured along an undrawn line at right angles thereto. These shall be the penalty-kick marks. From each penalty-kick mark an arc of a circle, having a radius of 10yd, shall be drawn outside the penalty-area.

(5) The Corner-Area

From each corner-flag post a quarter circle, having a radius of 1yd, shall be drawn inside the field of play.

(6) The Goals

The goals shall be placed on the centre of each goal-line and shall consist of two upright posts, equidistant from the corner-flags and 8yd apart (inside measurement), joined by a horizontal cross-bar, the lower edge of which shall be 8ft from the ground. The width and depth of the goal-posts and the width and depth of the cross-bars shall not exceed 5in (12cm). The goal-posts and the cross-bars shall have the same width.

Nets may be attached to the posts, cross-bars and ground behind the goals. They should be appropriately supported and be so placed as to allow the goalkeeper ample room.

INTERNATIONAL BOARD DECISIONS

(1) In International Matches the dimensions of the field of play shall be: maximum 110m × 75m; minimum 100m × 64m.

(2) National Associations must adhere strictly to these dimensions. Each National Assocation organising an International Match must advise the Visiting Association, before the match, of the place and the dimensions of the field of play.

(3) The Board has approved this table of measurements for the Laws of the Game:

Table of Metric Equivalents

130yd	120m	8ft		2.44m
120yd	110m	5ft		1.50m
110yd	100m	28in		0.71m
100yd	90m	27in		0.68m
80yd	75m	9in		0.22m
70yd	64m	5in		0.12m
50yd	45m	½in		12.7mm

12yd	.. ..	11m	14oz = 396g
10yd	.. ..	9.15m	16oz = 453g
8yd	.. ..	7.32m	8.5lb/sq in = 600g/cm^2
6yd	.. ..	5.50m	15.6lb/sq in = 1,100g/cm^2
1yd	.. ..	1m	

(4) The goal-line shall be marked the same width as the depth of the goal-posts and the cross-bar so that the goal-line and the goal-posts will conform to the same interior and exterior edges.

(5) The 6yd (for the outline of the goal-area) and the 18yd (for the outline of the penalty-area), which have to be measured along the goal-line, must start from the inner sides of the goal-posts.

(6) The space within the inside areas of the field of play includes the width of the lines marking these areas.

(7) All Associations shall provide standard equipment, particularly in International Matches, when the Laws of the Game must be complied with in every respect and especially with regard to the size of the ball and other equipment which must conform to the regulations. All cases of failure to provide standard equipment must be reported to FIFA.

(8) In a match played under the rules of a competition, if the cross-bar becomes displaced or broken play shall be stopped and the match abandoned unless the cross-bar has been repaired and replaced in position or a new one provided without such being a danger to the players. A rope is not considered to be a satisfactory substitute for a cross-bar.

In a friendly match, by mutual consent, play may be resumed without the cross-bar provided it has been removed and no longer constitutes a danger to the players. In these circumstances, a rope may be used as a substitute for a cross-bar. If a rope is not used and the ball crosses the goal-line at a point which in the opinion of the Referee is below where the cross-bar should have been he shall award a goal.

The game shall be restarted by the Referee dropping the ball at the place where it was when play was stopped, unless it was within the goal-area at that time, in which case it shall be dropped on that part of the goal-area line which runs parallel to the goal-line, at the point nearest to where the ball was when play was stopped.

(9) National Associations may specify such maximum and minimum dimensions for the cross-bars and goal-posts, within the limits laid down in Law 1, as they consider appropriate.

(10) Goal-posts and cross-bars must be made of wood, metal or other approved material as decided from time to time by the International FA Board. They may be square, rectangular, round, half round, or elliptical in shape. Goal-posts and cross-bars made of other materials and in other shapes are not permitted. The goal-posts must be of white colour.

(11) 'Curtain-raisers' to International Matches should only be played following agreement on the day of the match, and taking into account the condition of the field of play, between representatives of the two Associations and the Referee (of the International Match).

(12) National Associations, particularly in International Matches, should restrict the number of photographers around the field of play, have a line ('photographers' line') marked behind the goal-lines at least 2m from the corner-flag going through a point at least 3.5 m behind the intersection of the goal-line with the line marking the goal-area to a point situated at least 6m behind the goal-posts, prohibit photographers from passing over these lines and forbid the use of artificial lighting in the form of 'flash-lights'.

2. THE BALL

The ball shall be spherical; the outer casing shall be of leather or other approved materials. No material shall be used in its construction which might prove dangerous to the players. The circumference of the ball shall not be more than 28in nor less than 27in. The weight of the ball at the start of the game shall not be more than 16oz nor less than 14oz. The pressure shall be equal to 0.6–1.1 atmosphere ($= 600$–$1,100$ g/cm^2) at sea level. The ball shall not be changed during the game unless authorized by the Referee.

INTERNATIONAL BOARD DECISIONS

(1) The ball used in any match shall be considered the property of the Association or Club on whose ground the match is played, and at the close of play it must be returned to the Referee.

(2) The International Board, from time to time, shall decide what constitutes approved materials. Any approved material shall be certified as such by the International Board.

(3) The board has approved these equivalents of the weights specified in the Law:

14 to 16 ounces = 396 to 453 grammes.

(4) If the ball bursts or becomes deflated during the course of a match, the game shall be stopped and restarted by dropping the new ball at the place where the first ball became defective, unless it was within the goal-area at that time, in which case it shall be dropped on that part of the goal-area line which runs parallel to the goal-line, at the point nearest to where the ball was when play was stopped.

(5) If this happens during a stoppage of the game (place-kick, goal-kick, corner-kick, free-kick, penalty-kick or throw-in) the game shall be restarted accordingly.

3. NUMBER OF PLAYERS

(1) A match shall be played by two teams, each consisting of not more than 11 players, one of whom shall be the goalkeeper.

(2) Substitutes may be used in any match played under the rules of an official competition under the jurisdiction of FIFA, Confederations or National Associations, subject to the following conditions:

(*a*) That the authority of the International Association(s) or National Association(s) concerned has been obtained;

(*b*) That, subject to the restriction contained in the following paragraph (*c*), the rules of a competition shall state how many, if any, substitutes may be nominated and how many of these nominated may be used;

(*c*) That a team shall not be permitted to use more than two substitutes in any match who must be chosen from not more than five players whose names may (subject to the rules of the competition) be required to be given to the Referee prior to the commencement of the match.

(3) Substitutes may be used in any other match provided that the two teams concerned reach agreement on a maximum number, not exceeding five, and that the terms of such agreement are intimated to the Referee, before the match. If the Referee is not informed, or if the teams fail to reach agreement, no more than 2 substitutes shall be permitted. In all cases the substitutes must be chosen from not more than five players whose names may be required to be given to the Referee prior to the commencement of the match.

(4) Any of the other players may change places with the goalkeeper, provided that the Referee is informed before the change is made, and provided also that the change is made during a stoppage in the game.

(5) When a goalkeeper or any other player is to be replaced by a substitute, the following conditions shall be observed:

(*a*) The Referee shall be informed of the proposed substitution, before it is made;

(*b*) The substitute shall not enter the field of play until the player he is replacing has left, and then only after having received a signal from the Referee;

(*c*) He shall enter the field during a stoppage in the game, and at the halfway-line;

(*d*) A player who has been replaced shall not take any further part in the game;

(*e*) A substitute shall be subject to the authority and jurisdiction of the Referee whether called upon to play or not;

(*f*) The substitution is completed when the substitute enters the field of play, from which moment he becomes a player and the player whom he is replacing ceases to be a player.

Punishment: (*a*) Play shall not be stopped for an infringement of paragraph 4. The players concerned shall be cautioned immediately the ball goes out of play.

(*b*) If a substitute enters the field of play without the authority of the Referee, play shall be stopped. The substitute shall be cautioned and removed from the field or sent off according to the circumstances. The game shall be restarted by the Referee dropping the ball at the place where it was when he stopped play, unless it was within the goal-area at that time, in which case it shall be dropped on that part of the goal area line which runs parallel to the goal-line, at the point nearest to where the ball was when play was stopped.

(*c*) For any other infringement of this Law, the player concerned shall be cautioned, and if the game is stopped by the Referee to administer the caution, it shall be restarted by an indirect free-kick, to be taken by a player of the opposing team, from the place where the ball was when play was stopped, subject to the over-riding conditions imposed in Law 13.

(*d*) If a Competition's rules require the names of substitutes to be given to the Referee, prior to the commencement of the match, then failure to do so will mean that no substitutes can be permitted.

INTERNATIONAL BOARD DECISIONS
(1) The minimum number of players in a team is left to the discretion of National Associations.

(2) The Board is of the opinion that a match should not be considered valid if there are fewer than 7 players in either of the teams.

(3) A player who has been ordered off before play begins may only be replaced by one of the named substitutes. The kick-off must not be delayed to allow the substitute to join his team.

A player who has been ordered off after play has started may not be replaced. A named substitute who has been ordered off, either before or after play has started, may not be replaced. (This decision only relates to players who are ordered off under Law 12. It does not apply to players who have infringed Law 4.)

4. PLAYERS' EQUIPMENT
(1) (*a*) The basic compulsory equipment of a player shall consist of a jersey or shirt, shorts, stockings, shinguards and footwear.

(*b*) A player shall not wear anything which is dangerous to another player.

(2) Shinguards, which must be covered entirely by the stockings, shall be made of a suitable material (rubber, plastic, polyurethane or similar substance) and shall afford a reasonable degree of protection.

The goalkeeper shall wear colours which distinguish him from the other players and from the Referee.

Punishment: For any infringement of this Law, the player at fault shall be sent off the field of play to adjust his equipment and he shall not return without first reporting to the Referee, who shall satisfy himself that the player's equipment is in order; the player shall only re-enter the game at a moment when the ball has ceased to be in play.

INTERNATIONAL BOARD DECISIONS

(1) In International Matches, International Competitions, International Club Competitions and friendly matches between clubs of different National Associations, the Referee, prior to the start of the game, shall inspect the players' equipment, and prevent any player whose equipment does not conform to the requirements of this Law from playing until such time as it does comply.

The rules of any competition may include a similar provision.

(2) If the Referee finds that a player is wearing articles not permitted by the Laws and which may constitute a danger to other players, he shall order him to take them off. If he fails to carry out the Referee's instruction, the player shall not take part in the match.

(3) A player who has been prevented from taking part in the game or a player who has been sent off the field for infringing Law 4 must report to the Referee during a stoppage of the game and may not enter or re-enter the field of play unless and until the Referee has satisfied himself that the player is no longer infringing Law 4.

(4) A player who has been prevented from taking part in a game or who has been sent off because of an infringement of Law 4, and who enters or re-enters the field of play to join or rejoin his team in breach of the conditions of Law 12 (*j*), shall be cautioned.

If the Referee stops the game to administer the caution, the game shall be restarted by an indirect free-kick, taken by a player of the opposing side, from the place where the ball was when the Referee stopped the game, subject to the over-riding conditions imposed in Law 13.

5. REFEREES

A Referee shall be appointed to officiate in each game. His authority and the exercise of the powers granted to him by the Laws of the Game commence as soon as he enters the field of play.

His power of penalising shall extend to offences committed when play has been temporarily suspended, or when the ball is out of play. His decisions on points of fact connected with the play shall be final, so far as the result of the game is concerned.

He shall:

(*a*) Enforce the Laws.

(*b*) Refrain from penalising in cases where he is satisfied that, by doing so, he would be giving an advantage to the offending team.

(*c*) Keep a record of the game; act as timekeeper and allow the full or agreed time, adding thereto all time lost through accident or other cause.

(*d*) Have discretionary power to stop the game for any infringement of the Laws and to suspend or terminate the game whenever, by reason of the elements, interference by spectators, or other cause, he deems such stoppage necessary. In such a case he shall submit a detailed report to the competent authority, within the stipulated time*, and in accordance with the provisions set up by the National Association under whose jurisdiction the match was played. Reports will be deemed to be made when received in the ordinary course of post.

(*e*) From the time he enters the field of play, caution any player guilty of misconduct or ungentlemanly behaviour and, if he persists, suspend him from further participation in the game. In such cases the Referee shall send the name of the offender to the competent authority, within the stipulated time,* and in accordance with the provisions set up by the National Association under whose jurisdiction the match was played. Reports will be deemed to be made when received in the ordinary course of post.

(*f*) Allow no person other than the players and Linesmen to enter the field of play without his permission.

(*g*) Stop the game if, in his opinion, a player has been seriously injured; have the player removed as soon as possible from the field of play, and immediately resume the game. If a player is slightly injured the game shall not be stopped until the ball has ceased to be in play. A player who is able to go to the touch- or goal-line for attention of any kind shall not be treated on the field of play.

(*h*) Send off the field of play any player who, in his opinion, is guilty of violent conduct, serious foul play, or the use of foul or abusive language.

(*i*) Signal for recommencement of the game after all stoppages.

(*j*) Decide that the ball provided for a match meets with the requirements of Law 2.

INTERNATIONAL BOARD DECISIONS

(1) Referees in International Matches shall wear a blazer or blouse the colour of which is distinctive from the colours worn by the contesting teams.

(2) Referees for International Matches will be selected from a neutral

*In England, within two days, Sunday not included.

country unless the countries concerned agree to appoint their own officials.

(3) The Referee must be chosen from the official list of International Referees. This need not apply to Amateur and Youth International matches.

(4) The Referee shall report to the appropriate authority misconduct or any misdemeanour on the part of spectators, officials, players, named substitutes or other persons which take place either on the field of play or in its vicinity at any time prior to, during, or after the match in question so that appropriate action can be taken by the authority concerned.

(5) Linesmen are assistants of the Referee. In no case shall the Referee consider the intervention of a Linesman if he himself has seen the incident and, from his position on the field, is better able to judge. With this reserve, and the Linesmen neutral, the Referee can consider the intervention and if the information of the Linesman applies to that phase of the game immediately before the scoring of a goal, the Referee may act thereon and cancel the goal.

(6) The Referee, however, can only reverse his first decision so long as the game has not been restarted.

(7) If the Referee has decided to apply the advantage clause and to let the game proceed, he cannot revoke his decision if the presumed advantage has not been realised, even though he has not, by any gesture, indicated his decision. This does not exempt the offending player from being dealt with by the Referee.

(8) The Laws of the Game are intended to provide that games should be played with as little interference as possible, and in this view it is the duty of Referees to penalise only deliberate breaches of the Law. Constant whistling for trifling and doubtful breaches produces bad feeling and loss of temper on the part of the players and spoils the pleasure of spectators.

(9) By paragraph (*d*) of Law 5 the Referee is empowered to terminate a match in the event of grave disorder, but he has no power or right to decide, in such event, that either team is disqualified and thereby the loser of the match. He must send a detailed report to the proper authority who alone has the power to deal further with this matter.

(10) If a player commits two infringements of a different nature at the same time, the Referee shall punish the more serious offence.

(11) It is the duty of the Referee to act upon the information of neutral Linesmen with regard to incidents that do not come under the personal notice of the Referee.

(12) The Referee shall not allow any person to enter the field until play has stopped, and only then, if he has given him a signal to do so, nor shall he allow coaching from the boundary lines.

6. LINESMEN

Two Linesmen shall be appointed whose duty (subject to the decision of the Referee) shall be to indicate:

(*a*) When the ball is out of play;

(*b*) Which side is entitled to a corner-kick, goal-kick or throw-in;

(*c*) When a substitution is desired.

They shall also assist the Referee to control the game in accordance with the Laws. In the event of undue interference or improper conduct by a Linesman, the Referee shall dispense with his services and arrange for a substitute to be appointed. (The matter shall be reported by the Referee to the competent authority.) The Linesmen should be equipped with flags by the Club on whose ground the match is played.

INTERNATIONAL BOARD DECISIONS

(1) Linesmen where neutral shall draw the Referee's attention to any breach of the Laws of the Game of which they become aware if they consider that the Referee may not have seen it, but the Referee shall always be the judge of the decision to be taken.

(2) National Associations are advised to appoint official Referees of neutral nationality to act as Linesmen in International Matches.

(3) In International Matches, Linesmen's flags shall be of a vivid colour – bright reds and yellows. Such flags are recommended for use in all other matches.

(4) A Linesman may be subject to disciplinary action only upon a report of the Referee for unjustified interference or insufficient assistance.

7. DURATION OF THE GAME

The duration of the game shall be two equal periods of 45 minutes, unless otherwise mutually agreed upon subject to the following:

(*a*) Allowance shall be made in either period for all time lost through accident, substitution, the transport from the field of injured players, time-wasting or other cause, the amount of which shall be a matter for the discretion of the Referee.

(*b*) Time shall be extended to permit of a penalty-kick being taken at or after the expiration of the normal period in either half.

At half-time the interval shall not exceed 5 minutes, except by the consent of the Referee.

INTERNATIONAL BOARD DECISIONS

(1) If a match has been stopped by the Referee, before the completion of the time specified in the Rules, for any reason stated in Law 5, it must be

replayed in full unless the rules of the competition concerned provide for the result of the match at the time of such stoppage to stand.

(2) Players have a right to an interval at half-time.

8. THE START OF PLAY

(*a*) *At the beginning of the game* choice of ends and the kick-off shall be decided by the toss of a coin. The team winning the toss shall have the option of choice of ends or the kick-off.

The Referee having given a signal, the game shall be started by a player taking a place-kick (i.e. a kick at the ball while it is stationary on the ground in the centre of the field of play) into his opponents' half of the field of play. Every player shall be in his own half of the field and every player of the team opposing that of the kicker shall remain not less than 10yd from the ball until it is kicked-off; it shall not be deemed in play until it has travelled the distance of its own circumference. The kicker shall not play the ball a second time until it has been played or touched by another player.

(*b*) *After a goal has been scored* the game shall be restarted in like manner by a player of the team losing the goal.

(*c*) *After half-time*: When restarting after half-time, ends shall be changed and the kick-off shall be taken by a player of the opposite team to that of the player who started the game.

Punishment. For any infringement of this Law, the kick-off shall be retaken, except in the case of the kicker playing the ball again before it has been touched or played by another player; for this offence, an indirect free-kick shall be taken by a player of the opposing team from the place where the infringement occurred, subject to the over-riding conditions imposed in Law 13.

A goal shall not be scored direct from a kick-off.

(*d*) *After any other temporary suspension*: When restarting the game after a temporary suspension of play from any cause not mentioned elsewhere in these Laws, provided that immediately prior to the suspension the ball has not passed over the touch- or goal-lines, the Referee shall drop the ball at the place where it was when play was suspended, unless it was within the goal-area at that time, in which case it shall be dropped on that part of the goal-area line which runs parallel to the goal-line, at the point nearest to where the ball was when play was stopped. It shall be deemed in play when it has touched the ground; if, however, it goes over the touch- or goal-lines after it has been dropped by the Referee, but before it is touched by a player, the Referee shall again drop it. A player shall not play the ball until it has touched the ground. If this section of the Law is not complied with the Referee shall again drop the ball.

INTERNATIONAL BOARD DECISIONS

(a) If, when the Referee drops the ball, a player infringes any of the Laws before the ball has touched the ground, the player concerned shall be cautioned or sent off the field according to the seriousness of the offence, but a free-kick cannot be awarded to the opposing team because the ball was not in play at the time of the offence. The ball shall therefore be again dropped by the Referee.

(2) Kicking-off by persons other than the players competing in a match is prohibited.

9. BALL IN AND OUT OF PLAY

The ball is out of play:

(*a*) When it has wholly crossed the goal-line or touch-line, whether on the ground or in the air.

(*b*) When the game has been stopped by the Referee.

The ball is in play at all other times from the start of the match to the finish, including:

(*a*) If it rebounds from a goal-post, cross-bar or corner-flag post into the field of play.

(*b*) If it rebounds off either the Referee or Linesmen when they are in the field of play.

(*c*) In the event of a supposed infringement of the Laws, until a decision is given.

INTERNATIONAL BOARD DECISIONS

(1) The lines belong to the areas of which they are the boundaries. In consequence, the touch-lines and the goal-lines belong to the field of play.

10. METHOD OF SCORING

Except as otherwise provided by these Laws, a goal is scored when the whole of the ball has passed over the goal-line, between the goal-posts and under the cross-bar, provided it has not been thrown, carried or propelled by hand or arm, by a player of the attacking side, except in the case of a goalkeeper, who is within his own penalty-area.

The team scoring the greater number of goals during the game shall be the winner; if no goals or an equal number of goals are scored the game shall be termed a 'draw'.

INTERNATIONAL BOARD DECISIONS

(1) Law 10 defines the only method according to which a match is won or drawn; no variation whatsoever can be authorised.

(2) A goal cannot in any case be allowed if the ball has been prevented by some outside agency from passing over the goal-line. If this happens in the normal course of play, other than at the taking of a penalty-kick, the game must be stopped and restarted by the Referee dropping the ball at the place where the ball came into contact with the interference, unless it was within the goal-area at that time, in which case it shall be dropped on that part of the goal-area line which runs parallel to the goal-line, at the point nearest to where the ball was when play was stopped.

(3) If, when the ball is going into goal, a spectator enters the field before it passes wholly over the goal-line, and tries to prevent a score, a goal shall be allowed if the ball goes into goal, unless the spectator has made contact with the ball or has interfered with play, in which case the Referee shall stop the game and restart it by dropping the ball at the place where the contact or interference occurred, unless it was within the goal-area at that time, in which case it shall be dropped on that part of the goal-area line which runs parallel to the goal-line, at the point nearest to where the ball was when play was stopped.

11. OFF-SIDE

(1) A player is in an off-side position if he is nearer to his opponents' goal-line than the ball, unless:

    (*a*) He is in his own half of the field of play; or

    (*b*) He is not nearer to his opponents' goal-line than at least two of his opponents.

(2) A player shall only be declared off-side and penalised for being in an off-side position, if, at the moment the ball touches, or is played by, one of his team, he is, in the opinion of the Referee:

    (*a*) Interfering with play or with an opponent; or

    (*b*) Seeking to gain an advantage by being in that position.

(3) A player shall not be declared off-side by the Referee:

    (*a*) Merely because of his being in an off-side position; or

    (*b*) If he receives the ball, direct, from a goal-kick, a corner-kick, or a throw-in.

(4) If a player is declared off-side, the Referee shall award an indirect free-kick, which shall be taken by a player of the opposing team from the place where the infringement occurred, unless the offence is committed by a player in his opponents' goal-area, in which case, the free-kick shall be taken from a point anywhere within that half of the goal-area in which the offence occurred.

INTERNATIONAL BOARD DECISIONS

(1) Off-side shall not be judged at the moment the player in question receives the ball, but at the moment when the ball is passed to him by

one of his own side. A player who is not in an off-side position when one of his colleagues passes the ball to him, or takes a free-kick, does not therefore become off-side if he goes forward during the flight of the ball. (2) A player who is level with the second last opponent or with the last two opponents is not in an off-side position.

12. FOULS AND MISCONDUCT
A player who intentionally commits any of the following nine offences:

(*a*) Kicks or attempts to kick an opponent;

(*b*) Trips an opponent, i.e. throwing or attempting to throw him by the use of the legs or by stooping in front of or behind him;

(*c*) Jumps at an opponent;

(*d*) Charges an opponent in a violent or dangerous manner;

(*e*) Charges an opponent from behind unless the latter be obstructing;

(*f*) Strikes or attempts to strike an opponent or spits at him;

(*g*) Holds an opponent;

(*h*) Pushes an opponent;

(*i*) Handles the ball, i.e. carries, strikes or propels the ball with his hand or arm (this does not apply to the goalkeeper within his own penalty-area);

shall be penalised by the award of a *direct free-kick* to be taken by the opposing side from the place where the offence occurred, unless the offence is committed by a player in his opponents' goal-area, in which case the free-kick shall be taken from a point anywhere within that half of the goal-area in which the offence occurred.

Should a player of the defending side intentionally commit one of the above nine offences within the penalty-area he shall be penalised by a *penalty-kick*.

A penalty-kick can be awarded irrespective of the position of the ball, if in play, at the time an offence within the penalty-area is committed.

A player committing any of the five following offences:

1. Playing in a manner considered by the Referee to be dangerous, e.g. attempting to kick the ball while held by the goalkeeper;

2. Charging fairly, i.e. with the shoulder, when the ball is not within playing distance of the players concerned and they are definitely not trying to play it;

3. When not playing the ball, intentionally obstructing an opponent, i.e. running between the opponent and the ball, or interposing the body so as to form an obstacle to an opponent;

4. Charging the goalkeeper except when he:

(*a*) Is holding the ball;

(*b*) Is obstructing an opponent;

(*c*) Has passed outside his goal-area;

5. When playing as goalkeeper and within his own penalty-area:

(*a*) From the moment he takes control of the ball with his hands, he takes more than 4 steps in any direction whilst holding, bouncing or throwing the ball in the air and catching it again without releasing it into play, or, having released the ball into play before, during or after the 4 steps, he touches it again with his hands, before it has been touched or played by another player of the same team outside the penalty-area, or by a player of the opposing team either inside or outside of the penalty-area; or

(*b*) Indulges in tactics which, in the opinion of the Referee, are designed merely to hold up the game and thus waste time and so give an unfair advantage to his own team

shall be penalised by the award of an *indirect free-kick* to be taken by the opposing side from the place where the infringement occurred, subject to the over-riding conditions imposed in Law 13.

A player shall be *cautioned* if:

(*j*) He enters or re-enters the field of play to join or rejoin his team after the game has commenced, or leaves the field of play during the progress of the game (except through accident) without, in either case, first having received a signal from the Referee showing him that he may do so. If the Referee stops the game to administer the caution it shall be restarted by an indirect free-kick taken by a player of the opposing team from the place where the ball was when the Referee stopped the game, subject to the over-riding conditions imposed in Law 13. If, however, the offending player has committed a more serious offence he shall be penalised according to that section of the Law he infringed;

(*k*) He persistently infringes the Laws of the Game

(*l*) He shows, by word or action, dissent from any decision given by the Referee;

(*m*) He is guilty of ungentlemanly conduct.

For any of these last three offences, in addition to the caution, an *indirect free-kick* shall be awarded to the opposing side from the place where the offence occurred, subject to the over-riding conditions imposed in Law 13, unless a more serious infringement of the Laws of the Game was committed.

A player shall be sent off the field of play if in the opinion of the Referee, he:

(*n*) Is guilty of violent conduct, or serious foul play;

(*o*) Uses foul or abusive language;

(*p*) Persists in misconduct after having received a caution.

If play be stopped by reason of a player being ordered from the field for an offence without a separate breach of the Law having been committed, the game shall be resumed by an *indirect free-kick* awarded to the opposing side from the place where the infringement occurred, subject to the over-riding conditions imposed in Law 13.

INTERNATIONAL BOARD DECISIONS

(1) If the goalkeeper either intentionally strikes an opponent by throwing the ball vigorously at him, or pushes him with the ball while holding it, the Referee shall award a penalty-kick, if the offence took place within the penalty-area.

(2) If a player deliberately turns his back to an opponent when he is about to be tackled, he may be charged but not in a dangerous manner.

(3) In case of body-contact in the goal-area between an attacking player and the opposing goalkeeper not in possession of the ball, the Referee, as sole judge of intention, shall stop the game if, in his opinion, the action of the attacking player was intentional, and award an indirect free-kick.

(4) If a player leans on the shoulders of another player of his own team in order to head the ball, the Referee shall stop the game, caution the player for ungentlemanly conduct and award an indirect free-kick to the opposing side.

(5) A player's obligation when joining or rejoining his team after the start of the match to 'report to the Referee' must be interpreted as meaning to 'draw the attention of the Referee from the touch-line'. The signal from the Referee shall be made by a definite gesture which makes the player understand that he may come into the field of play; it is not necessary for the Referee to wait until the game is stopped (this does not apply in respect of an infringement of Law 4), but the Referee is the sole judge of the moment in which he gives his signal of acknowledgement.

(6) The letter and spirit of Law 12 do not oblige the Referee to stop a game to administer a caution. He may, if he chooses, apply the advantage. If he does apply the advantage, he shall caution the player when play stops.

(7) If a player covers up the ball without touching it in an endeavour not to have it played by an opponent, he obstructs but does not infringe Law 12, paragraph 3, because he is already in possession of the ball and covers it for tactical reasons whilst the ball remains within playing distance. In fact, he is actually playing the ball and does not commit an infringement; in this case, the player may be charged because he is in fact playing the ball.

(8) If a player intentionally stretches the arms to obstruct an opponent and steps from one side to the other, moving his arms up and down to delay his opponent, forcing him to change course, but does not make 'bodily contact' the Referee shall caution the player for ungentlemanly conduct and award an indirect free-kick.

(9) If a player intentionally obstructs the opposing goalkeeper, in an attempt to prevent him from putting the ball into play in accordance with Law 12, 5(*a*), the Referee shall award an indirect free-kick.

(10) If after a Referee has awarded a free-kick a player protests violently by using abusive or foul language and is sent off the field, the free-kick should not be taken until the player has left the field.

(11) Any player, whether he is within or outside the field of play, whose conduct is ungentlemanly or violent, whether or not it is directed towards an opponent, a colleague, the Referee, a Linesman or other person, or who uses foul or abusive language, is guilty of an offence, and shall be dealt with according to the nature of the offence committed.

(12) If in the opinion of the Referee a goalkeeper intentionally lies on the ball longer than is necessary, he shall be penalised for ungentlemanly conduct and:

(*a*) Be cautioned, and an indirect free-kick awarded to the opposing team;

(*b*) In case of repetition of the offence, be sent off the field.

(13) The offence of spitting at officials or other persons, or similar behaviour, shall be considered as violent conduct within the meaning of section (*n*) of Law 12.

(14) If, when a Referee is about to caution a player, and before he has done so, the player commits another offence which merits a caution, the player shall be sent off the field of play.

13. FREE-KICK

Free-kicks shall be classified under two headings:

'Direct' (from which a goal can be scored direct against the *offending side*), and 'Indirect' (from which a goal cannot be scored unless the ball has been played or touched by a player other than the kicker before passing through the goal).

When a player is taking a direct or an indirect free-kick inside his own penalty-area, all of the opposing players shall be at least 10yd (9.15m) from the ball and shall remain outside the penalty-area until the ball has been kicked out of the area. The ball shall be in play immediately it has travelled the distance of its own circumference and is beyond the penalty-area. The goalkeeper shall not receive the ball into his hands, in order that he may thereafter kick it into play. If the ball is not kicked direct into play, beyond the penalty-area, the kick shall be retaken.

When a player is taking a direct or an indirect free-kick outside his own penalty-area, all of the opposing players shall be at least 10yd from the ball, until it is in play, unless they are standing on their own goal-line, between the goal-posts. The ball shall be in play when it has travelled the distance of its own circumference.

If a player of the opposing side encroaches into the penalty-area, or within 10yd of the ball, as the case may be, before a free-kick is taken, the Referee shall delay the taking of the kick until the Law is complied with.

The ball must be stationary when a free-kick is taken, and the kicker shall not play the ball a second time, until it has been touched or played by another player.

Notwithstanding any other reference in these Laws to the point from which a free-kick is to be taken:

1. Any free-kick awarded to the defending side, within its own goal-area, may be taken from any point within that half of the goal-area in which the free-kick has been awarded.

2. Any indirect free-kick awarded to the attacking team within its opponent's goal-area shall be taken from the part of the goal-area line which runs parallel to the goal-line, at the point nearest to where the offence was committed.

Punishment. If the kicker, after taking the free-kick, plays the ball a second time before it has been touched or played by another player, an indirect free-kick shall be taken by a player of the opposing team from the spot where the infringement occurred, unless the offence is committed by a player in his opponents' goal-area, in which case the free-kick shall be taken from the point anywhere within that half of the goal-area in which the offence occurred.

INTERNATIONAL BOARD DECISIONS

(1) In order to distinguish between a direct and an indirect free-kick, the Referee, when he awards an indirect free-kick, shall indicate accordingly by raising an arm above his head. He shall keep his arm in that position until the kick has been taken and retain the signal until the ball has been played or touched by another player or goes out of play.

(2) Players who do not retire to the proper distance when a free-kick is taken must be cautioned and on any repetition be ordered off. It is particularly requested of Referees that attempts to delay the taking of a free-kick by encroaching should be treated as serious misconduct.

(3) If, when a free-kick is being taken, any of the players dance about or gesticulate in a way calculated to distract their opponents, it shall be deemed ungentlemanly conduct for which the offender(s) shall be cautioned.

14. PENALTY-KICK

A penalty-kick shall be taken from the penalty-mark and, when it is being taken, all players, with the exception of the player taking the kick, properly identified, and the opposing goalkeeper, shall be within the field of play but outside the penalty-area, and at least 10yd from the penalty-mark. The opposing goalkeeper must stand (without moving his feet) on his own goal-line, between the goal-posts, until the ball is kicked. The player taking the kick must kick the ball forward; he shall not play the ball a second time until it has been touched or played by another player. The ball shall be deemed in play directly it is kicked, i.e. when it has travelled the distance of its circumference. A goal may be scored direct from a penalty-kick. When a penalty-kick is being taken during the normal course of play, or when time has been extended at half-time or full-time to allow a penalty-kick to be taken or retaken, a goal shall not be nullified if, before passing between the posts and under the cross-bar, the ball touches either or both of the goal-posts, or the cross-bar, or the goalkeeper, or any combinations of these agencies, providing that no other infringement has occurred.

Punishment: For any infringement of this Law:

(*a*) By the defending team, the kick shall be retaken if a goal has not resulted;

(*b*) By the attacking team, other than by the player taking the kick, if a goal is scored the goal shall be disallowed and the kick retaken;

(*c*) By the player taking the penalty-kick, committed after the ball is in play, a player of the opposing team shall take an indirect free-kick from the spot where the infringement occurred, subject to the over-riding conditions imposed in Law 13.

INTERNATIONAL BOARD DECISIONS

(1) When the Referee has awarded a penalty-kick, he shall not signal for it to be taken until the players have taken up position in accordance with the Law.

(2) (*a*) If, after the kick has been taken, the ball is stopped in its course towards goal, by an outside agent, the kick shall be retaken.

(*b*) If, after the kick has been taken, the ball rebounds into play, from the goalkeeper, the cross-bar or a goal-post, and is then stopped in its course by an outside agent, the Referee shall stop play and restart it by dropping the ball at the place where it came into contact with the outside agent, unless it was within the goal-area at that time, in which case it shall be dropped on that part of the goal-area line which runs parallel to the goal-line, at the point nearest to where the ball was when play was stopped.

(3) (*a*) If, after having given the signal for a penalty-kick to be taken, the Referee sees that the goalkeeper is not in his right place on the goal-line, he shall, nevertheless, allow the kick to proceed. It shall be retaken, if a goal is not scored.

(*b*) If, after the Referee has given the signal for the penalty-kick to be taken, and before the ball has been kicked, the goalkeeper moves his feet, the Referee shall, nevertheless, allow the kick to proceed. It shall be retaken, if a goal is not scored.

(*c*) If, after the Referee has given the signal for a penalty-kick to be taken, and before the ball is in play, a player of the defending team encroaches into the penalty-area, or within 10yd of the penalty-mark, the Referee shall, nevertheless, allow the kick to proceed. It shall be retaken, if a goal is not scored.

The player concerned shall be cautioned.

(4) (*a*) If, when a penalty-kick is being taken, the player taking the kick is guilty of ungentlemanly conduct, the kick, if already taken, shall be retaken, if a goal is scored.

The player concerned shall be cautioned.

(*b*) If, after the Referee has given the signal for a penalty-kick to be taken, and before the ball is in play, a colleague of the player taking the kick encroaches into the penalty-area or within 10yd of the penalty-mark, the Referee shall, nevertheless, allow the kick to proceed. If a goal is scored, it shall be disallowed, and the kick retaken.

The player concerned shall be cautioned.

(*c*) If, in the circumstances described in the foregoing paragraph, the ball rebounds into play from the goalkeeper, the cross-bar or a goal-post, and a goal has not been scored, the Referee shall stop the game, caution the player and award an indirect free-kick to the opposing team from the place where the infringement occurred, subject to the over-riding conditions imposed in Law 13.

(5) (*a*) If, after the Referee has given the signal for a penalty-kick to be taken, and before the ball is in play, the goalkeeper moves from his position on the goal-line, or moves his feet, and a colleague of the kicker encroaches into the penalty-area or within 10yd of the penalty-mark, the kick, if taken, shall be retaken.

The colleague of the kicker shall be cautioned.

(*b*) If, after the Referee has given the signal for a penalty-kick to be taken, and before the ball is in play, a player of each team encroaches into the penalty-area, or within 10yd of the penalty-mark, the kick, if taken, shall be retaken.

The players concerned shall be cautioned.

(6) When a match is extended, at half-time or full-time, to allow a penalty-kick to be taken or retaken, the extension shall last until the moment that the penalty-kick has been completed, i.e. until the Referee has decided whether or not a goal is scored, and the game shall terminate immediately the Referee has made his decision.

After the player taking the penalty-kick has put the ball into play, no player other than the defending goalkeeper may play or touch the ball before the kick is completed.

(7) When a penalty-kick is being taken in extended time:

(*a*) The provisions of all the foregoing paragraphs, except paragraphs 2(*b*) and 4(*c*) shall apply in the usual way; and

(*b*) In the circumstances described in paragraphs 2(*b*) and 4(*c*) the game shall terminate immediately the ball rebounds from the goal-keeper, the cross-bar or the goal-post.

15. THROW-IN

When the whole of the ball passes over the touch-line, either on the ground or in the air, it shall be thrown in from the point where it crossed the line, in any direction, by a player of the team opposite to that of the player who last touched it. The thrower at the moment of delivering the ball must face the field of play and part of each foot shall be either on the touch-line or on the ground outside the touch-line. The thrower shall use both hands and shall deliver the ball from behind and over his head. The ball shall be in play immediately it enters the field of play, but the thrower shall not again play the ball until it has been touched or played by another player. A goal shall not be scored direct from a throw-in.

Punishment: (*a*) If the ball is improperly thrown in, the throw-in shall be taken by a player of the opposing team.

(*b*) If the thrower plays the ball a second time before it has been touched or played by another player, an indirect free-kick shall be taken by a player of the opposing team from the place where the infringement occurred, subject to the over-riding conditions imposed in Law 13.

INTERNATIONAL BOARD DECISIONS

(1) If a player taking a throw-in plays the ball a second time by handling it within the field of play before it has been touched or played by another player, the Referee shall award a direct free-kick.

(2) A player taking a throw-in must face the field of play with some part of his body.

(3) If, when a throw-in is being taken, any of the opposing players dance about or gesticulate in a way calculated to distract or impede the thrower, it shall be deemed ungentlemanly conduct, for which the offender(s) shall be cautioned.

(4) A throw-in taken from any position other than the point where the ball passed over the touch-line shall be considered to have been improperly thrown in.

16. GOAL-KICK

When the whole of the ball passes over the goal-line, excluding that portion between the goal-posts, either in the air or on the ground, having last been played by one of the attacking team, it shall be kicked direct into play beyond the penalty-area, from a point within that half of the goal-area nearest to where it crossed the line, by a player of the defending team. A goalkeeper shall not receive the ball into his hands from a goal-kick in order that he may thereafter kick it into play. If the ball is not kicked beyond the penalty-area, i.e. direct into play, the kick shall be retaken. The kicker shall not play the ball a second time until it has touched or been played by another player. A goal shall not be scored direct from such a kick. Players of the team opposing that of the player taking the goal-kick shall remain outside the penalty-area until the ball has been kicked out of the penalty-area.

Punishment: If a player taking a goal-kick plays the ball a second time after it has passed beyond the penalty-area, but before it has touched or been played by another player, an indirect free-kick shall be awarded to the opposing team, to be taken from the place where the infringement occurred, subject to the over-riding conditions imposed in Law 13.

INTERNATIONAL BOARD DECISIONS
(1) When a goal-kick has been taken and the player who has kicked the ball touches it again before it has left the penalty-area, the kick has not been taken in accordance with the Law and must be retaken.

17. CORNER-KICK
When the whole of the ball passes over the goal-line, excluding that portion between the goal-posts, either in the air or on the ground, having last been played by one of the defending team, a member of the attacking team shall take a corner-kick, i.e. the whole of the ball shall be placed within the quarter circle at the nearest corner-flag post, which must not be moved, and it shall be kicked from that position.

A goal may be scored direct from such a kick. Players of the team opposing that of the player taking the corner-kick shall not approach within 10yd of the ball until it is in play, i.e. it has travelled the distance of its own circumference, nor shall the kicker play the ball a second-time until it has been touched or played by another player.

Punishment: (*a*) If the player who takes the kick plays the ball a second time before it has been touched or played by another player, the Referee shall award an indirect free-kick to the opposing team, to be taken from the place where the infringement occurred, subject to the over-riding conditions imposed in Law 13.

(*b*) For any other infringement the kick shall be retaken.

NOTES: Subject to the agreement of the National Associations concerned and provided the principles of these Laws be maintained, they may be modified in their application.

1. For matches for players of under 16 years of age, as follows:

   (*a*) Size of playing pitch.

   (*b*) Size, weight and material of ball.

   (*c*) Width between the goal-posts and height of the cross-bar from the ground.

   (*d*) The duration of the periods of play.

   (*e*) Number of substitutions.

2. For matches played by women, as follows:

   (*a*) Size, weight and material of ball.

   (*b*) Duration of the periods of play.

Further modifications are only permissible with the consent of the International Board.

Reprinted by permission of the Football Association.

Athletics

Athletics

NOTES

The Associations draw attention to the fact that in the Rules the words 'must', 'shall' and 'should' are frequently employed. The variation in phrase is intentional. When the word 'must' or 'shall' is used the Rule is compulsory. Where 'should' is employed, while the Associations hope that the Rule will be complied with, strict compliance is not essential.

The Rules for Competition under AAA and WAAA Laws cover indoor as well as outdoor competition. The attention of Promoters and Officials is drawn to Appendix A on page 203 which sets out the principal requirements and modifications for indoor competitions.

The following terms used throughout the Rules have the following meanings:

Area Association: Northern Counties AA, Midland Counties AAA, Southern Counties AA, Welsh AAA, Northern Counties WAAA, Midland Counties WAAA, and Southern Counties WAAA, and such other 'Area' Associations as may be formed by the AAA or WAAA from time to time.

District: A District of the Northern CAA, a group of Counties or similar geographical sub-divisions of an 'Area' having a separate committee for administration purposes.

Club: Affiliated Club, Business House Club, University, College, School, Service Unit or Pre-Service Unit.

1. ELIGIBILITY TO COMPETE

All competitions held under the Laws of the Amateur Athletic Association or the Women's Amateur Athletic Association are confined to amateurs under the following definitions (hereinafter termed amateurs under AAA or WAAA Laws as appropriate).

1. Definition of Amateur
An amateur is a person who abides by the eligibility rules of the AAA/WAAA.

2. Restriction of Competition to Amateurs
Competition under AAA/WAAA Laws is restricted to amateur athletes who are under the jurisdiction of a Member of the IAAF and who are eligible under the rules laid down by the AAA/WAAA.

3. Ineligibility to Compete

4. Eligibility
Items 3 and 4 are given in full in AAA/WAAA Rules for Competition.

2. STATUS OF CLUB
(2) Athletics shall be divided into the following sections:
- (*a*) Track and Field
- (*b*) Race Walking
- (*c*) Road Running
- (*d*) Road Relay Running
- (*e*) Cross Country
- (*f*) Fell and Hill Running
- (*g*) Tug-of-War

Definitions of a Club (items 1 and 3 of Status of Club) are given in full in AAA/WAAA Rules for Competition.

3. CLUB MEMBERSHIP

4. CLAIM STATUS

5. HARDSHIP EXEMPTION

6. EXPENSES

7. COMPETITION CONDITIONS

8. REGISTRATION

9. PERMITS

10. ENTRIES

11. TRACK AND FIELD TEAM EVENTS

12. THE PROGRAMME AND PUBLISHED MATTER

13. PRIZES

14. CHALLENGE CUPS

15. DRESSING ACCOMMODATION

16. BETTING

GENERAL COMPETITION RULES

17. MIXED COMPETITIONS

18. TRACK AND FIELD COMPETITION CONFINED TO PARTICULAR CLASSES

Age groups (Ages at midnight August 31/September 1 in calendar year of competition)

(1) *Under 13 years*: AAA – Colts; WAAA – Minors.

(2) *Under 15 years*: AAA – Boys; WAAA – Girls.

(3) *Under 17 years*: AAA – Youths; WAAA – Intermediates.

(4) *Under 19/20 years*: AAA – Juniors; WAAA – Juniors.

(5) *Senior*.

(6) *Veterans*: AAA – at least 40 years of age on the day of competition; WAAA – at least 35 years of age on the day of competition.

Rules 3–18 are given in full in AAA/WAAA Rules for Competition.

19. CLOTHING

(1) In all events competitors must wear at least vest and shorts (or equivalent clothing) which are clean and so designed and worn as not to be objectionable, even if wet.

(2) When competing in any Team or Relay competition competitors shall wear the registered colours of the team they are representing, unless the Referee has given permission for a change to be made.
Note: AAA: Clubs are permitted to have two sets of colours registered at any one time. In Team or Relay Races all competitors should wear registered vests of the same design.

(3) In Individual National Championships athletes must wear the vest of their AAA/WAAA affiliated Club, or alternatively their County, Area or National vest.
Note: In exceptional circumstances the Referee may grant permission for an alternative vest to be worn.

(4) Advertising on competition clothing by the Sponsor of a Club or Association is permitted, subject to the following conditions:

(*a*) The specific design of the advertising material to be used, together with the name of the Sponsor(s) shall be submitted by the Club or Association to the AAA/WAAA for prior approval and registration;

(*b*) The advertising material may appear only on the vest of the Club or Association;

(*c*) Only one such advertisement, which must not exceed 3cm × 15cm in size, may appear on each vest.

(5) Subject to the provisions of 4. above or Rule 21.4, competitors are not allowed to take into an arena or course any form of advertising material, nor to display on their person any such advertising other than:

(*a*) The accepted name of their AAA/WAAA affiliated Club;

(*b*) A single trade mark of the manufacturer or supplier of the clothing they are wearing, which must not exceed 15 sq cm with a maximum height of 4cm.

(6) AAA: For use in races of 10km and over, Clubs may nominate alternative light coloured vests, including white with a Club badge, as an addition to the colours nominated in (2).

WAAA: Specialist type vests (approved by the WAAA) may be worn in middle and long distance races. The use of part mesh in such vests must comply with (1) above.

(7) AAA: In Fell or Hill Races competitors shall comply with any special conditions regarding clothing which may be laid down by the organisers for the safety of the competitors and their protection from exposure due to weather conditions.

20. FOOTWEAR

(1) Competitors may compete in bare feet or with footwear on one or both feet. The purpose of shoes for competition is to give protection and stability to the feet and a firm grip on the ground. Such shoes, however, must not be so constructed as to give the competitor any additional assistance, and no spring or device of any kind my be incorporated in the shoes. A shoe strap over the instep is permitted.

(2) The sole and the heel of the shoes shall be so constructed as to provide for the use of up to 11 spikes. Any number of spikes up to 11 may be used but the number of spike positions shall not exceed 11.

(3) When a competition is conducted on a synthetic surface that part of each spike which projects from the sole or the heel must not exceed 9mm except in the High Jump and Javelin events where it must not exceed 12mm. These spikes shall have a maximum diameter of 4mm. For non-synthetic surfaces the maximum length of spike shall be 25mm and the maximum diameter 4mm.

(4) The sole and/or heel may have grooves, ridges, indentations or protuberances provided these features are constructed of the same or similar material to the basic sole itself.

(5) In the High Jump the sole shall have a maximum thickness of 13mm and the heel shall have a maximum thickness of 19mm. In all other events shoes may be of any thickness.

21. NUMBER CARDS

(1) Competitors shall be supplied with and wear during competition a distinctive number card corresponding with their number in the programme. No competitor shall be allowed to take part in any competition without wearing the appropriate number cards and such cards must not be cut, folded or otherwise concealed in any way.

(2) Competitors should be supplied with two number cards to be displayed visibly, one on the breast and the other on the back. Competitors in the High Jump and Pole Vault may wear their number card on the back or the breast only. Where photo-finish equipment is in use, the meeting organisers may require competitors to wear additional numbers of an adhesive type on the side of their shorts facing the camera(s).

(3) In Team Races the entries should be numbered in consecutive order from beginning to end.

(4) In Field Events where competitors wish to take their trials while wearing their track suit, they must wear their number card or cards on the outside of their track suit (or other covering).

(5) Organisations which have contracts with commercial sponsors for the addition of lettering on number cards to be worn at meetings are not

to allow this lettering to exceed 4cm in height and 15cm in width or 48 sq cm in area. The sponsor's name may appear either above or below the number.

Organisations must ensure that the same style of number card is issued to, and worn by, all competitors taking part in the meeting.

22. ASSISTANCE

(1) Except as provided for in the AAA Road Race Handbook and in the Rules of the WCC and RRA for Road Races no competitor shall receive any advice or similar assistance during the progress of an event. 'Assistance' means direct help conveyed by any means including any technical device.

(2) Athletes receiving advice or similar assistance during a Field Event competition must be cautioned by the Referee and warned that for any repetition, they will be debarred from further participation in the competition. Any performance accomplished up to that time shall stand.

(3) 'Assistance' is also to be interpreted as including pacing by persons not participating in the race.

(4) Athletes receiving assistance as defined above are liable to be disqualified.

23. MISCONDUCT

(1) Any competitor (or other person) interfering, or attempting to interfere with the decision of an event official, or guilty of unfair practices or misbehaviour, including the use of offensive or abusive language shall, at the discretion of the Referee, be disqualified from the competition and, if necessary, reported to the appropriate Area Association of the AAA/WAAA as being guilty of misconduct.

(2) Athletes or officials who shall knowingly conduct themselves in a manner which, in the opinion of the General Committee/Executive Committee, may bring discredit to the sport of athletics shall be deemed to have committed an offence against the Association(s), for which offence they shall be liable to suspension.

24. PROTESTS

(1) (*a*) Any protest or objection by a competitor or team against the conduct or placing of another competitor or team in any competition, or relating to any matter which may develop during the carrying out of the programme, shall be made to the appropriate Referee or Judges immediately after that competition.

(*b*) Every protest or objection lodged under (*a*) shall be made verbally by the individual competitor or by a member of the protesting Club.

(c) The Referee shall decide any protest or objection made under (a) and that decision shall be final.

(d) In the event of a protest or objection being lodged against a successful competitor or team, the prize or prizes shall be withheld until the protest or objection has been disposed of in a manner provided for in this Rule.

(2) (a) Any protest or objection by a competitor, team or Club against the qualification to compete, or the statements in the entry form of another competitor, team or Club shall be made to the Referee, to the WAAA or to the Area Association of the AAA as appropriate, in the manner prescribed in (b) below. When practicable such protest or objection should be made before the date of the competition, or normally within 14 days of the date of the competition.

(b) Every protest or objection lodged under (a) shall be accompanied by a deposit of £2 and shall be made in writing and be signed by the individual objector, by a member of the protesting team, or by the Secretary of the protesting Club. If upon investigation, the protest or objection shall appear to have been made on no reasonable grounds, the deposit shall be forfeited to the appropriate Association.

(c) The Referee may decide any protest or objection made under (2) (a) on the ground, but if the decision is objected to at the time, he or she shall be required to refer the matter to the relevant Area Association of the AAA/WAAA. Any protest or objection referred in this manner shall be decided within one month of receipt, by the relevant Area Association.

(d) In the event of a protest or objection being lodged against a successful competitor, team or Club, the prize or prizes shall be withheld until the protest or objection shall have been finally disposed of in a manner provided for in this Rule. If within a period of three months from the date of the competition the protest or objection shall be sustained the prize or prizes shall be awarded as if the competitor, team or Club objected to had not taken part in the competition.

(e) AAA: Any competitor, team or Club may appeal against the decision of the Area Association of the AAA. Notice of Appeal must be sent to the General Secretary within 14 days of receipt of such decision and must be accompanied by a further deposit of £5. (See Procedure on Appeals – Law 14).

25. DOPING

(1) Doping is the use by, or the distribution to an athlete of certain

substances which could have the effect of improving artificially the athlete's physical and/or mental condition thereby augmenting athletic performance. Doping also includes the use by, or distribution to an athlete of substances which alter the integrity and validity of urine samples, or the use of any method which has the same effect.

(2) Doping is strictly forbidden, as is the practice of blood infusion ('blood doping').

(3) Doping substances for the purpose of this Rule are outlined in Appendix K. That list is not necessarily comprehensive and is subject to amendment at any time by the AAA/WAAA.

(4) Anti-doping tests shall be carried out only under the auspices of the Sports Council.

(5) An athlete who is requested to submit to a doping control by an authorised official must do so whether such a request is made during or outside an athletic competition. Failure to do so will constitute a breach of AAA/WAAA Rules and the athlete will be deemed to be ineligible as if a positive result had been obtained, will be disqualified from all competitions from that moment, and reported to the BAAB.

(6) A competitor found to have in the urine a doping substance and/or metabolite of a doping substance, or any other substance which is deemed to alter the integrity and validity of that urine sample, shall be disqualified from all competitions from that moment and reported to the BAAB, as shall any competitor found to have indulged in blood infusion. (Any performance established after the time of the test but before the notification of a positive result shall be declared null and void.)

(7) Any person assisting or inciting others to use doping substances as defined above shall be considered as having committed an offence and shall be subject to disciplinary action by the appropriate Association.
Note: The AAA/WAAA will not re-instate an athlete disqualified under (1) or (5) above.

26. MEDICAL EXAMINATION
A female athlete must submit herself for medical examination if so requested by the WAAA in order to determine her eligibility to compete in Women's events.

TRACK EVENTS

27. TRACK MEASUREMENTS
(1) Tracks should be level. For record purposes the maximum

allowance for lateral inclination of tracks shall not exceed 1:100, and in the running direction 1:1000 downwards; any inclination shall be uniform.

(2) The inner edge of all tracks must be distinctly marked, cinder and other permanent tracks preferably by a raised border of concrete or other suitable material, 5cm ± 1.25cm in height and at least 5cm in width. Where it is not possible to have a raised border the inner edge shall be marked with a white line or white tape 5cm in width. All other lanes shall be marked with a white line 5cm in width.

(3) For championship events (whether National, Area or County), or for any record to be accepted, the inside edge of the track must have a raised border, or be adequately flagged or coned to prevent any competitor running on the line itself. The flags shall be placed on the line at an angle of 60 degrees with the ground, pointing away from the track, at intervals of 5m.

(4) It is recommended that the direction of running be left hand inside.

(5) In all races where lanes are used the width of each lane shall be not less than 1.22m and not more than 1.25m. The lanes shall be measured for width from the outside edge of one marking line to the outside edge of the next line working outwards from the inner border of the track.

(6) (a) The track must be measured 30cm outwards from the track side of the inner edge if there is a raised border. If there is no raised border the track must be measured 20cm outwards from the track side of the inner edge.

(b) In measuring lanes for distance the inner lane shall be measured as stated in paragraph (a) and the outer lanes 20cm outwards from their respective inner borders.

(7) Races up to 110 metres must be run on a straight course in lanes so as to allow a separate course for each competitor.

(8) Individual races up to and including 400 metres should be run in lanes, with a separate lane for each competitor.

(9) Races over 400 metres and up to and including 800 metres may be run in lanes as far as the end of the first bend.

Note: The starting lines will be the same as for 200 metres plus the following distances:

Lane 1 + zero	Lane 5 + 0.145m
Lane 2 + 0.007m	Lane 6 + 0.224m
Lane 3 + 0.034m	Lane 7 + 0.325m
Lane 4 + 0.079m	Lane 8 + 0.444m

(10) In all races run wholly or partly in lanes the start shall be so staggered that the distance from start to finish shall be the same for each competitor.

28. STATIONS

(1) In all races stations for competitors shall be drawn. In straight sprint races the competitor drawing No. 1 shall take the station on the left facing the winning post, the competitor drawing No. 2 the next station and so on.

(2) In races on a circular track, the competitor drawing No. 1 shall take the station nearest the centre of the ground, the competitor drawing No. 2 the next station and so on.

Note: It is recommended that when a curved starting line is being used the inside lane is left unoccupied.

(3) It is recommended that a limit be placed on the number of competitors in races. In general the number should not be so great as to create possible danger or unfairness to any competitor, and if at the beginning of any race the number of competitors appears to the Referee to be excessive, dangerous or unfair, he or she shall have the power to order that the competitors be divided into such heats as he or she in his or her sole discretion considers necessary, and the event shall be run off accordingly.

Note: WAAA: For guidance, where races are started from a curved line the number of competitors in each heat should not normally exceed:

800m	10 where there are 6 lanes
	12 where there are 8 lanes
1500m	12 where there are 6 lanes
	14 where there are 8 lanes
3000m	14 where there are 6 lanes
	18 where there are 8 lanes

(4) In competitions where the compositions of heats is printed in the programme, competitors shall not be allowed to compete in any heat other than that in which their name appears; but the Referee, whose decision shall be final, shall have power, if he or she is of the opinion that it would be just and reasonable, to permit a departure from the rule.

29. STARTING BLOCKS

(1) The use of starting blocks is permitted in races up to and including 400 metres, including the first leg of a relay race, provided such leg does not exceed 400 metres.

(2) Their use is optional.

(3) Athletes may use their own starting blocks, but such starting blocks must be approved by the Starter.

Note: On all-weather tracks the organisers may insist that only starting blocks provided by them shall be used.

(4) The following rules apply to the construction and use of starting blocks:

(*a*) They must be constructed entirely of rigid materials

(*b*) They may be adjustable but must be without springs or other devices to give artificial aid to the runner

(*c*) They must be fixed to the track by a number of pins or spikes, arranged to cause minimum possible damage to the track surface. The arrangement must permit the starting blocks to be quickly and easily removed, and the anchorage must permit no movement during the actual start

(*d*) When in position on the track, no part of the starting block must overlap the starting line or extend beyond the lane for that athlete.

(5) When starting blocks are being used both hands must be in contact with the ground when the athlete is in the 'set' position.

30. THE START

(1) The start of a race shall be denoted by a line 5cm in width at right angles to the inner edge of the track. The distance of the race shall be measured from the edge of the starting line further from the finish, to the edge of the finish line nearer to the start.

(2) In all races not run in lanes the starting line shall be curved so that wherever it occurs on the track all the runners can cover the same distance in the race.

(3) All questions concerning the start shall be in the absolute discretion of the Starter, whose decision shall be final.

(4) Start Recallers should be appointed at National and Area Championships from within the appointed team of Starters. They may also be appointed at other meetings.

(5) Competitors must be placed in their respective stations by Marksmen (Starters' Assistants). An assembly line preferably marked in a distinctive colour should be drawn 3m behind the starting line (and in the case of races run in lanes behind each starting line). Marksmen shall place competitors on the assembly lines and signal to the Starter when all is ready.

If in the opinion of the Starter an athlete has failed to comply within a reasonable time with the instructions of the marksmen to prepare to come to the assembly line, then it may be considered a false start.

(6) Competitors must not touch the start line or the ground in front of it with their hands or feet when on their mark.

(7) All races (except Time Handicaps) shall be started by the report of a pistol or other similar apparatus and a start shall only be made to the actual report. The pistol or similar apparatus shall be fired upwards into the air and it is essential that it should give a satisfactory flash which can be clearly seen by the Timekeepers. The time shall be taken from the flash.

(8) (*a*) The Starter shall first receive a signal from the Chief Marksman that all competitors are ready.

(*b*) After the Starter has ascertained that the Timekeepers are ready, he shall give the competitors the following commands:

(i) For competitors running a distance up to and including 400 metres: 'On your marks', 'Set', and when all the competitors are set, i.e. motionless on their mark, the pistol shall be fired.

(ii) For competitors running or walking a distance greater than 400 metres: 'On your marks', and when all competitors are steady the pistol shall be fired.

(9) On the command 'On your marks' (for distances greater than 400m) or 'Set' (for distances up to and including 400m) all competitors shall at once and without delay assume their full and final Set position. Failure to comply with either command after a reasonable time shall constitute a false start.

(10) When a crouch start is being used, both hands must be in contact with the ground.

(11) If, for any reason, the Starter has to speak to any of the competitors after the command 'On your marks' and before the pistol is fired, or if the concentration of any competitor or the Starter is disturbed before the pistol is fired, he or she shall order all competitors to stand up and the Marksmen shall place them on the assembly lines again.

(12) If a competitor after the command 'On your marks' disturbs the other competitors in the race through sound or otherwise, it may be considered a false start.

(13) If a competitor commences a starting motion after assuming a full and final set position, and before the report of the gun, it shall be considered a false start.

(14) Any competitor making a false start must be warned. If a competitor is responsible for two false starts, or three in the case of a Combined Event (Pentathlon, Heptathlon, Octathlon or Decathlon) that athlete shall be disqualified.

(15) If in the opinion of the Starter, or the Start Recaller, the start was not fair, the competitors must be recalled with a second shot. If the Starter decides that the unfair start was due to one or more competitors 'beating the pistol', it shall be considered a false start and the Starter must warn the offender or offenders, who shall be disqualified if they continue to offend after one such warning, or two in the case of a Combined Event.

Note: In practice, when one or more competitors 'beat the pistol' others are inclined to follow and, strictly speaking, any competitor who does so has beaten the pistol. The Starter should warn only such competitor or competitors who in his or her opinion were responsible for beating the pistol. This may result in more than one competitor being warned. If the unfair start is not due to any competitor no warning shall be given.

31. THE RACE

(1) In all races run in lanes competitors should keep in their allotted lane from start to finish. If the Referee is satisfied, on the report of a Judge or Umpire, or otherwise, that a competitor has deliberately run out of lane, the Referee shall disqualify that competitor, but if the Referee considers that such action was unintentional, he or she may, at his or her discretion, disqualify if of the opinion that a material advantage was gained thereby. (The table below may be used for guidance in determining the advantage gained.) This Rule shall also apply to any portion of a race run in lanes.

Note: When an Umpire observes that an athlete has run out of his or her lane, it is recommended that the umpire marks the track where the infringement took place.

Track 400 metres Stride 2.30m	Advantage Gained by Encroaching *t* cm on Inside of Lane			
Number of Strides	t = 50mm	t = 100mm	t = 150mm	t = 300mm
	mm	mm	mm	mm
1	4	7	11	22
2	7	14	22	44
3	11	22	33	66
4	14	29	44	88
5	18	36	54	109
6	22	44	65	131
7	25	51	76	153
8	29	58	87	175
9	33	65	98	197
10	36	72	109	219

This table shows, mathematically, the theoretical advantage gained by taking from 1 to 10 strides inside the inner border of a lane. The distances are shown in millimetres, e.g. four strides 150mm inside gives an advantage of 44mm.

(2) Any competitor jostling, running or walking across, or obstructing another competitor so as to impede his or her progress shall be liable to disqualification.

(3) A competitor after voluntarily leaving the track or course shall not be allowed to continue in the race.

(4) In races longer than 1500 metres a lap scorer(s) shall be appointed by the Referee, who shall keep a record of the laps covered by each competitor.

(5) The Referee shall have the power to order a race to be re-held when he or she considers it just and reasonable to do so. If in any heat a competitor is disqualified the Referee shall have the power to permit any competitor affected by the act resulting in the disqualification to compete in a subsequent round of the event.

(6) No person except an official Timekeeper or other person appointed to do so by the Chief Timekeeper shall:

(a) indicate intermediate times to competitors;

(b) give times to be announced over the public address system.

(7) No attendant shall accompany any competitor on the mark or in the race.

(8) Except as provided for in Appendix F and in the Rules of the WCC and RRA for Road Races, no competitor shall receive any advice or similar assistance during the progress of a race. 'Assistance' means direct help or advice conveyed by any means, and pacing in running events by persons not participating in the race. Athletes receiving such assistance and advice are liable to be disqualified.

(9) In races of 200 metres or less the wind velocity should be measured and recorded whenever possible, and this is essential in the case of a record claim. The gauge should be set up half-way along the straight, not more than 2m from the edge of the track and at a height of approximately 1.22m.

(10) The periods for which the wind component should be measured are:

All distances up to and including 100m	10sec.
100m Hurdles and 110m Hurdles	13sec.
200m, commencing as the runners enter the straight	10sec.

See also Rule 62 (14) and (19).

(11) The wind gauge shall be read in metres per second, rounded to the next higher tenth of a metre per second in the positive direction. (For example: a reading of +2.03 m/sec. shall be recorded as +2.1 m/sec.; a reading of −2.03 m/sec. shall be recorded as −2.0 m/sec.)

32. THE FINISH

(1) The finish shall be a line 5cm in width drawn across the track at right angles to the inner edge.

(2) Two white posts shall denote the extremities of the finish line and shall be placed at least 30cm from the edge of the track. The finish posts

shall be of rigid construction of about 80mm in width and 20mm in thickness.

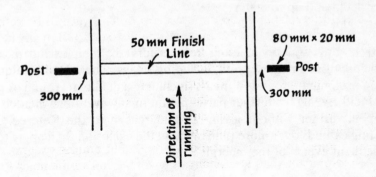

Diagram of Finish Posts

(3) The competitors shall be placed in the order in which any part of the body, i.e. the torso (as distinguished from head, neck, arms, hands, feet and legs), reaches the vertical plane of the edge of the finish line nearer to the start.

33. TIES
(1) In the event of a tie in any heat which affects the qualification of competitors to compete in the next round or final, where practicable, the tying competitors shall all qualify, failing which they shall compete again to decide the qualifiers.

(2) In the case of a tie for first place in any final, the Referee is empowered to decide whether it is practicable to arrange for the competitors so tying to compete again. If the Referee decides that it is not, the result shall stand. Ties in other placings shall remain.

34. QUALIFICATION FROM PRELIMINARY HEATS
(1) In the preliminary rounds of races, at least the winner, and preferably the winner and second, should qualify for the next round or final. Any other competitors to qualify shall be decided either according to their places or according to their times. Where any qualifying position is decided by time only one system of timing may be applied in determining times.

(2) The following minimum times must be allowed between the last heat of the round and the first heat of the subsequent round or final.

	Minimum minutes rest
Up to 100m	20
Over 100m and up to 200m	40
Over 200m and up to 400m	60
Over 400m and up to 800m	80
Over 800m	100

(3) In any athletic meeting competitors shall be excluded from participating in further events, including relays, when they have qualified in preliminary rounds or heats (including a qualifying round or pool in a Field Event) for further participation in any event but then do not compete further without giving a valid reason to the Referee. If a meeting extends over more than one day the exclusion shall apply to all subsequent events of the meeting.

35. HURDLE RACES

(1) All hurdle races shall be run in lanes and each competitor shall run in his or her lane throughout.

(2) A hurdle shall consist of two uprights, or standards, supporting a rectangular frame or gate and should have a level top rail.

(3) The total weight of the hurdle shall be not less than 10kg.

(4) The extreme width of the hurdle shall be 1.2m and the extreme length of the base shall be 70cm. The top bar shall be 70mm in width and should be between 10mm and 25mm thickness. The top bar should be striped in black and white, or in some other contrasting colours in such a manner that the lighter stripes appear at the end of the hurdle and that they shall be at least 225mm in width.

(5) The hurdle shall be made of wood or metal and shall consist of two bases and two uprights supporting the rectangular frame reinforced by one or more cross-bars, the uprights to be fixed at the extreme end of each base.

(6) The hurdle may be adjustable in height but should be rigidly fastened at the required height for each event.

(7) The hurdles shall be so placed on the track that the ends carrying the uprights shall be farthest from, with the counter-weights nearest to, the starting line.

(8) The hurdle shall be of such design that a force of at least 3.6kg applied to the centre of the top of the cross-bar is required to overturn it. Where an adjustable hurdle is used the counter-weights must be adjustable to the effect that in every position relating to the height of the hurdle the force required to overturn the hurdle when adjusted shall be at least 3.6kg and not more than 4kg.

Note: To check the resisting force of hurdles, a simple spring balance should be used by the application of a pulling force to the centre of the top of the cross-bar. Alternatively, use a cord with a hook, applied to the centre of the top of the cross-bar. Take the cord along over a pulley fixed conveniently and load the other end of the cord with the appropriate weights.

(9) The force required to overturn hurdles for Youths, Intermediate Women and younger age groups shall be at least 2.7kg and not more than 3kg.

(10) Where hurdles are used which overturn with less force than the minimum specified in (8) or (9) above as appropriate, the competitors shall be informed that an athlete knocking down three or more hurdles, or any part of three or more hurdles, shall be disqualified.

(11) Where hurdles comply with (8) or (9) above, as appropriate, knocking down any number of hurdles shall not disqualify, nor shall it disentitle a competitor from claiming a record.

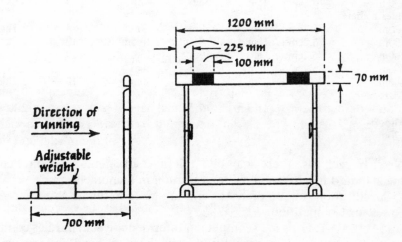

(adjustable weight may be inside or outside base)

Example of Approved Hurdle

(12) Competitors who trail a foot or leg below the plane of the top of the bar of the hurdle at the instant of clearance, or negotiate any hurdle not in their lane, or in the opinion of the Referee deliberately knock down any hurdle by hand or foot shall be disqualified.

(13) Specifications for particular hurdle events are:

Distance of race	Height of hurdle	Distance to 1st flight	Distance between flights	Distance to finish	Number of hurdles	Toppling weight
MEN'S EVENTS						
Senior Men						
110m	106.7cm	13.72m	9.14m	14.02m	10	3.6kg
400m	91.4cm	45m	35m	40m	10	3.6kg
Junior Men						
110m	99.0cm	13.72m	9.14m	14.02m	10	3.6kg
200m	76.2cm	18.29m	18.29m	17.1m	10	3.6kg
400m	91.4cm	45m	35m	40m	10	3.6kg
Youths						
100m	91.4cm	13m	8.5m	10.5m	10	2.7kg
400m	84.0cm	45m	35m	40m	10	2.7kg
Boys						
80m	84.0cm	12m	8m	12m	8	2.7kg
Colts						
80m	76.2cm	12m	8m	12m	8	2.7kg
WOMEN'S EVENTS						
Senior and Junior						
100m	84.0cm	13m	8.5m	10.5m	10	3.6kg
400m	76.2cm	45m	35m	40m	10	3.6kg
Intermediate						
80m	76.2cm	12m	8m	12m	8	2.7kg
100m	76.2cm	13m	8.5m	10.5m	10	2.7kg
200m	76.2cm	16m	19m	13m	10	2.7kg
300m	76.2cm	50m	35m	40m	7	2.7kg
400m	76.2cm	45m	35m	40m	10	2.7kg
Girls						
75m	76.2cm	11.5m	7.5m	11m	8	2.7kg
Minors						
70m	68.2cm	11m	7m	10m	8	2.7kg

Note: In each case there shall be a tolerance of 3mm above and below the standard heights to allow for variation in manufacture.

Specifications for Veterans' Events are given in full in AAA/WAAA Rules for Competition.

(14) *WAAA*: Girls may compete in Intermediate 80m hurdles competition but they may not compete in more than one hurdle age group in the course of the meeting.

(15) Specifications for Indoor Hurdle events are:

Distance of race	Height of hurdle	Distance to 1st flight	Distance between flights	Distance to finish	Number of hurdles	Toppling weight
MEN'S EVENTS						
Senior Men						
50m	106.7cm	13.72m	9.14m	8.86m	4	3.6kg
60m	106.7cm	13.72m	9.14m	9.72m	5	3.6kg
Junior Men						
60m	99.0cm	13.72m	9.14m	9.72m	5	3.6kg
Youths						
60m	91.4cm	13m	8.5m	13m	5	2.7kg
WOMEN'S EVENTS						
Senior and Junior						
50m	84.0cm	13m	8.5m	11.5m	4	3.6kg
60m	84.0cm	13m	8.5m	13m	5	3.6kg
Intermediate						
60m 'A'	76.2cm	12m	8m	16m	5	2.7kg
60m 'B'	76.2cm	13m	8.5m	13m	5	2.7kg
Girls						
60m	76.2cm	11.5m	7.5m	18.5m	5	2.7kg

36. STEEPLECHASE RACES

This event is only to be contested under AAA Rules and Laws.

(1) The hurdle may be made of heavy timber or of metal with a bar of heavy timber. In either case it must be constructed in such a way that it may not be easily overturned.

(2) The hurdle shall be 91.4cm in height and should be at least 3.96m in total width. The section of the top bar of the hurdle should be 12.7cm square.

(3) The weight of each hurdle should be between 80kg and 100kg.

(4) The hurdle shall be placed on the track so that about 30cm of the top bar, measured from the inside edge of the track, will be inside the field (i.e. the top bar will overlap the track edge).

(5) The top bar should be striped in black and white in such a manner that the white stripes appear at the end of each hurdle, and the stripes should be at least 30cm wide.

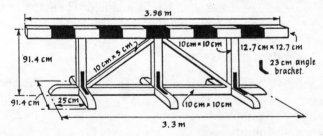

Specifications of Approved Heavy Timber Hurdle

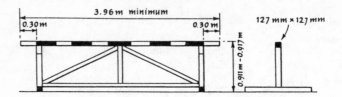

Specifications of Approved Hurdle with Metal Base

Note: In the case of all hurdle heights there shall be a tolerance of 3mm above and below the height of 91.4cm to allow for variation in manufacture.

(6) The hurdle at the water jump must be firmly fixed and be 91.4cm in height, 3.66m in total width, whilst the section of the top bar should be 12.7cm square.

(7) The water jump shall be 3.6m in width and length, the water being 70cm in depth at the hurdle end, remaining at this depth for a distance of 30cm and then sloping to the level of the track at the farther end.

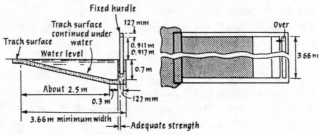

Steeplechase Water Jump – simplified diagrams

(8) Every competitor must go over or through the water. A competitor jumping to the right or left of the water jump, or trailing his leg or foot alongside any obstacle shall be disqualified. He may jump or vault over each hurdle and may place a foot or feet on each hurdle, including the one at the water jump.

(9) The standard events are:

Distance of Race	Age Group	Number of Hurdles	Number of Water Jumps	Distance from start to first hurdle
3000 metres	Senior	28	7	257.8m
2000 metres	Junior	18	5	203.8m
1500 metres	Youths	13	3	255.8m

Boys and Colts are not allowed to contest any steeplechase events.

Note: Owing to the water jump having to be constructed on the arena inside or outside the track, thereby shortening or lengthening the normal distance of the lap, it is not possible to lay down any rule specifying the exact length of the lap or to state precisely the position of the water jump.

It should be borne in mind that there must be enough distance from the starting line to the first hurdle to prevent competitors from overcrowding and there should be approximately 62.2m from the last hurdle to the finish line.

The water jump should be, where possible, the fourth jump in each lap. If necessary, the finish line should be moved to another part of the track.

The following measurements are given as a guide and any adjustments necessary should be made by lengthening or shortening the distance at the starting point of the race. It is assumed that a lap of 400m has been shortened by 6m by constructing the water jump inside the track.

(10) 3000 Metres

Distance from starting point to commencement of 1st lap, to be run without jumps	242.0m
Distance from commencement of 1st lap to 1st hurdle	15.8m
From 1st to 2nd hurdle	79.0m
From 2nd to 3rd hurdle	79.0m
From 3rd hurdle to water jump	79.0m
From water jump to 4th hurdle	79.0m
From 4th hurdle to finishing line	62.2m

$$7 \text{ laps of } 394m = 2758.0m$$
$$\text{plus} \qquad 242.0m$$
$$\overline{3000.0m}$$

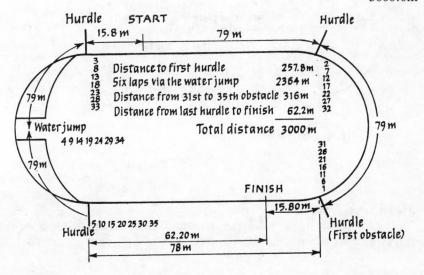

(11) 2000 Metres
    (If the course is laid out with a lap of 394m.)

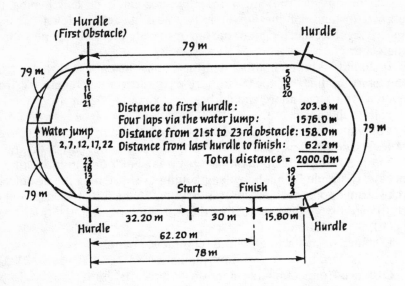

(12) 1500 Metres
    (If the course is laid out with a lap of 394m.)

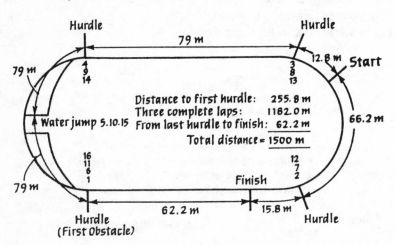

37. RELAY RACES

(1) Lines shall be drawn across the track to mark the distance of the stages and to denote the scratch line. Lines shall also be drawn 10m

before and after the scratch line to denote the take-over zone. These lines are to be included in the zonal measurements.

(2) Except for the first runner, where the stage to be run does not exceed 200 metres, the outgoing runners may commence their run not more than 10m outside the take-over zone; where the stage exceeds 200 metres the outgoing runners must commence their run within the take-over zone. Additional lines in a different colour from that used for the take-over zone markings should be drawn to indicate the additional 10m zone at all change-over points.

(3) The positions of the teams at the start of the race shall be drawn and shall be retained at each take-over zone, except that, in races where lanes are not used or have ceased to operate, waiting runners can move to an inner position on the track as incoming team-mates arrive, provided this can be done without fouling.

(4) When relay races up to and including 400 metres are contested on a circular track each team should, if possible, have a separate lane and each lane must be the full distance.

(5) Where the first section of a relay race is 200 metres or 400 metres, the first 400 metres section(s) should, if possible, be run in lanes with staggered starts. Alternatively, where the first section of a relay is 400 metres, lanes shall cease to operate at the beginning of the back straight on either the first or second lap.

(6) In events where the first lap only is run in lanes, competitors after leaving the take-over zone are free to take up any position on the track.

(7) In sprint relay races up and down a track the take-over is by touch, contact being made within a clearly defined area of 1m beyond, and at each end of, the relay distance.

(8) When a relay race is being run in lanes competitors may place a check mark on the track within their own lane but may not place, or cause to be placed, any marking object on or alongside the track.

(9) The baton must be carried in the hand throughout the race. If dropped, it must be recovered by the athlete who dropped it, who may leave the lane in order to retrieve the baton. Provided this procedure is adopted and no other athlete is impeded, dropping the baton shall not result in disqualification.

(10) The baton must be passed only within the take-over zone. The passing of the baton commences when it is first touched by the receiving runner and is completed the moment it is in the hands of the receiving runner only. Within the take-over zone it is only the position of the baton which is decisive, and not the position of the body or limbs of the competitors.

Note: To assist the judges, it is recommended that the batons be of distinctive colours.

(11) Competitors after handing over the baton should remain in their

lanes or zone until the course is clear to avoid obstruction to other competitors. Should any competitor wilfully impede a member of another team by running out of position or lane at the finish of a stage that competitor is liable to cause the disqualification of his or her own team.

(12) Assistance by pushing off or by any other methods will cause disqualification.

(13) On completion of the final leg the baton is to be handed to an official by the last runner. It is not to be dropped or thrown from the hand. Failure to comply with this instruction may lead to disqualification.

(14) Once a team has competed in the preliminary round(s) of an event the composition of the team must not be altered for any subsequent round or final, except in the case of injury or illness where the Referee is satisfied, on medical or other evidence, that a competitor is unfit to compete in a subsequent round, when permission may be given for the substitution of another competitor.

(15) It is permissible for the order of running to be changed between heats and succeeding round or final without reference to the Referee.

(16) No competitor may run two sections for a team.

(17) The relay baton shall be a smooth hollow tube circular in section made of any rigid material in one piece, the length of which shall not be more than 30cm or less than 28cm. The circumference shall be 12–13cm and the weight shall not be less than 50 grammes.

(18) The order of running in a 1600 metres Medley Relay for Women shall be – 200 metres, 200 metres, 400 metres, 800 metres.

38. TEAM RACES

(1) The composition of a team must not be changed after a heat has been run except in the case of injury or illness where the Referee is satisfied, on medical or other evidence, that a competitor is unfit to compete in a subsequent round, when permission may be given for the substitution of another competitor.

(2) Only competitors finishing the full distance are eligible to compete in the final.

(3) The entries should be numbered in consecutive order from beginning to end.

(4) At the discretion of the Referee a team may be permitted to start fewer competitors than the minimum number required to score.

(5) Stations shall be drawn and the members of each team shall, if necessary, be lined up behind each other at the start of the race.

(6) The team scoring the least number of points, according to the positions in which the members of the team finish whose positions are to

count, shall be the winner; the positions of the non-scoring members of a team, whether it finishes all its members or not, shall be scored in computing the scores of other teams.

(7) Alternatively team positions may be decided on the aggregate time of the scoring members of the team, the team having the lowest aggregate shall be the winner.

(8) In the case of a tie on points or on time aggregate, the team whose last scoring individual member finished nearest the first place shall be the winner.

(9) Time aggregates shall only be used if the organisers have announced in advance that this method will be used.

(10) In the case of a tie between two or more individual competitors each shall score for the team a number of points obtained by dividing the total sum of their positions numbers, reckoned as if they had, instead of being tied, finished regularly in a file, by the number of such competitors. (Thus, for instance, if two competitors finish tied for second place, each of them shall score $2\frac{1}{2}$ points.)

39. WALKING

The full rules relating to race walking are included in The Race Walking Association Handbook, available from the RWA Hon. General Secretary (Mrs Beryl Randle, 9 Whitehouse Court, Rectory Road, Sutton Coldfield B75 7SD. Tel: 021-329 3505).

40. TIMEKEEPING

Note: Manually operated electronic timers have generally superseded conventional watches. In the following Rule the terms 'timer' and 'watch' are used to distinguish between these two types.

General Conditions

(1) The Timekeepers must be in line with the finish. Wherever possible Timekeepers should be on the outside of the track and at least 5m from the outside lane. In order that they all have a good view of the finish line, and of the Starter, an elevated position should be provided.

(2) The time of an athlete shall be taken from the flash from the Starter's pistol or other device to the moment when the body of that competitor (i.e. the torso, as distinguished from the head, neck, hands, arms, feet or legs) reaches the vertical plane of the edge of the finish line nearer to the start (See Rule 32).

(3) It is desirable, wherever possible, to record lap times and the leader's number in races of 800 metres and over, and, in addition, times at each 1000 metres in races of 3000 metres and over. Such information is essential in the case of a record claim.

(4) No person except an official Timekeeper or other person appointed to do so by the Chief Timekeeper shall:

(*a*) Indicate intermediate times to competitors

(*b*) Give times to be announced over the public address system.

Manually Operated Timing

(5) Grade 1 Timekeepers must, and Grade 2 Timekeepers should use:

(*a*) Quartz crystal-controlled electronic timers which have obtained certificates of compliance with the requirements of NPL Test Leaflet TH42F, from a nationally recognised standardising organisation (e.g. the National Physical Laboratory or one of the accredited British Calibration Service Test Laboratories). Such a certificate requires renewal only if any timing component of the timer has been disturbed, modified, changed or adjusted.

Alternatively, or additionally, they may use:

(*b*) Conventional watches and dials and hands which have obtained certificates from a nationally recognised standardising organisation stating that the requirements of the NPL Test Leaflet TH42B have been met by a time-of-day chronograph watch, or NPL Test Leaflet TH42C for a stop watch. Such a certificate should be renewed every three years.

(6) Quartz crystal-controlled electronic timers may be used for hand timing in all races.

(7) Conventional watches with dials and hands may be used as follows:

(*a*) Stop watches must be used for timing races up to and including 1500 metres

(*b*) Stop watches may be used for timing races up to and including 3000 metres

(*c*) Time-of-day chronographs should be used for timing races longer than 3000 metres.

(8) For all hand timed races on the track the times shall be returned to 0.1 second by Timekeepers using manually operated electronic timers, conventional stop watches or time-of-day chronographs. Timings in 1/100th seconds not ending in zero shall be rounded up to the next longer 1/10th second e.g. 10.10s shall be returned as 10.1s but 10.11s shall be returned as 10.2s.

(9) For races contested partly or wholly outside the stadium timings will be returned to the next longer full second.

(10) Each Timekeeper shall time independently and declare the recorded time to the Chief Timekeeper immediately. The Chief Time-keeper may inspect the readings to verify the times and must do so if a record claim is involved.

(11) Unless satisfied that a mistake has been made the Chief

Timekeeper shall declare the time in accordance with the following conditions:

(a) When three Timekeepers are timing one placing and two agree but one disagrees the time shown by the two agreeing shall be the official time

(b) If all the Timekeepers disagree the middle time shall be the official time

(c) If, for any reason, only two times are taken the longer shall be the official time

(d) If the hand of an analogue display stops between the dial divisions the time read from it shall be to the longer of the two readings.

(12) In the event of a record claim the time should be taken by three Graded Timekeepers each of whom should be Grade 1 or 2, and using watches or timers certified as in paragraph (5) above. They shall show their timings to the Chief Timekeeper and certify these times on the appropriate Record Application Form.

If races longer than 3000 metres are concerned and only watches are used two of them shall be time-of-day chronographs certified in accordance with 5b above.

Fully Automated Timing

(13) A fully automated timing device approved by the AAA/WAAA may be used for timing all races. To be approved, such a device will require a certificate of accuracy from a nationally recognised standardising organisation showing an error of less than 0.001% (3.6 milliseconds per nominal hour) at 20°C and at its operating nominal voltage. The timing device must start within 2 milliseconds (0.002s) of the report and flash from the pistol or other starting device.

(14) Times shall be read from the photo-finish picture as follows:

(a) For events up to and including 10,000 metres the time shall be read to 1/100th second

(b) For events longer than 10,000 metres and held entirely on the track times shall be returned to the next longer 1/10th second

(c) For events held partly or entirely outside the stadium the time shall be returned to the next longer full second.

These times shall be the official times unless the Chief Timekeeper deems that an error has occurred when hand times shall be used in accordance with (7) and (8) above.

(15) In the event of a record claim the Chief Photo-finish Judge shall sign the Record Application Form and attach a copy of the photo-finish print. The Chief Timekeeper shall also sign the Form indicating acceptance of the time recorded. No details of the manually returned time are required on the Form.

FIELD EVENTS

41. GENERAL CONDITIONS

Draws, Trials and Qualifying Rounds
Rule 41 is given in full in AAA/WAAA Rules for Competition.

VERTICAL JUMPS (HIGH JUMP AND POLE VAULT)

42. GENERAL CONDITIONS
(1) Unless such details are specified in the programme, the Judge shall decide the height at which the competition shall start, and the different heights to which the bar will be raised at the end round. The competitors shall be informed of the details before the competition begins.

(2) Competitors may commence jumping/vaulting at any of the heights above the minimum height and may jump/vault at their own discretion at any subsequent height. Three consecutive failures, regardless of the height at which any such failure occurs, disqualify from further participation, except in the case of a jump-off of a first place tie.
Note: The effect of this Rule is that competitors may forgo their second and third jumps/vaults at a particular height (after failing once or twice) and still jump/vault at a subsequent height. If competitors forgo a trial at a certain height, they may not make any subsequent attempt at that height except in the resolution of a tie.

(3) Even after all the other competitors have failed, a competitor is entitled to continue until he or she has forfeited the right to compete further, and the best jump/vault shall be recorded as the winning height.

(4) After the competitor has won the competition the height or heights to which the bar is raised shall be decided after the Judge or Referee in charge of the event has consulted the wishes of the competitor.
Note: This does not apply for Combined Events Competitions.

(5) All measurements shall be made perpendicularly from the ground to the upper side of the cross-bar where it is lowest. A steel or fibre-glass measure should be used. Alternatively a scientific apparatus which has a

certificate of accuracy from a nationally recognised standardising organisation may be used. Any measurement of a new height shall be made before competitors attempt that height. In the case of a record claim the officials must check the measurement after the height has been cleared.

Note: Judges shall ensure, before commencing the competition, that the under-side and front of the cross-bar are distinguishable, and that the bar is always replaced in a similar manner.

(6) (*a*) The height shall be recorded to the nearest 1cm below the height measured if that distance is not a whole centimetre.

(*b*) Unless there is only one competitor remaining the bar shall not be raised by less than 2cm in the High Jump or 5cm in the Pole Vault after each round.

(7) Ties

Ties shall be decided as follows:

(*a*) The competitor with the lowest number of jumps/vaults at the height *at which the tie occurs* shall be awarded the higher place.

(*b*) If the tie still remains, the competitor with the lowest total of failures throughout the competition up to and including the height last cleared shall be awarded the higher place.

Example: High Jump

	1.67m	1.72m	1.75m	1.77m	1.80m	1.82m	1.85m	Total Failures	Position
Jones	—	xo	o	xo	—	xxo	All	4	2=
Smith	o	o	o	x—	xo	xxo	failed	4	2=
Brown	o	o	x—	o	xxo	xxo	three	5	4
Black	o	—	—	xxo	xxo	xo	times	5	1

Jones, Smith, Brown and Black all cleared 1.82m and failed at 1.85m
o = cleared   x = failed   — = did not jump

(*c*) if the tie still remains:
 (i) If it concerns first place, the competitors tying shall have one more jump/vault at the lowest height at which any of them finally failed, and if no decision is reached the bar shall be lowered or raised 2cm for the High Jump and 5cm for the Pole Vault. They shall then attempt one jump/vault at each height until one competitor clears a height and the remaining competitor(s) fail at the same height. Competitors so tying must jump/vault on each occasion when resolving the tie.
 (ii) If it concerns any other place, the competitors shall be awarded the same place in the competition.

Example:

	1.75m	1.80m	1.83m	1.86m	1.88m	Total Failures	Jump off 1.86m	1.84m	1.86m	Position
Green	o	xo	xo	xxx		2	x	o	x	2
Johnson	—	xo	xo	—	xxx	2	x	o	o	1
Baker	—	xxo	xo	xxx		3				3

o = cleared   x = failed   — = did not jump

Note: All competitors shall be credited with the best of all their jumps/vaults, including those taken in a jump-off of a first place tie.

43. HIGH JUMP
(1) Rules 41 and 42 apply.

(2) The uprights or posts shall not be moved during the competition unless the Referee considers the take-off or landing area has become unsuitable. Such a change shall be made only after a round has been completed.

(3) Competitors may place marks to assist them in their run-ups and take-off, and a handkerchief, or similar object, for sighting purposes may be placed on the cross-bar.

(4) The distance of the run-up is unlimited.

(5) Competitors fail if they:

(*a*) In the course of a jump dislodge the bar so that it falls from the pegs; or

(*b*) Take-off from both feet; or

(*c*) Touch the ground, including the landing area, beyond the plane of the uprights either between or outside the uprights with any part of the body, without first clearing the bar, unless in the opinion of the Judge no advantage is gained.

44. HIGH JUMP SPECIFICATIONS
(1) Any style or kind of uprights or posts may be used provided they are rigid. Uprights should be sufficiently tall so as to exceed the maximum height to which the bar can be raised by at least 10cm.

(2) The distance between the uprights should not be less than 4.0m or more than 4.04m.

(3) The cross-bar shall be of any suitable material.

(*a*) It shall be of uniform thickness, and should be circular with square ends provided it has a uniform section throughout, the diameter shall be at least 29mm but not more than 31mm.

(*b*) The ends of a circular bar shall be constructed in such a way that one flat or concave surface of 29–35mm × 150–200mm is obtained.

(*c*) The front of the bar should be painted. The length of the cross-bar should not be less than 3.98m and not more than 4.02m. The maximum weight of the cross-bar shall be 2kg.

(*d*) Those parts of the bar which rest on the supports shall be smooth; they may not be covered with any material which has the effect of increasing friction between them and the supports.

(4) Each peg supporting the cross-bar shall be flat and rectangular, 4cm wide and extending 6cm from the uprights *in the direction of the opposite upright*. The supports must be firmly fixed to the uprights and be without any kind of spring. The supports may not be covered with rubber or with any other material which has the effect of increasing the friction between the surface of the cross-bar and the supports. The ends of the cross-bar shall rest on the pegs in such a manner that it easily falls to the ground, either forwards or backwards, if touched by the competitor.

There shall be a space of at least 1cm between the ends of the cross-bar and the uprights.

(5) The ground round the take-off should be level but a maximum inclination of 1:250 in the direction of the centre of the cross-bar is permitted in the case of a synthetic take-off area.

(6) The minimum length of the runway shall be 15m but 25m is desirable if conditions permit.

(7) The landing area should measure not less than 5m long (that is at the take-off side) by 3m wide.

Note: The uprights and landing areas shall be so designed that there is a clearance of at least 10cm between them when in use to avoid displacement of the cross-bar through movement of the landing area causing contact with the uprights.

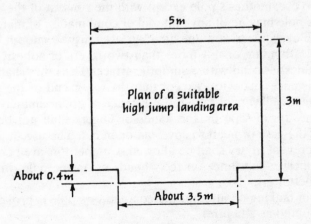

Plan of a suitable high jump landing area

45. POLE VAULT

This event is only to be contested under AAA Rules and Laws.

(1) Rules 41 and 42 apply.

(2) No marks may be placed on the runways, but a competitor may place marks alongside the runway.

(3) The distance of the run-up is unlimited.

(4) Competitors may have the uprights moved in either direction, but not more than 40cm in the direction of the runway, and not more than 80cm to the landing area from the prolongation of the inside edge of the top of the box.

Note: A white line 1cm wide may be drawn at right angles to the axis of the runway at the level of the inside edge of the top of the box. This line should be prolonged as far as the outside edge of the uprights.

(5) The take-off for the pole shall be from a wooden or metal box. A competitor is permitted to place sand in the box when it is his turn to vault.

(6) A competitor fails if he:

(*a*) In the course of a vault dislodges the bar so that it falls from the pegs; or

(*b*) Touches the ground, including the landing area beyond the vertical plane of the upper part of the box with any part of his body or with the pole, without first clearing the bar; or

(*c*) At the moment he makes a vault, or after leaving the ground, places his lower hand above the upper one, or moves the upper hand higher up on the pole.

(7) No one should touch the pole unless it is falling away from the bar or uprights; if it is so touched and the Referee or Judge is of the opinion it would have dislodged the bar so that it fell from the pegs the vault shall be recorded as a failure.

(8) Competitors may use their own poles. No competitor shall be allowed to use another's pole except with the consent of the owner.

(9) The pole may be of any material or combination of materials and any length or diameter, but the basic surface must be smooth. The pole may have a binding of not more than two layers of adhesive tape of uniform thickness and with a smooth surface. The poles shall have no other assistance or device, except that the lower end of the pole may have protective layers of tape for a distance of approximately 30cm

(10) The use of tape on the hands or fingers shall not be allowed except in the case of need to cover an open cut. The use of a forearm cover to prevent injury shall be allowed. Competitors are permitted to use an adhesive substance on their hands or on the pole, in order to obtain a better grip.

(11) If in making an attempt the competitor's pole is broken it shall not be counted as a failure.

46. POLE VAULT SPECIFICATIONS

(1) Any style or kind of uprights or posts may be used provided they are rigid.

(2) The distance between the uprights, or between extension arms where such are used, should be not less than 4.30cm or more than 4.37m wide.

(3) The cross-bar shall be of any suitable material.

(a) It shall be of uniform thickness, and should be circular with square ends provided it has a uniform section throughout, the diameter shall be at least 29mm but not more than 31mm.

(b) The ends of a circular bar shall be constructed in such a way that one flat or concave surface of 29–35mm × 150–200mm is obtained.

(c) The front of the bar should be painted. The length of the cross-bar should be not less than 4.48m and not more than 4.52m. The maximum weight of the cross-bar shall be 2.25kg.

(d) Those parts of the bar which rest on the supports shall be smooth. They may not be covered with rubber or any other material which has the effect of increasing friction between them and the supports.

(4) The pegs supporting the cross-bar shall extend horizontally not more than 7.5cm from the face of the uprights *on the side further from the runway* and must be without notches or indentations of any kind. The pegs must be of uniform thickness throughout and not more than 13mm in diameter. The pegs may not be covered with any material which has the effect of increasing the friction with the ends of the bar.

(5) As an alternative to (4) above, the pegs supporting the cross-bar may be placed upon extension arms 38cm in length permanently fixed to the uprights, thus allowing the uprights to be placed wider apart without increasing the length of the cross-bar.

(6) The box in which to plant the pole may be of wood or metal and shall be 1m in length, 60cm in width at the front end, tapering to 15cm in width at the bottom of the stopboard, where it shall be 20cm in depth. The front edge of the box must be level with the runway and firmly fixed

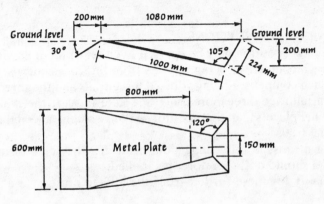

to the ground. If the box is constructed of wood, the bottom shall be lined with 2.5mm sheet metal for a distance of 80cm from the front of the box.

(7) The length of the runway is unlimited. The runway should be level and its minimum length shall be 40m but 45m is desirable if conditions permit. For record purposes the maximum allowance for lateral inclination of the runway must not exceed 1:100 and in the running direction of 1:1000 downwards. The minimum width of the runway shall be 1.22m.

(8) The landing area should measure not less than 5m by 5m, excluding the two protection pads on either side of the box.

Note: The contours of the bed around the edges of the box should allow for the bending of the lower part of the pole in the direction of the bed. This can be achieved if the bed maintains the angles produced by the box i.e. 105° between the base and the front edge of the box, and 120° between the base and the sides of the box.

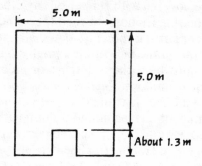

Plan of a suitable landing area

HORIZONTAL JUMPS (LONG JUMP AND TRIPLE JUMP)

47. GENERAL CONDITIONS
(1) The competition may be decided in either of the following ways:
(*a*) Each competitor being allowed from three to six trials; or
(*b*) Each competitor being allowed three trials and the three to eight best being allowed three more trials (See Rule 41.9). In the event of a tie for the final place(s), any competitor so tying shall be allowed the three additional trials.

(Tying means, in this connection, achieving the same distance and Rule 47.3 should not, therefore, be applied.)

To qualify for these further trials the athlete must have achieved a valid performance. The competition conditions must be explained to the competitors before the event begins.

(2) Competitors shall be credited with the best of all their trials, including jumps taken in resolving a first-place tie.

(3) In the case of a tie, the second-best performance of the competitors tying shall determine the result. If the tie remains, the third-best jump will be decisive and so on. If the tie still remains and it concerns first place, the competitors so tying shall have such additional extra trials as is required to determine the tie; if the tie concerns any other place, the competitors shall be awarded the same place in the competition.

(4) The take-off shall be from a board the edge of which nearer to the landing area shall be called the 'take-off line'. If a competitor takes off before reaching the board, it shall not for that reason be counted as a failure.

(5) The distance of the run is unlimited.

(6) No marks shall be placed on the runway, but a competitor may place marks alongside the runway. No competitor may place, or cause to be placed, any mark beyond the 'take-off line'.

(7) It shall be counted as a failure if any competitor:

(a) Touches the ground beyond the take-off line or take-off line extended with any part of the body, whether running up without jumping or in the act of jumping. Where there is any form of No Jump Indicator it is a failure if a visible impression is made.

(b) Takes off from outside either end of the board, whether beyond or behind the take-off line extended.

(c) In the course of landing, touches the ground outside the landing area nearer to the take-off line than the break in the sand to which the measurement of the jump would have been made.

(d) After a completed jump, walks back through the landing area.

(e) Employs any form of somersaulting.

(8) The measurement of the jump shall be made at right angles from the nearest break in the ground in the landing area made by any part of the body of the competitor to the take-off-line. Only valid trials shall be measured.

(9) The height shall be recorded to the nearest 1cm below the height measured if that distance is not a whole centimetre.

(10) If calibrated measuring equipment is used its accuracy must be checked with a steel or fibre-glass tape; otherwise a steel or fibre-glass tape should be used and the part of the tape showing the distance jumped must be held at the take-off line. Alternatively a scientific apparatus, which has a certificate of accuracy from a nationally recognised standardising organisation may be used.

(11) Whenever possible wind velocity should be measured and recorded.

(*a*) The gauge should be set up at 20m from the take-off line, not more than 2m from the edge of the runway and at a height of approximately 1.22m.

(*b*) The velocity shall be measured for a period of 5 seconds from the time a competitor passes a mark placed 40m (Long Jump) or 35m (Triple Jump) from the take-off line. If a competitor runs less than 40m or 35m as the case may be, the reading shall be taken from the time the athlete commences the run.

(*c*) The wind gauge shall be read in metres per second, rounded to the next higher tenth of a metre per second in the positive direction. (For example, a reading of +2.03m/sec. shall be recorded as +2.1m/sec.; a reading of −2.03m/sec. shall be recorded as −2.0m/sec.) (See also Rules 62.14 and 62.19.)

48. GENERAL SPECIFICATIONS

(1) A take-off board shall be rigidly fixed in the ground, flush therewith. It shall be made of wood 1.21–1.23m long, 19.8–20.2cm wide and maximum 10cm deep, and painted white.

(2) The runway should be level. The length of the runway is unlimited but its minimum length shall be 40m but 45m is desirable if conditions permit.

(3) The minimum width of the runway shall be 1.22m.

(4) For record purposes the maximum allowance for lateral inclination of the runway must not exceed 1:100 and in running direction 1:1000 downwards.

(5) In order that jumps can be measured accurately the sand in the landing area should be moistened before the competition.

(6) The surface of the sand in the landing area should be level with the top of the take-off board.

(7) Immediately beyond the the take-off line there shall be placed a board of plasticine or other suitable material for recording the athlete's footprint in the case of a foot fault. The specifications for the plasticine indicator board are as follows:

(*a*) The board shall be rigid, 98–102mm wide and 1.21–1.22m long, covered with plasticine or other suitable material on the top surface

(*b*) The surface shall rise from the level of the take-off board at an angle of 30° in the direction of running to a maximum height above the take-off board of 7mm

(*c*) The board shall be mounted in a recess or shelf in the runway, on the side of the take-off board nearer the landing area. When mounted in this recess, the whole assembly must be sufficiently rigid to accept the full force of the athlete's foot

(*d*) The surface of the board beneath the plasticine shall be of a material in which the spikes of an athlete's shoe will grip and not skid. *Note*: The layer of plasticine can be smoothed off my means of a roller or suitably shaped scraper for the purposes of removing the footprints of the competitors.

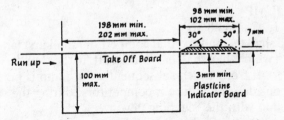

No-Jump Indicator for Long Jump and Triple Jump

(8) If it is not possible to install an Indicator Board as specified in (7), soft earth or damp sand should be sprinkled to a height of 7mm above the level of the take-off board over a width of 10cm beyond the edge of the board nearer to the landing area. At the take-off line the sand should be raised at an angle of 30° to the height of 7mm.

(9) The landing area should have a minimum width of 2.75m, a maximum width of 3m, and be at least 9m long. It should, if possible, be so placed that the middle of the runway, if extended, would coincide with the middle of the landing area.

Note: When the axis of the runway is not in line with the centre of the landing area this shall be achieved by placing a tape which shall delimit a landing area which has the same width on either side of the central axis of the runway prolonged.

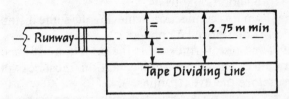

Centralised Long Jump/Triple Jump Landing Area

49. LONG JUMP
(1) Rules 41, 47 and 48 apply.
(2) A space of at least 1m but no more than 3m, of a similar surface to

the runway, should be left between the take-off board and the landing area.

(3) The distance between the take-off board and the end of the landing area should be at least 10m.

50. TRIPLE JUMP

(1) Rules 41, 47 and 48 apply.

(2) The hop shall be made so that competitors shall first land upon the same foot with which they shall have taken off, in the step they shall land on the other foot, from which subsequently the jump is performed. It shall not be considered a failure if competitors, during the step phase, touch the ground with the 'sleeping' leg.

(3) The ground between the take-off board and the landing area must be level.

(4) The distance between the take-off board and the landing area should be 13m or 11m for Senior competition, 9m for Junior competition, and as appropriate for Women's competition, but it must be appreciated that suitable distances will vary according to the standard of the competition.

THROWING EVENTS

51. GENERAL CONDITIONS

(1) The competition may be decided in either of the following ways:

(*a*) Each competitor being allowed from three to six trials; or

(*b*) Each competitor being allowed three trials and the three to eight best competitors being allowed three more trials (See Rule 41.9). In the event of a tie for the final place(s), any competitor so tying shall be allowed the three additional trials.

(Tying means in this connection achieving the same distance and Rule 51.3 should not, therefore be applied.)

To qualify for these further trials the athlete must have achieved a valid performance. The competition conditions must be explained to the competitors before the event begins.

(2) Competitors shall be credited with the best of all their trials, including throws taken in resolving a first place tie.

(3) In the case of a tie, the second-best performance of the competitors tying shall determine the result. If the tie remains, the third-best throw will be decisive and so on. If the tie remains and it concerns first place, the competitors so tying shall have such additional extra trials as is

required to determine the tie. If the tie concerns any other place, the competitors shall be awarded the same place in the competition.

(4) No competitor may place, or cause to be placed, any mark within the throwing sector .

(5) Competitors shall use only those implements provided for general use. Subject to any regulations laid down by the Promoting Body, competitors who wish to use their own implements must submit them to the Referee for approval and when they have been approved they shall be available for the use of all competitors.

(6) No device of any kind (e.g. the taping of the fingers) which in any way assists a competitor when making a throw shall be allowed.

Note: The use of tape to cover injuries to the hand will be allowed only if the Referee is satisfied on medical or other evidence that the tape is necessary. The use of tape on the wrist will be allowed.

(7) In order to obtain a better grip, competitors are permitted to use an adhesive substance on their hands only.

(8) In order to protect the spine from injury a competitor may wear a belt of leather or some other suitable material.

(9) When markers are used to indicate the best throw of each competitor and to show record distances they shall be placed on a line or tape outside the sector lines.

Note: The outer ends of the sector lines should be marked with flags.

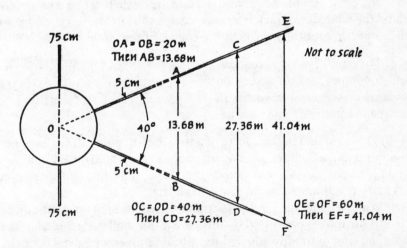

Note: The 40° sector may be laid out accurately and conveniently by making the distance between two points on the inside edge of the sector lines 20m from the centre of the circle exactly 13.68m apart.

52. PUTTING THE SHOT

(1) Rules 41 and 51 apply.

(2) *In order to avoid accidents throwing sectors should be roped off at a height of approximately 1m and at a minimum distance of 2m outside the sector lines.*

(3) Competitors must be given instructions that implements must be thrown during practice only from the circle. Implements must be returned by *hand* during practice or competition and must not be thrown back to the starting area. The Referee or other appropriate official shall disqualify from competing in the event any athletes who wilfully disobey the above instructions after having their attention drawn to them.

(4) No practice trials shall be allowed after a competition has begun.

(5) Gloves may not be worn.

(6) Competitors must not spray or spread any substance on the surface of a throwing circle nor on their shoes.

(7) A competitor must commence the throw from a stationary position within the circle.

(8) It shall be a foul throw if the competitor, after stepping into the circle and starting to make the throw, touches with any part of the body the ground outside the circle, the top of the stop-board or the top of the circle rim. A competitor is allowed to touch the inside of the iron band or stop-board.

(9) The competitor must not leave the circle until the implement has touched the ground. When leaving the circle the first contact with the top of the circle rim or the ground outside the circle must be completely behind the white line which is drawn outside the circle, the rear edge of which runs theoretically through the centre of the circle.

Note: To comply with this requirement a competitor's first step on leaving the circle must be wholly in the area marked 'A'.

Direction of Throw

(10) Provided that in the course of a trial the foregoing Rules have not been infringed, a competitor may interrupt a trial once started, may lay the implement down, may leave the circle, before returning to a stationary position and beginning a fresh trial.

Note: When leaving the circle the competitor must step out as required in 9. All the moves permitted by this paragraph shall be included in the maximum time normally allowed for a trial as given in Rule 41(5)(*a*).

(11) The shot shall be put from the shoulder with one hand only. At the time the competitor takes a stance in the ring to commence a put, the shot shall touch or be in close contact with the chin and the hand shall

not be dropped below this position during the act of putting. The shot must not be brought behind the line of the shoulders.

(12) In making a put the competitors may rest their feet against but not on top of the stop-board.

(13) A foul throw or letting go of the implement in an attempt shall be reckoned as a trial.

(14) For a valid put the shot must fall completely within the inner edges of lines marking a sector of 40° set out on the ground so that the radii lines cross at the centre of the circle. (See diagram below Rule 51.9.)

(15) All measurements must be made from the nearer edge of the first mark made in the ground by the implement to the inner edge of the circle rim along a line drawn from the mark to the centre of the circle.

(16) All measurements should be made immediately after each put. A steel or fibre-glass tape should be used for measurement, and that part of the tape showing the distance put must be held by the official at the circle. Alternatively, approved datum measurement equipment may be used, as may a scientific apparatus which has a certificate of accuracy from a nationally recognised standardising organisation.

(17) The distance shall be recorded to the nearest 1cm below the distance measured if that distance is not a whole centimetre.

53. PUTTING THE SHOT SPECIFICATIONS
Rule 53 is given in full in AAA/WAAA Rules for Competition.

54. THROWING THE HAMMER
This event is only to be contested under AAA Rules and Laws.

(1) Rules 41 and 51 apply.

(2) *In order to avoid accidents throwing sectors must be roped off at a height of approximately 1m and to make a 60° safety sector inside which the hammer throwing sector is centrally placed.*

(3) Competitors must be given instructions that implements must be thrown during practice only from the circle. Implements must be returned by *hand* during practice or competition and must not be thrown back to the starting area. The Referee or other appropriate official shall disqualify from competing in the event any athlete who wilfully disobeys the above instructions after having his attention drawn to them.

(4) No practice trials shall be allowed after a competition has begun.

(5) All throws shall be made from a cage (See Rule 58).

(6) Gloves may be worn. The gloves must be smooth on back and front, and the tip of the fingers, other than the thumb, must be exposed.

(7) A competitor must not spray or spread any substance on the surface of a throwing circle nor on his shoes.

(8) A competitor must commence the throw from a stationary position within the circle; he may adopt any position he chooses.

(9) It shall be a foul throw if the competitor, after he has stepped into the circle and started to make the throw, touches with any part of his body the ground outside the circle, or the top of the circle rim. A competitor is allowed to touch the inside of the iron band.

(10) The competitor must not leave the circle until the hammer has touched the ground. When leaving the circle the first contact with the top of the circle rim or the ground outside the circle must be completely behind the white line which is drawn outside the circle, the rear edge of which runs theoretically through the centre of the circle.

Note: To comply with this rule a competitor's first step on leaving the circle must be wholly in the area marked 'A'.

(11) The competitor in his starting position prior to the preliminary swings or turns is allowed to put the head of the hammer on the ground inside or outside the circle.

(12) It shall not be considered a foul throw if the head of the hammer touches the ground when the competitor makes the preliminary swings or turns, but if, having so touched the ground, he stops throwing so as to begin a trial again, this shall count as a failure.

(13) Provided that in the course of the trial the foregoing Rules have not been infringed, a competitor may interrupt a trial once started, may lay his hammer down, may leave the circle before returning to a stationary position and beginning a fresh trial.

Note: When leaving the circle the competitor must step out as required in 10. above. All the moves permitted by this paragraph shall be included in the maximum time normally allowed for a trial as given in Rule 41.5(*a*).

(14) If the hammer breaks during a throw or while in the air, it shall not be counted as a throw, provided it was made in accordance with the Rules. If the competitor thereby loses his balance and commits a foul, it shall not count against him.

(15) A foul throw or letting go of the hammer in an attempt shall be reckoned as a trial.

(16) For a valid throw the hammer head must fall completely within the inner edges of lines marking a sector of 40° set out on the ground so that the radii lines cross at the centre of the circle.

Note: The 40° sector may be laid out accurately and conveniently by making the distance between two points on the inside edge of the sector line 40m from the centre of the circle exactly 27.36m apart (See diagram below Rule 51.9). The outer ends of the sector lines should be marked with flags.

(17) All measurements must be made from the nearer edge of the mark first made in the ground by the head of the hammer to the inner edge of the circle along a line drawn from the mark to the centre of the circle.

(18) A steel or fibre-glass tape should be used for measurement, and that part of the tape showing the distance thrown must be held by the official at the circle. Alternatively, approved datum measurement equipment may be used, as may a scientific apparatus which has obtained a certificate of accuracy from a nationally recognised standardising organisation.

(19) The distance shall be recorded in even centimetre units to the nearest unit below the distance measured if that distance is not a whole even centimetre.

55. THROWING THE HAMMER SPECIFICATIONS

Rule 55 is given in full in AAA/WAAA Rules for Competition.

56. THROWING THE DISCUS

(1) Rules 41 and 51 apply.

(2) *In order to avoid accidents throwing sectors must be roped off at a height of approximately 1m and to make a 60° safety sector inside which the discus throwing sector is centrally placed.*

(3) Competitors must be given instructions that implements must be thrown during practice only from the circle. Implements must be returned by *hand* during practice or competition and must not be thrown back to the starting area. The Referee or other appropriate official shall disqualify from competing in the event any athletes who wilfully disobey the above instructions after having their attention drawn to them.

(4) No practice trials shall be allowed after a competition has begun.

(5) All throws shall be made from a cage (See Rule 58).

(6) Gloves may not be worn.

(7) Competitors must not spray or spread any substance on the surface of a throwing circle nor on their shoes.

(8) Competitors must commence the throw from a stationary position within the circle; they may adopt any position they choose.

(9) It shall be a foul throw if the competitor, after stepping into the circle and starting to make the throw, touches with any part of the body the ground outside the circle, or the top of the circle rim. A competitor is allowed to touch the inside of the iron band.

(10) The competitor must not leave the circle until the discus has touched the ground. When leaving the circle the first contact with the

top of the circle rim or the ground outside the circle must be completely behind the white line which is drawn outside the circle, the rear edge of which runs theoretically through the centre of the circle.

Note: To comply with this rule a competitor's first step on leaving the circle must be wholly in the area marked 'A'.

(11) Provided that in the course of a trial the foregoing Rules have not been infringed, a competitor may interrupt a trial once started, may lay down the discus, may leave the circle before returning to a stationary position and beginning a fresh trial.

Note: When leaving the circle the competitor must step out as required above. All the moves permitted by this paragraph shall be included in the maximum time normally allowed for a trial as given in Rule 41.5(*a*).

(12) A foul throw or letting go of the discus in an attempt shall be reckoned as a trial. If a discus breaks during a fair throw it shall not be counted as a trial.

(13) For a valid throw the discus must fall completely within the inner edges of lines marking a sector of 40° set out on the ground so that the radii lines cross at the centre of the circle.

Note: If the discus first hits the cage and then lands within the sector, the throw shall not, for that reason, be considered invalid.

Note: The 40° sector may be laid out accurately and conveniently by making the distance between two points on the inside edge of the sector lines 40m from the centre of the circle exactly 27.36m apart (See diagram below Rule 51.9). The outer ends of the sector lines should be marked with flags.

(14) All measurements must be made from the nearer edge of the mark first made in the ground by the discus to the inner edge of the circle along a line drawn from the mark to the centre of the circle.

(15) A steel or fibre-glass tape should be used for measurement, and that part of the tape showing the distance thrown must be held by the official at the circle. Alternatively, approved datum measurement equipment may be used, as may a scientific apparatus which has obtained a certificate of accuracy from a nationally recognised standardising organisation.

(16) The distance shall be recorded in even centimetre units to the nearest unit below the distance measured if that distance is not a whole even centimetre.

57. THROWING THE DISCUS SPECIFICATIONS
Rule 57 is given in full in AAA/WAAA Rules for Competition.

58. CAGES FOR HAMMER AND DISCUS
Hammer Throwing Cage

(1) All hammer throws shall be made from an enclosure or cage to ensure the safety of spectators, officials and competitors. Advice is available on request from the AAA General Secretary.

Rule 58 is given in full in AAA/WAAA Rules for Competition.

59. THROWING THE JAVELIN

(1) Rules 41 and 51 apply.

(2) *In order to avoid accidents a safety sector covering the landing area must be roped off at a height of approximately 1m and at a minimum distance of 2m outside the sector lines.*

(3) Competitors must be given instructions that implements must be thrown during practice only from the arc. Implements must be returned by *hand* during practice or competition and must not be thrown back to the starting area. The Referee or other appropriate official shall disqualify from competing in the event any athletes who wilfully disobey the above instruction after having their attention drawn to them.

(4) No practice throws shall be allowed after the competition has begun.

(5) Gloves may not be worn.

(6) The javelin must be held in one hand only, and at the grip, so that the little (or fourth) finger is nearest to the point.

(7) No marks shall be placed on the runway but the competitors may place marks at the side of the runway.

(8) In the course of running up to throw a competitor may not cross either of the parallel lines forming the runway.

(9) The javelin shall be thrown over the shoulder or upper part of the throwing arm, and must not be slung or hurled.

(10) At no time after preparing to throw, and until the javelin has been discharged into the air, may the competitor turn completely round so that the back is towards the throwing arc.

(11) Non-orthodox styles are not permitted.

(12) It is a foul throw if the competitor steps on or beyond the arc or extended scratch line on the ground marked 'N' on the diagram below.

(13) A throw shall be valid only if the tip of the metal head strikes the ground before any other part of the javelin.

(14) A competitor shall not leave the runway until the javelin has touched the ground. The competitor shall then, from a standing position, leave the runway from behind the arc and the lines drawn from the extremities of the arc at right angles to the parallel lines which define the runway.

(15) A foul throw or letting go of the javelin in an attempt shall be

reckoned as a trial. If a javelin breaks during a fair throw it shall not be counted as a trial.

(16) The arc must be clearly marked on the ground by chalk or otherwise, and all measurements must be made from the nearer edge of the mark first made in the ground by the tip of the metal head of the javelin to the inside edge of the javelin arc along a line from the point of the fall to the centre of the circle of which the arc is a part.

(17) For a valid throw the javelin must land so that the point from which the measurement is to be made is within the inner edges of lines marking the sector set out on the ground by extending the lines from the centre of the circle of which the arc is a part, through the points at which the arc joins the lines marking the runway.

(18) A steel or fibre-glass tape should be used for measurement, and the part of the tape showing the distance thrown must be held by the official at the arc. Alternatively, approved datum measurement equipment may be used, as may a scientific apparatus which has obtained a certificate of accuracy from a nationally recognised standardising organisation.

(19) The distance shall be recorded in even centimetre units to the nearest unit below the distance measured if that distance is not a whole even centimetre.

(20)

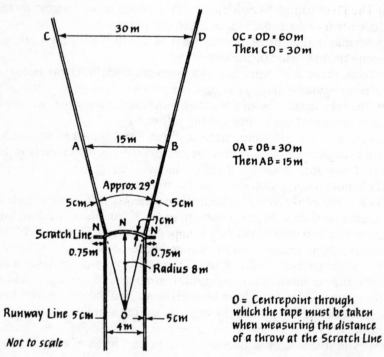

OC = OD = 60m
Then CD = 30m

OA = OB = 30m
Then AB = 15m

O = Centrepoint through which the tape must be taken when measuring the distance of a throw at the Scratch Line

60. THROWING THE JAVELIN SPECIFICATIONS
Rule 60 is given in full in AAA/WAAA Rules for Competition.

61. COMBINED EVENTS
(1) The Outdoor Pentathlon (Men) consists of five events which shall be held in the following order: Long Jump, Throwing the Javelin, 200 metres, Throwing the Discus and 1500 metres.

The Indoor Pentathlon (Men) consists of five events which shall be held on one day in the following order: 60 metres Hurdles, Long Jump, Shot Put, High Jump, 1000 metres.

(2) The Outdoor Pentathlon (Women) consists of five events which shall be held on one day, or on two consecutive days in the following order: First day – 100 metres Hurdles, Putting the Shot, High Jump; Second day – Long Jump, 800 metres.

Note: If practicable, there should be at least a 30 minute break between events. If the Pentathlon (Women) is held on one day, the competition shall be split into two sessions with a break of one hour between each session.

The Indoor Pentathlon (Women) consists of five events and shall be held on one day in the following order: 60 metres Hurdles, High Jump, Putting the Shot, Long Jump, 800 metres.

(3) The Heptathlon (Women) consists of seven events which shall be held over two days in the following order: 100 metres Hurdles, High Jump, Putting the Shot, 200 metres; Second day – Long Jump, Throwing the Javelin, 800 metres.

Note: This event is restricted to Intermediate and Senior competition only. Rest periods between events shall be as for Pentathlon (Women) above. No claim for a record will be considered if the order of events differs from that above.

(4) The Indoor Heptathlon (Men) consists of seven events which shall be held over two consecutive days in the following order: First day – 60 metres, Long Jump, Shot Put, High Jump. Second day – 60 metres, Hurdles, Pole Vault, 1000 metres.

(5) The Decathlon (Men) consists of ten events which shall be held on two consecutive days in the following order: First day – 100 metres, Long Jump, Putting the Shot, High Jump, 400 metres; Second day – 110 metres Hurdles, Throwing the Discus, Pole Vault, Throwing the Javelin, 1500 metres.

At the discretion of the organisers, it is permissible, where circumstances make it desirable, to decide all the events on the same day. If all the events are decided on the same day it is permissible to vary the order. No claim for a record will be considered if the order of events differs from that set about above.

(6) Three trials only are allowed in the Long Jump and Throwing Events.

(7) In track events run entirely in lanes, at least four competitors should start in each group whenever possible. In other track events at least five competitors should start in each group, and one such group should consist of those competitors occupying the leading positions prior to the final event.

(8) The time of each competitor should be taken by three Time-keepers independently. Where fully automatic timing is in operation, times shall be given to 1/100th of a second and scored by using the appropriate tables to 1/100th second.

(9) In the running and hurdles events competitors shall be disqualified in any event in which they have been responsible for three false starts.

(10) Any athlete failing to take part in any of the events shall not be allowed to take part in any subsequent event in that competition but shall be considered to have abandoned the competition. That athlete shall not figure in the final classification.

(11) Where the hurdles used do not comply with Rule 35 (8) or (9) a competitor knocking down three or parts of three or more hurdles shall score no points in that event.

(12) The winner shall be the competitor who has obtained the highest number of points in the five, seven, eight or ten events as the case may be, awarded on a basis of the IAAF Combined Events Scoring Tables.

(13) In the event of a tie, the winner shall be the competitor who has received the highest points in a majority of events. If this does not resolve the tie, the winner shall be the competitor who has scored the highest number of points in any one of the events. This procedure shall apply to ties for any place in the competition.

(14) *WAAA*: Intermediate Pentathlon and Heptathlon – Senior Scoring tables to be used, with 80 metres Hurdles (76.2cm).

Girls' Pentathlon – Events: Long Jump, 75 metres Hurdles (76.2cm), Putting the Shot, (Break of 1 hour), High Jump, 800 metres, or as for Seniors. (3.25kg shot to be used, but the score is to be the same as for the 4kg shot.) For 75 metres Hurdles points use 80 metre Hurdles table and add one second.

62. RULES FOR RECORDS
Rule 62 is given in full in AAA/WAAA Rules for Competition.

63. COUNTY QUALIFICATIONS
Rule 63 is given in full in AAA/WAAA Rules for Competition.

64. AREA CHAMPIONSHIPS QUALIFICATION
Rule 64 is given in full in AAA/WAAA Rules for Competition.

Appendix A
Indoor competitions – code of practice

A1 Events
Competitions may be held at race distances and in field events as are appropriate to the size of track and other facilities available. Hammer, discus and javelin are considered unsuitable for indoor competition.

A2 Tracks and Measurements
Tracks for indoor meetings should comply with Rule 27 with the following amendments:

(*a*) Banking of bends is permitted

(*b*) Races up to and including 60m must be run on a straight course in lanes, and it is recommended that races up to and including 200m should be run in lanes. In 400m races the first two complete bends on a track of 200m or less should be run in lanes, and a 'break' line shall be marked on the track in a distinctive colour

(*c*) Hurdle events are as specified in Rule 35

(*d*) 2000m Steeplechase shall be run over 19 barriers, one barrier on the first lap and 2 thereafter. The exact location of the barriers will be determined by local conditions, banking etc, but normally will be about 15m from the end of the home straight and 15m from the end of the back straight. There will be no hurdle at the end of the home straight on the first lap. Water jumps are not considered practical

(*e*) In events run in lanes or partly in lanes there shall be only one competitor per lane.

A3 Field Events
(*a*) **High Jump** Owing to the common use of banked tracks, a slope is acceptable in the approach run insofar as the banking forms part of the approach, but not less than the final 5m of an approach shall be on level ground. No competitor may use any other form of banking device or ramp.

(*b*) **Long Jump, Triple Jump and Pole Vault** In the long jump, triple jump and pole vault competitors may start their approach on the banking of the oval track provided that the last 40m is on the level runway.

(*c*) **Shot**
    (i) It is essential for safety reasons that a stopping device is provided at the end of the putting area
   (ii) Specifications for the indoor shot are the same as outdoor, but special plastic or rubber cased shots are permissible, which shall be spherical in shape with a smooth surface.
  (iii) The circle may be portable or permanent. If the circle is portable it shall not vary from the level of the landing area by more than ±3cm.
  (iv) The sector shall be 40° and shall be extended as far as the limitations of space allow.
   (v) Fibre boards may be used in the landing area to facilitate marking of the landing of the shot.

A4 Combined Events
The Combined Events are as specified in Rule 61.

A5 Records

A6 General Guidance
  Items A5 and A6 are given in full in AAA/WAAA Rules for Competition.

APPENDIX B
PHOTO-FINISH – CODE OF PRACTICE

APPENDIX C
HANDICAP EVENTS

APPENDIX D
OFFICIALS

APPENDIX E
JOINT ATHLETIC AND CYCLING MEETINGS (MEN)

APPENDIX F
ROAD RUNNING

APPENDIX G
CROSS-COUNTRY RUNNING

APPENDIX H
RACE WALKING FOR MEN AND WOMEN

APPENDIX I
UK RECORDS

APPENDIX J
UK INDOOR RECORDS

APPENDIX K
DRUGS

APPENDIX L
ELECTRONIC DISTANCE MEASUREMENT CODE OF PRACTICE

APPENDIX M
TIMEKEEPERS – CODE OF PRACTICE
   Appendices B–M are given in full in AAA/WAAA Rules for Competition.

Reprinted by permission of the AAA/WAAA. Some of the Rules given above have here been abbreviated for reasons of space. Copies of the current edition of the AAA/WAAA Handbook, containing the complete AAA/WAAA Rules for Competitions, are available from the Association.

THE LAWS OF

Badminton

Badminton

1. Court

1.1 The court shall be a rectangle and laid out as in the diagram on page 211 (except in the case provided for in Law 1.5) and to the measurements there shown, defined by lines 40mm wide.

1.2 The lines shall be easily distinguishable and preferably be coloured white or yellow.

1.3.1 To show the zone in which a shuttle of correct pace lands when tested (Law 4.4), an additional four marks 40mm by 40mm may be made inside each side-line for singles of the right service court, 530mm and 990mm from the back boundary line.

1.3.2 In making these marks, their width shall be within the measurement given, i.e. the marks will be from 530mm to 570mm and from 950mm to 990mm from the outside of the back boundary line.

1.4 All lines form part of the area which they define.

1.5 Where space does not permit the marking out of a court for doubles, a court may be marked out for singles only as shown in the diagram on page 213. The back boundary lines become also the long service lines, and the posts, or the strips of material representing them (Law 2.2), shall be placed on the side-lines.

2. Posts

2.1 The posts shall be 1.55m in height from the surface of the court. They shall be sufficiently firm to remain vertical and keep the net strained as provided in Law 3, and shall be placed on the doubles side-lines as shown in Diagram A.

2.2 Where it is not practicable to have posts on the side-lines, some method must be used to indicate the position of the side-lines where they pass under the net, e.g. by the use of thin posts or strips of material

40mm wide, fixed to the side-lines and rising vertically to the net cord.

2.3 On a court marked for doubles, the posts or strips of material representing the posts shall be placed on the side-lines for doubles, irrespective of whether singles or doubles is being played.

3. Net

3.1 The net shall be made of fine cord of dark colour and even thickness with a mesh not less than 15mm and not more than 20mm.

3.2 The net shall be 760mm in depth.

3.3 The top of the net shall be edged with a 75mm white tape doubled over a cord or cable running through the tape. This tape must rest upon the cord or cable.

3.4 The cord or cable shall be of sufficient size and weight to be firmly stretched flush with the top of the posts.

3.5 The top of the net from the surface of the court shall be 1.524m at the centre of the court and 1.55m over the side-lines for doubles.

3.6 There shall be no gaps between the ends of the net and the posts. If necessary, the full depth of the net should be tied at the ends.

4. Shuttle

Principles

The shuttle may be made from natural and/or synthetic materials. Whatever material the shuttle is made from, the flight characteristics, generally, should be similar to those produced by a natural feathered shuttle with a cork base covered by a thin layer of leather. Having regard to the Principles:

4.1 *General Design*

4.1.1 The shuttle shall have 16 feathers fixed in the base.

4.1.2 The feathers can have a variable length from 64mm to 70mm, but in each shuttle they shall be the same length when measured from the tip of the top of the base.

4.1.3 The tips of the feathers shall form a circle with a diameter from 58mm to 68mm.

4.1.4 The feathers shall be fastened firmly with thread or other suitable material.

4.1.5 The base shall be:

25mm to 28mm in diameter.

Rounded on the bottom.

4.2 *Weight*

The shuttle shall weigh from 4.74g to 5.50g.

4.3 *Non-feathered Shuttle*

4.3.1 The skirt, or simulation of feathers in synthetic materials, replaces natural feathers.

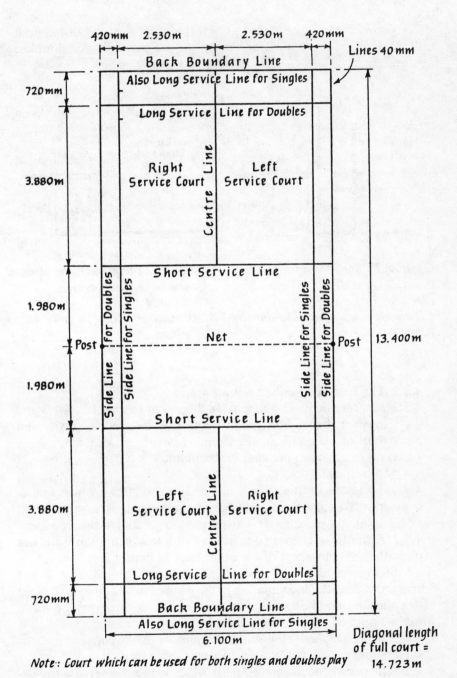

420mm   2.530m   2.530m   420mm

Lines 40 mm

Back Boundary Line
Also Long Service Line for Singles

720mm

Long Service | Line for Doubles

Right
Service Court

Centre Line

Left
Service Court

3.880m

Short Service Line

Side Line for Doubles
Side Line for Singles

1.980m

Net

Post

Side Line for Singles
Side Line for Doubles

Post

13.400m

1.980m

Short Service Line

Side Line

Left
Service Court

Centre Line

Right
Service Court

3.880m

Long Service | Line for Doubles

720mm

Back Boundary Line
Also Long Service Line for Singles

6.100m

Diagonal length
of full court =
14.723m

Note : Court which can be used for both singles and doubles play

**Optional testing marks are shown on page 212*

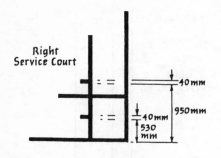

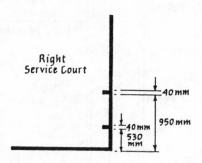

Optional Testing Marks for Doubles Court
(See Law 1.3)
NB measurement of marks 40mm by 40mm

Optional Testing Marks for Singles Court
(See Law 1.3)
NB measurements of marks 40mm by 40mm

4.3.2 The base is described in Law 4.1.5.

4.3.3 Measurements and weight shall be as in Laws 4.1.2, 4.1.3 and 4.2. However, because of the difference of the specific gravity and behaviour of synthetic materials in comparison with feathers, a variation of up to ten per cent is acceptable.

4.4 *Shuttle Testing*

4.4.1 To test a shuttle, use a full underhand stroke which makes contact with the shuttle over the back boundary line. The shuttle shall be hit at an upward angle and in a direction parallel to the side lines.

4.4.2 A shuttle of correct pace will land not less than 530mm and not more than 990mm short of the other back boundary line.

4.5 *Modifications*

Subject to there being no variation in the general design, pace and flight of the shuttle, modifications in the above specifications may be made with the approval of the National Organisation concerned:

4.5.1 In places where atmospheric conditions due to either altitude or climate makes the standard shuttle unsuitable; or

4.5.2 If special circumstances exists which make it otherwise necessary in the interests of the game.

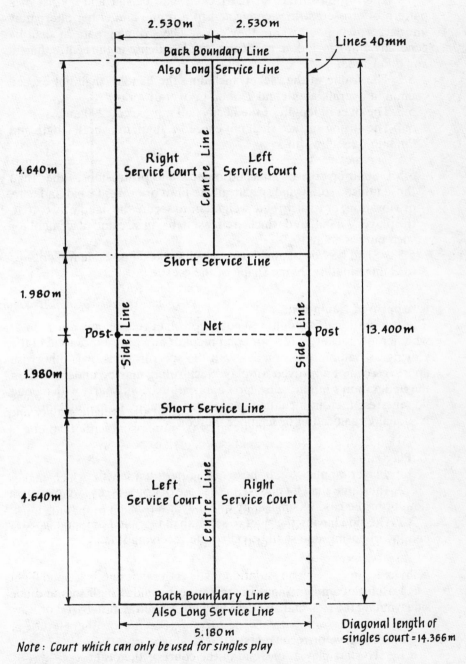

Note: Court which can only be used for singles play

**Optional testing marks are shown on the opposite page

5. Racket

5.1 The hitting surface of the racket shall be flat and consist of a pattern of crossed strings connected to a frame and either alternately interlaced or bonded where they cross. The stringing pattern shall be generally uniform and, in particular, not less dense in the centre than in any other area.

5.2 The frame of the racket, including the handle, shall not exceed 680mm in overall length and 230mm in overall width.

5.3 The overall length of the head shall not exceed 290mm.

5.4 The strung surface shall not exceed 280mm in overall length and 220mm in overall width.

5.5 *The racket*:

5.5.1 Shall be free of attached objects and protrusions, other than those utilised solely and specifically to limit or prevent wear and tear, or vibration, or to distribute weight, or to secure the handle by cord to the player's hand, and which are reasonable in size and placement for such purposes; and

5.5.2 Shall be free of any device which makes it possible for a player to change materially the shape of the racket.

6. Approved Equipment

The International Badminton Federation shall rule on any question of whether any racket, shuttle or equipment or any prototypes used in the playing of Badminton complies with the specifications or is otherwise approved or not approved for play. Such ruling may be undertaken on the Federation's initiative or upon application by any party with a bona fide interest therein including any player, equipment manufacturer or National Organisation or member thereof.

7. Players

7.1 'Player' applies to all those taking part in a match.

7.2 The game shall be played, in the case of doubles, by two players a side, or in the case of singles, by one player a side.

7.3 The side having the right to serve shall be called the serving side, and the opposing side shall be called the receiving side.

8. Toss

8.1 Before commencing play, the opposing sides shall toss and the side winning the toss shall exercise the choice in either Law 8.1.1 or Law 8.1.2.

8.1.1 To serve or receive first.

8.1.2 To start play at one end of the court or the other.

8.2 The side losing the toss shall then exercise the remaining choice.

9. Scoring

9.1 The opposing sides shall play the best of three games unless otherwise arranged.

9.2 Only the serving side can add a point to its score.

9.3 In doubles and Men's singles a game is won by the first side to score 15 points, except as provided in Law 9.6.

9.4 In Ladies' singles a game is won by the first side to score 11 points, except as provided in Law 9.6.

9.5.1 If the score becomes 13-all or 14-all (9-all or 10-all in Ladies' singles), the side which first scored 13 or 14 (9 or 10) shall have the choice of 'setting' or 'not setting' the game (Law 9.6).

9.5.2 This choice can only be made when the score is first reached and must be made before the next service is delivered.

9.5.3 The relevant side (Law 9.5.1) is given the opportunity to set at 14-all (10-all in Ladies' singles) despite any previous decision not to set by that side or the opposing side at 13-all (9-all in Ladies' singles).

9.6 If the game has been set, the score is called 'Love-all' and the side first scoring the set number of points (Law 9.6.1 to 9.6.4) wins the game.

9.6.1 13-all setting to 5 points

9.6.2 14-all setting to 3 points

9.6.3 9-all setting to 3 points

9.6.4 10-all setting to 2 points

9.7 The side winning a game serves first in the next game.

10. Change of Ends

10.1 Players shall change ends:

10.1.1 At the end of the first game;

10.1.2 Prior to the beginning of the third game (if any); and

10.1.3 In the third game, or in one-game match, when the leading score reaches:

– 6 in a game of 11 points

– 8 in a game of 15 points

10.2 When players omit to change ends as indicated by Law 10.1, they shall do so immediately the mistake is discovered and the existing score shall stand.

11. Service

11.1 In a correct service:

11.1.1 Neither side shall cause undue delay to the delivery of the service;

11.1.2 The server and receiver shall stand within diagonally opposite service courts without touching the boundary lines of these service courts; some part of both feet of the server and receiver must remain in contact with the surface of the court in a stationary position until the service is delivered (Law 11.4);

11.1.3 The server's racket shall initially hit the base of the shuttle while the whole of the shuttle is below the server's waist;

11.1.4 The shaft of the server's racket at the instant of hitting the shuttle shall be pointing in a downward direction to such an extent that the whole of the head of the racket is discernibly below the whole of the server's hand holding the racket;

11.1.5 The movement of the server's racket must continue forwards after the start of the service (Law 11.2) until the service is delivered; and

11.1.6 The flight of the shuttle shall be upwards from the server's racket to pass over the net, so that, if not intercepted, it falls in the receiver's service court.

11.2 Once the players have taken their positions, the first forward movement of the server's racket head is the start of the service.

11.3 The server shall not serve before the receiver is ready, but the receiver shall be considered to have been ready if a return of service is attempted.

11.4 The service is delivered when, once started (Law 11.2), the shuttle is hit by the server's racket or the shuttle lands on the floor.

11.5 In doubles, the partners may take up any positions which do not unsight the opposing server or receiver.

12. Singles

12.1 The players shall serve from, and receive in, their respective right service courts when the server has not scored or has scored an even number of points in that game.

12.2 The player shall serve from, and receive in, their respective left service courts when the server has scored an odd number of points in that game.

12.3 If a game is set, the total points scored by the server in that game shall be used to apply Laws 12.1 and 12.2.

12.4 The shuttle is hit alternately by the server and the receiver until a 'fault' is made or the shuttle ceases to be in play.

12.5.1 If the receiver makes a 'fault' or the shuttle ceases to be in play because it touches the surface of the court inside the receiver's court, the server scores a point. The server then serves again from the alternate service court.

12.5.2 If the server makes a 'fault' or the shuttle ceases to be in play because it touches the surface of the court inside the server's court, the server loses the right to continue serving, and the receiver then becomes the server, with no point scored by either player.

13. Doubles

13.1 At the start of a game, and each time a side gains the right to serve, the service shall be delivered from the right service court.

13.2 Only the receiver shall return the service: should the shuttle touch or be hit by the receiver's partner, the serving side scores a point.

13.3.1 After the service is returned, the shuttle is hit by either player of the serving side and then by either player of the receiving side, and so on, until the shuttle ceases to be in play.

13.3.2 After the service is returned, a player may hit the shuttle from any position on that player's side of the net.

13.4.1 If the receiving side makes a 'fault' or the shuttle ceases to be in play because it touches the surface of the court inside the receiving side's court, the serving side scores a point, and the server serves again.

13.4.2 If the serving side makes a 'fault' or the shuttle ceases to be in play because it touches the surface of the court inside the serving side's court, the server loses the right to continue serving, with no point scored by either side.

13.5.1 The player who serves at the start of any game shall serve from, or receive in, the right service court when that player's side has not scored or has scored an even number of points in that game, and the left service court otherwise.

13.5.2 The player who receives at the start of any game shall receive in, or serve from, the right service court when that player's side has not scored or has scored an even number of points in that game, and the left service court otherwise.

13.5.3 The reverse pattern applies to the partners.

13.5.4 If a game is set, the total points scored by a side in that game shall be used to apply Laws 13.5.1 to 13.5.3.

13.6 Service in any turn of serving shall be delivered from alternate service courts, except as provided in Laws 14 and 16.

13.7 The right to serve passes consecutively from the initial server in any game to the initial receiver in that game, and then consecutively from that player to that player's partner and then to one of the opponents and then the opponent's partner, and so on.

13.8 No player shall serve out of turn, receive out of turn, or receive two consecutive services in the same game, except as provided in Laws 14 and 16.

13.9 Either player of the winning side may serve first in the next game and either player of the losing side may receive.

14. Service-Court Errors

14.1 A service-court error has been made when a player:

14.1.1 Has served out of turn;

14.1.2 Has served from the wrong service court; or

14.1.3 Standing in the wrong service court, was prepared to receive the service and it has been delivered.

14.2 When a service-court error has been made, then:

14.2.1 If the error is discovered before the next service is delivered, it is a 'let' unless only one side was at fault and lost the rally, in which case the error shall not be corrected.

14.2.2 If the error is not discovered before the next service is delivered, the error shall not be corrected.

14.3 If there is a 'let' because of a service court error, the rally is replayed and the error corrected.

14.4 If a service-court error is not to be corrected, play in that game shall proceed without changing the players' new service courts (nor, when relevant, the new order of serving).

15. Faults

It is a 'fault':

15.1 If a service is not correct (Law 11.1).

15.2 If the server, in attempting to serve, misses the shuttle.

15.3 If, on service, the shuttle is caught on the net and remains suspended on top or, on service, after passing over the net is caught in the net.

15.4 If in play, the shuttle:

15.4.1 Lands outside the boundaries of the court;

15.4.2 Passes through or under the net;

15.4.3 Fails to pass the net;

15.4.4 Touches the roof, ceiling, or side walls;

15.4.5 Touches the person or dress of a player; or

15.4.6 Touches any other object or person outside the immediate surroundings of the court;

(*Where necessary, on account of the structure of the building, the local badminton authority may, subject to the right of veto of its National Organisation, make by-laws dealing with cases in which a shuttle touches an obstruction.*)

15.5 If when in play, the initial point of contact with the shuttle is not on the striker's side of the net. (The striker may, however, follow the shuttle over the net with the racket in the course of a stroke.)

15.6 If, when the shuttle is in play, a player:

15.6.1 Touches the net or its supports with racket, person or dress;

15.6.2 Invades an opponent's court with racket or person in any degree except as permitted in Law 15.5; or

15.6.3 Obstructs an opponent, i.e. prevents an opponent from making a legal stroke where the shuttle is followed over the net.

15.7 If, in play, a player deliberately distracts an opponent by any action such as shouting or making gesture.

15.8 If, in play, the shuttle:

15.8.1 Be caught and held on the racket and then slung during the execution of a stroke:

15.8.2 Be hit twice in succession by the same player with two strokes:

15.8.3 Be hit by a player and the player's partner successively; or

15.8.4 Touches a player's racket and continues towards the back of that player's court.

15.9 If a player is guilty of flagrant, repeated or persistent offences under Law 18.

16. Lets

'Let' is called by the Umpire, or by a player (if there is no Umpire) to halt play.

16.1 A 'let' may be given for any unforeseen or accidental occurrence.

16.2 If a shuttle is caught on the net and remains suspended on top, or after passing over the net is caught in the net, it is a 'let' except during service.

16.3 If during service, the receiver and server are both faulted at the same time, it shall be a 'let'.

16.4 If the server before the receiver is ready, it shall be a 'let'.

16.5 If during play, the shuttle disintegrates and the base completely separates from the rest of the shuttle, it shall be a 'let'.

16.6 If a Line Judge is unsighted and the Umpire is unable to make a decision, it shall be a 'let'.

16.7 When a 'let' occurs, the play since the last service shall not count, and the player who served shall serve again, except when Law 14 is applicable.

17. Shuttle not in Play

A shuttle is not in play when:

17.1 It strikes the net and remains attached there or suspended on top;

17.2 It strikes the net or post and starts to fall towards the surface of the court on the striker's side of the net;

17.3 It hits the surface of the court; or

17.4 A 'fault' or 'let' has occurred.

18. Continuous Play, Misconduct, Penalties

18.1 Play shall be continuous from the first service until the match is concluded, except as allowed in Laws 18.2 and 18.3.

18.2 An interval not exceeding 5 minutes is allowed between the second and third games of all matches in all of the following situations:

18.2.1 In international competitive events;

18.2.2 In IBF sanctioned events; and

18.2.3 In all other matches (unless the National Organisation has previously published a decision not to allow such an interval).

18.4 Under no circumstances shall play be suspended to enable a player to recover his strength or wind, or to receive instruction or advice.

18.5.1 Except in the intervals provided in Laws 18.2 and 18.3, no player shall be permitted to receive advice during a match.

18.5.2 Except at the conclusion of a match, no player shall leave the court without the Umpire's consent.

18.6 The Umpire shall be sole judge of any suspension of play.

18.7 A player shall not:

18.7.1 Deliberately cause suspension of play;

18.7.2 Deliberately interfere with the speed of the shuttle;

18.7.3 Behave in an offensive manner; or

18.7.4 Be guilty of misconduct not otherwise covered by the Laws of Badminton.

18.8 The Umpire shall administer any breach of Law 18.4, 18.5, or 18.7 by:

18.8.1 Issuing a warning to the offending side;

18.8.2 Faulting the offending side, if previously warned; or

18.8.3 In cases of flagrant offence or persistent offences, faulting the offending side and reporting the offending side immediately to the Referee, who shall have the power to disqualify.

18.9 Where a Referee has not been appointed, the responsible official shall have the power to disqualify.

19. Officials and Appeals

19.1 The Referee is in overall charge of the tournament or event of which a match forms part.

19.2 The Umpire, where appointed, is in charge of the match, the court and its immediate surrounds. The Umpire shall report to the Referee. In the absence of a Referee, the Umpire shall report instead to the responsible official.

19.3 The Service Judge shall call service faults made by the server should they occur (Law 11).

19.4 A Line Judge shall indicate whether a shuttle is 'in' or 'out'. An Umpire shall:

19.5 Uphold and enforce the Laws of Badminton, and especially call a 'fault' or 'let' should either occur, without appeal being made by the players;

19.6 Give a decision on any appeal regarding a point of dispute, if made before the next service is delivered;

19.7 Ensure players and spectators are kept informed of the progress of the match;

19.8 Appoint or remove Line Judges or a Service Judge in consultation with the Referee;

19.9 Not overrule the decisions of Line Judges and the Service Judge on points of fact;

19.10.1 Where another court official is not appointed, arrange for their duties to be carried out;

19.10.2 Where an appointed official is unsighted, carry out the official's duties or play a 'let';

19.11 Decide upon any suspension of play;

19.12 Record and report to the Referee all matters in relation to Law 18; and

19.13 Take to the Referee all unsatisfied appeals on questions of Law only. (Such appeals must be made before the next service is delivered, or, if at the end of a game, before the side that appeals has left the court.)

APPENDIX 1
Imperial Measurements

APPENDIX 2
Handicap Matches

APPENDIX 3
Games of Other than 11 or 15 Points

APPENDIX 4
Vocabulary

APPENDIX 5
Badminton for Disabled People

RECOMMENDATIONS TO COURT OFFICIALS
1. Introduction
2. Officials and their Decisions
3. Recommendations to Umpires
4. General Advice on Umpiring
5. Instructions to Service Judges
6. Instructions to Line Judges

Reprinted by permission of the Badminton Association of England. The Laws are as revised in 1987 by the International Badminton Federation. Appendixes 1 to 5 and the Recommendations to Court Officials are given in full in The Laws of Badminton, available from the Association.

THE RULES OF

Baseball

Baseball

1. Objectives of The Game

1.01 Baseball is a game between two teams of 9 players each, under direction of a manager, played on an enclosed field in accordance with these rules, under jurisdiction of one or more umpires.

1.02 The objective of each team is to win by scoring more runs than the opponent.

1.03 The winner of the game shall be that team which shall have scored, in accordance with these rules, the greater number of runs at the conclusion of a regulation game.

1.04 *The Playing Field.* The field shall be laid out according to the instructions below, supplemented by diagrams 1, 2 and 3 on pp. 227, 228 and 229.

The infield shall be a 90ft square. The outfield shall be the area between the two foul-lines formed by extending two sides of the square, as in diagram 1. The distance from home base to the nearest fence, stand or other obstruction on fair territory shall be 250ft or more. A distance of 320ft or more along the foul-lines, and 400ft or more to centre field is preferable. The infield shall be graded so that the base lines and home plate are level. The pitcher's plate shall be 10in above the level of home plate. The degree of slope from a point 6in in front of the pitcher's plate to a point 6ft towards home plate shall be 1in to 1ft and such degree of slope shall be uniform. The infield and outfield, including the boundary lines, are fair territory and all other area is foul territory.

It is desirable that the line from home base through the pitcher's plate to second base shall run east-northeast.

It is recommended that the distance from home base to the backstop, and from the base lines to the nearest fence, stand or other obstruction on foul territory shall be 60ft or more. See diagram 1.

When location of home base is determined, with a steel tape measure 127ft 3⅜in in desired direction to establish second base. From home base, measure 90ft towards first base; from second base, measure 90ft towards first base; the intersection of these lines establishes first base. From home base, measure 90ft towards third base; from second base, measure 90ft towards third base; the intersection of these lines establishes third base. The distance between first base and third base is 127ft 3⅜in. All measurements from home base shall be taken from the point where the first and third base-lines intersect.

The catcher's box, the batters' boxes, the coaches' boxes, the 3ft first base lines and the next batters' boxes shall be laid out as shown in Diagrams 1 and 2.

The foul-lines and all other playing lines indicated in the diagrams by solid black lines shall be marked with wet, unslaked lime, chalk or other white material.

The grass lines and dimensions shown on the diagrams are those used in many fields, but they are not mandatory and each club shall determine the size and shape of the grassed and bare areas of its playing field.

1.05 Home base shall be marked by a five-sided slab of whitened rubber. It shall be a 17in square with two of the corners removed so that one edge is 17in long, two adjacent sides are 8½in and the remaining two sides are 12in and set at an angle to make a point. It shall be set in the ground with the point at the intersection of the lines extending from home base to first base; with the 17in edge facing the pitcher's plate, and the two 12in edges coinciding with the first and third base lines. The top edges of home plate shall be bevelled and the base shall be fixed in the ground level with the ground surface.

1.06 First, second and third bases shall be marked by white canvas bags, securely attached to the ground as indicated in diagram 2. The first and third base bags shall be entirely within the infield. The second base bag shall be centred on second base. The bags shall be 15in square, not less than 3 nor more than 5 in thick, and filled with soft material.

1.07 The pitcher's plate shall be a rectangular slab of whitened rubber, 24in by 6in. It shall be set in the ground as shown in diagrams 1 and 2, so that the distance between the pitcher's plate and home base (the rear point of home plate) shall be 60ft 6in.

Diagram 1

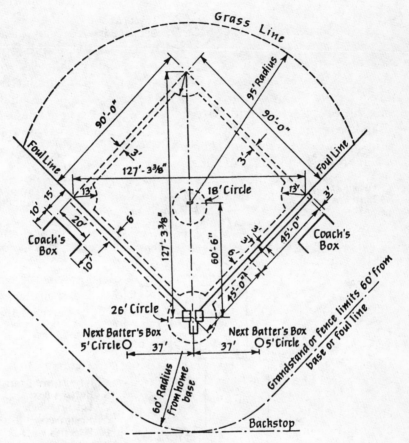

——— Base lines, Batter's box, Catcher's box,
Foul line, Pitcher's Plate, Coach's box
—·— Base lines
———— Grass lines

Diagram 2

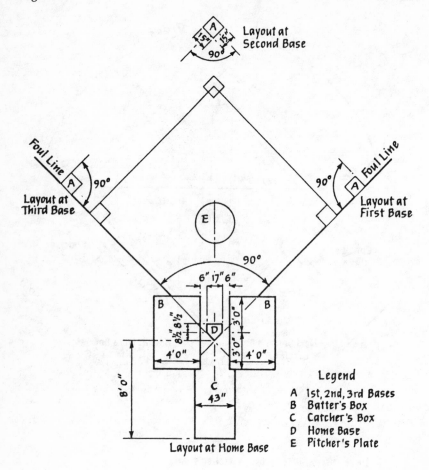

Layout at
Second Base

Foul Line
90°
Layout at
Third Base

90°
Foul Line
Layout at
First Base

E

90°

6" 17" 6"

B   B

8½" 8½"

D

4'0"   3'0" 3'0" 4'0"

8'0"

C
43"

Legend

A 1st, 2nd, 3rd Bases
B Batter's Box
C Catcher's Box
D Home Base
E Pitcher's Plate

Layout at Home Base

Diagram 3

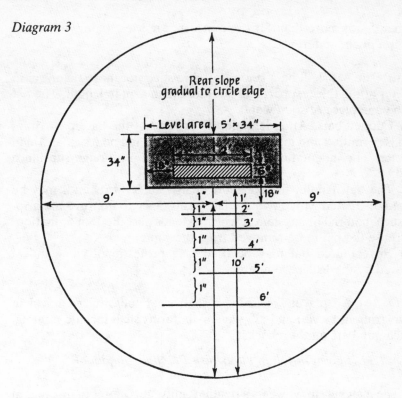

The degree of slope from a point 6″ in front of the pitcher's plate to a point 6′ towards the home plate shall be 1″ to 1′, and such degree of slope shall be uniform.

Pitching Mound – an 18″ diameter circle, the centre of which is 59′ from the back of the home plate. Locate the front edge of rubber 18″ behind the centre of the mound.

The front edge of rubber to the back point of home plate measures 60′6″.

The slope starts 6″ from the front edge of rubber.

The slope shall be 6″ from starting point, 6″ in front of rubber to a point 6″ in front of rubber, and the slope shall be uniform.

The level area surrounding rubber should be 6″ in front of rubber, 18″ to each side and 22″ to the rear of rubber. Total level area should be 5′ × 34″.

1.08 The home club shall furnish players' benches, one each for the home and visiting teams. Such benches shall not be less than 25ft from the base lines. They shall be roofed and enclosed at the back and ends.

1.09 The ball shall be a sphere formed by yarn wound around a small core of cork, rubber or similar material, covered with two stripes of white horsehide or cowhide, tightly stitched together. It shall weigh not less than 5 nor more than 5¼oz and measure not less than 9 nor more than 9¼in in circumference.

1.10 (*a*) The bat shall be a smooth, round stick not more than 2¾in in diameter at the thickest part and not more than 42in in length. The bat shall be one piece of solid wood.

(*b*) Cupped bats. An indentation in the end of the bat up to 1in in depth is permitted and may be no wider than 2in and no less than 1in in diameter. The indentation must be curved with no foreign substance added.

(*c*) The bat handle, for not more than 18in from its end, may be covered or treated with any material or substance to improve the grip. Any such material or substance, which extends past the 18in limitation, shall cause the bat to be removed from the game.

(*d*) No coloured bat may be used in a professional game unless approved by the Rules Committee.

1.11 (*a*) (1) All players on a team shall wear uniforms identical in colour, trim and style, and all players' uniforms shall include minimal six-inch numbers on their backs.

Section 1.11 is given in full in the British Baseball Handbook.

1.12 The catcher may wear a leather mitt not more than 38in in circumference, nor more than 15½in from top to bottom. Such limits shall include all lacing and any leather band or facing attached to the outer edge of the mitt. The space between the thumb section and the finger section of the mitt shall not exceed 6in at the top of the mitt and 4in at the base of thumb crotch. The web shall measure not more than 7in across the top or more than 6in from its top to the base of the thumb crotch. The web may be either a lacing or lacing through leather tunnels, or a centre piece of leather which may be an extension of the palm, connected to the mitt with lacing and constructed so that it will not exceed any of the above mentioned measurements.

1.13 The first baseman may wear a leather glove or mitt not more than 12in long from top to bottom and not more than 8in wide across the palm, measured from the base of the thumb crotch to the outer edge of the mitt. The space between the thumb section and the finger section of the mitt shall not exceed 4in at the top of the mitt and 3½in at the base of the thumb crotch. The mitt shall be constructed so that this space is permanently fixed and cannot be enlarged, extended, widened, or deepened by the use of any materials or process whatever. The web of the mitt shall measure not more than 5in from its top to the base of the thumb crotch. The web may be either a lacing, lacing through leather tunnels, or a centre piece of leather which may be an extension of the palm connected to the mitt with lacing and constructed so that it will not exceed the above-mentioned measurements. The webbing shall not be constructed of wound or wrapped lacing or deepened to make a net type of trap. The glove may be of any weight.

1.14 Each fielder, other than the first baseman or catcher, may use or wear a leather glove.

Section 1.14 is given in full in the British Baseball Handbook.

1.15 (*a*) The pitcher's glove shall be uniform in colour, including all stitching, lacing and webbing. The pitcher's glove may not be white or grey.
  (*b*) No pitcher shall attach to his glove any foreign material of a colour different from the glove.

1.16 *Section 1.16, concerning the use of helmets, is given in full in the British Baseball Handbook.*

1.17 Playing equipment, including but not limited to the bases, pitchers' plate, baseball, bats, uniforms, catcher's mitts, first baseman's gloves, infielders' and outfielders' gloves and protective helmets, as detailed in the provisions of this rule, shall not contain any undue commercialisation of the product. Designations by the manufacturer on any such equipment must be in good taste as to the size and content of the manufacturer's logo or the brand name of the item. The provisions of this Section 1.17 shall apply to professional leagues only.

2. Definitions of Terms
All definitions in rule 2 are listed alphabetically.
Adjudged is a judgement decision by the umpire.
An *Appeal* is the act of a fielder in claiming violation of the rules by the offensive team.
A *Balk* is an illegal act by the pitcher with a runner or runners on base, entitling all runners to advance one base.
A *Ball* is a pitch which does not enter the strike zone in flight and is not struck at by the batter.
A *Base* is one of four points which must be touched by a runner in order to score a run; more usually applied to the canvas bags and the rubber plate which mark the base points.
A *Base Coach* is a team member in uniform who is stationed in the coach's box at first or third base to direct the batter and the runners.

A *Base on Balls* is an award of first base granted to a batter who, during his time at bat, receives four pitches outside the strike zone.

A *Batter* is an offensive player who takes his position in the batter's box.

Batter-Runner is a term that identifies the offensive player who has just finished his time at bat until he is put out or until the play on which he became a runner ends.

The *Batter's Box* is the area within which the batter shall stand during his time at bat.

The *Battery* is the pitcher and the catcher.

Bench or Dugout is the seating facilities reserved for players, substitutes and other team members in uniform when they are not actively engaged on the playing field.

A *Bunt* is a batted ball not swung at, but intentionally met with the bat and tapped slowly within the infield.

A *Called Game* is one in which, for any reason, the umpire-in-chief terminates play.

A *Catch* is the act of a fielder in getting secure possession in his hand or glove of a ball in flight and firmly holding it; providing he does not use his cap, protector, pocket or any other part of his uniform in getting possession. It is not a catch, however, if simultaneously or immediately following his contact with the ball, he collides with a player, or with a wall, or if he falls down, and as a result of such collision or falling, drops the ball. It is not a catch if a fielder touches a fly ball which then hits a member of the offensive team or an umpire and then is caught by another defensive player. If the fielder has made the catch and drops the ball while in the act of making a throw following the catch, the ball shall be adjudged to have been caught. In establishing the validity of the catch, the fielder shall hold the ball long enough to prove that he has complete control of the ball and that his release of the ball is voluntary and intentional.

The *Catcher* is the fielder who takes his position back of the home base.

The *Catcher's Box* is that area within which the catcher shall stand until the pitcher delivers the ball.

The *Club* is a person or group of persons responsible for assembling the team personnel, providing the playing field and required facilities, and representing the team in relations with the league.

A *Coach* is a team member in uniform appointed by the manager to perform such duties as the manager may designate, such as but not limited to acting as base coach.

A *Dead Ball* is a ball out of play because of a legally created temporary suspension of play.

The *Defence (or Defensive)* is the team, or any player of the team, in the field.

A *Double Header* is two regularly scheduled or rescheduled games, played in immediate succession.

A *Double Play* is a play by the defense in which two offensive players are put out as a result of continuing action, providing there is no error between put-outs.

(*a*) A force double play is one in which both put-outs are force plays.

(*b*) A reverse force double play is one in which the first out is a force play and the second out is made on runner for whom the force is removed by reason of the first out.

Dugout (See definition of bench).

A *Fair Ball* is a batted ball that settles on fair ground between home and first base, or between home and third base, or that is on or over fair territory when bounding to the outfield past first or third base, or that touches first, second or third base, or that first falls on fair territory on or beyond first base or third base, or that, while on or over fair territory, touches the person of an umpire or player, or that, while over fair territory, passes out of the playing field in flight.

Fair Territory is that part of the playing field within, and including the first base and third base lines, from home base to the bottom of the playing field fence and perpendicularly upwards. All foul-lines are in fair territory.

A *Fielder* is any defensive player.

Fielder's Choice is the act of a fielder who handles a fair grounder and, instead of throwing to first base to put out the batter-runner, throws to another base in an attempt to put out a preceding runner.

A *Fly Ball* is a batted ball that goes high in the air in flight.

A *Force Play* is a play in which a runner legally loses his right to occupy a base by reason of the batter becoming a runner.

A *Forfeited Game* is a game declared ended by the umpire-in-chief in favour of the offended team by the score of 9 to 0, for violation of the rules.

A *Foul Ball* is a batted ball that settles on foul territory between home and first base, or between home and third base, or that bounds past first or third base on or over foul territory, or that first falls on foul territory, beyond first or third base, or that, while on or over foul territory, touches the person of an umpire or player, or any object foreign to the natural ground.

A foul fly shall be judged according to the relative position of the ball and the foul-line, including the foul-pole, and not as to whether the fielder is on foul or fair territory at the time he touches the ball.

Foul Territory is that part of the playing field outside the first and third base lines extended to the fence and perpendicularly upwards.

A *Foul Tip* is a batted ball that goes sharp and direct from the bat to the catcher's hands and is legally caught. It is not a foul tip unless caught and any foul tip that is caught is a strike, and the ball is in play. It is not a catch if it is a rebound, unless the ball has first touched the catcher's glove or hand.

A *Ground Ball* is a batted ball that rolls or bounces close to the ground.

The *Home Team* is the team on whose grounds the game is played, or if the game is played on neutral grounds, the home team shall be designated by mutual agreement.

Illegal (or Illegally) is contrary to these rules.

An *Illegal Pitch* is (1) A pitch delivered to the batter when the pitcher does not have his pivot foot in contact with the pitcher's plate; (2) A quick return pitch. An illegal pitch when runners are on base is a balk.

An *Infielder* is a fielder who occupies a position on the infield.

An *Infield Fly* is a fair fly ball (not including a line nor an attempted bunt) which can be caught by an infielder with ordinary effort, when first and second, or first, second and third bases are occupied, before two are out. The pitcher, catcher and any outfielder who stations himself in the infield on the play shall be considered infielders for the purpose of this rule.

When it seems apparent that a batted ball will be an infield fly, the umpire shall immediately declare 'infield fly' for the benefit of the runners. If the ball is near the base lines, the umpire shall declare 'infield fly, if fair'.

The ball is alive and runners may advance at the risk of the ball being caught, or retouch and advance after the ball is touched, the same as on any fly ball. If the hit becomes a foul ball, it is treated the same as any foul.

If a declared infield fly is allowed to fall untouched to the ground, and bounces foul before passing first or third base, it is a foul ball. If a declared infield fly falls untouched to the ground outside the baseline, and bounces fair before passing first or third base, it is an infield fly.

In Flight describes a batted, thrown or pitched ball which has not yet touched the grounds or some object other than a fielder.

In Jeopardy is a term indicating that the ball is in play and an offensive player may be put out.

An *Inning* is that portion of a game within which the teams alternate on offence and defence and in which there are three put-outs for each team. Each team's time at bat is a half-inning.

Interference

(*a*) Offensive interference is an act by the team at bat which interferes with, obstructs, impedes, hinders or confuses any fielder attempting to make a play. If the umpire declares the batter, batter-runner, or a runner out for interference, all other runners shall return to the last base that was, in the judgement of the umpire, legally touched at the time of the interference, unless otherwise provided by these rules.

(*b*) Defensive interference is an act by a fielder which hinders or prevents a batter from hitting a pitch.

(*c*) Umpire's interference occurs (1) When an umpire hinders, impedes or prevents a catcher's throw attempting to prevent a stolen base, or (2) When a fair ball touches an umpire on fair territory before passing a fielder.

(*d*) Spectator interference occurs when a spectator reaches out of the stands, or goes on the playing field, and touches a live ball.

On any interference the ball is dead.

The *League* is a group of clubs whose teams play each other in a pre-arranged schedule under these rules for the league championship.

The *League President* shall enforce the official rules, resolve any disputes involving the rules, and determine any protested games. The league president may fine or suspend any player, coach, manager or umpire for violation of these rules, at his discretion.

Legal (or Legally) is in accordance with these rules.

A *Live Ball* is a ball which is in play.

A *Line Drive* is a batted ball that goes sharp and direct from the bat to a fielder without touching the ground.

The *Manager* is a person appointed by the club to be responsible for the team's actions on the field, and to represent the team in communications with the umpire and the opposing team. A player may be appointed manager.

Offence is the team, or any play of the team, at bat.

Official Scorer. See Rule 10.

An *Out* is one of the three required retirements of an offensive team during its time at bat.

An *Outfielder* is a fielder who occupies a position in the outfield, which is the area of the playing field most distant from home base.

Overslide (or Oversliding) is the act of an offensive player when his slide to a base, other than when advancing from home to first base, is with such momentum that he loses contact with the base.

A *Penalty* is the application of these rules following an illegal act.

The *Person* of a player or an umpire is any part of his body, his clothing or his equipment.

A *Pitch* is a ball delivered to the batter by the pitcher.

A *Pitcher* is the fielder designated to deliver the pitch to the batter.

The pitcher's *Pivot Foot* is that foot which is in contact with the pitcher's plate as he delivers the pitch.

'*Play*' is the umpire's order to start the game or to resume action following any dead ball.

A *Quick Return* pitch is one made with obvious intent to catch a batter off balance. It is an illegal pitch.

Regulation Game. See Rules 4.10 and 4.11.

A *Retouch* is the act of a runner in returning to a base as legally required.

A *Run (or Score)* is the score made by an offensive player who advances from batter to runner and touches first, second, third and home bases in that order.

A *Run-Down* is the act of the defence in an attempt to put out a runner between bases.

A *Runner* is an offensive player who is advancing toward, or touching, or returning to any base.

'*Safe*' is a declaration by the umpire that a runner is entitled to the base for which he was trying.

Set Position is one of the two legal pitching positions.

Squeeze Play is a term to designate a play when a team, with a runner on third base, attempts to score that runner by means of a bunt.

A *Strike* is a legal pitch when so called by the umpire, which:

(*a*) Is struck at by the batter and missed;

(*b*) Is not struck at, if any part of the ball passes through any part of the strike zone;

(*c*) Is fouled by the batter when he has less than two strikes;

(*d*) Is bunted foul;

(*e*) Touches the batter as he strikes at it;

(*f*) Touches the batter in flight in the strike zone; or

(*g*) Becomes a foul tip.

The *Strike Zone* is that area over home plate the upper limit of which is a horizontal line at the midpoint between the top of the shoulders and the top of the uniform pants, and the lower level is a line at the top of the knees. The strike zone shall be determined from the batter's stance as the batter is prepared to swing at a pitched ball.

A *Suspended Game* is a called game which is to be completed at a later date.

A *Tag* is the action of a fielder in touching a base with his body while holding the ball securely and firmly in his hand or glove; or touching a runner with the ball, or with his hand or glove holding the ball, while holding the ball securely and firmly in his hand or glove.

A *Throw* is the act of propelling the ball with the hand and arm to a given objective and is to be distinguished, always, from the pitch.

A *Tie Game* is a regulation game which is called when each team has the same number of runs.

'*Time*' is the announcement by an umpire of a legal interruption of play, during which the ball is dead.

Touch. To touch a player or umpire is to touch any part of his body, his clothing or his equipment.

A *Triple Play* is a play by the defence in which three offensive players are put out as a result of continuous action, providing there is no error between put-outs.

A *Wild Pitch* is one so high, so low, or so wide of the plate that it cannot be handled with ordinary effort by the catcher.

Wind-Up Position is one of the two legal pitching positions.

3. Game Preliminaries
Section 3 is given in full in the British Baseball Handbook.

4. Starting and Ending a Game
4.01 Unless the home club shall have given previous notice that the game has been postponed or will be delayed in starting, the umpire, or umpires, shall enter the playing field 5 minutes before the hour set for the game to begin and proceed directly to home base where they shall be met by the managers of the opposing team.

In sequence:

(*a*) First, the home manager shall give his batting order to the umpire-in-chief, in duplicate.

(*b*) Next, the visiting manager shall give his batting order to the umpire-in-chief, in duplicate.

(*c*) The umpire-in-chief shall make certain that the original and copies of the respective batting orders are identical, and then tender a copy of each batting order to the opposing manager. The copy retained by the umpire shall be the official batting order. The tender of the batting order by the umpire shall establish the batting orders. Thereafter, no substitutions shall be made by either manager, except as provided in these rules.

(*d*) As soon as the home team's batting order is handed to the umpire-in-chief the umpires are in charge of the playing field and from that moment they shall have sole authority to determine when a game shall be called, suspended or resumed on account of weather or the condition of the playing field.

4.02 The players of the home team shall take their defensive positions, the first batter of the visiting team shall take his position in the batter's box, the umpire shall call 'Play' and the game shall start.

4.03 When the ball is put in play at the start of, or during a game, all fielders other than the catcher shall be on fair territory.

(*a*) The catcher shall station himself directly back of the plate. He may leave his position at any time to catch a pitch or make a play except that when the batter is being given an intentional base on balls, the catcher must stand with both feet within the lines of the catcher's box until the ball leaves the pitcher's hand.

Penalty: Balk.

(*b*) The pitcher, while in the act of delivering the ball to the batter, shall take his legal position;

(*c*) Except for the pitcher and the catcher, any fielder may station himself anywhere in fair territory.

(*d*) Except for the batter, or a runner attempting to score, no offensive player shall cross the catcher's lines when the ball is in play.

4.04 The batting order shall be followed throughout the game unless a player is substituted for another. In that case the substitute shall take the place of the replaced player in the batting order.

4.05 (*a*) The offensive team shall station two base coaches on the field during its term at bat, one near first and one near third base.

(*b*) Base coaches shall be limited to two in number and shall (1) be in team uniform, and (2) remain within the coach's box at all times.
Penalty: The offending base coach shall be removed from the game, and shall leave the playing field.

4.06 (*a*) No manager, player, substitute, coach, trainer or batboy shall at any time, whether from the bench, the coach's box or on the playing field, or elsewhere:

(1) Incite, or try to incite, by word or sign a demonstration from spectators;

(2) Use language which will in any manner refer to or reflect upon opposing players, an umpire or any spectator;

(3) Call 'Time' or employ any other word or phrase or commit any other act while the ball is alive and in play for the obvious purpose of trying to make the pitcher commit a balk;

(4) Make intentional contact with the umpire in any manner.

(*b*) No fielder shall take a position in batter's line of vision, and with deliberate unsportsmanlike intent, act in a manner to distract the batter.
Penalty: The offender shall be removed from the game, he shall leave the playing field, and, if a balk is made, it shall be nullified.

4.07 When a manager, player, coach or trainer is ejected from a game, he shall leave the field immediately and take no further part in that game. He shall remain in the club house or change to street clothes and either leave the park or take a seat in the grandstand well removed from the vicinity of his team's bench or bullpen.

4.08 When the occupants of a player's bench show violent disapproval of an umpire's decision the umpire shall first give warning that such disapproval shall cease.

Penalty: If such action continues the umpire shall order the offenders from the bench to the club house. If he is unable to detect the offender, or offenders, he may clear the bench of all substitute players. The manager of the offending team shall have the privilege of recalling to the playing field only those players needed for substitution in the game.

4.09 How a Team Scores

(*a*) One run shall be scored each time a runner legally advances and touches first, second, third and home base before three men are put out to end the inning. *Exception*: A run is not scored if the runner advances to home base during a play in which the third out is made (1) by the batter-runner before he touches first base; (2) by any runner being forced out; or (3) by a preceding runner who is declared out because he failed to touch one of the bases.

(*b*) When the winning run is scored in the last half-inning of a regulation game, or in the last half of an extra inning, as the results of a base on balls, hit batter or any other play with the bases full which forces the runner on third to advance, the umpire shall not declare the game ended until the runner forced to advance from third has touched home base and the batter-runner has touched first base.

Penalty: If the runner on third refuses to advance to the touch home base in a reasonable time, the umpire shall disallow the run, call out the offending player and order the game resumed. If, with two out, the batter-runner refuses to advance to and touch first base, the umpire shall disallow the run, call out the offending player, and order the game resumed. If, before two are out, the batter-runner refuses to advance to and touch first base, the run shall count, but the offending player shall be called out.

4.10 (*a*) A regulation game consists of nine innings, unless extended because of a tie score, or shortened (1) because the home team needs none of its half of the ninth inning or only a fraction of it, or (2) because the umpire calls the game.

Exception: National Association Leagues may adopt a rule providing that one or both games of a doubleheader shall be seven innings in length. In such games, any of these rules applying to the ninth innings shall apply to the seventh innings.

(*b*) If the score is tied after nine completed innings, play shall continue until (1) the visiting team has scored more total runs than the home team at the end of a completed inning, or (2) the home team scores the winning run in an uncompleted inning.

(*c*) If a game is called, it is a regulation game:

(1) If five innings have been completed;

(2) If the home team has scored more runs in four or four and a fraction half innings than the visiting team has scored in five completed half-innings;

(3) If the home team scores one or more runs in its half of the fifth inning to tie the scores.

(*d*) If each team has the same number of runs when the game ends, the umpire shall declare it a 'Tie Game'.

(*e*) If a game is called before it has become a regulation game, the umpire shall declare it 'No Game'.

(*f*) Rain checks will not be honoured for any regulation or suspended game which has progressed to or beyond a point of play described in 4.10(*c*).

4.11 The score of a regulation game is the total number of runs scored by each team at the moment the game ends.

(*a*) The game ends when the visiting team completes its half of the ninth inning if the home team is ahead.

(*b*) The game ends when the ninth inning is completed, if the visiting team is ahead.

(*c*) If the home team scores the winning run in its half of the ninth inning (or its half of an extra inning after a tie), the game ends immediately when the winning run is scored. *Exception*: If the batter in a game hits a home run out of the playing field, the batter-runner and all runners on base are permitted to score, in accordance with the base-running rules, and the game ends when the batter-runner touches home plate.

Approved Ruling: The batter hits a home run out of the playing field to win the game in the last half of the ninth or an extra inning, but is called out for passing a preceding runner. The game ends immediately when the winning run is scored.

(*d*) A called game ends at the moment the umpire terminates play. *Exception*: If the game is called while an inning is in progress and before it is completed, the game becomes a *suspended* game in each of the following situations:

(1) The visiting team has scored one or more runs to tie the score and the home team has not scored.

(2) The visiting team has scored one or more runs to take the lead and the home team has not tied the score or retaken the lead. National Association Leagues may also adopt the following rules for suspended games in addition to 4.11(*d*)(1) and (2) above. (If adopted by a National Association League, Rule 4.10(*c*), (*d*) and (*e*) would not apply to their games.)

(3) The game has not become a regulation game ($4\frac{1}{2}$ innings with the home team ahead, or 5 innings with the visiting club ahead or tied).

(4) Any regulation game tied at the point play is stopped because of weather, curfew or other reason.

(5) If a game is suspended before it becomes a regulation game, and is continued prior to another regularly scheduled game, the regularly scheduled game will be limited to seven innings.

(6) If a game is suspended after it is a regulation game, and is continued prior to another regularly scheduled game, the regularly schedule game will be a nine inning game.

Exception: The above sections (3), (4), (5) and (6) will not apply to the last scheduled game between the two teams during the championship season, or League Playoffs.

Any suspended game not completed prior to the last scheduled game between the two teams during the championship season, will become a called game.

4.12 Suspended Games

(*a*) A league shall adopt the following rules providing for completion at a future date of games terminated for any of the following reasons:

(1) A curfew imposed by law.

(2) A time limit permissible under league rules.

(3) Light failure or malfunction of a mechanical field device under control of the home club. (Mechanical field device shall include automatic tarpaulin or water removal equipment.)

(4) Darkness, when a law prevents the lights from being turned on.

(5) Weather, if the game is called while an inning is in progress, and before it is completed, and one of the following situations prevails:

    (i)   The visiting team has scored one or more runs to tie the score, and the home team has not scored.

    (ii) The visiting team has scored one or more runs to take the lead, and the home team has not tied the score or retaken the lead.

(*b*) Such games shall be known as suspended games. No game called because of a curfew, weather, or a time limit shall be a suspended game unless it has progressed far enough for it to be a regulation game under the provisions of Rule 4.10. A game called under the provisions of Rule 4.12 (*a*), (3) or (4) shall be a suspended game at any time after it starts.

Note: Weather and similar conditions – 4.12 (*a*) (1–5) – shall take precedence in determining whether a called game shall be a suspended game. A game can only be considered a suspended game if stopped for any of the five reasons specified in Section (*a*). Any regulation game called due to weather with the score tied (unless situation outlined in 4.12 (*a*) (5) (i) prevails) is a tie game and must be replayed in its entirety.

(*c*) A suspended game shall be resumed and completed as follows:

(1) Immediately preceding the next scheduled single game between the two clubs on the same grounds; or

(2) Immediately preceding the next scheduled doubleheader between the two clubs on the same grounds, if no single game remains on the schedule; or

(3) If suspended on the last scheduled date between the two clubs in that city, transferred and played on the grounds of the opposing club, if possible;

(i) Immediately preceding the next scheduled single game, or

(ii) Immediately preceding the next scheduled doubleheader, if no single game remains on the schedule.

(4) If a suspended game has not been resumed and completed on the last date scheduled for the two clubs, it shall be a called game.

(*d*) A suspended game shall be resumed at the exact point of suspension of the original game. The completion of a suspended game is a continuation of the original game. The lineup and batting order of both teams shall be exactly the same as the lineup and batting order at the moment of suspension, subject to the rules governing substitution. Any player may be replaced by a player who had not been in the game prior to the suspension. No player removed before the suspension may be returned to the lineup.

A player who was not with the club when the game was suspended may be used as a substitute, even if he has taken the place of a player no longer with the club who would not have been eligible because he had not been removed from the lineup before the game was suspended.

(*e*) Rain checks will not be honoured for any regulation or suspended game which has progressed to or beyond a point of play described in 4.10 (*c*).

4.13 Rules Governing Doubleheaders

(*a*) (1) Only two championship games shall be played on one date. Completion of a suspended game shall not violate this rule.

(2) If two games are scheduled to be played for one admission on one date, the first game shall be the regularly scheduled game for that date.

(*b*) After the start of the first game of a doubleheader, that game shall be completed before the second game of the doubleheader shall begin.

(*c*) The second game of a doubleheader shall start 20 minutes after the first game is completed, unless a longer interval (not to exceed 30 minutes) is declared by the umpire-in-chief and announced to the opposing managers at the end of the first game. *Exception*: If the league president has approved a request by the home club for a longer interval between games for some special event, the umpire-in-chief shall declare such longer interval and announce it to the opposing managers. The umpire-in-chief of the first game shall be the timekeeper controlling the interval between games.

(*d*) The umpire shall start the second game of a doubleheader, if at all possible, and play shall continue as long as ground conditions, local time restrictions, or weather permit.

(*e*) When a regularly scheduled doubleheader is delayed in starting for any cause, any game that is started is the first game of the doubleheader.

(*f*) When a rescheduled game is part of a doubleheader the rescheduled game shall be the second game, and the first game shall be the regularly scheduled game for that date.

4.14 The umpire-in-chief shall order the playing field lights turned on whenever in his opinion darkness makes further play in daylight hazardous.

4.15 A game may be forfeited to the opposing team when a team:

(*a*) Fails to appear upon the field, or being upon the field, refuses to start play within 5 minutes after the umpire has called 'Play' at the appointed hour for beginning the game, unless such delayed appearance is, in the umpire's judgement, unavoidable.

(*b*) Employs tactics palpably designed to delay or shorten the game.

(*c*) Refuses to continue play during a game unless the game has been terminated or suspended by the umpire.

(*d*) Fails to resume play, after suspension, within one minute after the umpire has called 'Play'.

(*e*) After warning by the umpire, wilfully and persistently violates any rules of the game.

(*f*) Fails to obey within a reasonable time the umpire's order for removal of a player from the game.

(*g*) Fails to appear for the second game of a doubleheader within 20 minutes after the close of the first game unless the umpire-in-chief of the first game shall have extended the time of the intermission.

4.16 A game shall be forfeited to the visiting team if, after it has been suspended, the order of the umpire to grounds-keepers respecting preparation for the field for resumption of play are not complied with.

4.17 A game shall be forfeited to the opposing team when a team is unable or refuses to place nine players on the field.

4.18 If the umpire declares a game forfeited, he shall transmit a written report to the league president within 24 hours thereafter, but failure of such transmittal shall not effect the forfeiture.

4.19 Protesting Games. Each league shall adopt rules governing the procedure for protesting a game, when a manager claims that an umpire's decision is in violation of these rules. No protest shall ever be permitted on judgement decisions by the umpire. In all protested games, the decision of the league president shall be final.

Even if it is held that the protested decision violated the rules, no replay of the game will be ordered unless in the opinion of the league president the violation adversely affected the protesting team's chances of winning the game.

5. Putting The Ball In Play.
Live Ball

5.01 At the time set for beginning the game the umpire shall call 'Play'.

5.02 After the umpire calls 'Play' the ball is live and in play and remains alive and in play until for legal cause, or at the umpire's call of 'Time' suspending play, the ball becomes dead. While the ball is dead no player may be put out, no bases may be run and no runs may be scored, except that runners may advance one or more bases as the results of acts which occurred while the ball was alive (such as, but not limited to a balk, an overthrow, interference, or a home run or other fair ball hit out of the playing field).

5.03 The pitcher shall deliver the pitch to the batter who may elect to strike the ball, or who may not offer at it, as he chooses.

5.04 The offensive team's objective is to have its batter become a runner, and its runners advance.

5.05 The defensive team's objective is to prevent offensive players from becoming runners, and to prevent their advance around the bases.

5.06 When a batter becomes a runner and touches all bases legally he shall score one run for his team.

5.07 When three offensive players are legally put out, that team takes the field and the opposing team becomes the offensive team.

5.08 If a thrown ball accidentally touches a base coach, or a pitched or thrown ball touches an umpire, the ball is alive and in play. However, if the coach interfers with a thrown ball, the runner is out.

5.09 The ball becomes dead and the runners advance one base, or return to their bases, without liability to put out, when:

(*a*) A pitched ball touches a batter, or his clothing, while in his legal batting position; runners, if forced, advance.

(*b*) The plate umpire interferes with the catcher's throw; runners may not advance.

Note: The interference shall be disregarded if the catcher's throw retires the runner.

(*c*) A balk is committed; runners advance (See Penalty 8.05).

(*d*) A ball is illegally batted; runners return.

(*e*) A foul ball is not caught; runners return. The umpire shall not put the ball in play until all runners have retouched their bases.

(*f*) A fair ball touches a runner or an umpire on fair territory before it touches an infielder, including the pitcher, or touches an umpire before it has passed an infielder other than the pitcher.

If a fair ball goes through, or by, an infielder, and touches a runner immediately back of him, or touches a runner after being deflected by an infielder, the ball is in play and the umpire shall not declare the runner out. In making such decision the umpire must be convinced that the ball passed through, or by, the infielder and that no other infielder had the chance to make a play on the ball; runners advance, if forced.

(*g*) A pitched ball lodges in the umpire's or catcher's mask or paraphernalia and remains out of play, runners advance one base.

(*h*) Any legal pitch touches a runner trying to score; runners advance.

5.10 The ball becomes dead when the umpire calls 'Time'. The umpire-in-chief shall call 'Time':

(*a*) When in his judgement weather, darkness or similar conditions make immediate further play impossible.

(*b*) When light failure makes it difficult or impossible for the umpires to follow the play.

Note: A league may adopt its own regulations governing games interrupted by light failure.

(*c*) When an accident incapacitates a player or an umpire.

(1) If an accident to a runner is such as to prevent him from proceeding to a base to which he is entitled, as on a home run hit out of the playing field, or an award of one or more bases, a substitute runner shall be permitted to complete the play.

(*d*) When a manager requests 'Time' for a substitution, or for a conference with one of his players.

(*e*) When the umpire wishes to examine the ball, to consult with either manager, or for any similar cause.

(*f*) When a fielder, after catching a fly ball, falls into a bench or stand, or falls across ropes into a crowd when spectators are on the field. As pertains to runners, the provisions of 7.04 (*c*) shall prevail.

If a fielder after making a catch steps into a bench, but does not fall, the ball is in play and runners may advance at their own peril.

(*g*) When an umpire orders a player or any other person removed from the playing field.

(*h*) Except in the cases stated in paragraphs (*b*) and (*c*) (1) of this rule, no umpire shall call 'Time' while a play is in progress.

5.11 After the ball is dead, play shall be resumed when the pitcher takes his place on the pitcher's plate with a new ball or the same ball in his possession and the plate umpire calls 'Play'. The plate umpire shall call 'Play' as soon as the pitcher takes his place on the plate with the ball in his possession.

6. The Batter
6.01

(*a*) Each play of the offensive team shall bat in the order that his name appears in his team's batting order.

(*b*) The first batter in each inning after the first inning shall be the player whose name follows that of the last player who legally completed his time at bat in the preceding inning.

6.02

(*a*) The batter shall take his position in the batter's box promptly when it is his time at bat.

(*b*) The batter shall not leave his position in the batter's box after the pitcher comes to Set Position, or starts his windup.
Penalty: If the pitcher pitches, the umpire shall call 'Ball' or 'Strike' as the case may be.

(*c*) If the batter refuses to take his position in the batter's box during his time at bat, the umpire shall order the pitcher to pitch, and shall call 'Strike' on each such pitch. The batter may take his proper position after any such pitch, and the regular ball and strike count shall continue, but if he does not take his proper position before three strikes are called, he shall be declared out.

6.03 The batter's legal position shall be with both feet within the batter's box.
Approved Ruling: The lines defining the box are within the batter's box.

6.04 A batter has legally completed his time at bat when he is put out or becomes a runner.

6.05 A batter is out when:

(*a*) His fair or foul fly ball (other than a foul tip) is legally caught by a fielder.

(*b*) A third strike is legally caught by the catcher.

(*c*) A third strike is not caught by the catcher when first base is occupied before two are out.

(*d*) He bunts foul on third strike.

(*e*) An infield fly is declared.

(*f*) He attempts to hit a third strike and the ball touches him.

(*g*) His fair ball touches him before touching a fielder.

(*h*) After hitting or bunting a fair ball, his bat hits the ball a second time in fair territory. The ball is dead and no runners may advance. If the batter-runner drops his bat and the ball rolls against the bat in fair territory and, in the umpire's judgement, there was no intention to interfere with the course of the ball, the ball is alive and in play.

(*i*) After hitting or bunting a foul ball, he intentionally deflects the course of the ball in any manner while running to first base. The ball is dead and no runners may advance.

(*j*) After a third strike or after he hits a fair ball, he or first base is tagged before he touches first base.

(*k*) In running the last half of the distance from home base to first base, while the ball is being fielded to first base, he runs outside (to the right of) the 3ft line, or inside (to the left of) the foul-line and, in the umpire's judgement, in so doing interferes with the fielder taking the throw at first base; except that he may run outside (to the right of) the 3ft line or inside (to the left of) the foul-line to avoid a fielder attempting to field a batted ball.

(*l*) An infielder intentionally drops a fair fly ball or line drive with first, first and second, first and third, or first, second and third base occupied before two are out. The ball is dead and runner or runners shall return to their original base or bases.

Approved Ruling: In this situation, the batter is not out if the infielder permits the ball to drop untouched to the ground, except when the Infield Fly Rule applies.

(*m*) A preceding runner shall, in the umpire's judgement, intentionally interfere with a fielder who is attempting to catch a thrown ball or to throw a ball in an attempt to complete any play.

(*n*) With two out, a runner on third base, and two strikes on the batter, the runner attempts to steal home base on a legal pitch and the ball touches the runner in the batter's strike zone. The umpire shall call 'Strike Three', the batter is out and the run shall not count; before two are out, the umpire shall call 'Strike Three', the ball is dead, and the run counts.

6.06 A batter is out for illegal action when:

(*a*) He hits a ball with one or both feet on the ground entirely outside the batter's box.

(*b*) He steps from one batter's box to the other while the pitcher is in position ready to pitch.

(*c*) He interferes with the catcher's fielding or throwing by stepping out of the batter's box or making any other movement that hinders the catcher's play at home base. *Exception*: Batter is not out if any runner attempting to advance is put out, or if runner trying to score is called out for batter's interference.

(*d*) He uses or attempts to use a bat that, in the umpire's judgement, has been altered or tampered with in such a way to improve the distance factor or cause an unusual reaction on the baseball. This includes bats that are filled, flat-surfaced, nailed, hollowed, grooved or covered with a substance such as paraffin, wax, etc.

No advancement on the bases will be allowed and any out or outs made during a play shall stand. In addition to being called out, the player shall be ejected from the game and may be subject to additional penalties as determined by his league president.

6.07 Batting out of Turn

(*a*) A batter shall be called out, on appeal, when he fails to bat in his proper turn, and another batter completes a time at bat in his place.

(1) The proper batter may take his place in the batter's box at any time before the improper batter becomes a runner or is put out, and any balls and strikes shall be counted in the proper batter's time at bat.

(*b*) When an improper batter becomes a runner or is put out, and the defensive team appeals to the umpire before the first pitch to the next batter of either team, or before any play or attempted play, the umpire shall (1) declare the proper batter out; and (2) nullify any advance or score made because of a ball batted by the improper batter or because of the improper batter's advance to first base on a hit, an error, a base on balls, a hit batter or otherwise.

Note: If a runner advances, while the improper batter is at bat, on a stolen base, balk, wild pitch or passed ball, such advance is legal.

(*c*) When an improper batter becomes a runner or is put out, and a pitch is made to the next batter of either team before an appeal is made, the improper batter thereby becomes the proper batter, and the results of his time at bat become legal.

(*d*) (1) When the proper batter is called out because he has failed to bat in turn, the next batter shall be the batter whose name follows that of the proper batter thus called out.

(2) When an improper batter becomes a proper batter because no

appeal is made before the next pitch, the next batter shall be the batter whose name follows that of such legalised improper batter. The instant an improper batter's actions are legalised, the batting order picks up with the name following that of the legalised improper batter.

6.08 The batter becomes a runner and is entitled to first base without liability to be put out (provided he advances to and touches first base) when:

(*a*) Four 'balls' have been called by the umpire.

(*b*) He is touched by a pitched ball which he is not attempting to hit unless: (1) The ball is in the strike zone when it touches the batter; or (2) The batter makes no attempt to avoid being touched by the ball.

If the ball is in the strike zone when it touches the batter, it shall be called a strike, whether or not the batter tries to avoid the ball. If the ball is outside the strike zone when it touches the batter, it shall be called a ball if he makes no attempt to avoid being touched.

Approved Ruling: When the batter is touched by a pitched ball which does not entitle him to first base, the ball is dead and no runner may advance.

(*c*) The catcher or any fielder interferes with him. If a play follows the interference, the manager of the offense may advise the plate umpire that he elects to decline the interference penalty and accept the play. However, if the batter reaches first base on a hit, an error, a base on balls, a hit batsman, or otherwise, and all other runners advance at least one base, the play proceeds without reference to the interference.

(*d*) A fair ball touches an umpire or a runner on fair territory before touching a fielder.

If a fair ball touches an umpire after having passed a fielder other than the pitcher, or having touched a fielder, including the pitcher, the ball is in play.

6.09 The batter becomes a runner when:

(*a*) He hits a fair ball.

(*b*) The third strike called by the umpire is not caught, providing (1) first base is unoccupied, or (2) first base is occupied with two out.

(*c*) A fair ball, after having passed a fielder other than a pitcher, or after having been touched by a fielder, including the pitcher, shall touch an umpire or runner on fair territory.

(*d*) A fair ball passes over a fence or into the stands at a distance from homebase of 250ft or more. Such a hit entitles the batter to a home run when he shall have touched all bases legally. A fair fly ball that passes out of the playing field at a point less than 250ft from home base shall entitle the batter to advance to second base only.

(*e*) A fair ball, after touching the ground, bounds into the stands, or passes through, over or under a fence, or through or under a score-board, or through or under a shrubbery, or vines on the fence, in which case the batter and the runners shall be entitled to advance two bases.

(*f*) Any fair ball which, either before or after touching the ground, passes through or under a fence, or through or under a scoreboard, or through any opening in the fence or scoreboard, or through or under a shrubbery, or vines on the fence, or which sticks in a fence or scoreboard, in which case the batter and the runners shall be entitled to advance two bases.

(*g*) Any bounding fair ball is deflected by the fielder into the stands, or over or under a fence on fair or foul territory, in which case the batter and all runners shall be entitled to advance two bases.

(*h*) Any fair fly ball is deflected by the fielder into the stands, or over the fence into foul territory, in which case the batter shall be entitled to advance to second base; but if deflected into the stands or over the fence in fair territory, the batter shall be entitled to a home run. However, should such a fair fly be deflected at a point less than 250ft from home plate, the batter shall be entitled to two bases only.

6.10. *Section 6.10, concerning the Designated Hitter Rule, is given in full in the British Baseball Handbook.*

7. The Runner

7.01 A runner acquires the right to an unoccupied base when he touches it before he is out. He is then entitled to it until he is put out, or forced to vacate it for another runner legally entitled to that base.

If a runner legally acquires title to a base, and the pitcher assumes his pitching position, the runner may not return to a previously occupied base.

7.02 In advancing, a runner shall touch first, second, third and home base in order. If forced to return, he shall retouch all bases in reverse order, unless the ball is dead under any provision of Rule 5.09. In such cases, the runner may go directly to his original base.

7.03 Two runners may not occupy a base, but if, while the ball is alive, two runners are touching a base, the following runner shall be out when tagged. The preceding runner is entitled to the base.

7.04 Each runner, other than the batter, may without liability to be put out, advance one base when:

(*a*) There is a ball.

(*b*) The batter's advance without liability to be put out forces the runner to vacate his base, or when the batter hits a fair ball that touches another runner or the umpire before such ball has been touched by, or has passed a fielder, if the runner is forced to advance.

(*c*) A fielder, after catching a fly ball, falls into a bench or stand, or falls across ropes into a crowd when spectators are on the field.

(*d*) While he is attempting to steal a base, the batter is interfered with by the catcher or any other fielder.

Note: When a runner is entitled to a base without liability to be put out, while the ball is in play, or under any rule in which the ball is in play after the runner reaches the base to which he is entitled, and the runner fails to touch the base to which he is entitled before attempting to advance to the next base, the runner shall forfeit his exemption from liability to be put out, and he may be put out by tagging the base or by tagging the runner before he returns to the missed base.

7.05 Each runner including the batter-runner may without liability to be put out, advance:

(*a*) To home base, scoring a run, if a fair ball goes out of the playing field and he touches all bases legally; or if a fair ball which, in the umpire's judgement, would have gone out of the playing field in flight, is deflected by the act of a fielder throwing his glove, cap or any article of his apparel.

(*b*) Three bases, if a fielder deliberately touches a fair ball with his cap, mask, or any part of his uniform detached from its proper place on his person. The ball is in play and the batter may advance to home base at his peril.

(*c*) Three bases, if a fielder deliberately throws his glove at and touches a fair ball. The ball is in play and the batter may advance to home base at his peril.

(*d*) Two bases, if a fielder deliberately touches a thrown ball with his cap, mask or any part of his uniform detached from its proper place on his person. The ball is in play.

(*e*) Two bases, if a fielder deliberately throws his glove at and touches a thrown ball. The ball is in play.

(*f*) Two bases, if a fair ball bounces or is deflected into the stands outside the first or third base lines; or if it goes through or under a field fence, or through or under a scoreboard, or through or under shrubbery or vines on the fence; or if it sticks in such fence, scoreboard, shrubbery or vines.

(*g*) Two bases when, with no spectators on the playing field, a thrown ball goes into the stands, or into a bench (whether or not the ball rebounds into the field), or over or under or through a field fence, or on a slanting part of the screen above the backstop, or remains in the meshes of a wire screen protecting spectators. The ball is dead. When such wild throw is the first play by an infielder, the umpire, in awarding such bases, shall be governed by the positions of the runners at the time the ball was pitched; in all other cases the umpire shall be governed by the position of the runners at the time the wild throw was made.

Approved Ruling: If all runners, including the batter-runner, have advanced at least one base when an infielder makes a wild throw on the first play after the pitch, the award shall be governed by the position of the runners when the wild throw was made.

(*h*) One base, if a ball, pitched to the batter, or thrown by the pitcher from his position on the pitcher's plate to a base to catch a runner, goes into a stand or bench, or over or through a field fence or backstop. The ball is dead.

Approved Ruling: When a wild pitch or passed ball goes through or by the catcher, or deflects off the catcher, and goes directly into the dugout, stands, above the break, or any area where the ball is dead, the awarding of bases shall be one base. One base shall also be awarded if the pitcher while in contact with the rubber throws to a base, and the throw goes directly into the stands or into any area where the ball is dead. If, however, the pitched or thrown ball goes through or by the catcher or through the fielder and remains on the playing field, and is subsequently kicked or deflected into the dugout, stands or other area where the ball is dead, the awarding of bases shall be two bases from position of runners at the time of the pitch or throw.

(*i*) One base, if the batter becomes a runner on Ball Four or Strike Three, when the pitch passes the catcher and lodges in the umpire's mask or paraphernalia.

If the batter becomes a runner on a wild pitch which entitles the runners to advance one base the batter-runner shall be entitled to first base only.

7.06 When obstruction occurs, the umpire shall call or signal 'Obstruction'.

(*a*) If a play is being made on the obstructed runner, or if the batter-runner is obstructed before he touches first base, the ball is dead and all runners shall advance, without liability to be put out, to the bases they would have reached, in the umpire's judgement, if there had been no obstruction. The obstructed runner shall be awarded at least one base beyond the base he had last legally touched before the obstruction. Any preceding runners, forced to advance by the award of bases as the penalty for obstruction, shall advance without liability to be put out.

(*b*) If no play is being made on the obstructed runner, the play shall proceed until no further action is possible. The umpire shall then call

'Time' and impose such penalties, if any, as in his judgement will nullify the act of obstruction.

7.07 If, with a runner on third base and trying to score by means of a squeeze play or a steal, the catcher or any other fielder steps on, or in front of home base without possession of the ball, or touches the batter or his bat, the pitcher shall be charged with a balk, the batter shall be awarded first base on the interference and the ball is dead.

7.08 Any runner is out when:

(*a*) (1) He runs more than 3ft away from a direct line between bases to avoid being tagged, unless his action is to avoid interference with a fielder fielding a batted ball; or (2) after touching first base, he leaves the baseline, obviously abandoning his effort to touch the next base.

Approved Ruling: When a batter becomes a runner on third strike not caught, and starts for his bench or position, he may advance to first base at any time before he enters the bench. To put him out, the defense must tag him or first base before he touches first base.

(*b*) He intentionally interferes with a thrown ball; or hinders a fielder attempting to make a play on a batted ball.

(*c*) He is tagged, when the ball is alive, while off his base. *Exception*: A batter-runner cannot be tagged out after overrunning or oversliding first base if he returns immediately to the base;

Approved Rulings: (1) If the impact of a runner breaks a base loose from its position, no play can be made on that runner at that base if he had reached the base safely. (2) If a base is dislodged from its position during a play, any following runner on the same play shall be considered as touching or occupying the base if, in the umpire's judgement, he touches or occupies the point marked by the dislodged bag.

(*d*) He fails to retouch his base after a fair or foul ball is legally caught before he, or his base, is tagged by a fielder. He shall not be called out for failure to retouch his base after the first following pitch, or any play or attempted play. This is an appeal play.

(*e*) He fails to reach the next base before a fielder tags him or the base, after he has been forced to advance by reason of the batter becoming a runner. However, if a following runner is put out on a force play, the force is removed and the runner must be tagged to be put out. The force is removed as soon as the runner touches the base to which he is forced to advance, and if he overslides or overruns the base, the runner must be tagged to be put out. However, if the forced runner, after touching the next base, retreats for any reason towards the base he had last occupied, the force play is reinstated, and he can again be put out if the defence tags the base to which he is forced.

(*f*) He is touched by a fair ball in fair territory before the ball has touched or passed an infielder. The ball is dead and no runner may score, nor runners advance, except runners forced to advance. *Exception*: If a runner is touching his base when touched by an infield fly, he is not out, although the batter is out.

If runner is touched by an infield fly when he is not touching his base, both runner and batter are out.

(*g*) He attempts to score on a play in which the batter interferes with the play at home base before two are out. With two out, the interference puts the batter out and no score counts.

(*h*) He passes a preceding runner before such runner is out.

(*i*) After he has acquired legal possession of a base, he runs the bases in reverse order for the purpose of confusing the defense or making a travesty of the game. The umpire shall immediately call 'Time' and declare the runner out.

(*j*) He fails to return at once to first base after overrunning or oversliding that base. If he attempts to run to second he is out when tagged. If, after overrunning or oversliding first base he starts toward the dugout, or toward his position, and fails to return to first base at once, he is out on appeal, when he or the base is tagged.

(*k*) In running or sliding for home base, he fails to touch home base and makes no attempt to return to the base, when a fielder holds the ball in his hand, while touching home base, and appeals to the umpire for the decision.

7.09 It is interference by a batter or runner when:

(*a*) After a third strike he hinders the catcher in his attempt to field the ball.

(*b*) After hitting or bunting a fair ball, his bat hits the ball a second time in fair territory. The ball is dead and no runners may advance. If the batter-runner drops his bat and the ball rolls against the bat in fair territory and, in the umpire's judgement, there was no intention to interfere with the course of the ball, the ball is alive and in play.

(*c*) He intentionally deflects the course of a foul ball in any manner.

(*d*) Before two are out and a runner on third base, the batter hinders a fielder in making a play at home base; the runner is out.

(*e*) Any member or members of the offensive team stand or gather round any base to which a runner is advancing, to confuse, hinder or add to the difficulty of the fielders. Such runner shall be declared out for the interference of his team-mate or team-mates.

(*f*) Any batter or runner who has just been put out hinders or impedes any following play being made on a runner. Such runner shall be declared out for the interference of his team-mate.

(*g*) If, in the judgement of the umpire, a base runner wilfully and deliberately interferes with a batted ball or a fielder in the act of fielding a batted ball with the obvious intent to break up a double play, the ball is dead. The umpire shall call the runner out for interference and also call out the batter-runner because of the action of his team-mate. In no event may bases be run or runs scored because of such action by a runner.

(h) If, in the judgement of the umpire, a batter-runner wilfully and deliberately interferes with a batted ball or a fielder in the act of fielding a batted ball, with the obvious intent to break up a double play, the ball is dead; the umpire shall call the batter-runner out for interference and shall also call out the runner who had advanced closest to the home plate regardless where the double play might have been possible. In no event shall bases be run because of such interference.

(i) In the judgement of the umpire, the base coach at third base, or first base, by touching or holding the runner, physically assists him in returning to or leaving third base or first base.

(j) With a runner on third base, the base coach leaves his box and acts in any manner to draw a throw by a fielder.

(k) In running the last half of the distance from home base to first base while the ball is being fielded to first base, he runs outside (to the right of) the 3ft line, or inside (to the left of) the foul-line and, in the umpire's judgement, interferes with the fielder taking the throw at first base, or attempting to field a batted ball.

(l) He fails to avoid a fielder who is attempting to field a batted ball, or intentionally interferes with a thrown ball, provided that if two or more fielders attempt to field a batted ball, and the runner comes in contact with one or more of them, the umpire shall determine which fielder is entitled to the benefit of this rule, and shall not declare the runner out for coming in contact with a fielder other than the one the umpire determines to be entitled to field such a ball.

(m) A fair ball touches him on fair territory before touching a fielder. If a fair ball goes through, or by, an infielder, and touches a runner immediately back of him, or touches the runner after having being deflected by a fielder, the umpire shall not declare the runner out for being touched by a batted ball. In making such decision the umpire must be convinced that the ball passed through, or by, the fielder, and that no other infielder had a chance to make a play on the ball. If, in the judgement of the umpire, the runner deliberately and intentionally kicks such a batted ball on which the infielder has missed a play, then the runner shall be called out for interference.

Penalty for interference: The runner is out and the ball is dead.

7.10 Any runner shall be called out, on appeal, when:

(a) After a fly ball is caught, he fails to retouch his original base before he or his original base is tagged.

(*b*) With the ball in play, while advancing or returning to a base, he fails to touch each base in order before he, or a missed base, is tagged. *Approved Rulings*: (1) No runner may return to touch a missed base after a following runner has scored. (2) When the ball is dead, no runner may return to touch a missed base or one he has left after he has advanced to and touched a base beyond the missed base.

(*c*) He overruns or overslides first base and fails to return to the base immediately, and he or the base is tagged:

(*d*) He fails to touch home base and makes no attempt to return to that base, and home base is tagged.

Any appeal under this rule must be made before the next pitch, or any play or attempted play. If the violation occurs during a play which ends a half-inning, the appeal must be made before the defensive team leaves the field.

An appeal is not to be interpreted as a play or an attempted play.

Successive appeals may not be made on a runner at the same base. If the defensive team on its first appeal errs, a request for a second appeal on the same runner at the same base shall not be allowed by the umpire. (Intended meaning of the word 'err' is that the defensive team in making an appeal threw the ball out of play. For example, if the pitcher threw to first base to appeal and threw the ball into the stands, no second appeal would be allowed.)

Appeal plays may require an umpire to recognise an apparent 'fourth out'. If the third out is made during a play in which an appeal play is sustained on another runner, the appeal play decision takes precedence in determining the out. If there is more than one appeal during a play that ends a half-inning, the defence may elect to take the out that gives it the advantage. For the purpose of this rule, the defence team has 'left the field' when the pitcher and all infielders have left fair territory on their way to the bench or clubhouse.

7.11 The players, coaches or any member of an offensive team shall vacate any space (including both dugouts) needed by a fielder who is attempting to field a batted or thrown ball.
Penalty: Interference shall be called and the batter or runner on whom the play is being made shall be declared out.

7.12 Unless two are out, the status of a following runner is not affected by a preceding runner's failure to touch or retouch a base. If, upon appeal, the preceding runner is the third out, no runners following him shall score. If such third out is the result of a force play, neither preceding runners shall score.

8. The Pitcher

8.01 Legal pitching delivery. There are two legal pitching positions, the windup position and the set position, and either position may be used at any time.

Pitchers shall take signs from the catchers while standing on the rubber.

(*a*) *The Windup Position.* The pitcher shall stand facing the batter, his entire pivot foot on, or in front of and touching and not off the end of the pitcher's plate, and the other foot free. From this position any natural movement associated with his delivery of the ball to the batter commits him to the pitch without interruption or alteration. He shall not raise either foot from the ground, except that in his actual delivery of the ball to the batter, he may take one step backward, and one step forward with his free foot.

When a pitcher holds the ball with both hands in front of his body, with his entire pivot foot on, or in front of and touching but not off the end of the pitcher's plate, and his other foot free, he will be considered in the windup position.

(*b*) *The Set Position* Set position shall be indicated by the pitcher when he stands facing the batter with his entire pivot foot on, or in front of, and in contact with, and not off the end of the pitcher's plate, and his other foot in front of the pitcher's plate, holding the ball in both hands in front of his body and coming to a complete stop. From such set position he may deliver the ball to the batter, throw to a base or step backward off the pitcher's plate with his pivot foot. Before assuming set position, the pitcher may elect to make any natural preliminary motion such as that known as 'the stretch'. But if he so elects, he shall come to set position before delivering the ball to the batter. After assuming set position, any natural motion associated with his delivery of the ball to the batter commits him to the pitch without alteration or interruption.

(*c*) At any time during the pitcher's preliminary movement and until his natural pitching motion commits him to the pitch, he may throw to any base provided he steps directly toward such base before making the throw.

(*d*) If the pitcher makes an illegal pitch with the bases unoccupied, it shall be called a ball unless the batter reaches first base on a hit, an error, a base on balls, a hit batter or otherwise.

(*e*) If the pitcher removes his pivot foot from contact with the pitcher's plate by stepping backward with that foot, he thereby becomes an infielder and if he makes a wild throw from that position, it shall be considerd the same as a wild throw by any other fielder.

8.02 The pitcher shall not:

(*a*) (1) Bring his pitching hand in contact with his mouth or lips while

in the 18ft circle surrounding the pitching rubber. *Exception*:
Provided it is agreed by both managers, the umpire, prior to the start
of the game played in cold weather, may permit the pitcher to blow on
his hand.

Penalty: For violation of this part of this rule the umpire shall
immediately call a ball. However, if the pitch is made and the batter
reaches first base on a hit, an error, a hit batsman or otherwise, and no
other runner is put out before advancing at least one base, the play
shall proceed without reference to the violation. Repeated offenders
shall be subject to a fine by the league president.

(2) Apply a foreign substance of any kind to the ball:

(3) Expectorate on the ball, either hand or his glove.

(4) Rub the ball on his glove, person or clothing.

(5) Deface the ball in any manner.

(6) Deliver what is called the 'shine' ball, 'spit' ball, 'mud' ball or
'emery' ball. The pitcher, of course, is allowed to rub the ball between
his bare hands.

Penalty: For violation of any part of this rule 8.02 (*a*) (2–6) the umpire
shall:

(*a*) Call the pitch a ball, warn the pitcher and have announced on the
public address system the reason for the action.

(*b*) In the case of a second offence by the same pitcher in the same
game, the pitcher shall be disqualified from the game.

(*c*) If a play follows the violation called by the umpire, the manager
of the offence may advise the plate umpire that he elects to accept the
play. Such election shall be made immediately at the end of the play.
However, if the batter reaches first base on a hit, an error, a base on
balls, a hit batsman, or otherwise, and no other runner is out out
before advancing at least one base, the play shall proceed without
reference to the violation.

(*d*) Even though the offence elects to take the play, the violation shall
be recognised and the penalties in (*a*) and (*b*) will still be in effect.

(*e*) The umpire shall be sole judge on whether any portion of this rule
has been violated.

(*b*) Have on his person, or in his possession, any foreign substance.
For such infraction of this section (*b*) the penalty shall be immediate
ejection from the game.

(*c*) Intentionally delay the game by throwing the ball to players other
than the catcher, when the batter is in position, except in an attempt to
retire a runner.

Penalty: If, after warning by the umpire, such delaying action is
repeated, the pitcher shall be removed from the game.

(*d*) Intentionally pitch at the batter. If in the umpire's judgement,
such a violation occurs, the umpire may elect either to:

1. Expel the pitcher, or the manager and the pitcher, from the game; or

2. May warn the pitcher and the manager of both teams that another such pitch will result in the immediate expulsion of that pitcher (or a replacement) and the manager.

8.03 When a pitcher takes his position at the beginning of each inning, or when he relieves another pitcher, he shall be permitted to pitch not to exceed eight preparatory pitches to his catcher during which play shall be suspended. A league by its own action may limit the number or preparatory pitches to less than eight preparatory pitches. Such preparatory pitches shall not consume more than one minute of time. If a sudden emergency causes a pitcher to be summoned into the game without any opportunity to warm up, the umpire-in-chief shall allow him as many pitches as the umpire deems necessary.

8.4 When the bases are unoccupied, the pitcher shall deliver the ball to the batter within 20 seconds after he receives the ball. Each time the pitcher delays the game by violating this rule, the umpire shall call 'Ball'.

8.05 If there is a runner, or runners, it is a balk when:

(*a*) The pitcher, while touching his plate, makes any motion naturally associated with his pitch and fails to make such delivery.

(*b*) The pitcher, while touching his plate, feints a throw to first base and fails to complete the throw.

(*c*) The pitcher, while touching his plate, fails to step directly toward a base before throwing to that base.

(*d*) The pitcher, while touching his plate, throws, or feints a throw to an unoccupied base, except for the purpose of making a play.

(*e*) The pitcher makes an illegal pitch.

(*f*) The pitcher delivers the ball to the batter while he is not facing the batter.

(*g*) The pitcher makes any motion naturally associated with his pitch while he is not touching the pitcher's plate.

(*h*) The pitcher unnecessarily delays the game.

(*i*) The pitcher, without having the ball, stands on or astride the pitcher's plate or while off the plate, he feints a pitch.

(*j*) The pitcher, after coming to a legal pitching position, removes one hand from the ball other than in an actual pitch, or in throwing to a base.

(*k*) The pitcher, while touching his plate, accidentally or intentionally drops the ball.

(*l*) The pitcher, while giving an intentional base on balls, pitches when the catcher is not in the catcher's box.

(*m*) The pitcher delivers the pitch from set position without coming to a stop.

Penalty: The ball is dead, and each runner shall advance one base without liability to be put out, unless the batter reaches first on a hit, an error, a base on balls, a hit batter, or otherwise, and all other runners advance at least one base, in which case the play proceeds without reference to the talk.

Approved Ruling: In cases where a pitcher balks and throws wild, either to a base or homeplate, a runner or runners may advance beyond the base to which he is entitled at his own risk.

Approved Ruling: A runner who misses the first base to which he is advancing and who is called out on appeal shall be considered as having advanced one base for the purpose of this rule.

Section 8.06, concerning the visit of the manager or coach to the pitcher, is given in full in the British Baseball Handbook.

9. The Umpire

9.01 (*a*) The league president shall appoint one or more umpires to officiate at each league championship game. The umpire shall be responsible for the conduct of the game in accordance with these official rules and for maintaining discipline and order on the playing field during the game.

Rule 9 is given in full in the British Baseball Handbook.

Section 10.01 is given in full in the British Baseball Handbook.

10.02 The official score report prescribed by the league president shall make provisions for entering the information listed below, in a form convenient for the compilation of permanent statistical records:

(*a*) The following records for each batter and runner:

(1) Number of times he batted, except that no time at bat shall be charged against a player when:

  (i) He hits a sacrifice bunt or fly;
 (ii) He is awarded first base on four called balls;
(iii) He is hit by a pitched ball;
 (iv) He is awarded first base because of interference or obstruction;

(2) Number of runs scored;
(3) Number of safe hits;
(4) Number of runs batted in;
(5) Two-base hits;
(6) Three-base hits;

(7) Home runs;
(8) Total bases on safe hits;
(9) Stolen bases;
(10) Sacrifice bunts;
(11) Sacrifice flies;
(12) Total number of bases on balls;
(13) Separate listing of any intentional bases on balls;
(14) Number of times hit by a pitched ball;
(15) Number of times awarded first base for interference or obstruction;
(16) Strikeouts.

(*b*) The following records for each fielder:
(1) Number of putouts;
(2) Number of assists;
(3) Number of errors;
(4) Number of double plays participated in;
(5) Number of triple plays participated in.

(*c*) The following records for each pitcher:
(1) Number of innings pitched;
(2) Total number of batters faced;
(3) Number of batters officially at bat against pitcher computed according to 10.02 (*a*) (1);
(4) Number of hits allowed;
(5) Number of runs allowed;
(6) Number of earned runs allowed;
(7) Number of home runs allowed;
(8) Number of sacrifice hits allowed;
(9) Number of sacrifice flies allowed;
(10) Total number of bases on balls allowed;
(11) Separate listing of any intentional bases on balls allowed;
(12) Number of batters hit by pitched balls;
(13) Number of strikeouts;
(14) Number of wild pitches;
(15) Number of balks.

(*d*) The following additional data:
(1) Name of the winning pitcher;
(2) Name of the losing pitcher;
(3) Names of the starting pitcher and the finishing pitcher for each team;
(4) Name of pitcher credited with save.

(*e*) Number of passed balls allowed by each catcher.
(*f*) Number of players participating in double plays and triple plays.
(*g*) Number of runners left on base by each team. This total shall include all runners who get on base by any means and who do not score

and are not put out. Include in this total a batter-runner whose batted ball results in another runner being retired for the third out.

(*h*) Names of batters who hit home runs with bases full.

(*i*) Names of batters who ground into force double plays and reverse force double plays.

(*j*) Names of runners caught stealing.

(*k*) Number of outs when winning run scored, if game is won in last half-inning.

(*l*) The score by innings for each team.

(*m*) Names of umpires, listed in this order (1) plate umpire, (2) first base umpire, (3) second base umpire, (4) third base umpire.

(*n*) Time required to play the game, with delays for weather or light failure deducted.

The Official Baseball Rules have been reprinted by permission of the Commissioner of Baseball. The copyright in the Rules is owned and registered by the Commissioner of Baseball.

Sections 10.03–10.24 are given in full in the British Baseball Handbook, concerning How to Prove a Box Score, When a Player Bats out of Turn, Called and Forfeited Games, Runs Batted In, Base Hits, Determining the Value of Base Hits, Game-ending Hits, Stolen Bases, Caught Stealing, Sacrifices, Putouts, Assists, Double Plays, Triple Plays, Errors, Wild Pitches – Passed Balls, Base on Balls, Strikeouts, Earned Runs, Winning and Losing Pitcher, Saves for Relief Pitchers, Statistics, Determining Percentage Records, Minimum Standards for Individual Championships, and Guidelines for Cumulative Performance Records.

Basketball

Basketball

RULE 1

The Game

Art 1. Definition
Basketball is played by two teams of five players each. The purpose of each team is to throw the ball into the opponents' basket and to prevent the other team from securing the ball or scoring. The ball may be passed, thrown, tapped, rolled or dribbled in any direction, subject to the restrictions laid down in the following Rules.

RULE 2

Equipment

Art. 2. Court – Dimension
The playing court shall be a rectangular, flat, hard surface free from obstructions.

For the Olympic Tournaments and World Championships, the dimensions shall be 28m in length by 15m in width, measured from the inside edge of the boundary line.

For all other events, the appropriate entity of FIBA, such as the Zone

Commission in the case of Zone or continental competitions, or the National Federation for all domestic competitions, has the authority to approve existing playing courts with dimensions which fall within the following limits: minus 4m on the length and minus 2m on the width, provided that the variations are proportional to each other.

All new courts shall be constructed in accordance with the requirements for the main official competitions of FIBA, that is: 28m by 15m.

The height of the ceiling or lowest obstruction should be at least 7.00m. The playing surface should be uniformly and adequately lighted. The light units should be placed where they will not hinder the vision of the players.

Art. 3. Boundary Lines
The playing court shall be marked by well-defined lines which shall be at every point at least 2m from the spectators, advertising boards or any other obstruction.

The lines of the long sides of the court shall be termed the side-lines, those of the short sides, the end-lines.

The lines mentioned in this and in the following articles must be drawn so as to be perfectly visible and be 0.05m in width.

Art. 4. Centre Circle
The centre circle shall have a radius of 1.80m and shall be marked in the centre of the court. The radius shall be measured to the outer edge of the circumference.

Art. 5. Centre Line – Front Court, Back Court
A centre line shall be drawn parellel to the end lines from the mid-points of the side-lines and shall extend 0.15m beyond each side line.

A team's Front Court is that part of the court between the end line behind the opponents' basket and the nearer edge of the centre line. The other part of the court, including the centre line, is the Team's Back Court.

Art. 6. Three-point Field Goal Areas
The three-point field goal-areas shall be the floor areas marked on the court limited by the lines forming two arcs, each constructed as a semi-circle with a radius of 6.25m to the outer edge, taking as its centre the point on the floor directly perpendicular to the exact centre of the basket and, continuing parellel to the side-lines, terminating at the end-lines. The distance from the inside edge of the mid-point of the end of the centre point from which the arc is constructed is 1.575m.

Art. 7. Restricted Areas, Free-throw Lanes and Lines

The restricted areas shall be the floor area marked on the court limited by the end lines, the free-throw lines and the lines which originate at the end lines, their outer edges being 3m from the mid-points of the end-lines and terminating at the outer edge of the free-throw lines.

The free-throw lanes are the restricted areas extended in the playing court by semi-circles with a radius of 1.80m, their centres at the mid-points of the free-throw lines. Similar semi-circles shall be drawn with a broken line within the restricted areas.

Lane places along the free-throw lanes to be used by players during free throws shall be marked as follows: the first line shall be marked 1.75m from the inside edge of the end line, measured along the line at the side of the free-throw lane. The first lane place shall be limited by a line 0.85m away. Next to this line will be a neutral zone 0.30m in width. The second lane place shall be adjacent to the neutral zone and shall be 0.85m in width. Adjacent to the line limiting the second lane place shall be the third lane place which shall also be 0.85m in width. All lines used to mark these lane places shall be 0.10m long and 0.05m wide, perpendicular to the side line of the free-throw lane and shall be drawn outside the places they are delimiting.

A free-throw line shall be drawn parellel to each end-line. It shall have its further edge 5.80m from the inner edge of the end line and shall be 3.60m long and its mid-point shall lie on the line joining the mid-points of the two end-lines.

Art. 8. Team Bench Areas

Team bench areas shall be marked outside the court on the same side as the Scorer's Table and the Team Benches (see diagram of full-size regulation court). Each area shall be limited by a line 2m in length, extending from the end-line, and by another line 2m in length, drawn 5m from the centre line and perpendicular to the side-line.

The lines, 2m in length, shall be of a contrasting colour to that of the side- and end-lines.

Art. 9. Back-boards – Size, Material and Position

Each of the two back-boards shall be made of hard wood, 0.03m thick, or suitable transparent material (made in one piece and of the same degree of rigidity as those made of wood).

For the Olympic Tournaments and World Championships, the dimensions shall be 1.80m horizontally and 1.05m vertically with the lower edges 2.90m above the floor.

For all other events, the appropriate entity of FIBA such as the Zone Commission in the case of Zone or continental competitions, or the

Full-size Regulation Court

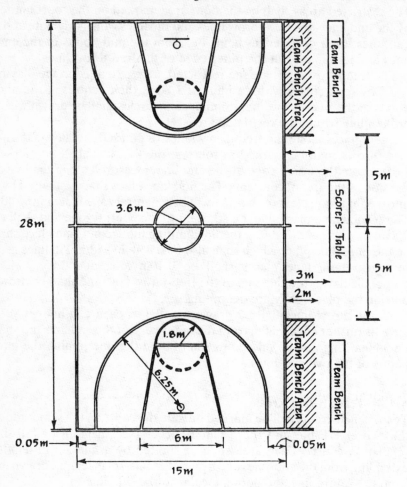

Regulation Free-throw Line

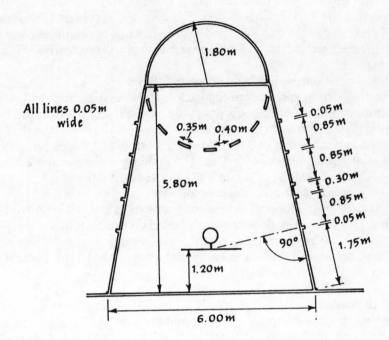

All lines 0.05m wide

1.80m

0.35m   0.40m

5.80m

0.05m
0.85m
0.85m
0.30m
0.85m
0.05m

90°

1.75m

1.20m

6.00m

National Federation for all domestic competitions, has the authority to approve back-board dimensions of either 1.80m horizontally and 1.20m vertically, with their lower edges 2.75m above the floor, or 1.80m horizontally, 1.05m vertically, with their lower edges 2.90m above the floor.

All new back-boards constructed shall be the same as those described for the Olympic Tournaments and World Chamionships, that is, 1.80m by 1.05m.

The front surface shall be flat and, unless it is transparent, shall be white. This surface shall be marked as follows: a rectangle shall be drawn behind the ring and marked by a line 0.05m in width. The rectangle shall have outside dimensions of 0.59m horizontally and 0.45m vertically. The rop of its base-line shall be level with the ring.

The borders of the back-boards shall be marked with a line 0.05m in width. If the back-board is transparent it shall be marked in white; in other cases, in black. The edges of the back-boards and the rectangles marked on them should be of the same colour.

The back-boards shall be firmly mounted in a position at each of the court at right angles to the floor, parallel to the end-lines. Their centres shall lie in the perpendiculars erected at the points on the court 1.20m from the inner edge of the mid-point of each end-line. The uprights supporting the back-boards shall be at a distance of at least 1.00m from the outer edge of the end-lines and shall be of a bright colour, in contrast with the background, in such a manner that they will be clearly visible to the players.

Both back-boards shall be padded as follows:

For the bottom and sides of the back-boards, the padding shall cover the bottom surface of the board and the side surface to a distance of a minimum of 0.35m from the bottom. The front and back surface shall be covered to a minimum of 0.02m from the bottom and the padding shall be a minimum thickness of 0.02m. The padding of the bottom edge of the backboard shall be of a minimum thickness of 0.05m.

The supports shall be padded as follows:

Any back-board support behind the back-board and at a height of less than 2.75m above the floor shall be padded on the bottom surface to a distance of 0.60m from the face of the back-board.

All portable back-boards must have the bases padded to a height of 2.15m on the court side surface.

Art. 10. Baskets

The baskets shall comprise the rings and the nets.

The rings shall be constructed of solid iron, with a 0.45m inside diameter, painted orange. The metal of the rings shall be of a minimum diameter of 0.017m and of a maximum diameter of 0.020m with the possible addition of small gauge loops on the under edge or similar device for attaching the nets. They should be rigidly attached to the back-boards and should hang horizontally 3.05m above the floor, equidistant from the two vertical edges of the back-board. The nearest point of the inside edge of the rings shall be 0.15m from the faces of the back-boards.

The nets shall be of white cord suspended from the rings and constructed in such a way so that they check the ball momentarily as it passes through the basket. They shall be 0.40m in length.

Art. 11. Ball – Material, Size and Weight

The ball shall be spherical and of an approved orange shade in colour; it shall be made with an outer surface of leather, rubber or synthetic material; it shall not be less than 0.749m and not more than 0.780m in circumference; it shall weight not less than 567g nor more than 650g; it shall be inflated to an air pressure such that when it is dropped on to a solid wooden floor or the playing surface from a height of about 1.80m measured from the bottom of the ball, it will rebound to a height, measured at the top of the ball, of not less than about 1.20m nor more than about 1.40m. The width of the seams and/or channels of the ball shall not exceed 0.635cm.

The home team shall provide at least one used ball that meets the above specifications. The Referee shall be the sole judge of the legality of the ball and he may select for use a ball provided by the visiting team.

Art. 12. Technical Equipment
The following technical equipment shall be provided by the home team and shall be at the disposal of the Officials and their assistants:

(a) The game clock and the time-out watch; the Timekeeper shall be provided with at least a game clock and a stop-watch. The clock used for timing periods of play and the intervals between them and the stop-watch used for timing time-outs shall be placed so that they may be clearly seen by both the Timekeeper and Scorer.

(b) A suitable device, visible to all players and spectators, shall be provided for the administration of the 30-seconds Rule and shall be operated by the 30-seconds Operator.

(c) The official scoresheet shall be the one approved by the International Basketball Federation and shall be filled in by the Scorer before and during the game as provided for in these Rules.

(d) There shall be equipment for at least the three signals provided for in these Rules. In addition, there shall be a scoreboard visible to players, spectators and Table Officials.

(e) Markers numbered 1 to 5 shall be at the disposal of the Scorer. Every time a player commits a foul, the Scorer shall raise, in a manner visible to both Coaches, the marker with the number corresponding to the number of fouls committed by that player. The markers shall be white with numbers of a minimum size of 0.2m in length and 0.1m in width, numbered from 1 to 4 in black, with the number 5 in red.

(f) The Scorer shall be provided with two team foul markers. These shall be red, constructed in such a way that when positioned on the Scorer's Table they are clearly visible to players, Coaches and Officials. The moment the ball goes into play following the seventh player foul by a team, a marker shall be positioned on the Scorer's table at the end nearer the bench of the team that has committed the seventh player foul.

(g) A suitable device to indicate team fouls.

RULE 3

Players, Substitutes and Coaches

Art. 13. Teams
Each team shall consist of not more than 10 players and a Coach. One of

the players shall be the Captain. Each team may have an Assistant Coach (see also Art. 16). In tournaments in which a team has to play more than three games the number of players on each team may be increased to 12.

Five players from each team shall be on the court during playing time and may be substituted in accordance with the provisions contained in these Rules.

A member of the team is a player when he is on the court and is entitled to play. Otherwise he is a substitute. A substitute becomes a player when the Official beckons him to enter the court and a player becomes a substitute at the time when the Official beckons that player's replacement on to the floor.

Each player shall be numbered on the front and back of his shirt with plain numbers of a solid colour contrasting with the colour of the shirt. The numbers shall be clearly visible: those on the back at least 0.20m high, those on the front at least 0.10m high and made of material not less than 0.02m wide. Teams shall use numbers from 4 to 15. Players on the same teams shall not wear duplicate numbers.

The uniform of the players shall consist of:

Shirts of the same, single, solid colour – on both the back and front shall be worn by all players of the same team. Striped shirts are not permitted.

Shorts of the same, single, solid colour shall be worn by all players of the same team.

T-shirts may be worn under the shirts. However, if T-shirts are worn, they must be of the same, single colour as the shirt.

Undergarments that extent below the shorts may be worn provided they are of the same, single colour as the shorts.

Art. 14. Player Leaving Court
A player may not leave the playing court to gain an unfair advantage (see Art. 70).

Art. 15. Captain – Duties and Powers
When necessary, the Captain shall be the representative of his team on the court. He may address an Official on matters of interpretation or to obtain essential information. This shall be done in a courteous manner.

Before leaving the playing court for any reason, the Captain shall inform the Referee regarding the player who will replace him as Captain during his absence.

Art. 16. Coaches
At least 20 minutes before the game is scheduled to begin, each Coach shall furnish the Scorer with the names and numbers of the players who

are to play in the game, as well as the names of the Captain of the team, the Coach and the Assistant Coach.

At least 10 minutes before the game the Coaches will confirm their agreement with the names and numbers of their players and Coaches inscribed by signing the scoresheet and at the same time shall indicate the five players who are to start the game. The Coach of Team 'A' will be the first to provide this information.

If a player changes his number during the game he (the player) shall report the change to the Scorer and to the Referee. Requests for charged time-outs shall be made by the Coach or Assistant Coach. When a Coach or Assistant Coach requires a substitution to be effected, the substitute must report to the Scorer to make the request and be ready to play immediately (see Art. 13, 40, 43 and Procedure before the game).

If there is an Assistant Coach his name must be inscribed on the scoresheet before the beginning of the game. He shall assume the responsibilities of the Coach if for any reason the Coach is unable to continue.

The team Captain may act as Coach. If he must leave the playing court for any reason, he may continue to act as Coach. However, if he must leave following a disqualifying foul, or if he is unable to act as Coach because of severe injury, his substitute as Captain shall also replace him as Coach.

RULE 4
Officials and their Duties

Art. 17. Officials and their Assistants
The officials shall be a Referee and an Umpire, who shall be assisted by a Timekeeper, a Scorer and a 30-seconds Operator. A Technical Commissioner may also be present.

The Officials and their Assistants shall conduct the game in accordance with the Rules and official FIBA interpretations of such Rules.

It cannot be too strongly emphasised that the Referee and the Umpire of a given game should not be connected in any way with either of the organisations represented on the court and that they should be thoroughly competent and impartial. The Officials, their Assistants or the Technical Commissioner have no authority to agree to changes to the Rules. Officials shall wear a uniform consisting of black basketball shoes, long grey trousers and grey shirt.

Art. 18. Duties and Powers of Referee
The Referee shall inspect and approve all equipment, including all the

signals used by the Table Officials and their Assistants. He shall designate the official timepiece and recognise its operator and shall also recognise the Scorer and the 30-seconds Operator. He shall not permit any player to wear objects which, in his judgement, are dangerous.

The Referee shall toss the ball at centre to start the game. He shall decide whether a goal shall count if the Officials disagree. He shall have the power to stop a game when conditions warrant it, and to determine that a team shall forfeit the game if it refuses to play after being instructed to do so by the Referee or if it, by its actions, prevents the game from being played. He shall decide matters upon which the Timekeeper and Scorer disagree. At the end of each half and of each extra period or at any time he feels it is necessary, he shall carefully examine the scoresheet, approve the score and confirm the time that remains to be played. His approval at the end of the game terminates the connection of the Officials with the game.

The Referee shall have the power to make decisions on any point not specifically covered in the Rules.

Art. 19. Duties of Officials

The Officials shall blow their whistles and simultaneously give the signal (No. 5 or No. 19) to stop the clock, followed by all the signals to make clear their decision. The Officials shall not blow their whistles after a goal from the field or resulting from a free throw, but shall clearly indicate that a goal has been scored by using signal No. 1 or No. 3.

If verbal communication is necessary to make a decision clear, this must be done in English for all international games.

After each foul or jump ball decision the Officials shall exchange their positions on the court.

The duty of the Technical Commissioner during the game is primarily to supervise the work of the Table Officials and to assist the Referee and Umpire in the smooth functioning of the game.

Art. 20. Time and Place for Decisions

The Officials shall have powers to make decisions for infractions of the Rules committed either within or outside the boundary lines. These powers shall start when they arrive on the court, which shall be 20 minutes before the game is scheduled to begin, and shall terminate with the expiration of playing time as approved by the Referee.

Penalties for fouls committed during intervals of play shall be administered as descibed in Art. 72.

If, during the period between the end of playing time and the signing of the scoresheet, there is any unsportsmanlike behaviour by players, Coaches, Assistant Coaches or Team Followers, the Referee must record on the scoresheet that an incident has occurred and ensure that a detailed report is submitted to the responsible authority which shall deal with the matter with appropriate severity.

Neither Official shall have the authority to set aside or question decisions made by the other within the limits of his respective duties as outlined in these Rules.

Art. 21. Duties of Scorer
The Scorer shall keep a chronological running summary of points scored and shall record the field goals made and the free throws made or missed. He shall record the personal and technical fouls called on each player and shall notify the Referee immediately when the fifth foul is called on any player. He shall record the time-outs charged to each team and shall notify a Coach through an Official when he has taken a second time-out in each half. He shall also indicate the number of fouls committed by each player using the numbered markers as provided in Art. 12e.

The Scorer shall keep a record of the names and numbers of players who are to start the game and of all substitutes who enter the game. When there is an infraction of the Rules pertaining to submission of line-up, substitutions or numbers of players, he shall notify the nearest Official as soon as possible when the infraction is discovered.

The sounding of the Scorer's signal does not stop the clock or the game, nor does it cause the ball to become dead. The scorer should be careful to sound his signal only when the ball is dead and the game clock is stopped, and before the ball goes again into play.

It is essential that the sound of the Scorer's signal be different from that of any other sounding signal.

Art. 22. Duties of Timekeeper
The Timekeeper shall note when each half is to start and shall notify the Referee more than 3 minutes before this time so that he may notify the teams, or cause them to be notified, at least 3 minutes before the half is to start. He shall keep a record of playing time and time of stoppage as provided in these Rules.

The signal of the Timekeeper causes the ball to become dead and the game clock to be stopped.

For a charged time-out (see Art. 40) the Timekeeper shall start a time-out watch and shall direct the Scorer to signal when 50 seconds have elapsed after the start of the time-out.

The Timekeeper shall indicate with a loud signal the expiration of playing time in each half or extra period.

If the Timekeeper's signal fails to sound or if it is not heard, the

Timekeeper shall use other means to notify the Referee immediately. If in the meantime a field goal has been scored or a foul has been called, the Referee, if in doubt whether to award the field goal or administer the foul penalty, shall consult the Umpire. If further consultation proves necessary, the Referee shall seek advice from the Technical Commissioner, if present, as well as the Timekeeper and Scorer. However, the Referee shall make the final decision.

Art. 23. Duties of the 30-seconds Operator

The 30-seconds Operator shall operate the 30-seconds device or clock (see Art. 12b) as provided in Art. 57 of these Rules.

The signal of the 30-seconds Operator causes the ball to become dead and the game clock to be stopped (see Art. 39, exception 1).

The 30-seconds device shall be started by the Operator as soon as a player gains control of a live ball on the court.

The device shall be stopped as soon as team control is ended (see Art. 46) when:

(*a*) A shot for goal is attempted and the ball is no longer in contact with the hand of the shooter; or

(*b*) An opponent secures control; or

(*c*) The ball becomes dead.

The device shall be re-set to 30 seconds and restarted only when a new 30-seconds period begins as player control is next established on the court.

A new 30-seconds period, however, does not begin following a throw-in from out-of-bounds at the side line when:

(*a*) The ball has gone out-of-bounds and the throw-in is taken by a player from the same team that was previously in control of the ball; or

(*b*) The officials have suspended play to protect an injured player and the throw-in taken by a player from the same team as the injured player.

Under such circumstances the 30-seconds Operator will restart the device from the time it was stopped, when a player of the same team gains control of the ball on the court after the throw-in has been made.

If the team in control of the ball fails to shoot for goal within 30-seconds, this shall be indicated by the sounding of the 30-seconds signal.

RULE 5

Playing Regulations

Art. 24. Playing Time

The game shall consist of two halves of 20 minutes each, with an interval of 10 minutes between halves.

Art. 25. Beginning of a Game

The game shall be started by a jump ball in the centre circle. The Referee shall make the toss between any two opponents.

The same procedure shall be followed at the beginning of the second half and, if necessary, of each extra period.

The visiting team shall have its choice of basket and team benches. On neutral courts the teams shall toss. For the second half the teams shall change baskets.

The game cannot begin if one of the teams is not on the court with five players ready to play. If, 15 minutes after the starting time, the defaulting team is not present or is not able to field five players, the other team wins the game by forfeit.

Art. 26. Jump Ball

A jump ball takes place when the Official tosses the ball between two opposing players.

During a jump ball the two jumpers shall stand with their feet inside that half of the circle which is nearer to their own baskets, with one foot near the centre of the line that is between them. The Official shall then toss the ball upward (vertically) between the jumpers to a height greater than either of them can reach by jumping and such that it will drop between them. The ball must be tapped by one or both of the jumpers after it reaches its highest point. If it touches the floor without being tapped by at least one of the jumpers, the jump ball shall be re-taken.

Neither jumper shall tap the ball before it reaches its highest point, nor leave their positions until the ball has been tapped. Neither jumper may catch the ball or touch it more than twice until it has touched one of the eight non-jumpers, the floor, the basket or the backboard.

Under this provision four taps are possible, two by each jumper. When a jump ball takes place, the eight non-jumpers shall remain outside the circle (cylinder) until the ball has been tapped. Team-mates may not occupy adjacent positions around the circle if an opponent desires one of the positions.

Art. 27. Violation during a Jump Ball

A player shall not violate the provisions governing a jump ball. If, before the ball is tapped, a jumper leaves the jumping position, or, if a non-jumper enters the circle (cylinder), it is a violation which shall be called immediately by one of the Officials. If there is a violation by both teams, or if the Official makes a bad toss, the jump ball shall be re-taken.

Penalty: The ball is awarded to an opponent for a throw-in from the sideline nearest the place where the violation occurred (see Art. 62).

Art. 28. Goal – When Made and its Value

A goal is made when a live ball enters the basket from above and remains within or passes through.

A goal from the field counts 2 points unless attempted from the 3-point field-goal-area, when it counts 3 points; a goal from a free throw counts 1 point. A goal from the field counts for the team attacking the basket into which the ball is thrown.

If the ball accidentally enters the basket from below, it shall become dead and the game shall be resumed by a jump ball at the nearest free throw line.

If, however, a player deliberately causes the ball to enter the basket from below, it is a violation and the game shall be resumed by an opponent throwing the ball in from the side-line out-of-bounds at the point nearest to where the violation occurred.

Art. 29. Interference with the Ball on Offence

An offensive player may not touch the ball when it is on its downward flight and completely above the level of the ring and is directly above the restricted area, whether it is a shot for a field goal or a pass. This restriction applies only until the ball touches the ring.

An offensive player shall not touch his opponent's basket or back-board while the ball is on the ring during a shot for a field goal or during a pass.

Penalty: The ball becomes dead when the violation occurs. No point can be scored and the ball is awarded to the opponents for a throw-in from out-of-bounds at a position on the side line nearest the place where the violation occurred (see Art. 62).

For interference with the ball on offence during a free-throw, see penalty, Art. 67.

Art. 30. Interference with the Ball on Defence

A defensive player shall not touch the ball after it has started on its downward flight during an opponent's shot for a field goal and while the ball is completely above the level of the ring. This restriction applies only until the ball touches the ring or until it is apparent that is shall not touch it.

A defensive player shall not touch his own basket or backboard while the ball is on the ring during a shot for a field goal, or touch the ball or basket while the ball is within such basket.

Penalty: The ball becomes dead when the violation occurs. The shooter is awarded 2 points, unless the shot was attempted from the three-point field goal area when 3 points are awarded.

The game is restarted from out-of-bounds behind the end line as though the shot for goal has been successful and there had been no violation.

For interference with the ball on defence during a free throw see penalty, Art. 67.

Art 31. Throw-in After a Field Goal or a Successful Last Free Throw

After a field goal or successful last free throw, any opponent of the team credited with the score shall be entitled to throw the ball in from any point out-of-bounds at the end of the court where the goal was made. He may throw it from any point on or behind the end line or he may pass it to a team-mate on or behind the end line. Not more than 5 seconds shall be taken when throwing the ball in, the count starting the instant the ball is at the disposal of the first player out-of-bounds. (Penalty: violation, see Art. 65).

The Official should not handle the ball unless, by so doing, the game can be resumed more quickly. Opponents of the player who is to throw the ball in shall not touch the ball. Allowance may be made for touching the ball accidentally or instinctively, but if a player delays the game by interfering with the ball, it is a technical foul.

Exception: Following a technical foul charged against the Coach, an intentional or disqualifying foul committed by a player, the ball shall be thrown in from out-of-bounds at mid-court, opposite the Scorer's table, whether or not the last free throw is successful (see penalties Art. 70 Penalty ii, 71, 75 and 76).

Art. 32. Decision of a Game

A game shall be decided by the scoring of the greater number of points during the playing time.

Art. 33. Game To Be Forfeited

A team shall forfeit the game if it refuses to play after being instructed to do so by the Referee or, by its actions, prevents the game from being played.

When, during a game, the number of players of a team on the court is less than 2, the game shall end and the team shall lose the game by forfeit.

If the team to which the game is awarded is ahead, the score at the time of forfeiture shall stand. If the team is not ahead, the score shall be recorded as 2 to 0 in its favour.

Art. 34. Tied Score and Extra Periods

If the score is tied at the expiration of the second half, the game shall be continued for an extra period of 5 minutes or as many such periods of 5 minutes as are necessary to break the tie. Before the first extra period, the teams shall toss for baskets and shall change baskets at the beginning of each additional extra period. An interval of 2 minutes shall be allowed before each extra period. At the beginning of each extra period, the game shall be restarted with a jump ball at the centre circle.

Art. 35. When a Game is Terminated

The game shall terminate at the sounding of the Timekeeper's signal indicating the end of playing time.

When a foul is committed simultaneously with or just prior to the Timekeeper's signal ending a half or an extra period, any eventual free throw or throws as a result of the foul shall be taken.

When a shot (see Art. 53) is taken near the end of playing time, the goal, if made, shall count if the ball was in the air before time expired. All provisions contained in Art 29 and 30 shall apply until the ball touches the ring. If the ball strikes the ring, rebounds and then enters the basket, the goal shall count. If, after the ball has touched the ring, a player of either team touches the ball, it is a violation. If a defensive player commits such a violation, the goal shall count and either 2 or 3 points awarded. If an offensive player commits such a violation, the ball becomes dead and the goal, if scored, shall not count. These provisions apply until it is apparent the shot will not be successful.

RULE 6

Timing Regulations

Art. 36. Game Clock Operations

The game clock shall be started:

(*a*) When the ball, after having reached its highest point on a toss during a jump ball, is tapped by the first player; or

(*b*) If a free throw is not successful and the ball is to continue in play, when the ball touches a player on the court; or

(*c*) If the game is resumed by a throw-in from out-of-bounds, when the ball touches a player on the court.

The game clock shall be stopped:

(*a*) At the end of each half or extra period; or

(*b*) When an Official blows his whistle; or

(*c*) When the 30-second signal is sounded; or

(*d*) When a field goal is scored against the team of a Coach who has requested a charged time-out prior to the ball being released from the hands of the shooter on a try for a field goal.

Art. 37. Ball Goes Into Play
The ball goes into play (is in play) when:

(*a*) The Official enters the circle to administer a jump ball; or

(*b*) The Official enters the free-throw lane to administer a free throw (see Art. 66); or

(*c*) In an out-of-bounds situation, the ball is at the disposal of the player who is at the point of the throw-in.

Art. 38. Ball Becomes Alive
The ball becomes alive when:

(*a*) After having reached its highest point in a jump ball, it is tapped by the first player; or

(*b*) The Official places it at the disposal of a free throw shooter (see Art. 66); or

(*c*) After a throw-in from out-of-bounds, it touches a player on the court.

Art. 39. Dead Ball
The ball becomes dead when:

(*a*) Any goal is made (see Art. 28); or

(*b*) An Official's whistle is blown while the ball is alive or in play; or

(*c*) It is apparent that the ball will not go into the basket, on a free throw for a technical foul by the Coach, Assistant Coach, substitute, or Team Follower, an intentional or disqualifying foul committed by a player, or a free throw which is to be followed by another free throw; or

(*d*) The 30-seconds Operator's signal is sounded while the ball is alive; or

(*e*) Time expires for a half or an extra period; or

(*f*) The ball already in flight on a shot for goal is touched by a player of either team after time has expired for a half or extra period, or after a foul has been called. The provisions of Article 29, 30 and 35 still apply.

Exception: The ball does not become dead at the time of the listed act and the field goal, if made, counts, if:

(1) The ball is in flight on a free throw or a shot for a field goal when (b), (d), or (e) occurs: or

(2) An opponent fouls while the ball is still in the control of a player who is in the act of shooting for goal and who finishes his shot with a continuous motion which started before the foul occurred. The goal does not count if he makes an entirely new effort after the whistle blows.

This does not apply at the end of a period (see Art. 35).

Art. 40. Charged Time-out
Two charged time-outs may be granted to each team during each half of playing time and one charged time-out for each extra period.

Unused time-outs may not be carried over to the next half or extra period.

A Coach or Assistant Coach has the right to request a charged time-out. He shall do so by going in person to the Scorer and asking clearly for a 'time-out', making the proper conventional sign with his hands.

The Scorer shall indicate to the Officials that a request for a charged time-out has been made by sounding his signal as soon as the ball is dead and the game clock is stopped but before the ball goes again into play (see Art. 37).

A Coach or Assistant Coach may also be granted a charged time-out if, after a request from him for a time-out, a field goal is scored by his opponents, provided that the request was made before the ball left the hand of the shooter. In this case, the Timekeeper shall immediately stop the game clock. The Scorer shall then sound his signal and indicate to the Officials that a charged time-out has been requested.

A charged time-out is not permitted from the moment the ball goes into play for the first or only free throw, until the ball becomes dead again after a clock running phase of the game, except:

(*a*) When a foul occurs between free throws, in which case the free throws will be completed and the time-out taken before the ball goes into play for the new foul penalty; or

(*b*) A violation is called before the clock starts, the penalty for which is a jump ball or a throw-in from out-of-bounds at the side line.

A time-out of 1 minute's duration shall be charged to a team under these provisions. If the team responsible for the time-out is ready to play before the end of the charged time-out, the Referee shall start the game immediately. During the time-out, the players are permitted to leave the playing court and sit on the team bench.

Exception: No time-out is charged if an injured player is ready to play immediately without receiving treatment, or is substituted as soon as possible, or if a disqualified player or a player who has committed his fifth foul is replaced within one minute, or if an Official permits a delay.

Art. 41. In Case of Injury to Players or Officials

The Officials may stop the game in case of injury to players or for any other reason. If the ball is alive when an injury occurs, the Officials shall withhold their whistles until the play has been completed, that is, the team in control of the ball has shot for goal, lost control of the ball, has withheld the ball from play, or the ball has become dead.

When necessary to protect an injured player, the Officials may suspend play immediately.

If the injured player cannot continue to play immediately and receives treatment, he must be substituted within one minute, or as soon as possible should the injury prevent an earlier substitution. If free throws have been awarded to the injured player, they must be attempted by his substitute; in the event the last free throw is successful, the substitute for the injured player may not be substituted until the next substitution opportunity for his team.

If an injured player is not substituted as set out in this article, his team shall be charged with a time-out, except in the case of a team having to continue with fewer than five players. If his team has no charged time-outs left, a technical foul shall be charged against the Coach.

Art. 42. How the Game is Resumed
After the ball has become dead for any reason, the game is resumed as follows:

(*a*) If a team had control of the ball, any player of that team shall throw it in from the point out-of-bounds at the side line nearest the place where the ball became dead.

(*b*) If neither team had control, by a jump ball in the circle nearest the place where the ball become dead.

(*c*) After a foul, as provided in Art. 63.

(*d*) After a held ball, as provided in Art. 52.

(*e*) After the ending of a half or extra period, as provided in Art 25 and 34.

(*f*) After a field goal, as provided in Art. 31.

(*g*) After a free throw, as provided in Art. 31, 66, 67, 71, 75 and 76.

(*h*) After an out-of-bounds, as provided in Art. 62.

(*j*) After a violation, as provided in Art. 62.

RULE 7

Players' Regulations

Art. 43. Substitutions
A substitute, before entering the court, shall report to the Scorer and must be ready to play immediately.

The Scorer shall sound his signal as soon as the ball becomes dead and the game clock is stopped, but before the ball goes again into play (see Art. 37).

Following a violation, only the non-violating team who is to make the throw-in from out-of-bounds may effect a substitution. If such a situation occurs, the opponents may also then effect a substitution. The substitute shall remain outside the boundary line until an Official beckons him on to the court whereupon he shall enter immediately.

Substitutions shall be completed as quickly as possible. If, in the opinion of the Official, there is an unreasonable delay, a time-out shall be charged against the offending team.

A player involved in a jump ball may not be substituted by another player.

The player who has been substituted may not re-enter the court during the same period of substitution.

A substitution is not permitted:

(*a*) After a field goal has been scored, unless a charged time-out is granted or a foul has been called; or

(*b*) From the moment the ball goes into play for the first or only free throw, until the ball becomes dead again after a clock-running phase of the game, or until a foul or a violation is called before the clock starts, the penalty for which is a free throw or throws, a jump ball or a throw-in from out-of-bounds on the side line.

Exception: In the event that a foul occurs between free throws, substitutions will be permitted, but only after the free throws for the earlier foul have been completed and before the ball goes into play for the new foul penalty. After a successful last or only free throw, only the player who was attempting the free throw may be substituted, provided that such substitution was requested before the ball went into play for the first or only free throw, in which case the opponents may then be granted one substitution provided the request is made before the ball goes into play for the last or only free throw.

Art. 44. Location of a Player and of an Official

The location of a player is determined by where he is touching the floor. When he is in the air from a leap, he retains the same status as when he last touched the floor as far as the boundary lines, the centre line, the 3-point line, the free-throw line or the lines delimiting the free-throw lanes are concerned (except as provided in Art. 65*c*).

The location of an Official is determined in the same manner as that of a player. When the ball touches an Official, it is the same as touching the floor at the Official's location.

Art. 45. How the Ball is Played

In basketball, the ball is played with the hands. It is a violation to run with the ball, kick it or strike it with the fist. For penalty, see Art. 62.

Kicking the ball or blocking it with any part of a player's leg is a violation only when it is done deliberately.

To accidentally touch the ball with the foot or leg is not a violation.

Art. 46. Control of the Ball

A player is in control when he is holding or dribbling a live ball or in an out-of-bounds situation, when the ball is at his disposal for a throw-in (see Art. 37c).

A team is in control when a player of that team is in control and also when the ball is being passed between team-mates.

Team control continues until an opponent secures control, the ball becomes dead or on a shot for goal, when the ball is no longer in contact with the hand of the shooter.

Art. 47. Player Out-of-Bounds – Ball Out-of-Bounds
A player is out-of-bounds when any part of his body is in contact with the floor on or outside the boundary lines.

The ball is out-of-bounds when it touches:
(a) A player or any other person who is out of bounds; or
(b) The floor or any object on or outside a boundary line; or
(c) The supports or the back of the back-boards.

Art. 48. How the Ball Goes Out-of-Bounds
The ball is caused to go out-of-bounds by the last player to touch it before it goes out, even in the event of the ball going out-of-bounds by touching something other than a player.

An Official shall clearly indicate the team which shall take the throw-in from out-of-bounds.

To cause the ball to go out-of-bounds is a violation. For penalty, see Art. 62.

Officials should declare a held ball when they are in doubt as to which team caused the ball to go out-of-bounds (see Art. 52).

Art. 49. Dribbling
A dribble is made when a player, having gained control of the ball, gives impetus on it by throwing, tapping or rolling it and touches it again before it touches another player. In a dribble the ball must come in contact with the floor. After giving impetus to the ball as described in the foregoing, the player completes his dribble the instant he touches the ball simultaneously with both hands or permits the ball to come to rest in one or both hands. There is no limit to the number of steps a player may take when the ball is not in contact with his hand.

A player shall not dribble a second time after his first dribble has ended, unless it is after he has lost control because of:
(a) A shot for goal; or
(b) A tap by an opponent; or
(c) A pass or fumble that has then touched or been touched by another player.

A player who throws the ball against a backboard and touches it before it touches another player commits a violation unless, in the opinion of the Official, it was a shot.

Exception: The following are *not* dribbles:

(*a*) Successive shots for goal.

(*b*) Accidentally losing and then regaining player control (fumble) at the beginning or at the end of a dribble.

(*c*) Attempts to gain control of the ball by tapping it from the vicinity of other players striving for it.

(*d*) Tapping it from the control of another player.

(*e*) Blocking a pass and recovering the ball.

(*f*) Tossing the ball from hand(s) to hand(s) and permitting it to come to rest before touching the floor, provided he does not commit a progressing with the ball violation.

To make a second dribble is a violation.

Penalty: The ball is awarded to an opponent for a throw-in from the side line nearest the place where the violation occurred.

Art. 50. Pivot

A pivot takes place when a player who is holding the ball steps once or more than once in any direction with the same foot; the other foot, called the pivot foot, being kept at its point of contact with the floor.

Art. 51. Progressing with the Ball

A player may progress with the ball in any direction within the following limits:

Item I – A player who receives the ball while standing still may pivot, using either foot as the pivot foot.

Item II – A player who receives the ball while he is progressing or upon completion of a dribble, may use a two-count rhythm in coming to a stop or in getting rid of the ball.

The first count occurs:

(*a*) As he receives the ball if either foot is touching the floor at the time he receives it; or

(*b*) As either foot touches the floor or as both feet touch the floor simultaneously after he receives the ball, if both feet are off the floor when he receives it.

The second count occurs when, after the count of one, either foot touches the floor or both feet touch the floor simultaneously.

A player who has come to a stop at the first count of the two-count rhythm, is not entitled to a new movement within the second count.

When a player comes to a legal stop, if one foot is in advance of the other, he may pivot, but the rear foot only may be used as the pivot foot.

However, if neither foot is in advance of the other, he may use either foot as the pivot foot.

Item III – A player who receives the ball while standing still or who comes to a legal stop while holding the ball:

(*a*) May lift the pivot foot or jump when he shoots for goal or passes, but the ball must leave his hands before one or both feet again touch the floor, even if a defensive player makes contact with the ball with one or both hands. If the hand or hands are so firmly on the ball that neither player can gain possession without undue roughness, a held ball shall be called; or

(*b*) May not lift the pivot foot in starting a dribble before the ball leaves his hands.

To progress with the ball in excess of these limits is a violation.

Penalty: The ball is awarded to an opponent for a throw-in from the side line nearest the place where the violation occurred.

Art. 52. Held Ball

A held ball should not be called too quickly, thereby interrupting the continuity of the game and unjustly taking the ball from the player who has gained or is about to gain possession. It should only be called when one or more players of opposing teams have one or both hands firmly on the ball so that neither player could gain possession without undue roughness.

A held ball decision is not warranted merely on the grounds that the defensive player gets his hands on the ball. Usually such a decision is unfair to the player who has firm possession of the ball.

A jump ball shall take place:

(*a*) When held ball is called. If there are more than two players involved, the ball shall be tossed up between two opposing players of approximately the same height.

(*b*) If the ball goes out-of-bounds and was last touched simultaneously by two opponents, or if the Official is in doubt as to who last touched the ball, or if the Officials disagree, the game shall be resumed by a jump ball between the two players involved at the nearest circle.

(*c*) Whenever the ball lodges on the basket support the game shall be resumed by a jump ball between any two opponents on the nearer free-throw line. (Exceptions: see Art 71, 75, 76 and 79).

Art. 53. Player in the Act of Shooting

A player is in the act of shooting when, in the judgement of an Official, he has started an attempt to score by throwing, dunking or tapping the ball and the attempt continues until the ball has left the player's hand(s).

Exceptions: Players who tap the ball towards the basket directly from a jump ball are not considered to be in the act of shooting.

Art. 54. Three-seconds Rule

A player shall not remain for more than 3 consecutive seconds in that part of the opponent's restricted area, between the end-line and the farther edge of the free-throw line, while his team is in control of the ball.

The 3-seconds restriction is in force in all out-of-bounds situations, and the count shall start at the moment the player taking the throw-in is out-of-bounds and has control of the ball.

The lines bounding the restricted area are part of the restricted area and a player touching one of these lines is in the area. The 3-seconds restriction does not apply while the ball is in the air during a shot for goal, during a rebound, or is dead because neither team has control of the ball at such times. Allowance may be made for a player who, having been in the restricted area for less then 3 seconds, dribbles in to shoot for goal.

An infraction of this Rule is a violation.

Penalty: The ball is awarded to an opponent for a throw-in from the side line nearest the place where the violation occurred.

Art. 55. Five-seconds Rule

A violation shall be called when a closely guarded player who is holding the ball does not pass, shoot, roll or dribble the ball within 5 seconds.

Penalty: The ball is awarded to an opponent for a throw-in from the side line nearest the place where the violation occurred.

Art. 56. Ten-seconds Rule

When a player gains control of a live ball in his back court, his team must, within 10 seconds, cause the ball to go into its front court.

The ball goes into a teams's front court when it touches the court beyond the centre line or touches a player of that team who has part of his body in contact beyond the centre line.

An infraction of this Rule is a violation.

Penalty: The ball is awarded to an opponent for a throw-in from the side-line nearest the place where the violation occurred.

Art. 57. Thirty-seconds Rule

When a player gains control of a live ball on the court, a shot for goal must be by his team within 30 seconds.

An infraction of this Rule is a violation.

Penalty: The ball is awarded to an opponent for a throw-in from the side-line nearest the place where the violation occurred.

A new 30-seconds period, however, does not begin following a throw-in from out-of-bounds at the side-line when:

(*a*) The ball has gone out-of-bounds and the throw-in is taken by a player from the same team that was previously in control of the ball.

(*b*) The officials have suspended play to protect an injured player and the throw-in is taken by a player from the same team as the injured player.

Under such circumstances, the 30-seconds Operator will restart the device from the time it was stopped when a player of the same team gains control of the ball on the court after the throw-in has been made.

All regulations concerning the end of playing time shall apply to violations of the 30-seconds Rule (see Art. 35 and 39).

Art. 58. Ball Returned to the Back Court

A player whose team is in control of the ball in the front court may not cause the ball to go into his back court. It is caused to go into the back court by the last player of the team in control to touch it before it goes into the back court. This restriction applies to all situations occurring in a teams's front court, including a throw-in from out-of-bounds.

It does not apply, however, to a throw-in from the mid-point of a side-line in accordance with Art. 58 (Penalty), Art. 70 (Penalty ii), Art. 71 (Penalty), Art. 75 (Penalty) and Art. 76 (Penalty).

The ball goes into a team's back court when it touches a player of that team who has part of his body in contact with the centre line or with the court beyond the centre line, or is first touched by a player of that team after it has touched the back court.

Penalty: The ball is awarded to an oppenent for a throw-in from the mid-point of a side-line. He shall have one foot on either side of the extended centre line and be entitled to pass the ball to a player at any point on the playing court.

Exception: It is not a violation when, during a jump ball at centre, a player jumps from his front court, gains control of the ball while in the air directly from a jump ball and lands with one or both feet in the back court.

RULE 8

Infractions and Penalties

Art. 59. Violations

A violation is an infraction of the Rules, the penalty for which is the loss of the ball by the team that committed the violation. (Exception, see Art. 30.)

Art. 60. Fouls

A foul is an infraction of the Rules involving personal contact with an opponent or unsportsmanlike behaviour, charged against the offender and consequently penalised according to the provisions of the relevant articles of the Rules.

Art. 61. How the Game is Resumed following a Violation or a Foul

After the ball has become dead, following an infraction of the Rules, the game is resumed by:

   (*a*) A throw-in from out-of-bounds; or
   (*b*) A jump ball at one of the circles; or
   (*c*) One or more free throws; or
   (*d*) One or more throws followed by a throw-in from out-of-bounds

at the mid-point of the side line opposite the Scorer's table.

Art. 62. Procedure when a Violation is Committed

When a violation is committed, the official shall blow his whistle and simultaneously give the signal (No.5) to stop the clock, causing the ball to become dead. The ball is awarded to an opponent for a throw-in from the side line nearest the place where the violation occurred. If the ball enters the basket while the ball is dead following a violation, no point can be scored.

Art. 63. Procedure when a Foul is Committed

When a personal foul is committed, the Official shall blow his whistle and simultaneously give the signal (No.19) to stop the clock. He shall then indicate to the offender that a foul has been committed. The offending player is required to acknowledge this by raising his hand in the air only if requested to do so by the Official. The Official shall then move into a position to establish clear visual contact with the Scorer and signal the number of the offender, the nature of the offence, and the penalty that is to follow. When the foul has been acknowledged by the Scorer, inscribed on the scoresheet and the foul marker raised, the Officials shall exchange positions. The game shall be resumed by one of the Officials handing the ball to the player who is to take the throw-in from out-of-bounds at the side line or end line, or take the free throw(s) from the free-throw line. (Exception, see Art. 77.)

If the act is flagrant, the Officials shall penalise the offender by disqualifying him from the game (signal No.32) and banishing him from the proximity of the court.

When a technical foul is committed, the Official shall blow his whistle and, simultaneously, give the signal (No.30) to stop the clock.

Art. 64. Throw-in from Out-of-Bounds at the Side Line

The player who is to throw the ball in from out-of-bounds shall stand out-of-bounds at the side line at the place nearest the point where the ball left the court, or where the violation occurred or the foul was committed. Within five seconds from the time the ball is at his disposal, he shall throw, bounce or roll the ball to another player within the court. While the ball is being passed into the court, no other player shall have any part of his body over the boundary line.

Whenever the ball is awarded to a team for a throw-in from out-of-bounds at the side line, an Official must hand the ball directly to the player, or place it at his disposal. The player who is to take the throw-in must do so from the place designated by the official.

Art. 65. Violations of the Throw-in from Out-of-Bounds
A player shall not violate provisions governing a throw-in from out-of-bounds. These provisions forbid:

(a) A player who has been awarded the ball, or had the ball placed at his disposal for a throw-in, to touch it in the court before it has touched another player, or to step on the court while releasing the ball, or to consume more than 5 seconds before releasing the ball, in order to throw, bounce or roll it to another player on the court.

(b) Any player who has been awarded the ball, or had the ball placed at his disposal for a throw-in, to take more than one normal step along the side line from the place designated by the Official before releasing the ball for the throw-in.

(c) Any other player to have any part of his body over the boundary line before the ball has been thrown across the line.

(d) The ball touching out-of-bounds before contacting a player on the court following the release of the ball for the throw-in.

An infraction of this Rule is a violation.

Penalty: The ball is awarded to the oppenents for a throw-in from out-of-bounds at the side-line at the point of the original throw-in.

Art. 66. Free Throws
A free throw is an opportunity given to a player to score one point from an unhindered shot for goal from a position directly behind the free-throw line.

When a personal foul is called and the penalty is the awarding of free throw(s), the player against whom the foul was committed shall be designated by the Official to attempt the free throw(s).

The player who is to attempt a free throw(s) has 5 seconds from the time the ball is placed at his disposal by one of the officials to release the ball on a shot for goal.

The free-throw shooter shall take a position immediately behind the free-throw line and may use any method to shoot for goal, provided he does not touch the free-throw line or the playing court beyond the line until the ball has touched the ring. It is a violation by the free-throw shooter to take a free throw.

In the event that a player by mistake executes a free throw towards the wrong basket, the free throw shall be annulled, whether successful or not, and a new attempt shall be granted at the correct basket (see Art. 68).

In the event that the wrong player attempts a free throw(s), it shall not count whether successful or not, and the correct free thrower shall attempt the throw(s) (see Art. 68).

If the designated player must leave the game because of injury, his substitute must attempt the free throw(s). When there is no substitute available, the free throw(s) may be attempted by the Captain or by the player designated by him. If there is a request for the player who has been fouled to be substituted, he must attempt the free throws before leaving (see Art. 43).

When a technical foul is called, the free throws may be attempted by any player of the opposing team.

Players may not attempt to disconcert the free-throw shooter by their actions. Neither Official shall stand in the restricted area or behind the back-board.

During a free throw, the other players shall be entitled to take a position:

(*a*) In one of the designated six lane places along both sides of the restricted area, provided they do not enter the restricted area or neutral zone until the ball has left the hand of the free-throw shooter. Players who occupy the lane places shall take up alternate positions, with the defensive team only having the privilege to occupy the first lane place on both sides of the restricted area. The lane places are considered to be 1m in depth and shall only be occupied by a player of the team entitled to that place, otherwise they shall remain unoccupied.

(*b*) Anywhere else on the court, except in the free-throw lane and between the end-line and first lane place, and in such a way that they do not disturb the free-throw shooter. They are entiltled to move into the restricted area or neutral zone after the ball has touched the ring following the free throw.

During free throws which are to be followed by a throw-in from out-of-bounds at mid-court on the side line, the players shall not be entitled to occupy the lane places, and all players, are required to be behind the free-throw line extended and not in the free-throw lanes.

In all other situations, the game shall be restarted following the last free throw:

(*a*) By a throw-in from the end line by the opponents, if the free throw is successful; or (*b*) By continuing play, if the free throw is unsuccessful and no violation has occurred; or

(*c*) In accordance with the procedure in Art. 67, in case of a violation of the free-throw provisions.

Art. 67. Violation of free Throw Provisions

After the ball has been placed at the disposal of the free-throw shooter:

(*a*) He shall shoot for goal within 5 seconds and in such a way that the ball enters the basket or touches the ring before it is touched by a player.

(*b*) (i) Neither he or any other player shall touch the ball while it is on its way to the basket nor touch the ball, the basket or the back-board while the ball is on the ring during a free throw. An opponent shall not touch the ball or the basket while the ball is within such basket.

(ii) On the first free throw, to be followed by a further free throw(s), the restriction on touching the ball is applicable as long as the ball has an opportunity to enter the basket.

(iii) During the first of a one-and-one or the last or only free throw, neither he nor any other player shall touch the ball until such time as it has touched the ring and rebounded from it.

(*c*) (i) He shall not touch the floor on or across the free-throw line, until the ball touches the ring, nor purposely fake a free throw.

(ii) No player from either team along the free-throw lane may enter the restricted area until the ball has left the hand of the free throw shooter.

(iii) No other player from either team may enter the restricted area until the ball has touched the ring following the free throw or it is apparent it will not touch it.

(iv) No opponent may disconcert the free-throw shooter.

Penalty

1. If the violation is by the free-throw shooter only, no point can be scored. The ball becomes dead when the violation occurs. The ball is awarded to the opponents for a throw-in from out-of-bounds at the side-line opposite the free-throw line, except after a technical foul charged against the Coach, Assistant Coach, substitute or Team Follower, an intentional or disqualifying foul committed by a player, when the throw-in from out-of-bounds at the mid-court of the side line opposite the Scorer's table taken by the free-throw shooter's team.

2. If the violation of (*b*) is by a team-mate of the free-throw shooter, no point can be scored and the violation shall be penalised as above. If the violation of (*b*) is by both teams, no point can be scored and the game is resumed by a jump ball at the free-throw line.

If the violation of (*b*)i or (*b*)ii is by the opponents of the free-throw shooter, the free throw will be considered successful and one point awarded.

If the violation of (*b*)iii is by the opponents of the free-throw shooter, the free throw will be considered successful, one point awarded and a technical foul shall be charged to the player who has committed the violation.

3. If the violation of (*c*) is by a team-mate of the free-throw shooter and the free throw is successful, the goal shall count and the violation be disregarded. If the free throw is not successful, or of the ball misses the ring, goes out-of-bounds or falls within bounds the violation shall be penalised by awarding the ball to the opponents for a throw-in from out-of-bounds at the sideline opposite the free-throw line.

4. If the violation of (*c*) is by the opponents of the free-throw shooter only, and the shot for goal is successful, the goal shall count and the violation be disregarded; if it is not successful, a substitute free throw shall be attempted by the free-throw shooter.

5. If there is a violation of (*c*) by both teams and the free throw is successful, the goal shall count and the violation be disregarded. If the free throw is not successul, the game shall be resumed by a jump ball at the free-throw line.

If more than one free throw is taken, the out-of-bounds and jump ball provisions apply only to a violation during the last free throw.

Art. 68. Correctable error
Officials may correct an error if a rule is inadvertently set aside and results in *only* the following situations:

(*a*) Failure to award a merited free throw(s); or
(*b*) Awarding an unmerited free throw(s); or
(*c*) Permitting a wrong player to attempt a free throw(s); or
(*d*) Attempting a free throw(s) at the wrong basket; or
(*e*) Erroneously counting or cancelling a score.

To be correctable, errors listed in items (*a*), (*b*), (*c*), (*d*) and (*e*) must be discovered by an official before the ball becomes alive following the first dead ball after the clock has started following the error.

If the error is a free throw by the wrong player or at the wrong basket or the awarding of an unmerited free throw, the free throw and all the activity accompanying it shall be cancelled, unless there is unsportsman-like conduct or disqualifying, intentional or technical fouls. However, other points scored, consumed time and additional activity, which may occur prior to the recognition of a mistake, shall not be nullified. Errors because of free-throw attempts by the wrong player or at the wrong basket shall be corrected according to Art. 66.

After the correction of an error, the game shall be restarted at the point at which it was interrupted to correct the error. The ball will be awarded to the team entitled to the ball at the time the error was discovered.

An Official may stop the game immediately upon discovering a correctable error, as long as it does not place either team at a disadvantage.

Other errors or mistakes shall be dealt with according to the appropriate Rule or protest procedure.

RULE 9

Rules of Conduct

A. RELATIONSHIPS

Art. 69. Definition
The proper conduct of the Game demands the full and loyal cooperation of members of both teams, including Coaches and substitutes, with the Official and their assistants.

Both teams are entitled to do their best to secure victory, but this must be done in a spirit of sportsmanship and fair play.

An infringement of this cooperation or of this spirit, when deliberate or repeated, should be considered as a technical foul and penalised as provided in the following articles of these Rules.

Art. 70. Technical Foul by a Player
A player shall not disregard admonitions by Officials or use unsportsmanlike tactics, such as:

(*a*) Disrespectfully addressing or contacting an Official; or

(*b*) Using language or gestures likely to give offence; or

(*c*) Baiting an opponent or obstructing his vision by waving his hands near his eyes; or

(*d*) Delaying the game by preventing the throw-in from being taken promptly; or

(*e*) Not raising his hand properly after being requested to do so by an Official when a foul is called on him (see Art. 63); or

(*f*) Changing his playing number without reporting to the Scorer and Referee; or

(*g*) Entering the court as a substitute without reporting to the Scorer; or

(*h*) Leaving the court to gain an unfair advantage; or

(*j*) Grasping the ring in such a way that the weight of the player is supported by the ring. However, a player may grasp the ring if, in the judgement of the Official, the player is trying to prevent injury to himself or to another player.

Technical infractions, which are obviously unintentional and have no effect on the game or are of an administrative character, are not considered technical fouls, unless there is repetition of the same infraction after a warning by an Official to the offending player and to his Captain.

Technical infractions, which are deliberate or unsportsmanlike or give the offender an unfair advantage, should be penalised promptly with a technical foul.

Penalty:

(i) A foul shall be charged and recorded for each offence and two free throws awarded to the opponents. The Captain shall designate the free-throw shooter.

(ii) For flagrant or persistent infraction of this Article, a player shall be disqualified, removed from the game, and the same penalty as in Art. 76 applied.

If the discovery of such a foul is made after the ball is in play following the foul, the penalty should be administered as if the foul had occurred at the time of discovery. Whatever occurred in the interval between the foul and its discovery shall be valid.

Art. 71. Technical Foul by Coaches, Substitutes or Team Followers

The Coaches, Assistant Coaches, Substitutes, and Team Followers must stay within their team bench area, except:

(*a*) A Coach, Assistant Coach or Team Follower may enter the playing court to attend to an injured player after receiving permission from an Official to do so.

(*b*) A substitute may request a substitution at the Scorer's table.

(*c*) A Coach or Assistant Coach may request a charged time-out.

(*d*) When the clock is stopped, courteously and without interfering with the normal progress of the game, he may seek information from the Scorer's table concerning the score, time, scoreboard or number of fouls.

A Coach, Assistant Coach, Substitute or Team Follower shall not disrespectfully address Officials (including Technical Commissioner if present), Scorer, Timekeeper, 30-seconds Operator or opponents.

A Coach, or Assistant Coach, may address his players during the game and during a charged time-out providing he is within the team bench area.

A foul by a player who has previously committed his fifth foul is inscribed against the Coach and penalised accordingly.

Penalty: A foul shall be charged and inscribed against the Coach and two free throws awarded. The opposing Captain shall designate the free-throw shooter. During the free throws, players shall not line up along the free-throw lanes. After the free throws, the ball shall be thrown in by any player of the free-throw shooter's team from out-of-bounds at mid-court on the side line opposite the Scorer's table, whether or not the free throws are successful (see Art. 85).

The player taking the throw-in shall have one foot on either side of the extended centre line and be entitled to pass the ball to a player at any point on the playing court.

For a flagrant infraction of this Article, or when a Coach is charged with three technical fouls as a result of unsportsmanlike conduct by the Coach, Assistant Coach, substitute or Team Follower, the Coach shall be disqualified and banished from the proximity of the court, which includes the team bench area and the area surrounding the playing court, and may no longer be in communication in any way, with his team.

He shall be replaced by the Assistant Coach inscribed on the scoresheet or, in the event of there not being an Assistant Coach, by the Captain.

For a flagrant infraction of this Article by the Assistant Coach, Substitutes or Team Followers, they may also be disqualified and banished from the proximity of the court.

Art. 72. Technical Foul during an Interval of Play

Technical fouls may be called during an interval of play. An interval of play is the period prior to the start of the game, the half-time interval and the interval prior to all extra periods.

If the foul is called against a player or substitute, it is inscribed against his name and the penalty shall be two free throws.

If the foul is called against a Coach, Assistant Coach or Team Follower, it is inscribed against the Coach and the penalty shall be two free throws.

After the two free throws have been attempted, the game shall be started or resumed with a jump ball in the centre circle (see Art. to 25 and Art. 85b).

If more than one technical foul is called, see also Art. 85.

A charged time-out is not considered to be an interval of play.

B. PERSONAL CONTACT

Art. 73. Contact

Although Basketball is, theoretically, a non-contact game, it is obvious that personal contact cannot be avoided entirely when ten players are moving with great rapidity over a limited space. If personal contact results from a bona fide attempt to play the ball, provided the players are in such positions that they could reasonably expect to obtain possession of the ball without contact and if they use due care to avoid contact, such contact may be considered incidental and need not be penalised, unless it puts the player who has been contacted at a disadvantage (see Art. 74).

On the other hand, if a player is about to catch the ball and an opponent behind him jumps in an attempt to get the ball and contacts him in the back, the opponent commits a foul, even though he is playing the ball. In such cases, the player behind is usually responsible for the contact because of his unfavourable position in relation to the ball and his opponent.

Comment: Many decisions related to personal contact must result from a judgement which must be exercised with the following basic principles in mind:

(*a*) It is the duty of each player to avoid contact in any possible way.

(*b*) Any player is entitled to a normal floor position not occupied by an opponent, provided he does not cause personal contact in taking up such a position.

(*c*) If a contact foul occurs, the foul is caused by the player responsible for the contact.

Art. 74. Personal Foul

A personal foul is a player foul which involves contact with an opponent, whether the ball is in play, alive or dead.

A player shall not block, hold, push, charge, trip, impede the progress of an opponent by extending his arm, shoulder, hip or knee, or by bending his body into other than a normal position, nor use any rough tactics.

Definitions

Blocking: is personal contact which impedes the progress of an opponent.

Charging: is personal contact, with or without the ball, by pushing or moving into an opponent's torso.

Guarding from the rear: which results in personal contact is a personal foul. Officials should give special attention to this type of infraction. The mere fact that the defensive player is attempting to play the ball does not justify him in making contact with an opponent who controls the ball.

Handchecking: is the action by a defensive player in a guarding situation where the hand(s) are used to contact an opponent to either impede his progress or to assist the defensive player in guarding his opponent. Such contact is illegal as it gives an unfair advantage to the defensive player (see Comment).

Holding: is personal contact with an opponent that interferes with his freedom of movement.

Illegal use of hand(s): occurs when a player contacts an opponent with his hand(s) in an attempt to play the ball, unless such contact is only with the opponent's hand while it is on the ball and is incidental.

Pushing: is personal contact that takes place when a player forcibly moves or attempts to move an opponent. Contact with a player holding the ball by an opponent approaching from the rear may be a form of pushing.

Screening: is an attempt to prevent an opponent who does not control the ball from reaching a desired position.

A dribbler shall not charge into or contact an opponent in his path, nor attempt to dribble between opponents or between an opponent and a boundary line, unless there is a reasonable chance for him to go through without contact. If a dribbler, without causing contact, passes an opponent sufficiently to have head and shoulders in advance of him, the greater responsibility for subsequent contact is on the opponent. If a dribbler has established a straight line path, he may not be forced out of that path, but if an opponent is able to establish a legal guarding position in that path, the dribbler must avoid contact by stopping or changing direction (see Comment).

A player who screens has the greater responsibility if contact occurs when:

(*a*) He takes an illegal position so near an opponent and outside the field of vision that pushing or charging occurs when normal movements are made by the opponent; or

(*b*) He takes a position so quickly in a moving opponent's path that the opponent is not able to stop or change direction.

Penalty: A personal foul shall be to the offender in all cases. In addition:

1. If the foul is committed on a player who is not in the act of shooting. The game shall be resumed by a throw-in by the non-offending team from out-of-bounds on the side line nearest the place of the foul.

After the foul is called and administered, the Official shall hand the ball to the opponents for a throw-in from the side line (for exceptions, see Art. 31, 82 and 83).

2. If the foul is committed on a player who is in the act of shooting:

(i) If the goal is made, it shall count, and in addition, one free throw shall be awarded; or

(ii) If the shot for goal for 2 points is unsuccessul, two free throws shall be awarded; or

(iii) If the shot for goal for 3 points is unsuccessful, three free throws shall be awarded.

After the foul is called and administered, the Official shall hand the ball to the free-thrower for the appropriate number of shots as in (i), (ii) and (iii) above.

Comment – Legal Guarding Position

A defensive player has taken a legal guarding position when he is facing his opponent and has both feet on the floor in a normal straddle position.

The distance between his feet is generally proportional to his height but he must not assume an abnormal straddle position.

Furthermore, the legal guarding position extends vertically above him. He may raise his arms above his head but he must maintain them in a vertical position.

A legal guarding position may be considered as a vertical plane, rectangular in shape, with one short side on the floor limited by the two feet of the player, two long sides vertical from the location of his feet and the other short side in the air, higher than any player on the court can jump.

Screening – Illegal Screening

Screening occurs when a player attempts to prevent an opponent who does not control the ball from reaching a desired position on the court. Screening may be legal or illegal.

Legal screening occurs when the player who is attempting to screen an opponent is not in motion but standing still and has both feet on the floor. Illegal screening occurs when the player who is attempting to screen an opponent is moving when contact occurs with the player who is being screened. If that occurs, the screener is guilty of blocking, and blocking is a foul.

If a player establishes a stationary legal screen in the direct field of vision (frontal or lateral) of the player who is being screened and who is in motion and contact occurs, the player who is being screened is responsible for it and a foul may be called on him.

If the screen is set outside the field of vision of a stationary opponent, the screener must permit the opponent to take one normal step toward the screen without making contact.

When a player is taking a stationary screening position within the field of vision of a stationary opponent, he may establish it as close to him as he desires, short of contact. If the opponent is in motion, however, the screener must leave enough space so that the player who is being screened is able to avoid the screen by stopping or changing direction in order to go around him.

A player who is legally screened is responsible for any contact with the player who has set up the screen.

Blocking

A player who is attempting to screen is blocking if contact occurs when he is moving and his opponent is stationary or retreating from him. In other cases of contact resulting from an attempt to screen when both players are in motion, the greater responsibility is on the player who is attempting to screen.

If a player disregards the ball, faces an opponent and shifts his position as the opponent shifts, such player is primarily responsible for any contact that ensues, unless other factors are involved.

The expression 'unless other factors are involved' in the foregoing statement refers to deliberate pushing, charging or holding of the player who is being screened. This player must make a reasonable effort to avoid contact, and any deliberate act on his part which causes contact should be penalised.

It is legal for one or more players to run down the court close to a team-mate who has the ball with the apparent intention of preventing opponents from approaching the player with the ball. If, however, they run into an opponent who has taken a legal position in their path, and charging or blocking occurs, the greater responsibility is on the offensive team in case of contact in such a play.

It is legal for a player to extend his arm or elbow in taking position on the floor, but the arm or elbow must be lowered when an opponent attempts to go by, otherwise blocking or holding by that player usually occurs.

The Principle of Verticality

On the basketball court, players have a right to the space immediately above them. This principle of verticality protects the air space above the player, but, as soon as he leaves his vertical position and body contact occurs, he is responsible and a foul may be called on him.

Thus, a defensive player cannot prevent an offensive player from jumping vertically and shooting for goal by placing his arms above the offensive player, unless, in doing so, he makes contact with the ball or the hand(s) of the offensive player which is (are) in contact with the ball. If body contact occurs, the defensive player is responsible.

An offensive player may dribble the ball close to the end line under the opponents' basket and then jump obliquely in order to attempt a shot for goal. If, in doing so, he lands in a place not already occupied by an opponent and no body contact occurs, this is legal play. But if contact occurs, the dribbler is responsible.

An offensive player who, while in the act of shooting for goal, leans on an opponent who is legally guarding him from behind, thereby losing his vertical position and causing body contact, commits a foul.

Guarding a Player who does not Control the Ball

A player who does not control the ball is entitled to move freely on the court and take any position not already occupied by another player. However, such a player and any opponent guarding him must take into account the elements of time and distance. This means that players who do not control the ball, either belonging to the defensive or offensive team, cannot take a position so near an opponent in motion (and the distance is directly proportional to the speed of the opponent, neither less than one nor more than two paces), or too quickly in the path of a moving opponent that the latter does not have sufficient time or distance to either stop or change his direction. If a player disregards the elements of time and distance in taking his position and body contact occurs, he is responsible for the contact and a foul may be called on him.

Once a defensive player has taken a legal guarding position, he may not prevent his opponent from passing him by extending his arms, shoulders, hips or legs in his path. He may, however, turn or place his arm in front of his body to avoid injury in case of a charge.

Once a defensive player has taken a legal guarding position, he may shift or move laterally or backwards in order to remain in the path of his opponent. He may not move forward toward his opponent: if body contact occurs, he is responsible for it. He must respect the element of space, in this case the distance between himself and his opponent.

Guarding a Player who Controls the Ball

In guarding a player who controls the ball, the elements of time and distance should be disregarded. The player with the ball must expect to be guarded and therefore must be prepared to stop or change his direction immediately when an opponent takes a legal guarding position in front of him, even if this was done within a fraction of a second. Of course, the guarding player must do so without causing body contact prior to taking his position, otherwise a foul may be called on him.

Once the defensive player has taken a legal guarding position, he may not extend his arms, shoulders, hips or legs to prevent the dribbler from passing by him.

Position of Players with Respect to the Ball

When two or more players of both teams try to reach for the ball and body contact occurs, the Official in calling the foul must take into consideration the relative position of players with respect to the ball. If a player tries to reach for the ball from a position at the side or rear of an opponent who is in a more favourable position to catch the ball and body contact occurs, that player is responsible and a foul may be called on him. Such a situation occurs very often when two or more players of both teams try to catch a rebound. The player who is in a less favourable position (behind an opponent) may indeed try to reach the ball without causing contact with his arms or hands but, generally he contacts his opponent with his chest or hips. One must not overlook the fact that, in a rebound situation, both players are not in control of the ball and that the player who is behind, therefore, must leave a certain space between his body and that of his opponent.

If both players face one another and both are in a favourable position to catch the ball and contact occurs, it may be disregarded unless one of the players uses his arms, shoulders, hips or legs to push the opponent out of his position, in which case a foul may be called on him. If the contact is particularly violent and both players are involved, a double foul may be called.

The principle described above in a rebound situation is of course also valid elsewhere on the court, whenever two or more opponents try to reach for the ball simultaneously.

Who is There First has the Right to Pass
If a dribbler is closely guarded by an opponent and, without causing body contact, passes his guard and has his head and shoulders past him and contact occurs, the defensive player is generally responsible and a foul may be called on him. However, if the offensive player contacts the guard on the chest or shoulders, then the offensive player is responsible for the contact and a charging foul may be called on him. This, of course, assumes that the guard was in a legal guarding position and was not moving forward toward the dribbler.

The Player who is in the air
A player who has jumped in the air from a spot on the court is entitled to land again at the same spot without hindrance by opponents. He may also land at another spot on the court, provided the landing spot was not already occupied by an opponent at the time of the take-off and that the direct path between the take-off and landing spot was not already occupied by opponents.

A player may not move in the path of an opponent after the latter has jumped into the air. Moving under a player who is in the air is always an intentional foul (if there is contact) and in certain cases it may be a disqualifying foul.

However, if a player has taken off and landed but his momentum causes him to contact an opponent who has taken a legal guarding position near the landing spot, then the jumper is responsible for the contact, and a foul may be called on him.

Touching Opponents with the Hands
The touching of an opponent with a hand or hands, in itself, is not necessarily an infraction. However, if the contact in any way restricts the freedom of movement of an opponent, such contact is a foul. Likewise, a dribbler may not use an extended forearm or hand to prevent an

opponent from securing the ball. Situations of this nature can result in an advantage not intended by the Rules and should be discouraged as it will lead to increased contact between opponents.

Some players have tendency to touch an opponent while they are moving on the court. This is generally done in order to identify the position of an opponent. When the opponent is in the field of vision of a player, there is no justification in touching with the hands and such action should be considered illegal personal contact.

Post Play

The principle of verticality also applies to post play. Both the player in the post position and an opponent guarding him must respect each other's vertical right.

The pivot player should not be allowed to shoulder or hip his opponent out of position, nor interfere with the latter's freedom of movement by the use of extended elbows or arms. On the other hand, the defensive player should not be allowed to interfere with the pivot player's freedom of movement by the illegal use of arms, knees or other parts of the body.

Art. 75. Intentional Foul

An intentional foul is a personal foul on a player with or without the ball which, in the opinion of the Official, was deliberately committed by a player against an opponent. It is not determined by the severity of the act, but is the contact which appears to be premeditated or designed.

A player who repeatedly commits intentional fouls may be disqualified.

Penalty: A personal foul shall be charged to the offender. Free throw(s) shall be awarded to the non-offending team, followed by possession of the ball for a throw-in from out-of-bounds at the mid-point of the sideline opposite the Scorer's table.

The number of free throws to be awarded shall be as follows:

(i) If the foul is committed on a player not in the act of shooting, 2 free throws shall be awarded.

(ii) If the foul is committed on a player who is in the act of shooting, the goal, if made, shall count and in addition one free throw shall be awarded.

(iii) If the foul is committed on a player in the act of shooting who fails to score, two or three free throws shall be awarded (see Art. 63 and 74, Penalty), according to the place from where the shot for goal was attempted.

During the free throw(s), players shall not line up along the free-throw lanes. After the free throw(s), the ball shall be thrown in by any player of the free-throw shooter's team from out-of-bounds at mid-court on the side line opposite the Scorer's table, whether or not the free throw(s) are successful (see Art. 85).

The player taking the throw-in shall have one foot on either side of the extended centre line, and be entitled to pass the ball to a player at any point on the playing court.

Art. 76. Disqualifying Foul
Any flagrantly unsportsmanlike infraction of Art. 70 or 74 is a disqualifying foul.
Penalty: Two free throws and possession of the ball for a throw-in from out-of-bounds at the mid-point of the side-line opposite the Scorer's table.

A player who commits such a foul must be charged with the foul, disqualified and banned from the proximity of the court, which includes the team bench and playing court areas, and may no longer, in any way, be in communication with the team.

Art. 77. Double Foul
A double foul is a situation in which two opposing players commit fouls against each other at the same time.
Penalty: In case of a double foul, no free throws are awarded but a personal foul shall be charged against each offending player.

The game shall be resumed at the nearest circle by a jump ball between the two players involved, unless a valid field goal is scored at the same time, in which case the ball shall be put into play from the end-line.

Art. 78. Double and Additional Foul
When a double foul and another foul are committed at the same time, the game shall be resumed, after the fouls have been charged and the eventual penalty administered, as though the double foul had not occurred.

Art. 79. Foul on a player in the Act of Shooting
Whenever a foul is committed against a player after he has started his shooting action, the goal shall count if made, even if the ball leaves the player's hand after the whistle has blown. The goal does not count if he makes an entirely new effort after the whistle has blown.

This does not apply at the end of a period (see Art. 35).

C. GENERAL PROVISIONS

Art. 80. Basic Principle
Each Official has the power to call fouls independently from the other, at any time during the game, whether the ball is in play, alive or dead.

Any number of fouls may be called at the same time against one or both teams. Irrespective of the penalty, a foul shall be inscribed on the score sheet against the offender for each foul.

Art. 81. Five Fouls by a Player
A player who has committed five fouls either personal or technical, must automatically leave the game.

Art. 82. Seven Fouls by a Team
After a team has committed seven player fouls, personal or technical, in a half, all subsequent player fouls shall be penalised by the one and one rule, unless a penalty or greater severity is involved.

In the event that the foul is committed by a player while his team is in control of the ball, Art. 84 is applied.

Art. 83. One and One Rule
When a player commits a subsequent personal foul after his team has committed seven player fouls, personal or technical, in a half, the one and one rule comes into effect, whereby the player against whom the foul has been committed is given the opportunity to shoot one free throw.

If this free throw is successful, it is followed by a further free throw taken by the same player. If, however, the first free throw is unsuccessful, the game shall continue in accordance with Art. 66.

In the event that the foul is committed by a player while his team is in control of the ball, Art. 84 is applied.

Art. 84. Foul by a player while his Team is in Control of the Ball
A foul committed by a player while his team is in control of the ball shall always be penalised by recording the foul against the offender and awarding the ball for a throw-in to an opponent at the nearest point out-of-bounds at a side-line (for exceptions, see Art. 70, 75, 76, 77 and 78).

Note: For definition of team in control of the ball, see Art. 46.

Art. 85. Fouls in Special Situations
Situations other than those foreseen in these Rules may occur when fouls are committed at approximately the same time or during the dead ball period which follows a foul or a double foul.

In such situations, the following principles shall be applied:

(*a*) A foul shall be charged for each offence.

(*b*) Fouls against both teams that involve the same penalties shall not be penalised by awarding free throws or possession of the ball for a throw-in from the side-line. For this purpose, the one and one and the two free throws penalties shall be regarded as being the same. The game shall be restarted by a jump ball at the nearest circle unless a field goal has been scored, in which case the game shall be restarted by a throw-in from out-of-bounds on or behind the end-line.

(*c*) Fouls against both teams that do not involve the same penalties shall be penalised and administered according to the order in which they occurred. If fouls are called against both teams at approximately the same time, the Officials must determine the order in which the fouls occurred. This does not apply to a double foul situation, the penalty for which shall be administered according to Art. 77.

(*d*) The right to possession of the ball for a throw-in as the result of a previous foul penalty shall be forfeited in the event that another foul is called before the throw-in is taken.

Art. 86. Fighting

Any bench personnel who leave the confines of the team bench area during a fight, or during any situation which may lead to a fight, shall be disqualified from the game and shall be banned from the proximity of the court, which includes the team bench area and the playing court area, and may no longer, in any way, be in communication with his team.

In addition, for any incident of this nature, a single technical foul shall be charged against the Coach.

However, the Coach may leave the confines of the team bench area during a fight or during any situation which may lead to fight in order to assist the Officials to maintain or restore order.

If a Coach leaves the confines of the team bench area and fails to assist, in any way, in maintaining or restoring order, he shall be disqualified and shall be banned from the proximity of the court, which includes the team bench area and the playing court area and may no longer, in any way, be in communication with his team.

The disqualifying foul(s) will not be recorded as team fouls.

Reprinted by permission of the English Basket Ball Association. Some of the Rules have been abbreviated and Comments omitted for reasons of space. Copies of the complete Official Rules, including those for FIBA Competitions, Mini Basketball and Wheelchair Basketball can be obtained from the Association.

Bowls and Crown Green Bowls

Bowls

DEFINITIONS

1. (*a*) 'Controlling Body' means the body having immediate control of the conditions under which a match is played. The order shall be:

(i) The International Bowling Board;

(ii) The National Bowling Authority;

(iii) Divisions within National Authorities;

(iv) The Club on whose Green the Match is played.

(*b*) 'Skip' means the Player, who, for the time being, is in charge of the head on behalf of the team.

(*c*) 'Team' means either a Four, Triples or a Pair.

(*d*) 'Side' means any agreed number of Teams, whose combined scores determine the results of the match.

(*e*) 'Four' means a team of four players whose positions in order of playing are named Lead, Second, Third, Skip.

(*f*) 'Bowl in Course' means a Bowl from the time of its delivery until it comes to rest.

(*g*) 'End' means the playing of the Jack and all the Bowls of all the opponents in the same direction on a rink.

(*h*) 'Head' means the Jack and such Bowls as have come to rest within the boundary of the rink and are not dead.

(*i*) 'Mat Line' means the edge of the Mat which is nearest to the front ditch. From the centre of the Mat Line all necessary measurements to Jack or Bowls shall be taken.

(*j*) 'Master Bowl' means a Bowl which has been approved by the IBB as having the minimum bias required, as well as in all other respects complying with the Laws of the Game and is engraved with the words 'Master Bowl'.

(i) A Standard Bowl of the same bias as the Master Bowl shall be kept in the custody of each National Authority.

(ii) A Standard Bowl shall be provided for the use of each official Licensed Tester.

(*k*) 'Jack High' means that the nearest portion of the Bowl referred to is in line with and at the same distance from the Mat Line as the nearest portion of the Jack.

(*l*) 'Pace of Green' means the number of seconds taken by a bowl from the time of its delivery to the moment it comes to rest, approximately 90ft (27.43m) from the Mat line.

(*m*) 'Displaced' as applied to a Jack or Bowl means 'disturbed' by any agency that is not sanctioned by these laws.

(*n*) 'A set of Bowls' means four Bowls all of a matched set which are of the same manufacture and are of the same weight, colour, bias and where applicable serial number and engraving.

THE GREEN

2. The Green – Area and Surface
The green should form a square of not less than 120ft (36.58m) and not more than 132ft (40.23m) a side. It shall have a suitable natural playing surface which shall be level. It shall be provided with suitable boundaries in the form of a ditch and bank.

3. The Ditch
The green shall be surrounded by a ditch which shall have a holding surface not injurious to bowls and be free from obstacles. The ditch shall be not less than 8in (203mm) nor more than 15in (381mm) wide and it shall be not less than 2in (51mm) nor more than 8in (203mm) below the level of the green.

4. Banks
The banks shall be not less than 9in (229mm) above the level of the green, preferably upright, or alternatively at an angle of not more than 35° from the perpendicular. The surface of the face of the bank shall be non-injurious to bowls. No steps likely to interfere with play shall be cut in the banks.

5. Division of the Green
The green shall be divided into spaces called rinks, each not more than 19ft (5.79m) nor less than 18ft (5.48m) wide. They shall be numbered consecutively, the centre line of each rink being marked on the bank at each end by a wooden peg or other suitable device. The four corners of the rink shall be marked by pegs made of wood or other suitable material, painted white, and fixed to the face of the bank and flush

therewith, or alternatively fixed on the bank not more than 4in (102mm) back from the face thereof. The corner pegs shall be connected by a green thread drawn tightly along the surface of the green, with sufficient loose thread to reach the corresponding pegs on the face or surface of the bank, in order to define the boundary of the rink.

White pegs or discs shall be fixed on the side banks to indicate a clear distance of 76ft (23.16m) from the ditch on the line of play. Under no circumstances shall the boundary thread be lifted while the Bowl is in motion. The boundary pegs of an outside rink shall be placed at least 2ft (61cm) from the side ditch.

6. Permissible Variations of Laws 2 and 5

(*a*) National Associations may admit greens not longer than 132ft (40.23m) nor shorter than 99ft (30.17m) in the direction of play.

(*b*) For domestic play the green may be divided into Rinks not less than 14ft (4.27m) nor more than 19ft (5.79m) wide. National Authorities may dispense with the use of boundary threads.

(*c*) National Authorities may approve artificial surfaces for domestic play.

MAT, JACK, BOWLS, FOOTWEAR

7. Mat
The mat shall be of a definite size, namely 24in (61cm) long and 14in (35.6cm) wide.

8. Jack
The Jack shall be round and white, with a diameter of not less than $2\frac{15}{32}$in (63mm) nor more than $2\frac{17}{32}$in (64mm), and not less than 8oz (227g), nor more than 10oz (283g) in weight.

9. Bowls
(*a*) (i) Bowls shall be made of wood, rubber or composition and shall be black or brown in colour, and each Bowl of the set shall bear the member's individual and distinguishing mark on each side. The provision relating to the distinguishing mark on each side of the Bowl need not apply other than in International Matches, World Bowls Championships and Commonwealth Games. Bowls made of wood (Lignum Vitae) shall have a maximum diameter of $5\frac{1}{4}$in (133.35mm) and a minimum diameter of $4\frac{5}{8}$in (117mm) and the weight shall not exceed 3lb 8oz (1.59kg). Loading of Bowls made of wood is strictly prohibited.

(ii) For all International and Commonwealth Games Matches a Bowl made of rubber or composition shall have a maximum diameter of 5⅛in (130mm) and a minimum diameter of 4⅝in (117mm) and the weight shall not exceed 3lb 8oz (1.59kg).

Subject to Bowls bearing a current stamp of the Board, and/or a current stamp of a Member National Authority, and/or the current stamp of the BIBC and provided they comply with the Board's Laws, they may be used in all matches controlled by the Board, or by any Member National Authority.

Notwithstanding the aforegoing provisions, any Member National Authority may adopt a different scale of weights and sizes of Bowls to be used in matches under its own control – such bowls may not be validly used in International Matches. World Bowls Championships, Commonwealth Games, or other matches controlled by the Board if they differ from the Board's Laws, and unless stamped with a current stamp of the Board or any Member National Authority or the BIBC.

(iii) The controlling body may, at its discretion, supply and require players to temporarily affix an adhesive marking to their Bowls in any competition game. Any temporary marking under this Law shall be regarded as part of the Bowl for all purposes under these Laws.

(*b*) *Bias of Bowls*. The master bowl shall have a bias approved by the International Bowling Board. A Bowl shall have a bias not less than that of the master bowl and shall bear the imprint of the Stamp of the International Bowling Board, or that of its National Authority. National Authorities may adopt a standard which exceeds the bias of the Master Bowl. To ensure accuracy of bias and visibility of stamp, all bowls shall be re-tested and re-stamped at least once every ten years, or earlier if the date of the stamp is not clearly legible.

(*c*) *Objection to Bowls*

A challenge may be lodged by an opposing player and/or by the Official Umpire and/or the Controlling Body.

A challenge or any intimation thereof shall not be lodged with any opposing player during the progress of the Match.

A challenge may be lodged with the Umpire at any time during a Match, provided the Umpire is not a Player in that or any other match of the same competition.

If a challenge be lodged it shall be made not later than 10 minutes after the completion of the final end in which the Bowl was used.

Once a challenge is lodged with the Umpire, it cannot be withdrawn.

The challenge shall be based on the grounds that the Bowl does not comply with one or more of the requirements set out in Law 9(*a*) and (*b*).

The Umpire shall request the user of the Bowl to surrender it to him for forwarding to the Controlling Body. If the owner of the challenged Bowl refuses to surrender it to the Umpire, the Match shall thereupon be forfeited to the opponent. The user or owner, or both, may be disqualified from playing in any match controlled or permitted by the Controlling Body, so long as the Bowl remains untested by a Licensed Tester.

On receipt of the Bowls, the Umpire shall take immediate steps to hand them to the Secretary of the Controlling Body, who shall arrange for a table test to be made as soon as practicable, and in the presence of a representative of the Controlling Body.

If a table test be not readily available, and any delay would unduly interfere with the progress of the competition, then, should an approved green testing device be available, it may be used to make an immediate test on the green. If a green test be made, it shall be done by, or in the presence of, the Umpire over a distance of not less than 70ft (21.35m). The comparison shall be between the challenged Bowl and a standard Bowl, or if it be not readily available then a recently stamped Bowl, of similar size or nearly so, should be used.

The decision of the Umpire, as a result of the test, shall be final and binding for that match.

The result of the subsequent table test shall not invalidate the decision given by the Umpire on the green test.

If a challenged Bowl, after an official table test, be found to comply with all the requirements of Law 9(a) and (b), it shall be returned to the user or owner.

If a Bowl in the hands of a Licensed Tester has been declared as not complying with the Law 9(b), it shall be altered, if possible, so as to comply, before being returned. The owner of the Bowl shall be responsible for the expense involved.

If the Bowl cannot be altered to comply with Law 9(a) and (b), any current official stamp appearing thereon shall be cancelled prior to its return. The stamp shall be cancelled by the Tester by stamping an X over any current official stamp.

(d) *Alteration to Bias*. A player shall not alter, or cause to be altered, other than by an Official Bowl Tester, the bias of any Bowl bearing the imprint of the official stamp of the Board, under penalty of suspension from playing for a period to be determined by the Council of the National Authority of which his club is a member. Such suspension shall be subject to confirmation by the Board or a Committee thereof appointed for that purpose and shall be operative among all Authorities in membership with the Board.

10. Footwear
Players, Umpires and Markers shall wear white, brown or black smooth-soled, heel-less footwear while playing on the green or acting as Umpires or Markers.

ARRANGING A GAME

11. General Form and Duration
A game of Bowls shall be played on one rink or on several rinks. It shall consist of a specified number of shots or ends, or shall be played for any period of time as previously arranged. The ends of the game shall be played alternatively in opposite directions excepting as provided in Laws 38, 42, 44, 46 and 47.

12. Selecting the Rinks for Play
When a match is to be played, the draw for the rinks to be played on shall be made by the Skips or their representatives.

In a match for a trophy or where competing Skips have previously been drawn, the draw to decide the numbers of the rinks to be played on shall be made by the visiting Skips or their representatives.

No player in a competition or match shall play on the same rink on the day of such competition or match before play commences, under penalty of disqualification.

This law shall not apply in the case of open Tournaments.

13. Play Arrangements
Games shall be organised in the following play arrangements:
  (a) As a single game.
  (b) As a team game.
  (c) As a sides game.
  (d) As a series of single games, team games, or side games.
  (e) As a special tournament of games.
14. A single game shall be played on one rink of a Green as a single-handed game by two contending players, each playing two, three or four Bowls singly and alternately.
15. (a) A Pairs game shall be played by two contending teams of two players called Lead and Skip according to the order in which they play, and who at each end shall play four Bowls, alternately, the Leads first, then the Skips similarly.

(For other than Internationals and Commonwealth Games, players in a pairs game may play two, three or four bowls each, as previously arranged by the controlling body.)

(b) A Pairs game shall be played by two contending teams of two players called Lead and Skip according to the order in which they play, and who at each end shall play four Bowls and may play alternatively in the following order: Lead 2 Bowls, Skip 2 Bowls then repeat this order of play.
16. A Triples game shall be played by two contending teams of three

players, who shall play two or three Bowls singly and in turn, the Leads playing first.

17. A Fours game shall be played by two contending teams of four players, each member playing two Bowls singly and in turn.

18. A side game shall be played by two contending sides, each composed of an equal number of teams/players.

19. Games in series shall be arranged to be played on several and consecutive occasions, as:

(*a*) A series or sequence of games organised in the form of an eliminating competition, and arranged as Singles, Pairs, Triples or Fours.

(*b*) A series or sequence of side matches organised in the form of a league competition, or an eliminating competition, or of Inter-Association matches.

20. A special tournament of games

Single games and team games may also be arranged in group form as a special tournament of games in which the contestants play each other in turn; or they may play as paired-off teams of players on one or several greens in accordance with a common timetable, success being adjudged by the number of games won, or by the highest net score in shots in accordance with the regulations governing the tournament.

21. For International Matches, World Bowls Championships and Commonwealth Games in matches where played:

(i) Singles shall be 21 shots up (shots in excess of 25 shall not count), four Bowls each player, played alternately;

(ii) Pairs shall be 21 ends, four Bowls each player, played alternately;

(iii) Triples shall be 18 ends, three Bowls each player, played alternately;

(iv) Fours shall be 21 ends, two Bowls each player, played alternately;

Provided that Pairs, Triples and Fours may be of a lesser number of ends, but in the case of Pairs and Fours there shall not be less than 18 ends, but in the case of Triples not less than 15 ends, subject in all cases to the express approval of the Board as represented by its most senior officer present. If there be no officer of the Board present at the time, the decision shall rest with the 'Controlling Body' as defined in Law 1. Any decision to curtail the number of ends to be played shall be made before the commencement of any game, and such decision shall only be made on the grounds of climatic conditions, inclement weather, or shortage of time to complete a programme.

22. Awards
Cancelled.

STARTING THE GAME

23. (*a*) **Trial Ends** Before start of play in any competition, match or game, or on the resumption of an unfinished competition, match or game on another day, not more than one trial end each way shall be played.

(*b*) **Tossing for Opening Play** The Captain in a side game or Skips in a team game shall toss to decide which side or team shall play first, but in all singles games the Opponents shall toss, the winner of the toss to have the option of decision. In the event of a tied (no score) or a dead end, the first to play in the tied end or dead end shall again play first.

In all ends subsequent to the first the winner of the preceding score end shall play first.

24. Placing the Mat

At the beginning of the first end the player to play first shall place the centre line of the mat lengthwise on the centre line of the rink, the front edge of the mat to be 6ft (1.84m) from the ditch. (Where groundsheets are in use they shall be placed with the back edge 6ft (1.84m) from the ditch. The mat at the first and every subsequent end shall be placed at the back edge of the sheet – the mat's front edge being 6ft (1.84m) from the ditch.)

25. The Mat and its Replacement

After play has commenced in any end the mat shall not be moved from its first position.

If the mat be displaced during the progress of an end it shall be replaced as nearly as is practicable in the same position.

If the mat be out of alignment with the centre line of the rink it may be straightened at any time during the end.

After the last Bowl in each end has come to rest in play, or has sooner become dead, the mat shall be lifted and placed wholly beyond the face of the rear bank. Should the mat be picked up by a player before the end has been completed, the opposing player shall have the right of replacing the mat in its original position.

26. The Mat and Jack in Subsequent Ends

(*a*) In all subsequent ends the front edge of the mat shall be not less than 6ft (1.84m) from the rear ditch and the front edge of the mat not less than 76ft (23.16m) from the front ditch and on the centre line of the rink of play.

(*b*) Should the Jack be improperly delivered under Law 30, the opposing player may then move the mat in the line of play, subject to Clause (*a*) above, and deliver the Jack, but shall not play first. Should the Jack be improperly delivered twice by each player in any end, it shall not be delivered again in that end but shall be centred so that the front of the Jack is a distance of 6ft (1.84m) from the opposite ditch, and the mat placed at the option of the first to play.

If, after the Jack is set at regulation length from the ditch (6ft or 1.84m), both players each having improperly delivered the Jack twice, the end is made dead, the winner of the preceding scoring end shall deliver the Jack when the end is played anew.

(c) No one shall be permitted to challenge the legality of the original position of the mat after the first to play has delivered the first Bowl.

27. Stance on Mat
A player shall take his stance on the mat and, at the moment of delivering the Jack or his bowl, shall have one foot remaining entirely within the confines of the mat. The foot may be either in contact with, or over, the mat. Failure to observe this Law constitutes foot-faulting.

28. Foot-faulting
Should a player infringe the Law of foot-faulting, the Umpire may, after having given a warning, have the Bowl stopped and declared dead. If the Bowl has disturbed the head, the opponents shall have the option of either resetting the head, leaving the head as altered, or declaring the end dead.

29. Delivering the Jack
The player to play first shall deliver the Jack. If the Jack in its original course comes to rest at a distance of less than 6ft (1.84m) from the opposite ditch, it shall be moved out to a mark at that distance so that the front of the Jack is 6ft (1.84m) from the front ditch, with the nearest portion of the Jack to the mat line being 6ft (1.84m) from the edge of the opposite ditch.

If the Jack during its original course be obstructed or deflected by a neutral object or neutral person, or by a Marker, Opponent, or member of the opposing team, it shall be re-delivered by the same player. If it be obstructed or deflected by a member of his own team, it shall be re-delivered by the Lead of the opposing team, who shall be entitled to reset the mat.

30. Jack Improperly Delivered
Should the Jack in any end be not delivered from a proper stance on the mat, or if it ends its original course in the ditch or outside the side boundary of the rink, or less than 70ft (21.35m) in a straight line of play

from the front edge of the mat, it shall be returned and the opposing player shall deliver the Jack, but shall not play first.

The Jack shall be returned if it is improperly delivered, but the right of the player first delivered the Jack in that end, to play the first Bowl of the end, shall not be affected.

No one shall be permitted to challenge the legality of the original length of the Jack after the first to play has delivered the first Bowl.

31. Variations to Laws 24, 26, 29 and 30

Notwithstanding anything contained in Laws 24, 26, 29 and 30, any National Authority may for domestic purposes, but not in any International Matches, World Bowls Championships or Commonwealth Games, vary any of the distances mentioned in these Laws.

MOVEMENT OF BOWLS

32. 'Live' Bowl

A Bowl which, in its original course on the Green, comes to rest within the boundaries of the rink, and not less than 45ft (13.71m) from the front edge of the mat, shall be accounted as a 'live' Bowl and shall be in play.

33. 'Touchers'

A Bowl which, in its original course on the green, touches the Jack, even though such Bowl passes into the ditch within the boundaries of the rink, shall be accounted as a 'live' Bowl, and shall be called a 'toucher'. If after having come to rest a Bowl falls over and touches the Jack before the next succeeding Bowl is delivered, or if in the case of the last Bowl of an end it falls and touches the Jack within the period of 30 seconds invoked under Law 53, such Bowl shall also be a 'toucher'. No Bowl shall be accounted a 'toucher' by playing on to, or by coming into contact with, the Jack while the Jack is in the ditch. If a 'toucher' in the ditch cannot be seen from the mat, its position may be marked by a white or coloured peg about 2in (51mm) broad placed upright on the top of the bank and immediately in line with the place where the 'toucher' rests.

34. Marking a 'toucher'

A 'toucher' shall be clearly marked with a chalk mark by a member of the player's team. If, in the opinion of either Skip, or Opponent in Singles, a 'toucher' or a wrongly chalked Bowl comes to rest in such a position that the act of making a chalk mark, or of erasing it, is likely to move the Bowl or to alter the head, the Bowl shall not be marked or have its mark erased but shall be 'indicated' as a 'toucher' or 'non-toucher' as the case may be. If a Bowl is not so marked or not so 'indicated' before the succeeding Bowl comes to rest, it ceases to be a 'toucher'. If both Skips or Opponents agree that any subsequent movement of the Bowl eliminates the necessity for continuation of the 'indicated' provision, the Bowl shall thereupon be marked or have the chalk mark erased as the case may be. Care should be taken to remove 'toucher' marks from all Bowls before they are played, but should a player fail to do so, and should the Bowl not become a 'toucher' in the end in play, the marks shall be removed by the opposing Skip or his deputy or Marker immediately the Bowl comes to rest, unless the Bowl is 'indicated' as a 'non-toucher' in circumstances governed by earlier provisions of this Law.

35. Movement of 'Touchers'

A 'toucher' in play in the ditch may be moved by the impact of a Jack in play or of another 'toucher' in play, and also by the impact of a 'non-toucher' which remains in play after the impact, and any movement of the 'toucher' by such incidents shall be valid. However, should the 'non-toucher' enter the ditch at any time after the impact, it shall be dead, and the 'toucher' shall be deemed to have been displaced by a dead Bowl, and provisions of Law 38(*e*) shall apply.

36. Bowl Accounted 'Dead'

(*a*) Without limiting the application of any other of these Laws, a bowl shall be accounted dead if:

(i) Not being a 'toucher', comes to rest in the ditch or rebounds on the playing surface of the rink after contact with the bank or with the Jack or a 'toucher' in the ditch; or

(ii) After completing its original course, or after being moved as a result of play, it comes to rest wholly outside the boundaries of the playing surface of the rink, or within 45ft (13.71m) of the front of the mat; or

(iii) In its original course, passes beyond a side boundary of the rink on a bias which would prevent its re-entering the rink. (A Bowl is not rendered 'dead' by a player carrying it whilst inspecting the head.)

(*b*) Skips or the Opponents in Singles shall agree on the question as to whether or not a Bowl is 'dead'. Any member of either team may request a decision from the Skips but no member shall remove any Bowl prior to agreement by the Skips. Once their attention has been drawn to the matter, the Skips by agreement must make a decision. If they cannot reach agreement, the Umpire must make an immediate decision.

37. Bowl Rebounding

Only 'touchers' rebounding from the face of the bank to the ditch or the rink shall remain in play.

38. Bowl Displacement

(*a*) Displacement by rebounding 'non-toucher' – bowl displaced by a 'non-toucher' rebounding from the bank shall be restored as near as possible to its original position, by a member of the opposing team.

(*b*) Displacement by participating player – if a Bowl, while in motion or at rest on the green, or a 'toucher' in the ditch, be interfered with or displaced by one of the players, the opposing Skip shall have the option of:

(i) Restoring the Bowl as near as possible to its original position;

(ii) Letting it remain where it rests;

(iii) Declaring the Bowl 'dead'; or

(iv) Declaring the end 'dead'.

(*c*) Displacement by a neutral object or neutral person (other than as provided in Clause (*d*) hereof):

(i) Of a bowl in its original course – if such a Bowl be displaced within the boundaries of the rink of play without having disturbed the head, it shall be replayed. If it be displaced and it has disturbed the head, the Skips, or the Opponents in Singles, shall reach agreement on the final position of the displaced Bowl and on the replacement of the head, otherwise the end shall be 'dead'.

These provisions shall also apply to a Bowl in its original course displaced outside the boundaries of the rink of play provided such a Bowl was running on a bias which would have enabled it to re-enter the rink.

(ii) Of a Bowl at rest, or in motion as a result of play after being at rest – if such a bowl be displaced, the Skips or Opponents in Singles, shall come to an agreement as to the position of the Bowl and of the replacement of any parts of the head disturbed by the displaced Bowl, otherwise the end shall be 'dead'.

(*d*) Displacement inadvertently produced – if a Bowl be moved at the time of its being marked or measured it shall be restored to its former position by an opponent. If such displacement is caused by a Marker or an Umpire, the Marker or Umpire shall replace the Bowl.

(*e*) Displacement by a 'dead' Bowl – if a 'toucher' in the ditch be displaced by a 'dead' Bowl from the rink of play, it shall be restored to its original position by a player of the opposite team or by the Marker.

39. 'Line bowls'

A Bowl shall not be accounted as outside the line unless it be entirely clear of it. This shall be ascertained by looking perpendicularly down upon the Bowl or by placing a square on the green.

MOVEMENT OF JACK

40. A 'live' Jack in the Ditch
A Jack moved by a Bowl in play into the front ditch within the boundaries of the rink shall be deemed to be 'live'. It may be moved by the impact of a 'toucher' in play and also by the impact of a 'non-toucher' which remains in play after the impact; any movement of the Jack by such incidents shall be valid. However, should the 'non-toucher' enter the ditch after impact, it shall be 'dead' and the Jack shall be deemed to have been 'displaced' by a 'dead' Bowl and the provisions of Law 48 shall apply. If the Jack in the ditch cannot be seen from the mat its position shall be marked by a 'white' peg about 2in (51mm) broad and not more than 4in (102mm) in height, placed upright on top of the bank and immediately in line from the place where the Jack rests.

41. A Jack Accounted 'Dead'
Should the Jack be driven by a Bowl in play and come to rest wholly beyond the boundary of the rink, i.e. over the bank or over the side boundary, or into any opening or inequality of any kind in the bank, or rebound to a distance less than 61ft (18.59m) in a direct line from the centre of the front edge of the mat to the Jack in its rebounded position, it shall be accounted 'dead'.

(National Associations have the option to vary the distance to which a Jack may rebound and still be playable for games other than International and Commonwealth Games.)

42. 'Dead' End
When the Jack is 'dead', the end shall be regarded as a 'dead' end and shall not be accounted as a played end, even though all the Bowls in that end have been played. All 'dead' ends shall be played anew in the same direction unless both Skips or Opponents in Singles agree to play in the opposite direction.

43. Playing to a Boundary Jack
The Jack, if driven to the side boundary of the rink and not wholly beyond its limits, may be played to on either hand and if necessary a Bowl may pass outside the side limits of the rink. A Bowl so played, which comes to rest within the boundaries of the rink, shall not be accounted 'dead'.

If the Jack be driven to the side boundary line and comes to rest partly within the limits of the rink, a Bowl played outside the limits of the rink and coming to rest entirely outside the boundary line, even though it has made contact with the Jack, shall be accounted 'dead' and shall be removed to the bank by a member of the player's team.

44. A Damaged Jack
In the event of a Jack being damaged, the Umpire shall decide if another Jack is necessary and, if so, the end shall be regarded as a 'dead' end and another Jack shall be substituted and the end shall be replayed anew.

45. A Rebounding Jack
If the Jack is driven against the face of the bank and rebounds on to the rink, or after being played into the ditch it be operated on by a 'toucher' so as to find its way on to the rink, it shall be played to in the same manner as if it had never left the rink.

46. Jack Displacement
(a) *By a player*: If the Jack be diverted from its course while in motion on the green, or displaced while at rest on the green, or in the ditch, by any one of the players, the opposing Skip shall have the Jack restored to its former position, or allow it to remain where it rests and play the end to a finish, or declare the end 'dead'.

(b) *Inadvertently produced*: If the Jack be moved at the time of measuring by a player it shall be restored to its former position by an opponent.

47. Jack Displaced by Non-player
(a) If the Jack, whether in motion or at rest on the rink, or in the ditch, be displaced by a Bowl from another rink, or by any object or by an individual not a member of the team, the two Skips shall decide as to its original position, and if they are unable to agree, the end shall be declared 'dead'.

(b) If a Jack be displaced by a Marker or Umpire, it shall be restored by him to its original position, of which he shall be the sole judge.

48. Jack Displaced by 'Non-toucher'
A Jack displaced in the rink of play by a 'non-toucher' rebounding from the bank shall be restored, or as near as possible, to its original position by a player of the opposing team, or by the Marker in a Singles game. Should a Jack, however, after having been played into the ditch, be displaced by a 'dead Bowl', it shall be restored to its marked position by a player of the opposing side or by the Marker.

FOURS PLAY

The basis of the game of bowls is fours play.

49. The Rink and Fours Play

(a) *Designation of players*: A team shall consist of four players, named respectively Lead, Second, Third and Skip, according to the order in which they play, each playing two Bowls.

(b) *Order of play*: The Leads shall play their two Bowls alternately, and so on, each pair of players in succession to the end. No one shall play until his opponent's Bowl shall have come to rest. Except under circumstances provided for in Law 63, the order of play shall not be changed after the first end has been played, under penalty of disqualification, such penalty involving the forfeiture of the match or game to the opposing team.

50. Possession of the Rink

Possession of the rink shall belong to the team whose Bowl is being played. The players in possession of the rink for the time being shall not be interfered with, annoyed, or have their attention distracted in any way by their opponents.

As soon as each Bowl shall have come to rest, possession of the rink shall be transferred to the other team, time being allowed for marking a 'toucher'.

51. Position of Players

Players of each team not in the act of playing or controlling play shall stand behind the Jack and away from the head or 3ft (92cm) behind the mat. As soon as the Bowl is delivered, the Skip or player directing, if in front of the Jack, shall retire behind it.

52. Players and their Duties

(a) *The Skip* shall have sole charge of his team and his instructions shall be observed by his players. With the opposing Skip he shall decide all disputed points, and when both agree their decision shall be final.

If both Skips cannot agree, the point in dispute shall be referred to and considered by an Umpire, whose decision shall be final.

A Skip may at any time delegate his powers and any of his duties to other members of his team, provided that such delegation is notified to the opposing Skip.

(b) *The Third*: The Third player may have deputed to him the duty of measuring any and all disputed shots.

(c) *The Second*: The Second player shall keep a record of all shots scored for and against his team and shall at all times retain possession of the score card whilst play is in progress. He shall see what the names of all players are entered on the score card, shall compare his record of the game with that of the opposing Second player as each end is declared, and at the close of the game shall hand his score card to his Skip.

(*d*) *The Lead*: The Lead shall place the mat, and shall deliver the Jack, ensuring that the Jack is properly centred before playing his first Bowl.

(*e*) In addition to the duties specified in the preceding clauses, any player may undertake such duties as may be assigned to him by the Skip in Clause 52(*a*) hereof.

RESULT OF END

53. 'The Shot'
A shot or shots shall be adjudged by the Bowl or Bowls nearer to the Jack than any Bowl played by the opposing player or players.

When the last Bowl has come to rest, 30 seconds shall elapse, if either team desires, before the shots are counted.

Neither Jack nor Bowls shall be moved until each Skip has agreed as to the number of shots, except in circumstances where a Bowl has to be moved to allow the measuring of another Bowl.

54. Measuring Conditions to be Observed
No measuring shall be allowed until the end has been completed.

All measurements shall be made to the nearest point of each object. If a Bowl requiring to be measured is resting on another Bowl which prevents its measurement, the best available means shall be taken to secure its position, whereupon the other Bowl shall be removed. The same course shall be followed where more than two Bowls are involved, or where, in the course of measuring, a single Bowl is in danger of falling or otherwise changing its position.

When it is necessary to measure to a Bowl or Jack in the ditch, and another Bowl or Jack on the green, and measurement shall be made with the ordinary flexible measure. Calipers may be used to determine the shot when the Bowls in question and the Jack are on the same plane.

55. 'Tie' – No Shot
When at the conclusion of play in any end the nearest Bowl of each team is touching the Jack, or is deemed to be equidistant from the Jack, there shall be no score recorded. The end shall be declared 'drawn' and shall be counted a played end.

56.
Nothing in these Laws shall be deemed to make it mandatory for the last player to play his last Bowl in any end, but he shall declare to his

Opponent or opposing Skip his intention to refrain from playing it before the commencement of determining the result of the end and this declaration shall be irrevocable.

GAME DECISIONS
57. In the case of a single game or a team game or a side game played on one occasion, or at any stage of an eliminating competition, the victory decision shall be awarded to the player, team or side of players producing at the end of the game the higher total score of shots, or in the case of a 'game of winning ends', a majority of winning ends.

58. Tournament Games and Games in Series
In the case of tournament games or games in series, the victory decisions shall be awarded to the player, team or side of players producing at the end of the tournament or series of contests either the largest number of winning games or the highest net score of shots in accordance with the regulations governing the tournament or series of games.

Points may be used to indicate game successes.

Where points are equal, the aggregate shots scored against each team (or side) shall be divided into the aggregate shots it has scored. The team (or side) with the highest result shall be declared the winner.

59. Playing to a Finish and Possible Drawn Games
If in an eliminating competition, consisting of a stated or agreed upon number of ends, it be found, when all the ends have been played, that the scores are equal, an extra end or ends shall be played until a decision has been reached.

The Captains or Skips shall toss and the winner shall have the right to decide who shall play first. The extra end shall be played from where the previous end was completed, and the mat shall be placed in accordance with Law 24.

DEFAULTS OF PLAYERS IN FOURS PLAY

60. Absentee Players in any Team or Side
(*a*) *In a single fours game*, for a trophy, prize or other competitive award, where a club is represented by only one Four, each member of such Four shall be a bona fide member of the club. Unless all four players appear and are ready to play at the end of the maximum waiting period of 30 minutes, or should they introduce an ineligible player, then that team shall forfeit the match to the opposing team.

(*b*) *In a domestic Fours game*: Where, in a domestic Fours game the number of players cannot be accommodated in full teams of four players, three players may play against three players, but shall suffer the deduction of one-fourth of the total score of each team.

A smaller number of players than six shall be excluded from that game.

(*c*) *In a side game*: If, within a period of 30 minutes from the time fixed for the game, a single player is absent from one or both teams in a side game, whether a friendly club match or a match for a trophy, prize or other award, the game shall proceed, but in the defaulting team, the number of Bowls shall be made up by the Lead and Second players playing three Bowls each, but one-fourth of the total shots scored by each 'four' playing three men shall be deducted from their score at the end of the game.

Fractions shall be taken into account.

(*d*) *In a side game*: Should such default take place where more Fours than one are concerned, or where a Four has been disqualified for some other infringement, and where the average score is to decide the contest, the scores of the non-defaulting Fours only shall be counted, but such average shall, as a penalty in the case of the defaulting side, be arrived at by dividing the aggregate score of that side by the number of Fours that should have been played and not, as in the case of the other side, by the number actually engaged in the game.

61. Play Irregularities

(*a*) *Playing out of turn*: When a player has played before his turn, the opposing Skip shall have the right to stop the Bowl in its course and it shall be played in its proper turn, but, in the event of the bowl so played having moved or displaced the Jack or a Bowl, the opposing Skip shall have the option of allowing the end to remain as it is after the Bowl so played has come to rest, or of having the end declared 'dead'.

(*b*) *Playing the wrong Bowl*: A Bowl played by mistake shall be replaced by the player's own Bowl.

(*c*) *Changing Bowls*: A player shall not be allowed to change his Bowls during the course of a game, or in a resumed game, unless they be objected to as provided in Law 9(*d*), or when a Bowl has been so damaged in the course of play as, in the opinion of the Umpire, to render the Bowl (or Bowls) unfit for play.

(*d*) *Omitting to play*:

(i) If the result of an end has been agreed upon, or the head has been touched in the agreed process of determining the result, then a player who forfeits or has omitted to play a Bowl, shall forfeit the right to play it.

(ii) A player who has neglected to play a Bowl in the proper sequence shall forfeit the right to play such Bowl, if a Bowl has been played by each team before such mistake was discovered.

(iii) If before the mistake be noticed, a Bowl has been delivered in the reversed order and the head has not been disturbed, the opponent shall then play two successive Bowls to restore the correct sequence. If the head has been disturbed, Law 61(a) shall apply.

62. Play Interruptions

(a) *Game stoppages*: When a game of any kind is stopped, either by mutual arrangement or by the Umpire, after appeal to him on account of darkness or the conditions of the weather, or any other valid reason, it shall be resumed with the scores as they were when the game stopped. An end commenced, but not completed, shall be declared null.

(b) *Substitutes in a resumed game*: If in a resumed game any one of the four original players be not available, one substitute shall be permitted as stated in Law 63 below. Players, however, shall not be transferred from one team to another.

INFLUENCES AFFECTING PLAY

63. Leaving the Green

If during the course of a side Fours, Triples or Pairs game a player has to leave the green owing to illness, or other reasonable cause, his place shall be filled by a substitute, if in the opinion of both Skips (or failing agreement by them, then in the opinion of the Controlling Body) such substitution is necessary. Should the player affected be a Skip, his duties and position in a Fours game shall be assumed by the Third player, and the substitute shall play either as Lead, Second or Third. In the case of Triples the substitute may play either as Lead or Second but not a Skip, and in the case of Pairs the substitute shall play as Lead only. Such substitute shall be a member of the club to which the team belongs. In domestic play National Authorities may decide the position of any substitute.

If during the course of a single-handed game a player has to leave the green owing to illness, or reasonable cause, the provisions of Law 62(a) shall be observed.

No player shall be allowed to delay the play by leaving the rink or team, unless with the consent of his opponent, and then only for a period not exceeding 10 minutes.

Contravention of this Law shall entitle the Opponent or opposing team to claim the game or match.

64. Objects on the Green

Under no circumstances, other than as provided in Laws 29, 33 and 40, shall any extraneous object to assist a player be placed on the green, or on the bank, or on the Jack, or on a Bowl, or elsewhere.

65. Unforeseen Incidents
If during the course of play the position of the Jack or Bowls be disturbed by wind, storm or by any neutral object, the end shall be declared 'dead', unless the Skips are agreed as to the replacement of Jack or Bowls.

DOMESTIC ARRANGEMENTS
66. In addition to any matters specifically mentioned in these Laws. National Authorities may, in circumstances dictated by climate or other local conditions, make such other regulations as are deemed necessary and desirable, but such regulations must be submitted to the IBB for approval. For this purpose the Board shall appoint a committee, to be known as the 'Laws Committee', with powers to grant approval or otherwise to any proposal, such decision being valid until the proposal is submitted to the Board for a final decision.

67. Local Arrangements
Constituent clubs of National Authorities shall also, in making their domestic arrangements, make such regulations as are deemed necessary to govern their club competitions, but such regulations shall comply with the Laws of the Game and be approved by the Council of their National Authority.

68. National Visiting Teams or Sides
No team or side of bowlers visiting overseas or the British Isles shall be recognised by the International Bowling Board unless it first be sanctioned and recommended by the National Authority to which its members are affiliated.

69. Contracting Out
No club or club management committee or any individual shall have the right or power to contract out of any of the Laws of the Game as laid down by the International Bowling Board.

REGULATING SINGLE-HANDED, PAIRS AND TRIPLES GAMES
70. The foregoing Laws, where applicable, shall also apply to Single-Handed, Pairs and Triples games.

SPECTATORS
71. Persons not engaged in the game shall be situated clear of and beyond the limits of the rink of play and clear of the verges. They shall

neither by word nor act disturb or advise the players. This shall not apply to advice given by a Manager or in his absence his delegated deputy of a team or side.

Betting or gambling in connection with any game or games shall not be permitted or engaged in within the grounds of any constituent club.

DUTIES OF MARKER

72. (*a*) In the absence of the Umpire the Marker shall control the game in accordance with the IBB Basic Laws. He shall, before play commences, examine all Bowls for the imprint of the IBB stamp, or that of its National Authority, such imprint to be clearly visible, and shall ascertain by measurement the width of the rink of play (see note on Stamp Details on page 332).

(*b*) He shall centre the Jack and shall place a full-length Jack 6ft (1.84m) from the ditch.

(*c*) He shall ensure that the Jack is not less than 70ft (21.35m) from the front edge of the mat, after it has been centred.

(*d*) He shall stand at one side of the rink, and to the rear of the Jack.

(*e*) He shall answer affirmatively or negatively a player's enquiry as to whether a Bowl is Jack high. If requested he shall indicate the distance of any Bowl from the Jack, or from any other Bowl, and also, if requested, indicate which Bowl he thinks is shot and/or the relative position of any other Bowl.

(*f*) Subject to contrary directions from either opponent under Law 34, he shall mark all 'touchers' immediately they come to rest, and remove chalk marks from 'non-touchers'. With the agreement of both opponents he shall remove all 'dead' Bowls from the green and the ditch. He shall mark the positions of the Jack and 'touchers' which are in the ditch (See Laws 33 and 40).

(*g*) He shall not move, or cause to be moved, either Jack or Bowls until each player has agreed to the number of shots.

(*h*) He shall measure carefully all doubtful shots when requested by either player. If unable to come to a decision satisfactory to the players, he shall call in an Umpire. If an official Umpire has not been appointed, the Marker shall select one. The decision of the Umpire shall be final.

(*i*) He shall enter the score at each end and shall intimate to the players the state of the game. When the game is finished, he shall see that the scorecard, containing the names of the players, is signed by the players, and disposed of in accordance with the rules of the competition.

DUTIES OF UMPIRE

73. An Umpire shall be appointed by the Controlling Body of the Association, Club or Tournament Management Committee. His duties shall be as follows:

(a) He shall examine all bowls for the imprint of the IBB stamp or that of its National Authority and ascertain by measurement the width of the rinks of play.

(b) He shall measure any shot or shots in dispute, and for this purpose shall use a suitable measure. His decision shall be final.

(c) He shall decide all questions as to the distance of the mat from the ditch and the Jack from the mat.

(d) He shall decide as to whether or not Jack and/or Bowls are in play.

(e) He shall enforce the Laws of the Game.

(f) In World Bowls Championships and Commonwealth Games the Umpire's decision shall be final in respect of any breach of a Law, except that, upon questions relating to the meaning of interpretation of any Law there shall be a right of appeal to the Controlling Body.

INTERNATIONAL BOWLING BOARD BY-LAWS

Professional Bowler

All players are eligible for selection for Commonwealth Games except those whose principal source of income is derived from playing the Game of Bowls.

Stamping of Bowls

Manufacturers will be entitled to use the registered IBB stamp, to facilitate the imprint between the inner and outer rings of Bowls. Imprints on running surfaces should be avoided wherever possible.

Stamp Details

BIB – International Bowling Board.

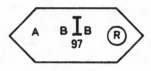

A – Denotes factory of Manufacture.
Numerals – Denotes year of expiry.
R – Denotes that the stamp is a registered trade mark.

Metric Equivalents

In connection with the manufacture of Bowls there is no objection to manufacturers using metric equivalents in lieu of the present figures, always provided that Law 9 of the Board's Laws is complied with.

Furthermore, there is no objection to manufacturers indicating various sizes of Bowls by numerals, and the manufacturers will be entitled to use the following table if they so desire.

Size in inches	Size number	Actual Metric (mm)	May be rounded off Metric (mm)
$4\frac{9}{16}$	00	115.9	116
$4\frac{5}{8}$	0	117.4	117
$4\frac{3}{4}$	1	120.7	121
$4\frac{13}{16}$	2	122.2	122
$4\frac{7}{8}$	3	123.8	124
$4\frac{15}{16}$	4	125.4	125
5	5	127.0	127
$5\frac{1}{16}$	6	128.6	129
$5\frac{1}{8}$	7	130.2	131

If size numbers are utilised and size measurements omitted, then no Bowl in diameter shall be less than $4\frac{9}{16}$ inches (115.9mm) nor more than $5\frac{1}{8}$ inches (130.2mm) and no Bowl shall weigh more than 3lb 8oz (1.59kg).

These Laws are reprinted by permission of the International Bowling Board. Originally formulated by the Scottish Bowling Association and last revised in 1990, they may not be published without the consent of the Board.

Crown Green Bowls

1. The game shall be played on grass or on an artificial surface as approved by the BCGBA. The game shall be played by two players, each having two Bowls, the players playing alternately until each shall have delivered both Bowls, except in the event of one player having forfeited his first Bowl, in which case his opponent will then be allowed to deliver his two Bowls consecutively. A Bowl must be played at least 3m from the Footer to count, except when an opponent's Bowls are out of play. Before commencing play the number of points to be scored to make the game shall be fixed. (Where more than two players take part in a game, these Laws shall operate when applicable.) The entrance (which must be near the centre of any one side) shall be plainly marked.

2. Method of Scoring

The winner of each end shall score one point for each Bowl he has nearer to the Jack than his opponent's nearest Bowl, and he shall lead out the Jack at the succeeding end.

3. Commencement of Games

On commencing a game, the Footer must be placed by the leader within 3m of the entrance to the Green on either right or left side, and 1m from the edge, and from there play shall commence.

4. The Footer

Every player must place his toe on the Footer when bowling either Jack or Bowl. A player bowling the Jack with his right hand must play his Bowls with the right hand and must have his right toe on the Footer, and a player bowling the Jack with his left hand must play his Bowls with the left hand and must have his left toe on the Footer. Nothing in this rule shall apply to any player who suffers a disability. A player must Bowl with the same hand throughout the game. Any Bowl not so played may be stopped by the Referee, and shall then be played again. If a player shall again transgress during the course of the game, the Bowl wrongly played shall be deemed dead. A player may retain possession of the Footer until his Bowl has ceased running. At no time may the Footer be used within 1m from the edge of the Green. The Footer, which shall be round, shall have a diameter of not less than 5in (128mm) and not more than 6in (154mm).

5. Replacing Footer

If a player shall have taken up the Footer after playing a Bowl, which for any reason has to be replayed, the Footer shall be replaced as nearly as possible in its former position.

6. After each end is concluded, the Footer shall be placed at the Jack by the last player. The leader in the succeeding end may, however, before bowling the Jack, remove the Footer anywhere he pleases within the space of 1m from the spot where the Jack lay at the termination of the preceding end (subject to the provisions of Law 4).

7. A Mark

The leader shall bowl the Jack to set a Mark, the object of the players being to play their Bowls as near as possible to the Jack. To set a Mark, the Jack must be bowled and if it rests on the Green at all (except as Laws and Law 30), it shall be deemed a Mark.

8. Not a Mark

The following shall be deemed 'not a Mark':

(*a*) If, after objection, the Jack is proved by measurement to be less than 19m from the Footer, the measurement to be taken from the nearest point of the Jack to the centre of the Footer.

(*b*) If, when bowled, the Jack shall go off the Green.

9. Who Shall Set Mark

If the leader in one trial shall fail to set a Mark, his opponent is then entitled to set the Mark with the same Jack, but not to play first at it. If the opponent fails in one trial to set a Mark, the original leader shall then have one trial, and so on alternately, until a Mark has been set by one of them, the original leader to play the first bowl at it.

10. Objection to a Mark

Objection to a Mark must be made verbally *after* the first Bowl has come to rest. Any player objecting to a Mark must raise his hand as an indication to the Referee that an objection has been made.

11. If (after objection to a Mark has been made) it is proved by measurement to be a Mark, the Jack and Bowl shall remain.

12. If the original leader fails to set a Mark, and objects to the Mark set by his opponent, he shall not be allowed to bowl his wood until the objection has been settled, and if the measurement shall prove that a legitimate mark has been set, it must be accepted.

13. A tape or other certified measure (at least 19m long) must be used for the purpose of carrying out these Laws.

14. The Jack
Standard Jacks as defined in Appendix A shall be used in all Competitions.

15. Delivery of Jack
A player shall not bowl the Jack without allowing his opponent the opportunity of seeing with what bias he bowls it, and of watching its course from a point near the Footer.

16. Jack Struck off Green
If the Jack is struck off the Green that end shall be deemed to have been played. Play shall resume, 1m from the point where the Jack left the Green, the same player setting the Mark.

17. Jack Impeded
If the Jack in its course is impeded in any way, or stops on the land of other players, it must under all circumstances be returned, and if two Jacks are bowled near the same place, the one that is last stationary must be pronounced not a mark and be returned, no penalty being incurred.

18. Jack Displaced
If the Jack is displaced by a Bowl or the Jack of any other players, or by any exterior cause, and the players agree as to the spot of replacement, the end must be continued, otherwise the end is void.

19. Jack or Bowl in Danger of Striking Still Bowl or Jack
If a running Jack or Bowl appears to be in danger of striking a still Bowl or Jack belonging to another set, such running Jack or Bowl should be stopped and returned to be replayed.

20. When, after delivery of the Jack and a Mark is set, the leader is prevented from delivering his first Bowl through the tape being on the Green during the measure of another Mark, the leader may have the Jack returned and again set the Mark.

21. If a player strikes the Jack with his Bowl, and the Jack comes in contact with a Bowl or Jack not belonging to the playing party, or if it comes in contact with any person on the Green the end becomes void; but if the Jack comes in contact with a Bowl belonging to the playing party, it must remain at the place to which it is removed by the strike.

22. Changing Jack or Bowls

No player shall be allowed to change the Jack or Bowls during the progress of a game except with the consent of the Referee and then only if in his opinion the Jack or Bowls are so damaged as to be unplayable. No player shall be permitted to play with Bowls or Jack which have a device for adjusting the bias, nor shall any player be permitted to alter the bias of Bowls or Jack, by any means, during the course of play.

23. No player shall deliver a Bowl while the Jack or a preceding Bowl is in motion, otherwise his Bowl shall be deemed dead and must be taken out of play.

24. Approaching Running Bowl

A player must not approach nearer than 1m to a running Bowl, nor follow it up in such a manner as to obstruct the view of his opponent. He must not endeavour to accelerate or impede its progress. If he offends the Bowl shall be taken out of play and in the case of a further offence, his Bowls shall be taken off the Green and the game shall be awarded to his opponent, the defaulter's score at that point to count.

25. Running Bowl Impeded

If a running Bowl is impeded in any way (except by either player), it must be played again. If a running Bowl is impeded by either player, both the offending player's Bowls shall be forfeited at the end concerned. If, however, the leader's first Bowl is impeded, he may, if he so desires, have the Jack returned to him to set another Mark. If a running Bowl comes into contact with the Jack or any of the Bowls in the set, such Jack and/or Bowls must remain where they stop.

26. Playing out of Turn or with a Bowl Other than Own

If a Bowl is played out of turn it must be returned and played again in its proper turn. If a Bowl other than the player's own is delivered whether by mistake or otherwise, it shall be deemed a dead Bowl to that player and be returned to the proper owner to be played, the defaulter losing one of his Bowls as a penalty. If, however, the Jack or a Bowl already played is disturbed by the Bowl wrongly played, it shall be replaced as nearly as possible in its original position.

27. Disturbing a Still Bowl
If a still Bowl is disturbed by any person other than the players concerned, or by a Bowl or Jack of any other players, it must be replaced as near as possible to its original position, but should either player touch or displace a still Bowl before the end is completed, both the offending player's Bowls shall be forfeited at the end concerned.

28. Bowl Falling From Player's Hand
If a player has taken up his position, and a Bowl falls from his hand (even by accident) and runs so far that he cannot recover it without quitting the Footer, such Bowl shall be considered dead and must be taken out of play.

29. Blocking Opponent's Course
A player may play his Bowl so as to block his opponent's course whenever he thinks proper, but he must not play his Bowl a less distance than 3m from the Footer, otherwise it shall be deemed dead and must be taken out of play. A Bowl must be played, not placed, or it becomes a dead Bowl.

30. Dead Bowls
A bowl or Jack played or struck off the green or prevented from going off by resting against anything at the edge or in the channel, shall be dead.

31. Moving Jack or Bowls Before Opponent Agrees
At the conclusion of an end, neither the Jack nor a Bowl claimed to count may be moved without the consent of the opponent until the points are counted and both players are satisfield, otherwise the opponent shall score one point for each of his Bowls in play.

32. A player, when at the end where the Jack lies, must not stand directly behind the Jack or obstruct the view of his opponent.

33. Instructions to Referees and Measurers
The Referee or Measurer is not permitted to place either his thumb or finger on either the Jack or Bowl when measuring an end.

No measuring is permitted until the end is finished. In the event of the displacement of the Jack during a measure the points already given shall stand.

34. When measuring, the adjustable end of the pegs or permitted metal measures as approved by the British Crown Green Bowling Association must be taken to the Jack. Only the winner of the end shall signal the result to the Scorers who must sit together, and initial each other's score cards every third end to signify agreement. Where the score cannot be agreed it shall revert to the end where both Markers show the score to be agreed as correct.

35. Displacing Jack or Bowl During Measure, Bowl Resting on Another

If, during a measure, the Jack or Bowl is displaced by a player, he shall lose the point claimed. When a Bowl rests on another, or is touching the Jack, and the Bowl rested on has to be removed to allow a measure it must be removed by the Referee and the measure made after such removal.

36. Referee not to Wait for an Objection

Referees are instructed to insist on and see that the games are carried out strictly in accordance with the Laws of the Game.

37. No person, other than the players and the Referee, are allowed on the Green (except Measurers when their services are required).

38. Refusal, or Inability to Continue Game

If, after commencing a game any player shall refuse or is unable to continue, the Referee shall decide on the point at issue. Should a player leave the Green without informing his opponent and obtaining the permission of the Referee, he shall forfeit the game, no score to be given. Any incident which necessitates a player having to stop play or leave the green and is unable to resume before the finish of the match, his opponent shall receive the maximum points and the score of the player who left the Green to remain as it stood, but in the case of refusal of a player to continue the game, his opponent shall be awarded the maximum score and he shall receive no score.

39. Ungentlemanly Conduct

In case of wilful breach of the Laws of the Game or any unfair play or ungentlemanly conduct, the Referee may caution the offending players or spectators or order them to retire from the game or green, and, if a player, no substitute shall be allowed to take his place. The game shall be awarded to his opponent, who will receive the maximum score and the offending player to receive no score. If a player receives a second caution, he shall forfeit the game, his opponent receiving the maximum score and the offending player to receive no score.

40. Bad Light and Postponement of Game
If, during the course of a game, it becomes so dark that the Jack cannot be distinctly seen from the Footer, any player may have a light exhibited at the Jack if he so requests, or he may appeal to the Referee, whose decision shall be final, for the game to be postponed. In the event of a postponement, owing to the above cause or any other unforseen circumstances, the points scored by each player shall count and the position of the Jack shall be marked.

41. Warnings Before Striking
All players are required to give a verbal warning and to take every precaution before striking to eliminate the possibility of causing injury to other players, Referees, Measurers and spectators by being struck with Bowls or Jack.

42. Alteration of Laws
The British Crown Green Bowling Association is the interpreter of these Laws, and from its decision there shall be no appeal either at Law or otherwise. None of these Laws shall be altered except as provided by the Association's By-Laws numbered 16 and 17 for the alteration of Rules and By-Laws.

43. Dispute not Provided for in Laws
Any dispute arising which is not provided for in the foregoing Laws, shall be decided by the Referee whose decision shall be final.

APPENDIX A

A Standard Jack
1. Standard Jacks of 2 Full bias as approved by the British Crown Green Bowling Association, shall weigh a minimum of 567g (20oz) and a maximum of 680g (24oz) and the diameter shall be a minimum of 95mm ($\frac{3}{4}$in) and a maximum of 98mm ($3\frac{7}{8}$in). They shall be black in colour with white mounts and spots or white in colour with black mounts and spots. In place of mounts, composing Jacks may have engraved circles of approximately the diameter of the mounts or spots and filled in the appropriate colour.

2. The mounts shall be approximately 20mm ($\frac{13}{16}$in) diameter and bias side mounts shall not be hollow. The spots shll be approximately 6mm ($\frac{1}{4}$in) diameter and there shall be three spots on the non-bias side at a radius of approximately 19mm ($\frac{3}{4}$in) from the centre of the mount.

3. They shall not be numbered or lettered. Evidence of ownership shall be made on the non-bias side.

4. They shall be branded BCGBA and the Code letter of the Official Tester. All new standard Jacks shall bear the manufacturer's name.

5. New and renovated Jacks shall be stamped with the year of expiry and for this purpose the year shall be reckoned from 1 October to 30 September the next year. (i.e. Jacks manufactured or re-tested between 1 October and 31 December will bear the stamp of expiry from the following year). All Jacks shall be re-tested at not more than seven-yearly intervals.

Reprinted by permission of the British Crown Green Bowling Association.

Boxing

Boxing

RULE 1

Ring

In all tournaments, the ring shall conform with the following requirements:

(*a*) The minimum size shall be 12ft (3.66m) square and the maximum size 20ft (6.10m) square, measured inside the line of the ropes. In senior Championships the minimum size of the ring must be 16ft (4.88m).

(*b*) The platform shall be safely constructed, level and free from any obstructing projections and shall extend for at least 18in (50cm) outside the line of the ropes. It shall be fitted with four corner posts which shall be well padded or otherwise so constructed as to prevent injury to the boxers.

(*c*) The floor shall be covered with felt, rubber or other suitable, ABA-approved material having the same quality of elasticity, not less than ½in (1.5cm) and not more than ¾in (1.9cm) thick over which canvas shall be stretched and secured in place. The felt, rubber or other approved material, and canvas shall cover the entire platform.

(*d*) There shall be three ropes of a thickness of 3cm (1.18in) minimum to 5cm (1.96in) maximum tightly drawn from the corner posts at 40cm (1ft 3.7in), 80cm (2ft 7½in) and 1.30m (4ft 3in) high respectively. The ropes shall be covered with a soft or smooth material.

The ropes shall be joined on each side, at equal intervals, by two pieces of close textured canvas 3 to 4cm (1½in) wide. The pieces must not slide along the rope.

(*e*) The ring shall be provided with suitable steps at opposite corners for the use of the contestants, officials and seconds.

(*f*) At all Dinner/Boxing Tournaments a minimum distance of 2m shall be clear of all tables, excluding those required for use by officials.

(g) The only persons authorised to enter the Ring shall be boxer, coach, Referee, MC and Medical Officer on the instruction of the Referee.

RULE 2

Gloves

(i) For boxers 67kg and below, all will wear 8oz.

(ii) All boxers over 67kg will wear 10oz.

(iii) During Championships weight allowance will be discounted when deciding the weight of gloves to be used.

(iv) In Club Tournaments, if one boxer is over 67kg both boxers will wear 10oz gloves.

RULE 3

Head Guards

On all International Tournaments home and away, headguards will be worn.

(a) **Bandages**

A soft surgical bandage, not to exceed 8ft 4in (2.5m) in length and 2in (5cm) in width, or a bandage of the Velpeau type or crepe not to exceed 2m (6ft 6in) in length, may be worn on each hand. No other kind of bandage may be used. The use of any kind of tapes, rubber or adhesive plaster, as bandages, is strictly forbidden, but a single strap of adhesive 3in (7.5cm) long and 1in (2.5cm) wide must be used at the upper wrists to secure the bandages.

(b) **Number of Contests**

Boxers may box in a maximum of 18 contests per season, excluding Championships and Internationals.

(c) **Three Day Rule**

There shall be 3 clear days between contests. During Championships and Internationals the 3-day rule will not apply.

RULE 4

Dress

Competitors shall be dressed in accordance with the following:

(a) Competitors shall box in light boots or shoes (without spikes and without any heels), socks, shorts reaching at least half-way down the thigh, and a vest covering the chest and back. Where trunks and vests are of the same colour the belt line must be clearly indicated by marking of a distinctive colour.

Note: The belt is an imaginary line from the navel to the top of the hips.

(*b*) Gum shields must be worn. If the gum shield comes out during a bout for any reason, the first time it is washed and replaced. If it comes out again for any reason during the bout the second, third and fourth time a warning will be given. Senior boxers must wear cup protector. Junior and under 15 boxers must wear a jock strap or other protection.

(*c*) No other objects may be worn during the competition.

(*d*) The use of grease, vaseline or products likely to be harmful or objectionable to an opponent, on the face, arms or any other part of the body is forbidden.

(*e*) Beards and long hair are forbidden, the fringe in front must not extend below the level of the eye-brows.

(*f*) Every Association will arrange for their boxers to have an ME3, which must contain a record of the boxers' bouts, name of opponents and showing the result, how won or lost.

(*g*) Competitors must wear distinguishing colours, such as red or blue sashes round the waist.

A Referee shall exclude from competing any senior or junior A and B boxer who does not wear a cup-protector or who is not clean and properly dressed.

In the event of a boxer's glove or dress becoming undone during boxing, a Referee shall stop the contest to have it attended to.

RULE 5

Weights for all International Competitions
See Appendix 15 of the *Rules of Boxing*, available from the Amateur Boxing Association.

RULE 6

Weigh-in
Senior Competitors to weigh-in on the day of competition, stripped. Juniors to weigh-in in boxing shorts only.

RULE 7

Draws and Byes
The draw shall take place after the weigh-in and medical examination. In competitions where there are more than four competitors a sufficient

number of byes shall be drawn in the first series to reduce the number of competitors in the second series to 4, 8, 16 or 32. Bouts shall be drawn first.

Competitors drawing a bye in the first series shall be the first to box in the second series. If there is an odd number of byes, the boxer who draws the last bye will compete in the second series against the winner of the first bout in the first series.

Where the number of byes is even the boxers drawing byes shall box the first bouts in the second series in the order in which they are drawn.

No competitor may receive a bye in the first series and a 'walk-over' in the second series or two consecutive 'walk-overs'. Should such a situation arise a fresh draw shall be made of the other boxers remaining in the series who have not received a bye or a walk-over in the preceding series. The first boxer to be drawn will meet the boxer who has benefited from a bye or walk-over in the preceding series, and the new draw shall then proceed in the normal way.

Table for Drawing Bouts and Byes

No. of Entries	Bouts	Byes
5	1	3
6	2	2
7	3	1
8	4	–
9	1	7

RULE 8

Duration of Rounds

The number and duration of rounds for senior contests shall be as follows:

Contests:

Between open-class boxers – 3 rounds of 3 minutes each.

Between an open-class boxer and an intermediate-class boxer – 3 rounds of 3 minutes each.

Between intermediate-class boxers – 3 rounds of 3 minutes each.

Between an intermediate-class boxer and a novice-class boxer – 3 rounds of 2 minutes each.

Between novice-class boxers – 3 rounds of 2 minutes each.

In every case, there shall be an interval of one minute between the rounds.

Note: The number and duration of rounds for junior boxers are laid down in Appendix 14 of the *Rules of Boxing*, available from the Amateur Boxing Association.

RULE 9

The Second

Each competitor is entitled to one second and one assistant second who shall be governed by the following rules:

(*a*) Only the second and assistant second shall mount the ring platform, but only the chief second can enter the ring to service the boxer. The assistant second must not touch or speak to the boxer.

(*b*) No advice, assistance or encouragement shall be given to the competitor by his second or assistant during the progress of the rounds.

(*c*) A second may retire his boxer, and may, when he considers his boxer to be in difficulty, throw the towel into the ring, except when the Referee is in course of counting.

(*d*) During the boxing, neither second nor assistant second shall remain on the platform of the ring. The second or assistant second shall, before a round begins, remove from the platform of the ring, seats, towels, buckets, etc.

(*e*) Any second, assistant second or official encouraging or inciting spectators by words or signs to advise or encourage a boxer during the progress of a round or infringing the rules in any other way may be warned or disqualified from acting as a second, assistant second or official for the remainder of the contest concerned. If a second, assistant second or official is disqualified from acting in that capacity by the Referee for a second time at the same tournament, he will be suspended from taking any further part in that tournament. This action shall be recorded on the OIC's Report Form.

(*f*) No stimulant of any kind other than water may be administered to a boxer immediately prior to or during a bout.

A boxer may also be cautioned, warned or disqualified by the Referee for offences committed by his second or assistant second.

Seconds must wear white or plain grey trousers, and white vest or white shirt or a white sweater. Training shoes or boxing boots must be worn. Track suits and white jackets are permitted.

If a second or his assistant infringes the Rules he may be warned or disqualified. His boxer may also be cautioned, warned or disqualified by the Referee for offences committed by the second or assistant second.

RULE 10

Dressing Rooms

Suitable dressing-room accommodation must be provided for competitors at all tournaments. Whenever possible, separate dressing-room accomodation should be provided for appointed officials.

RULE 11

The 'Break'
When a Referee orders the two competitors to 'break' both boxers must step back one pace before recommencing to box. A boxer shall not attempt to strike his opponent on the 'break'. A competitor breaking this Rule shall be liable to disqualification.

RULE 12

Control of Bouts: Referees, Judges and Timekeepers
All contests shall be controlled by a Referee, three judges and a time-keeper. The Referee shall officiate in the ring. When less than 3 judges are available the Referee shall complete a scoring paper.

Referees shall use a score pad or introduction slip to record the names and colours of the boxers. In all cases when a bout is terminated through injury or other cause, the Referee shall record the reason thereon and give it to the official-in-charge.

The timekeeper shall be seated at one side of the ring and the judges at the remaining three sides. The seats shall afford them a satisfactory view of the boxing and shall be apart from the spectators. The Referee shall be solely responsible for the control of the bout in accordance with the Rules and the three judges shall independently award points.

When the bell/gong sounds to indicate the end of the contest both boxers must return immediately to their own corners. The Referee shall ensure that this is obeyed.

The Referee shall be attired in white when officiating at major tournaments.

RULE 13

Announcement of Decision and Disposal of Scoring Papers
(a) At the end of each bout where the stipulated number of rounds has been completed, the Referee shall collect and verify the judges' scoring papers and instruct the MC to announce the decision stating whether this is a unanimous or majority decision and the judges' scores shall be made known to the public. The Referee will raise the hand of the winner.

(b) If a bout be terminated in favour of one boxer, the Referee shall instruct the MC to announce the name of the winner and the reason for the stoppage, then collect the judges' scoring papers.

(c) If both boxers be unable to continue boxing due to injury or simultaneous knock-out, the judges' scoring papers will be collected and the verdict awarded to the boxer who was leading on points when the bout was stopped. In such cases, should the bout be terminated during a round the judges shall award points as though it had been a completed round.

(*d*) If a boxer be disqualified the Referee shall instruct the MC to announce the reason for disqualification and the name of the winner. If both boxers be disqualified the Referee shall instruct the MC to announce the reason(s). The judges' scoring papers shall then be collected by the Referee.

(*e*) When there are only two judges the Referee shall first complete his scoring paper and then collect the Judges' scoring papers. Should there be less than two judges the Referee alone shall officiate; on no account shall he officiate with only one judge.

(*f*) At the termination of each bout the Referee shall hand the scoring papers to the MC who will be responsible for giving them to the official-in-charge, unless other arrangements for their disposal have been made by the ABA or other appropriate Association.

RULE 14

The Referee
1. The Referee shall officiate in the ring. He shall be dressed in white trousers, white shirt and light shoes or boots without raised heels.
2. He shall:
(*a*) Check the gloves and dress.
(*b*) Prevent a boxer from receiving undue and unnecessary punishment.
(*c*) See that the Rules and fair play are strictly observed.
(*d*) At the end of the contest collect and check the papers of the three judges; after checking he shall hand these papers to the adjudicator, OIC or announcer.

The Referee shall not indicate the winner, by raising a boxer's hand or otherwise, until the announcement has been made.
3. (*a*) He shall use three words of command:
'Stop' when ordering the boxers to stop boxing.
'Box' when ordering them to continue.
'Break' when breaking a clinch, upon which command each boxer shall step back before continuing boxing.
(*b*) When the winner of a bout is announced the Referee shall raise the hand of the winning boxer.
4. He shall indicate to a boxer by suitable explanatory signs or gestures any infringement of the Rules. Such signs or gestures may be accompanied by verbal cautions or warnings.

5. *Powers of the Referee*
The Referee is empowered:

(*a*) To terminate a contest at any stage if he considers it too one-sided.

(*b*) To terminate a contest at any stage if one of the boxers has received any injury on account of which the Referee decides he should not continue.

(*c*) To terminate a contest at any stage if he considers the contestants are not in earnest. In such cases he may disqualify one or both contestants.

(*d*) To caution a boxer or to stop the boxing during a contest and administer a warning to a boxer against fouls or for any other reason in the interests of fair play, or to ensure compliance with the Rules.

(*e*) To disqualify a boxer who fails to comply immediately with his orders, or behaves towards him in an offensive or aggressive manner at any time.

(*f*) To disqualify a second or assistant who has infringed the Rules, and the boxer himself if the second or assistant does not comply with the Referee's orders.

(*g*) With or without previous warning to disqualify a contestant for committing a foul.

(*h*) In the event of a knock-down, to suspend a count, if a boxer deliberately fails to retire to a neutral corner or delays to do so.

(*i*) To interpret the Rules in so far as they are applicable or relevant to the actual contest or to decide and take action on any circumstance of the contest which is not covered by a Rule.

6. Should a boxer receive 3 counts in any one round or 4 during a contest, the Referee must terminate the contest.

7. (*a*) If a boxer infringes the Rules but does not merit disqualification for such infringement, the Referee shall stop the contest and shall issue a warning to the offender. As a preliminary to a warning the Referee shall order the boxers to stop. The warning shall be clearly given and in such a way that the boxer understands the reason and the purpose of the warning. The Referee shall signal with his hand to each of the judges that a warning has been given and shall clearly indicate to them the boxer whom he has warned.

After giving the warning, the Referee shall order the boxers to 'Box'. If a boxer is given three warnings in a contest, he shall be disqualified.

(*b*) A Referee may caution a boxer. A caution is in the nature of advice or admonishment given by the Referee to a boxer to check or prevent undesirable practices or the less serious infringements of the Rules. To do so he will not necessarily stop the contest but may avail of a suitable safe opportunity during a round to admonish a boxer for an infringement of the Rules.

8. *Medical Examination of Referees for International Tournaments*
A Referee, before officiating in any international tournament conducted under these Rules shall undergo a medical examination as to his
physical fitness for carrying out his duties in the ring. His vision shall be
at least 6 dioptres in each eye.

The wearing of spectacles by a Referee during the progress of a bout is
not permitted, but contact lenses are allowed. For tournaments other
than Internationals Referees can wear spectacles or contact lenses.

It will be compulsory for the Referees to take part in a meeting before
each Championship, arranged by the Medical Jury.

RULE 15

Judges

(*a*) Each judge shall independently judge the merits of the two
contestants and shall decide the winner according to the Rules.

(*b*) He shall not speak to a contestant, nor to another judge, nor to
anyone else except the Referee during the contest, but may, if
necessary, at the end of a round, bring to the notice of the Referee any
incident which he (the Referee) may appear not to have noticed, such as
the misconduct of a second, loose ropes, etc.

(*c*) The number of points awarded to each competitor shall be
entered by a judge on his scoring paper immediately after the end of
each round.

(*d*) At the end of the bout a judge shall total the points, nominate a
winner and sign his scoring paper, and the unanimous/majority verdict
shall be made known to the public.

(*e*) He shall not leave his seat until the verdict has been announced to
the public.

RULE 16

The Timekeeper
The main duty of the timekeeper is to regulate the number and duration
of the rounds and the intervals between rounds.

(*a*) He shall be seated directly at the ringside.

(*b*) Five seconds before the commencement of each round he shall
clear the ring by ordering 'seconds out'.

(*c*) He shall commence and end each round by striking the gong or
bell.

(*d*) He shall announce the number of each round immediately prior
to commencing it.

(*e*) He shall take off time for temporary stoppages, or when instructed to do so by the Referee.

(*f*) He shall regulate all periods of time and counts by a watch or clock.

(*g*) At a 'knock-down' he shall signal to the Referee with his hand the passing of the seconds while the Referee is counting.

(*h*) If at the end of any round a boxer is 'down' and the Referee is in the course of counting, the gong indicating the end of the round will not be sounded. The gong will be sounded only when the Referee gives the command 'Box' indicating the continuation of the contest.

The intervals between rounds shall be of a full minute's duration.

RULE 17

Decisions
Decisions shall be as follows:

(*a*) *Win on points*
At the end of a contest the boxer who has been awarded the decision by a majority of the judges shall be declared the winner. If both boxers are injured, or are knocked out simultaneously, and cannot continue the contest, the judges shall record the points gained by each boxer up to its termination, and the boxer who was leading on points up to the actual end of the contest shall be declared the winner.

(*b*) *Win by retirement*
If a boxer retires voluntarily owing to injury or other cause, or if he fails to resume boxing immediately after the rest between rounds, his opponent shall be declared the winner.

(*c*) *Win by Referee stopping contest*
 (i) *Outclassed*: If a boxer in the opinion of the Referee is being outclassed, or is receiving excessive punishment, the bout shall be stopped and his opponent declared the winner.

(ii) *Injury*: If a boxer in the opinion of the Referee is unfit to continue because of injury or other physical reasons, the bout shall be stopped and his opponent declared the winner. The right to make this decision rests with the Referee, who may consult the doctor. Having consulted the doctor, the Referee must follow his advice. When a Referee calls a doctor into the ring to examine a boxer, only these two officials should be present. No seconds should be allowed into the ring, nor on the apron.

(*d*) *Win by disqualification*: If a boxer is disqualified his opponent shall be declared the winner. If both boxers are disqualified the decision shall be announced accordingly.

The decision of the judges or Referee, as the case may be, shall be final and without appeal.

The Referee shall have power to caution, warn, or disqualify without warning.

(*e*) *Win by knock-out*: If a boxer is 'down' and fails to resume boxing within 10 seconds, his opponent shall be declared the winner by a knock-out.

(*f*) *No contest*: A bout may be terminated by the Referee inside the scheduled distance owing to a material happening outside the responsibility of the boxers, or the control of the Referee, such as the ring becoming damaged, the failure of the lighting supply, exceptional weather conditions, etc. In such circumstances the bout shall be declared 'no contest' and the official-in-charge shall decide the necessary further action.

RULE 18

Awarding of Points
In awarding points the following directives shall be observed:
Directive 1 – Concerning hits

(*a*) During each round a judge shall assess the respective scores of each boxer according to the number of hits obtained by each. Each hit to have scoring value must, without being blocked or guarded, land directly with the knuckle part of the closed glove of either hand on any part of the front or sides of the head or body above the belt with force. Swings landing as described above are scoring hits.

(*b*) The value of hits scored in a rally of infighting shall be assessed at the end of such rally and shall be credited to the boxer who has had the better of the exchanges according to the degree of his superiority.

(*c*) Hits which are struck by a boxer:

  (i) While infringing any of the rules; or

  (ii) With the side, the heel, the inside of the glove or with the open glove than the knuckle part of the closed glove; or,

  (iii) Which land on the arms; or

  (iv) Which merely connect, without the weight of the body or shoulder, are not scoring hits.

Directive 2 – Concerning fouls

(*a*) During each round a judge shall assess the seriousness of and shall impose a commensurate scoring penalty for any foul witnessed by him irrespective of the fact whether the Referee has observed such foul or not.

(*b*) If the Referee warns one of the competitors, the judges may award a point to the other competitor. When a judge decides to award a point to a competitor for a foul committed by his opponent for which the latter has been warned by the Referee, he shall place a 'W' in the appropriate column against the points of the warned competitor to show that he has done so. If he decides not so to award a point he shall in the appropriate column place the letter 'X' against the points allotted for that round to the warned competitor.

(c) If a Judge observes a foul apparently unnoticed by the Referee, and imposes an appropriate penalty on the offending competitor, he shall indicate that he has done so by placing in the appropriate column the letter 'J' against the points of the offending competitor and indicating the reason why he has done so.

Directive 3 – Concerning the award of points

(a) 20 points shall be awarded for each round. No fraction of points may be given. At the end of each round the better (more skilful) boxer shall receive 20 points and his opponent proportionately less. When boxers are equal in merit, each shall receive 20 points.

(b) If at the end of a contest and having marked each round in accordance with Directives 1 and 2 a judge shall find that the boxers are equal in points he shall award the decision to the boxer:

(i) Who has done most of the leading off or who has shown the better style;

or if equal in that respect,

(ii) Who has shown the better defence (blocking parrying, ducking side-stepping etc.) by which the opponent's attacks have been made to miss.

A winner must be nominated.

(c) No extra points shall be awarded for a knock-down.

RULE 19

Fouls

The competitor who does not obey the instructions of the Referee, acts against the boxing Rules, boxes in any unsportsmanlike manner, or commits fouls, can at the discretion of the Referee be cautioned, warned or disqualified without warning. Only three warnings may be given to the same boxer in one contest. A third warning brings automatic disqualification.

Each boxer is responsible in the same way for his second.

A Referee may, without stopping a contest caution a boxer at some safe opportunity.

If he intends to warn a boxer, he shall stop the contest, and will demonstrate the infringement. He will then point to the boxer and to each of the three judges.

The following are fouls:

(1) Holding or hitting below the belt, tripping, kicking and butting with foot or knee.

(2) Hits or blows with head, shoulder, forearm, elbow, throttling of the opponent, pressing with arm or elbow in opponent's face, pressing the head of the opponent back over the ropes.

(3) Hitting with open glove, the inside of the glove, wrist or side of the hand.

(4) Hits landing on the back of the opponent, and especially any blow on the back of the neck or head or kidneys.

(5) Pivot blows.

(6) Attack whilst holding the ropes or making any unfair use of the ropes.

(7) Lying on, wrestling and throwing in the clinch.

(8) An attack on an opponent who is down or who is in the act of rising.

(9) Holding.

(10) Holding and hitting or pulling and hitting.

(11) Holding, or locking, of the opponent's arm or head, or pushing an arm underneath the arm of the opponent.

(12) Ducking below the belt of the opponent in a manner dangerous to his opponent.

(13) Completely passive defence by means of double cover and intentionally falling to avoid a blow.

(14) Useless, aggressive, or offensive utterances during the round.

(15) Not stepping back when ordered to break.

(16) Attempting to strike opponent immediately after the Referee has ordered 'Break' and before taking a step back.

(17) Assaulting or behaving in an aggressive manner towards a Referee at any time.

Or any other act the Referee may deem improper.

If a Referee has any reason to believe that a foul has been committed which he himself has not seen he may consult the judges.

RULE 20
Down

(1) A boxer is considered 'down':

(i) If he touches the floor with any part of his body other than his feet; or

(ii) If he hangs helplessly on the ropes; or

(iii) If he is outside or partly outside the ropes; or

(iv) If following a hard punch he has not fallen and is not lying on the ropes, but is in a distressed state and cannot, in the opinion of the Referee, continue the bout.

(2) In the case of a knock-down the Referee shall immediately begin to count the seconds. If a boxer is down his opponent must at once go to

the corner indicated by the Referee. He may only continue against the opponent who is knocked down after the latter has got up and on the command 'Box' of the Referee. If the opponent should not go to the corner indicated, on the command of the Referee, the Referee shall stop counting until the opponent has done so. The counting shall then be continued where it has been interrupted.

(3) When a boxer is 'down' the Referee shall count aloud from 1 to 10 with intervals of a second between the numbers, and shall indicate each second with his hand in such a manner that the boxer who has been knocked down may be aware of the count. Before the number 1 is counted, an interval of 1 second must have elapsed from the time when the boxer has fallen to the floor, and the time of announcing '1'.

(4) When a boxer is 'down' as the result of a blow the bout shall not be continued until the Referee has reached the count of 8, even if the boxer is ready to continue before then. After the Referee has said '10' the bout ends and shall be decided as a 'knock-out'.

(5) In the event of a boxer being 'down' at the end of a round the Referee shall continue to count. Should the Referee count up to 10, such boxer shall be deemed to have lost the bout by a 'knock-out'. If the boxer is fit to resume boxing before the count of 10 is reached, the Referee shall immediately use the command 'Box'.

(6) If a boxer is 'down' as the result of a blow and the bout is continued after the count of 8 has been reached, but the boxer falls again without having received a fresh blow, the Referee shall continue the counting from the count of 8 at which he had stopped.

(7) If both boxers go down at the same time, counting will be continued as long as one of them is still down. If both boxers remain down until '10' the bout will be stopped and the decision given in accordance with the points awarded up to the time of the knock-down.

(8) A boxer who fails to resume boxing immediately after the termination of the rest interval, or who, when knocked down by a blow, fails to resume within 10 seconds, shall lose the contest.

RULE 21

Procedure After Knock-outs and RSC (H)

(1) If a boxer is rendered unconscious, then only the Referee and the doctor summoned should remain in the ring, unless the doctor needs extra help.

(2) A boxer who has been knocked out during a contest or wherein the Referee has stopped the contest due to a boxer having received hard blows to the head, making him defenceless or incapable of continuing, shall be examined by a doctor immediately afterwards and accompanied

to his home or suitable accommodation by one of the officials on duty at the event.

(3) A boxer who has been knocked out during a contest or wherein the Referee has stopped the contest due to a boxer having received hard blows to the head, making him defenceless or incapable of continuing shall not be permitted to take part in competitive boxing or sparring for a period of at least 28 clear days after he has been knocked out.

(4) A boxer who has been knocked out during a contest or wherein the Referee has stopped the contest due to a boxer having received hard blows to the head, making him defenceless or incapable of continuing twice in a period of 84 days shall not be permitted to take part in competitive boxing or sparring during a period of 84 days from the second knock-out or RSC (H).

(5) A boxer who has been knocked out during a contest or wherein the Referee has stopped the contest due to a boxer having received hard blows to the head, making him defenceless or incapable of continuing three times in a period of 12 months shall not be allowed to take part in competitive boxing or sparring for a period of one year from the third knock-out or RSC (H).

(6) The Referee will indicate to the OIC and judges to annotate the score card 'RSCH' when he has stopped the contest as a result of a boxer being unable to continue as a result of blows to the head.

RULE 22

Shaking of Hands

Before beginning and after a bout, boxers shall shake hands in a proper manner, as a sign of purely sporting and friendly rivalry in accordance with the boxing rules. The shaking of hands takes place before beginning the first round and after the announcing of the result.

Any further shaking of hands between the rounds is prohibited.

RULE 23

Administration of Drugs etc.

The administration to a boxer of drugs or chemical substances not forming part of the usual diet of a boxer (i.e. doping) is prohibited.

Any boxer or official infringing this prohibition shall be liable to disqualification or suspension by the ABA.

Any boxer who refuses after a bout to undergo any medical test to ascertain if he has committed any breach of this rule shall be liable to disqualification or suspension. The same shall apply to any official encouraging such a refusal.

Drug abuse in Amateur Boxing is strictly forbidden and is the use by a boxer or certain substances, which artificially affect and improve the boxer's physical and/or mental state so improving his performance.

Any boxer must submit to drug testing if requested by a responsible ABA official. Refusal will be taken as if a positive result has been obtained, and will be dealt with accordingly. If a boxer withdraws from a contest, after being selected for testing he will be required to undergo testing.

The finding of a banned drug or one of its metabolites in the body fluid will constitute an offence and the offender will be penalised.

The penalty imposed by the ABA Council if a boxer is found to have positive test of a drug will be to ban the boxer for life. The case may be reviewed in five years.

There may be mitigating circumstances after a first offence, but this is up to the Disciplinary Committee.

Any person assisting or inciting others to drug abuse shall be considered to have committed an offence of the ABA Rules, and will be subject to disciplinary action.

RULE 24

Medical Aptitude
As laid down in the ABA Medical Scheme, Appendix 12 of the *Rules of Boxing*, available from the Amateur Boxing Association.

RULE 25

Attendance of Doctor
It is desirable that a qualified Doctor of Medicine so approved, shall be in attendance throughout the tournament.

RULE 26

Failure to Resume Bout
In all bouts, any competitor failing to resume sparring when time is called shall lose the bout.

RULE 27

Breach of these Rules
The breaking of any of these Rules by a competitor or his second shall render such competitor liable to disqualification.

RULE 28

Suspected Foul
If the Referee suspects a foul which he himself has not clearly seen, he shall consult the judges and give his decision accordingly.

RULE 29
Match Secretaries shall be allowed to see boxers' records as listed on ME3 (Boxers Medical/Record Card) on request.

Reprinted by permission of the Amateur Boxing Association. Some of the Rules have been abbreviated and the Appendixes omitted for reasons of space. Copies of the complete Rules of Boxing can be obtained from the Amateur Boxing Association.

THE LAWS OF

Cricket

Cricket

1. THE PLAYERS

1. Number of Players and Captain

A match is played between two sides each of eleven players, one of whom shall be captain. In the event of the captain not being available at any time a deputy shall act for him.

2. Nomination of Players

Before the toss for innings, the captain shall nominate his players who may not thereafter be changed without the consent of the opposing captain.

NOTE

    (a) *More or Less than Eleven Players a Side.*

A match may be played by agreement between sides of more or less than eleven players but not more than eleven players may field.

2. SUBSTITUTES AND RUNNERS: BATSMAN OR FIELDSMAN LEAVING THE FIELD: BATSMAN RETIRING: BATSMAN COMMENCING INNINGS

1. Substitutes

In normal circumstances, a Substitute shall be allowed to field only for a player who satisfies the Umpires that he has become injured or become ill during the match. However, in very exceptional circumstances, the Umpires may use their discretion to allow a Substitute for a player who has to leave the field or does not take the field for other wholly acceptable reasons, subject to consent being given by the opposing Captain. If a player wishes to change his shirt, boots, etc., he may leave the field to do so (no changing on the field) but no Substitute will be allowed.

2. Objection to Substitutes
The opposing captain shall have no right of objection to any player acting as Substitute in the field, nor as to where he shall field, although he may object to the substitute acting as wicket-keeper.
Experimental Law: The opposing captain shall have no right of objection to any player acting as substitute on the field, nor as to where he shall field; however, no substitute shall act as wicket-keeper. (It has been recommended that this Experimental Law should apply in all levels of cricket from April, 1989.)

3. Substitute Not to Bat or Bowl
A substitute shall not be allowed to bat or bowl.

4. A Player for whom a Substitute has acted
A player may bat, bowl or field even though a substitute has acted for him.

5. Runner
A runner shall be allowed for a batsman who during the match is incapacitated by illness or injury. The player acting as runner shall be a member of the batting side and shall, if possible, have already batted in that innings.

6. Runner's Equipment
The player acting as runner for an injured batsman shall wear the same external protective equipment as the injured batsman.

7. Transgression of the Laws by an Injured Batsman or Runner
An injured batsman may be out should his runner break any one of Laws 33 (Handled the Ball), 37 (Obstructing the Field) or 38 (Run Out). As striker he remains himself subject to the Laws. Furthermore, should he be out of his ground for any purpose and the wicket at the wicket-keeper's end be put down he shall be out under Law 38 (Run Out) or Law 39 (Stumped) irrespective of the position of the other batsman or the runner and no runs shall be scored.

When not the striker, the injured batsman is out of the game and shall stand where he does not interfere with the play. Should he bring himself into the game in any way then he shall suffer the penalties that any transgression of the Laws demands.

8. Fieldsman Leaving the Field

No fieldsman shall leave the field or return during a session of play without the consent of the Umpire at the bowler's end. The Umpire's consent is also necessary if a substitute is required for a fieldsman, when his side returns to the field after an interval. If a member of the fielding side leaves the field or fails to return after an interval and is absent from the field for longer than 15 minutes, he shall not be permitted to bowl after his return until he has been on the field for at least that length of playing time for which he was absent. This restriction shall not apply at the start of a new day's play.

9. Batsman Leaving the Field or Retiring

A batsman may leave the field or retire at any time owing to illness, injury or other unavoidable cause, having previously notified the Umpire at the bowler's end. He may resume his innings at the fall of a wicket, which for the purposes of this Law shall include the retirement of another batsman.

If he leaves the field or retires for any other reason he may only resume his innings with the consent of the opposing captain.

When a batsman has left the field or retired and is unable to return owing to illness, injury or other unavoidable cause, his innings is to be recorded as 'retired, not out'. Otherwise it is to be recorded as 'retired, out'.

10. Commencement of a Batsman's Innings

A batsman shall be considered to have commenced his innings once he has stepped onto the field of play.

3. THE UMPIRES

1. Appointment

Before the toss for innings two Umpires shall be appointed, one for each end, to control the game with absolute impartiality as required by the Laws.

2. Change of Umpire

No Umpire shall be changed during a match without the consent of both captains.

3. Special Conditions

Before the toss for innings, the Umpires shall agree with both captains on any special conditions affecting the conduct of the match.

4. The Wickets
The Umpires shall satisfy themselves before the start of the match that the wickets are properly pitched.

5. Clock or Watch
The Umpires shall agree between themselves and inform both captains before the start of the match on the watch or clock to be followed during the match.

6. Conduct and Implements
Before and during a match the Umpires shall ensure that the conduct of the game and the implements used are strictly in accordance with the Laws.

7. Fair and Unfair Play
The Umpires shall be the sole judges of fair and unfair play.

8 Fitness of Ground, Weather and Light
(*a*) The Umpires shall be the sole judges of the fitness of the ground, weather and light for play.

(i) However, before deciding to suspend play or not to start play or not to resume play after an interval or stoppage, the Umpires shall establish whether both captains (the batsmen at the wicket may deputise for their captain) wish to commence or to continue in the prevailing conditions; if so, their wishes shall be met.

(ii) In addition, if during play the Umpires decide that the light is unfit, only the batting side shall have the option of continuing play. After agreeing to continue to play in unfit light conditions, the captain of the batting side (or a batsman at the wicket) may appeal against the light to the Umpires, who shall uphold the appeal only if, in their opinion, the light has deteriorated since the agreement to continue was made.

(*b*) After any suspension of play, the Umpires, unaccompanied by any of the players or officials shall, on their own initiative, carry out an inspection immediately the conditions improve and shall continue to inspect at intervals. Immediately the Umpires decide that play is possible they shall call upon the players to resume the game.

9. Exceptional Circumstances
In exceptional circumstances, other than those of weather, ground or light, the Umpires may decide to suspend or abandon play. Before making such a decision the Umpires shall establish, if the circumstances allow, whether both captains (the batsmen at the wicket may deputise

for their captain) wish to continue in the prevailing conditions; if so their wishes shall be met.

10. Position of Umpires
The Umpires shall stand where they can best see any act upon which their decision may be required.

Subject to this over-riding consideration the Umpire at the bowler's end shall stand where he does not interfere with either the bowler's run up or the striker's view.

The Umpire at the striker's end may elect to stand on the off instead of the leg side of the pitch, provided he informs the captain of the fielding side and the striker of his intention to do so.

11. Umpires Changing Ends
The Umpires shall change ends after each side has had one innings.

12. Disputes
All disputes shall be determined by the Umpires and if they disagree the actual state of things shall continue.

13. Signals
The following code of signals shall be used by Umpires who will wait until a signal has been answered by a scorer before allowing the game to proceed.

Boundary — by waving the arm from side to side.

Boundary 6 — by raising both arms above the head.

Bye — by raising an open hand above the head.

Dead Ball — by crossing and re-crossing the wrists below the waist.

Leg Bye — by touching a raised knee with the hand.

No Ball — by extending one arm horizontally.

Out — by raising the index finger above the head. If not out the Umpire shall call 'not out'.

Short Run — by bending the arm upwards and by touching the nearer shoulder with the tips of the fingers.

Wide — by extending both arms horizontally.

14. Correctness of Scores
The Umpires shall be responsible for satisfying themselves on the correctness of the scores throughout and at the conclusion of the match. See Law 21.6 (Correctness of Result).

4. THE SCORERS

1. Recording Runs
All runs scored shall be recorded by scorers appointed for the purpose.

Where there are two scorers they shall frequently check to ensure that the score sheets agree.

2. Acknowledging Signals
The scorers shall accept and immediately acknowledge all instructions and signals given to them by the Umpires.

5. THE BALL

1. Weight and Size
The ball, when new, shall weigh not less than 5½oz (155.9g), nor more than 5¾oz (163g): and shall measure not less than 8$\frac{13}{16}$in (22.4cm), nor more than 9in (22.9cm) in circumference.

2. Approval of Balls
All balls used in matches shall be approved by the Umpires and captains before the start of the match.

3. New Ball
Subject to agreement to the contrary, having been made before the toss, either captain may demand a new ball at the start of each innings.

4. New Ball in Match of 3 or more Days' Duration
In a match of 3 or more days' duration, the captain of the fielding side may demand a new ball after the prescribed number of overs has been bowled with the old one. The Governing Body for cricket in the country concerned shall decide the number of overs applicable in that country which shall be not less than 75 six-ball overs (55 eight-ball overs).

5. Ball Lost or Becoming Unfit for Play
In the event of a ball during play being lost or, in the opinion of the Umpires, becoming unfit for play, the Umpires shall allow it to be replaced by one that in their opinion has had a similar amount of wear. If a ball is to be replaced, the Umpires shall inform the batsmen.

6. THE BAT

1. Width and Length
The bat overall shall not be more than 38in (96.5cm) in length; the blade of the bat shall be made of wood and shall not exceed 4¼in (10.8cm) at the widest part.

7. THE PITCH

1. Area of Pitch
The pitch is the area between the bowling creases – See Law 9 (The Bowling, Popping and Return Creases). It shall measure 5ft (1.52m) in width on either side of a line joining the centre of the middle stumps of the wickets – See Law 8 (The Wicket).

2. Selection and Preparation
Before the toss for innings, the Executive of the Ground shall be responsible for the selection and preparation of the pitch; thereafter the Umpires shall control its use and maintenance.

3. Changing Pitch
The pitch shall not be changed during a match unless it becomes unfit for play, and then only with the consent of both captains.

4. Non-Turf Pitches
In the event of a non-turf pitch being used, the following shall apply:
   (*a*) *Length*: That of the playing surface to a minimum of 58ft (17.68m).
   (*b*) *Width*: That of the playing surface to a minimum of 6ft (1.83m).

8. THE WICKETS

1. Width and Pitching
Two sets of wickets, each 9in (22.86cm) wide, and consisting of three wooden stumps with two wooden bails upon the top, shall be pitched opposite and parallel to each other at a distance of 22yd (20.12m) between the centres of the two middle stumps.

2. Size of Stumps
The stumps shall be of equal and sufficient size to prevent the ball from passing between them. Their tops shall be 28in (71.1cm) above the ground, and shall be dome-shaped except for the bail grooves.

3. Size of Bails
The bails shall be each 4⅜in (11.1cm) in length and when in position on the top of the stumps shall not project more than ½in (1.3cm) above them.

9. THE BOWLING, POPPING AND RETURN CREASES

1. The Bowling Crease
The bowling crease shall be marked in line with the stumps at each end and shall be 8ft 8in (2.64m) in length, with the stumps in the centre.

2. The Popping Crease
The popping crease, which is the back edge of the crease marking, shall be in front of and parallel with the bowling crease. It shall have the back edge of the crease marking 4ft (1.22m) from the centre of the stumps and shall extend to a minimum of 6ft (1.83m) on either side of the line of the wicket.

The popping crease shall be considered to be unlimited in length.

3. The Return Crease
The return crease marking, of which the inside edge is the crease, shall be at each end of the bowling crease and at right angles to it. The return crease shall be marked to a minimum of 4ft (1.22m) behind the wicket and shall be considered to be unlimited in length. A forward extension shall be marked to the popping crease.

10. ROLLING, SWEEPING, MOWING, WATERING THE PITCH AND RE-MARKING OF CREASES

1. Rolling
During the match the pitch may be rolled at the request of the captain of the batting side, for a period of not more than 7 minutes before the start of each innings, other than the first innings of the match, and before the start of each day's play. In addition, if, after the toss and before the first innings of the match, the start is delayed, the captain of the batting side shall have the right to have the pitch rolled for not more than 7 minutes.

The pitch shall not otherwise be rolled during the match.

The 7 minutes' rolling permitted before the start of a day's play shall take place not earlier than half an hour before the start of play and the captain of the batting side may delay such rolling until 10 minutes before the start of play should he so desire.

If a captain declares an innings closed less than 15 minutes before the resumption of play, and the other captain is thereby prevented from exercising his option of 7 minutes rolling or if he is so prevented for any other reason the time for rolling shall be taken out of the normal playing time.

2. Sweeping

Such sweeping of the pitch as is necessary during the match shall be done so that the 7 minutes allowed for rolling the pitch provided for in 1 above is not affected.

3. Mowing

(a) *Responsibilities of Ground Authority and of Umpires*. All mowings which are carried out before the toss for innings shall be the responsibility of the Ground Authority. Thereafter they shall be carried out under the supervision of the Umpires – See Law 7.2 (Selection and Preparation).

(b) *Initial Mowing*. The pitch shall be mown before play begins on the day the match is scheduled to start or in the case of a delayed start on the day the match is expected to start. See 3 (a) above (Responsibilities of Ground Authority and of Umpires).

(c) *Subsequent Mowings in a Match of 2 or More Days' Duration*. In a match of two or more days' duration, the pitch shall be mown daily before play begins. Should this mowing not take place because of weather conditions, rest days or other reasons the pitch shall be mown on the first day on which the match is resumed.

(d) *Mowing of the Outfield in a Match of 2 or More Days' Duration*. In order to ensure that conditions are as similar as possible for both sides, the outfield shall normally be mown before the commencement of play on each day of the match, if ground and weather conditions allow.

4. Watering

The pitch shall not be watered during a match.

5. Re-Marking Creases

Whenever possible the creases shall be re-marked.

6. Maintenance of Foot Holes

In wet weather, the Umpires shall ensure that the holes made by the bowlers and batsmen are cleaned out and dried whenever necessary to facilitate play. In matches of 2 or more days' duration, the Umpires shall allow, if necessary, the re-turfing of foot holes made by the bowler in his delivery stride, or the use of quick-setting filings for the same purpose, before the start of each day's play.

7. Securing of Footholes and Maintenance of Pitch

During play, the Umpires shall allow either batsman to beat the pitch with his bat and players to secure their footholds by the use of sawdust, provided that no damage to the pitch is so caused, and Law 42 (Unfair Play) is not contravened.

11. COVERING THE PITCH

1. Before the Start of a Match
Before the start of a match complete covering of the pitch shall be allowed.

2. During a Match
The pitch shall not be completely covered during a match unless prior arrangement or regulations so provide.

3. Covering Bowlers' Run-Up
Whenever possible, the Bowlers' run-up shall be covered, but the covers so used shall not extend further than 4ft/1.22m in front of the popping crease.

12. INNINGS

1. Number of Innings
A match shall be of one or two innings of each side according to agreement reached before the start of play.

2. Alternate Innings
In a two-innings match each side shall take their innings alternately except in the case provided for in Law 13 (The Follow-on).

3. The Toss
The captains shall toss for the choice of innings on the field of play not later than 15 minutes before the time scheduled for the match to start, or before the time agreed upon for play to start.

4. Choice of Innings
The winner of the toss shall notify his decision to bat or to field to the opposing captain not later than 10 minutes before the time scheduled for the match to start, or before the time agreed upon for play to start. The decision shall not thereafter be altered.

5. Continuation After One Innings of Each Side
Despite the terms of 1 above, in a one-innings match, when a result has been reached on the first innings the captains may agree to the

continuation of play if, in their opinion, there is a prospect of carrying the game to a further issue in the time left. See Law 21 (Result).

13. THE FOLLOW-ON

1. Lead on First Innings
In a two-innings match the side which bats first and leads by 200 runs in a match of five days or more, by 150 runs in a three-day or four-day match, by 100 runs in a two-day match, or by 75 runs in a one-day match, shall have the option of requiring the other side to follow their innings.

2. Day's Play Lost
If no play takes pace on the first day of a match of 2 or more days' duration, 1 above shall apply in accordance with the number of day's play remaining from the actual start of the match.

14. DECLARATIONS

1. Time of Declaration
The captain of the batting side may declare an innings closed at any time during a match irrespective of its duration.

2. Forfeiture of Second Innings
A captain may forfeit his second innings, provided his decision to do so is notified to the opposing captain and umpires in sufficient time to allow 7 minutes rolling of the pitch. See Law 10 (Rolling, Sweeping, Mowing, Watering the Pitch and Re-Marking of Creases). The normal 10-minute interval between innings shall be applied.

15. START OF PLAY

1. Call of Play
At the start of each innings and of each day's play and on the resumption of play after any interval or interruption the Umpire at the bowlers' end shall call 'play'.

2. Practice on the Field
At no time on any day of the match shall there be any bowling or batting practice on the pitch.

No practice may take place on the field if, in the opinion of the Umpires, it could result in a waste of time.

3. Trial Run-Up

No bowler shall have a trial run-up after 'play' has been called in any session of play, except at the fall of a wicket when an umpire may allow such a trial run-up if he is satisfied that it will not cause any waste of time.

16. INTERVALS

1. Length

The Umpire shall allow such intervals as have been agreed upon for meals, and 10 minutes between each innings.

2. Luncheon Interval – Innings Ending or Stoppage within 10 Minutes of Interval

If an innings ends or there is a stoppage caused by weather or bad light within 10 minutes of the agreed time for the luncheon interval, the interval shall be taken immediately.

The time remaining in the session of play shall be added to the agreed length of the interval but no extra allowance shall be made for the 10 minutes interval between innings.

3. Tea Interval – Innings Ending or Stoppage within 30 Minutes of Interval

If an innings ends or there is a stoppage caused by weather or bad light within 30 minutes of the agreed time for the tea interval, the interval shall be taken immediately.

The interval shall be of the agreed length and, if applicable, shall include the 10-minute interval between innings.

4. Tea Interval – Continuation of Play

If at the agreed time for the tea interval, nine wickets are down, play shall continue for a period not exceeding 30 minutes or until the innings is concluded.

5. Tea Interval – Agreement to Forgo

At any time during the match, the captains may agree to forgo a tea interval.

6. Intervals for Drinks

If both captains agree before the start of a match that intervals for drinks may be taken, the option to take such intervals shall be available to either side. These intervals shall be restricted to one per session, shall be kept as short as possible, shall not be taken in the last hour of the match and in any case shall not exceed 5 minutes.

The agreed times for these intervals shall be strictly adhered to except that if a wicket falls within 5 minutes of the agreed time then drinks shall be taken out immediately.

If an innings ends or there is a stoppage caused by weather or bad light within 30 minutes of the agreed time for a drinks interval, there will be no interval for drinks in that session.

At any time during the match the captains may agree to forgo any such drinks interval.

17. CESSATION OF PLAY

1. Call of Time
The Umpire at the bowler's end shall call 'time' on the cessation of play before any interval or interruption of play, at the end of each day's play, and at the conclusion of the match. See Law 27 (Appeals).

2. Removal of Bails
After the call of 'time', the Umpires shall remove the bails from both wickets.

3. Starting a Last Over
The last over before an interval or the close of play shall be started provided the Umpire, after walking at his normal pace, has arrived at his position behind the stumps at the bowler's end before time has been reached.

4. Completion of the Last Over of a Session
The last over before an interval or the close of play shall be completed unless a batsman is out or retires during that over within 2 minutes of the interval or the close of play or unless the players have occasion to leave the field.

5. Completion of the Last Over of a Match
An over in progress at the close of play on the final day of a match shall be completed at the request of either captain even if a wicket falls after time has been reached.

If during the last over the players have occasion to leave the field the Umpires shall call 'time' and there shall be no resumption of play and the match shall be at an end.

6. Last Hour of Match – Number of Overs
The Umpires shall indicate when one hour of playing time of the match remains according to the agreed hours of play. The next over after that

moment shall be the first of a minimum of 20 six-ball overs, (15 eight-ball overs), provided a result is not reached earlier or there is no interval or interruption of play.

7. Last Hour of Match – Intervals Between Innings and Interruptions of Play

If, at the commencement of the last hour of the match, an interval or interruption of play is in progress or if, during the last hour there is an interval between innings or an interruption of play, the minimum number of overs to be bowled on the resumption of play shall be reduced in proportion to the duration, within the last hour of the match, of any such interval or interruption.

The minimum number of overs to be bowled after a resumption of play shall be calculated as follows:

(*a*) In the case of an interval or interruption of play being in progress at the commencement of the last hour of the match, or in the case of a first interval or interruption a deduction shall be made from the minimum of 20 six-ball overs (or 15 eight-ball overs).

(*b*) If there is a later interval or interruption a further deduction shall be made from the minimum number of overs which should have been bowled following the last resumption of play.

(*c*) These deductions shall be based on the following factors:

(i) The number of overs already bowled in the last hour of the match or, in the case of a later interval or interruption in the last session of play.

(ii) The number of overs lost as a result of the interval or interruption allowing one six-ball over for every full three minutes (or one eight-ball over for every full four minutes) of interval or interruption.

(iii) Any over left uncompleted at the end of an innings to be excluded from these calculations.

(iv) Any over left uncompleted at the start of an interruption of play to be completed when play is resumed and to count as one over bowled.

(v) An interval to start with the end of an innings and to end 10 minutes later; an interruption to start on the call of 'time' and to end on the call of 'play'.

(*d*) In the event of an innings being completed and a new innings commencing during the last hour of the match, the number of overs to be bowled in the new innings shall be calculated on the basis of one six-ball over for every three minutes or part thereof remaining for play (or one eight-ball over for every four minutes or part thereof remaining for play); or alternatively on the basis that sufficient overs be bowled to enable the full minimum quota of overs to be completed under circumstances governed by (*a*), (*b*), and (*c*) above. In all such cases the alternative which allows the greater number of overs shall be employed.

8. Bowler Unable to Complete an Over During Last Hour of the Match

If, for any reason, a bowler is unable to complete an over during the period of play referred to in 6 above, Law 22.7 (Bowler Incapacitated or Suspended during an Over) shall apply.

18. SCORING

1. A Run

The score shall be reckoned by runs. A run is scored:

(a) So often as the batsmen, after a hit or at any time while the ball is in play, shall have crossed and made good their ground from end to end.

(b) When a boundary is scored. See Law 19 (Boundaries).

(c) When penalty runs are awarded. See 6 below.

2. Short Runs

(a) If either batsman runs a short run, the Umpire shall call and signal 'one short' as soon as the ball becomes dead and that run shall not be scored. A run is short if a batsman fails to make good his ground on turning for a further run.

(b) Although a short run shortens the succeding one, the latter, if completed shall count.

(c) If either or both batsmen deliberately run short the Umpire shall, as soon as he sees that the fielding side have no chance of dismissing either batsman, call the signal 'dead ball' and disallow any runs attempted or previously scored. The batsmen shall return to their original ends.

(d) If both batsmen run short in one and the same run, only one run shall be deducted.

(e) Only if three or more runs are attempted can more than one be short and then, subject to (c) and (d) above, all runs so called shall be disallowed. If there has been more than one short run the Umpires shall instruct the Scorers as to the number of runs disallowed.

3. Striker Caught

If the striker is caught, no run shall be scored.

4. Batsman Run Out

If a batsman is run out, only that run which was being attempted shall not be scored. If, however, an injured striker himself is run out no runs shall be scored. See Law 2.7 (Transgression of the Laws by an Injured Batsman or Runner).

5. Batsman Obstructing the Field

If a batsman is out obstructing the field, any runs completed before the obstruction occurs shall be scored unless such obstruction prevents a catch being made in which case no runs shall be scored.

6. Runs Scored for Penalties

Runs shall be scored for penalties under Laws 20 (Lost Ball), 24 (No-ball), 25 (Wide-ball), 41.1 (Fielding the Ball) and for boundary allowances under Law 19 (Boundaries).

7. Batsman Returning to Wicket he has Left

If, while the ball is in play, the batsmen have crossed in running, neither shall return to the wicket he has left even though a short run has been called or no run has been scored as in the case of a catch. Batsmen, however, shall return to the wickets they originally left in the cases of a boundary and of any disallowance of runs and of an injured batsman being, himself, run out. See Law 2.7 (Transgression of the Laws by an Injured Batsman or Runner).

19. BOUNDARIES

1. The Boundary of the Playing Area

Before the toss for innings, the Umpires shall agree with both captains on the boundary of the playing area. The boundary shall, if possible, be marked by a white line, a rope laid on the ground, or a fence. If flags or posts only are used to mark a boundary, the imaginary line joining such points shall be regarded as the boundary. An obstacle, or person, within the playing area shall not be regarded as a boundary unless so decided by the Umpires before the toss for innings. Sightscreens within, or partially within, the playing area shall be regarded as the boundary and when the ball strikes or passes within or under or directly over any part of the screen, a boundary shall be scored.

2. Runs Scored for Boundaries

Before the toss for innings, the Umpires shall agree with both captains the runs to be allowed for boundaries, and in deciding the allowance for them, the Umpires and captains shall be guided by the prevailing custom of the ground. The allowance for a boundary shall normally be 4 runs, and 6 runs for all hits pitching over the clear of the boundary line or fence, even though the ball has been previously touched by a fieldsman.

6 runs shall also be scored if a fieldsman, after catching a ball, carries it over the boundary. 6 runs shall not be scored when a ball struck by the striker hits a sightscreen full pitch if the screen is within, or partially within, the playing area, but if the ball is struck directly over a sightscreen so situated, 6 runs shall be scored.

3. A Boundary
A boundary shall be scored and signalled by the Umpire at the bowler's end whenever, in his opinion:

(*a*) A ball in play touches or crosses the boundary, however marked.

(*b*) A fieldsman with ball in hand touches or grounds any part of his person on or over a boundary line.

(*c*) A Fieldsman with ball in hand grounds any part of his person over a boundary fence or board. This allows the fieldsman to touch or lean on or over a boundary fence or board in preventing a boundary.

4. Runs Exceeding Boundary Allowance
The runs completed at the instant the ball reaches the boundary shall count if they exceed the boundary allowance.

5. Overthrows or Wilful Act of a Fieldsman
If the boundary results from an overthrow or from the wilful act of a fieldsman, any runs already completed and the allowance shall be added to the score. The run in progress shall count provided that the batsman have crossed at the instant of the throw or act.

20. LOST BALL

1. Runs Scored
If a ball in play cannot be found or recovered any fieldsman may call 'lost ball' when 6 runs shall be added to the score; but if more than 6 have been run before 'lost ball' is called, as many runs as have been completed shall be scored. The run in progress shall count provided that the batsmen have crossed at the instant of the call of 'lost ball'.

2. How Scored
The runs shall be added to the score of the striker if the ball has been struck, but otherwise to the score of byes, leg-byes, no-balls or wides as the case may be.

21. THE RESULT

1. A Win – Two-Innings Matches
The side which has scored a total of runs in excess of that scored by the opposing side in its two completed innings shall be the winners.

2. A Win – One-Innings Matches

(a) One-innings matches, unless played out as in 1 above, shall be decided on the first innings, but see Law 12.5 (Continuation After One Innings of Each Side).

(b) If the captains agree to continue play after the completion of one innings of each side in accordance with Law 12.5 (Continuation After One Innings of Each side) and a result is not achieved on the second innings, the first innings result shall stand.

3. Umpires Awarding a Match

(a) A match shall be lost by a side which, during the match, (i) refuses to play, or (ii) concedes defeat, and the Umpires shall award the match to the other side.

(b) Should both batsmen at the wickets or the fielding side leave the field at any time without the agreement of the Umpires, this shall constitute a refusal to play and, on appeal, the Umpires shall award the match to the other side in accordance with (a) above.

4. A Tie

The result of a match shall be a tie when the scores are equal at the conclusion of play, but only if the side batting last has completed its innings.

If the scores of the completed first innings of a one-day match are equal, it shall be a tie but only if the match has not been played out to a further conclusion.

5. A Draw

A match not determined in any of the ways as in 1, 2, 3 and 4 above shall count as a draw.

6. Correctness of Result

Any decision as to the correctness of the scores shall be the responsibility of the Umpires. See Law 3.14 (Correctness of Scores).

If, after the Umpires and players have left the field, in the belief that the match has been concluded, the Umpires decide that a mistake in scoring has occurred, which affects the result, and provided time has not been reached, they shall order play to resume and to continue until the agreed finishing time unless a result is reached earlier.

If the Umpires decide that a mistake has occurred and time has been reached, the Umpires shall immediately inform both captains of the necessary corrections to the scores and, if applicable, to the results.

7. Acceptance of Result

In accepting the scores as notified by the scorers and agreed by the Umpires, the captains of both sides thereby accept the result.

22. THE OVER

1. Number of Balls
The ball shall be bowled from each wicket alternately in overs of either six or eight balls according to agreement before the match.

2. Call of 'Over'
When the agreed number of balls has been bowled, and as the ball becomes dead or when it becomes clear to the Umpire at the bowler's end that both the fielding side and the batsmen at the wicket have ceased to regard the ball as in play, the Umpire shall call 'over' before leaving the wicket.

3. No-ball or Wide-ball
Neither a no-ball nor a wide-ball shall be reckoned as one of the over.

4. Umpire Miscounting
If an Umpire miscounts the number of balls, the over as counted by the Umpire shall stand.

5. Bowler Changing Ends
A bowler shall be allowed to change ends as often as desired provided only that he does not bowl two overs consecutively in an innings.

6. The Bowler Finishing an Over
A bowler shall finish an over in progress unless he be incapacitated or be suspended under Law 42.8 (The Bowling of Fast Short-pitched Balls), 42.9 (The Bowling of Fast High Full Pitches), 42.10 (Time Wasting) and 42.11 (Players Damaging the Pitch). If an over is left incomplete for any reason at the start of an interval or interruption of play, it shall be finished on the resumption of play.

7. Bowler Incapacitated or Suspended During an Over
If, for any reason, a bowler is incapacitated while running up to bowl the first ball of an over, or is incapacitated or suspended during an over, the Umpire shall call the signal 'dead ball' and another bowler shall be allowed to bowl or complete the over from the same end, provided only that he shall not bowl two overs, or part thereof, consecutively in one innings.

8. Position of Non-Striker
The batsman at the bowler's end shall normally stand on the opposite

side of the wicket to that from which the ball is being delivered, unless a request to do otherwise is granted by the Umpire.

23. DEAD BALL

1. The Ball Becomes Dead, when:
(a) It is finally settled in the hands of the wicket-keeper or the bowler.
(b) It reaches or pitches over the boundary.
(c) A batsman is out.
(d) Whether played or not, it lodges in the clothing or equipment of a batsman or the clothing of an Umpire.
(e) A ball lodges in a protective helmet worn by a member of the fielding side.
(f) A penalty is awarded under Law 20 (Lost Ball) or Law 41.1 (Fielding the Ball).
(g) The Umpire calls 'over' or 'time'.

2. Either Umpire Shall Call and Signal 'Dead Ball', when:
(a) He intervenes in a case of unfair play.
(b) A serious injury to a player or Umpire occurs.
(c) He is satisfied that, for an adequate reason, the Striker is not ready to receive the ball and makes no attempt to play it.
(d) The bowler drops the ball accidentally before delivery, or the ball does not leave his hand for any reason.
(e) One or both bails fall from the Striker's wicket before he receives delivery.
(f) He leaves his normal position for consultation.
(g) He is required to do so under Laws 26.3 (Disallowance of Leg-byes), etc.

3. The Ball Ceases to be Dead, when:
The bowler starts his run up or bowling action.

4. The Ball is Not Dead, when:
(a) It strikes an Umpire (unless it lodges in his dress).
(b) The wicket is broken or struck down (unless a batsman is out thereby).
(c) An unsuccessful appeal is made.
(d) The wicket is broken accidentally either by the bowler during his delivery or by a batsman in running.
(e) The Umpire has called 'no ball' or 'wide'.

24. NO-BALL

1. Mode of Delivery
The Umpire shall indicate to the striker whether the bowler intends to bowl over or round the wicket, overarm or underarm, or right- or left-handed. Failure on the part of the bowler to indicate in advance a change in his mode of delivery is unfair and the Umpire shall call and signal 'no-ball'.

2. Fair Delivery – The Arm
For a delivery to be fair the ball must be bowled not thrown. If either Umpire is not entirely satisfied with the absolute fairness of a delivery in this respect he shall call the signal 'no-ball' instantly upon delivery.

3. Fair Delivery – The Feet
The Umpire at the bowler's wicket shall call and signal 'no-ball' if he is not satisfied that in the delivery stride:

(a) The bowler's back foot has landed within and not touching the return crease or its forward extension; or

(b) Some part of the front foot whether grounded or raised was behind the popping crease.

4. Bowler Throwing at Striker's Wicket Before Delivery
If the Bowler, before delivering the ball, throws it at the striker's wicket in an attempt to run him out, the Umpire shall call and signal 'no-ball'. See Law 42.12 (Batsman Unfairly Stealing a Run) and Law 38 (Run Out).

5. Bowler Attempting to Run Out Non-Striker Before Delivery
If the bowler, before delivering the ball, attempts to run out the non-Striker, any runs which result shall be allowed and shall be scored as no-balls. Such an attempt shall not count as a ball in the over. The Umpire shall not call 'no-ball'. See Law 42.12 (Batsman Unfairly Stealing a Run).

6. Infringement of Laws by a Wicket-Keeper or Fieldsman
The Umpire shall call and signal 'no-ball' in the event of the wicket-keeper infringing Law 40.1 (Position of Wicket-Keeper) or a fieldsman infringing Law 41.2 (Limitation of On-Side Fieldsman) or Law 41.3 (Position of Fieldsman).

7. Revoking a Call
An Umpire shall revoke the call 'no-ball' if the ball does not leave the

bowler's hand for any reason. See Law 23.2 (Either Umpire Shall Call and Signal 'Dead Ball').

8. Penalty
A penalty of one run for a no-ball shall be scored if no runs are made otherwise.

9. Runs From a No-ball
The striker may hit a no-ball and whatever runs result shall be added to his score. Runs made otherwise from a no-ball shall be scored no balls.

10. Out From a No-ball
The striker shall be out (from a no-ball if he breaks Law 34 (Hit the Ball Twice) and either batsman may be run out or shall be given out if either breaks Law 33 (Handled the Ball) or Law 37 (Obstructing the Field).

11. Batsman Given Out Off a No-ball
Should a batsman be given out off a no-ball the penalty for bowling it shall stand unless runs are otherwise scored.

25. WIDE-BALL

1. Judging a Wide
If the bowler bowls the ball so high over or so wide of the wicket that, in the opinion of the Umpire it passes out of reach of the striker, standing in a normal guard position, the Umpire shall call the signal 'wide-ball' as soon as it has passed the line of the Striker's wicket.

The Umpire shall not adjudge a ball as being a wide if:

(*a*) The striker, by moving from his guard position, causes the ball to pass out of his reach.

(*b*) The striker moves and thus brings the ball within his reach.

2. Penalty
A penalty of one run for a wide shall be scored if no runs are made otherwise.

3. Ball Coming to Rest in Front of the Striker
If a ball which the Umpire considers to have been delivered comes to rest in front of the line of the striker's wicket, 'wide' shall not be called. The striker has a right, without interference from the fielding side, to make one attempt to hit the ball. If the fielding side interfere, the Umpire shall replace the ball where it came to rest and shall order the

fieldsmen to resume the places they occupied in the field before the ball was delivered.

The Umpire shall call the signal 'dead ball' as soon as it is clear that the striker does not intend to hit the ball, or after the striker has made one unsuccessful attempt to hit the ball.

4. Revoking a Call
The Umpire shall revoke the call if the striker hits a ball which has been called 'wide'.

5. Ball Not Dead
The ball does not become dead on the call of 'wide-ball' – see Law 23.4 (The Ball is Not Dead).

6. Runs Resulting from a Wide
All runs which are run or result from a wide ball which is not a no ball shall be scored wide balls, or if no runs are made one shall be scored.

7. Out from a Wide
The striker shall be out from a wide ball if he breaks Law 35 (Hit Wicket) or Law 39 (Stumped). Either batsman may be run out and shall be out if he breaks Law 33 (Handled the Ball) or Law 37 (Obstructing the Field).

8. Batsman Given Out Off a Wide
Should a batsman be given out off a wide, the penalty for bowling it shall stand unless runs are otherwise made.

26. BYE AND LEG-BYE

1. Byes
If the ball, not having been called 'wide' or 'no-ball' passes the striker without touching his bat or person, and any runs are obtained, the Umpire shall signal 'bye' and the run or runs shall be credited as such to the batting side.

2. Leg-byes
If the ball, not having been called 'wide' or 'no-ball' is unintentionally deflected by the striker's dress or person, except a hand holding the bat, and any runs are obtained the Umpire shall signal 'leg-bye' and the run or runs so scored shall be credited as such to the batting side.

Such leg-byes shall only be scored if, in the opinion of the Umpire, the striker has:

(*a*) Attempted to play the ball with his bat; or

(*b*) Tried to avoid being hit by the ball.

3. Disallowance of Leg-byes

In the case of a deflection by the striker's person, other than in 2(*a*) and (*b*) above, the Umpire shall call and signal 'dead ball' as soon as one run has been completed or when it is clear that a run is not being attempted or the ball has reached the boundary.

On the call and signal of 'dead ball' the batsmen shall return to their original ends and no runs shall be allowed.

27. APPEALS

1. Time of Appeals

The Umpires shall not give a batsman out unless appealed to by the other side which shall be done prior to the bowler beginning his run-up or bowling action to deliver the next ball. Under Law 23.1 (*g*) (The Ball Becomes Dead) the ball is dead on 'over' being called; this does not, however, invalidate an appeal made prior to the first ball of the following over provided 'time' has not been called. See Law 17.1 (Call of Time).

2. An Appeal 'How's That?'

An appeal 'How's That?' shall cover all ways of being out.

3. Answering Appeals

The Umpire at the bowler's wicket shall answer appeals before the other Umpire in all cases except those arising out of Law 35 (Hit Wicket) or Law 39 (Stumped) or Law 38 (Run Out) when this occurs at the striker's wicket.

When either Umpire has given a batsman not out, the other Umpire shall, within his jurisidction, answer the appeal or a further appeal, provided it is made in time in accordance with 1 (Time of Appeals) above.

4. Consultation by Umpires

An Umpire may consult with the other Umpire on a point of fact which the latter may have been in a better position to see and shall then give his decision. If, after consultation, there is still doubt remaining the decision shall be in favour of the Batsman.

5. Batsman Leaving his Wicket under a Misapprehension

The Umpires shall intervene if satisfied that a batsman, not having been given out, has left his wicket under a misapprehension that he has been dismissed.

6. Umpire's Decision
The Umpire's decision is final. He may alter his decision, provided that such alteration is made promptly.

7. Withdrawal of an Appeal
In exceptional circumstances the captain of the fielding side may seek permission of the Umpire to withdraw an appeal providing the outgoing batsman has not left the playing area. If this is allowed, the Umpire shall cancel his decision.

28. THE WICKET IS DOWN

1. Wicket Down
The wicket is down if:
   (a) Either the ball or the striker's bat or person completely removes either bail from the top of the stumps. A disturbance of a bail, whether temporary or not, shall not constitute a complete removal, but the wicket is down if a bail in falling lodges between two of the stumps.
   (b) Any player completely removes with his hand or arm a bail from the top of the stumps, providing that the ball is held in that hand or in the hand of the arm so used.
   (c) When both bails are off, a stump is struck out of the ground by the ball, or a player strikes or pulls a stump out of the ground, providing that the ball is held in the hand(s) or in the hand of the arm so used.

2. One Bail Off
If one bail is off, it shall be sufficient for the purpose of putting the wicket down to remove the remaining bail, or to strike or pull any of the three stumps out of the ground in any of the ways stated in 1 above.

3. All the Stumps Out of the Ground
If all the stumps are out of the ground, the fielding side shall be allowed to put back one or more stumps in order to have an opportunity of putting the wicket down.

4. Dispensing with Bails
If owing to the strength of the wind, it has been agreed to dispense with the bails, the decision as to when the wicket is down is one for the Umpires to decide on the facts before them. In such circumstances and if

the Umpires so decide the wicket shall be held to be down even though a stump has not been struck out of the ground.

29. BATSMAN OUT OF HIS GROUND

1. When out of his Ground
A batsman shall be considered to be out of his ground unless some part of his bat in his hand or of his person is grounded behind the line of the popping crease.

30. BOWLED

1. Out Bowled
The striker shall be out bowled if:

(a) His wicket is bowled down, even if the ball first touches his bat or person.

(b) He breaks his wicket by hitting or kicking the ball on to it before the completion of a stroke, or as a result of attempting to guard his wicket. See Law 34.1 (Out Hit the Ball Twice).

31. TIMED OUT

1. Out Timed Out
An incoming Batsman shall be out timed out if he wilfully takes more than two minutes to come in – the two minutes being timed from the moment a wicket falls until the new batsman steps on to the field of play.

If this is not complied with and if the Umpire is satisfied that the delay was wilful and if an appeal is made, the new batsman shall be given out by the Umpire at the bowler's end.

2. Time to be Added
The time taken by the Umpires to investigate the cause of the delay shall be added at the normal close of play.

32. CAUGHT

1. Out Caught
The striker shall be out caught if the ball touches his bat or if it touches

below the wrist his hand or glove, holding the bat, and is subsequently held by a fieldsman before it touches the ground.

2. A Fair Catch
A catch shall be considered to have been fairly made if:

(*a*) The fieldsman is within the field of play throughout the act of making the catch.

(i) The act of making the catch shall start from the time when the fieldsman first handles the ball and shall end when he both retains complete control over the further disposal of the ball and remains within the field of play.

(ii) In order to be within the field of play, the fieldsman may not touch or ground any part of his person on or over a boundary line. When the boundary is marked by a fence or board the fieldsman may not ground any part of his person over the boundary fence or board, but may touch or lean over the boundary fence or board in completing the catch.

(*b*) The ball is hugged to the body of the catcher or accidentally lodges in his dress or, in the case of the wicket-keeper, in his pads. However, a striker may not be caught if a ball lodges in a protective helmet worn by a fieldsman, in which case the Umpire shall call the signal 'dead ball'. See Law 23 (Dead Ball).

(*c*) The ball does not touch the ground even though a hand holding it does so in effecting the catch.

(*d*) A fieldsman catches the ball, after it has been lawfully played a second time by the striker, but only if the ball has not touched the ground since being first struck.

(*e*) A fieldsman catches the ball after it has touched an Umpire, another fieldsman or the other batsman. However, a striker may not be caught if a ball has touched a protective helmet worn by a fieldsman.

(*f*) The ball is caught off an obstruction within the boundary provided it has not previously been agreed to regard the obstruction as a boundary.

3. Scoring of Runs
If a striker is caught, no runs shall be scored.

33. HANDLED THE BALL

1. Out Handled the Ball
Either batsman on appeal shall be out handled the ball if he wilfully touches the ball while in play with the hand not holding the bat unless he does so with the consent of the opposite side.

34. HIT THE BALL TWICE

1. Out Hit the Ball Twice
The striker, on appeal, shall be out hit the ball twice if, after the ball is struck or is stopped by any part of his person, he wilfully strikes it again with his bat or person except for the sole purpose of guarding his wicket: this he may do with his bat or any part of his person other than his hands, but see Law 37.2 (Obstructing a Ball From Being Caught).

For the purpose of this Law, a hand holding the bat shall be regarded as part of the bat.

2. Returning the Ball to a Fieldsman
The striker, on appeal, shall be out under this Law, if, without the consent of the opposite side he uses his bat or person to return the ball to any of the fielding side.

3. Runs from Ball Lawfully Struck Twice
No runs except those which result from an overthrow or penalty, see Law 41 (The Fieldsman), shall be scored from a ball lawfully struck twice.

35. HIT WICKET

1. Out Hit Wicket
The striker shall be out hit wicket if, while the ball is in play:

(a) His wicket is broken with any part of his person, dress, or equipment as a result of any action taken by him in preparing to receive or in receiving a delivery, or in setting off for his first run, immediately after playing, or playing at, the ball.

(b) He hits down his wicket whilst lawfully making a second stroke for the purpose of guarding his wicket within the provisions of Law 34.1 (Out Hit the Ball Twice).

36. LEG BEFORE WICKET

1. Out LBW
The striker shall be out LBW in the circumstances set out below:

(a) *Striker Attempting to Play the Ball.* The striker shall be out LBW if he first intercepts with any part of his person, dress or equipment a fair ball which would have hit the wicket and which has not previously touched his bat or a hand holding the bat, provided that:

(i) The ball pitched in a straight line between wicket and wicket or on the off side of the striker's wicket, or in the case of a ball intercepted full pitch would have pitched in a straight line between wicket and wicket; and

(ii) the point of impact is in a straight line between wicket and wicket, even if above the level of the bails.

(b) *Striker Making No Attempt to Play the Ball.* The striker shall be out LBW even if the ball is intercepted outside the line of the off-stump, if, in the opinion of the Umpire, he has made no genuine attempt to play the ball with his bat, but has intercepted the ball with some part of his person and if the circumstances set out in (a) above apply.

37. OBSTRUCTING THE FIELD

1. Wilful Obstruction
Either batsman, on appeal, shall be out obstructing the field if he wilfully obstructs the opposite side by word or action.

2. Obstructing a Ball from Being Caught
The striker, on appeal, shall be out should wilful obstruction by either batsman prevent a catch being made.

This shall apply even though the striker causes the obstruction in lawfully guarding his wicket under the provisions of Law 34. See Law 34.1 (Out Hit the Ball Twice).

38. RUN OUT

1. Out Run Out
Either batsman shall be out run out if in running or at any time while the ball is in play – except in the circumstances described in Law 39 (Stumped) he is out of his ground and his wicket is put down by the opposite side. If, however, a batsman in running makes good his ground he shall not be out run out, if he subsequently leaves his ground, in order to avoid injury, and the wicket is put down.

2. 'No-ball' Called
If a no-ball has been called, the striker shall not be given run out unless he attempts to run.

3. Which Batsman is Out
If the batsmen have crossed in running, he who runs for the wicket which is put down shall be out; if they have not crossed, he who has left the wicket which is put down shall be out. If a batsman remains in his ground

or returns to his ground and the other batsman joins him there, the latter shall be out if his wicket is put down.

4. Scoring of Runs
If a batsman is run out, only that run which is being attempted shall not be scored. If however an injured striker himself is run out, no runs shall be scored. See Law 2.7 (Transgression of the Laws by an Injured Batsman or Runner).

39. STUMPED

1. Out Stumped
The striker shall be out stumped if, in receiving a ball, not being a no-ball, he is out of his ground otherwise than in attempting a run and the wicket is put down by the wicket-keeper without the intervention of another fieldsman.

2. Action by the Wicket-Keeper
The wicket-keeper may take the ball in front of the wicket in an attempt to stump the striker only if the ball has touched the bat or person of the striker.

40. THE WICKET-KEEPER

1. Position of Wicket-Keeper
The wicket-keeper shall remain wholly behind the wicket until a ball delivered by the bowler touches the bat or person of the striker, or passes the wicket, or until the striker attempts a run.

In the event of the wicket-keeper contravening this Law, the Umpire at the striker's end shall call and signal 'no-ball' at the instant of delivery or as soon as possible thereafter.

2. Restriction on Actions of the Wicket-Keeper
If the wicket-keeper interferes with the striker's right to play the ball and to guard his wicket, the striker shall not be out, except under Laws 33 (Handled the Ball), 34 (Hit the Ball Twice), 37 (Obstructing the Field) and 38 (Run Out).

3. Interference with the Wicket-Keeper by the Striker
If in the legitimate defence of his wicket, the striker interferes with the wicket-keeper, he shall not be out, except as provided for in Law 37.2 (Obstructing a Ball From Being Caught).

41. THE FIELDSMAN

1. Fielding the Ball
The fieldsman may stop the ball with any part of his person, but if he wilfully stops it otherwise, 5 runs shall be added to the run or runs already scored; if no run has been scored 5 penalty runs shall be awarded. The run in progress shall count provided that the batsmen have crossed at the instant of the act. If the ball has been struck, the penalty shall be added to the score of the striker, but otherwise to the score of byes, leg-byes, no-balls or wides as the case may be.

2. Limitation of On-Side Fieldsmen
The number of on-side fieldsmen behind the popping crease at the instant of the bowler's delivery shall not exceed two. In the event of infringement by the fielding side the Umpire at the striker's end shall call and signal 'no-ball' at the instant of delivery or as soon as possible thereafter.

3. Position of Fieldsmen
Whilst the ball is in play and until the ball has made contact with the bat or the striker's person or has passed his bat, no fieldsman, other than the bowler, may stand on or have any part of his person extended over the pitch [measuring 22yd (20.12m) × 10ft (3.05m)]. In the event of a fieldsman contravening this Law, the Umpire at the bowler's end shall call and signal 'no-ball' at the instant of delivery or as soon as possible thereafter. See Law 40.1 (Position of Wicket-Keeper).

4. Fieldsmen's Protective Helmets
Protective helmets, when not in use by members of the fielding side, shall only be placed, if above the surface, on the ground behind the wicket-keeper. In the event of the ball, when in play, striking a helmet whilst in this position, 5 penalty runs shall be awarded, as laid down in Law 41.1 and Note (a).
Note
   (a) **Batsmen Changing Ends**
The 5 runs referred to in 1 and 4 above are a penalty and the batsmen do not change ends solely by reason of this penalty.

42. UNFAIR PLAY

1. Responsibility of Captains
The captains are responsible at all times for ensuring that play is conducted within the spirit of the game as well as within the Laws.

2. Responsibility of Umpires
The Umpires are the sole judges of fair and unfair play.

3. Intervention by the Umpire
The Umpires shall intervene without appeal by calling and signalling 'dead ball' in the case of unfair play, but should not otherwise interfere with the progress of the game except as required to do so by the Laws.

4. Lifting the Seam
A player shall not lift the seam of the ball for any reason. Should this be done, the Umpires shall change the ball for one of similar condition to that in use prior to the contravention.

5. Changing the Condition of the Ball
Any member of the fielding side may polish the ball provided that such polishing wastes no time and that no artificial substance is used. No one shall rub the ball on the ground or use any artificial substance or take any other action to alter the condition of the ball.

In the event of a contravention of this Law, the Umpires, after consultation, shall change the ball for one of similar condition to that in use prior to the contravention.

This Law does not prevent a member of the fielding side from drying a wet ball, or removing mud from the ball.

6. Incommoding the Striker
An Umpire is justified in intervening under this Law and shall call and signal 'dead ball' if, in his opinion, any player of the fielding side incommodes the striker by any noise or action while he is receiving a ball.

7. Obstruction of a Batsman in Running
It shall be considered unfair if any fieldsman wilfully obstructs a batsman in running. In these circumstances the Umpire shall call and signal 'dead ball' and allow any completed runs and the run in progress or alternatively any boundary scored.

8. The Bowling of Fast Short-Pitched Balls
The bowling of fast short-pitched balls is unfair if, in the opinion of the Umpire at the bowler's end, it constitutes an attempt to intimidate the striker.

Umpires shall consider intimidation to be the deliberate bowling of fast short-pitched balls which by their length, height and direction are intended or likely to inflict physical injury on the striker. The relative skill of the striker shall also be taken into consideration.

In the event of such unfair bowling, the Umpire at the Bowler's end shall adopt the following procedure:

(*a*) In the first instance the Umpire shall call and signal 'no-ball', caution the bowler and inform the other Umpire, the captain of the fielding side and the batsmen of what has occurred.

(*b*) If this caution is ineffective, he shall repeat the above procedure and indicate to the bowler that this is a final warning.

(*c*) Both the above caution and final warning shall continue to apply even though the bowler may later change ends.

(*d*) Should the above warnings prove ineffective the Umpire at the bowler's end shall:

(i) At the first repetition call and signal 'no-ball' and when the ball is dead direct the captain to take the bowler off forthwith and to complete the over with another bowler, provided that the bowler does not bowl two overs or part thereof consecutively. See Law 22.7 (Bowler Incapacitated or Suspended during an Over).

(ii) Not allow the bowler, thus taken off, to bowl again in the same innings.

(iii) Report the occurrence to the captain of the batting side as soon as the players leave the field for an interval

(iv) Report the occurrence to the executive of the fielding side and to any governing body responsible for the match who shall take any further action which is considered to be appropriate against the bowler concerned.

9. The Bowling of Fast High Full Pitches
The bowling of fast high full pitches is unfair.

In the event of such unfair bowling the Umpire at the bowler's end shall adopt the procedures of caution, final warning action against the bowler and reporting as set out in 8, above.

10. Time Wasting
Any form of time wasting is unfair.

(*a*) In the event of the captain of the fielding side wasting time or allowing any member of his side to waste time, the Umpire at the bowler's end shall adopt the following procedure:

(i) In the first instance he shall caution the captain of the fielding side and inform the other Umpire of what has occurred.

(ii) If this caution is ineffective he shall repeat the above procedure and indicate to the captain that this is a final warning.

(iii) The Umpire shall report the occurrence to the captain of the batting side as soon as the players leave the field for an interval.

(iv) Should the above procedure prove ineffective the Umpire shall report the occurrence to the executive of the fielding side and to any governing body responsible for that match who shall take appropriate action against the captain and the players concerned.

(*b*) In the event of a bowler taking unnecessarily long to bowl an over the Umpire at the bowler's end shall adopt the procedures, other than the calling of 'no-ball', of caution, final warning, action against the bowler and reporting.

(*c*) In the event of a batsman wasting time other than in the manner described in Law 31 (Timed Out), the Umpire at the bowler's end shall adopt the following procedure:

(i) In the first instance he shall caution the batsman and inform the other Umpire at once, and the captian of the batting side, as soon as the players leave the field for an interval, of what has occurred.

(ii) If this proves ineffective, he shall repeat the caution, indicate to the batsman that this is a final warning and inform the other Umpire

(iii) The Umpire shall report the occurrence to both captains as soon as the players leave the field for an interval.

(iv) Should the above procedure prove ineffective, the Umpire shall report the occurrence to the executive of the batting side and to any governing body responsible for that match who shall take appropriate action against the player concerned.

11. Players Damaging the Pitch

The Umpires shall intervene and prevent players from causing damage to the pitch which may assist the bowlers of either side.

(*a*) In the event of any member of the fielding side damaging the pitch the Umpire shall follow the procedure of caution, final warning and reporting as set out in 10 (*a*) above.

(*b*) In the event of a bowler contravening this Law by runninng down the pitch after delivering the ball, the Umpire at the bowler's end shall first caution the bowler. If this caution is ineffective the Umpire shall adopt the procedures as set out in 8, other than the calling and signalling of 'no-ball'.

(*c*) In the event of a batsman damaging the pitch the Umpire at the bowler's end shall follow the procedures of caution, final warning and reporting as set out in 10 (*c*) above.

12. Batsman Unfairly Stealing a Run

Any attempt by the batsman to steal a run during the bowler's run-up is unfair. Unless the bowler attempts to run out either batsman – see Law 24.4 (Bowler Throwing at Striker's Wicket Before Delivery) and Law 24.5 (Bowler Attempting to Run Out Non-Striker Before Delivery) –

the Umpire shall call and signal 'dead ball' as soon as the batsmen cross in any such attempt to run. The batsmen shall then return to their original wickets.

13. Players' Conduct
In the event of a player failing to comply with the instructions of an Umpire, criticising his decisions by word or action, or showing dissent, or generally behaving in a manner which might bring the game into disrepute, the Umpire concerned shall, in the first place, report the matter to the other Umpire and to the player's captain requesting the latter to take action. If this proves ineffective, the Umpire shall report the incident as soon as possible to the executive of the player's team and to any governing body responsible for the match, who shall take any further action which is considered appropriate against the player or players concerned.

Reprinted by permission of MCC. Copies of the current edition of the official Laws of Cricket with full notes and interpretations can be obtained from MCC at Lord's Cricket Ground, London NW8 8QN.

THE RULES OF

Curling

'The Rink'

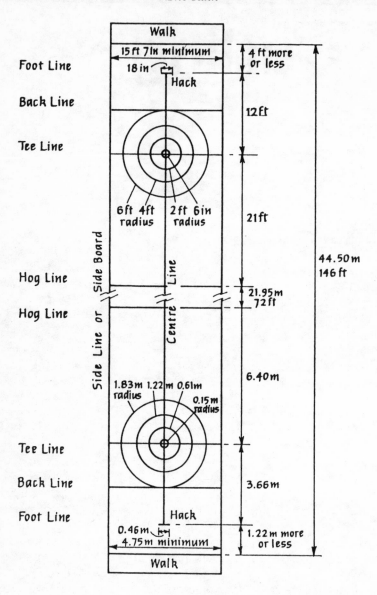

Curling

SECTION A. THE RINK

1. The length of the playing area shall be 42.06m (138ft). It is recommended that the width of the playing area shall be a minimum of 4.75m (15ft 7in) and that, where possible, the ice be continued a further 1.22m (4ft) or more behind each Foot Line.

2. The length of the Rink from the Foot Line to the Tee shall, subject to the provisions of Rules 5 (Section A) and 1 and 2 (Section H) be 38.40m (126ft).

3. The Tees shall be 34.75m (114ft) apart and – with the Tees as centres – Circles having radii of 1.22m (4ft) and 1.83m (6ft) shall be drawn.

4. Additional inner Circles may also be drawn. Dividing lines must be drawn from Back Line or barriers placed between adjoining Rinks.

5. In alignment with the Tees, lines, to be called Centre Lines, shall be drawn from Foot Line to Foot Line and through each Tee; the Foot Line, to be 45.72cm (18in) in length, shall be drawn at right angles, on which at 7.62cm (3in) from the Centre Line, the inside edge of the Hack shall be placed. When Hack and Crampit are both being used in the same Rink, the Crampit shall be placed immediately behind the Hack except on outdoor ice when the heel of the Crampit will be placed on the Foot Line and the Hack, if used, placed immediately in front of the Crampit.

6. Other lines shall be drawn across the Rink at right angles to the Centre Lines as in the diagram, viz:

(*a*) A 'Hog Line', distant from each Tee, one-sixth part of the distance between the 'Foot Line' and the further Tee.

(*b*) A 'Tee Line', from Dividing Line to Dividing Line or Barrier to Barrier (or Side Board to Side Board) and through each Tee.

(*c*) A 'Back Line' – the back edge of the Back Line shall be at a tangent to the 6ft Circle at the point where the Centre Line crosses the Back Line.

7. All lines shall be as in the diagram which shall form part of these Rules subject to Rules 1 and 2 (Section H).

SECTION B – THE CURLING STONE

1. Shape, Weight and Dimensions of Stone

(*a*) Curling Stones shall be of a circular shape.

(*b*) No Stone, including handle and bolt, shall be of greater weight than 19.96kg (44lb), or of greater circumference than 91.44cm (36in), or of less height than 11.43cm (4.5in).

2. Substitution and Breaking of Stone

(*a*) No Stone shall be substituted for another (except under Rules 2 (*b*) (Section B) or 5 (Section C)) after a game has started.

(*b*) Should a Stone be broken, the largest fragment shall be counted for that End, the player using another Stone, or another pair, thereafter.

3. Stone Rolling Over, Handle Quitting

(*a*) Any Stone which rolls over in its course, or comes to rest on its side or top, shall be removed from play immediately.

(*b*) Should the handle quit the Stone in delivery, the player is entitled to replay the shot.

SECTION C – DELIVERY OF STONE

1. Left-handed players shall play from the Hack or Crampit placed on the right-hand side of the Centre-Line and right-handed players shall play from the Hack or Crampit placed on the left-hand side of the Centre Line.

2. Delivery from Wrong Hack or Crampit

(*a*) A Stone delivered from the wrong Hack or Crampit should, if possible, be stopped in its progress and removed from the ice.

(*b*) However, if the Stone so played has come to rest or struck another Stone, the played Stone shall be removed from play and the displaced Stone or Stones be placed as nearly as possible where they originally were, to the satisfaction of the opposing Skip; both Skips should agree upon the position, but failing agreement, the Umpire shall decide.

3. Release of Stone

(*a*) In the delivery of the Stone, the Stone shall be clearly seen to be released from the hand before the Stone reaches the nearer Hog Line.

(*b*) If the player fails to so release the Stone, it shall be removed from play immediately by the playing team. If the Stone has struck another Stone, the played Stone shall be removed from play by the playing team and any displaced Stone shall be placed as nearly as possible where it orginally lay to the satisfaction of the opposing Skip.

4. Holding Stone, Returning for Another Delivery

No player may hold his Stone and return to the Hack or Crampit for another delivery if the Stone has reached the nearer Tee Line, in which event the Stone be removed from play by the playing side.

5. Playing Wrong Stone

Should a player play a wrong Stone, a Stone belonging to his team shall be put in its place.

6. Playing Out of Turn

(*a*) If a player should play out of turn in his team, the Stone so played should, if possible, be stopped in its progress and returned to the player.

(*b*) Should the mistake not be discovered until after the Stone has come to rest or has struck another Stone, the end shall be continued, as if it had been played properly from the beginning, but the missed Stone shall be played by the player missing his turn as the last Stone for his side for that end.

(*c*) Where the Skips agree that a Stone has been missed but are unable to agree as to which player missed his turn, the Lead of the team which made the mistake shall play the last Stone for his team at that end.

(*d*) Where two Stones of a team are delivered in succession at the same end, the opposite Skip shall remove the Stone played by mistake, replace to his satisfaction any Stone displaced by the Stone played by mistake and continue the end as if the mistake had not occurred, and the player who delivered the Stone played by mistake shall redeliver it as the last Stone for his team at that end.

(*e*) Where a player delivers three Stones at one end, the end shall be continued as if the mistake had not occurred and the fourth player of his team shall deliver one Stone only at that end.

7. Wrongful Delivery

No player shall deliver a Stone, until the Stone delivered by the previous player has come to rest or until such time as any Stone whose movement has been generated by that Stone comes to rest. In case of infringement, the Stone shall be returned to the offending player who shall deliver that Stone correctly.

SECTION D – THE GAME

1. All games shall be:
(*a*) Of a certain number of ends; or
(*b*) By time
as may be agreed on, or as fixed by the Umpire at the outset (see Section I).

2. Composition of Team, Order of Play, Disqualification, Accident

(*a*) Every team of players shall be composed of four-a-side, each player using two Stones, and play each Stone alternately with his opponent.

(*b*) Any team not having its full complement of four players shall be disqualified except in the case of illness or accident during the game, in which case the first and second players shall play three Stones each.

(*c*) When, in a competition, owing to illness, accident or any other valid reason, a player is unable to play in any round, he may be replaced by another player as substitute, provided this substitute has not already taken part in that competition in any other team. A substitute may play in any position in any round but not higher than the position of the Curler he is replacing. The Skip shall declare any substitute in the first round of a competition or the team in the first round will be understood to be the entered team. No team shall take into play more than two substitutes, in any game, match or competition. All substitutes must be eligible in terms of the rules of the competition.

(*d*) The teams opposing each other shall settle by lot which side shall lead at the first end, after which the winners of the preceding end shall lead, and shall continue to do so if any extra ends be played.

(*e*) The rotation of play observed during the first end of a game shall not be changed.

(*f*) The Royal Club may modify the above Rules to meet with requirements of a specific competition.

3. Finishing of Games Played by Time

(*a*) When a game is being played by time, no end shall be started after the finishing time signal has been given, except where extra ends are required.

(*b*) If a time signal has not been given when the last Stone of the last played end has come to rest, then another end shall be played. (The intention of this Rule is that another end will not be started if, when the time signal is given, the Stone delivered by the previous player has not come to rest or any Stone whose movement has been generated by that Stone, has not come to rest.)

4. Stone Not Clearing Hog Line
A Stone which does not clear the farther Hog Line shall be a Hog and shall be removed from play immediately except where it has struck another Stone lying in play.

5. Stone Crossing Back Line
A Stone having crossed the Back Line, and lying clear of it, shall be removed from play immediately.

6. Stone Touching Sides of Rink
Any Stone which in its progress touches dividers on either side of the Rink shall be removed from play. But, if a Stone crosses a Dividing line drawn on the ice between Rinks or sheets and returns to finish within the Rink clear of the Dividing Line, it remains in play, provided it has not touched any object in the adjoining Rink (see 10(*b*)).

7. Running Stone Touched
(*a*) If, in sweeping or otherwise, a running Stone be touched by any of the side to which it belongs, or by their equipment, it shall be removed from play, but if by any of the opposing side it shall be placed where the Skip of the side to which it belongs shall direct, in a position as nearly as possible where he estimates it would have come to rest.

(*b*) Should the position of any Stone be altered by such affected Stone, the Skip opposed to the side at fault shall have the right to replace it in a position as nearly as possible where he estimates it rested before its position was altered.

8. Displaced Stones
(*a*) If a Stone which would have affected the course of a running Stone is displaced by the playing team, the running Stone shall be removed from play and any affected Stone shall be placed as nearly as possible where the opposing Skip considers it originally lay.

(*b*) If a Stone which would have affected the course of a running Stone is displaced by the opposing team the Skip of the playing team shall replace any affected Stone as nearly as possible where he considers it originally lay or would have come to rest.

(*c*) If displaced in a way other than stated in (*a*) and (*b*) of this rule, both Skips should agree on the positions to which the Stones are to be returned.

9. Measuring of Shots

(*a*) No Stone shall be measured by instrument until the last Stone of the end has come to rest except by the Umpire when requested by a Skip to decide whether or not a Stone is in play.

(*b*) Measurements shall be taken from the Tee to the nearest part of the Stone.

(*c*) If two or more Stones are so close to the Tee that the Umpire finds it impossible to make a decision, the end shall be scored as a blank end.

10. Scoring

(*a*) Games shall be decided by a majority of shots. A Team shall score one shot for every Stone which is nearer the Tee than any Stone of the opposing team.

(*b*) Every Stone which is not clearly outside the Outer Circle shall be eligible to count, even if touching a Dividing Line.

(*c*) In the event of the scores being equal, play may be continued for one or more ends, as may be agreed on, or as provided for by the conditions of the Game or Match, or as may be fixed by the Umpire.

(*d*) An end is decided when the Skips (or Acting Skips) in charge of the House at the time agree upon the score for that end.

SECTION E – THE SKIP: HIS AUTHORITY, PRIVILEGES, AND RESPONSIBILITIES

1. (*a*) The Skip has the exclusive direction of the game for his team.

(*b*) Subject to Rule 2 (*e*) Section D, he may play in any position in the game he pleases.

(*c*) When his turn to play comes, he shall select one of his players as Acting Skip.

(*d*) He may, however, return to the House for brief consultation.

(*e*) The Skip of the playing side has the choice of place, and he shall not be obstructed by the other Skip.

(*f*) Only Skips (or Acting Skips) are entitled to stand within or behind the Circle.

SECTION F – THE PLAYERS: THEIR DUTIES AND RESPONSIBILITIES

1. (*a*) Players, during the course of each end, shall be arranged along the sides, but well off the centre of the Rink.

(*b*) No player, except when sweeping acording to Rule, shall go upon the centre of the Rink.

(*c*) No player shall cross the Rink when:

(i) A player is about to play; or

(ii) In front of a Stone which is in motion.

(*d*) No player, other than the Skips and Acting Skips, shall stand within or behind the Circle while play is proceeding.

(*e*) Each player shall be ready to play immediately when his turn comes.

(*f*) A player shall not take more than a reasonable time to play.

(*g*) Where the Chief Umpire considers that play is unnecessarily slow, he shall notify the Skip of the team at fault that if their next Stone is not delivered within 30 seconds from the time he gives a signal, he will order the Stone to be removed from play immediately.

(*h*) No player shall use footwear or equipment which may damage the surface of the ice.

SECTION G – SWEEPING

1. The sweeping shall be under the direction of the Skips.

2. Method of Sweeping

The sweeping motion shall be from side to side across the entire running surface in front of the Stone and clearly finish to either side of the Stone.

3. Limitations of Sweeping

(*a*) The player's side may sweep the ice from Tee Line to Tee Line but any Stone set in motion by a played Stone may only be swept by the side to which it belongs, except behind the Tee Line, where both Skips have an equal right to sweep.

(*b*) Only the player in charge of the head shall be allowed to sweep behind the Tee Line and shall not start to sweep an opposing Stone until the Stone reaches the Line.

SECTION H – OUTDOOR GAMES

1. Shortening or Changing Rink

(*a*) If from any change of weather after a game has begun, or from any other reasonable cause, one side should desire to shorten the Rink, or to change to another, and if the two Skips cannot agree, the Umpire shall, after seeing one end played, determine whether and by how much the Rink shall be shortened, or whether it shall be changed, and his decision shall be final.

(*b*) In no case, however, shall the Rink be shortened to less than 29.26m (96 ft) from the Foot Line to the Tee.

(*c*) Should there be no Umpire, or should he be otherwise engaged, the two Skips may call in any neutral Curler to decide, and his powers shall be equal with those of an Umpire.

2. Stopping, Postponing a Game

(*a*) Should the Skips not agree, the Umpire shall, in the event of the ice appearing to him to be dangerous, stop the game.

(*b*) He shall postpone the game, even if begun, when the state of the ice is, in his opinion, not fitted for testing the Curling skill of the players.

(*c*) Except in very special circumstances, of which the Umpire shall be judge, the game or match shall not proceed, or be continued:

(i) When a thaw has fairly set in;

(ii) When snow is falling and likely to continue during the game or match; or

(iii) If darkness comes on to prevent the played Stones being well seen by players at the other end of the Rink.

(*d*) In every case of such postponement to another day the game or match, when renewed, must be begun anew.

3. Cleaning Rink

(*a*) At the completion of any end, either of the Skips may call upon all the players to clean and sweep the entire Rink.

(*b*) If objected to, this shall be subject to the approval of the Umpire.

4. Sweeping

When snow is falling or drifting, both Skips have equal right to clean and sweep the ice behind the Tee Line.

5. Reversing of Stone

During a game, the sole of a Stone may be reversed provided the player be ready when his turn comes.

SECTION I – THE UMPIRE

1. An Umpire may be appointed in any game, match or competition. He shall be a Member of the Royal Club and shall be acquainted with these Rules.

2. The duties and powers of an Umpire shall be the general superintendence of a game, match or competition, the power of settling disputed shots, enforcing these Rules and other questions that may arise in course of play.

3. He shall satisfy himself that all the players are duly qualified.

4. He may depute a neutral Curler who is a Member of the Royal Club and acquainted with the Rules to act in his stead.

5. His decision in respect of all questions affecting the game, match or competition shall be final.

SECTION J – THE CHIEF UMPIRE

1. The Chief Umpire shall hear and determine any appeals from a decision of an Umpire and his decision is final.

2. Where the Royal Club has authorised the Chief Umpire to do so he may intervene in any game at any time and give such directions concerning the conduct of the game as he considers proper.

THE SPIRIT OF CURLING

Curling is a game of skill and of traditions. A shot well executed is a delight to see and so, too, it is a fine thing to observe the time-honoured traditions of curling being applied in the true spirit of the game. Curlers play to win but never to humble their opponents. A true Curler would prefer to lose rather than win unfairly.

A good Curler never attempts to distract an opponent or otherwise prevent him from playing his best.

No Curler ever deliberately breaks a rule of the game or any of its traditions. But, if he should do so inadvertently and be aware of it, he is the first to divulge the breach.

While the main object of the game of curling is to determine the relative skill of the players, the spirit of the game demands good sportsmanship, kindly feeling and honurable conduct. This spirit should influence both the interpretation and application of the rules of the game and also the conduct of all participants on and off the ice.

Reprinted by permission of the Royal Caledonian Curling Club, to whom copyright in these Rules belongs.

THE RULES OF

Golf

Golf

SECTION I ETIQUETTE: COURTESY ON THE COURSE

Safety

Prior to playing a stroke or making a practice swing, the player should ensure that no one is standing close by or in a position to be hit by the club, the ball or any stones, pebbles, twigs or the like which may be moved by the stroke or swing.

Consideration for Other Players

The player who has the honour should be allowed to play before his opponent or fellow-competitor tees his ball.

No one should move, talk or stand close to or directly behind the ball or the hole when a player is addressing the ball or making a stroke.

In the interest of all, players should play without delay.

No player should play until the players in front are out of range.

Players searching for a ball should signal the players behind them to pass as soon as it becomes apparent that the ball will not easily be found. They should not search for 5 minutes before doing so. They should not continue play until the players following them have passed and are out of range.

When the play of a hole has been completed, players should immediately leave the putting green.

Priority on the Course

In the absence of special rules, two-ball matches should have precedence over and be entitled to pass any three- or four-ball match.

A single player has no standing and should give way to a match of any kind.

Any match playing a whole round is entitled to pass a match playing a shorter round.

If a match fails to keep its place on the course and loses more than one clear hole on the players in front, it should invite the match following to pass.

Care of the Course

Holes in Bunkers
Before leaving a bunker, a player should carefully fill up and smooth over all holes and footprints made by him.

Replace Divots; Repair Ball-Marks and Damage by Spikes
Through the green, a player should ensure that any turf cut or displaced by him is replaced at once and pressed down and that any damage to the putting green made by a ball is carefully repaired. Damage to the putting green caused by golf shoe spikes should be repaired on *completion of the hole*.

Damage to Green – Flagsticks, Bags, etc.
Players should ensure that, when putting down bags or the flagstick, no damage is done to the putting green and that neither they nor their caddies damage the hole by standing close to it, in handling the flagstick or in removing the ball from the hole. The flagstick should be properly replaced in the hole before the players leave the putting green. Players should not damage the putting green by leaning on their putters, particularly when removing the ball from the hole.

Golf Carts
Local notices regulating the movement of golf carts should be strictly observed.

Damage Through Practice Swings
In taking practice swings, players should avoid causing damage to the course, particularly the tees, by removing divots.

SECTION II DEFINITIONS

Addressing the Ball
A player has 'addressed the ball' when he has taken his stance and has also grounded his club, except that in a hazard a player has addressed the ball when he has taken his stance.

Advice
'Advice' is any counsel or suggestion which could influence a player in determining his play, the choice of a club or the method of making a stroke.

Information on the Rules or on matters of public information, such as the position of hazards or the flagstick on the putting green, is not advice.

Ball Deemed to Move
See 'Move or Moved'.

Ball Holes
See 'Holed'.

Ball Lost
See 'Lost Ball'.

Ball in Play
A ball is 'in play' as soon as the player has made a stroke on the teeing ground. It remains in play until holed out, except when it is lost, out of bounds or lifted, or another ball has been substituted under an applicable Rule, whether or not such Rule permits substitution; a ball so substituted becomes the ball in play.

Bunker
A 'bunker' is a hazard consisting of a prepared area of ground, often a hollow, from which turf or soil has been removed and replaced with sand or the like. Grass-covered ground bordering or within a bunker is not part of the bunker. The margin of a bunker extends vertically downwards, but not upwards.

Caddie
A 'caddie' is one who carries or handles a player's clubs during play and otherwise assists him in accordance with the Rules.

When one caddie is employed by more than one player, he is always deemed to be the caddie of the player whose ball is involved, and equipment carried by him is deemed to be that player's equipment, except when the caddie acts upon specific directions of another player, in which case he is considered to be that other player's caddie.

Casual Water
'Casual water' is any temporary accumulation of water on the course which is visible before or after the player takes his stance and is not in a

water hazard. Snow and ice are either casual water or loose impedi-ments, at the option of the player, except that manufactured ice is an obstruction. Dew is not casual water.

Committee
The 'Committee' is the committee in charge of the competition or, if the matter does not arise in a competition, the committee in charge of the course.

Competitor
A 'competitor' is a player in a stroke competition. A 'fellow-competitor' is any person with whom the competitor plays. Neither is partner of the other.

In stroke play foursome and four-ball competitions, where the context so admits, the word 'competitor' or 'fellow-competitor' includes his partner.

Course
The 'course' is the whole area within which play is permitted (see Rule 33-2).

Equipment
'Equipment' is anything used, worn or carried by or for the player except any ball he has played at the hole being played and any small object, such as a coin or a tee, when used to mark the position of a ball or the extent of an area in which a ball is to be dropped. Equipment includes a golf cart, whether or not motorised. If such a cart is shared by more than one player, its status under the Rules is the same as that of a caddie employed by more than on player. See 'Caddie'.

Fellow-Competitor
See 'Competitor'.

Flagstic
The 'flagstick' is a movable straight indicator, with or without bunting or other material attached, centred in the hole to show its position. It shall be circular in cross-section.

Forecaddie
A 'forecaddie' is one who is employed by the Committee to indicate to players the position of balls during play. He is an outside agency.

Ground Under Repair

'Ground under repair' is any portion of the course so marked by order of the Committee or so declared by its authorised representative. It includes material piled for removal and a hole made by a greenkeeper, even if not so marked. Stakes and lines defining ground under repair are in such ground. The margin of ground under repair extends vertically downwards, but not upwards.

Note 1: Grass cuttings and other material left on the course which have been abandoned and are not intended to be removed are not ground under repair unless so marked.

Note 2: The Committee may make a Local Rule prohibiting play from ground under repair.

Hazards

A 'hazard' is any bunker or water hazard.

Hole

The 'hole' shall be 4¼in (108mm) in diameter and at least 4in (100mm) deep. If a lining is used, it shall be sunk at least 1in (25mm) below the putting green surface unless the nature of the soil makes it impracticable to do so; its outer diameter shall not exceed 4¼in (108mm).

Holed

A ball is 'holed' when it is at rest within the circumference of the hole and all of it is below the level of the lip of the hole.

Honour

The side entitled to play first from the teeing ground is said to have the 'honour'.

Lateral Water Hazard

A 'lateral water hazard' is a water hazard or that part of a water hazard so situated that it is not possible or is deemed by the Committee to be impracticable to drop a ball behind the water hazard in accordance with Rule 26-1(*b*).

That part of a water hazard to be played as a lateral water hazard should be distinctively marked.

Note: Lateral water hazards should be defined by red stakes or lines.

Loose Impediments

'Loose impediments' are natural objects such as stones, leaves, twigs, branches and the like, dung, worms and insects and casts or heaps made by them, provided they are not fixed or growing, are not solidly embedded and do not adhere to the ball.

Sand and loose soil are loose impediments on the <u>putting green</u>, but not elsewhere.

Snow and ice are either <u>casual water</u> or loose impediments, at the option of the player, except that manufactured ice is an <u>obstruction</u>.

Dew is not a loose impediment.

Lost Ball
A ball is 'lost' if:

(*a*) It is not found or identified as his by the player within five minutes after the player's side or his or their caddies have begun to search for it; or

(*b*) The player has put another ball into play under the Rules, even though he may not have searched for the original ball; or

(*c*) The player has played any stroke with a <u>provisional ball</u> from the place where the original ball is likely to be or from a point nearer the hole than that place, whereupon the provisional ball becomes the <u>ball in play</u>.

Time spent in playing a <u>wrong ball</u> is not counted in the five-minute period allowed for search.

Marker
A 'marker' is one who is appointed by the Committee to record a <u>competitor's</u> score in stroke play. He may be a <u>fellow-competitor</u>. He is not a <u>referee</u>.

Matches
See 'Sides and Matches'.

Move or Moved
A ball is deemed to have 'moved' if it leaves its position and comes to rest in any other place.

Observer
An 'observer' is one who is appointed by the Committee to assist a <u>referee</u> to decide questions of fact and to report to him any breach of a Rule. An observer should not attend the flagstick, stand at or mark the position of the hole, or lift the ball or mark its position.

Obstructions
An 'obstruction' is anything artificial including the artificial surfaces and sides of roads and paths and manufactured ice, except:

(*a*) Objects defining <u>out of bounds</u>, such as walls, fences, stakes and railings;

(*b*) Any part of an immovable artificial object which is out of bounds; and

(*c*) Any construction declared by the Committee to be an integral part of the course.

Out of Bounds
'Out of bounds' is ground on which play is prohibited.

When out of bounds is defined by reference to stakes or a fence or as being beyond stakes or a fence, the out of bounds line is determined by the nearest inside points of the stakes or fence posts at ground level excluding angled supports.

When out of bounds is defined by a line on the ground, the line itself is out of bounds.

The out of bounds line is deemed to extend vertically upwards and downwards.

A ball is out of bounds when all of it lies out of bounds.

A player may stand out of bounds to play a ball lying within bounds.

Outside Agency
An 'outside agency' is any agency not part of the match or, in stroke play, not part of a competitor's side, and includes a referee, a marker, an observer or a forecaddie. Neither wind nor water is an outside agency.

Partner
A 'partner' is a player associated with another player on the same side.

In a threesome, foursome or a four-ball match, where the context so admits, the word 'player' includes his partner or partners.

Penalty Stroke
A 'penalty stroke' is one added to the score of a player or side under certain Rules. In a threesome or foursome, penalty strokes do not affect the order of play.

Provisional Ball
A 'provisional ball' is a ball played under Rule 27-2 for a ball which may be lost outside a water hazard or may be out of bounds.

Putting Green
The 'putting green' is all ground of the hole being played which is specially prepared for putting or otherwise defined as such by the Committee. A ball is on the putting green when any part of it touches the putting green.

Referee
A 'referee' is one who is appointed by the Committee to accompany

players to decide questions of fact and apply the Rules of Golf. He shall act on any breach of a Rule which he observes or is reported to him.

A referee should not attend the flagstick, stand at or mark the position of the hole, or lift the ball or mark its position.

Rub of the Green
A 'rub of the green' occurs when a ball in motion is accidentally deflected or stopped by any outside agency (See Rule 19-1).

Rule
The term 'Rule' includes Local Rules made by the Committee under Rule 33-8(*a*).

Side and Matches
Side: A player, or two or more players who are partners.

Single: A match in which one plays against another.

Threesome: A match in which one plays against two, and each side plays one ball.

Foursome: A match in which two play against two, and each side plays one ball.

Three-ball: A match play competition in which three play against one another, each playing his own ball. Each player is playing two distinct matches.

Best-ball: A match in which one plays against the better ball of two or the best ball of three players.

Four-ball: A match in which two play their better ball against the better ball of two other players.

Stance
Taking the 'stance' consists in a player placing his feet in position for the preparatory to making a stroke.

Stipulated Round
The 'stipulated round' consists of playing the holes of the course in their correct sequence unless otherwise authorised by the Committee. The number of holes in a stipulated round is 18 unless a small number is authorised by the Committee. As to extension of stipulated round in match play, see Rule 2-3.

Stroke
A 'stroke' is the forward movement of the club made with the intention of fairly striking at and moving the ball, but if a player checks his downswing voluntarily before the clubhead reaches the ball he is deemed not to have made a stroke.

Teeing Ground
The 'teeing ground' is the starting place for the hole to be played. It is a rectangular area two club-lengths in depth, the front and the sides of which are defined by the outside limits of two tee-markers. A ball is outside the teeing ground when all of it lies outside the teeing ground.

Through the Green
'Through the green' is the whole area of the course except:
   (*a*) The teeing ground and putting green of the hole being played; and
   (*b*) All hazards on the course.

Water Hazard
A 'water hazard' is any sea, lake, pond, river, ditch, surface drainage ditch or other open water course (whether or not containing water) and anything of a similar nature.
   All ground or water within the margin of a water hazard is part of the water hazard. The margin of a water hazard extends vertically upwards and downwards. Stakes and lines defining the margins of water hazards are in the hazards.
   Note: Water hazards (other than lateral water hazards) should be defined by yellow stakes or lines.

Wrong Ball
A 'wrong ball' is any ball other than:
   (*a*) The ball in play,
   (*b*) A provisional ball or
   (*c*) In stroke play, a second ball played under Rule 3-3 or Rule 20-7(*b*).
Note: Ball in play includes a ball substituted for the ball in play when the player is proceeding under an applicable Rule which does not permit substitution.

SECTION III THE RULES OF PLAY

RULE 1

The Game

1-1 General
The Game of Golf consists in playing a ball from the teeing ground into the hole by a stroke or successive strokes in accordance with the Rules.

1-2 Exerting Influence on Ball

No player or caddie shall take any action to influence the position or the movement of a ball except in accordance with the Rules.

PENALTY FOR BREACH OF RULE 1–2:

Match play – Loss of hole; Stroke play – Two strokes.

Note: In the case of a serious breach of Rule 1–2, the Committee may impose a penalty of disqualification.

1-3 Agreement to Waive Rules

Players shall not agree to exclude the operation of any Rule or to waive any penalty incurred.

PENALTY FOR BREACH OF RULE 1–3:

Match play – Disqualification of both sides; Stroke play – Disqualification of competitors concerned.

(Agreeing to play out of turn in stroke play – See Rule 10-2c.)

1-4 Points Not Covered by Rules

If any point in dispute is not covered by the Rules, the decision shall be made in accordance with equity.

RULE 2

Match Play

2-1 Winner of Hole; Reckoning of Holes

In match play the game is played by holes.

Except as otherwise provided in the Rules, a hole is won by the side which holes its ball in the fewer strokes. In a handicap match the lower net score wins the hole.

2-2 Halved Hole

A hole is halved if each side holes out in the same number of strokes.

When a player has holed out and his opponent has been left with a stroke for the half, if the player thereafter incurs a penalty, the hole is halved.

2-3 Winner of Match

A match (which consists of a stipulated round, unless otherwise decreed by the Committee) is won by the side which is leading by a number of holes greater than the number of holes remaining to be played.

The Committee may, for the purpose of settling a tie, extend the stipulated round to as many holes as are required for a match to be won.

2-4 Concession of Next Stroke, Hole or Match

When the opponent's ball is at rest or is deemed to be at rest under Rule 16-2, the player may concede the opponent to have holed out with his next stroke and the ball may be removed by either side with a club or otherwise.

A player may concede a hole or a match at any time prior to the conclusion of the hole or the match.

Concession of a stroke, hole or match may not be declined or withdrawn.

2-5 Claims

In match play, if a doubt or dispute arises between the players and no duly authorised representative of the Committee is available within a reasonable time, the players shall continue the match without delay. Any claim, if it is to be considered by the Committee, must be made before any player in the match plays from the next teeing ground or, in the case of the last hole of the match, before all players in the match leave the putting green.

No later claim shall be considered unless it is based on facts previously unknown to the player making the claim and the player making the claim had been given wrong information (Rules 6-2(*a*) and 9) by an opponent. In any case, no later claim shall be considered after the result of the match has been officially announced, unless the Committee is satisfied that the opponent knew he was giving wrong information.

2-6 General Penalty

The penalty for a breach of a Rule in match play is loss of hole except when otherwise provided.

RULE 3

Stroke Play

3-1 Winner

The competitor who plays the stipulated round or rounds in the fewest strokes is the winner.

3-2 Failure to Hole Out

If a competitor fails to hole out at any hole and does not correct his mistake before he plays a stroke from the next teeing ground or, in the case of the last hole of the round, before he leaves the putting green, *he shall be disqualified.*

3-3 Doubt as to Procedure

(a) Procedure

In stroke play only, when during play of a hole a competitor is doubtful of his rights or procedure, he may, without penalty, play a second ball. After the situation which caused the doubt has arisen, the competitor should, before taking further action, announce to his marker or a fellow competitor his decision to invoke this Rule and which ball with which he will score if the Rules permit.

The competitor shall report the facts to the Committee before returning his score card unless he scores the same with both balls; if he fails to do so, *he shall be disqualified*.

(b) Determination of Score for Hole

If the Rules allow the procedure selected in advance by the competitor, the score with the ball selected shall be his score for the hole.

If the competitor fails to announce in advance his decision to invoke this Rule or his selection, the score with the original ball or, if the original ball is not one of the balls being played, the first ball put into play shall count if the Rules allow the procedure adopted for such ball. *Note*: A second ball played under Rule 3-3 is not a provisional ball under Rule 27-2.

3-4 Refusal to Comply with a Rule

If a competitor refuses to comply with a Rule affecting the rights of another competitor, *he shall be disqualified*.

3-5 General Penalty

The penalty for a breach of a Rule in stroke play is two strokes except when otherwise provided.

CLUBS AND THE BALL

The Royal and Ancient Golf Club of St Andrews and the United States Golf Association reserve the right to change the Rules and make and change the interpretations relating to clubs, balls and other implements at any time.

RULE 4

Clubs

If there may be any reasonable basis for doubt as to whether a club which is to be manufactured conforms with Rule 4 and Appendix II, the manufacturer should submit a sample to the Royal and Ancient Golf Club of St Andrews for a ruling, such sample to become its propery for reference purposes. If a manufacturer fails to do so, he assumes the risk of a ruling that the club does not conform with the Rules of Golf.

A player in doubt as to the conformity of a club should consult the Royal and Ancient Golf Club of St Andrews.

4.1 Form and Make of Clubs

A club is an implement designed to be used for striking the ball.

A putter is a club designed primarily for use on the putting green.

The player's clubs shall conform with the provisions of this Rule and with the specifications and interpretations set forth in Appendix II.

(*a*) **General**

The club shall be composed of a shaft and a head. All parts of the club shall be fixed so that the club is one unit. The club shall not be designed to be adjustable except for weight. The club shall not be substantially different from the traditional and customary form and make.

(*b*) **Shaft**

The shaft shall be generally straight, with the same bending and twisting properties in any direction, and shall be attached to the clubhead at the heel either directly or through a single plain neck or socket. A putter shaft may be attached to any point in the head.

(*c*) **Grip**

The grip consists of that part of the shaft designed to be held by the player and any material added to it for the purpose of obtaining a firm hold. The grip shall be substantially straight and plain in form and shall not be moulded for any part of the hands.

(*d*) **Clubhead**

The distance from the heel to the toe of the clubhead shall be greater than the distance from face to back. The clubhead shall be generally plain in shape.

The clubhead shall have only one face designed for striking the ball, except that a putter may have two such faces if their characteristics are the same, they are opposite each other and the loft of each is the same and does not exceed ten degrees.

(*e*) **Club Face**

The face shall not have any degree of concavity and, in relation to the ball, shall be hard and rigid. It shall be generally smooth except for such markings as are permitted by Appendix II. If the basic structural material of the head and face of a club, other than a putter, is metal, no inset or attachment is permitted.

(*f*) **Wear**

A club which conforms to Rule 4-1 when new is deemed to conform after wear through normal use. Any part of a club which has been purposely altered is regarded as new and must conform, in the altered state, to the Rules.

(g) **Damage**

If a player's club ceases to conform with Rule 4-1 because of damage sustained in the normal course of play, the player may:

(i) Use the club in its damaged state, but only for the remainder of the stipulated round during which such damage was sustained; or

(ii) Without unduly delaying play, repair it.

A club which ceases to conform because of damage sustained other than in the normal course of play shall not subsequently be used during the round.

(Damage changing playing characteristics of club – See Rule 4-2.)

4-2 Playing Characteristics Changed

During a stipulated round, the playing characteristics of a club shall not be purposely changed.

If the playing characteristics of a player's club are changed during a round because of damage sustained in the normal course of play, the player may:

(i) Use the club in its altered state; or

(ii) Without unduly delaying play, repair it.

If the playing characteristics of a player's club are changed because of damage sustained other than in the normal course of play, the club shall not subsequently be used during the round.

Damage to a club which occurred prior to a round may be repaired during the round, provided the playing characteristics are not changed and play is not unduly delayed.

4-3 Foreign Material

No foreign material shall be applied to the club face for the purpose of influencing the movement of the ball.

PENALTY FOR BREACH OF RULE 4-1, 4-2 or 4-3:
Disqualification.

4-4 Maximum of Fourteen Clubs

(a) **Selection and Replacement of Clubs**

The player shall start a stipulated round with no more than fourteen clubs. He is limited to the clubs thus selected for that round except that, without unduly delaying play, he may:

(i) If he started with fewer than fourteen, add as many as will bring his total to that number; and

(ii) Replace, with any club, a club which becomes unfit for play in the normal course of play.

(*b*) **Borrowing or Sharing Clubs**

The addition or replacement of a club or clubs may be made by borrowing from anyone; only the borrower may use such club or clubs for the remainder of the round.

The sharing of a club or clubs is prohibited except that partners may share clubs, provided that the total number of clubs carried by the partners so sharing does not exceed fourteen.

PENALTY FOR BREACH OF RULE 4-4(*a*) or (*b*), REGARDLESS OF NUMBER OF EXCESS CLUBS CARRIED:

Match play – At the conclusion of the hole at which the breach is discovered, the state of the match shall be adjusted by deducting one hole for each hole at which a breach occurred. Maximum deduction per round: two holes.

Stroke play – Two strokes for each hole at which any breach occurred; maximum penalty per round: four strokes.

Bogey and par competitions – Penalties as in match play.

Stableford competition – See Rule 32-1(b).

(*c*) **Excess Club Declared Out of Play**

Any club carried or used in breach of this Rule shall be declared out of play by the player immediately upon discovery that a breach has occurred and thereafter shall not be used by the player during the round.

PENALTY FOR BREACH OF RULE 4-4(*c*):

Disqualification.

RULE 5

The Ball

5-1 General

The ball the player uses shall conform to specifications set forth in Appendix III on maximum weight, minimum size, spherical symmetry, initial velocity and overall distance when tested under specified conditions.

Note: In laying down the conditions under which a competition is to be played (Rule 33-1), the Committee may stipulate that the ball to be used shall be of certain specifications, provided these specifications are within the limits prescribed by Appendix III, and that it be of a size, brand and marking as detailed on the current List of Conforming Golf Balls issued by the Royal and Ancient Golf Club of St Andrews.

5-2 Foreign Material

No foreign material shall be applied to a ball for the purpose of changing its playing characteristics.

PENALTY FOR BREACH OF RULE 5-1 or 5-2:
Disqualification.

5-3 Ball Unfit for Play
A ball is unfit for play if it is visibly cut, cracked or out of shape. A ball is not unfit for play solely because mud or other materials adhere to it, its surface is scratched or its paint is damaged or discoloured.

If a player has reason to believe his ball has become unfit for play during play of the hole being played, he may during the play of such hole lift his ball without penalty to determine whether it is unfit, provided he announces his intention in advance to his opponent in match play or his marker or a fellow-competitor in stroke play and gives his opponent, marker or fellow-competitor an opportunity to examine the ball. If he lifts the ball without announcing his intention in advance or giving his opponent, marker or fellow-competitor an opportunity to examine the ball, *he shall incur a penalty of one stroke*.

If it is determined that the ball has become unfit for play during play of the hole being played, the player may substitute another ball, placing it on the spot where the original ball lay. Otherwise, the original ball shall be replaced.

If a ball breaks into pieces as a result of a stroke, the stroke shall be replayed without penalty (see Rule 20-5).

*PENALTY FOR BREACH OF RULE 5-3:
Match play – Loss of hole; Stroke play – Two strokes.

If a player incurs the general penalty for breach of Rule 5-3, no additional penalty under the Rule shall be applied.
Note 1: The ball may not be cleaned to determine whether it is unfit for play – See Rule 21.
Note 2: If the opponent, marker or fellow-competitor wishes to dispute a claim of unfitness, he must do so before the player plays another ball.

RULE 6

The Player

Definition
A 'marker' is one who is appointed by the Committee to record a competitor's score in stroke play. He may be a fellow-competitor. He is not a referee.

6-1 Conditions of Competition
The player is responsible for knowing the conditions under which the competition is to be played (Rule 33-1).

6-2 Handicap

(a) Match Play

Before starting a match in a handicap competition, the players should determine from one another their respective handicaps. If a player begins the match having declared a higher handicap which would affect the number of strokes given or received, *he shall be disqualified*; otherwise, the player shall play off the declared handicap.

(b) Stroke Play

In any round of a handicap competition, the competitor shall ensure that his handicap is recorded on his scorecard before it is returned to the Committee. If no handicap is recorded on his scorecard before it is returned, or if the recorded handicap is higher than that to which he is entitled and this affects the number of strokes received, *he shall be disqualified* from that round of the handicap competition; otherwise, the score shall stand.

Note: It is the player's responsibility to know the holes at which handicap strokes are to be given or received.

6-3 Time of Starting and Groups

(a) Time of Starting

The player shall start at the time laid down by the Committee.

(b) Groups

In stroke play, the competitor shall remain throughout the round in the group arranged by the Committee unless the Committee authorises or ratifies a change.

PENALTY FOR BREACH OF RULE 6-3: *Disqualification*.

(Best-ball and four-ball play – See Rules 30-3(*a*) and 31-2.)

Note: The Committee may provide in the conditions of a competition (Rule 33-1) that, if the player arrives at his starting point, ready to play, within five minutes of his starting time, in the absence of circumstances which warrant waiving the penalty of disqualification as provided in Rule 33-7, the penalty for failure to start on time is *loss of the first hole in match play or two strokes at the first hole in stroke play* instead of disqualification.

6-4 Caddie

The player may have only one caddie at any one time, *under penalty of disqualification*.

For any breach of a Rule by his caddie, the player incurs the applicable penalty.

6-5 Ball

The responsibility for playing the proper ball rests with the player. Each player should put an identification mark on his ball.

6-6 Scoring in Stroke Play

(*a*) Recording Scores

After each hole the <u>marker</u> should check the score with the competitor. On completion of the round the marker shall sign the card and hand it to the competitor. If more than one marker records the scores, each shall sign for the part for which he is responsible.

(*b*) Signing and Returning Card

After completion of the round, the competitor should check his score for each hole and settle any doubtful points with the Committee. He shall ensure that the marker has signed the card, countersign the card himself and return it to the Committee as soon as possible.

PENALTY FOR BREACH OF RULE 6-6b: *Disqualification.*

(*c*) Alteration of Card

No alteration may be made on a card after the competitor has returned it to the Committee.

(*d*) Wrong Score for Hole

The competitor is responsible for the correctness of the score recorded for each hole. If he returns a score for any hole lower than actually taken, *he shall be disqualified.* If he returns a score for any hole higher than actually taken, the score as returned shall stand.

Note 1: The Committee is responsible for the addition of scores and application of the handicap recorded on the card – See Rule 33-5.

Note 2: In four-ball stroke play, see also Rule 31-4 and 31-7(*a*).

6-7 Undue Delay

The player shall play without undue delay. Between completion of a hole and playing from the next teeing ground, the player shall not unduly delay play.

PENALTY FOR BREACH OF RULE 6-7:

Match play – Loss of hole; Stroke play – Two strokes. For repeated offence – Disqualification. If a player unduly delays play between holes, he is delaying the play of the next hole and the penalty applies to that hole.

6-8 Discontinuance of Play

(*a*) When Permitted

The player shall not discontinue play unless:

(i) The Committee has suspended play;

(ii) He believes there is danger from lightning;

(iii) He is seeking a decision from the Committee on a doubtful or disputed point (see Rules 2-5 and 34-3); or

(iv) There is some other good reason such as sudden illness.

Bad weather is not of itself a good reason for discontinuing play.

If the player discontinues play without specific permission from the

Committee, he shall report to the Committee as soon as practicable. If he does so and the Committee considers his reason satisfactory, the player incurs no penalty. Otherwise, *the player shall be disqualified.*

Exception in match play: Players discontinuing match play by agreement are not subject to disqualification unless by so doing the competition is delayed.

Note: Leaving the course does not of itself constitute discontinuance of play.

(*b*) **Procedure When Play Suspended by Committee**

When play is suspended by the Committee, if the players in a match or group are between the play of two holes, they shall not resume play until the Committee has ordered a resumption of play. If they are in the process of playing a hole, they may continue provided they do so without delay. If they choose to continue, they shall discontinue either before or immediately after completing the hole, and shall not thereafter resume play until the Committee has ordered a resumption of play.

PENALTY FOR BREACH OF RULE 6-8(*b*): *Disqualification.*

(*c*) **Lifting Ball When Play Discontinued**

When during the play of a hole a player discontinues play under Rule 6-8(*a*), he may lift his ball. A ball may be cleaned when so lifted. If a ball has been so lifted, the player shall, when play is resumed, place a ball on the spot from which the original ball was lifted.

PENALTY FOR BREACH OF RULE 6-8(*c*):

Match play – Loss of hole; Stroke play – Two strokes.

RULE 7

Practice

7-1 Before or Between Rounds

(*a*) **Match Play**

On any day of a match play competition, a player may practise on the competition course before a round.

(*b*) **Stroke Play**

On any day of a stroke competition or play-off, a competitor shall not practise on the competition course or test the surface of any putting green on the course before a round or play-off. When two or more rounds of a stroke competition are to be played over consecutive days, practice between those rounds on any competition course remaining to be played is prohibited.

Exception: Practice putting or chipping on or near the first teeing ground before starting a round or play-off is permitted.

PENALTY FOR BREACH OF RULE 7-1*b*: *Disqualification.*

Note: The Committee may in the conditions of a competition (Rule 33-1) prohibit practice on the completion course on any day of a match play competition or permit practice on the competition course or part of the course (Rule 33-2(*c*) on any day of or between rounds of a stroke competition.

7-2 During Round

A player shall not play a practice <u>stroke</u> either during the play of a hole or between the play of two holes except that, between the play of two holes, the player may practise putting or chipping on or near the <u>putting</u> <u>green</u> of the hole last played, any practice putting green or the <u>teeing</u> <u>ground</u> of the next hole to be played in the round, provided such practice stroke is not played from a hazard and does not unduly delay play (Rule 6-7).

Exception: When play has been suspended by the Committee, a player may, prior to resumption of play, practise (*a*) as provided in this Rule, (*b*) anywhere other than on the competition course and (*c*) as otherwise permitted by the Committee.

PENALTY FOR BREACH OF RULE 7-2:
Match play – Loss of hole; Stroke play – Two strokes.
In the event of a breach between the play of two holes, the penalty applies to the next hole.
Note 1: A practice swing is not a practice <u>stroke</u> and may be taken at any place, provided the player does not breach the Rules.
Note 2: The Committee may prohibit practice on or near the <u>putting</u> <u>green</u> of the hole last played.

RULE 8

Advice; Indicating Line of Play

Definition

'Advice' is any counsel or suggestion which could influence a player in determining his play, the choice of a club or the method of making a <u>stroke</u>.

Information on the Rules or on matters of public information, such as the position of hazards or the flagstick on the putting green, is not advice.

8-1 Advice

A player shall not give advice to anyone in the competition except his partner. A player may ask for advice from only his partner or either of their caddies.

8-2 Indicating Line of Play
(a) Other Than on Putting Green
Except on the putting green, a player may have the line of play indicated to him by anyone, but no one shall stand on or close to the line while the stroke is being played. Any mark placed during the play of a hole by the player or with his knowledge to indicate the line shall be removed before the stroke is played.

Exception: Flagstick attended or held up – See Rule 17-1.

(b) On the Putting Green
When the player's ball is on the putting green, the player, his partner or either of their caddies may, before but not during the stroke, point out a line for putting, but in so doing the putting green shall not be touched. No mark shall be placed anywhere to indicate a line for putting.

PENALTY FOR BREACH OF RULE:

Match play – Loss of hole; Stroke play – Two strokes.

Note: In a team competition without concurrent individual competition, the Committee may in the conditions of the competition (Rule 33-1) permit each team to appoint one person, e.g. team captain or coach, who may give advice (including pointing out a line for putting) to members of that team. Such person shall be identified to the Committee prior to the start of the competition.

RULE 9

Information as to Strokes Taken

9-1 General
The number of strokes a player has taken shall include any penalty strokes incurred.

9-2 Match Play
A player who has incurred a penalty shall inform his opponent as soon as practicable. If he fails to do so, he shall be deemed to have given wrong information, even he was not aware that he had incurred a penalty.

An opponent is entitled to ascertain from the player, during the play of a hole, the number of strokes he has taken and, after play of a hole, the number of strokes taken on the hole just completed.

If during the play of a hole the player gives or is deemed to give wrong information as to the number of strokes taken, he shall incur no penalty if he corrects the mistake before his opponent has played his next stroke. If the player fails so to correct the wrong information, *he shall lose the hole.*

If after play of a hole the player gives or is deemed to give wrong information as to the number of strokes taken on the hole just completed and this affects the opponent's understanding of the result of the hole, he shall incur no penalty if he corrects his mistake before any player plays from the next teeing ground or, in the case of the last hole of the match, before all players leave the putting green. If the player fails so to correct the wrong information, *he shall lose the hole*.

9-3 Stroke Play

A competitor who has incurred a penalty should inform his marker as soon as practicable.

RULE 10

Order of Play

10.1 Match Play

(*a*) **Teeing Ground**

The side entitled to play first from the teeing ground is said to have the 'honour'.

The side which shall have the honour at the first teeing ground shall be determined by the order of the draw. In the absence of a draw, the honour should be decided by lot.

The side which wins a hole shall take the honour at the next teeing ground. If a hole has been halved, the side which had the honour at the previous teeing ground shall retain it.

(*b*) **Other Than on Teeing Ground**

When the balls are in play, the ball farther from the hole shall be played first. If the balls are equidistant from the hole, the ball to be played first should be decided by lot.

Exception: Rule 30-3(*c*) (best-ball and four-ball match play).

(*c*) **Playing Out of Turn**

If a player plays when his opponent should have played, the opponent may immediately require the player to cancel the stroke so played and play a ball in correct order, without penalty (See Rule 20-5).

10-2 Stroke Play

(*a*) **Teeing Ground**

The competitor entitled to play first from the teeing ground is said to have the 'honour'.

The competitor who shall have the honour at the first teeing ground shall be determined by the order of the draw. In the absence of a draw, the honour should be decided by lot.

The competitor with the lowest score at a hole shall take the honour at the next teeing ground. The competitor with the second lowest score shall play next and so on. If two or more competitors have the same score at a hole, they shall play from the next teeing ground in the same order as at the previous teeing ground.

(*b*) **Other Than on Teeing Ground**

When the balls are in play, the ball farthest from the hole shall be played first. If two or more balls are equidistant from the hole, the ball to be played first should be decided by lot.

Exceptions: Rules 22 (ball interfering with or assisting play) and 31-5 (four-ball stroke play).

(*c*) **Playing Out of Turn**

If a competitor plays out of turn, no penalty is incurred and the ball shall be played as it lies. If, however, the Committee determines that competitors have agreed to play in an order other than that set forth in Clauses 2(*a*) and 2(*b*) of this Rule to give one of them an advantage, *they shall be disqualified.*

(Incorrect order of play in threesomes and foursomes stroke play – See Rule 29-3.)

10-3 Provisional Ball or Second Ball from Teeing Ground

If a player plays a provisional ball or a second ball from a teeing ground, he should do so after his opponent or fellow-competitor has played his first stroke. If a player plays a provisional ball or a second ball out of turn, Clauses 1(*c*) and 2(*c*) of this Rule shall apply.

10-4 Ball Moved in Measuring

If a ball is moved in measuring to determine which ball is farther from the hole, no penalty is incurred and the ball shall be replaced.

TEEING GROUND
RULE 11

Teeing Ground

Definition

The 'teeing ground' is the starting place for the hole to be played. It is a rectangular area two club-lengths in depth, the front and the sides of which are defined by the outside limits of two tee-markers. A ball is outside the teeing ground when all of it lies outside the teeing ground.

11-1 Teeing

In teeing, the ball may be placed on the ground, on an irregularity of surface created by the player on the ground or on a tee, sand or other substance in order to raise it off the ground.

A player may stand outside the teeing ground to play a ball within it.

11-2 Tee-Markers

Before a player plays his first stroke with any ball from the teeing ground of the hole being played, the tee-markers are deemed to be fixed. In such circumstances, if the player moves or allows to be moved a tee-marker for the purpose of avoiding interference with the stance, the area of his intended swing or his line of play, *he shall incur the penalty for a breach of Rule 13-2.*

11-3 Ball Falling Off Tee

If a ball, when not in play, falls off a tee or is knocked off a tee by the player in addressing it, it may be re-teed without penalty, but if a stroke is made at the ball in these circumstances, whether the ball is moving or not, the stroke counts but no penalty shall be incurred.

11-4 Playing Outside Teeing Ground

(*a*) **Match Play**

If a player, when starting a hole, plays a ball from outside the teeing ground, the opponent may immediately require the player to cancel the stroke so played and play a ball from within the teeing ground, without penalty.

(*b*) **Stroke Play**

If a competitor, when starting a hole, plays a ball from outside the teeing ground, *he shall incur a penalty of two strokes* and shall then play a ball from within the teeing ground.

If the competitor plays a stroke from the next teeing ground without first correcting his mistake or, in the case of the last hole of the round, leaves the putting green without first declaring his intention to correct his mistake, *he shall be disqualified.*

Strokes played by a competitor from outside the teeing ground do not count in his score.

PLAYING THE BALL
RULE 12

Searching for and Identifying Ball

Definitions

A 'hazard' is any bunker or water hazard.

A 'bunker' is a hazard consisting of a prepared area of ground, often a hollow, from which turf or soil has been removed and replaced with sand or the like. Grass-covered ground bordering or within a bunker is not part of the bunker. The margin of a bunker extends vertically downwards, but not upwards.

A 'water hazard' is any sea, lake, pond, river, ditch, surface drainage ditch or other open water course (whether or not containing water) and anything of a similar nature.

All ground or water within the margin of a water hazard is part of the water hazard. The margin of a water hazard extends vertically upwards and downwards. Stakes and lines defining the margins of water hazards are in the hazards.

12-1 Searching for Ball; Seeing Ball

In searching for his ball anywhere on the course, the player may touch or bend long grass, rushes, bushes, whins, heather or the like, but only to the extent necessary to find and identify it, provided that this does not improve the lie of the ball, the area of his intended swing or his line of play.

A player is not necessarily entitled to see his ball when playing a stroke.

In a hazard, if a ball is covered by loose impediments or sand, the player may remove by probing, raking or other means as much thereof as will enable him to see a part of the ball. If an excess is removed, no penalty is incurred and the ball shall be re-covered so that only a part of the ball is visible. If the ball is moved in such removal, no penalty is incurred; the ball shall be replaced and, if necessary, re-covered. As to removal of loose impediments outside a hazard, see Rule 23.

If a ball lying in casual water, ground under repair or a hole, cast or runway made by a burrowing animal, a reptile or a bird is accidentally moved during search, no penalty is incurred; the ball shall be replaced, unless the player elects to proceed under Rule 25-1(b).

If a ball is believed to be lying in water in a water hazard, the player may probe for it with a club or otherwise. If the ball is moved in so doing, no penalty is incurred; the ball shall be replaced, unless the player elects to proceed under Rule 26-1.

PENALTY FOR BREACH OF RULE 12-1:
Match play – Loss of hole; Stroke play – Two strokes.

12-2 Identifying Ball

The responsibility for playing the proper ball rests with the player. Each player should put an indentification mark on his ball.

Except in a hazard, the player may, without penalty, lift a ball he believes to be his own for the purpose of identification and clean it to the extent necessary for identification. If the ball is the player's ball, he shall replace it. Before the player lifts the ball, he shall announce his intention to his opponent in match play or his marker or a fellow-competitor in stroke play and given his opponent, marker or fellow-competitor an opportunity to observe the lifting and replacement. If he lifts the ball without announcing his intention in advance or giving his opponent, marker or fellow-competitor an opportunity to observe, or if he lifts his ball for identification in a hazard, *he shall incur a penalty of one stroke* and the ball shall be replaced.

If a player who is required to replace a ball fails to do so, *he shall incur the penalty* for a breach of Rule 20-3(*a*), but no additional penalty under Rule 12-2 shall be applied.

RULE 13

Ball Played As it Lies; Lie, Area of Intended Swing and Line of Play; Stance

Definitions
A 'hazard' is any bunker or water hazard.

A 'bunker' is a hazard consisting of a prepared area of ground, often a hollow, from which turf or soil has been removed and replaced with sand or the like. Grass-covered ground bordering or within a bunker is not part of the bunker.

A 'water hazard' is any sea, lake, pond, river, ditch, surface drainage ditch or other open water course (whether or not containing water) and anything of a similar nature.

All ground or water within the margin of a water hazard is part of the water hazard. The margin of a water hazard is deemed to extend vertically upwards and downwards. Stakes and lines defining the margins of water hazards are in the hazards.

13-1 Ball Played As It Lies
The ball shall be played as it lies, except as otherwise provided in the Rules. (Ball at rest moved – See Rule 18.)

13-2 Improving Lie, Area of Intended Swing or Line of Play
Except as provided in the Rules, a player shall not improve or allow to be improved:

the position or lie of his ball,

the area of his intended swing, or

his line of play, or

the area in which he is to drop or place a ball

by any of the following actions:

moving, bending or breaking anything growing or fixing (including objects defining out of bounds), or

removing or pressing down sand, loose soil, replaced divots, other cut turf placed in position or other irregularities of surface

except as follows:

as may occur in fairly taking his stance,

in making a stroke or the backward movement of his club for a stroke,

on the teeing ground in creating or eliminating irregularities of surface, or

on the putting green in removing sand and loose soil as provided in Rule 16-1(*a*) or in repairing damage as provided in Rule 16-1(*c*).

The club may be grounded only lightly and shall not be pressed on the ground.

Exception: Ball lying in or touching hazard – Rule 13-4.

13-3 Building Stance

A player is entitled to place his feet firmly in taking his stance, but he shall not build a stance.

13-4 Ball Lying in or Touching Hazard

Except as provided in the Rules, before making a stroke at a ball which lies in or touches a hazard (whether a bunker or a water hazard), the player shall not:

(*a*) Test the condition of the hazard or any similar hazard;

(*b*) Touch the ground in the hazard or water in the water hazard with a club or otherwise; or

(*c*) Touch or move a loose impediment lying in or touching the hazard.

Exceptions:

1. At address or in the backward movement for the stroke, the club may touch any obstruction or any grass, bush, tree or other growing thing.

2. The player may place his clubs in a hazard, provided nothing is done which may constitute testing the soil or improving the lie of the ball.

3. The player after playing the stroke, or his caddie at any time without the authority of the player, may smooth sand or soil in the hazard, provided that, if the ball still lies in the hazard, nothing is done which improves the lie of the ball or assists the player in his subsequent play of the hole.

PENALTY FOR BREACH OF RULE:
Match play – Loss of hole; Stroke play – two strokes.
(Searching for ball – See Rule 12-1.)

RULE 14

Striking the Ball

Definition
A 'stroke' is the forward movement of the club made with the intention of fairly striking at and moving the ball, but if a player checks his downswing voluntarily before the clubhead reaches the ball he is deemed not to have made a stroke.

14-1 Ball to be Fairly Struck At
The ball shall be fairly struck at with the head of the club and must not be pushed, scraped or spooned.

14-2 Assistance
In making a stroke, a player shall not accept physical assitance or protection from the elements.
PENALTY FOR BREACH OF RULE 14-1 or 14-2:
Match play – Loss of hole; Stroke play – Two strokes.

14-3 Artificial Devices and Unusual Equipment
Except as provided in the Rules, during a stipulated round the player shall not use any artificial device or unusual equipment:
   (*a*) For the purpose of gauging or measuring distance or conditions which might affect his play; or
   (*b*) Which might assist him in gripping the club, in making a stroke or in his play, except that plain gloves may be worn, resin, tape or gauze may be applied to the grip (provided such application does not render the grip non-conforming under Rule 4-1(*c*) and a towel or handkerchief may be wrapped around the grip.
PENALTY FOR BREACH OF RULE 14-3: *Disqualification.*

14-4 Striking the Ball More than Once
If a player's club strikes the ball more than once in the course of a stroke, the player shall count the stroke and *add a penalty stroke*, making two strokes in all.

14-5 Playing Moving Ball
A player shall not play while his ball is moving.

Exceptions:

Ball falling off tee – Rule 11-3.

Striking the ball more than once – Rule 14-4.

Ball moving in water – Rule 14-6.

When the ball begins to move only after the player has begun the stroke or the backward movement of his club for the stroke, he shall incur no penalty under this Rule for playing a moving ball, but he is not exempt from any penalty incurred under the following Rules:

Ball at rest moved by player – Rule 18-2(*a*).

Ball at rest moving after address – Rules 18-2(*b*)

Ball at rest moving after loose impediment touched – Rule 18-2(*c*).

14-6 Ball Moving in Water

When a ball is moving in water in a water hazard, the player may, without penalty, make a stroke, but he must not delay making his stroke in order to allow the wind or current to improve the position of the ball. A ball moving in water in a water hazard may be lifted if the player elects to invoke Rule 26.

PENALTY FOR BREACH OF RULE 14-5 or 14-6:

Match play – Loss of hole; Stroke play – Two strokes.

RULE 15

Playing a Wrong Ball

Definition

A 'wrong ball' is any ball other than:

(*a*) The ball in play;

(*b*) A provisional ball; or

(*c*) In stroke play, a second ball played under Rule 3-3 or Rule 20-7(*b*).

Note: Ball in play includes a ball substituted for the ball in play when the player is proceeding under an applicable Rule which does not permit substitution.

15-1 General

A player must hole out with the ball played from the teeing ground unless a Rule permits him to substitute another ball. If a player substitutes another ball when proceeding under an applicable Rule which does not permit substitution, that ball is not a wrong ball; it becomes the ball in play and, if the error is not corrected as provided in Rule 20-6, *the player shall incur a penalty of loss of hole in match play or two strokes in stroke play.*

15-2 Match Play

If a player plays a stroke with a <u>wrong ball</u> except in a <u>hazard</u>, *he shall 'ose the hole*.

If a player plays any strokes in a hazard with a wrong ball, there is no penalty. Strokes played in a hazard with a wrong ball do not count in the player's score. If the wrong ball belongs to another player, its owner shall replace a ball on the spot from which the wrong ball was first played.

If the player and opponent exchange balls during the play of a hole, the first to play the wrong ball other than from a hazard shall lose the hole; when this cannot be determined, the hole shall be played out with the balls exchanged.

15-3 Stroke Play

If a competitor plays a stroke with a <u>wrong ball</u>, *he shall incur a penalty of two strokes*, unless the only stroke or strokes played with such ball were played when it was lying in a hazard, in which case no penalty is incurred.

The competitor must correct his mistake by playing the correct ball. If he fails to correct his mistake before he plays a stroke from the next <u>teeing ground</u> or, in the case of the last hole of the round, fails to declare his intention to correct his mistake before leaving the <u>putting green</u>, *he shall be disqualified*.

Strokes played by a competitor with a wrong ball do not count in his score.

If the wrong ball belongs to another competitor, its owner shall place a ball on the spot from which the wrong ball was first played.

(Lie of ball to be placed or replaced altered – see Rule 20-3*b*.)

THE PUTTING GREEN
RULE 16

The Putting Green

Definitions

The 'putting green' is all ground of the hole being played which is specially prepared for putting or otherwise defined as such by the Committee. A ball is on the putting green when any part of it touches the putting green.

A ball is 'holed' when it is at rest within the circumference of the hole and all of it is below the level of the lip of the hole.

16-1 General
   (*a*) **Touching Line of Putt**

The line of putt must not be touched except:

   (i) The player may move sand, loose soil and other loose impediments by picking them up or by brushing them aside with his hand or a club without pressing anything down;

  (ii) In addressing the ball, the player may place the club in front of the ball without pressing anything down;

 (iii) In measuring – Rule 10-4;

 (iv) In lifting the ball – Rule 16-1(*b*);

  (v) In pressing down a ball-marker;

 (vi) In repairing old hole plugs or ball marks on the putting green – Rule 16-1(*c*), and

(vii) In removing movable obstructions – Rule 24-1.

   (Indicating line for putting on putting green – See Rule 8-2*b*.)

   (*b*) **Lifting Ball**

A ball on the putting green may be lifted and, if desired, cleaned. A ball so lifted shall be replaced on the spot from which it was lifted.

   (*c*) **Repair of Hole Plugs and Ball Marks**

The player may repair an old hole plug or damage to the putting green caused by the impact of a ball, whether or not the player's ball lies on the putting green. If the ball is moved in the process of such repair, it shall be replaced, without penalty.

   (*d*) **Testing Surface**

During the play of a hole, a player shall not test the surface of the putting green by rolling a ball or roughening or scraping the surface.

   (*e*) **Standing Astride or on Line of Putt**

The player shall not make a stroke on the putting green from a stance astride, or with either foot touching, the line of the putt or an extension of that line behind the ball. For the purpose of this Clause only, the line of putt does not extend beyond the hole.

   (*f*) **Position of Caddie or Partner**

While making the stroke, the player shall not allow his caddie, his partner or his partner's caddie to position himself on or close to an extension of the line of putt behind the ball.

   (*g*) **Playing Stroke While Another Ball in Motion**

A player shall not play a stroke while another ball is in motion after a stroke on the putting green.

   (Lifting ball interfering with or assisting play while another ball in motion – See Rule 22.)

PENALTY FOR BREACH OF RULE 16-1:

Match play – Loss of hole; Stroke play – Two strokes.

16.2 Ball Overhanging Hole

When any part of the ball overhangs the lip of the hole, the player is allowed enough time to reach the hole without unreasonable delay and an additional ten seconds to determine whether the ball is at rest. If by then the ball has not fallen into the hole, it is deemed to be at rest. If the ball subsequently falls into the hole, the player is deemed to have holed out with his last stroke, and *he shall add a penalty stroke to his score* for the hole; otherwise there is no penalty under this Rule.

(Undue delay – see Rule 6-7.)

RULE 17

The Flagstick

17-1 Flagstick Attending, Removed or Held Up
Before and during the stroke, the player may have the flagstick attended, removed or held up to indicate the position of the hole. This may be done only on the authority of the player before he plays his stroke.

If the flagstick is attended or removed by an opponent, a fellow-competitor or the caddie of either with the player's knowledge and no objection is made, the player shall be deemed to have authorised it. If a player or a caddie attends, removes or holds up the flagstick or stands near the hole while a stroke is being played, he shall be deemed to be attending the flagstick until the ball comes to rest.

If the flagstick is not attended before the stroke is played, it shall not be attended or removed while the ball is in motion.

17-2 Unauthorised Attendance
(*a*) **Match Play**
In match play, an opponent or his caddie shall not attend, remove or hold up the flagstick without the player's knowledge or authority while the player is making a stroke or his ball is in motion.

(*b*) **Stroke Play**
In stroke play, if a fellow-competitor or his caddie attends, removes or holds up the flagstick without the competitor's knowledge or authority while the competitor is making a stroke or his ball is in motion, *the fellow-competitor shall incur the penalty* for breach of this Rule. In such circumstances, if the competitor's ball strikes the flagstick or the person attending it, the competitor incurs no penalty and the ball shall be played as it lies, except that, if the stroke was played from the putting green, the stroke shall be replayed.

PENALTY FOR BREACH OF RULE 17-1 or 17-2:
Match play – Loss of hole; Stroke play – Two strokes.

17-3 Ball Striking Flagstick or Attendant
The player's ball shall not strike:

(*a*) The flagstick when attended, removed or held up by the player, his partner or either of their caddies, or by another person with the player's knowledge or authority; or

(*b*) The player's caddie, his partner or his partner's caddie when attending the flagstick, or another person attending the flagstick with the player's knowledge or authority, or <u>equipment</u> carried by any such person; or

(*c*) The flagstick in the hole, unattended, when the ball has been played from the <u>putting green</u>.

PENALTY FOR BREACH OR RULE 17-3:

Match play – Loss of hole; Stroke play – Two strokes, and the ball shall be played as it lies.

17-4 Ball Resting Against Flagstick

If the ball rests against the flagstick when it is in the hole, the player or another person authorised by him may move or remove the flagstick and if the ball falls into the hole, the player shall be deemed to have holed out at his last stroke; otherwise the ball, if <u>moved</u>, shall be placed on the lip of the hole, without penalty.

RULE 18

Ball at Rest Moved

Definitions

A ball is deemed to have 'moved' if it leaves its position and comes to rest in any other place.

An 'outside agency' is any agency not part of the match or, in stroke play, not part of a competitor's side, and includes a referee, a marker, an observer or a forecaddie. Neither wind nor water is an outside agency.

'Equipment' is anything used, worn or carried by or for the player except any ball he has played at the hole being played and any small object, such as a coin or a tee, when used to mark the position of a ball or the extent of an area in which a ball is to be dropped. Equipment includes a golf cart, whether or not motorised. If such a cart is shared by more than one player, its status under the Rules is the same as that of a caddie employed by more than one player. See 'Caddie'.

A player has 'addressed the ball' when he has taken his <u>stance</u> and has also grounded his club, except that in a <u>hazard</u> a player has addressed the ball when he has taken his stance.

Taking his 'stance' consists in a player placing his feet in position for and preparatory to making a stroke.

18-1 By Outside Agency
If a ball at rest is moved by an outside agency, the player shall incur no penalty and the ball shall be replaced before the player plays another stroke.

(Player's ball at rest moved by another ball – See Rule 18-5.)

18-2 By Player, Partner, Caddie or Equipment
(*a*) **General**
When a player's ball is in play, if:

(i) The player, his partner or either of their caddies lifts or moves it, touches it purposely (except with a club in the act of addressing it) or causes it to move except as permitted by a Rule; or

(ii) Equipment of the player or his partner causes the ball to move;
the player shall incur a penalty stroke. The ball shall be replaced unless the movement of the ball occurs after the player has begun his swing and he does not discontinue his swing.

Under the Rules no penalty is incurred if a player accidentally causes his ball to move in the following circumstances:

In measuring to determine which ball farther from hole – Rule 10-4;
In searching for covered ball in hazard or for ball in casual water, ground under repair, etc. – Rule 12-1;
In the process of repairing hole plug or ball mark – Rule 16-1(*c*);
In the process of removing loose impediment on putting green – Rule 18-2(*c*)
In the process of lifting ball under a Rule – Rule 20-1
In the process of placing or replacing ball under a Rule – Rule 20-3(*a*)
In complying with Rule 22 relating to lifting ball interfering with or assisting play
In removal of movable obstruction – Rule 24-1.

(*b*) **Ball Moving After Address**
If a player's ball in play moves after the player has addressed it (other than as a result of a stroke), the player shall be deemed to have moved the ball and *shall incur a penalty stroke*. The player shall replace the ball unless the movement of the ball occurs after he has begun his swing and he does not discontinue his swing.

(*c*) **Ball Moving After Loose Impediment Touched**
Through the green, if the ball moves after any loose impediment lying within a club-length of it has been touched by the player, his partner or either of their caddies, and before the player has addressed it, the player shall be deemed to have moved the ball and *shall incur a penalty stroke*. The player shall replace the ball unless the movement of the ball occurs after he has begun his swing and he does not discontinue his swing.

On the putting green, if the ball moves in the process of removing any loose impediment, it shall be replaced without penalty.

18-3 By Opponent, Caddie or Equipment in Match Play

(*a*) **During Search**

If, during search for a player's ball, it is moved by an opponent, his caddie or his <u>equipment</u>, no penalty is incurred and the player shall replace the ball.

(*b*) **Other Than During Search**

If, other than during search for a ball, the ball is touched or moved by an opponent, his caddie or his <u>equipment</u>, except as otherwise provided in the Rules, *the opponent shall incur a penalty stroke*. The player shall replace the ball.

(Ball moved in measuring to determine which ball farther from the hole – See Rule 10-4.)

(Playing a wrong ball – See Rule 15-2.)

(Ball moved in complying with Rule 22 relating to lifting ball interfering with or assisting play.)

18-4 By Fellow-Competitor, Caddie or Equipment in Stroke Play

If a competitor's ball is moved by a fellow-competitor, his caddie or his <u>equipment</u>, no penalty is incurred. The competitor shall replace his ball.

(Playing a wrong ball – See Rule 15-3.)

18-5 By Another Ball

If a ball in play and at rest is moved by another ball in motion after a stroke, the moved ball shall be replaced.

*PENALTY FOR BREACH OF RULE:

Match play – Loss of hole; Stroke play – Two strokes.

   **If a player who is required to replace a ball fails to do so, he shall incur the general penalty for breach of Rule 18 but no additional penalty under Rule 18 shall be applied.*

Note 1: If a ball to be replaced under this Rule is not immediately recoverable, another ball may be substituted.

Note 2: If it is impossible to determine the spot on which a ball is to be placed, see Rule 20-3(*c*).

RULE 19

Ball in Motion Deflected or Stopped

Definitions

An 'outside agency' is any agency not part of the match or, in stroke play, not part of a competitor's side, and includes a referee, a marker, an observer or a forecaddie. Neither wind nor water is an outside agency.

'Equipment' is anything used, worn or carried by or for the player except any ball he has played at the hole being played and any small object, such as a coin or a tee, when used to mark the position of a ball or the extent of an area in which a ball is to be dropped. Equipment includes a golf cart, whether or not motorised. If such a cart is shared by more than one player, its status under the Rules is the same as that of a caddie employed by more than one player. See 'Caddie'.

19-1 By Outside Agency

If a ball in motion is accidentally deflected or stopped by any outside agency, it is a rub of the green, no penalty is incurred and the ball shall be played as it lies except:

(*a*) If a ball in motion after a stroke other than on the putting green comes to rest in or on any moving or animate outside agency, the player shall, through the green or in a hazard, drop the ball, or on the putting green place the ball, as near as possible to the spot where the outside agency was when the ball came to rest in or on it; and

(*b*) If a ball in motion after a stroke on the putting green is deflected or stopped by, or comes to rest in or on, any moving or animate outside agency except a worm or an insect, the stroke shall be cancelled and the ball shall be replaced.

If the ball is not immediately recoverable, another ball may be substituted.

(Player's ball deflected or stopped by another ball at rest – See Rule 19-5.)

Note: If the referee or the Committee determines that a competitor's ball has been deliberately deflected or stopped by an outside agency, Rule 1-4 applies to the competitor. If the outside agency is a fellow-competitor or his caddie, Rule 1-2 applies to the fellow-competitor.

19-2 By Player, Partner, Caddie or Equipment

(*a*) **Match Play**

If a player's ball is accidentally deflected or stopped by himself, his partner or either of their caddies or equipment, *he shall lose the hole.*

(*b*) **Stroke Play**

If a competitor's ball is accidentally deflected or stopped by himself, his partner or either of their caddies or equipment, *the competitor shall incur a penalty of two strokes.* The ball shall be played as it lies, except when it comes to rest in or on the competitor's, his partner's or either of their caddies' clothes or equipment, in which case the competitor shall through the green or in a hazard drop the ball, or on the putting green place the ball, as near as possible to where the article was when the ball came to rest in or on it.

Exception: Dropped Ball – See Rule 20-2(*a*).

(Ball purposely deflected or stopped by player, partner or caddie – See Rule 1-2.)

19-3 By Opponent, Caddie or Equipment in Match Play

If a player's ball is accidentally deflected or stopped by an opponent, his caddie or his equipment, no penalty is incurred. The player may play the ball as it lies or, before another stroke is played by either side, cancel the stroke and replay it (See Rule 20-5). If the player elects to replay the stroke and the original ball is not immediately recoverable, another ball may be substituted.

If the ball has come to rest in or on the opponent's or his caddie's clothes or equipment, the player may through the green or in a hazard drop the ball, or on the putting green place the ball, as near as possible to where the article was when the ball came to rest in or on it.

Exception: Ball striking person attending flagstick – See Rule 17-3(*b*).

(Ball purposely deflected or stopped by opponent or caddie – See Rule 1-2.)

19-4 By Fellow-Competitor, Caddie or Equipment in Stroke Play

See Rule 19-1 regarding ball deflected by outside agency.

19.5 By Another Ball

If a player's ball in motion after a stroke is deflected or stopped by a ball at rest, the player shall play his ball as it lies. In stroke play, if both balls lay on the putting green prior to the stroke, *the player incurs a penalty of two strokes*. Otherwise, no penalty is incurred.

If a player's ball in motion after a stroke is deflected or stopped by another ball in motion, the player shall play his ball as it lies. There is no penalty unless the player was in breach of Rule 16-1(*g*), in which case *he shall incur the penalty for breach of that Rule*.

Exception: Ball in motion after a stroke on the putting green deflected or stopped by moving or animate outside agency – See Rule 19-1(*b*).

PENALTY FOR BREACH OF RULE

Match play – Loss of hole; Stroke play – Two strokes.

RULE 20

Lifting, Dropping and Placing; Playing from Wrong Place

20-1 Lifting

A ball to be lifted under the Rules may be lifted by the player, his partner or another person authorised by the player. In any such case, the player shall be responsible for any breach of the Rules.

The position of the ball shall be marked before it is lifted under a Rule which requires it to be replaced. If it is not marked, *the player shall incur a penalty of one stroke* and the ball shall be replaced. If it is not replaced, *the player shall incur the general penalty* for breach of this Rule but no additional penalty under Rule 20-1 shall be applied.

If a ball or a ball-marker is accidentally moved in the process of lifting the ball under a Rule or marking its position, no penalty is incurred and the ball or the ball-marker shall be replaced.

Note: The position of a ball to be lifted should be marked by placing a ball-marker, a small coin or other similar object immediately behind the ball. If the ball-marker interferes with the play, stance or stroke of another player, it should be placed one or more clubhead-lengths to one side.

20-2 Dropping and Re-dropping

(*a*) **By whom and How**

A ball to be dropped under the rules shall be dropped by the player himself. He shall stand erect, hold the ball at shoulder height and arm's length and drop it. If a ball is dropped by any other person or in any other manner and the error is not corrected as provided by Rule 20-6, *the player shall incur a penalty stroke.*

If the ball touches the player, his partner, either of their caddies or their equipment before or after it strikes the ground, the ball shall be re-dropped, without penalty. There is no limit to the number of times a ball shall be re-dropped in such circumstances.

(Taking action to influence position or movement of ball – See Rule 1-2.)

(*b*) **Where to Drop**

When a ball is to be dropped, it shall be dropped as near as possible to the spot where the ball lay, but not nearer the hole, except when a Rule permits or requires it to be dropped elsewhere. If a ball is to be dropped in a hazard, the ball shall be dropped in and come to rest in that hazard.

Note: A ball when dropped must first strike the ground where the applicable Rule requires it to be dropped. If it is not so dropped, Rules 20-6 and -7 apply.

(*c*) **When to Re-Drop**

A dropped ball shall be re-dropped without penalty if it:

   (i) Rolls into a hazard;

  (ii) Rolls out of a hazard;

 (iii) Rolls on to a putting green;

 (iv) Rolls out of bounds;

(v) Rolls back into the condition from which relief was taken under Rule 24-2 (immovable obstruction) or Rule 25 (abnormal ground conditions and wrong putting green);

(vi) Rolls and comes to rest more than two club-lengths from where it first struck the ground; or

(vii) Rolls and comes to rest nearer the hole than its original position unless otherwise permitted by the Rules.

If the ball again rolls into such position, it shall be placed as near as possible to the spot where it first struck the ground when re-dropped.

If a ball to be re-dropped or placed under this Rule is not immediately recoverable, another ball may be substituted.

20-3 Placing and Replacing

(a) By Whom and Where

A ball to be placed under the Rules shall be placed by the player or his partner. A ball to be replaced shall be replaced by the player, his partner or the person who lifted or moved it. In any such case, the player shall be responsible for any breach of the Rules.

If a ball or ball-marker is accidentally moved in the process of placing or replacing the ball, no penalty is incurred and the ball or the ball-marker shall be replaced.

(b) Lie of Ball to Be Placed or Replaced Altered

If the original lie of a ball to be placed or replaced has been altered:

(i) Except in a hazard, the ball shall be placed in the nearest lie most similar to the original lie which is not more than one club-length from the original lie, not nearer the hole and not in a hazard;

(ii) In a water hazard, the ball shall be placed in accordance with Clause (i) above, except that the ball must be placed in the water hazard;

(iii) In a bunker, the original lie shall be recreated as nearly as possible and the ball shall be placed in that lie.

(c) Spot Not Determinable

If it is impossible to determine the spot where the ball is to be placed:

(i) Through the green, the ball shall be dropped as near as possible to the place where it lay but not nearer the hole or in a hazard;

(ii) In a hazard, the ball shall be dropped in the hazard as near as possible to the place where it lay but not nearer the hole;

(iii) On the putting green, the ball shall be placed as near as possible to the place where it lay but not nearer the hole or in a hazard.

(d) Ball Fails to Remain on Spot

If a ball when placed fails to remain on the spot on which it was placed, it shall be replaced without penalty. If it still fails to remain on that spot:

(i) Except in a <u>hazard</u>, it shall be placed at the nearest spot not nearer the hole or in a hazard where it can be placed at rest;

(ii) In a hazard, it shall be placed in the hazard at the nearest spot not nearer the hole where it can be placed at rest.

PENALTY FOR BREACH OF RULE 20-1, 20-2 or 20-3:

Match play – Loss of hole; Stroke play – Two strokes.

20-4 When Ball Dropped or Placed Is in Play

If the player's <u>ball in play</u> has been lifted, it is again in play when dropped or placed.

A substituted ball becomes the ball in play if it is dropped or placed under an applicable Rule, whether or not such Rule permits substitution. A ball substituted under an inapplicable Rule is a <u>wrong ball</u>.

20-5 Playing Next Stroke from Where Previous Stroke Played

When, under the Rules, a player elects or is required to play his next <u>stroke</u> from where a previous stroke was played, he shall proceed as follows:

If the stroke is to be played from the <u>teeing ground</u>, the ball to be played shall be played from anywhere within the teeing ground and may be teed;

If the stroke is to be played from <u>through the green</u> or a hazard, it shall be dropped;

If the stroke is to be played on the <u>putting green</u>, it shall be placed.

PENALTY FOR BREACH OF RULE 20-5:

Match play – Loss of hole; Stroke play – Two strokes.

20-6 Lifting Ball Wrongly Dropped or Placed

A ball dropped or placed in a wrong place or otherwise not in accordance with the Rules but not played may be lifted, without penalty, and the player shall then proceed correctly.

20-7 Playing from Wrong Place

For a ball played outside teeing ground, see Rule 11-4.

(*a*) **Match Play**

If a player plays a stroke with a ball which has been dropped or placed in a wrong place, *he shall lose the hole.*

(*b*) **Stroke Play**

If a competitor plays a stroke with:

(i) His original ball which has been dropped or placed in a wrong place;

(ii) A substituted ball which has been dropped or placed under an applicable Rule but in a wrong place; or

(iii) His ball in play when it has been moved and not replaced in a case where the Rules require replacement,

he shall, provided a serious breach has not occurred, *incur the penalty prescribed by the applicable Rule* and play out the hole with the ball.

If, after playing from a wrong place, a competitor becomes aware of that fact and believes that a serious breach may be involved, he may, provided he has not played a stroke from the next teeing ground or, in the case of the last hole of the round, left the putting green, declare that he will play out the hole with a second ball dropped or placed in accordance with the Rules. The competitor shall report the facts to the Committee before returning his score card; if he fails to do so, *he shall be disqualified*. The Committee shall determine whether a serious breach of the Rule occurred. If so, the score with the second ball shall count and *the competitor shall add two penalty strokes to his score with that ball*.

If a serious breach has occurred and the competitor has failed to correct it as prescribed above, *he shall be disqualified*.

Note: If a competitor plays a second ball, penalty strokes incurred by playing the ball ruled not to count and strokes subsequently taken with that ball shall be disregarded.

RULE 21

Cleaning Ball

A ball on the putting green may be cleaned when lifted under Rule 16-1b. Elsewhere, a ball may be cleaned when lifted except when it has been lifted:

(*a*) To determine if it is unfit for play (Rule 5-3);

(*b*) For identification (Rule 12-2), in which case it may be cleaned only to the extent necessary for identification; or

(*c*) Because it is interfering with or assisting play (Rule 22).

If a player cleans his ball during play of a hole except as provided in this Rule, *he shall incur a penalty of one stroke* and the ball, if lifted, shall be replaced.

If a player who is required to replace a ball fails to do so, *he shall incur the penalty* for breach of Rule 20-3(*a*), but no additional penalty under Rule 21 shall be applied.

Exception: If a player incurs a penalty for failing to act in accordance with Rule 5-3, 12-2 or 22, no additional penalty under Rule 21 shall be applied.

RULE 22

Ball Interfering with or Assisting Play

Any player may:

(*a*) Lift his ball if he considers that it might assist any other player; or

(*b*) Have any other ball lifted if he considers that it might interfere with his play or assist the play of any other player, but this may not be done while another ball is in motion. In stroke play, a player required to lift his ball may play first rather than lift. A ball lifted under this Rule shall be replaced.

If a ball is accidentally moved in complying with this Rule, no penalty is incurred and the ball shall be replaced.

PENALTY FOR BREACH OF RULE:

Match play – Loss of hole; Stroke play – Two strokes.

RULE 23

Loose Impediments

Definition

'Loose impediments' are natural objects such as stones, leaves, twigs, branches and the like, dung, worms and insects and casts or heaps made by them, provided they are not fixed or growing, are not solidly embedded and do not adhere to the ball.

Sand and loose soil are loose impediments on the putting green but not elsewhere.

Snow and ice are either casual water or loose impediments, at the option of the player, except that manufactured ice is an obstruction.

Dew is not a loose impediment.

23-1 Relief

Except when both the loose impediment and the ball lie in or touch a hazard, any loose impediment may be removed without penalty. If the ball moves, see Rule 18-2(*c*).

When a player's ball is in motion, a loose impediment on his line of play shall not be removed.

PENALTY FOR BREACH OF RULE:

Match play – Loss of hole) Stroke play – Two strokes.

(Searching for ball in hazard – See Rule 12-1.)

(Touching line of putt – See Rule 16-1*a*.)

RULE 24

Obstructions

Definition

An 'obstruction' is anything artificial, including the artificial surfaces and sides of roads and paths, except:

(a) Objects defining out of bounds, such as walls, fences, stakes and railings;

(b) Any part of an immovable artificial object which is out of bounds; and

(c) Any construction declared by the Committee to be an integral part of the course.

24.1 Movable Obstruction

A player may obtain relief from a movable obstruction as follows:

(a) If the ball does not lie in or on the obstruction, the obstruction may be removed; if the ball moves, no penalty is incurred and the ball shall be replaced.

(b) If the ball lies in or on the obstruction, the ball may be lifted, without penalty, and the obstruction removed. The ball shall through the green or in a hazard be dropped, or on the putting green be placed, as near as possible to the spot directly under the place where the ball lay in or on the obstruction, but not nearer the hole.

The ball may be cleaned when lifted under Rule 24-1.

When a ball is in motion, an obstruction on the player's line of play other than an attended flagstick and equipment of the players shall not be removed.

24-2 Immovable Obstruction

(a) **Interference**

Interference by an immovable obstruction occurs when a ball lies in or on the obstruction, or so close to the obstruction that the obstruction interferes with the player's stance or the area of his intended swing. If the player's ball lies on the putting green, interference also occurs if an immovable obstruction on the putting green intervenes on his line of putt. Otherwise, intervention on the line of play is not, of itself, interference under this Rule.

(b) **Relief**

Except when the ball lies in or touches a water hazard or a lateral water hazard, a player may obtain relief from interference by an immovable obstruction, without penalty, as follows:

(i) **Through the Green:** If the ball lies through the green, the point on the course nearest to where the ball lies shall be determined (without crossing over, through or under the obstruction) which (*a*) is not nearer the hole, (*b*) avoids interference (as defined) and (*c*) is not in a hazard or on a putting green. The player shall lift the ball and drop it within one club-length of the point thus determined on ground which fulfils (*a*), (*b*) and (*c*) above.

Note: The prohibition against crossing over, through or under the obstruction does not apply to the artificial surfaces and sides of roads and paths or when the ball lies in or on the obstruction.

  (ii) **In a Bunker:** If the ball lies in or touches a bunker, the player shall lift and drop the ball in accordance with Clause (i) above, except that the ball must be dropped in the bunker.

(iii) **On the Putting Green:** If the ball lies on the putting green, the player shall lift the ball and place it in the nearest position to where it lay which affords relief from interference, but not nearer the hole nor in a hazard.

  The ball may be cleaned when lifted under Rule 24-2(*b*).

  (Ball rolling back into condition from which relief taken – See Rule 20-2(*c*)(v).)

  Exception: A player may not obtain relief under Rule 24-2(*b*) if (*a*) it is clearly unreasonable for him to play a stroke because of interference by anything other than an immovable obstruction or (*b*) interference by an immovable obstruction would occur only through use of an unnecessarily abnormal stance, swing or direction of play.

Note: If a ball lies in or touches a water hazard including a lateral water hazard), the player is not entitled to relief without penalty from interference by an immovable obstruction. The player shall play the ball as it lies or proceed under Rule 26-1.

PENALTY FOR BREACH OF RULE:

Match play – Loss of hole; Stroke play – Two strokes.

RULE 25

Abnormal Ground Conditions and Wrong Putting Green

Definitions

'Casual water' is any temporary accumulation of water on the course which is visible before or after the player takes his stance and is not a water hazard. Snow and ice are either casual water or loose impediments, at the option of the player, except that manufactured ice is an obstruction. Dew is not casual water.

'Ground under repair' is any portion of the course so marked by order of the Committee or so declared by its authorised representative. It includes material piled for removal and a hole made by a greenkeeper, even if not so marked. Stakes and lines defining ground under repair are in such ground. The margin of ground under repair extends vertically downwards, but not upwards.

Note 1: Grass cuttings and other material left on the course which have been abandoned and are not intended to be removed are not ground under repair unless so marked.

Note 2: The Committee may make a Local Rule prohibiting play from ground under repair.

25.1 Casual Water, Ground Under Repair and Certain Damage to Course

(*a*) **Interference**

Interference by casual water, ground under repair or a hole, cast or runway made by a burrowing animal, a reptile or a bird occurs when a ball lies in or touches any of these conditions or when the condition interferes with the player's stance or the area of his intended swing.

If the player's ball lies on the putting green, interference also occurs if such condition on the putting green intervenes on his line of putt.

If interference exists, the player may either play the ball as it lies (unless prohibited by Local Rule) or take relief as provided in Clause (*b*).

(*b*) **Relief**

If the player elects to take relief, he shall proceed as follows:

(i) **Through the Green:** If the ball lies through the green, the point on the course nearest to where the ball lies shall be determined which (*a*) is not nearer the hole, (*b*) avoids interference by the condition, and (*c*) is not in a hazard or on a putting green. The player shall lift the ball and drop it without penalty within the club-length of the point thus determined on ground which fulfils (*a*), (*b*), and (*c*) above.

(ii) **In a Hazard:** If the ball lies in or touches a hazard, the player shall lift and drop the ball either:

(*a*) Without penalty, in the hazard, as near as possible to the spot where the ball lay, but not nearer the hole, on ground which affords maximum available relief from the condition; or

(*b*) *Under penalty of one stroke*, outside the hazard, keeping the point where the ball lay directly between the hole and the spot on which the ball is dropped.

Exception: If a ball lies in or touches a water hazard (including a lateral water hazard), the player is not entitled to relief without penalty from a hole, cast or runway made by a burrowing animal, a reptile or a bird. The player shall play the ball as it lies or proceed under Rule 26-1.

(iii) On the Putting Green: If the ball lies on the <u>putting green</u>, the player shall lift the ball and place it without penalty in the nearest position to where it lay which affords maximum available relief from the condition, but not nearer the hole nor in a <u>hazard</u>.

The ball may be cleaned when lifted under Rule 25-1(*b*).

(Ball rolling back into condition from which relief taken – See Rule 20-2(*c*)(v).)

Exception: A player may not obtain relief under Rule 25-1(*b*) if (*a*) it is clearly unreasonable for him to play a stroke because of interference by anything other than a condition covered by Rule 25-1(*a*), or (*b*) interference by such a condition would occur only through use of an unnecessarily abnormal stance, swing or direction of play.

(*c*) Ball Lost Under Condition Covered by Rule 25-1

It is a question of fact whether a ball lost after having been struck toward a condition covered by Rule 25-1 is lost under such condition. In order to treat the ball as lost under such condition, there must be reasonable evidence to that effect. In the absence of such evidence, the ball must be treated as a lost ball and Rule 27 applies.

(i) Outside a Hazard – If a ball is lost outside a <u>hazard</u> under a condition covered by Rule 25-1, the player may take relief as follows: the point on the <u>course</u> nearest to where the ball last crossed the margin of the area shall be determined which (*a*) is not nearer the hole than where the ball last crossed the margin, (*b*) avoids interference by the condition, and (*c*) is not in a hazard or on a <u>putting green</u>. He shall drop a ball without penalty within one club-length of the point thus determined on ground which fulfils (*a*), (*b*) and (*c*) above.

(ii) In a Hazard – If a ball is lost in a <u>hazard</u> under a condition covered by Rule 25-1, the player may drop a ball either:

(*a*) Without penalty, in the hazard as near as possible to the point at which the original ball last crossed the margin of the area, but not nearer the hole, on ground which affords maximum available relief from the condition;

or

(*b*) *Under penalty of one stroke*, outside the hazard, keeping the spot at which the original ball last crossed the margin of the hazard directly between the hole and the spot on which the ball is dropped.

Exception: If a ball lies in a <u>water hazard</u> (including a <u>lateral water hazard</u>), the player is not entitled to relief without penalty for a ball lost in a hole, cast or runway made by a burrowing animal, a reptile or a bird. The player shall proceed under Rule 26-1.

25-2 Embedded Ball

A ball embedded in its own pitch-mark in the ground in any closely mown area <u>through the green</u> may be lifted, cleaned and dropped, without penalty, as near as possible to the spot where it lay but not nearer the hole. 'Closely mown area' means any area of the <u>course</u>, including paths through the rough, cut to fairway height or less.

25-3 Wrong Putting Green

If a ball lies on a <u>putting green</u> other than that of the hole being played, the point on the <u>course</u> nearest to where the ball lies shall be determined which (*a*) is not nearer the hole, and (*b*) is not in a *hazard* or on a putting green. The player shall lift the ball and drop it without penalty within one club-length of the point thus determined on ground which fulfils (*a*) and (*b*) above. The ball may be cleaned when so lifted.

Note: Unless otherwise prescribed by the Committee, the term 'a putting green other than that of the hole being played' includes a practice putting green or pitching green on the course.

PENALTY FOR BREACH OF RULE:
Match play – Loss of hole; Stroke play – Two strokes.

RULE 26

Water Hazards (including Lateral Water Hazards)

Definitions

A 'water hazard' is any sea, lake, pond, river, ditch, surface drainage ditch or other open water course (whether or not containing water) and anything of a similar nature.

A ground or water within the margin of a water hazard is part of the water hazard. The margin of a water hazard extends vertically upwards and downwards. Stakes and lines defining the margins of water hazards are in the hazards.

Note: Water hazards (other than <u>lateral water hazards</u>) should be defined by yellow stakes or lines.

A 'lateral water hazard' is a <u>water hazard</u> or that part of a water hazard so situated that it is not possible or is deemed by the Committee to be impracticable to drop a ball behind the water hazard in accordance with Rule 26-1(*b*).

That part of a water hazard to be played as a lateral water hazard should be distinctively marked.

Note: Lateral water hazards should be defined by red stakes or lines.

26-1 Ball in Water Hazard

It is a question of fact whether a ball lost after having been struck toward a water hazard is lost inside or outside the hazard. In order to treat the ball as lost in the hazard, there must be reasonable evidence that the ball lodged in it. In the absence of such evidence, the ball must be treated as a lost ball and Rule 27 applies.

If a ball lies in, touches or is lost in a water hazard (whether the ball lies in water or not), the player may *under penalty of one stroke*:

(*a*) Play his next stroke as nearly as possible as the spot from which the original ball was last played (See Rule 20-5); or

(*b*) Drop a ball behind the water hazard, keeping the point at which the original ball last crossed the margin of the water hazard directly between the hole and the spot on which the ball is dropped, with no limit to how far behind the water hazard the ball may be dropped; or

(*c*) *As additional options available only if the ball lies in, touches or is lost in a lateral water hazard*, drop a ball outside the water hazard within two club-lengths of (i) the point where the original ball last crossed the margin of the water hazard, or (ii) a point on the opposite margin of the water hazard equidistant from the hole. The ball must be dropped and come to rest not nearer the hole than the point where the original ball last crossed the margin of the water hazard.

The ball may be cleaned when lifted under this Rule.

(Ball moving in water in a water hazard – See Rule 14-6.)

26-2 Ball Played Within Water Hazard

(*a*) Ball comes to Rest in Hazard

If a ball played from within a water hazard comes to rest in the hazard after the stroke, the player may:

(i) proceed under Rule 26-1; or

(ii) *under penalty of one stroke*, play his next stroke as nearly as possible at the spot from which the last stroke from outside the hazard was played (see Rule 20-5).

(*b*) Ball Lost or Unplayable Outside Hazard or Out of Bounds

If a ball played from within the water hazard is lost or declared unplayable outside the hazard or is out of bounds, the player, after taking *a penalty of one stroke* under Rule 27-1 or 28(*a*), may:

(i) play a ball as nearly as possible at the spot from which the original ball was last played by him (see Rule 20-5); or

(ii) *under an additional penalty of one stroke*, proceed under Rule 26-1(*b*) or, if applicable, Rule 26-1(*c*), using as the reference point the point where the original ball last crossed the margin of the hazard before it came to rest in the hazard; or

(iii) *under an additional penalty of one stroke*, play his next stroke as nearly as possible at the spot from which the last stroke from outside the hazard was played (see Rule 20-5).

Note: If a ball played from within a water hazard is declared unplayable outside the hazard, nothing in Rule 26-2(*b*) precludes the player from proceeding under Rule 28(*b*) or (*c*).

PENALTY FOR BREACH OF RULE:
Match play – Loss of hole; Stroke play – Two strokes.

RULE 27

Ball Lost or Out of Bounds; Provisional Ball

If the original ball is lost under a condition covered by Rule 25-1 (casual water, ground under repair and certain damage to the course), the player may proceed under that Rule. If the original ball is lost in a water hazard, the player shall proceed under Rule 26.

Such Rules may not be used unless there is reasonable evidence that the ball is lost under a condition covered by Rule 25-1 or in a water hazard.

Definitions
A ball is 'lost' if:

(*a*) It is not found or identified as his by the player within five minutes after the player's side or his or their caddies have begun to search for it; or

(*b*) The player has put another ball into play under the Rules, even though he may not have searched for the original ball; or

(*c*) The player has played any stroke with provisional ball from the place where the original ball is likely to be or from a point nearer the hole than that place, whereupon the provisional ball becomes the ball in play.

Time spent in playing a wrong ball is not counted in the five-minute period allowed for search.

'Out of bounds' is ground on which play is prohibited.

When out of bounds is defined by reference to stakes or a fence, or as being beyond stakes or a fence, the out of bounds line is determined by the nearest inside points of the stakes or fence posts at ground level excluding angled supports.

When out of bounds is defined by a line on the ground, the line itself is out of bounds.

The out of bounds line extends vertically upwards and downwards.

A ball is out of bounds when all of it lies out of bounds.

A player may stand out of bounds to play a ball lying within bounds.

A 'provisional ball' is a ball played under Rule 27-2 for a ball which may be <u>lost</u> outside a <u>water hazard</u> or may be <u>out of bounds</u>.

27-1 Ball Lost or Out of Bounds

If a ball is <u>lost</u> outside a <u>water hazard</u> or is <u>out of bounds</u>, the player shall play a ball, *under penalty of one stroke*, as nearly as possible at the spot from which the original ball was last played (see Rule 20-5).

PENALTY FOR BREACH OF RULE 27-1:
Match play – Loss of hole; Stroke play – Two strokes.

27.2 Provisional Ball

(*a*) **Procedure**

If a ball may be <u>lost</u> outside a <u>water hazard</u> or may be <u>out of bounds</u>. to save time the player may play another ball provisionally as nearly as possible at the spot from which the original ball was played (see Rule 20-5). The player shall inform his opponent in match play or his marker or a fellow competitor in stroke play that he intends to play a <u>provisional ball</u>, and he shall play it before he or his partner goes forward to search for the original ball. If he fails to do so and plays another ball, such ball is not a provisional ball and becomes the <u>ball in play</u> *under penalty of stroke and distance* (Rule 27-1); the original ball is deemed to be lost.

(*b*) **When Provisional Ball Becomes Ball in Play**

The player may play a provisional ball until he reaches the placed where the original ball is likely to be. If he plays a stroke with the provisional ball from the place where the original ball is likely to be or from a point nearer the hole than that place, the original ball is deemed to be <u>lost</u> and the provisional ball becomes the ball in play under *penalty of stroke and distance* (Rule 27-1).

If the original ball is lost outside a water hazard or is out of bounds, the provisional ball becomes the ball in play, *under penalty of stroke and distance* (Rule 27-1).

(*c*) **When Provisional Ball to Be Abandoned**

If the original ball is neither lost outside a water hazard nor out of bounds, the player shall abandon the provisional ball and continue play with the original ball. If he fails to do so, any further strokes played with the provisional ball shall constitute playing a <u>wronged ball</u> and the provisions of Rule 15 shall apply.

Note: If the original ball lies in a water hazard, the player shall play the ball as it lies or proceed under Rule 26. If it is lost in a water hazard or unplayable, the player shall proceed under Rule 26 or 28, whichever is applicable.

RULE 28

Ball Unplayable

The player may declare his ball unplayable at any place on the course except when the ball lies in or touches a <u>water hazard</u>. The player is the sole judge as to whether his ball is unplayable.

If the player deems his ball to be unplayable, he shall, *under penalty of one stroke*:

(*a*) Play his next stroke as nearly as possible at the spot from which the original ball was last played or moved by him (see Rule 20-5); or

(*b*) Drop a ball within two club-lengths of the spot where the ball lay, but not nearer the hole; or

(*c*) Drop a ball behind the spot where the ball lay, keeping that point directly between the hole and the spot on which the ball is dropped, with no limit to how far behind that point the ball may be dropped.

If the unplayable ball lies in a <u>bunker</u> and the player elects to proceed under Clause (*b*) or (*c*), a ball must be dropped in the bunker.

The ball may be cleaned when lifted under this Rule.

PENALTY FOR BREACH OF RULE:
Match play – Loss of hole; Stroke play – Two strokes.

RULE 29

Threesomes and Foursomes

Definitions

Threesome: A match in which one plays against two, and each side plays one ball.

Foursome: A match in which two play against two, and each side plays one ball.

29-1 General
In a threesome or a foursome, during any <u>stipulated round</u> the partners shall play alternately from the teeing grounds and alternately during the play of each hole. <u>Penalty strokes</u> do not affect the order of play.

29-2 Match Play
If a player plays when his partner should have played, *his side shall lose the hole.*

29-3 Stroke Play

If the partners play a stroke or strokes in incorrect order, such stroke or strokes shall be cancelled and *the side shall incur a penalty of two strokes*. The side shall correct the error by playing a ball in correct order at the spot from which it first played in incorrect order (see Rule 20-5). If the side plays a stroke from the next teeing ground without first correcting the error or, in the case of the last hole of the round, leaves the putting green without declaring its intention to correct the error, *the side shall be disqualified*.

RULE 30

Three-Ball, Best-Ball and Four-Ball Match Play

Definitions

Three-Ball: A match play competition in which three play against one another, each playing his own ball. Each player is playing two distinct matches.

Best-Ball: A match in which one plays against the better ball of two or the best ball of three players.

Four-Ball: A match in which two play their better ball against the better ball of two other players.

30-1 Rules of Golf Apply

The Rules of Golf, so far as they are not at variance with the following special Rules, shall apply to three-ball, best-ball and four-ball matches.

30-2 Three-Ball Match Play

(*a*) Ball at Rest Moved by an Opponent

Except as otherwise provided in the Rules, if the player's ball is touched or moved by an opponent, his caddie or equipment other than during search, Rule 18-3(*b*) applies. *That opponent shall incur a penalty stroke in this match with the player*, but not his match with the other opponent.

(*b*) Ball Deflected or Stopped by an Opponent Accidentally

If a player's ball is accidentally deflected or stopped by an opponent, his caddie or equipment, no penalty shall be incurred. In his match with that opponent the player may play the ball as it lies or, before another stroke is played by either side, he may cancel the stroke and replay it (see Rule 20-5). In his match with the other opponent, the ball shall be played as it lies.

Exception: Ball striking person attending flagstick – See Rule 17-3(*b*). (Ball purposely deflected or stopped by opponent – See Rule 1-2.)

30-3 Best-Ball and Four-Ball Match Play

(*a*) Representation of Side

A side may be represented by one partner for all or any part of a match; all partners need not be present. An absent partner may join a match between holes, but not during play of a hole.

(*b*) Maximum of Fourteen Clubs

The side shall be penalised for a breach of Rule 4-4 by any partner.

(*c*) Order of Play

Balls belonging to the same side may be played in the order the side considers best.

(*d*) Wrong Ball

If a player plays a stroke with a <u>wrong ball</u> except in a <u>hazard</u>, *he shall be disqualified for that hole*, but his partner incurs no penalty even if the wrong ball belongs to him. The owner of the ball shall replace it on the spot from which it was played, without penalty. If the ball is not immediately recoverable, another ball may be substituted.

(*e*) Disqualification of Side

(i) *A side shall be disqualified* for a breach of any of the following by any partner:

Rule 1-3	Agreement to Waive Rules.
Rule 4-1, -2 or -3	Clubs.
Rule 5-1 or -2	The Ball.
Rule 6-2a	Handicap (playing off higher handicap).
Rule 6-4	Caddie.
Rule 6-7	Undue Delay (repeated offence).
Rule 14-3	Artificial Devices and Unusual Equipment.

(ii) *A side shall be disqualified* for a breach of any of the following by all partners:

Rule 6-3	Time of Starting and Groups.
Rule 6-8	Discontinuance of Play.

(*f*) Effect of Other Penalties

If a player's breach of a Rule assists his partner's play or adversely affects an opponent's play, *the partner incurs the relative penalty in addition to any penalty incurred by the player*.

In all other cases where a player incurs a penalty for breach of a Rule, the penalty shall not apply to his partner. Where the penalty is stated to be loss of hole, the effect shall be to disqualify the player for that hole.

(*g*) Another Form of Match Played Concurrently

In a best-ball or four-ball match when another form of match is played concurrently, the above special Rules shall apply.

RULE 31

Four-Ball Stroke Play

In four-ball stroke play two competitors play as partners, each playing his own ball. The lower score of the partners is the score for the hole. If one partner fails to complete the play of a hole, there is no penalty.

31-1 Rules of Golf Apply
The Rules of Golf, so far as they are not at variance with the following special Rules, shall apply to four-ball stroke play.

31-2 Representation of Side
A side may be represented by either partner for all or any part of a stipulated round; both partners need not be present. An absent competitor may join his partner between holes, but not during play of a hole.

31-3 Maximum of Fourteen Clubs
The side shall be penalised for a breach of Rule 4-4 by either partner.

31-4 Scoring
The marker is required to record for each hole only the gross score of whichever partner's score is to count. The gross scores to count must be individually identifiable; otherwise *the side shall be disqualified.* Only one of the partners need by responsible for complying with Rule 6-6(*b*).
    (Wrong score – See Rule 31-7*a*.)

31-5 Order of Play
Balls belonging to the same side may be played in the order the side considers best.

31-6 Wrong Ball
If a competitor plays a stroke with a wrong ball except in a hazard, *he shall add two penalty strokes to his score for the hole* and shall then play the correct ball. His partner incurs no penalty even if the wrong ball belongs to him.
    The owner of the ball shall replace it on the spot from which it was played, without penalty. If the ball is not immediately recoverable, another ball may be substituted.

31-7 Disqualification Penalties
  (*a*) **Breach by One Partner**
A side shall be disqualified from the competition for a breach of any of the following by either partner:

Rule 1-3	Agreement to Waive Rules.
Rule 3-4	Refusal to Comply with Rule.
Rule 4-1, 4-2 or 4-3	Clubs.
Rule 5-1 or 5-2	The Ball.
Rule 6-2(*b*)	Handicap (playing off higher handicap; failure to record handicap).
Rule 6-4	Caddie.
Rule 6-6(*b*)	Signing and Returning Card.
Rule 6-6(*d*)	Wrong Score for Hole, i.e. when the recorded lower score of the partners is lower than actually played. If the recorded lower score of the partners is higher than actually taken, it must stand as returned.
Rule 6-7	Undue Delay (repeated offence).
Rule 7-1	Practice Before or Between Rounds.
Rule 14-3	Artificial Devices and Unusual Equipment.
Rule 31-4	Gross Scores to count Not Individually Identifiable.

(*b*) **Breach by Both Partners**

A side shall be disqualified:

(i) For a breach by both partners of Rule 6-3 (Time of Starting and Groups) or Rule 6-8 (Discontinuance of Play); or

(ii) If, at the same hole, each partner is in breach of a Rule the penalty for which is disqualification from the competition or for a hole.

(*c*) **For the Hole Only**

In all other cases where a breach of a Rule would entail disqualification, *the competitor shall be disqualified only for the hole at which the breach occurred*.

31-8 Effect of Other Penalties

If a competitor's breach of a Rule assists his partner's play, *the partner incurs the applicable penalty in addition to any penalty incurred by the competitor*.

In all other cases where a competitor incurs a penalty for breach of a Rule, the penalty shall not apply to his partner.

RULE 32

Bogey, Par and Stableford Competitions

32-1 Conditions

Bogey, par and Stableford competitions are forms of stroke competition in which play is against a fixed score at each hole. The Rules for stroke play, so far as they are not at variance with the following special Rules, apply.

(*a*) Bogey and Par Competitions

The reckoning for bogey and par competitions is made as in match play. Any hole for which a competitor makes no return shall be regarded as a loss. The winner is the competitor who is most successful in the aggregate of holes.

The marker is responsible for marking only the gross number of strokes for each hole where the competitor makes a net score equal to or less than the fixed score.

Note: Maximum of fourteen Clubs – Penalties as in match play – see Rule 4-4.

(*b*) Stableford Competitions

The reckoning in Stableford competitions is made by points awarded in relation to a fixed score at each hole as follows:

Holes Played in	*Points*
More than one over fixed score or no score returned	0
One over fixed score	1
Fixed score	2
One under fixed score	3
Two under fixed score	4
Three under fixed score	5

The winner is the competitor who scores the highest number of points.

The marker shall be responsible for marking only the gross number of strokes at each hole where the competitor's net score earns one or more points.

Note: Maximum of fourteen Clubs (Rule 4-4) – Penalties applied as follows: From total points scored for the round, deduction of two points for each hole at which any breach occurred; maximum deduction per round: four points.

32-2 Disqualification Penalties

(*a*) From the Competition

A competitor shall be disqualified from the competition for a breach of any of the following:

Rule 1-3	Agreement to Waive Rules.
Rule 3-4	Refusal to Comply with Rule.
Rule 4-1, 4-2 or 4-3	Clubs.
Rule 5-1 or 5-2	The Ball.
Rule 6-2(*b*)	Handicap (playing off higher handicap; failure to record handicap).
Rule 6-3	Time of Starting and Groups.

Rule 6-4	Caddie.
Rule 6-6(*b*)	Signing and Returning Card.
Rule 6-6(*d*)	Wrong Score for Hole, except that penalty shall be incurred when a breach of this Rule does not affect the result of the hole.
Rule 6-7	Undue Delay (repeated offence).
Rule 6-8	Discontinuance of Play.
Rule 7-1	Practice Before or Between Rounds.
Rule 14-3	Artificial Devices and Unusual Equipment.

(*b*) **For a Hole**

In all other cases where a breach of a Rule would entail disqualification, *the competitor shall be disqualified only for the hole at which the breach occurred.*

RULE 33

The Committee

33-1 Conditions; Waiving Rule

The Committee shall lay down the conditions under which a competition is to be played.

The Committee has no power to waive a Rule of Golf.

Certain special rules governing stroke play are so substantially different from those governing match play that combining the two forms of play is not practicable and is not permitted. The results of matches played and the scores returned in these circumstances shall not be accepted.

In stroke play the Committee may limit a referee's duties.

33.2 The Course

(*a*) **Defining Bounds and Margins**

The Committee shall define accurately:

   (i) the course and out of bounds,
   (ii) the margins of water hazards and lateral water hazards,
   (iii) ground under repair, and
   (iv) obstruction and integral parts of the course.

(*b*) **New Holes**

New holes should be made on the day on which a stroke competition begins and at such other times as the Committee considers necessary, provided all competitors in a single round play with each hole cut in the same position.

Exception: When it is impossible for a damaged hole to be repaired so that it conforms with the Definition, the Committee may make a new hole in a nearby similar position.

(*c*) **Practice Ground**

Where there is no practice ground available outside the area of a competition course, the Committee should lay down the area on which players may practise on any day of a competition, if it is practicable to do so. On any day of a stroke competition, the Committee should not normally permit practice on or to a putting green or from a hazard of the competition course.

(*d*) **Course Unplayable**

If the Committee or its authorised representative considers that for any reason the course is not in a playable condition or that there are circumstances which render the proper playing of the game impossible, it may, in match play or stroke play, order a temporary suspension of play or, in stroke play, declare play null and void and cancel all scores for the round in question. When play has been temporarily suspended, it shall be resumed from where it was discontinued, even though resumption occurs on a subsequent day. When a round is cancelled, all penalties incurred in that round are cancelled.

(Procedure is discontinuing play – Rule 6-8.)

33-3 Times of Starting and Groups

The Committee shall lay down the times of starting and, in stroke play, arrange the groups in which competitors shall play.

When a match play competition is played over an extended period, the Committee shall lay down the limit of time within which each round shall be completed. When players are allowed to arrange the date of their match with these limits, the Committee should announce that the match must be played at a stated time on the last day of the period unless the players agree to a prior date.

33-4 Handicap Stroke Table

The Committee shall publish a table indicating the order of holes at which handicap strokes are to be given or received.

33-5 Score Card

In stroke play, the Committee shall issue for each competitor a scorecard containing the date and the competitor's name or, in foursome or four-ball stroke play, the competitors' names.

In stroke play, the Committee is responsible for the addition of scores and application of the handicap recorded on the card.

In four-ball stroke play, the Committee is responsible for recording the better-ball score for each hole and in the process applying the handicaps recorded on the card, and adding the better-ball scores.

In bogey, par and Stableford competitions, the Committee is responsible for applying the handicap recorded on the card and determining the results of each hole and the overall result or points total.

33-6 Decision of Ties

The Committee shall announce the manner, day and time for the decision of a halved match or of a tie, whether played on level terms or under handicap.

A halved match shall not be decided by stroke play. A tie in stroke play shall not be decided by a match.

33-7 Disqualification Penalty; Committee Discretion

A penalty of disqualification may in exceptional individual cases be waived, modified or imposed if the Committee considers such action warranted.

33-8 Local Rules

  (*a*) **Policy**

The Committee may make and publish Local Rules for abnormal conditions if they are consistent with the policy of the Governing Authority for the country concerned as set forth in Appendix I to these Rules.

  (*b*) **Waiving Penalty**

A penalty imposed by a Rule of Golf shall not be waived by a Local Rule.

RULE 34

Disputes and Decisions

34-1 Claims and Penalties

  (*a*) **Match Play**

In match play if a claim is lodged with the Committee under Rule 2-5, a decision should be given as soon as possible so that the state of the match may, if necessary, be adjusted.

If a claim is not made within the time limit provided by Rule 2-5, it shall not be considered unless it is based on facts previously unknown to the player making the claim and the player making the claim had been given wrong information (Rules 6-2*a* and 9) by an opponent. In any case, no later claim shall be considered after the result of the match has been officially announced, unless the Committee is satisfied that the opponent knew he was giving wrong information.

(*b*) **Stroke Play**

Except as provided below, in stroke play no penalty shall be rescinded, modified or imposed after the competition is closed. A competition is deemed to have closed when the result has been officially announced or, in stroke play qualifying followed by match play, when the player has teed off in his first match.

A penalty of disqualification shall be imposed at any time if a competitor:

(i) Returns a score for any hole lower than actually taken (Rule 6-6*d*) for any reason other than failure to include a penalty which he did not know he had incurred; or

(ii) Returns a scorecard on which he has recorded a handicap which he knows is higher than that to which he is entitled, and this affects the number of strokes received (Rule 6-2*b*).

34-2 Referee's Decision

If a referee has been appointed by the Committee, his decision shall be final.

34-3. Committee's Decision

In the absence of a referee, the players shall refer any dispute to the Committee, whose decision shall be final.

If the Committee cannot come to a decision, it shall refer the dispute to the Rules of Golf Committee of the Royal and Ancient Golf Club of St Andrews, whose decision shall be final.

If the point in doubt or dispute has not been referred to the Rules of Golf Committee, the player or players have the right to refer an agreed statement through the Secretary of the Club to the Rules of Golf Committee for an opinion as to the correctness of the decision given. The reply will be sent to the Secretary of the Club or Clubs concerned.

If play is conducted other than in accordance with the Rules of Golf, the Rules of Golf Committee will not give a decision on any question.

NOTE. RULES OF GOLF (The Royal and Ancient Golf Club of St Andrews) includes Appendixes dealing in some detail with 'Local Rules', 'Design of Clubs' and 'The Ball', plus 'Rules of Amateur Status'.

Reprinted by permission of the Royal and Ancient Golf Club of St Andrews and the United States Golf Association, by whom these Rules have been approved. For reasons of space the Appendixes to the Rules of Golf have been omitted. Copy of those Appendixes and the complete Rules of Golf can be obtained from the Royal and Ancient Golf Club of St Andrews.

THE RULES OF

Handball

The Playing Area

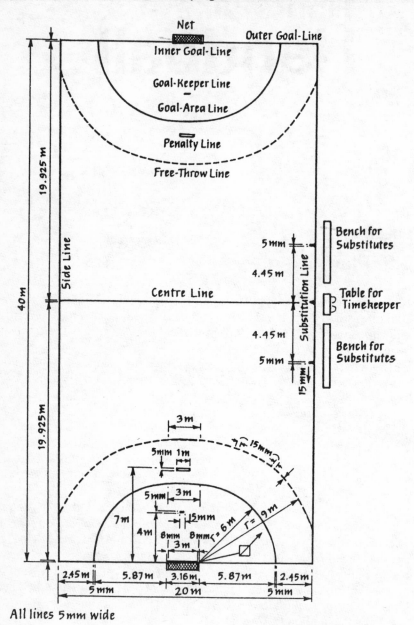

All lines 5mm wide

Handball

RULE 1

The Playing Area

1. The playing area (the court) shall be rectangular, 40m in length and 20m in width. The playing court shall be divided, by means of a centre-line, into two equal halves, as shown in the diagram on the opposite page.

 (i) Where possible a safety area should be included outside the playing area at least 1m beyond the side-lines, and 2m behind the goal-lines.

 (ii) The condition of the court must never be altered in any way to favour one of the playing teams.

2. The goals must be placed in the centre of the goal-line. Each goal consists of two upright posts equidistant from the corners of the playing area, 3m apart and 2m in height, measured from the inside of the goal-posts. The outer edge of the goal-line and the back of the goal-post shall be in line. The posts should be firmly placed on the ground and joined by a horizontal cross-bar. The posts and the cross-bar shall be square 8cm × 8cm, made of wood, light metal or synthetic material. They shall be painted on all sides in two colours that contrast effectively with the background. Where the goal-posts and the cross-bar join, they shall be painted in the same colour, and the rectangles of colour shall be 28cm long. All other rectangles of colour shall be 20cm in length.

 Each goal shall have a net attached in such a way that the ball when thrown into it, cannot rebound immediately into the playing court.

3. The goal-area is measured by marking a line 3m long at a distance of 3m from the goal and parallel to the goal-line. The ends of this line are connected to the goal-line by means of two quarter circles, each having a

radius of 6m, measured from the back inside corner of the goal-posts. This line is known as the goal-area line. Inside the goal-area at a distance of 4m, measured from outside of the goal-line, and from the centre of the goal, is drawn a line 15cm in length. (This line shall mark the limit of the goalkeeper's advance when a penalty throw is being executed.)

4. A second line is drawn at a distance of 9m from the goal-line and it is drawn in such a manner that it is a constant distance of 3m from the goal-area line (See 1.3). This is achieved by connecting the line with two quarter-circles each with a radius of 9m, measured from the rear inside corner of the goalposts. This line is called the free-throw line and it is drawn on the court as a broken line. The solid parts of this line measure 15cm and the gaps between also measure 15cm.

5. At 7m from the rear edge of the goal-line and parallel to it is drawn a line (the penalty-line), 1m long, the ends of this line being equidistant from the side-lines of the court.

6. The centre-line is drawn at a point exactly half-way between the two goal-lines. This line should be drawn across the court and must connect with the inner edges of the side-lines.

7. On each side of the centre-line and at a distance of 4.50m shall be drawn on line at right angles to the side-line. Each line shall measure 15cm in length and shall protrude into the court. The area encompassed by these lines shall be known as the area for substitution.

8. All lines form part of the area they enclose. They shall measure 5cm in width and be clearly visible (See, however, 1.9).

9. Between the goal-posts and goal-line shall measure the same width as each of the goal-posts, i.e. 8cm.

RULE 2

Duration of Play

1. For both male and female players, and where the age of the players is in excess of 18 years, each game shall consist of two periods of 30 minutes, with an interval of 10 minutes between each period.

2. Before the commencement of a game the referee shall toss a coin and the team winning the toss shall be entitled to decide whether to begin the game with the throw-off or alternatively decide which goal they wish to defend. In the event of a decision being made to take the throw-off, the team losing the toss shall have the choice of which goal they wish to defend. The court Referee shall start the game by blowing his whistle and the timing of the game shall begin when this whistle signal is made (See Rules 10.1, 18.4, 18.5, 10.3). The signal for both the ends of the

first half of time and of the end of the game shall be made by the timekeeper (See 19.2).

3. The teams change ends for the second period of play.

4. The Referees shall decide if play is to be interrupted and when play shall be restarted. Where necessary, they shall signal to the timekeeper if they wish the timing clock to be stopped (time-out).

Note: Where possible a clock that is publicly visible shall be utilised. However, such clock must be controlled from the timekeeper's table. Where it is impossible to exercise such control, the timekeeper shall use a table-clock or stopwatch.

5. The timekeeper shall stop the clock only when instructed so to do by the Referee. The Referee shall indicate such time-out by three short blasts on his whistle and by forming his hands into a 'T' shape. The clock is restarted following a whistle signal from the referee to indicate the resumption of play (See 16.3*a*).

6. If immediately before the expiry of the first half, or the completion of the game, a free throw or penalty is awarded, the throw must be executed and the result of the throw ascertained, before the timekeeper shall signal for the end of the period. Should the timekeeper inadvertently signal time too early, the throw must still be executed and the result ascertained, before the Referee shall make the appropriate signal to end the period (See 19.5).

7. If the Referees determine that the timekeeper has signalled the end of a period or the end of the game too early, they shall keep the two teams on the court, restart the game, and play the unexpired period of time. The play is restarted by a whistle signal, and by the team who were in possession of the ball at the time of the faulty decision by the timekeeper. The play must restart from the position where it was interrupted.

8. Where it is apparent that the timekeeper has signalled the end of the first period too late, the second half should be shortened accordingly.

9. Where the rules of a competition determine that a match must be won by one of the teams, and at the end of normal time the result is a tie, extra time shall be played after an interval of 5 minutes has elapsed. The Referee shall toss a coin to decide which team shall begin the period of extra time, and to determine which goal a team shall defend. The extra time shall consist of two periods of 5 minutes, without interval, for all categories of players. At the end of extra time, and where the result is still a tie, two further periods of 5 minutes, without interval, shall be played following a break of 5 minutes. The Referee shall once again toss a coin to determine which team shall have the throw off and which goal shall be defended.

10. Where even after a second period of extra time, the scores are level,

the regulations governing the competition shall be applied to determine the winner.

RULE 3

The Ball

1. The ball must be spherical and consist of an outer casing of leather or synthetic material. The outer casing must not be too shiny or slippery, and the ball should not be inflated too hard.
2. At the start of play the ball for Men and Youths shall weigh not more than 475g and not less than 425g. The circumference shall be not more than 60cm and not less than 58cm.

The ball for Women and Juniors shall weigh not more than 400g and not less than 325g, and the circumference shall be not more than 56cm and not less than 54cm.
3. Two balls which conform to the Rules must be available at the beginning of every game. Both balls shall be checked by the Referees and they shall decide which of the two shall be used in the game.
4. The ball chosen shall be used throughout the whole of the game and shall only be changed for the most compelling of reasons.

Note: Where it is found necessary to change the ball for whatever reason, the original ball should be brought back into use at the first interruption of the game following its substitution, provided it is still conforming to the Rules.
5. Only balls marked with Official International Handball Federation logo shall be used for International events and for all International matches.

RULE 4

The Players

1. Each team shall consist of 12 players (10 court players and 2 goalkeepers), of which a maximum of 7 (6 court players and 1 goalkeeper) may be present on the court at any one time. The remaining players are substitutes.

Substitutions, suspended players and 4 Officials are allowed in the substitution area. The Officials must be listed on the scoresheet and one shall be appointed as responsible for his team. Only this named Official shall have the right to address the timekeeper and if necessary, the Referee.

Note: A team must play with a goalkeeper at *all* times.

2. When a match begins, each team must have at least 5 players present on the playing court. The number of players on the court may be increased, at any time during the game, to 7, and the total complement of the team increased to 12. After a game has begun, it is permitted for numbers on the playing court to drop below 5 and for play to continue.

3. Prior to a game beginning, each player shall have his/her name recorded on the official scoresheet. Each player so recorded and present at the commencement of the game shall be 'entitled to participate'. Players entitled to participate may enter the court at any time providing such entry is in accordance with the Rules, and provided the player entering the court does so from within the area set aside for substitutions (See 1.7).

Note: When entering the court the player must do so within the substitution area inside his team's half of the court. Players who arrive late shall only be 'entitled to participate' after explicit permission has been granted by the timekeeper. If a player who is not 'entitled to participate' enters the court, the opposing team shall be awarded a free throw and the offending player shall be disqualified (See 17.5).

4. Substitutes may enter the game at any time without notifying the timekeeper. However, they shall only enter the playing court after the player they are replacing has left the playing court. The substitution of players must be made within the boundaries of the substitution area and within the players' own half of the court (See 4.4, 4.5, 13.1*a*).

Note: This Rule shall also apply when the substitution of goalkeepers is taking place.

During a time-out, a player may only enter the court from the substitution area with the permission of the Referee.

Any player who leaves the court or who enters the court and in so doing, commits an infringement of the substitution rule, shall be punished, unless such act is committed unintentionally.

5. A faulty substitution shall be penalised by a free throw (13.1.*a*) taken from the place where the substitute entered the court. In addition the offending player shall be suspended for 2 minutes. (The offending player is the player entering the court.) (See 17.3.*a*.)

Where the faulty substitution takes place during a stoppage of the game, the offending player shall be suspended and the game restarted by the throw appropriate to the original stoppage.

If, in connection with a faulty substitution an act of blatant unsportsmanlike conduct, is committed by the offending player, the player shall be either disqualified or excluded (See 17.5.*d*, 17.7).

6. If an extra player enters the court against the Rules and as a consequence his team have 8 players on the playing court, the offending

player shall be suspended and in addition another member of the team shall also leave the court for the suspension period.

Where a player serving a period of suspension enters the court before the suspension period has expired, he shall be suspended for a further period of 2 minutes. In addition another member of the team present on the court shall leave the court to serve the remainder of the original period of suspension.

Note: Where a decision has to be made as to which player must leave the court such decision shall be the responsibility of the team official. In the event of the official refusing so to choose, the decision as to which player shall leave the court will be made by the Referee.

7. All the court players in a team shall be uniformly dressed. The goalkeepers shall wear colours that distinguish them from the court players of both teams (See 18.3). The captain of each team must wear an armlet around an upper arm. The armlet should be approximately 4cm wide and must contrast with the colour of the shirt.

Players shall be numbered from 1 to 20; the numbers 1, 12 and 16 being reserved for the goalkeepers. Each player shall have a number clearly visible on the back of his shirt, at least 20cm high and a number at least 10cm high on the front of the shirt. The number should contrast with the colour of the shirt.

All players shall wear sports shoes.

Bracelets, wrist watches, rings, necklaces, frameless or rimless spectacles and any other item which in the opinion of the Referee might be dangerous or harmful to other players, shall be prohibited (See 18.3). It is the duty of the Referee to examine the equipment of the players prior to the commencement of the game. Equipment that is contrary to the Rules or which in the opinion of the Referee might constitute a hazard shall be removed before a player is allowed to participate in the game.

RULE 5

The Goalkeeper

1. The numbers reserved for the goalkeepers are 1, 12 and 16. Any player recorded upon the scoresheet under one of those three numbers shall be considered a goalkeeper for the duration of the game. Whereas it is permitted for a court player to substitute for a goalkeeper, it is not allowed for a player recorded upon the scoresheet as a goalkeeper to play as a court player.

In the event of a court player replacing the goalkeeper the timekeeper must be informed before the substitution can take place. The court player must change his uniform before entering the court (See 4.7, 17.3.*a*).

Note: The court player who substitutes the goalkeeper *is* allowed to play again as a court player at any time during the game.

The goalkeeper is allowed to:

2. Touch the ball with any part of the body, in the act of defence, when inside the goal-area.

3. Move around with the ball inside the goal-area without restriction (See, however, 16.3.*b*).

4. Leave the goal-area provided he is not at the time in possession of the ball. After leaving the goal-area the goalkeeper is considered to be a court player and the Rules applying to court players shall also apply to the goalkeeper. The goalkeeper is considered to have left the goal-area as soon as any part of his body touches the ground outside the goal-area line (See 5.12).

5. The goalkeeper shall not be penalised if, in the act of defence, he leaves the goal-area wholly or parially whilst trying to get the ball under control. Where the goalkeeper in this situation leaves or partially leaves the goal area, he shall be permitted to play the ball from outside of the goal without infringing the Rules of the game.

The goalkeeper is not allowed to:

6. Commit an act that might endanger an opponent whilst defending the goal (See 8.12).

7. Play the ball intentionally over the goal-line, outside the goal, once he has got the ball under control (See 13.1.*b*).

8. Leave the goal-area with the ball under control (See 13.1.*b*).

9. Make contact with the ball outside the goal-area, following a goal throw, until the ball has been touched by another player (See 13.1.*b*).

10. Touch the ball when it is lying or rolling on the floor outside the goal-area line, whilst he is inside the goal-area (See 13.1.*b*).

11. Take the ball into the goal-area whilst it is lying or rolling on the floor outside the goal-area line (See 14.1.*b*).

12. Re-enter the goal-area from the playing area whilst in possession of the ball (See 14.1.*b*).

13. Touch the ball with the feet or the legs below the knee whilst it is moving outwards in the direction of the playing area or is stationary within the goal-area (See 13.1.*b*).

14. Touch or cross the 4m line marked in the goal-area before the ball has left the thrower's hand, when a penalty throw is being executed (See 1.3, 14.8).

Note: When a penalty throw is executed, and the goalkeeper places himself at the 4m line, he is allowed, provided one foot is placed firmly on the the ground and behind the line, to move the other foot or any part of his body, in the air and in front of the 4m line.

RULE 6

The Goal-Area

The goal-area is that part of the court bounded by the goal-area line. Only the goalkeeper is allowed to enter the goal-area (See, however, 6.3).

The goal-area line is considered to be part of the goal area. The area is considered to have been entered when a court player touches it with any part of his body.

2. Court players who enter the goal-area shall be penalised as follows:

(*a*) Free throw when the player is in possession of the ball (See 13.1.*c*).

(*b*) Free throw if the player is not in possession of the ball, but by entering the goal-area gains advantage (See 6.2.*c*).

(*c*) Penalty throw, when a player of the defending team, by entering the goal-area, gains an advantage over the attacking opponent, who is in possession of the ball.

3. A court player who enters the goal-area shall not be penalised:

(*a*) If he enters the goal-area after playing the ball, provided such entry causes no disadvantage to the opposing team

(*b*) If he enters the goal-area without with ball and thereby does not gain advantage

(*c*) If, during or following a genuine defensive action, a defending player enters the goal-area, he shall not be penalised unless such action causes a disadvantage to the opposing team.

4. When the ball is inside the goal-area, it belongs to the goalkeeper. No court player shall be allowed to touch the ball whilst it is stationary or rolling along the floor, or when the ball is in the possession of the goalkeeper (See 13.1.*c*).

Note: The goal-area is recognised to be that area of the playing court floor bounded by the goal-area line. The air above that floor area is not considered to be part of the goal-area. Therefore, players may legitimately make contact with a ball not in contact with the floor.

5. When at the end of its momentum, the ball comes to rest in the goal-area, it shall be returned to the field of play by the goalkeeper.

6. Play is not interrupted when a defending player legitimately and in the act of defence, touches or deflects the ball into the goal-area, where the ball comes to rest or ultimately is taken by the goalkeeper.

7. Where a player intentionally plays the ball into his own goal-area, the Referee shall decide as follows:

(*a*) Goal, if the ball goes into the goal.

(*b*) Penalty throw if the goalkeeper touches the ball and a goal is not scored (See 14.1.*d*).

(*c*) Free throw if the ball finally comes to rest within the goal-area or the ball goes over the goal line, outside of the goal.

(*d*) Play to continue uninterrupted if the ball enters the goal-area, and returns into the field of play without being touched by the goalkeeper.

Play continues uninterrupted if the ball enters the goal-area and returns into the playing court without having been touched by the goalkeeper and without having gone out of play.

RULE 7

Playing the Ball

A player is permitted:

1. To catch, stop, push, hit or throw the ball with the hands (the hands may be open or closed) in any direction, or to play the ball with arms, head, torso, thigh and knees.

2. To hold the ball for a maximum of 3 seconds, either in his hands or holding the ball against the floor.

3. To take a maximum of 3 steps with the ball.

One step is considered taken when:

(*a*) A player who is standing with both feet in contact with the ground lifts one foot and puts it down again, or moves one foot from one place to another.

(*b*) A player who is in contact with the floor with one foot only, catches the ball and then makes contact with the ground with the other foot.

(*c*) A player, after a jump, touches the ground with one foot only, and then hops on the same foot or touches the ground with the other foot.

(*d*) A player after a jump, touches the ground with both feet simultaneously and then lifts one foot and puts it down again, or moves one foot from one place to another.

Note: When one foot is moved from one place to another, the player is allowed to move the other foot until it is level with the first without this being counted as a step.

4. Whilst standing or moving:

(*a*) To bounce the ball once and catch it with one or both hands.

(*b*) To bounce the ball or roll the ball on the ground repeatedly with one hand, and thereafter catch or pick up the ball in one or both hands.

As soon as the player takes possession of the ball in one or both hands, it must be played within 3 seconds or after taking no more than 3 steps.

The act of bouncing or dribbling the ball shall be deemed to have begun when the player touches the ball with any part of his body and in so doing, directs the ball towards the ground.

Once the ball has touched another player or the goal, the player is allowed to take possession of the ball again.

5. To place the ball from one hand to the other. (It is not allowed to throw the ball from one hand into the other.)

6. To play the ball whilst kneeling, sitting or lying on the ground.

A player is not permitted:

7. To touch the ball more than once unless it has touched the ground, or another player, or any part of the goal (See 13.1*d*.).

Note: Where a player, in the act of catching or stopping the ball, does not control the ball cleanly at the first attempt, and therefore fumbles in his efforts, such action shall not be penalised.

8. To touch the ball with any part of the leg, below the knee (See 13.1.d)

Note: In the event of a player touching the ball below the knee due to an opposing player throwing the ball against the legs of the player concerned, no offence shall be deemed to have taken place. In addition, if the Referee should consider that the striking of the ball below the knee does not lead to an advantage being gained, the offending player shall not be penalised.

9. To dive for the ball whilst it lying or rolling on the ground (See 13.1.*d*).

   Note: This Rule does not apply to the goalkeeper whilst he is in his own goal area.

10. To play the ball intentionally over the side-lines or the goal-lines outside the goal (See 13.1).

Note: This Rule does not apply to the goalkeeper who, from his own area and in the act of defence, fails to control the ball and thereby directs the ball over his own goal-lines outside the goal (goal throw).

11. To keep the ball in the team's possession without making any recognisable attempt to attack or to score a goal.

   Note: Such action is considered to be 'passive play' and is penalised by a free throw against the offending team. The throw is executed from the place where the ball was, when the play was interrupted.

12. Where the ball makes contact with one of the Referees, the play

shall continue as the Referee in this instance is considered to be part of the field of play.

RULE 8

Approach to an Opponent

A player is permitted:
1. To use his hands and arms to gain possession of the ball.
2. To use an open hand, in any direction, to dispossess an opponent.
3. To obstruct an opponent with the torso even if the opponent is not in possession of the ball.
A player is not permitted:
4. To obstruct an opponent with arms or legs.
5. To push or force an opponent into the goal-area.
6. To pull or hit the ball, with one or both hands, from the hands of an opponent.
7. To use the fist to dispossess an opponet.
8. To throw the ball intentionally or dangerously at an opponent or to feint with the ball in such a manner that the Referee might consider likely to endanger an opponent.
9. To endanger the goalkeeper.
10. To hold an opponent with one or both arms, or push him.
11. To run into, jump into, trip, hit or threaten an opponent in any other way.
12. Infringements of the Rules governing Approach to an Opponent (See 5.6, 8.4-11) shall be penalised by the award of a free throw against the offending players(s) (See 13.1.g) or by a penalty throw (See 14.1.a, 17.1.a).
13. Infringements of Rules 8.4-11, and where the action is mainly or exclusively directed at the opponent and not at the ball, shall be penalised progressively (See 17.16, 17.3.b). Where a player is considered guilty of performing in an unsportsmanlike manner (Unsporting Conduct), such action shall also be penalised progressively (See 17.1.d, 17.3.c).
14. Serious infringements of the Rules governing approach to an opponent or any serious occurrence of unsporting conduct shall be penalised by the disqualification of the offending player (See 17.5.b, 17.5.d).
15. A player who commits an assault upon another player or an official whilst on the court shall be excluded (See 17.7).

RULE 9

Scoring

1. A goal is scored when the *whole* of the ball has crossed the goal-line, between the goal-posts and underneath the cross-bar, provided that no infringement of the Rules had been committed by the scoring player or any of his team colleagues prior to the ball entering the goal.

When a defending player commits an infringement of the Rules in an attempt to prevent a goal being scored, but the ball still enters the goal, the goal shall be awarded. However, if a Referee or the timekeeper has blown the whistle before the whole of the ball has entered into the goal, then the goal *cannot* be awarded.

In the event of a defender, including the goalkeeper, throwing the ball into his own goal, the goal shall be awarded to the opposing team.

If the ball is prevented from entering the goal by someone or something that is not authorised to be on the court, e.g. a team official or a spectator, the Referees shall award a goal if in their opinion a goal would have been the inevitable result, had the throw not been interrrupted.

2. After a goal has been scored and the game resumed by means of a throw-off, that goal cannot subsequently be disallowed.

Note: Where a goal is scored immediately before half-time or the end of the game, and play cannot continue by means of a throw-off, because of a signal by the timekeeper to end the period of play, the goal shall be counted and the Referees shall ensure that both the timekeeper and team officials are made aware of the validity of the goal.

3. The team scoring the most goals in a match shall be declared the winner.

4. In the event of each team scoring the same number of goals the match shall be declared drawn.

RULE 10

Throw-Off

1. A game is begun by the execution of a throw-off taken by the team which wins the toss and decide to begin the game with the ball. However (See 2.2), where the team winning the toss opts to choose the end they wish to defend, rather than to start the game, the throw-off shall be taken by the team that did not win the toss. The second period of play is

begun by a throw-off taken by that team which did not start the first period of the game.

In the event of extra time being deemed necessary, the teams shall toss a coin again to decide which team should begin the extra period (See 2.7).

2. After a goal has been scored, play is resumed by a throw-off taken by the team conceding the goal.

3. The throw-off shall be taken from the centre of the court and may be executed in any direction. The throw shall only be made after the Referee has blown his whistle and it must be executed within 3 seconds of the blowing of the whistle (See 13.1.*h*).

4. At the moment the throw-off is executed, all players present on the court, shall be in their own half of the court. The players of the team that is not in possession of the ball shall be positioned at least 3m away from the player taking the throw (See 13.1.*h*).

RULE 11

Throw-In

1. A throw-in is awarded if the whole of the ball has crossed the side-line, either on the ground or in the air. Additionally, a throw-in is also awarded if a defending player, other than the goalkeeper, deflects or causes the ball to cross the goal-line on either side of the goal (See, however, 7.10).

2. The throw-in is taken without any whistle signal from the Referee, by a member of the team whose players did not last touch the ball before it went out of play.

3. The throw-in is taken from the place where the ball crossed the side-line. Where, however, the throw is awarded for the ball crossing the goal-line, the throw is taken from the corner point of the court, where the side-line and goal-line connect, and from the side of the goal from which the ball left the field of play.

4. The player taking the throw-in must have one foot placed on the side-line until the ball has left his hand.

Note: Whilst taking the throw the player is not allowed to place the ball on the ground and take it up again or to bounce the ball and catch it again (See 13.1.*i*).

5. Whilst the throw is being taken, all members of the opposing team shall position themselves at least 3m from the thrower. However, players of the opposing teams are entitled at *all* times to position

themselves immediately outside their own goal-area line, irrespective of whether this position is 3m from the thrower or not.

RULE 12

Goal Throw

1. A goal throw is awarded when the ball crosses the goal-line outside the goal, having last been touched with a member of the team attacking the goal or by the goalkeeper in the act of defending his goal (See, however, 5.7, 7.10).
2. When executing the goal throw, the goalkeeper shall throw the ball into the playing court from a position within the goal-area. The throw is made without any whistle signal from the Referee (See, however 16.3.*b*). The throw is considered taken, when the ball thrown by the goalkeeper, has crossed the goal-area line.
3. If the ball comes to rest in the goal-area, the goalkeeper shall bring the ball back into play by throwing the ball into the playing court (See, however, 6.7.*c*).
4. Once the goalkeeper has executed the goal throw, he is not allowed to make contact with ball again until it has been touched by another player (See 5.9, 13.1.*k*).

RULE 13

Free Throw

1. A free throw is awarded for:
   (*a*) Incorrect substitution or entering the court in a manner contrary to the Rules (See 4.6).
   (*b*) Infringements by the goalkeeper (See 5.7-10, 5.13).
   (*c*) Infringements by court players in the goal-area (See 6.2*a*, 6.2*b*, 6.2.4).
   (*d*) Incorrectly playing the ball (See 7.2-4, 7.7-9).
   (*e*) Deliberately playing the ball across the goal-line outside the goal, or playing the ball deliberately over the side-line (See 6.7.*c*, 7.10).
   (*f*) Passive play (See 7.11).
   (*g*) Offences relating to approach to opponents (See 8.12).
   (*h*) Infringements connected with a throw-off (See 10.3-4).
   (*i*) Infringements connected with a throw-in (See 11.4).
   (*k*) Infringements connected with a goal throw (See 12.4).
   (*l*) Infringements connected with a free throw (See 13.3).

(*m*) Interruption of play without infringement of the Rules (See 13.7).
(*n*) Infringements relating to the penalty throw (See 14.2-4, 14.6).
(*o*) Infringements connected with a Referee's throw (See 15.3).
(*p*) Taking throws incorrectly (See 16.2-5).
(*q*) Unsporting conduct (See 8.13-14).
(*r*) Assault (8.15).

2. A free throw is normally taken without any whistle signal from the Referee, and from the place where the offence took place. However, were the offence was committed by the defending team between their goal area line and the free-throw line, the throw shall be taken from the nearest point outside the free-throw line (See, however, 16.3.*a-h*).

3. Once the player executing the throw has taken up his position from which to make the throw, he is not allowed to bounce the ball or to put it down and take it up again (See 13.1.*l*).

4. Players of the attacking team must not cross or touch their opponents' free-throw line until the throw is taken (See 16.3.*c*).

The Referee shall correct the positions of any attacking players contravening the Rule, and who in his opinion are interfering with the play or gaining an advantage from the position they have adopted. Where such action is deemed necessary by the Referee, the throw shall only be taken following a whistle signal from the Referee.

5. When a free throw is taken members of the team not in possession of the ball shall position themselves at least 3m from the thrower. However, where the throw is executed from the free-throw line, the defending team are allowed to position themselves immediately outside their own goal-area line.

6. The Referee shall not award a free throw if by so doing, an advantage would be gained by the team causing the infringement.

Where the infringement causes the attacking team to lose possession or be placed at a disadvantage a free throw, at least, shall be awarded.

If, in spite of an infringement, an attacking player retains full control of both his ball and body, a free throw shall not be awarded.

7. In the event of the game being interrupted without any infringement of the Rules, and one of the teams is in possession of the ball, the game shall be restarted by means of a free throw executed by the team that was in possession, and from the place where the ball was at the time of the interruption. Where neither team was in possession, play will restart with the throw appropriate to the situation. In both instances, the play will re-commence upon a whistle signal being made by the Referee (See 13.1.*m*, 16.3.*a*).

8. The ball must be put down *immediately* by the player in possession when a decision is made against him or his team (See 17.3.*d*).

RULE 14

Penalty Throw

1. Penalty throw shall be awarded:

(*a*) When a clear chance of scoring a goal is prevented by an infringement, in any part of the court, and even when the offender is an official.

(*b*) When the goalkeeper enters his goal-area in possession of the ball, or takes it into the goal-area (See 5.11-12).

(*c*) When a court player enters his own area to gain an advantage over an attacking opponent who is in possession of the ball.

(*d*) When a court player deliberately plays the ball to his own goalkeeper and the goalkeeper is inside the goal-area.

2. The penalty throw must be taken as a shot propelled towards the goal and within 3 seconds of the whistle signal given by the court Referee (See 13.1.*n*).

3. The player taking the penalty throw must not touch or cross the penalty-line before the ball has left his hand (See 13.1.*n*).

4. Once the penalty thrown has been executed, the ball may not be played again until it has touched the goalkeeper or the goal (See 13.1.*n*).

5. Whilst the penalty throw is being taken, *all* players with the exception of the thrower, shall take up a position outside the free-throw line.

6. If a player of the attacking team touches the free-throw line or crosses into the zone between the free-throw line and the goal-area line before the ball has left the thrower's hand, a free throw shall be awarded to the defending team (See 13.1.*n*).

7. Whilst the penalty throw is being taken all members of the defending team, with the exception of the goalkeeper, shall position themselves at least 3m from the thrower. Where a member of the defending team touches or crosses the free-throw line or is nearer than 3m from the thrower, the Referee shall decide as follows:

(*a*) Goal, if the ball goes into the goal.

(*b*) The penalty throw to be retaken where a goal is not the result of the throw.

8. Whilst the penalty throw is being taken the goalkeeper is not allowed to advance any nearer to the thrower than the 4-m line (See 1.6, 5.14) before the ball has left the hand of the thrower. Where the goalkeeper contravenes this Rule, and a goal does not result from the penalty throw, the throw must be retaken.

9. The Referee must not award a penalty throw for an infringement of

the Rules by the defending team, if by so doing he causes a disadvantage to the attacking team.

Note: This Rule refers to a situation whereby an attacking player might be impeded in a manner preventing a shot being made. However, it may be possible in certain instances for the attacking player to break free and ultimately make the goal-scoring attempt. In such circumstances the Referee should wait until absolutely convinced that the momentum of the attacking player is ended due to illegal action on the part of the defending team, before awarding a penalty throw. Similarly, where a player is impeded but is nevertheless able to throw at the goal, the Referee should not award a penalty until the absolute result of the throw is ascertained. Where a goal does not result in these circumstances, a penalty at least should be awarded.

If in spite of any infringement, the attacking player retains *full* control of the ball and the body, a penalty throw should not be awarded.

RULE 15

Referee's Throw

1. A game shall be restarted by a Referee's throw when:

(*a*) The Rules have been infringed simultaneously by players of both teams.

(*b*) The ball has touched the roof or fixed equipment in place above the playing court.

(*c*) An interruption of the game is caused through no infringement of the Rules, and whilst neither team is in possession of the ball.

2. The *court* Referee executes the throw by throwing the ball vertically into the air and between two players, one from each of the teams. The throw is made from that place where the ball was when the game was stopped, and it is executed without a whistle signal from the Referee.

If, when the stoppage of the game takes place, the ball is to be found between the goal-area line and the free-throw line, the Referee's throw shall be made from the nearest point outside the free-throw line.

Where a Referee's throw is required to restart the game, following a time-out, a whistle signal must be given (See 16.3.*a*).

3. With the exception of the two active players (See 15.2) all other players shall be positioned at least 3m from the Referee, and shall remain so until the throw is executed (See 13.10).

The two players participating in the action relating to the throw shall stand next to the Referee and on that side of the Referee that is nearest to their respective goals. The Referee shall throw the ball into the air between the two players, both of whom shall jump in an attempt to gain possession. The ball, however, may only be played after it has reached its highest point.

RULE 16

Taking the Throws

1. Before a throw is taken, the ball must rest in the hand of the thrower. All other players must take up a position on the court that is in accordance with the Rules governing the throw in question (See, however, 16.7).
2. During the execution of the throw-off, throw-in, free throw and penalty throw, the thrower, must keep at least a part of one of his feet in contact with the floor. It is permitted, however, for the player to repeatedly lift and put down the other foot.
3. The Referee must give a whistle signal:

(*a*) When a game or period is to begin and to restart play after a stoppage during the game (See 2.4, 10.3, 13.7, 14.2, 15.2).

(*b*) When the execution of a throw-in, a goal throw or a free throw is delayed (See 11.2-12.2, 13.2).

(*c*) After a correction or caution (See 13.4, 16.7).

(*d*) Following a warning (See 17.1).

(*e*) Following the award of a period of suspension (See 17.3).

(*f*) Following a disqualification (See 17.5).

(*g*) Following an exclusion (See 17.7).

(*h*) Where there is a failure to agree on the part of the Referees as to which team should be punished (See 18.9).

In the execution of a throw and where a whistle signal has been given by the Referee, the thrower must play the ball within 3 seconds.
4. A throw is considered to have been executed once the ball has left the hand of the thrower (See, however, 12.2, 15.3).

Note: Once a player is considered to be in position for the execution of the throw, and the ball is under control, the player must not place the ball on the ground and then take it up again, neither shall he bounce the ball and catch it again.

In taking the throw, the player concerned, must actually release the ball. It is not permitted for the ball to be placed into the hands of a team colleague or touched by a player other than the thrower (See 13.1).
5. Once the player taking the throw has released the ball he is not allowed to play the ball again until it has touched another player or the goal (See 13.1).
6. A goal may be scored directly from any throw. (See, however, 9.1).

7. When a throw-in or free throw is being taken, players of the defending team shall be 3m from the thrower. However, the Referee does not correct the position of players contravening the Rules if no advantage is gained, and the attacking team are in a position to play the ball quickly. The Referee does, however, correct any wrong position, if he feels an advantage is being gained. Where the Referee is involved in such correction, he must resume the play with a whistle signal.

If the Referee blows his whistle for a throw to be taken, despite the incorrect positions of defenders, those players are fully entitled to participate immediately. They cannot be penalised.

If a defending player deliberately causes delay, or interferes in the taking of the throw and thereby infringes the Rules, that player shall be cautioned, and where the offence is repeated, shall be suspended (See 17.1.c, 17.3.c, but also see 12.2).

RULE 17

Punishment

1. *Caution (Yellow Card)*
A caution can be given for:
   (*a*) Infringements of the Rules concerning approach to an opponent (See 8.4, 8.11, 17.5.c).
A caution shall be given for:
   (*b*) Infringements concerning the approach to an opponent and which are to be punished progressively.
   (*c*) Infringements of the Rules, where an opponent is attempting to execute a throw (See 16.7).
   (*d*) Unsporting conduct by a player or official (See 17.11, 17.12.a, 17.12.c).
2. The Referee shall indicate his decision to issue a caution to an offending player by holding up a yellow card. The card shall be visible to the player and the timekeeper and scorer.
   Note: The yellow card should measure approximately 12cm × 9cm.
   Individual players are only entitled to receive one caution and not more than three cautions may be awarded against the team as a whole.
   Where a player has served a period of suspension, he cannot, during any part of the game, receive a caution.
   The Referee shall only give one caution to the officials of a team.
3. *Suspension*
A suspension shall be given:
   (*a*) For an incorrect substitution or entering the court contrary to the Rules (See 4.4, 4.6).

(*b*) For repetitive infringements of the Rules in connection with the approach to the opponent including progressive punishment (See 8.13).

(*c*) For continuous unsporting conduct by a player on the court (See 8.13, 17.11).

(*d*) When a player fails to place the ball down immediately, when a decision for an infringement has been made against his team (See 8.13, 17.11).

(*e*) For repetitive infringement of the Rules when the opposing team is executing a throw.

In exceptional circumstances, a suspension can be awarded without recourse to an initial caution.

4. The decision to suspend a player must be clearly indicated to the player concerned by the Referee raising his arm in the air with two fingers extended. The action of the Referee shall be clearly visible to the timekeeper and scorer.

In all cases the period of suspension shall be of 2 minutes' duration. A player may be suspended for two periods of 2 minutes. The player may rejoin the game after each of these periods have been completed. However, if a player is suspended for a third time, he shall be disqualified (See 17.5.*c*).

Whilst a player is serving a period of suspension his team shall play with its strength reduced until the period of suspension has expired.

Where a player is suspended for a third time and is ultimately disqualified, the team shall play at reduced strength until the period of suspension has expired. Following the period of suspension, the team may bring the number of players on the court to full strength, but the disqualified player shall take no further part in the game.

A period of suspension shall begin immediately the Referee blows the whistle to restart the game.

If a period of suspension has not expired by the end of the first period, the unexpired time shall be carried forward into the second period. Similarly, where a game goes into extra time, any unexpired period of suspension at the end of normal time, shall be carried forward into the extra period to be played.

5. *Disqualification (Red Card)*
A disqualification shall be given:

(*a*) If a player who is not entitled to take part enters the court (See 4.3).

(*b*) For serious infringements relating to the approach to an opponent (See 8.14).

(*c*) For repeated unsporting conduct by an official or a player outside the court (See 17.11, 17.12*d*).

(*d*) For serious unsporting conduct by players or officials (17.11, 17.12.*b* and 17.12.*d*).

(*e*) For a third period of suspension (See 17.4).

(*f*) In the event of assault by a player or official outside the court.

(*g*) Disqualification of a player on the court is always accompanied by a period of suspension.

6. When awarding a disqualification the Referee shall signal a time-out and the clock should be stopped by the timekeeper. The Referee shall indicate the punishment to the player by the holding up of a red card.

The disqualified player or official shall take no further part in the game and must leave the court and the substitution area immediately.

When a player is disqualified the number of players available to a team is reduced by one. The team may, however, continue to play at full strength on the court following the expiry of the suspension time.

7. *Exclusion*

An exclusion shall be given in the event of an assault on the court.

Note: Assault is a deliberate and particularly violent physical action (See 18.5) made against the Rules and inflicted upon the person of a player, Referee, scorer/timekeeper, official or spectator.

8. When an exclusion is to be awarded, it shall be indicated clearly to the player in question and to his team official and the scorer/timekeeper. An exclusion shall only be given after a time-out has been called by the Referee. The Referee shall signal the exclusion to the offending player, by crossing his arms at head height.

The excluding player shall take no further part in the game and he must leave the court and the substitution area immediately. Throughout the remainder of the game, the team of the excluded player shall play at reduced strength as an excluded player cannot be replaced.

9. A player who is suspended and who commits an assault on the court shall be excluded. However, if a suspended player commits a serious offence or an assault within the substitution area, he shall be disqualified.

10. In the event of a goalkeeper being suspended, disqualified or excluded, he may be replaced by the second goalkeeper named on the scoresheet. Where such action takes place, a court player shall leave the court.

11. A player deemed guilty of unsporting conduct, both on or off the playing court shall be cautioned by the Referees (See 17.1.*d*).

If the offence is repeated and the player is on the court, he shall be suspended. However, where the player repeats the offence outside the court he shall be disqualified (See 17.5.*c*).

An official committing an offence deemed unsporting conduct by the Referee shall first be cautioned (17.1.*d*), and where any such action is repeated he shall be disqaulified (See 17.5.*c*.).

On the occasion where serious infringements occur, concerning assault or unsportsmanlike conduct, and the game has already been interrupted or a time-out has been called, the game shall be resumed by the throw appropriate to the original interruption, following the necessary disciplinary action by the Referees.

Note: Unsportsmanlike conduct shall include verbal or physical abuse and any other action considered incompatible to the spirit of good sportsmanship.

An official who enters the court without permission (see 4.4) shall be punished for unsportsmanlike conduct.

Where a series of offences is committed by a player or official, either simultaneously or in succession, and such offences incur a different punishment, e.g. suspension, disqualification, exclusion etc., only the most severe of punishments shall be imposed.

12. Unsportsmanlike conduct or assault within the sports hall shall be penalised as follows:

Prior to the game:

(*a*) For the offence of unsportsmanlike conduct a caution shall be issued (See 17.1.*d*).

(*b*) Serious unsportsmanlike conduct or assault shall be punished by disqualification of the offending player (See 17.5.*d*, 17.5.*f*). The team of the disqualified individual is allowed, however, to begin the game with 12 players.

During the half-time interval:

(*c*) In the case of unsportmanlike conduct a caution shall be issued to the offender (See 17.1.*d*).

(*d*) Serious unsportsmanlike conduct or assault shall be punished by disqualification (See 17.5.*c*, 17.5.*d*, 17.5.*f*).

After the game has been completed:

Written report.

RULE 18

The Referees

1. Each game shall be conducted by two Referees. Both shall have equal authority and they shall be assisted by a scorer and a timekeeper.
2. The Referees shall monitor the conduct of both players and officials from the moment they enter the premises where the game is to be played until the moment they leave.
3. Prior to a game the Referees shall examine the playing court, the goals and the balls (See 3.1). They decide which ball shall be used. Where there is failure to agree, the decision of the Referee officially named first shall prevail.

The Referees shall check the scoresheet and ensure that all details recorded are correct, including the uniforms of the players, and establish the presence and identity of the officials responsible for the teams, together with the manning of the substitute area.

Where any discrepancy occurs such shall be corrected by the Referees (See 4.7).

4. The Referee officially named first shall toss a coin before the beginning of the game in the presence of his colleague and the two team captains (See 10.1).

5. At the start of the game, the Referee officially named second shall take up the position of court Referee, behind the team taking the throw-off and in their half of the court. The court Referee shall give the whistle signal for the game to begin (See 10.3).

Note: The Referees shall be known as the court Referee and the goal-line Referee. The court Referee is so named because he is always in a position on the court and behind the attacking team. The other official will have adopted a position on the goal-line outside the goal whilst an attack is mounted and thus will be positioned behind the defence.

When the team defending ultimately gains possession, they become the attacking team and their opponents fall back upon their own goal-area for the purpose of defence. The position of the Referees is now reversed. The Referee who was the court Referee shall retreat before the team now defending and assume a position on their goal-line outside the goal, to become the new goal-line Referee. His colleague moves forward behind the team now attacking and thus becomes the court Referee. This action is repeated in reverse when possession of the ball is once more exchanged.

From time to time the Referees should change their positions to ensure they are not always goal-line and court Referee for the same team throughout the game.

6. In principle a game shall be conducted by the same two Referees. Jointly they must ensure that the game is played in accordance with the Rules, and they must penalise infringements (See, however, 13.6, 14.9).

In the circumstances of one Referee being unable to Referee throughout the game the other Referee shall continue alone.

7. The court Referee shall assume responsibility for:

   (*a*) The throw-off.

   (*b*) The taking of a penalty.

   (*c*) The execution of all throws relating to the rule 16 and to restart the game following a time-out.

The goal-line Referee shall signal:

   (*d*) When a goal has been scored (See 9.1).

8. If on occasion both Referees decide simultaneously that an infringement shall be penalised, but display different opinions as to the punishment, the more severe shall be applied.

9. Where both Referees interrupt the game simultaneously and differ as to which team shall be penalised, the decision of the court Referee shall prevail.

Note: Where such occasion arises and to avoid confusion, and either team gaining an advantage, the court Referee after giving clear hand signals shall restart the game by means of a whistle signal (See 16.3.*h*).

10. The Referees shall keep a record of the goals scored by both teams and they shall also record cautions, suspensions, disqualifications and exclusions.

11. Both Referees shall be responsible for controlling the playing time. Where there is disagreement about the accuracy of the time-keeping, the decision of the first-named Referee shall apply.

12. Upon completion of the game the Referees shall assume responsibility for ensuring that all information recorded on the score sheet is correct.

Disqualifications outside the playing court, offences against the Referee, and exclusion shall be explained in written form upon the scoresheets by the Referees (See 17.5.(*d*), 17.7).

RULE 19

The Scorer and the Timekeeper

1. The scorer shall be responsible for the keeping of a scoresheet and such journal shall be provided for every game. The scoresheet shall record the names of the players, together with cautions, suspensions, disqualifications and exclusions awarded during the game by the Referees. It shall also record the number of goals scored.

Prior to the game the scorer shall examine the team lists and only those players recorded shall be entitled to participate. Whilst a game is in progress, the scorer shall assist the timekeeper in organising the entry of players arriving late, or entering the court following a period of suspension. (Players arriving late must have their names included on the scoresheet before they are allowed to enter the court.)

2. The timekeeper shall control:

(*a*) The playing time (See 2.1, 2.4-7 – the Referees shall decide when the clocks are to be stopped and restarted).

(*b*) The number of players and officials on the substitutes bench.

(*c*) Players arriving late to participate on the game. (In exercising this responsibility the timekeeper shall be assisted by the scorer.) (See also 4.1.)

(*d*) Ensuring the correct execution of the Rule governing substitution (See 4.4, 4.5).

(e) The entering of players not entitled to do so (See 4.6).

(f) The suspension time of players (See 17.4).

The timekeeper shall stop the game at the end of the first period (half-time) and at the end of the game with a clearly emitted signal (See, however, 2.2, 2.5).

3. At any interruption of the play (time-out) and where no publicly visible clock is available, the timekeeper shall inform team officials of the time that elapsed and the time that is remaining before completion of the game (See 2.4).

4. The timekeeper shall, upon completion of a period of suspension, inform either the player or the team official that the suspension has expired (See 17.4).

5. The timekeeper shall not signal the end of the first half or the end of the game if an award has been made for an infringement of the Rules by the Referee immediately before the time for the signal. The final signal shall only be made after the result of the throw awarded by the Referees has been ascertained.

The signal to end a period shall be given if the ball enters the goal without an infringement of the Rules taking place. The timekeeper must be careful to allow for the ball hitting the goal-posts, the goalkeeper or another player deflecting the ball into the goal. Only when the result of the throw is known and the ball has come to rest shall the signal be given to end the play,

When the ball does not enter the goal, or the thrower propels the ball away from the direction of the goal, the signal shall be given to end the play.

Where an infringement occurs before or during the execution of the penalty or free throw, such must be penalised and the termination signal delayed further.

Reprinted by permission of the Commonwealth Handball Association. For reasons of space a Commentary on these Rules, and the Regulations Governing the Substitution Rule, have been omitted but are included in the complete Rules of Handball, available from the Association.

Hockey

The Field of Play

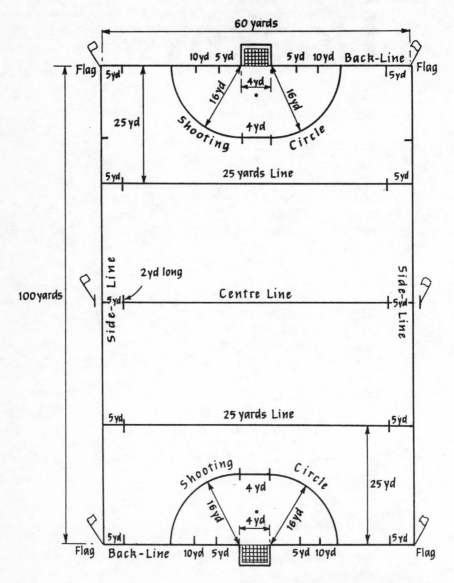

The front of the goal-posts must be touching the outer edge of the goal-line.
All lines must be 3in wide.
A spot 6in in diameter shall be marked 7yd in front of the centre of each goal.
All short indication marks must be inside the field only and shall be 12in in length.

Hockey

1. Teams and Duration of Play

(a) A game shall be played between two teams. Not more than eleven players of each team shall be on the field at the same time. Each team shall have one goalkeeper on the field or shall indicate a field player who has the privileges of a goalkeeper.

(b) Each team is permitted to substitute not more than three players during the game.

(c) No player once substituted shall be permitted on the field again, and no substitute shall be permitted for a suspended player during his suspension.

(d) (i) Substitution of players shall only take place with the permission of an umpire and during any stoppage of play other than following the award of a penalty corner or penalty stroke subject to (ii).

(ii) After the award of a penalty corner or penalty stroke any player who is injured and has to leave the field of play can be substituted subject to Rule 1(c). Rules 9(b), 15(b)(ii) and 16(b)(i) shall apply. Time may be added for completion of substitutions.

(e) The duration of the game shall be two periods of 35 minutes each unless otherwise agreed before the game.

(f) At half-time the teams shall change ends, and the duration of the interval shall not exceed 5 minutes, unless otherwise agreed before the game, but in no case shall it exceed 10 minutes.

(g) The game starts when the umpire blows his whistle for the opening pass back. See also Rule 10(a).

2. Captains

Each team must have a captain on the field who may wear a distinctive arm-band and who shall:

(*a*) Toss for choice of start. The winner of the toss shall have:

(i) the right to choose which end his team will attack in the first half;
or

(ii) the right to have possession of the ball at the start of the game.

The winner of the toss having made his choice, the opposing side will automatically have the second option. The team not having started the game will have possession of the ball for re-starting after half-time.

(*b*) Before the start of play and on any change, indicate, if necessary, to each other and to the umpires, their respective goalkeepers subject to Rules 15(*c*)(ii) and 16(*b*)(i).

(*c*) In case he is substituted or suspended, indicate to the umpires the player who will replace him as captain.

3. Umpires and Timekeepers

(*a*) There shall be two umpires to control the game and to administer the rules. These umpires shall be the sole judges of fair and unfair play during the game.

(*b*) Unless otherwise provided, each team shall be responsible for providing one umpire.

(*c*) Each umpire shall be:

(i) Primarily responsible for decisions in his own half of the field, for the whole of the game without changing ends.

(ii) Solely responsible for decisions on the hit-in for the full length of his nearer side-line.

(iii) Solely responsible for decisions on corners, penalty corners, penalty strokes and goals in his own half and free hits in his own circle.

(*d*) The umpires shall be responsible for keeping time for the duration of the game. It shall be permissible to have a timekeeper or timekeepers. Such timekeepers shall take over those duties of the umpires which concern the keeping of time and the indication of the end of each half.

(*e*) Umpires shall allow the full or agreed time and shall keep a written record of the goals as they are scored.

(*f*) Time shall be allowed for all enforced stoppages and such time shall be added to that half in which the stoppage occurred.

(*g*) Umpires and timekeepers shall be debarred from coaching during a game and during the interval.

(*h*) Umpires shall only blow the whistle to:

(i) Start and end each half of the game.

(ii) Enforce a penalty.

(iii) Start and end a penalty stroke.

(iv) Indicate, when necessary, that the ball has passed wholly outside the field of play.

(v) Signal a goal.

(vi) Restart the game after a goal has been scored.

(vii) Suspend the game for any reason and restart after a suspension.

(*i*) Umpires shall satisfy themselves before the game that, as far as is practicable, Rules 4 to 9 inclusive are observed.

Umpires shall refrain from enforcing a penalty in cases where they are satisfied that by enforcing it an advantage would be given to the offending team.

4. Field of Play
(*See page 504*)

(*a*) All lines used in the measurements of the field are to be 3in wide. The side-lines and back-lines including the goal-lines are part of the field of play.

(*b*) The field shall be rectangular, 100yd long and 60yd wide. Its boundaries shall be clearly marked out with lines in accordance with the plan on page 504. The longer lines shall be called the side-lines and the shorter the back-lines, including that part of the back-line between the goal-posts called the goal-line.

(*c*) A centre-line and two 25-yards lines shall be marked throughout their length on the field; the middle of these lines to be 50yd and 25yd respectively from the outer edge of the back-lines.

(*d*) To assist in the control of the hit-in, across the centre-line and each 25-yards line, parallel to and 5yd from the outer edge of the side-lines a mark of 2yd in length shall be made.

(*e*) A mark 12in in length shall be placed inside the field of play on each side-line and parallel to the back-line and 16yd from its inner edge.

(*f*) For penalty corner hits, the field shall be marked inside the field of play on the back-lines on both sides of the goal at 5yd and 10yd from the outer edge of the nearer goal-post such distance being to the further edge of those lines. For corner hits the field shall be marked inside the field of play on the back-lines 5yd from the outer edge of the side-line. All these marks to be 12in in length.

(*g*) A spot 6in in diameter shall be marked in front of the centre of each goal; the centre of the spot shall be 7 yd from the inner edge of the goal-line.

(*h*) No marks other than those shown on the plan are permissible on the playing surface.

(*i*) Flagposts of not more than 5ft nor less than 4ft in height shall be placed for the whole game at each corner of the field, and at the centre; those at the centre shall be 1yd outside the side-lines.

5. Goals, Posts, etc.

(*a*) There shall be a goal at the centre of each back-line consisting of two perpendicular posts 4yd apart, joined together by a horizontal cross-bar 7ft from the ground (inside measurements). The front base of the goal-posts shall touch the outer edge of the back-line. The goal-posts shall not extend upwards beyond the cross-bar, nor the cross-bar extend sideways beyond the goal-posts.

(*b*) The goal-posts and cross-bar shall be rectangular and shall be 2in wide and not more than 3in nor less than 2in deep, and shall be painted white.

(*c*) Nets shall be attached firmly to the goal-posts and the cross-bar at intervals of not more than 6in, and shall be attached firmly to the ground behind the goal or to the back-board/side-boards.

(*d*) A back-board, 18in in height and 4 yd in length, shall be placed at the foot of and inside the goal-nets. Side-boards 18in in height and a minimum 4ft in length shall be placed at right angles to the back-lines. The side-boards shall be fixed to the back of the goal-posts, so that the width of the goal-posts is not effectively increased.

(*e*) No chocks shall be placed inside the goal to support any of the boards.

6. Shooting Circles

In front of each goal shall be drawn a line, 4 yd long, parallel to and 16yd from the back-line. The 16yd shall be measured from the inside front corner of the goal-posts to the outer edge of that line. This line shall be continued each way to meet the back-lines by quarter circles having the inside front corner of the goal-posts as centres. The space enclosed by these lines, including the lines themselves, shall be called the shooting circle (hereinafter referred to as 'the circle').

7. The Ball

(*a*) The ball shall be spherical with the specifications mentioned in this Rule.

(*b*) The weight of the ball shall be not more than $5\frac{3}{4}$oz (163g), and not less than $5\frac{1}{2}$oz (156g).

(*c*) The circumference of the ball shall be not more than $9\frac{1}{4}$in (23.5cm) nor less than $8\frac{13}{16}$in (22.4cm).

(*d*) (i) The ball shall be hard; it may be solid or hollow, provided it meets the other specifications in this Rule.

(ii) The ball shall have an outer surface of any natural or artificial material. The surface shall be smooth, but a seam or indentations are permitted provided they do not alter the shape of the ball.

(iii) The inner portion of a solid ball may consist of any natural or artificial material in any composition or mixture, as long as it meets the other specifications in this Rule.

(e) The traditional colour of the ball is white, but the team captains may agree upon the use of a ball of any other colour, as long as it contrasts with the colour of the field of play.

(f) Umpires shall not permit the use of a ball that does, in their opinion, not comply with this Rule. Should a ball during a game deteriorate in such a way that it not longer meets the specifications of this Rule, it shall be replaced immediately. If the game has not been stopped for any reason and the ball is in play when it becomes unusable, the game shall be stopped and restarted using a new ball in accordance with Rule 10(b). See also Rule 11(a) and Rule 17.I and II.

8. The Stick

(a) The stick shall have a flat face on its left-hand side only. The face of the stick is the whole of the flat side and that part of the handle for the whole of the length which is above the flat side.

(b) The head (i.e. the part below the lower end of the splice) shall be curved and shall be of wood and shall not be edged with or have any insets or fittings of metal or any other substance, nor shall there be any sharp edges or dangerous splinters. The maximum length of the curved head of the stick, as measured from the lowest part of the flat face, shall not exceed 4in. It shall not be cut square or pointed, but shall have rounded edges.

(c) The total weight of the stick shall not exceed 28oz, nor be less than 12oz, and it shall be of such a size, inclusive of any covering, that it can be passed through a ring having an interior diameter of 5.10cm.

(d) Umpires shall forbid the use of any stick which in their opinion does not comply with this Rule. See Rule 3(i).

Penalty: For any breach of this Rule any player concerned shall not be allowed on the field of play until such time as he complied with this Rule.

9. Players' Dress and Equipment

(a) Each player shall wear the dress approved by his Association or Club, unless varied to avoid confusion in a particular game. Goal-keepers shall wear a colour different from that of their own team and that of their opponents. Players shall not have dangerous spikes, studs or protruding nails in footwear, or wear anything that may be dangerous to other players.

(b) The following equipment is permitted for use by goalkeepers only: Body Protectors, Pads, Kickers, Gauntlet Gloves, Protective Headgear, Facemasks and Elbow Pads.

Penalty: For any breach of this Rule any player concerned shall not be allowed on the field of play until such time as he has complied with this Rule.

10. To Start or Restart the Game

(*a*) To start the game, restart it after half-time and after each goal scored, a 'pass-back' shall be played at the centre of the field. The pass-back for the start of the game shall be made by a player of the team which did not make a choice of ends (see Rule 2*a*), after half-time by a player of the opposing team, and after a goal has been scored by a player of the team against whom the goal has been awarded. The pass-back, which may be pushed or hit, must not be directed over the centre-line. At the moment when the pass-back is taken, no player of the opposing team shall be within 5yd of the ball and all players of both teams other than the player making the pass-back must be in their own half of the field. If the striker hits at but misses the ball, the pass-back still has to be taken. After taking the pass-back, the striker shall not play the ball nor remain or approach within playing distance until it has been touched or played by another player of either team. Time wasting shall not be permitted.

(*b*) (i) To restart the game in accordance with Rule 7(*f*), Rule 12 III, Rule 12 Penalties 4 or Rule 18(*b*)(i) a bully shall be played on a spot to be chosen by the umpire in whose half of the ground the incident occurred.

(ii) To bully, a player of each team shall stand squarely facing the side-lines, each with his own back-line on his right. The ball shall be placed on the ground between the two players. Each player shall tap with his stick, first the ground between the ball and his own back-line, and then, with the flat face of his stick, his opponent's stick, over the ball, three times alternately, after which one of these two players shall play the ball with his stick to put it into play.

(iii) Until the ball is in play, all other players shall not stand within 5yd of the ball.

(iv) A bully shall not be played within 16 yd of the back-line or goal-line.

Penalties. 1. For a breach of Rule 10(*a*) a free hit shall be awarded to the opposing team.

2. For a breach of Rule 10(*b*)(ii) or (iii) the bully shall be played again.

3. For persistent breaches of Rule 10(*b*)(ii) and (iii), the umpire may award a free hit to the opposing team; or, for such breaches in the circle by a defender, a penalty corner.

11. Scoring a Goal

(*a*) A goal is scored when the whole ball, having been hit or deflected by the stick of an attacker whilst in the circle and not having gone outside the circle, passes completely over the goal-line between the goal-posts and under the cross-bar – except in circumstances detailed in Rule 15(*g*) and Rule 16. 15(*e*) and 15(*h*), when a goal may not be awarded, and in circumstances detailed in Rule 16 Penalty 1, when a goal may be awarded. It is immaterial if the ball subsequently touches, or is played by one or more defenders. If, during the game, the goal-posts and/or the cross-bar becomes displaced, and the ball passes completely over the goal-line at a point which, in the umpire's opinion, is between where the goal-posts and/or under where the cross-bar, respectively, should have been, a goal shall be awarded.

(*b*) The team scoring the greater number of goals shall be the winner.

12. Conduct of Play

I. A player shall not:

(*a*) Play the ball with the rounded side of his stick.

(*b*) Take part in or interfere with the game unless he has his own stick in his hand, or change his stick for the purpose of taking part in the game under Rules 14, 15, 16 and 17.

'Own stick' means the stick with which the player began to play, or any stick that he legitimately substitutes for it.

(*c*) Raise his stick in a manner that is dangerous, intimidating or hampering to another player when approaching, attempting to play, playing or stopping the ball. A ball above the height of a player's shoulder shall not be played or played at by any part of the stick. For goalkeepers see Rule 12II(*c*).

(*d*) Stop the ball with his hand or catch it. For goalkeepers, see Rule 12II(*c*). *There is nothing in this Rule which prevents a player using his hand to protect himself from a dangerously raised ball.*

(*e*) Hit wildly into an opponent or play or raise or kick the ball in such a way as to be dangerous in itself, or likely to lead to dangerous play or play the ball intentionally into an opponent's foot, leg or body.

(*f*) Stop or deflect the ball on the ground or in the air with any part of the body *to his or his team's advantage*, save as provided for in Rule 12II(*c*).

(*g*) Deliberately raise the ball from a *hit*, except for a shot at goal.

(*h*) Deliberately raise the ball so that it will fall into the circle.

(*i*) Use the foot or leg to support the stick in order to resist an opponent.

(*j*) Kick, pick up, throw, carry or propel the ball in any manner or direction except with the stick. But see guidance 12I(*f*), 12I(*i*) and Rule 12II(*c*).

(*k*) Hit, hook, hold, strike at or interfere with an opponent's stick.

(*l*) Charge, kick, shove, trip, strike at or personally handle an opponent or his clothing.

(*m*) Obstruct by running between an opponent and the ball nor interpose himself or his stick as an obstruction.

II. A player may:

(*a*) Play the ball only with the flat side of his stick, which includes that part of the handle above the flat side.

(*b*) Tackle from the left of an opponent provided that he plays the ball without previous interference with the stick or person of his opponent. See Rule 12 I, particularly (*k*), (*l*), (*m*).

(*c*) If he is a goalkeeper and the ball is inside his circle be allowed – contrary to the provisions of Rule 12.1(*c*), (*d*), (*f*) and (*j*) – to kick the ball, stop it with any part of his body including his hand and stop it with his stick above his shoulder, unless dangerous. No penalty shall be incurred if when stopping a shot at goal, the ball rebounds off any part of the goalkeeper's body or his stick.

III. (*a*) If the ball becomes lodged in one of the pads of a goalkeeper, or in the clothing of any player or umpire, the umpire shall stop the game and restart it by a bully on the spot where the incident occurred, subject to Rule 10(*b*)(iv).

(*b*) If the ball strikes an umpire or any loose object on the pitch, including any piece of playing equipment dropped accidentally, the game shall continue. Any deliberate action by a player in throwing his stick or other piece of playing equipment on to the pitch, at the ball, at an opponent or at an umpire, should be penalised under Rule 12, IV.

IV. *Misconduct. Rough or dangerous play, time-wasting, deliberate breaches of any rule, or any other behaviour which in the umpire's opinion amounts to misconduct shall not be permitted.*

Penalties.

1. *Outside the circle*: A free hit shall be awarded to the opposing team. An umpire shall award a penalty corner for an offence by any defender inside his own 25yd area, when, in the umpire's opinion, the offence was deliberate.

2. *Inside the circle – by an attacker*: A free hit shall be awarded to the defending team.

3. *Inside the circle – by a defender*: For a breach inside the circle by a defender a penalty corner shall be awarded or a penalty stroke if in the umpire's opinion, Rule 16(*a*) applies.

4. *Inside and Outside the circle*: For a simultaneous breach of this Rule by two opponents, the umpire shall order a bully to be played on the spot where the breach occurred, subject to Rule 10(*b*) (iv).

5. *Inside and Outside the circle*: For rough or dangerous play or misconduct, in addition to awarding the appropriate penalty, the umpire may:

(i) Warn the offending player(s), which may also be indicated by showing a green card;

(ii) Suspend him (them) temporarily, for not less than 5 minutes, which may also be indicated by showing a yellow card;

(iii) Suspend him (them) from further participation in the game which may also be indicated by showing a red card.

A temporarily suspended player shall remain behind his own goal or in such other places as designated before the game, until allowed by the umpire by whom he was suspended to resume play; when necessary changing ends at the start of the second half of the game.

13. Off-side

(*a*) *At the moment when the ball is played*, a player of the same team as the pusher or striker is in an off-side position if he is in his opponents' 25-yd area unless:

(i) He is behind the ball; or

(ii) There are at least two opponents nearer to their own back-line or goal-line than he is.

For the purpose of this Rule, a player of either team shall be deemed to be on the field of play even though he is outside the side-line or behind the back-line or goal-line.

(*b*) A player who is in an off-side position shall not play or attempt to play the ball or gain any advantage for his team or influence the play of an opponent.

Penalty: A free hit shall be awarded to the defending team.

14. Free Hit

(*a*) A free hit shall be taken on the spot where the breach occurred except that:

(i) *for a breach by an attacker within the circle* it shall be taken:
either from any spot within that circle,
or from any spot within 16 yd of the inner edge of the defending team's back-line or goal-line on a line drawn through the place where the breach occurred and parallel to the side-line.

(ii) *for a breach by an attacker outside the circle but within 16yd of the defending team's back-line* it shall be taken from any spot within 16yd of the inner edge of the defending team's back-line on a line drawn through the place where the breach occurred and parallel to the side-line.

(*b*) The ball shall be stationary and the striker shall push or hit it. The ball must be moved and shall not be raised intentionally in such a way as to be dangerous in itself, or likely to lead to dangerous play.

(*c*) At the moment when the free hit is taken, no player of the opposing team shall remain within 5yd of the ball. However, for a free hit to the attacking team within 5yd of the circle, players of both teams, except the striker, shall be at least 5yd from the ball. Should the umpire consider that a player is standing within 5yd of the ball in order to gain time, the free hit shall not be delayed.

(*d*) If the striker hits at but misses the ball, provided that Rule 12I(*c*) has not been contravened, the free hit still has to be taken.

(*e*) After taking the free hit, the striker shall not play the ball again nor remain or approach within playing distance until it has been touched or played by another player of either team.

Penalties.

1. *Inside the circle*: A penalty corner or a penalty stroke shall be awarded to the attacking team.

2. *Outside the circle*: A free hit shall be awarded to the opposing team. An umpire shall award a penalty corner for an offence by any defender in his own 25yd area, when, in the umpire's opinion, the offence was deliberate.

15. Penalty Corner

(*a*) A penalty corner shall be awarded to the opposing team if, in the umpire's opinion:

(i) There has been an *intentional* breach of Rules 12, 14 or 17 inside the 25yd area but outside the circle by a player of the defending team; or

(ii) An *unintentional* breach of Rule 12, 14 or 17.II(*b*) inside the circle by a player of the defending team; or

(iii) For persistent breaches of Rule 10(*b*)(ii) or (iii) in the circle by a defender.

(*b*) A player of the attacking team shall push or hit the ball from a spot on the back-line not less than 10yd from the goal-post, on whichever side of the goal the attacking team prefers. The player concerned is not required to be wholly inside or outside the field of play when taking the penalty corner. The ball shall not be raised intentionally, but the hit shall not be penalised if the ball lifts off the ground without causing danger or appearing likely to lead to dangerous play.

(*c*) (i) At the moment when such push or hit is made, no other player shall be within 5yd of the ball. The rest of the attacking team shall be in the field of play with both sticks and feet outside the circle. Not more than 5 of the defending team shall stand with both sticks and feet behind their own goal-line or back-line. The rest of the defending team shall be beyond the centre-line.

(ii) In the event of the defending goalkeeper being incapacitated he shall be replaced immediately by another goalkeeper. If the defending goalkeeper be suspended, his team captain shall immediately nominate another goalkeeper. Replacement goalkeepers shall be permitted to put on protective equipment without undue delay (See Rule 9(*b*)).

(*d*) Until the ball is pushed or hit no attacker shall enter the circle, nor shall a defender cross the goal-line, back-line or centre-line.

(*e*) (i) No shot at goal shall be made from a penalty corner until the ball has stopped or come to rest on the ground or touched the stick or person of a defender. The defending goalkeeper shall remain on his feet until the first shot at goal has been made.

(ii) If the first shot at goal is a hit, the ball shall not cross the goal-line at a height higher than the back-board/side-boards (18in) unless it has touched the stick or person of a defender.

(iii) If the ball travels beyond 5yd from the outer edge of the circle-line, the penalty corner is ended and the special provisions mentioned in (i) and (ii) no longer apply.

(*f*) The player taking the penalty corner hit or push from the back-line shall not, after striking the ball, play the ball again, nor approach or remain within playing distance of the ball, until it has been touched or played by another player of either team.

(*g*) If the striker of the penalty corner hits at or pushes at but misses the ball, the penalty corner still has to be taken.

(*h*) No goal shall be scored directly by the player taking the penalty corner hit or push from the back-line, even if the ball is played into goal by a defender.

Penalties.

1. *For a breach of Rules* 15(*c*) (i) *or* 15(*d*), *viz*:

Attacker(s) entering the circle or defender(s) crossing the goal-line, back-line or centre-line too soon or coming from 5yd of the ball too soon – the penalty may, at the discretion of the umpire, be taken again.

2. *For persistent breaches of Rule* 15(*b*) (i) *or* 15(*d*) *by the attackers* – The umpire may award a free hit.

3. *For persistent breaches of Rules* 15(*c*) (i) *or* 15(*d*) *by the defenders* – The umpire may award a penalty stroke.

4. *For an unintentional breach of Rule* 15(*e*) (i) *by the goalkeeper* – The penalty corner may, at the discretion of the umpire, be taken again.

5. *For intentional or persistent breaches of Rule* 15(*e* (i) *by the goalkeeper* – The umpire shall award a penalty stroke.

6. *For any other breach of Rule* 15 – A free hit shall be awarded to the defending team.

16. Penalty Stroke

(*a*) A penalty stroke shall be awarded to the opposing team if that team has possession or the opportunity to gain possession of the ball in the circle and, in the opinion of the umpire:

(i) There has been an *intentional* breach of Rules 12, 14 or 17 II (*g*) (v) inside the circle by a player of the defending team; or

(ii) A goal would probably have been scored had an *unintentional* breach of Rule 12 inside the circle by a player of the defending team not occurred.

(iii) Rules 15(*c*)(i) and/or 15(*d*) are persistently breached by the defenders.

(*b*) (i) The penalty stroke shall be either a push, flick or scoop stroke taken from a spot 7yd in front of the centre of the goal by a player of the attacking team and defended by the goalkeeper of the opposing team on the field at the time the breach occurred. In the event of the goalkeeper being incapacitated or suspended, the captain of the defending team shall immediately nominate another goalkeeper. This goalkeeper shall be permitted to put on or remove, without undue delay, protective equipment. Under the provisions of this Rule, before the taking of the stroke, a goalkeeper may also remove his face mask, headgear and/or his gauntlet gloves. See Rule 9(*b*).

(ii) Whichever stroke is used, the ball may be raised to any height.

(iii) During the taking of a penalty stroke all the other players of both teams shall stand beyond the nearer 25-yd line and shall not influence or attempt to influence the conduct of the penalty stroke.

(*c*) (i) The attacking player shall not take the penalty stroke until the umpire, having satisfied himself that both defender and attacker are ready, has indicated that he may do so by blowing his whistle.

(ii) When taking the stroke the attacker shall stand close to and behind the ball and shall be permitted in making the stroke to take one stride forward. Dragging or lifting the rear foot is not a breach of this Rule, provided that it does not pass the front foot before the ball is moved.

(iii) The attacker shall touch the ball once only and thereafter shall not approach either the ball or the goalkeeper.

(*d*) (i) The goalkeeper shall stand on the goal-line. After the player taking the stroke and the goalkeeper are in position and the umpire has blown his whistle, the goalkeeper may not leave the goal-line or move either of his feet until the ball has been played.

(ii) The usual privileges of the goalkeeper shall be allowed to him, but he shall not be allowed to delay the taking of the stroke by making unnecessary changes or modifications of clothing. If the ball be caught and held by the goalkeeper, the penalty stroke is ended. See also clause (*e*) (iii). He shall not be penalised, if, in stopping a shot at goal, the ball, in the umpire's opinion, rebounds off his body, stick or his hand.

(iii) If any deliberate action by the attacker prior to striking the ball induces the goalkeeper to move either of his feet or, if the attacker feints at striking the ball, the attacker shall be penalised.

(*e*) If, as a result of the penalty stroke:

(i) The whole ball passes completely over the goal-line between the goal-posts and under the cross-bar, a goal is scored.

(ii) The ball should come to rest inside the circle, be lodged in the goalkeeper's pads, be caught by the goalkeeper, or pass outside the circle, in all cases the penalty stroke is ended. Unless a goal has been scored or awarded, the game shall be restarted by a push or hit to be taken by a defender from a spot in front of the centre of the goal and 16yd from the inner edge of that line.

(*f*) All time taken between the award of a penalty stroke and resumption of play shall be added to the time of play.

Penalties.

1. For a breach of any rule by the goalkeeper which prevents a goal from being scored, a goal shall be awarded to the opposing team. (See penalty 3 below).

2. For a breach of any Rule by an attacker, the game shall be restarted with a free hit to be taken by a defender from a spot in front of the centre of the goal-line and 16yd from the inner edge of that line.

3. For a breach of clause (*b*) (iii) or (*d*) (i), the umpire may order the stroke to be taken again.

17. Ball Outside Field of Play

When the whole ball passes completely over the back-line, and no goal is scored, or over the side-line, it is out of play and the game shall be restarted as in Rules 17 I and 17 II.

I. *Over side-line*

(*a*) When the whole ball passes completely over the side-line, it or another ball shall be placed on the line at the spot at which it crossed the side-line. The ball shall be pushed or hit without undue delay by a player of the team opposed to the player who last touched it in play. This player is not required to be wholly inside or outside the side-line when making his push or hit.

(*b*) The ball shall be stationary and the striker shall push or hit it. The ball must be moved and shall not be raised intentionally or in such a way as to be dangerous in itself or likely to lead to dangerous play.

(*c*) At the moment when the push or hit is taken no player of the opposing team shall be within 5yd of the ball. If any player of the opposing team be within 5yd of the ball, the umpire may require the push or hit to be taken again. If, however, in the umpire's opinion, a player of the opposing remains within 5yd of the ball to gain time, the push or hit shall not be delayed.

(*d*) If the striker hits at but misses the ball, provided that Rule 12 I(*c*) has not been contravened, the push or hit still has to be taken.

(*e*) After taking a push or hit the player shall not play the ball again, nor remain or approach within playing distance of the ball until it has been touched or played by another player of either team.

Penalty. For any breach of this Rule, a free hit shall be awarded to the opposing team.

II. *Over back-line*

(*a*) By an attacker.

(i) When the ball passes completely over the opponents' back-line by or off one of the attacking team and no goal is scored, it or another ball shall be placed on a spot opposite the place where it crossed the back-line and not more than 16yd from the inner edge of that line. The ball shall be pushed or hit without undue delay by one of the defending team.

(ii) The ball shall be stationary and the striker shall push or hit it. The ball must be moved and shall not be raised intentionally or in such a way as to be dangerous in itself or likely to lead to dangerous play.

(iii) No player of the opposing team shall be within 5 yd of the ball when the push or hit is taken.

(iv) If the striker hits at but misses the ball, provided that Rule 12 I(*c*) has not been contravened, the push or hit still has to be taken.

(v) After taking the push or hit, the striker shall not play the ball again nor remain nor approach within playing distance of the ball until it has been touched or played by another player of either team.

(*b*) *By a defender*.

(i) When the ball has been unintentionally hit by, or glanced off, the stick or person of a defender and has gone over his own back-line or goal-line from within his own 25-yd area, a push or hit shall be taken by the attacking team as follows, unless a goal has been scored.

(*a*) The player shall push or hit the ball from a spot on the back-line within 5yd of the corner flag nearer to the point where the ball crossed the back-line.

(*b*) The ball shall be stationary and the striker shall push or hit it. The ball must be moved and shall not be raised intentionally or in such a way as to be dangerous in itself or likely to lead to dangerous play.

(*c*) No player of the opposing team shall be within 5yd of the ball when the push or hit is taken.

(*d*) If the striker hits at but misses the ball, provided that Rule 12 I(*c*) has not been contravened, the push or hit still has to be taken.

(*e*) After taking the push or hit, the striker shall not play the ball again nor remain or approach within playing distance of the ball until it has been touched or played by another player of either team.

(ii) When the ball, in the umpire's opinion, is sent over his own back-line or goal-line by or off one of the defending team who is more than 25yd from the back-line, the game shall be restarted by a push or hit by one of the defending team from a spot opposite the place where it crossed the back-line or goal-line and not more than 16yd from the inner edge of that line.

(*a*) The ball shall be stationary and the striker shall push or hit it. The ball must be moved and shall not be raised intentionally or in such a way as to be dangerous in itself or likely to lead to dangerous play.

(*b*) No player of the opposing team shall be within 5yd of the ball when the push or hit is taken.

(*c*) If the striker hits at but misses the ball, provided that Rule 12 I(*c*) has not been contravened, the push or hit has to be taken.

(*d*) After taking the push or hit, the striker shall not play the ball again nor remain nor approach within playing distance of the ball until it has been touched or played by another player of either team.

Penalties:

1. For a breach of this Rule by an attacker, a free hit shall be awarded to the defending team.

2. For a ball raised dangerously from a free hit within the circle by a defender, a penalty corner shall be awarded.

3. For an unintentional breach of this Rule by a defender outside the circle a free hit shall be awarded to the attacking team.

4. For an unintentional breach of this Rule inside the circle or for an intentional breach of this Rule by a defender within the 25yd area but outside the circle, a penalty corner shall be awarded.

5. For an intentional breach of this Rule by a defender within the circle, a penalty stroke shall be awarded.

III. No player may deliberately play or deflect the ball over his own back-line or goal-line from an area enclosed by the 25yd line, including the circle.

Penalty: For a breach of this Rule, a penalty corner shall be awarded to the opposing team.

18. Accidents

(*a*) If a player or an umpire be incapacitated, the umpire or other umpire shall stop the game temporarily noting the time lost. See Rule 3(*f*).

In either case, if a goal be scored before the game be stopped it shall be allowed if, in the umpire's opinion, it would have been scored had the accident not occurred.

(*b*) The umpire shall restart the game as soon as possible, by:

(i) A bully – subject to Rule 10(*b*)(iv) – on a spot to be chosen by the umpire in whose half of the ground the accident occurred; or

(ii) The appropriate penalty when the accident was the result of a breach of the rules; or

(iii) The implementation of a decision given before the game was stopped.

(*c*) If the umpire concerned cannot continue, the other umpire or a replacement or reserve umpire shall restart the game.

METRIC EQUIVALENTS

Imperial	Metric	Imperial	Metric
100yd	91.40m	18in	46.00cm
60yd	55.00m	12in	30.00cm
25yd	22.90m	$9\frac{1}{4}$in	23.50cm
16yd	14.63m	$8\frac{13}{16}$in	22.40cm
10yd	9.14m	6in	15.00cm
7yd	6.40m	3in	7.50cm
5yd	4.55m	2in	5.10cm
4yd	3.66m	28oz	794g
2yd	1.83m	23oz	652g
1yd	0.91m	12oz	340g
7ft	2.14m	$5\frac{3}{4}$oz	163g
5ft	1.50m	$5\frac{1}{2}$oz	156g
4ft	1.20m		

Issued under the Authority of the Hockey Rules Board and reprinted here with their permission. Guidance for Players and Umpires, Advice to Umpires and Equipment Specifications have been omitted for reasons of space but are given in the complete Rules of the Game of Hockey, available from the Board.

Ice Hockey

The Rink

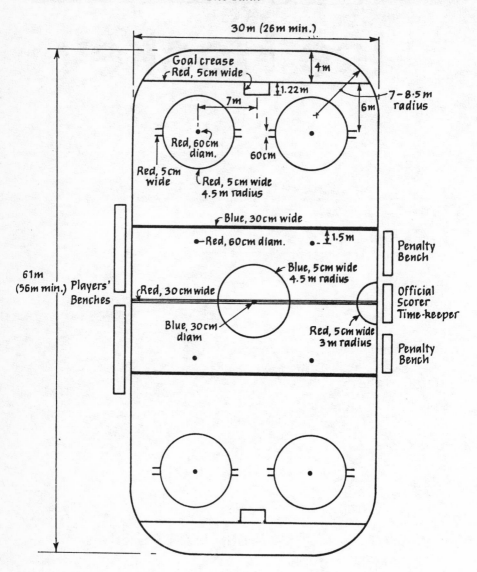

Ice Hockey

1. THE RINK
A glossary of terms may be found on pages 567-69.

101. Rink
The game of Ice Hockey shall be played on an ice surface known as a **rink**.

102. Dimensions of Rink (see diagram on opposite page)
(*a*) The maximum size of the rink shall be 61m long and 30m wide with a minimum size of 56m long and 26m wide. The corners shall be rounded in the arc of a circle with a radius of 7 to 8.5m.

The rink shall be surrounded by a wooden or plastic wall or fence known as the **boards** which shall extend not less than 1.20m and not more than 1.22m in height above the level of the ice surface.

Except for the official markings provided for in these rules, the entire playing surface and the boards shall be white in colour.

(*b*) The boards shall be constructed in such manner that the surface facing the ice shall be smooth and free of any obstruction or any object that could cause injury to players.

All doors giving access to the playing surface must swing away from the ice surface.

All protective screens and gear used to hold them in position shall be mounted on the boards on the side away from the playing surface.

It is recommended that above the boards of the rink there be:

1. Protective glass 160–200cm in height on the ends between the goal-lines and 80–100cm along the sides.

2. Nets at the ends behind the goals above the glass to protect the spectators.

For the IIHF Championships the protective glass is obligatory.

103. Goals

(*a*) 4.00m from each end of the rink and in the centre of a red line 5cm wide drawn completely across the width of the ice and continued vertically up the side of the boards, regulation goal-posts and nets shall be set in such manner as to remain stationary during the progress of a game.

(*b*) The goal-posts shall be of approved design and material, extending vertically 1.22m above the surface of the ice and 1.83m apart, measured from the inside of the posts. A cross-bar of the same material as the goal-posts shall extend from the top of one post to the top of the other.

1. The inside measurement of the goal from the front of the goal-line to the rear of the net, at its deepest point, shall not be more than 1.12m or less than 60cm.

2. There shall be attached to the back of each goal-frame a net which is constructed in such a manner as to keep the puck within the confines of the goal.

(*c*) The goal-posts, cross-bar and the exterior surface of other supporting framework for the goal shall be painted entirely in red. The surface of the base plate inside the goal and supports other than the goal-posts shall be painted white.

(*d*) The red line, 5cm wide, between the goal-posts on the ice and extended completely across the rink, shall be known as the **goal-line**.

(*e*) The goal-area, enclosed by the goal-line and the base of the goal, shall be painted white.

104. Goal-Crease

(*a*) In front of each goal a **goal-crease** area shall be marked by a red line 5cm in width.

(*b*) The goal-crease shall be laid out as follows: 30cm from the outside of each goal-post, lines 1.22m in length and 5cm in width shall be drawn at right angles to the goal-line and the points of these lines farthest from the goal-line shall be joined by another line, 5cm in width.

(*c*) The goal-crease area shall include all the space outlined by the crease-lines and extended vertically 1.22m to the level of the top of the goal-frame.

105. Division of Ice Surface

(*a*) The ice area between the two goal-lines shall be divided into three equal parts by lines 30cm in width and blue in colour, extending completely across the rink, parallel with the goal-lines, and continuing vertically up the side of boards.

(*b*) That portion of the ice surface in which the goal is situated shall be called the **defending zone** of the team defending that goal; the central portions shall be known as the **neutral zone**, and the portion farthest from the defending goal as the **attacking zone**. The zone-line shall be considered part of the zone that the puck is in.

(*c*) There shall also be a line, known as the **centre line**, 30cm in width and red in colour, drawn completely across the rink in centre ice, parallel with the goal-lines, continuing vertically up the side of the boards.

106. Centre Ice Spot and Circle
A circular blue spot, 30cm in diameter, shall be marked exactly in the centre of the rink; and with this spot as a centre, a circle of 4.5m radius shall be marked with a blue line 5cm in width.

107. Face-off Spots in Neutral Zone
Two spots 60cm in diameter shall be marked with a red line 5 cm wide on the ice in the Neutral Zone 1.5m from each blue line, and the same distance from the boards as the end zone face-off spots. Within each face-off spot draw two parallel lines 7.5cm from the top and bottom of the spot. The area within the two lines shall be painted red, the remainder shall be painted white.

108. End Zones Face-off Spots and Circles
(*a*) Face-off spots and circles shall be marked on the ice in both end zones and on both sides of each goal. The face-off spots shall be 60cm in diameter and drawn with a red line 5cm wide. Within each face-off spot draw two parallel lines 7.5cm from the top and bottom of the spot. The area within the two lines shall be painted red, the remainder shall be painted white. The circles shall have a radius of 4.5m from the centre of the face-off spots and marked with a red line 5cm wide. Extending from the outer edge of both sides of each face-off circle shall be two lines 5.5m and 6.5m from the parallel to the goal-line, 60cm long and 5cm wide.

(*b*) The location of the face-off spots shall be fixed in the following manner.

Establish the imaginary point 6m directly in front of the centre of each goal; 7m on each side of this point, parallel to and 6m from the goal-line, shall be the centre of the end zone face-off spots.

109. Players' Benches
(*a*) Each rink shall be provided with seats or benches for the use of both teams, and the accommodations provided including benches and doors shall be uniform for both teams. Such seats or benches shall have accommodation for at least 16 persons of each team and shall be placed

immediately alongside the ice, in the Neutral Zone, as near to the centre of the rink as possible, and convenient to the dressing-rooms.

The players' benches should be on the same side of the playing surface opposite the penalty bench and should be separated by a substantial distance.

Where physically possible, each players' bench shall have two doors opening in the Neutral Zone, and all doors opening to the playing surface shall be constructed so that they swing inward.

(*b*) None but players in uniform, and not more than 6 team officials, shall be permitted to occupy the players' bench area so provided.

(*c*) For the choice of players' benches, see Section B under Rule 632, Start of Game and Periods.

110. Penalty Bench

(*a*) Each rink must be provided with benches or seats to be known as the **penalty bench**. It is preferable to have separate penalty benches for each team separated from each other and substantially separated from either players' bench. The penalty bench(es) must be situated opposite the Neutral Zone.

(*b*) A semi-circle, 3m in radius, to be known as the **referees' crease**, shall be marked on the ice by a line 5cm wide immediately in front of the Penalty Timekeeper.

111. Signal and Timing Devices

(*a*) Each rink shall be provided with a siren, or other suitable sound device, for the use of Timekeepers.

(*b*) Each rink shall have some form of electrical clock for the purpose of keeping the spectators, players and game officials accurately informed as to all time elements at all stages of the game, including the time played in any period and the time remaining to be served by at least two penalised players on each team.

(*c*) Behind each goal there shall be electrical lights for the use of the Goal Judges. A red light shall signify the scoring of a goal. Where automatic lights are available, a green light will signify the end of a period only.

112. Dressing-rooms and Rink Lighting

(*a*) Each rink shall provide a suitable room, equipped with sanitary toilet and shower suitable for 25 persons with equipment, for the use of the visiting team.

(*b*) A separate dressing-room equipped with sanitary toilet and shower shall be provided for the use of the Referees and Linesmen.

(*c*) No officer, manager, player or employee of any team may enter into an acrimonious discussion with any Referee or Linesman, during or after a game and no person, except as authorised by the Association concerned, shall be allowed to enter the Referees' dressing-room during the course of, or immediately following a game. For any infraction of this Rule the matter shall be reported by the Referee to the proper authorities for further action.

(*d*) All rinks shall be sufficiently well lighted so that the players and spectators may conveniently follow play at all times.

Note: If, in the opinion of the Referee, there is not sufficient light to continue the game, the Referee shall have the authority to postpone the remainder of the game or take time out pending the necessary improvement to the lights. If one team is being handicapped to a greater extent by failure of lights and in the opinion of the Referee the game should not be cancelled, he shall have the authority to alternate the teams so as each team will play the same amount of time in each end of the rink.

2. TEAMS

201. Composition of Teams

(*a*) A team shall not have more than 6 players on the ice at any one time while the play is in progress. These 6 players shall be designated as follows: Goalkeeper, Right Defence, Left Defence, Centre, Right Wing and Left Wing.

(*b*) If at any time a team has more than 6 players on the ice, or the number to which they are entitled by reason of penalties, during the progress of play, they shall be assessed a bench minor penalty.

202. Captain of Team

(*a*) Each team shall appoint a Captain and not more than two Alternate Captains. On the ice, only the Captain or Alternate Captain shall have the privilege of discussing any questions with the Referee relating to interpretation of rules that may arise during the progress of a game. Only the Captain or an Alternate Captain may come off the bench if invited by the Referee when none are on the ice. If the Captain or Alternate Captain comes off the bench when not invited by the Referee, a bench minor penalty is to be assessed upon the team. When the Captain and an Alternate Captain are on the ice, only the Captain may talk to the Referee.

The Captain shall wear the letter 'C' and the Alternate Captain(s) the letter 'A' in a conspicuous position on the front of the sweater. The letters should be in a contrasting colour approximately 8cm in height.

If the letters are not worn, the privileges under this section will not be granted.

(*b*) The Referee and Official Scorer shall be advised, prior to the start of each game, the names and numbers of the Captain of the team and Alternate Captain(s).

(*c*) No goalkeepers shall be entitled to exercise the privileges of Captain or Alternative Captain.

(*d*) Only the Captain or Alternate Captain shall have the privilege of discussing with the Referee any point relating to the interpretation of rules. Any other player who comes off the bench and makes any protest or intervention with the officials for any purpose shall be assessed a misconduct penalty in addition to a minor penalty under Rule 601(*a*), Abuse of Officials.

A complaint about a penalty is *not* a matter 'relating to the interpretation of the rules' and a minor penalty under Rule 601(*a*) Abuse of Officials, shall be imposed against any Captain or Alternate Captain or other player making such a complaint.

(*e*) No playing Coach or playing Manager shall be permitted to act as Captain.

203. Players in Uniform

(*a*) At the beginning of each game the Manager or Coach of each team shall list the players and goalkeepers who shall be eligible to play in the game. A maximum of 20 players, plus 2 goalkeepers, shall be permitted.

(*b*) Each player shall wear an individual number at least 25cm in height on the back of his sweater.

All players of each team shall be dressed uniformly in colour of their helmet, sweaters, pants and stockings. Any player not complying with this provision shall not be permitted to participate in the game.

(*c*) A list of names and numbers of all eligible players and goalkeepers shall be handed to the Referee or Official Scorer before the game, and no change in the list or addition thereto shall be permitted after the commencement of the game.

(*d*) Each team shall be allowed one goalkeeper on the ice at one time. The goalkeeper may be removed and another 'player' substituted. Such a 'player' substitute shall not be permitted the privileges of the goalkeeper.

(*e*) Each team shall have on its bench, or on a chair immediately beside the bench, a substitute goalkeeper who shall at all times be fully dressed and equipped ready to play.

The substitute goalkeeper may enter the game at any time following a stoppage of play, but no warm-up shall be permitted (see Rule 205, Change of Players).

(*f*) Except when both goalkeepers are incapacitated, no player on the playing roster in that game shall be permitted to wear the equipment of the goalkeeper.

(*g*) In all games, where in the opinion of the Referee, the colours of the competing teams are so much alike that there is a possibility of a miscall by the Referee or Linesmen, it is the responsibility of the home team to change its sweaters if the Referee so orders.

204. Starting Line-up

(*a*) Prior to the start of the game, at the request of the Referee, the Manager or Coach of the visiting team is required to name the starting line-up to the Referee or the Official Scorer. At any time in the game, at the request of the Referee, made to the Captain, the visiting team must place a playing line-up on the ice and promptly commence play.

(*b*) Prior to the start of the game the Manager or Coach of the home team, having been advised by the Official Scorer or the Referee of the names of the starting line-up of the visiting team, shall name the starting line-up of the home team, which information shall be conveyed by the Official Scorer or the Referee to the Coach of the visiting team.

(*c*) No change in the starting line-up of either team, as given to the Referee or Official Scorer, or in the playing line-up on the ice, shall be made until the game is actually in progress. For an infraction of this rule, a bench minor penalty shall be imposed upon the offending team, provided such infraction is called to the attention of the Referee by the Captain of the opposing team before the second face-off in the first period takes place.

(*d*) Following a stoppage of play, the visiting team shall promptly place a line-up on the ice ready for play and no substitution shall be made for that time until play has been resumed. The home team may then make any desired substitution which does not result in the delay of the game.

If there is any undue delay by either team in changing lines, the Referee shall order the offending team or teams to take their positions immediately and not permit a line change.

Note: In the application of this rule, the change of one or more player(s) shall constitute a line change.

205. Change of Players

(*a*) Players may be changed at any time from the players' bench, provided that the changing players shall be within an imaginary area limited by the length of the respective players' bench and 3m from the boards and out of the play before any change is made.

A goalkeeper may be changed for another player at any time under the conditions set out in this section.

(*b*) If, in the last 2 minutes of the game, a bench minor penalty is imposed for deliberate illegal substitution (too many men on the ice), a penalty shot shall be awarded against the offending team. The bench minor will not be served – see Rule 406(*d*), Penalty Shot.

(*c*) A player serving a penalty on the penalty bench, who is to be changed after the penalty has been served, must proceed at once, by way of the ice, and be at his own players' bench before any change can be made.

For any violation of this rule, a bench minor penalty shall be imposed.

(*d*) When a substitution for the goalkeeper has been made during a stoppage of play, the goalkeeper who left the game may not re-enter the game until the first stoppage of play thereafter.

There shall be no warm-up for any substitute goalkeeper. For violation of this rule a minor penalty shall be assessed to the goalkeeper returning to the game illegally.

(*e*) For player changes taking place during a stoppage of play, the Referee will assume the normal position for the ensuing face-off. The Referee will then allow a 5-second period during which the visiting team may make a player change. After this 5-second period has elapsed, the Referee will raise an arm to indicate that the visiting team may no longer change any player(s).

With the arm still up, the Referee will allow a 5-second period during which the home team may make a player change. After this 5-second period has elapsed, the Referee will drop the arm to indicate that the home team may no longer change any player(s).

Where a team attempts to make a player-change after their allotted period of time, the Referee shall send the player(s) back to their bench. Any subsequent infraction to this procedure at any time during the course of the game shall incur a bench minor penalty under this rule. A change of players may include from 1 to 6 players. A change of one player is considered a change under this rule.

206. Injured Players

(*a*) When a player, other than a goalkeeper, is injured or compelled to leave the ice during the game, he may retire from the game and be replaced by a substitute, but play must continue without the teams leaving the ice.

(*b*) If a goalkeeper sustains an injury or becomes ill, he must be ready to resume play immediately or be replaced by a substitute goalkeeper and no additional time shall be allowed by the Referee for the purpose of enabling the injured or ill goalkeeper to resume play – see also section (*d*).

If both goalkeepers of the team are incapacitated and unable to play, the team shall have 10 minutes to prepare and dress another player in uniform to act as the goalkeeper. In this case, neither of the two regular goalkeepers may return to that game.

No warm-up shall be permitted for a substitute goalkeeper.

(*c*) The substitute goalkeeper shall be subject to the regular rules governing goalkeepers and shall be entitled to the same privileges.

(*d*) If a penalised player has been injured, he may proceed to the dressing-room without the necessity of taking a seat on the penalty bench. If the injured player receives a minor, major or match penalty, the penalised team shall immediately put a substitute player on the penalty bench who shall serve the penalty without change, except by the injured penalised player. For violation of this rule, a bench minor penalty shall be imposed.

The penalised player who has been injured and been replaced on the penalty bench shall not be eligible to play until his penalty has expired.

(*e*) When a player is injured so that he cannot continue play or go to his bench, the play shall not be stopped until the injured player's team has secured possession of the puck. If the player's team is in possession of the puck at the time of injury, play shall be stopped immediately, unless his team is in a scoring position.

Note: In the case where it is obvious that a player has sustained a serious injury, the Referee and/or Linesmen may stop the play immediately.

3. EQUIPMENT

301. Sticks

(*a*) The sticks shall be made of wood or other material approved by the IIHF such as aluminium or plastic and must not have any projections. The shaft of a player's stick must be straight. Adhesive tape of any colour may be wrapped around the stick at any place.

(*b*) No stick shall exceed 147cm in length, from the heel to the end of the shaft, nor more than 32cm from the heel to the end of the blade.

The blade of the stick shall not be more than 7.5cm and less than 5cm in width at any point.

All edges of the blade shall be bevelled.

The curvature of the blade of the stick shall be restricted in such a way that the distance of a perpendicular line measured from a straight line drawn from any point at the heel to the end of the blade to the point of maximum curvature shall not exceed 1.5cm.

(*c*) The blade of the goalkeeper's stick shall not exceed 9cm in width at any point, except at the heel where it must not exceed 11.5cm in width, nor shall the goalkeeper's stick exceed 39cm in length from the heel to the end of the blade.

The widened portion of the goalkeeper's stick extending up the shaft from the blade shall not extend more than 71cm from the heel and shall not exceed 9cm in width.

(*d*) A player who participates in the play while taking a replacement stick to his goalkeeper shall incur a minor penalty under this rule.

302. Skates

(*a*) All skates (except goalkeepers') shall be equipped with safety heel tips.

When the Referee becomes aware that any person is wearing a skate on which the protective heel tip is missing or broken, he shall direct its replacement at the next intermission between periods. If such replacement is not carried out and the player re-enters the game, the Referee shall assess a minor penalty to the offending player.

(*b*) The use of speed skates or fancy skates or any skate so designed that it may cause injury is prohibited.

303. Goalkeeper's Equipment

(*a*) With the exception of skates and stick, all the equipment worn by the goalkeeper must be constructed solely for the purpose of protection of head or body, and must not include any garment or contrivance which would give the goalkeeper undue assistance in keeping goal.

(*b*) The leg-guards worn by goalkeepers shall not exceed 30cm in extreme width when on the leg of the goalkeeper.

(*c*) Protective padding attached to the back or forming part of the goalkeeper's blocker glove shall not exceed 20.3cm in width nor 40.6cm in length at any point.

Cages on catching gloves are prohibited. A 'cage' shall mean any lacing or webbing or other material in the goalkeeper's catching glove joining the thumb and the index finger which is in excess of the minimum necessary to fill the gap when the goalkeeper's thumb and index finger in the glove are fully extended and spread and includes any pocket or pouch effect produced by excess lacing or webbing or other material between the thumb and index finger when fully extended.

304. Protective Equipment

(*a*) All protective equipment, except gloves, headgear or goalkeeper's leg guards, must be worn *entirely* under the uniform. For violation of this rule, after one warning by the Referee, a minor penalty shall be imposed on the offending player.

(*b*) All players must wear a hockey helmet, with chin-strap properly fastened.

(*c*) All goalkeepers must wear a full face-mask and a goalkeeper's full head protector or hockey helmet.

(*d*) Full face-masks shall be worn in all IIHF sanctioned games and tournaments in classifications of 20 years and younger. It is recommended that all senior players also wear full face-masks or at least eye protectors.

Full face-masks shall be worn in the IIHF Women's championships and in Women's international games.

(*e*) Full face-masks must be constructed in such a way that neither the puck nor the stick blade might get through it.

(*f*) Referees and Linesmen shall wear a black hockey helmet.

305. Dangerous Equipment

(*a*) The use of pads or protectors made of metal or any other material likely to cause injury to a player is prohibited.

Note: The Referee has the authority to prohibit a player from participating in the game while using or wearing any equipment that he considers dangerous to a player or game official.

(*b*) A glove from which all or part of the palm has been intentionally removed or cut to permit the use of the bare hand shall be considered illegal equipment and if any player wears such a glove in play, a minor penalty shall be imposed.

306. Puck

The puck shall be made of vulcanised rubber or other approved material, 2.54cm thick and 7.62cm in diameter, and be primarily black in colour. The puck shall weigh not less than 156g nor more than 170g.

4. PENALTIES

401. Penalties

Penalties shall be actual playing time and shall be divided into the following classes:

(1) Minor penalties
(2) Bench minor penalties
(3) Major penalties
(4) Misconduct penalties
(5) Match penalties
(6) Penalty shot

Where coincident penalties are imposed on players of both teams, the penalised players of the visiting team shall take their positions on the penalty bench first in the place designated for visiting players, or where there is no special designation, then on the bench farthest from the gate.

When penalties are imposed after the conclusion of any game and until the players have left the ice, such penalties shall be reported to the proper authorities by the Referees on the official game report.

In cases when any rule states that the Manager or Coach shall designate a player to serve any penalty and if the Manager or Coach refuses to name a player, the Referee shall have the authority to name any player of the offending team that he desires to serve the penalty.

402. Minor Penalties

(a) For a **minor penalty**, any player, other than a goalkeeper, shall be ruled off the ice for 2 minutes, during which time no substitute shall be permitted.

(b) A **bench minor** penalty involves the removal from the ice of one player of the team against which the penalty is imposed for a period of 2 minutes. Any player, except the goalkeeper of the team, may be designated to serve the penalty by the Manager or the Coach, through the Captain, and such player shall take his place on the penalty bench promptly and serve the penalty as if it was a minor penalty imposed on him.

(c) If, while a team is **short-handed** by one or more minor or bench minor penalties, the opposing team scores a goal, the first of such penalties served or assessed shall automatically terminate.

Note: 'Short-handed' means that the team must be below the numerical strength of its opponents on the ice at the time the goal is scored. The minor or bench minor penalty which terminates automatically is the one which causes the team scored against to be short-handed. Thus, an equal number of penalties to an equal number of players of both teams does not cause either team to be short-handed.

(d) When a team is short-handed by one player and an equal number of players on each team are assessed penalties of equal duration, the penalised players shall take their places on the penalty benches and such penalised players shall not leave the penalty bench until the first stoppage of play following the expiry of their respective penalties. Immediate substitution shall be made for the penalised players and such penalties shall not be taken into account for the purpose of the delayed penalty rule (408).

403. Major Penalties

(a) For the first **major penalty** in any one game, except to the goalkeeper, the offender shall be ruled off the ice for 5 minutes, during which time no substitute shall be permitted.

(b) For the second major penalty in the same game to the same player, or a major penalty for cross-checking, butt-ending, high-sticking, slashing, spearing and boarding the player, he shall be ruled off the ice for the balance of the playing time, but a substitute shall be permitted after 5 minutes' major penalty plus game misconduct penalty (See Rules 604, 607, 615, 630, 631.)

404. Misconduct Penalties

(*a*) A **misconduct penalty** to any player, except the goalkeeper, involves removal from the game for a period of 10 minutes. A substitute player is permitted to replace, immediately, a player serving a misconduct penalty. A player whose misconduct penalty has expired shall remain on the penalty bench until the next stoppage of play.

When a player receives a minor or major penalty and a misconduct penalty at the same time, the penalised team shall immediately put a substitute player on the penalty bench and he shall serve the minor or major penalty without change.

Any player receiving two misconduct penalties in one game shall automatically be assessed a game misconduct.

(*b*) A **game misconduct** penalty involves removal for the balance of the game and the offender shall be ordered to the dressing-room for the remainder of the game, but a substitute shall be permitted immediately.

(*c*) A **gross misconduct** penalty involves the suspension of a player or team official for the balance of the game, but a substitution shall be permitted immediately.

Any player or team official incurring a gross misconduct penalty shall be suspended from participating in any further games until his case has been dealt with by the proper authorities.

Note: For game misconduct or gross misconduct penalties, regardless of when imposed, a total of 20 minutes shall be charged in the records against the player. Such penalties shall be reported by the Referee to the proper authorities immediately following the game.

405. Match Penalties

(*a*) A **match** penalty involves the suspension of a player for the balance of the game, and the offender shall be ordered to the dressing-room immediately. A substitute player is permitted to replace the penalised player after 5 minutes' playing time has elapsed.

Note: For all match penalties, regardless of when imposed, a total of 20 minutes shall be charged in the records against the offending player.

(*b*) A player incurring a match penalty shall be suspended from playing in any further games until his case has been dealt with by the proper authorities.

406. Penalty Shot

(*a*) When there is an infraction of the rules that calls for a penalty shot not involving a major, misconduct, game misconduct, or match penalty, the non-offending team shall be given the option of accepting the penalty shot or having a minor penalty assessed to the offending player. If, however, a major, misconduct, game misconduct, or match penalty is incurred with the penalty shot, the shot shall be awarded and the penalty for the prescribed infraction shall be assessed.

(*b*) Any infraction of the rules which calls for a penalty shot shall be taken as follows:

The Referee shall cause to be announced over the public address system the name of the player designated by him or selected by the team entitled to take the shot (as appropriate). He shall then place the puck on the centre face-off spot and the player taking the shot will, on the instruction of the Referee, play the puck from there and shall attempt to score on the goalkeeper. Once the player taking the shot has possession of the puck he must proceed towards his opponent's goal-line, and once the puck is shot, the play shall be considered complete. No goal can be scored by a second shot of any kind, and any time the puck crosses the goal-line the shot shall be considered complete.

Only the goalkeeper or alternate goalkeeper or a player designated as a goalkeeper or alternate goalkeeper, may defend against the penalty shot.

(*c*) The goalkeeper must remain in his crease until the player taking the penalty shot has touched the puck, and in the event of violation of this rule or any foul committed by the goalkeeper, the Referee shall allow the shot to be completed, signalling such violation by raising his arm, and if the shot fails, he shall permit the penalty shot to be taken over again. If the goalkeeper leaves the goal crease too early:
 – The first time: warning and a new penalty shot
 – The second time: misconduct penalty and a new penalty shot
 – The third time: award a goal.

The goalkeeper may attempt to stop the shot in any manner except by throwing his stick or any other object in which case a goal shall be awarded.

Note: See Rule 633. Throwing Stick.

(*d*) In cases where a penalty shot has been awarded, the penalty shot shall be taken by any player selected by the Captain of the non-offending team except a player serving a penalty or a player to be assessed a delayed penalty. Such selection shall be reported to the Referee and cannot be changed.

If, at the time a penalty shot is awarded, the goalkeeper of the penalised team has been removed from the ice and substituted for by another player, including the substitute goalkeeper, the goalkeeper shall be permitted to return to the ice before the penalty shot is taken.

(*e*) While the penalty shot is being taken, players of both sides shall withdraw to the sides of the rink and behind the centre red line.

(*f*) If, while the penalty shot is being taken, any player of the opposing team shall have by some action interfered with or distracted the player taking the shot and, because of such action, the shot should have failed, a second attempt shall be permitted and the Referee shall impose a misconduct penalty on the player so interfering or distracting.

(*g*) If a goal is scored from a penalty shot, the puck shall be faced at centre ice in the usual way. If a goal is not scored, the puck shall be faced at either of the end face-off spots in the zone in which the penalty shot has been attempted.

(*h*) Should a goal be scored from a penalty shot, a further penalty to the offending player shall not be assessed unless the offence for which the penalty shot was awarded was such as to incur a major, misconduct, game misconduct, match or gross misconduct penalty, in which case the penalty prescribed for the particular offence shall be served.

If the offence for which the penalty shot was awarded was such as would normally incur a minor penalty, then regardless of whether the penalty shot results in a goal or not, the minor penalty shall not be served.

(*i*) If the foul upon which the penalty shot is based occurs during actual playing time, the penalty shot shall be awarded and taken immediately in the usual manner, notwithstanding any delay occasioned by a slow whistle by the Referee to permit the play to be completed which delay results in the expiry of the regular playing time in any period.

The time required for the taking of a penalty shot shall not be included in the regular playing time or any overtime.

407. Goalkeeper's Penalties

(*a*) A goalkeeper shall not be sent to the penalty bench for an offence which results in a minor, major or misconduct penalty, but instead the penalty shall be served by another member of his own team who was on the ice when the offence was committed, said player to be designated by the Manager or Coach of the offending team, through the Captain, and such substitute shall not be changed.

(*b*) Should a goalkeeper incur two major penalties in one game, he shall also receive a game misconduct penalty.

(*c*) Should a goalkeeper incur a game misconduct penalty, his place shall be taken by the substitute goalkeeper, if available, otherwise by a member of his team, who shall be permitted 10 minutes to dress in the goalkeeper's full equipment.

(*d*) Should a goalkeeper incur a match penalty, his place shall then be taken by the substitute goalkeeper, if available, otherwise by a member of his team, and such player will be allowed the goalkeeper's equipment. However, any additional penalties as specifically called for by the individual rules covering match penalties will apply, and the offending team shall be penalised accordingly. Such additional penalty shall be served by another member of the team on the ice at the time the offence was committed, said player to be designated by the Manager or Coach of the offending team through the Captain.

(*e*) A minor penalty shall be imposed on a goalkeeper who leaves the immediate vicinity of his crease during an altercation.

(*f*) If a goalkeeper participates in the play in any manner when he is beyond the centre red line, he shall be assessed a minor penalty.

408. Delayed Penalties

(*a*) If a third player of any team is penalised while two players of the same team are serving penalties, the penalty time of the third player shall not commence until the penalty time of one of the two players already penalised shall have elapsed. Nevertheless, the third player penalised shall at once proceed to the penalty bench, but may be replaced on the ice by a substitute, until such time as the penalty time of the penalised player shall commence.

(*b*) When any team has three or more players serving penalties at the same time and because of the delayed penalty rule, a substitute for the third offender on the ice, none of the three penalised players on the penalty bench may return to the ice until play has been stopped unless, by reason of the expiration of penalties, the penalised team is entitled to have more than four players, including the goalkeeper, on the ice in which case the penalised player shall be permitted to return in the order of the expiry of their penalties. Otherwise, when play is stopped the player(s) whose penalty has expired may return to the game.

(*c*) If the penalties of two players of the same team will expire at the same time, the Captain of the team will designate to the Referee which of such players will return will designate to the Referee which of such players will return to the ice first and the Referee will instruct the penalty Timekeeper accordingly.

(*d*) When a major and a minor penalty are imposed at the same time on two or more players of the same team, the Penalty Timekeeper shall record the minor as being the first of such penalties.

409. Calling of Penalties

(*a*) Should an infraction of the rules which would call for a penalty be committed by a player of the side in possession of the puck, the Referee shall immediately blow his whistle and assess the penalty to the offending player. The resulting face-off shall be made at the place where the play was stopped, unless the stoppage occurs in the Attacking Zone of the player penalised, in which case the face-off shall be made at the nearest face-off spot in the Neutral Zone.

(*b*) Should an infraction of the rules, which would call for a penalty, be committed by a player of team *not* in possession of the puck, the Referee shall signify the calling of a penalty by raising his arm and, upon completion of the play (as defined in Note 2 below) by the team in possession, will immediately blow his whistle and give the penalty to the offending player.

Note 1: The subsequent face-off shall be made at the place where the play was stopped, unless during the period of a delayed whistle due to a foul by a player of the side not in possession, the side in possession ices the puck, shoots the puck from its defensive zone so that it goes out of bounds or is unplayable, then the face-off following the stoppage shall take place in the Neutral Zone near the defending blue line of the team shooting the puck.

If the penalty or penalties to be imposed are minor penalties, and a goal is scored on the play by the non-offending team, the first minor penalty shall not be imposed, but all other minor, major or match penalties shall be imposed in the normal manner.

Note 2: 'Completion of the play by the team in possession' in this Rule means that the puck must have come into the possession and control of or been intentionally directed by an opposing player or goalkeeper, or has been 'frozen'. This does not mean a rebound off the goalkeeper, the goal or the boards, or any accidental contact with the body or equipment of an opposing player.

Note 3: If after the Referee has signalled a penalty, but before the whistle has been blown, the puck shall enter the goal of the non-offending team as the direct result of the action of a player of that team, the goal shall be allowed and the penalty signalled shall be imposed in the normal manner.

If, when a team is short-handed by reason of one or more minor cr bench minor penalties, the Referee signals a further minor penalty or penalties against the short-handed team a goal is scored by the non-offending team before the whistle is blown, then the goal shall be allowed, the penalty signalled shall be waived and one of the minor penalties already being served shall automatically terminate under Rule 402, Minor Penalties.

(*c*) Should the same offending player commit other fouls on the same play, either before or after the Referee has blown his whistle, the offending player shall serve such penalties consecutively.

(*d*) If any fouls are committed after the play has been stopped, the offending players shall be penalised as though play were actually in progress.

401. Supplementary Discipline

In addition to the suspensions imposed under these rules, the proper disciplinary authority may, at any time after conclusion of the game, at their discretion investigate any incident that occurs in connection with any game, and may, if done before the next game of the offending team, assess additional suspensions for any offence committed during the pre-game warm-up, on the way between the dressing-room and the ice surface, during the course of a game or any aftermath thereof by a player or team official, whether or not such offence has been penalised by the Referee.

5. OFFICIALS

501. Appointment of Officials
For all International matches there shall be appointed one Referee and two Linesmen, one Game Timekeeper, one Penalty Timekeeper, one Official Scorer and two Goal Judges for each game.

National Associations have the authority to use the Two Referee system in games which are completely under their jurisdiction.

502. Referee
(*a*) The Referee shall have general supervision of the game, and shall have full control of game officials and players during the game, including stoppages; and in case of any dispute, his decision shall be final. The Referee shall remain on the ice at the conclusion of each period until all players have proceeded to their dressing-rooms.

(*b*) All Referees and Linesmen shall be garbed in black trousers and official sweaters.

They shall be equipped with approved whistles and metal tape-measures with minimum length of 2m.

(*c*) The Referee shall order the teams on the ice at the appointed time for the beginning of a game, and at the commencement of each period. If for any reason there be more than 15 minutes' delay in the commencement of the game or any undue delay in resuming play after the 15-minute interval between periods, the Referee shall state in his report to the proper authorities the cause of the delay and the team or teams which were at fault.

(*d*) The Referee may, at his own discretion, measure any equipment. The Referee shall check or measure the equipment worn by any player when requested to do so by the Captain of either team.

(*e*) The Referee shall, before starting the game, see that the appointed Game Timekeeper, Penalty Timekeeper, Official Scorer and Goal Judges are in their respective places, and satisfy himself that the timing and signalling equipment are in order.

(*f*) It shall be his duty to impose such penalties as are prescribed by the rules for infractions thereof, and to give the final decision in matters of disputed goals. The Referee, in matters of disputed goals, may consult with the Linesmen or Goal Judge before making his decision.

(g) The Referee shall announce to the Penalty Timekeeper all penalties, and for what such penalties are imposed. The infraction of the rules for which each penalty has been imposed will be announced correctly, as reported by the Referee, over the public address system. Where players of both teams are penalised on the same play, the penalty to the visiting player will be announced first.

(h) The Referee shall report to the Official Scorer the name or number of the goal scorer and any players entitled to assists. (In IIHF 'A' Pool Championships, assists will be determined by the Official Scorer.)

The Referee shall cause to be announced over the public address system the reason for not allowing a goal whenever the goal signal light is turned on in the course of play. This shall be done at the first stoppage of play regardless of any standard signal given by the Referee when the goal signal light was put on in error.

(i) The Referee shall see to it that players of opposing teams are separated on the penalty bench to prevent feuding.

(j) Should a Referee accidentally leave the ice or receive an injury which incapacitates him from discharging his duties while play is in progress, the game shall be stopped immediately by the Linesman, unless one of the teams has the puck in a scoring position, in which case the play shall be allowed to be completed. If it is obvious that the injury sustained is of a serious nature, play shall be stopped immediately.

(k) If, through misadventure or sickness, the Referees or Linesmen appointed are prevented from appearing, the team leaders of the two teams shall agree on a Referee or Linesman. If they are unable to agree, the proper authorities shall appoint the Officials.

If the regularly appointed officials appear during the progress of the game, they shall at once replace the temporary officials.

(l) Should a Linesman appointed be unable to act at the last minute or through sickness or accident be unable to finish the game, the Referee shall have the power to appoint a replacement, if he deems it necessary.

(m) If, owing to illness or accident, the Referee is unable to continue to officiate, one of the Linesmen shall perform such duties of the Referee during the balance of the game, the Linesman to be selected by the Referee, or, if necessary, by the team leaders of the competing teams.

(n) The Referee shall secure, from the Official Scorer, the Game Report immediately following each game. He shall sign and check this report and return same to the Official Scorer.

(o) The Referee is required to report on the official game report all game misconducts, gross misconducts, and match penalties immediately following the game involved giving full details to the Proper Authorities concerned.

503. Linesman

(*a*) The duty of the Linesman is to determine any infractions of the rules concerning:

Off-side – Rule 624, Off-side;

Off-side Pass – Rule 625, Passes;

Icing – Rule 618, Icing the Puck.

He shall stop the play when the puck:

(i) Goes out of playing area – Rule 626(*a*), Puck Out of Bounds or Unplayable;

(ii) When it is interfered with by an ineligible person – Rule 620, Interference by Spectators;

(iii) When the goal-post has been displaced from its normal position – Rule 608, Delaying the Game.

He shall stop the play:

(i) For off-sides occurring on face-off circles – Rule 610, Face-Offs;

(ii) When there has been a premature substitution for a goalkeeper – Rule 205, Change of Players;

(iii) For injured player(s) – Rule 206, Injured Players;

(iv) Interference by spectators – Rule 620, Interference by Spectators.

(*b*) He shall stop play if the puck has been batted with the hand from one player to a team-mate or again when the puck has been struck with a high stick and it has become obvious the Referee did not observe the infraction.

(*c*) He shall conduct the face-off at all times, except at the start of the game, at the beginning of each period and after a goal has been scored.

The Referee may call upon a linesman to conduct a face-off at any time.

(*d*) He shall, when requested to do so by the Referee, give his version of any incident that may have taken place during the playing of the game.

(*e*) He shall not stop play to impose any penalty except for violations of:

(i) Too many men on the ice – Rule 201(*b*), Composition of Teams;

(ii) Articles thrown on the ice from vicinity of the players' or penalty bench – Rule 601(*j*), Abuse of Officials and other Misconduct;

(iii) Stick thrown on to the ice from the players' or penalty bench – Rule 605, Broken Stick;

and he shall report such violations to the Referee, who shall impose a bench minor penalty against the offending team.

He shall report immediately to the Referee his version of the circumstances with respect to deliberately displacing the goal-post from its normal position – Rule 608, Delaying the Game.

He shall report immediately to the Referee his version of any infraction of the Rules constituting a bench minor penalty, a major or match foul, misconduct, game misconduct or gross misconduct penalty.

504. Two Referees

(a) The Referees shall have general supervision of the game, and shall have full control of all game officials and players during the game, including stoppages; and in case of any dispute, their decision shall be final. The Referees shall remain on the ice at the conclusion of each period until all players have proceeded to their dressing-rooms.

(b) All Referees shall be garbed in black trousers and official sweaters.

They shall be equipped with approved whistles and metal tape-measures with minimum length of 2m.

(c) The Referees shall order the teams on the ice at the appointed time for the beginning of a game, and at the commencement of each period. If, for any reason, there be more than 15 minutes' delay in the commencement of the game or any undue delay in resuming play after the 15-minute interval between periods, the Referees shall state in their report to the proper authorities the cause of the delay, and the team or teams which were at fault.

(d) The Referees may, at their own discretion, measure any equipment, the Referee shall check the equipment worn by any player when requested to do by the Captain of either team.

(e) The Referees shall, before starting the game, see that the appointed Game Timekeeper, Penalty Timekeeper, Official Scorer and Goal Judges are in their respective places, and satisfy themselves that the timing and signalling equipment are in order.

(f) It shall be their duty to impose such penalties as are prescribed by the rules for infractions thereof, to stop play for any other infractions of the Rules, and to give the final decision in matters of disputed goals. The Referees may, in matters of disputed goals, consult with the Goal Judge before making a decision.

(g) The Referees shall announce to the Penalty Timekeeper all penalties, and for what infractions such penalties are imposed.

The infraction of the Rules for which each penalty has been imposed will be announced correctly, as reported by the Referees, over the public address system. Where players of both teams are penalised at the same time, the penalty to the visiting player will be announced first.

(h) The Referees shall report to the Official Scorer the name or number of the goal scorer and any players entitled to assists.

The Referees shall cause to be announced over the public address system the reason for not allowing a goal whenever the goal signal light is turned on in the course of play. This shall be done at the first stoppage of play regardless of any standard signal given by the Referees when the goal signal light was put on in error.

(*i*) The Referees shall see to it that players of opposing teams are separated on the penalty bench to prevent feuding.

(*j*) Should a Referee accidentally leave the ice or receive an injury which incapacitates him from discharging his duties while play is in progress the game shall be stopped immediately by the other Referee, unless one of the teams has the puck in a scoring position, in which case the play shall be allowed to be completed. If it is obvious that the injury sustained is of a serious nature, play shall be stopped immediately.

(*k*) If, through misadventure or sickness, both Referees appointed are prevented from appearing, the team leaders of the two clubs shall agree on Referees.

If they are unable to agree, the proper authorities shall appoint the officials.

If the regularly appointed officials appear during the progress of the game, they shall at once replace the temporary officials.

(*l*) Should one of the appointed Referees be unable to act at the last minute or through sickness or accident be unable to finish the game, the other Referee shall have no power to appoint a replacement, if he deems it necessary.

(*m*) The Referees shall secure from the Official Scorer the Game Report immediately following each game. They shall sign and check this report and return it to the Official Scorer.

(*n*) The Referees are required to report on the official game report all game misconducts, gross misconducts and match penalties immediately following the game involved, giving full details to the proper authorities concerned.

505. Goal Judges

(*a*) There shall be one Goal Judge at each goal. They shall not be members of either team engaged in the game, nor shall they be replaced during its progress, unless after the commencement of the game it becomes apparent that either Goal Judge, on account of partisanship or any other cause, is guilty of giving unjust decisions, in which case the Referee may appoint a replacement Goal Judge.

(*b*) Goal Judges shall be stationed behind the goals, during the progress of play, in properly screened cages, so that there can be no interference with their activities. They shall not change goals during the game.

(*c*) The Goal Judge shall decide if the puck has passed between the goal-posts and completely over the goal-line and give the appropriate signal.

The Referee shall give the final decision in matters of a disputed goal. He may consult with the Goal Judge or Linesman before making his decision.

506. Penalty Timekeeper

(a) The Penalty Timekeeper shall keep, on the official forms provided, a correct record of all penalties imposed by the officials, including the names of the players penalised, the infractions penalised, the duration of each penalty and the time at which each penalty was imposed. He shall report in the penalty record each penalty shot awarded, the name of the player taking the shot and the result of the shot.

(b) The Penalty Timekeeper shall check and ensure that the time served by all penalised players is correct. He shall be responsible for the correct posting of penalties on the scoreboard at all times and shall promptly call to the attention of the Referee any discrepancy between the time recorded on the clock and the official correct time, and he shall be responsible for making any adjustments ordered by the Referee.

He shall, upon request, give a penalised player correct information as to the unexpired time of his penalty.

(c) The Penalty Timekeeper shall advise the Referee(s) when the same player has received his second major or misconduct penalty in the same game.

507. Official Scorer

(a) Before the start of the game, the Official Scorer shall obtain from the Manager or Coach of both teams a list of all eligible players and the starting line-up of each team, which information shall be made known to the opposing team Manager and Coach before the start of play, either personally or through the Referee. (See Rule 203, Players in Uniform, and Rule 204, Starting Line-up.)

The Official Scorer shall secure the names of the Captain from the Manager or Coach at the time the line-ups are collected and will so indicate by placing the letter 'C' opposite their names on the score-sheet. The information shall be presented to the Referee for his signature at the completion of the game.

(b) The Official Scorer shall keep a record of the goals scored, the scorers, the players to whom assists have been credited, and shall indicate those players on the lists who have actually taken part in the game. He shall also record the time of entry into the game of any substitute goalkeeper. He shall record on the official score-sheet a notation where a goal is scored when the goalkeeper has been removed from the ice.

(*c*) The awards of points for goals and assists shall be announced over the public address system and all changes in such awards shall also be announced in the same manner.

No request for changes in any award of points, shall be considered unless they are made at, or before, the conclusion of actual play in the game by the team Captain.

(*d*) The Official Scorer shall also prepare the official score-sheet for signature by the Referee and forward it to the Proper Authorities.

508. Game Timekeeper

(*a*) The Game Timekeeper shall record the time of the starting and finishing of each game and all actual playing time during the game.

(*b*) The Game Timekeeper shall signal the Referee(s) for the commencement of the game, for the start of second and third periods, and any overtime period or periods. He shall allow 15 minutes' intermission between each period after which Referee(s) shall start play. He shall also signal by ringing a gong, siren or by blowing a whistle, the ending of each period, any overtime period or periods and the ending of the game. This applies in rinks that are not provided with an automatic gong or siren, or if the automatic gong or siren should fail to operate.

(*c*) Where a public address system is used, the Game Timekeeper shall announce when only *1 minute* of actual playing time remains in the first and second period and *2 minutes* remain in the third period and overtime.

(*d*) In the event of any dispute regarding time, the Referee's decision shall be final.

509. Proper Authorities

The term 'proper authorities' or 'proper disciplinary authority' as applied under these Rules is defined as the immediate governing body of the games involved.

6. PLAYING RULES

601. Abuse of Officials and Other Misconducts

Note: In the enforcement of this rule, the Referee has, in many instances, the opinion of imposing a misconduct penalty or a bench minor penalty. In principle, the Referee is directed to impose a bench minor penalty in respect to the violations which occur on or in the immediate vicinity of the players' bench but off the playing surface, and in all cases affecting non-playing personnel or players. A misconduct penalty should be imposed for violations which occur on the playing surface or in the penalty bench area and where the penalised player is readily identifiable.

(*a*) Any player who challenges or disputes the rulings of any official during the game shall be assessed a minor penalty for unsportsmanlike conduct. If the player persists in such a challenge or dispute, he shall be assessed a misconduct penalty, and any further dispute will result in a game misconduct penalty being assessed.

(*b*) If any player is guilty of any one of the following, his team shall be assessed a bench minor penalty:

1. After being penalised he does not proceed directly and immediately to the penalty bench and take his place on the penalty bench, or to the dressing-room when so ordered by the Referee.

2. While off the playing surface, uses obscene, profane or abusive language to any person, or uses the name of any official coupled with any such remarks.

3. While off the playing surface, interferes in any manner with any game official, including the Referee, Linesmen, Timekeepers or Goal Judges in the performance of their duties.

(*c*) Any player who is guilty of any one of the following shall be assessed a misconduct penalty:

1. Using obscene, profane or abusive language to any person on the ice or anywhere in the rink before, during or after the game, except in the immediate vicinity of the players' bench – see 601(*b*)2.

2. Intentionally knocking or shooting the puck out of reach of an official who is retrieving it.

3. Deliberately throwing any equipment, except the stick (see Rule 633*c*, Throwing Stick) out of the playing area.

4. Banging the board with his stick or any other instrument at any time.

5. Failing to proceed directly and immediately to the penalty bench following a fight or other altercation in which he has been involved and which has been broken up, and for which he is penalised or causes any delay by retrieving his equipment. His gloves, stick, etc. shall be delivered to him at the penalty bench by a team-mate (this misconduct penalty shall be in addition to any other penalties incurred).

6. After a warning by the Referee, persisting in any course of conduct (including threatening or abusive language or gestures or similar actions) designated to incite an opponent into incurring a penalty.

7. Entering or remaining in the Referee's crease while the Referee is reporting to, or consulting with, any game official, including Linesmen, Timekeeper, Penalty Timekeeper, Official Scorer or

Announcer, except for the purpose of taking his place on the penalty bench.

(*d*) Any player who is guilty of any of the following shall, at the discretion of the Referee, be assessed a misconduct or game misconduct:

1. Touching or holding with his stick or hands, tripping or body-checking a Referee, Linesman or any game official.

2. Throwing a stick out of the rink – Rule 633(*c*). Throwing Stick.

3. Continuing or attempting to continue a fight or altercation after he has been ordered by the Referee to stop, or resisting a Linesman in the discharge of his duties.

(*e*) Any player who is guilty of any of the following shall be assessed a game misconduct:

1. Persisting in any course of conduct for which he has previously been assessed a misconduct penalty.

2. Using obscene gestures on the ice or anywhere in the rink before, during or after the game.

(*f*) Any player who is guilty of any manner of behaviour which makes a travesty of, interferes with or is detrimental to the conducting of the game shall be assessed a gross misconduct penalty.

(*g*) If any team official is guilty of any of the following, his team shall be assessed a bench minor penalty:

1. Banging the boards with a stick or other instrument at any time.

2. Using obscene, profane or abusive language to any person or uses the name of any official coupled with such remarks anywhere in the rink.

3. Interfering in any manner with any game official, including the Referee, Linesmen, Timekeepers or Goal Judges in the performance of their duties.

(*h*) Any team official who is guilty of any type of misconduct shall be assessed a game misconduct penalty plus a bench minor penalty.

(*i*) Any team official who is guilty of holding or striking an official, or any manner of behaviour which makes a travesty of or interferes with or is detrimental to the conducting of the game, shall be assessed a gross misconduct penalty.

(*j*) Throwing anything on to the ice from anywhere in the rink is prohibited.

If this rule is violated by:

1. A player – he shall be assessed a minor plus game misconduct penalty.

2. A team official – he shall be assessed a game misconduct and his team a bench minor penalty.

3. A unidentified person of the team in the vicinity of the players' bench – the team shall be assessed a bench minor penalty.

If the player or team is penalised under Rule 633, Throwing Stick, this Rule shall not apply.

(*k*) Any player or team official who deliberately spits on or at an opponent, team official or game official shall be assessed a gross misconduct penalty. When a team official is assessed a gross misconduct under this section the team shall also be assessed a bench minor penalty.

602. Adjustment of Equipment

(*a*) Play shall not be stopped nor the game delayed by reason of adjustments to clothing, equipment, shoes, skates or sticks.

(*b*) The onus of maintaining clothing and equipment in proper condition shall be upon the player. If adjustments are required, the player shall retire from the ice and play shall continue.

(*c*) No delay shall be permitted for the repair or adjustment of goalkeeper's equipment. If adjustments are required, the goalkeeper shall retire from the ice and his place shall be taken by the substitute goalkeeper immediately and no warm-up shall be permitted.

(*d*) For an infraction of this rule, a minor penalty shall be imposed.

603. Attempt to Injure or Deliberate Injury

(*a*) A match penalty shall be imposed on any player who attempts to injure or deliberately injures an opponent. The circumstances shall be reported to the proper authorities for further action. A substitute for the penalised player shall be permitted at the end of the fifth minute.

(*b*) A gross misconduct penalty shall be imposed on any player who attempts to injure or deliberately injures a team official or game official.

604. Boarding

A minor or major penalty, at the discretion of the Referee based upon the degree of violence of the impact with the boards, shall be imposed on any player who body-checks, cross-checks, elbows, charges or trips an opponent in such manner that causes the opponent to be thrown violently into the boards. When a major penalty is assessed under this rule, the player shall automatically be assessed in addition a game misconduct penalty.

Note: Any unnecessary contact with a player playing the puck on an obvious icing or off-side play which results in that player being knocked into the boards is *boarding* and must be penalised as such. In other instances where there is no contact with the boards, it should be treated as *charging*.

Rolling an opponent (if he is the puck carrier) along the boards where he is endeavouring to go through too small an opening is not boarding. However, if the opponent is not the puck carrier, then such action shall be penalised as boarding, charging, interference or if the arms or stick are employed it shall be called holding or hooking.

605. Broken Stick

(*a*) A player without a stick may participate in the game. A player whose stick is broken may participate in the game provided he drops the broken portion. A minor penalty shall be imposed for an infraction of this rule.

Note: A broken stick is one which, in the opinion of the Referee, is unfit for normal play.

(*b*) A goalkeeper may continue to play with a broken stick until stoppage of play or until he has been legally provided with a stick.

(*c*) A player or goalkeeper whose stick is broken may not receive a stick thrown on to the ice from any part of the rink, but may receive a stick from a team-mate without proceeding to his player's bench.

For an infraction of this rule penalties will be assessed under Rule 601(*j*), Abuse of Officials and Other Misconducts.

(*d*) A goalkeeper whose stick is broken may not go to the players' bench during a stoppage of play for a replacement, but must receive his stick from a team-mate.

For an infraction of this rule a minor penalty shall be imposed on the goalkeeper.

606. Charging

(*a*) A minor or major penalty shall be imposed on a player who runs, jumps into or charges an opponent.

A minor or major penalty shall be assessed any player who pushes, bodychecks or hits an opponent from behind in any manner, anywhere on the ice.

A major plus a game misconduct penalty shall be assessed any player who injures an opponent as a result of checking that player from behind.

Where a layer is high-sticked, cross-checked, body-checked, pushed, hit or propelled in any manner from behind into the boards in such a way that the player is unable to protect or defend himself, a major penalty plus a game misconduct penalty shall be assessed.

(*b*) A double minor or major penalty shall be imposed on a player who commits any foul against a goalkeeper while the goalkeeper is within the goal-crease.

A goalkeeper is *not* 'fair game' just because he is outside the goal-crease area. A penalty for interference or charging (minor or major) should be called in every case where an opposing player makes unnecessary contact with a goalkeeper.

Likewise, Referees should be alert to penalise goalkeepers for tripping, slashing or spearing in the vicinity of the goal.

(*c*) A minor or major penalty at the discretion of the Referee shall be imposed on a player who makes physical contact with an opponent after the whistle has been blown, if in the opinion of the Referee, the player has had sufficient time after the whistle to avoid such contact.
Note: In women's ice hockey a direct body-check shall be penalised by a minor penalty.

607. Cross-Checking
(*a*) A minor or major penalty, at the discretion of the Referee, shall be imposed on a player who cross-checks an opponent.
Note: 'Cross-check' shall mean a check delivered with both hands on the stick and no part of the stick on the ice.
(*b*) A major penalty shall be imposed on any player who injures an opponent by cross-checking.
(*c*) When a major penalty is assessed under this Rule, the player shall automatically be assessed in addition a game misconduct penalty.

608. Delaying the Game
(*a*) A minor penalty shall be assessed on a goalkeeper who shoots the puck directly outside the playing area. A minor penalty shall be assessed on any player who deliberately shoots the puck outside the playing area. A minor penalty shall be assessed on any player or goalkeeper who throws or deliberately bats the puck with his hand or stick outside the playing area.
A bench minor penalty shall be imposed upon a team that, after scoring a goal, has more than one change of players on the ice.
(*b*) A minor penalty shall be imposed on any player (including the goalkeeper) who delays the game by deliberately displacing a goal-post from its normal position.
The Referee or Linesman shall stop play immediately when a goal-post has been displaced.
If the above mentioned delay is caused by any player or goalkeeper from the defending team in its defensive zone during the last 2 minutes of a game, or overtime, a penalty shot shall be awarded.
If the goal is deliberately displaced by a goalkeeper or player during the course of a break-away (see note), a penalty shot will be awarded to the non-offending team. Should this violation occur after the goalkeeper has been removed for another player, a goal shall be awarded to the non-offending team.
Note: A player with a 'break-away' is defined as a player in control of the puck with no opposition between him and the opposing goal and with a reasonable scoring opportunity.
(*c*) A bench minor penalty shall be imposed upon any team which,

after warning by the Referee to its Captain to place the correct number of players on the ice and commence play, fails to comply with the Referee's direction and thereby causes any delay by making additional substitutions, by persisting in having players off-side, or in any other manner.

(*d*) The puck must be kept in motion at all times.

(*e*) Except to carry the puck behind its goal once, a team in possession of the puck in its own defence area shall advance the puck towards the opposing goal, except if it is prevented from so doing by players of the opposing team.

For the first infraction of this rule, play shall be stopped and a face-off shall be made at either end face-off spot adjacent to the goal of the team causing the stoppage, and the Referee shall warn the Captain of the offending team of the reason for the face-off. For a second violation by any player of the same team in the same period, a minor penalty shall be imposed on the player violating the rule.

(*f*) A minor penalty shall be imposed on any player including the goalkeeper who holds, freezes or plays the puck with his stick, skates or body along the boards in such a manner as to cause a stoppage of play unless he is actually being checked by an opponent.

(*g*) A player beyond his defensive zone shall not pass nor carry the puck backward into his defensive zone for the purpose of delaying the game, except when his team is below the numerical strength of the opponents on the ice.

(*h*) For an infringement of this rule, the face-off shall be at the nearest end face-off spot in the Defending Zone of the offending team.

(*i*) If a team is not on the ice and prepared to start play in 15 minutes after the start of the intermission (or previous period) a bench minor penalty shall be assessed under this rule.

609. Elbowing or Kneeing

(*a*) A minor or major penalty, at the discretion of the Referee, shall be imposed on any player who uses his elbow or knee to foul an opponent.

(*b*) A major penalty shall be imposed on any player who injures an opponent as the result of a foul committed by using his elbow or knee.

(*c*) A match penalty shall be imposed on any player who deliberately head-butts or attempts to head-butt an opponent.

610. Face-Offs

(*a*) The puck shall be faced-off by the Referee or the Linesman by dropping the puck on the ice between the sticks of the players facing-off. Players facing-off will stand squarely facing their opponents' end of the rink, approximately one stick length apart, with the blade of their sticks touching the ice.

When the face-off takes place at any of the end or Neutral Zone face-off spots, the players taking part shall take their positions so that they will stand squarely facing their opponent's end of the rink. The sticks of both players facing-off shall have the blade touching the ice in contact with the designated white area. The player of the attacking team in his attacking half of the rink shall place his stick within the designated white area first.

No other players shall be allowed to enter the face-off circle or come within 4.5m of the players facing-off and must stand on-side on all face-offs.

If a violation of this sub-section of this Rule occurs, the Referee or Linesman shall re-face the puck, *unless* the non-offending team gained possession of the puck in which case the face-off will be considered valid and play shall be permitted to continue.

(*b*) If a player facing-off fails to take his proper position immediately when directed by the official, the official may order him replaced for that face-off by any team-mate on the ice.

No substitution of players shall be permitted until the face-off has been completed and play has been resumed, except when a penalty is imposed that will affect the on-ice strength of either team.

(*c*) In the conduct of any face-off anywhere on the playing surface, no player facing-off shall make any physical contact with his opponent's body by means of his own body or by his stick, except in the course of playing the puck after the face-off has been completed.

For violation of this rule the Referee shall impose a minor penalty or penalties on the player(s) whose action(s) caused the physical contact.

(*d*) Where a player has been removed from a face-off by an official, and another player of the same team delays taking up his proper position after a warning by the official, a bench minor penalty shall be assessed that team.

A second violation of this section by a player of the same team during the same face-off shall be penalised with a minor penalty to that player who commits the second violation of this section by his team.

(*e*) When an infringement of a rule has been committed or a stoppage of play has been caused by any player of the attacking side in the Attacking Zone, the ensuing face-off shall be made in the Neutral Zone at the nearest face-off spot.

Note: This includes stoppage of play caused by a player of the attacking side shooting the puck on the back of the defending team's goal without any intervening action by the defending team.

(*f*) When an infringement of a rule has been committed by players of both teams the ensuing face-off will be made at the place where the puck was when the play was stopped.

(*g*) When stoppage occurs between the end face-off spots and the near end of the rink, the puck shall be faced-off at the end face-off spot, on the side where the stoppage occurs, unless otherwise expressly provided by these Rules.

(*h*) All face-offs shall be conducted at the designated face-off spots as dictated by reason for the stoppage of play or on an imaginary line parallel to the side boards from one end-zone face-off spot to the other end-zone spot.

(*i*) When a goal is illegally scored as a result of a puck being deflected directly off or by an official, the resulting face-off shall be made at the end face-off spot in the defending zone.

(*j*) When the game is stopped for any reason not specifically covered in the official rules, the puck shall be faced-off where it was last played.

(*k*) The whistle shall not be blown by the official to start play. Playing time shall commence from the instant the puck is faced-off and shall stop when the whistle is blown.

(*l*) Following a stoppage of play, should one or both defencemen, who are playing near their attacking blue line, or any player coming from the bench of the attacking team enter into the attacking zone beyond the outer edge of the corner face-off circle, the ensuing face-off shall take place at the nearest face-off spot in the Neutral Zone near the blue line of the defending team.

611. Falling on the Puck

(*a*) A minor penalty shall be imposed on a player other than the goalkeeper who deliberately falls on or gathers a puck into his body.
Note: Any player who drops to his knees to block shots should not be penalised if the puck is shot under him or becomes lodged in his clothing or equipment, but any use of the hands to make the puck unplayable should be penalised promptly.

(*b*) A minor penalty shall be imposed on a goalkeeper who deliberately falls on or gathers the puck into his body or who holds or places the puck against any part of the goal or against the boards, when the puck is behind the goal-line and the goalkeeper's body is entirely outside the boundaries of his goal-crease.

(*c*) No defending player, except the goalkeeper, will be permitted to fall on the puck or hold the puck or gather the puck into his body or hands when the puck is within the goal creases.

For infringement of this rule, play shall immediately be stopped and a penalty shot shall be imposed against the offending team, but no other penalty shall be given.

612. Fisticuffs or Roughing

(*a*) A match penalty shall be imposed on any player who starts fisticuffs.

(*b*) A minor penalty shall be imposed on a player who, having been struck, shall retaliate with a blow or attempted blow. However, at the discretion of the Referee, a double minor, major or match penalty may be imposed if such player continues the altercation.

Note 1: It is the intent and purpose of this Rule that the Referee shall impose the match penalty in all cases when the instigator or retaliator of the fight is the aggressor.

Note 2: The Referee is provided very wide latitude in the penalties which he may impose under this rule. This is done intentionally to enable him to differentiate between the obvious degrees of responsibility of the participants, either for starting the fighting or persisting in continuing the fighting. The discretion provided should be exercised realistically.

(*c*) At the discretion of the Referee a minor or double minor penalty may be imposed on any player deemed guilty of unnecessary roughness.

(*d*) A misconduct or game misconduct penalty shall be imposed on any player involved in fisticuffs off the playing surface. If one player is on the ice and one is off the ice, both shall be considered on the ice for the application of this Rule (*a*) and (*b*) above.

(*e*) A game misconduct penalty shall be imposed on any player or goalkeeper who is the first to intervene in an altercation already in progress. This penalty is in addition to any other penalty incurred in the same incident.

613. Goal and Assist

(*a*) A goal shall be scored when the puck shall have been put between the goal-posts below the cross-bar, and entirely across the goal-line by the stick of a player of the attacking side.

(*b*) A goal shall be scored if the puck is put into the goal in any way by a player of the defending side. The player of attacking side who last played the puck shall be credited with the goal but no assist shall be awarded.

(*c*) If an attacking player kicks the puck and it is deflected into the goal by any player or goalkeeper the goal shall not be allowed.

(*d*) If the puck shall have been deflected into the goal from the shot of an attacking player by striking any part of the person of a player of the same side, the goal shall be allowed. The player who deflected the puck shall be credited with the goal. The goal shall not be allowed if the puck has been kicked, thrown or otherwise deliberately directed into the goal by any means other than a stick.

(*e*) A goal shall not be allowed if the puck has been deflected directly into the goal off an official.

(*f*) Should a player legally propel a puck into the goal-crease of the opposing team and the puck should become loose and available to another player of the attacking side, a goal scored on the play shall be valid.

(*g*) Unless the puck is on the goal-crease area, a player of the attacking side may not stand on the goal-crease line or in the goal-crease or hold his stick in the goal-crease area, and if the puck should enter the goal while such condition prevails except as in section (*h*) of this rule – a goal shall not be allowed, and the puck shall be faced in the neutral zone at the face-off spot nearest the Attacking Zone of the offending team.

(*h*) If a player of the attacking side has been physically interfered with by the action of any defending player so as to cause him to be in the goal-crease, and the puck should enter the goal while the player so interfered with is still within the goal-crease, the goal shall be allowed, unless, in the opinion of the Referee, he had sufficient time to get out of the crease, but stayed there of his own accord.

(*i*) Any goal scored, other than as covered by the official Rules, shall not be allowed.

(*j*) A goal shall be credited in the scoring records to a player who shall have propelled the puck into the opponents' goal. Each goal shall count one point in the player's record.

(*k*) When a player scores a goal, an assist shall be credited to the player or players taking part in the play immediately preceeding the goal, but not more than two assists can be given in any goal. Each assist so credited shall count one point in the player's record.

(*l*) Only one point can be credited to any one player on a goal.

(*m*) Where a player not listed on the Game Report scored a goal or is awarded an assist, the goal is to be disallowed, the player is to be removed from the game and no penalty is to be assessed.

614. Handling the Puck with the Hands

(*a*) A player, except the goalkeeper, shall not close his hand on the puck.

(*b*) A goalkeeper shall not:
1. Hold the puck in his hand(s) for longer than 3 seconds or in any manner which in the opinion of the Referee causes a stoppage of play; or
2. Throw the puck forward towards his opponent's goal which is first played by a team-mate; or
3. Deliberately drop the puck into his pads or on to the goal-net.

(*c*) For a violation of this rule, the offending player shall be assessed a minor penalty.

(*d*) A defending player, other than the goalkeeper, shall not pick up the puck from the ice with his hands. For a violation of this rule, the player shall be assessed a minor penalty. However, if the puck was in the goal-crease at the time of the violation, a penalty shot shall be awarded the opposing team.

(*e*) A player shall be permitted to stop or 'bat' a puck in the air with his open hand, or push it along the ice with his hand. However, the play shall be stopped if, in the opinion of the Referee, he has deliberately and intentionally directed the puck to a team-mate, and the puck faced-off at the spot where the offence occurred. If this violation is committed by an attacking player in his Attacking Zone, the face-off shall take place at the nearest Neutral Zone face-off spot.

Note: The object of this rule is to ensure continuous action and the Referee should not stop play unless he is satisfied that the directing of the puck to a team-mate was in fact deliberate and intentional.

The goal shall be disallowed if the puck was batted with the hand by an attacking player and deflected off any player or goalkeeper into the goal.

615. High-sticks

(*a*) The carrying of sticks above the normal height of the shoulder is prohibited, and a minor penalty may be imposed on any player violating this rule, at the discretion of the Referee.

(*b*) A goal scored from a stick so carried except by a player of the defending team shall not be allowed.

(*c*) When a player carries or holds any part of his stick above the height of his shoulders that causes an injury to an opposing player, the Referee shall have no alternative but to impose a major penalty plus a game misconduct penalty on the offending player.

If, however, such high-sticking action that causes the injury was judged to be accidental, a major penalty shall be imposed.

(*d*) Batting the puck above the normal height of the shoulders with the stick is prohibited and when it occurs play shall be stopped and a face-off conducted at one of the end face-off spots adjacent to the goal of the team committing the high-stick violation unless:

1. The puck is batted to an opponent, in which case the play shall continue; or

2. A player of the defending team bats the puck into his own goal, in which case the goal shall be allowed.

616. Holding an Opponent

(*a*) A minor penalty shall be imposed on a player who holds an opponent with his hands or stick or in any other way.

(*b*) A minor or major penalty plus a misconduct penalty shall be imposed on a player who grabs or holds the face mask, helmet, or pulls the hair of an opponent with his hand.

617. Hooking
(*a*) A minor penalty shall be imposed on a player who impedes or seeks to impede the progress of an opponent by hooking with his stick.

(*b*) A major penalty shall be imposed on any player who injures an opponent by hooking.

(*c*) When a player, in control of the puck on the opponent's side of the centre red line and having no opponent to pass other than the goalkeeper, is hooked or otherwise fouled from behind, thus preventing a reasonable scoring opportunity, a penalty shot shall be awarded to the non-offending team. The Referee, however, shall not stop the play until the attacking team has lost possession of the puck to the defending team.

(*d*) If, when the opposing goalkeeper has been removed from the ice, a player in control of the puck is hooked or otherwise foulded with no opposition between him and the opposing goal, thus preventing a reasonable scoring opportunity, the Referee shall immediately stop the play and award a goal to the attacking team.

618. Icing the Puck
(*a*) For the purpose of this Rule, the centre line will divide the ice into halves. Should any player of a team, equal or superior in numerical strength to the opposing team, shoot, bat, or deflect the puck from his own half of the ice, beyond the goal-line of the opposing team, play shall be stopped and the puck faced-off at the end face-off spot of the offending team nearest to where they last touched the puck, unless on the play the puck shall have entered the goal of the opposing team, in which case the goal shall be allowed.

For the purpose of this rule, the point of last contact with the puck by the team in possession shall be used to determine whether or not icing has occurred.

(*b*) If the puck was so shot by a player of a side below the numerical strength of the opposing team, play shall continue and icing shall not be called.

(*c*) If, however, the puck shall go beyond the goal-line in the opposite half of the ice directly from either of the players participating in a face-off, it shall not be considered a violation of this Rule.

(*d*) If, in the opinion of the Linesman, a player of the opposing team, except the goalkeeper, is able to play the puck before it passes his goal-line, but has not done so, icing shall not be called and play shall continue. If, in the opinion of the Referee, the defending side intentionally abstains from playing the puck promptly when they are in a position to do so, he shall stop the play and order a face-off on the end-zone face-off spot nearest the goal of the offending team.

(*e*) If the puck shall touch any part of a player of the opposing side, or his skates or his stick, or if it passes through any part of the goal-crease before it shall have reached the goal-line, or shall have touched the goalkeeper, or his skates or his stick, before crossing the goal-line, it shall not be considered as icing the puck and play shall continue.

(*f*) If the Linesman shall have erred in calling an icing the puck infraction (regardless of whether either team is short-handed) the puck shall be faced-off on the centre ice face-off spot.

619. Interference

(*a*) A minor penalty shall be imposed on a player who interferes with or impedes the progress of an opponent who is not in possession of the puck, or who deliberately knocks a stick out of an opponent's hand or who prevents a player who has dropped his stick or any other piece of equipment from regaining possession of it, or who knocks or shoots any abandoned or broken stick or illegal puck or other debris towards an opposing puck carrier in a manner that could cause him to be distracted – see also Rule 633(*a*), Throwing Stick.

(*b*) A minor penalty shall be imposed on any player on the players' bench or on the penalty bench who by means of his stick or his body interferes with the movements of the puck or of any opponent on the ice during the progress of play.

(*c*) If an attacking player deliberately stands in the goal-crease, the Referee shall stop play, and the ensuing face-off shall take place in the Neutral Zone.

(*d*) A minor penalty shall be imposed on a player who, by means of his stick or body, interferes with or impedes the movements of the goalkeeper while he is in his goal-crease area, unless the puck is already in that area.

(*e*) If, when the goalkeeper has been removed from the ice, any member of his team (including the goalkeeper) not legally on the ice, including any team official, interferes by means of his body or stick or any other object with the movements of the puck or an opposing player, the Referee shall immediately award a goal to the non-offending team.

(*f*) When a player in control of the puck on the opponent's side of the centre red line, and having no opponent to pass other than the goalkeeper, is interfered with by a stick or part thereof or any other object thrown or shot by any member of the defending team including a team official, a penalty shot shall be awarded to the non-offending side.

620. Interference by Spectators

(*a*) In the event of a player being held or interfered with by a spectator, play shall be stopped by the Referee or Linesman. If the team of the player interfered with is in possession of the puck at this time, the play shall be allowed to be completed before play is stopped. The puck shall be faced at the spot where last played at the time of the stoppage.

(*b*) Any player who physically interferes with a spectator shall, at the discretion of the Referee, be assessed a gross misconduct penalty and the Referee shall report all such infractions to the proper authorities.

(*c*) In the event that objects are thrown on to the ice which interfere with the progress of the game, the Referee shall stop the play and the puck shall be faced-off at the spot where play is stopped.

621. Kicking a Player

A match penalty shall be imposed on any player who kicks or attempts to kick another player.

622. Kicking the Puck

Kicking the puck shall be permitted in all zones, but a goal may not be scored by the kick of an attacking player. If an attacking player kicks the puck and it is deflected into the goal by any player (other than off a player's stick), or goalkeeper, the goal shall not be allowed.

623. Leaving the Players' or Penalty Bench

(*a*) No player may leave the players' bench or penalty bench at any time during the altercation. Substitutions made prior to the altercation shall be permitted provided the players so substituting do not enter the altercation.

(*b*) The first player to leave the players' or penalty bench during an altercation shall be assessed a double minor penalty and a game misconduct. If players of both teams leave their respective benches at the same time, the first identifiable player of each team to do so shall be penalised under this rule.

(*c*) Any other player or players (those not penalised under *b* above) who leave the players' bench during an altercation shall be assessed a misconduct penalty up to a maximum of five misconducts per team as designated by the Referee.

(*d*) Any player or players (other than in *b* above) that leaves the players' bench and incurs a minor, major or misconduct for his actions shall be automatically assessed a game misconduct.

(*e*) Except at the end of each period, or on expiration of a penalty, no player may at any time leave the penalty bench.

(*f*) A penalised player who leaves the penalty bench, whether play is in progress or not, before his penalty time has expired shall be assessed:

1. A minor penalty (except for *g* below) to be served at the expiration of his previous penalty.

2. If the violation occurred during a stoppage of play and an altercation was taking place, he shall also be assessed a game misconduct in addition to the minor penalty.

3. If the player is penalised under Rule 623(*b*) above, as the first player off the players' or penalty bench, he shall not be assessed any penalties under paragraphs 1 and 2 above.

(*g*) If a player leaves the penalty bench before his penalty is fully served, the Penalty Timekeeper shall note the time and advise the Referee at the first stoppage of play.

If the player returned to the ice prematurely because of an error of the Penalty Timekeeper, he shall not be assessed an additional penalty but must serve the amount of time remaining in his penalty when he re-entered the game.

(*h*) If a player shall illegally enter the game from his own players' bench or from the penalty bench by his own error or the error of the Penalty Timekeeper, any goal scored by his own team while he is illegally on the ice shall be disallowed, but all penalties imposed against either team shall be served as regular penalties.

(*i*) If a player is in possession of the puck and in such a position as to have no opposing player between himself and the opposing goalkeeper and he is interfered with by a player of the opposing team who has illegally entered the game, he shall be awarded a penalty shot.

(*j*) If, when the opposing goalkeeper has been removed from the ice, a player of the side attacking the unattended goal is interfered with by a player who shall have entered the play illegally, the Referee shall immediately award a goal to the non-offending team.

(*k*) Any team official who goes on the ice during any period, without permission of the Referees, shall be assessed a game misconduct.

624. Off-Sides

(*a*) Players of an attacking team may not precede the puck into the Attacking Zone.

(*b*) For a violation of this Rule, play shall be stopped and a face-off conducted.

If the puck was carried over the blue line at the time of the violation, the face-off shall take place at the nearest neutral zone face-off spot to where the puck crossed the line. If the puck was passed or shot over the blue line, the face-off shall take place where the pass or shot originated. *Note*: A player actually propelling and in control of the puck who shall cross the line ahead of the puck shall not be considered off-side.

(*c*) The position of the player's skates and not that of his stick shall be the determining factor in deciding an off-side violation. A player is off-side when both skates are completely over the blue line into his Attacking Zone.

(*d*) If (an) attacking player(s) precedes the puck that is shot, passed or deflected into the attacking zone by a team-mate, or again deflected into the attacking zone off a defending player, but a defending player is able to play the puck, the Linesman shall signal a delayed off-side. The Linesman shall drop his arm to nullify the off-side violation and allow play to continue if:

1. The defending team passes or carries the puck into the neutral zone; or

2. All attacking players in the attacking zone (at the time the puck crosses the blue line) clear the attacking zone by making skate contact with the blue line.

If the puck is shot on goal, causing the goalkeeper to play the puck, play shall be stopped immediately for an off-side violation under this Rule. If any attacking player touches the puck or attempts to gain possession of a loose puck while the puck is still in the attacking zone or forces the defending puck carrier further back in the attacking zone, the Linesman shall stop play.

(*e*) If a player legally carries or passes the puck back into his own Defending Zone while a player of the opposing team is in such Defending Zone, the off-side shall be waived and play permitted to continue. (No delayed whistle.)

(*f*) If, in the opinion of the Linesman, a player has intentionally caused an off-side play, the puck shall be faced-off at the end face-off spot in the Defending zone of the offending team.

Note: An intentional off-side is one which is made for the purpose of securing a stoppage of play, regardless of the reason, or where an off-side play is made under conditions where there is no possibility of competing a legal play.

625. Passes

(*a*) The puck may be passed by any player to a team-mate within any one of the three zones into which the ice is divided.

The puck, however, may not be passed by a player from his Defensive Zone to a team-mate who is on the opposite side of the centre red line unless the puck preceded the receiving player across the centre line.

(*b*) For a violation of this Rule, play shall be stopped and a face-off shall take place at the place where the pass originated or the nearest face-off location.

(*c*) Should the puck, having been passed, touch any player's body, stick or skates, between the passing player's Defensive Zone and the centre red line, it shall nullify any violation of this rule.

(*d*) If the Linesman errs in calling an off-side pass infraction, the puck shall be faced-off at the centre face-off spot.

626. Puck Out of Bounds or Unplayable

(*a*) When the puck goes outside the playing area at either end, or either side of the rink or strikes any obstacles above the playing surface other than the boards, glass or wire, it shall be faced-off at the place from where it was shot or deflected, unless otherwise expressly provided in these Rules.

(*b*) When the puck becomes lodged in the netting on the outside of either goal so as to make it unplayable, or if it is frozen against the goal between opposing players intentionally or otherwise, the Referee shall stop the play and face-off the puck at the nearest end-zone face-off spots unless, in the opinion of the Referee, the stoppage was caused by a player of the attacking team, in which case the resulting face-off shall be conducted in the Neutral Zone.

Note: This includes the stoppage of play caused by a player of the attacking team shooting the puck on to the back of the defending team's goal without any intervening action by a defending player.

(*c*) A minor penalty shall be imposed on a goalkeeper who deliberately drops the puck on the goal netting to cause a stoppage of play.

(*d*) If the puck comes to rest on top of the boards surrounding the playing area, it shall be considered to be in play and may be played legally by hand or stick.

627. Puck Out of Sight and Illegal Puck

(*a*) Should a scramble take place, or a player accidentally fall on the puck, and the puck is out of sight of the Referee, he shall immediately stop the play. The puck shall then be faced-off at the point where the play was stopped unless otherwise provided for in the Rules.

(*b*) If, at any time while play is in progress, a puck other than the one legally in play shall appear on the playing surface, the play shall not be stopped, but shall continue with the legal puck until the play then in progress is completed by change of possession.

628. Puck Striking Official

Play shall not be stopped because the puck touches a Referee or Linesman anywhere on the rink, regardless of whether or not a team is short-handed, except when the puck has entered the goal in which case a face-off shall take place at the nearest end zone face-off spot.

629. Refusing to Start Play

(*a*) If, when both teams are on the ice, one team for any reason shall refuse to play when ordered to do so by the Referee, he shall warn the Captain and allow the team so refusing 30 seconds within which to begin the game or resume play. If at the end of that time the team shall still refuse to play, the Referee shall impose bench minor penalty on the offending team, and the case shall be reported to the proper authorities for further action.

Should there be a recurrence of the same incident, the Referee shall have no alternative but to declare that the game is forfeited to the non-offending team, and the case shall be reported to the proper authorities for further action.

(*b*) If a team, when ordered to do so by the Referee, through its Captain, Manager or Coach, fails to go on the ice and start play within 2 minutes, the game shall be forfeited, and the case shall be reported to the proper authorities for further action.

630. Slashing

(*a*) A minor or major penalty, at the discretion of the Referee, shall be imposed on any player who impedes or seeks to impede the progress of an opponent by slashing with his stick.

(*b*) A major penalty shall be imposed on any player who injures an opponent by slashing.

Note: Referees should penalise as slashing any player who swings his stick at any opposing player (whether in or out of range) without actually striking him or where a player on the pretext of playing the puck makes a wild swing at the puck with the object of intimidating an opponent.

(*c*) Any player who swings his stick at another player in the course of any altercation shall be subject to a major or match penalty.

(*d*) When a major penalty is assessed under this Rule, the player shall be automatically assessed a game misconduct penalty.

631. Spearing or Butt-ending

(*a*) A minor or major penalty shall be imposed on a player who spears, attempts to spear, butt-ends, or attempts to butt-end an opponent.

When a penalty is imposed under this Rule, the offending player shall automatically also be assessed a misconduct penalty.

When a major penalty is imposed under this Rule, the offending player shall automatically be assessed a game misconduct penalty.

(*b*) If any injury results from spearing or butt-ending, a match penalty shall be imposed.

632. Start of Game and Periods

(*a*) The game shall be commenced at the time scheduled by a face-off at the centre face-off spot and shall be renewed promptly at the conclusion of each intermission in the same manner.

(*b*) Home teams shall have the choice of goals to defend at the start of the game, except where both players' benches are on the same side of the rink, in which case the home team shall start the game, defending the goal nearest to its own players' bench. The teams shall change ends for each succeeding regular or overtime period.

(*c*) During the pre-game warm-up (which shall not exceed 20 minutes in duration) and before the commencement of play in any period, each team shall confine its activity to its own end of the rink so as to leave clear an area 9m wide across the centre of the Neutral Zone.

Note: Players shall not be permitted to come on the ice during a stoppage of play or at the end of the first and second periods for the purpose of warming-up.

(*d*) Fifteen minutes before the time scheduled for the start of the game, both teams shall vacate the ice and proceed to their dressing-room while the ice is being flooded. Both teams shall be signalled by the Game Timekeeper to return to the ice together in time for the scheduled start of the game.

633. Throwing a Stick

(*a*) When any player or goalkeeper or team official of the defending team deliberately throws or shoots a stick or any part thereof, or any other objects, in the direction of the puck in his Defending Zone, the Referee shall allow the play to be completed, and if a goal is not scored, a penalty shot shall be awarded to the non-offending team, which shot shall be taken by any player designated by the team Captain.

If, however, the goal being unattended and the attacking player having no defending player to pass and having a chance to score on an open goal, a stick or part thereof or any other object, be thrown or shot by any member of the defending team, including a team official, thereby preventing a shot on the open goal, a goal shall be awarded to the attacking team.

(*b*) A major penalty shall be imposed on any player or goalkeeper on the ice who throws his stick or any part thereof, or any other object in the direction of the puck in any zone, except when such act has been penalised by the assessment of a penalty shot, the awarding of a goal or a goal is scored on the play by the non-offending team.

Note: When a player or goalkeeper discards the broken portion of a stick by tossing it to the side of the ice (and not over the boards) in such a way as will not interfere with play or opposing player, no penalty will be imposed for so doing.

(*c*) A misconduct or game misconduct penalty, at the discretion of the Referee, shall be imposed on a player or goalkeeper who throws his stick, or any part thereof, within or outside the playing area, unless a penalty was imposed under 633(*a*) or (*b*) above. If the offence is committed in protest at an official's decision, a minor penalty under Rule 601(*a*), Abuse of Officials, plus a game misconduct shall be assessed to the offending player.

(*d*) If the goalkeeper intentionally leaves his stick or part thereof in front of his goal and if the puck hits the stick, while the goalkeeper is on or off the ice, the Referee shall stop play immediately and award a goal to the opposing team.

634. Time of Match

(*a*) The game shall consist of three 20 minute periods of actual play with a rest intermission between periods. Play shall be resumed promptly following each intermission upon the expiry of 15 minutes from the completion of play in the preceding period. A preliminary warning shall be given by the Game Timekeeper to the officials and to both teams 3 minutes prior to the resumption of play in each period and the final warning shall be given in sufficient time to enable the teams to resume play promptly.

In games played in outside or uncovered rinks, teams shall change ends at the mid-way period of the third period and overtime period. Goalkeepers shall not be permitted to go to the players' bench, except to be replaced. For a violation of this rule, a minor penalty shall be assessed.

(*b*) The team scoring the greatest number of goals during the three 20-minute periods shall be the winner, and shall be credited with 2 points in the standings.

(*c*) In the intervals between periods, the ice surface shall be flooded unless mutually agreed to by the teams to the contrary.

(*d*) If any unusual delay occurs within 5 minutes of the end of the first or second periods, the Referee may order the next regular intermission to be taken immediately and the balance of play with the teams defending the same goals, after which the teams will change ends and resume play of the ensuing period without delay.

(*e*) Each team shall be permitted to take one time-out of 30 seconds' duration during the course of regular time or over-time and which must be taken during a normal stoppage of play. Any player designated by the Coach will indicate to the Referee who will report the time-out to the Game Timekeeper who shall be reponsible for signalling the termination of the time-out.

Note: All players including goalkeepers on the ice at the time of the time-out will be allowed to go to their respective benches. Only one time-out per stoppage of play is allowed.

635. Tied Game

Generally if, at the end of the three regular 20-minute periods, the score of both teams shall be equal, the game shall be called a tie with the points being shared equally between the two teams. This Rule is subject to any Regulation of the IIHF or a National Association.

636. Tripping

(*a*) A minor penalty shall be imposed on any player who shall place his stick, knee, foot, arm, hand or elbow in such a manner that it shall cause his opponent to trip or fall.

Note 1: If, in the opinion of the Referee, a player is unquestionably hook-checking the puck and obtains possession of it, thereby tripping the puck carrier, no penalty shall be imposed.

Note 2: Accidental trips accurring simultaneously with, or after, stoppage of play will not be penalised.

(*b*) When a player, in control of the puck in the opponent's side of the centre red line, and having no other opponent to pass than the goalkeeper, is tripped or otherwise fouled from behind, thus preventing a reasonable scoring opportunity, a penalty shot shall be awarded to the non-offending team. Nevertheless, the Referee shall not stop the play until the attacking team has lost possession of the puck to the defending team.

By 'control of the puck' is meant the act of propelling the puck with the stick. If, while it is being propelled, the puck is touched by another player or his equipment or hits the goal or goes free, the player shall no longer be considered to be in control of the puck.

(*c*) If, when the opposing goalkeeper has been removed from the ice, a player in control of the puck is tripped or otherwise fouled with no opposition between him and opposing goal, thus preventing a reasonable scoring opportunity, the Referee shall immediately stop the play and award a goal to the attacking team.

7. DOPING

Doping is prohibited.
Rule 7 is given in full in the IIHF Official Rule Book.

GLOSSARY

Altercation is defined as any incident involving players leading to a penalty or penalties.

Attempt to or deliberate injury identifies an action by a player or team official who by use of a stick, skate or other object, or by use of his body, hits or attempts to hit an opposing player or team official or game official with the intention of causing injury.

Break-away can be defined as a player in full control of the puck and having no opposing player between himself and the opposing goalkeeper (or goal, if the goalkeeper has been removed).

Broken stick is one which, in the opinion of the Referee, is unfit for normal play.

Butt-ending identifies the condition whereby a player uses the shaft of the stick, above the upper hand, to check an opposing player in any manner or jabs or attempts to jab an opposing player with this part of the stick. A butt-ending penalty shall be called when any of these conditions arises.

Captain is a player, exclusive of a goalkeeper, who is selected or named by the team to represent the team with the Officials in accordance with the rules. Wherever the word 'Captain' appears in the rule book, it defines those players who have been designated as Captain or Alternate Captain on the official game report.

Charging identifies the act of taking more than two steps or strides to contact an opposing player.

Coach is a person primarily responsible for directing and guiding the actions and efforts of his team. Along with the Manager he is responsible for the conduct of the players before, during and after the game in the arena.

Creases are the enclosed areas designed for the protection of the goalkeeper and the use of the Referee in the discharge of their respective duties. The lines which designate these areas are to be considered as part of the creases.

Cross-checking: Where a stick is being held with both hands, the action of using the shaft of the stick between the two hands and no part of the stick on the ice to check an opponent at any height shall constitute cross-checking.

Delayed off-side is a situation where an attacking player has preceded the puck across the attacking blue line, but the defending team is in a position to bring the puck back out of its defending zone without any delay or contact with an attacking player. The puck shall not have proceeded beyond the top of the circles.

Face-off is identified as a result of the action of the Referee or Linesman in dropping the puck between the sticks of two opposing players to start or resume play. The conduct of a face-off begins when the Referee indicates the location of the face-off and the official and the players take their appropriate positions, and ends when the puck has been legally dropped.

Game is a meeting of two teams playing for a specific length of time for the purpose of declaring a winner through the scoring of goals. The game consists of regular playing time and overtime, if such is required.

Game ejection means that a player or team official has been removed from the game by the Referee and must leave the area of the players' bench and must in no way direct, coach or assist the team in any manner for the remainder of the game.

Goalkeeper is a person designated as such on the game report, who is identified by the use of special and legal equipment and privileges to prevent the puck from entering the goal.

Goalkeepers' skates are specifically designed for the use of goalkeepers only. The blade of the skate is closed at both ends and is specially constructed so as to prevent the puck from passing through the blade.

Kicking is the motion of a player's foot towards an opponent with no intent to play the puck.

High-sticking is the action of the player carrying the stick or any part of the stick above the normal height of the shoulders.

Holding is any action by a player that impedes the progress of an opposing player who is in possession of the puck.

Hooking is the action of using the blade of the stick in a pulling or tugging motion to impede the progress of an opponent. The hooking action may apply to any part of an opponent's body or stick.

Heel of the stick is the portion between the straight part of the shaft and the flat part on the bottom of the blade.

Interference is any action which impedes the progress of an opponent who is not in possession of the puck.

Players are the members of the team physically participating in a game in accordance with the rules. Except where special rules apply to him, the goalkeeper is to be considered as one of the players.

Protective equipment is defined as the equipment worn by a player for the sole purpose of protecting himself from an injury.

Slashing is the action of hitting an opponent with a stick while holding the stick with one or both hands. Tapping the stick of the puck carrier is not considered slashing inasmuch as it is limited to hitting the stick of the opponent for the sole purpose of taking the puck. A player who swings his stick at an opponent and makes no contact shall still be guilty of slashing.

Spearing is the act of poking or attempting to poke an opponent with the point of the blade of the stick while holding the stick with one or both hands.

The term **Team Official** applies to all persons involved in the management of a team and includes coach, manager, trainers, stick boy, team doctor or any other non-playing member of teams' organisation.

Time-out: see Rule 634.

Reprinted by permission of the International Ice Hockey Federation. Copies of the complete Rules with Notes and Referees' Signals can be obtained from the Federation.

THE RULES OF

Korfball

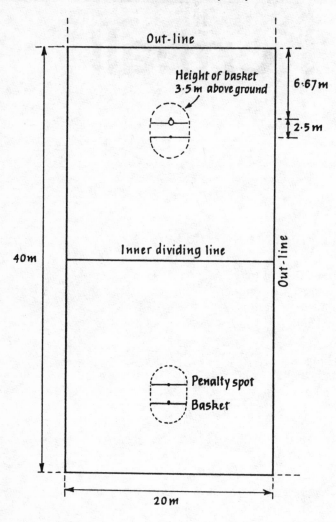

Out-line

Height of basket
3·5 m above ground

6·67 m

2·5 m

40m

Inner dividing line

Out-line

Penalty spot

Basket

20 m

Korfball: Indoor

1: HALL, GROUND AND MATERIAL

1. Hall and field of play
The dimensions of the field of play are 40m × 20m. The free height is preferably 9m, but must be at least 7m. The field of play is divided into two equal zones by a line parallel to the width of the field.

2. Marking
The whole field of play is marked out by clearly visible lines, which should be at least 3–5cm wide. The line separating the two zones is marked in the same way.

The penalty spots must be marked 2.5m in front of the post as seen from the centre of the field.

3. Posts
Posts are erected in both zones on the longitudinal axes of the field, at a distance from the ends equal to 1/6th of the length of the field. The posts are round and may consist of solid wood or metal tubing with an external diameter of 4.5–8cm. They are fixed perpendicularly in or on the ground.

4. Baskets
A basket is fitted to each post. The basket must face towards the centre and all of its top edge must be 3.5m above the ground. The baskets are cylindrical without a bottom; they are 25cm high and have an inner diameter of 39–41cm. The rim (top edge) of the basket has a width of 2–3cm. The baskets are made of osier twigs or rotan; they must be one colour and must be similar.

The method of fixing the baskets to the post must satisfy the following conditions:

(i) No movement of the basket with respect to the post is permitted.

(ii) The post must not protrude above the basket.

(iii) No fixture of more than 1cm may protrude inside or outside.

(iv) A metal support underneath the basket is only permitted over not more than one quarter of the circumference nearest to the post; metal strips against the outside of the basket are only permitted over one third of the circumference.

5. Ball

Korfball is played with a round ball consisting of a rubber pneumatic bladder in a two-coloured outer casing from leather of synthetic material. The circumference is 68–71cm. It must be inflated hard.

At the start of a match the weight of the ball must be not less than 425g and not more than 475g.

2. PERSONS

6. Players

(*a*) *Numbers and position*. The game is played by two teams, each consisting of 4 male and 4 female players, of whom 2 men and 2 ladies are placed in each zone.

(*b*) *Incomplete teams*. When one or both teams are incomplete, the game can only start, or be continued, if a line-up is possible which ensures that no zone has less than 3 players from each side and that in no division one female and two males players are opposed by one male and two female players.

(*c*) *Substitution of players*. Up to 2 players of a team can be substituted without the approval of the Referee. After the afore-mentioned two substitutions, players can only be substituted when they are injured and can no longer take part in the match. In these cases the Referee must decide whether the substitution shall be allowed.

Once a player has been substituted he cannot return to the match.

A player sent off by the Referee cannot be replaced.

(*d*) *Equipment of players*. The players of each side must be dressed in a uniform sports costume which is sufficiently different from that of the other side. The players must wear shoes. Players are prohibited to wear objects which can cause injuries during the game.

7. Captain and Coach

(*a*) *Captain*. One player of each team is captain. He* wears a clearly visible band on the upper part of his left arm. He represents the team and is responsible for the proper conduct of his players. In the absence of the team coach, he informs the Referee of any change in the team. He has the right to draw the Referee's attention to anything he thinks desirable in the interest of the good progress of the match.

(*b*) A coach is permitted to accompany his team to a match. When the coach is present at a match, it is his task to inform the Referee of all changes in his team.

* *Whenever the word 'he' is used, it should be understood that this could be 'she'.*

8. Referee

The Referee controls the game. His task is:

(*a*) To decide the suitability of the ball, field of play and material.

The Referee ascertains before the match that hall and field of play are not unsuitable, that the materials satisfy the stipulations and that everything is ready for the commencement of the game. He pays attention to any changes which might occur during the game.

(*b*) To enforce the Rules.

The Referee punishes infringements of the Rules, except when the punishment would be to the disadvantage of the non-offending side (Advantage Rule).

He takes action when one side obtains an unfair advantage from circumstances outside the game.

He decides in cases of doubt.

(*c*) To indicate the starting, stopping and restarting of the game by means of blowing a whistle.

To start or restart the game, the Referee blows his whistle as soon as the player taking the throw is ready and all the requirements (Rules 19 and 20) are satisfied.

(*d*) To take action against misbehaviour by the players or interference by the public.

In the case of misbehaviour the Referee can warn the person concerned formally, or he can send the player in question off. The Referee has the power to withdraw all authority from the coach for the duration of the match and send him off the field

When it appears necessary to him, he can let the public be warned, or removed, or he can cancel or terminate the match.

9. Timekeeper

If at all possible the Referee will appoint a timekeeper whose duty it is to warn the Referee just before the end of each half of the game.

3. THE GAME

10. Linesmen
In each match there are two Linesmen whose duty is to make sure whether the ball is out, whether Rule 16(*m*) has been infringed and to draw attention to any foul made in their vicinity.

The Linesmen indicate the spot where the free pass should be taken after the ball has gone out of play or after an infringement of Rule 16(*m*) on, or outside, the field of play.

The Referee will tell the Linesmen their positions. In the case of unpermitted interference, partiality, improper conduct, showing approval, disapproval or encouragement of one of the teams by a Linesman, the Referee has the right to deprive him of his function and to appoint a substitute.

11. Duration
A game normally lasts 2 × 30 minutes with 5 to 15 minutes' rest.

12. Goals
 (*a*) A team scores a goal when:
 (i) The ball has fallen completely through the basket which is positioned in the attack zone of that team, except for the cases mentioned under (*c*).
 (ii) It is sure that the ball would have fallen completely through the basket, but it is tapped back from underneath by a defender, except for the cases mentioned under (*c*).
 (*b*) A goal stands even when the Referee has previously blow for an infringement committed by a defender, provided the ball had left the hands of the shooting attacker at the moment of whistling and was outside the reach of any defender, except for the cases mentioned under (*c*).
 (*c*) The Referee does not allow the goal when:
 (i) He has blown his whistle before the ball has fallen through the basket and the infringement was committed by an attacker, or because he has blown for the end of the first or the second half of the match.
 (ii) He has observed an infringement committed by the attacking side but has not blown for the infringement until after the ball has gone through the basket.
 (iii) He has previously observed an unfair advantage to the attacking side.
 (iv) The ball is first thrown from underneath through the basket and then falls back again through the basket.

(*d*) The team scoring the most goals wins the match.

13. Line-up

(*a*) *Choice of line-up*. The home team decides into which basket they will shoot in the first half. They arrange their players in the 2 zones and the visiting team arranges their side accordingly.

(*b*) *Change in line-up*. Normally the same line-up is maintained throughout the match. If, however, during the game circumstances alter owing to the dropping out of a player, the Referee can, at the request of a coach and after consulting the other coach, permit a change. He will order a change when this is necessary to comply with the conditions mentioned in Rule 6(*b*), or when the number of players with a direct opponent is less than absolutely necessary.

14. Zone changes and changes of end

Each time that two goals have been scored the players change zone. At half-time there is a change of ends. The players move to the other zone.

15. Throw-off

The throw-off is taken by an attacker from a point inside his zone near the centre of the field. A throw-off takes place at the start of the game, at the start of the second half and after every goal; in the first case the throw-off is taken by the home team, in the second case by the visiting team and in the last case by the team against which the goal has been scored.

The same stipulations apply as for a free pass (see Rule 19).

16. Infringements of the rules

During the game it is prohibited:

(*a*) To touch the ball with leg or foot. If the touching is unintentional and exerts no important influence upon the game, it will not be punished.

(*b*) To hit the ball with the fist.

(*c*) To take hold of the ball in a fallen position.

(*d*) To run with the ball. Running with the ball is contrary to the requirement of co-operation. Change of position with the ball is therefore only permitted when otherwise it would be impossible to throw the ball correctly or to stop with the ball.

In applying these principles, three cases are to be distinguished:

1. When seizing the ball the player stands at rest. In this case he may move one leg at will, provided the other one remains in its place.

Turning on the latter is permitted. It is also permitted to jump, provided that the leg which did not move is used for the take-off. If after a jump the player comes down with the ball still in his hands, this will only be an infringement of the Rules if, in doing so, he has moved from his former position. In general, there can be no question of running with the ball if it did not result in a clear change of position.

2. When seizing the ball the player is running or jumping; first he stops and afterwards passes the ball. The requirement is that, after seizing the ball, he has immediately and fully tried to come to a stop. After coming to a stop, the same rules apply as mentioned under 1, above.

3. After seizing the ball while running or jumping, the player throws the ball before he has come to a stop. This is permitted provided the catching and throwing have only taken a very short time, or have been combined into one flowing movement, or if the player has tried hard to lessen his speed immediately after catching the ball.

(e) To avoid co-operation (solo-play).

Note: Solo-play is the deliberate avoidance of co-operation, i.e. a player tries to change his position with the ball in his possession without the help of another player.

Solo-play is not punishable:

1. When the player does not change his position appreciably.

2. When the avoidance of co-operation was not intentional.

(f) To hand the ball to another player of one's own team.

(g) To delay the game unnecessarily.

(h) To knock, take or run the ball out of an opponent's hand.

(i) To push, to cling to, or to hold off an opponent.

This unlawful hindering of an opponent has to be punished no matter whether this opponent does or does not possess the ball even if the ball is in another zone.

Every impediment of the free movement of an opponent is forbidden whether this is done deliberately or not.

This rule does not force a player to give way for another player, i.e. each player is allowed to position himself just as he pleases. He will only be punished when he jumps so suddenly in the path of a moving opponent that a collision becomes inevitable.

(j) To hinder an opponent excessively. This rule applies when the opponent has the ball in his possession.

The hindering player is allowed to hinder the throwing of the ball in the desired direction by actions which result in the ball being thrown against his hand or arm.

He is allowed to block the ball by bringing his arm in the path of the ball, but he must not:

1. Hinder his opponent in the free use of his body by blocking the arm instead of the ball.

2. Beat the ball or hit the throwing arm, i.e. the hindering arm or hand must not move towards the ball at the instant of contact.

Unexpected movements by an opponent will often cause a restriction in a player's freedom of movement. Such cases will not be punished, provided immediate action is taken by the opponent to restore the player's freedom of movement.

(*k*) To hinder an opponent of the opposite sex in throwing the ball.

(*l*) To hinder an opponent who is already being hindered by another player.

(*m*) To play outside one's zone.

(*n*) To shoot from a defended position.

The shot must be considered defended when the hindering defender satisfies each of the following three conditions:

1. He must be within arm's length of the attacker and must have his face turned towards him.

2. He must actually try to block the ball.

3. He must be nearer the post than the attacker, except when he and the attacker are near and on opposite sides of the post. In the latter case conditions 1 and 2 alone are sufficient.

(*o*) To shoot after cutting past another attacker.

'Cutting' occurs when a defender cannot follow an attacker, because the attacker runs so close past another attacker, that the defender collides with or is likely to collide with this attacker and therefore is forced to give up his defending position. If at that instant the defender is at a considerable distance from the attacker, then there can be no question of 'cutting' and the shot must be allowed.

(*p*) To shoot from the defence zone, from a free pass or from a referee-throw (throw-up).

(*q*) To shoot when one plays without a personal opponent.

This occurs when the defence has only three players against an attack of four players. In that case the captain of the attacking side must inform the Referee and the other captain which of his attackers will not shoot.

The captain is entitled to change his decision during the match, but only after informing the Referee and the other captain at a time when the ball is dead, i.e. the Referee has blown for an infringement, goal etc. This change of attacker is only allowed twice between a change of zones. A goal can be made from a penalty by an attacker without a personal opponent.

(*r*) To influence a shot by moving the post.

(*s*) To take hold of the post when jumping, running or in order to move away quickly.

(*t*) To violate the conditions laid down for a free pass or a penalty.

17. Out-ball

The ball is out as soon as it touches a boundary line of the field of play, the ground, a person or an object outside the field of play.

The ball is also out when it touches the ceiling or an object above the field of play.

In the case of an out-ball a free pass is awarded against the side who touched the ball last.

18. Referee-throw (throw-up)

When two opponents seize the ball simultaneously, the Referee will stop play and will throw the ball up.

The same applies when play must be restarted without one side being entitled to the ball. For this purpose the Referee chooses two players from the zone concerned, who must be of the same sex and if possible of about the same height. These two players may touch the ball after the ball has reached its highest point during the throw-up. The other players must observe a distance of 2.5m and may only touch the ball after one of the two selected players has touched the ball or after the ball has been in contact with the ground.

The attacker, selected by the Referee for the throw-up, is not allowed to shoot directly from the throw-up.

19. Free pass

(*a*) *When to award a free pass.* A free pass is awarded to the opposing side after the Referee has indicated that one of Rules 16 or 17 has been violated.

(*b*) *Place of the free pass.* The free pass is taken from the spot where the infringement was committed. If the infringement was committed against a certain person (Rule 16, *h, i, j, k, l* and sometimes *m*), then the free pass is taken from the spot where the person was standing.

In the case of an out-ball or when Rule 16(*m*) has been violated on or outside the boundaries of the field of play then the free pass is taken from outside the field near the boundary line where the ball or the offending player touched or crossed the line.

When the ball is out because it touches the ceiling or an object above the field of play, the free pass is taken near one of the long boundaries and nearest to the spot where the ball touches the ceiling or the object.

(*c*) *How to take a free pass.* The player taking the free pass must bring the ball into play within no more than 4 seconds after the whistle has gone for the commencement of play – see Rule 8(*c*).

The players of the opposing team must keep a distance of at least 2.5m until the taker of the free pass moves the ball. The players of the same team as the taker of the free pass must keep a distance of at least 2.5m until the ball is brought into play. The ball is brought into play when a player of the opposing team touches the ball, or when a player of the same team as the player taking the free pass touches the ball whilst standing at least 2.5m from the spot at which the pass is taken, or when the ball has travelled at least 2.5m from the place of the free pass. When after 4 seconds the taker of the free pass is still in possession of the ball, then the Referee blows his whistle and awards a free pass to the other side.

Shooting after the taking of a free pass is only allowed after the ball has moved freely through the air and afterwards has been touched by another player.

When the person taking the free pass touches a boundary line, or the playing area on the other side of the boundary line before the ball has left his hands and after the Referee has blown his whistle to indicate that the free pass can be taken, then the Referee awards a free pass to the opposing side on the other side of the boundary line.

20. Penalty

(a) *When to award a penalty*. Infringements which result in the loss of a scoring chance, are punished by the award of a penalty to the other side. A penalty can also be awarded for other infringements which repeatedly hinder the attack unfairly.

(b) *Place of penalty*. The penalty must be taken from the penalty spot (see Rule 2) which is 2.5m from the post as seen from the centre of the field.

(c) *How to take a penalty*. It is permitted to score directly from a penalty. The person taking the penalty must not touch the ground between the post and the penalty spot with any part of his body before the ball has left his hands. The penalty must be retaken if it is taken before the Referee has blown his whistle to indicate that the penalty can be taken.

All other players must observe a distance of 2.5m (in all directions) from any point on the imaginary line between spot and post. They must refrain from any action or comments disturbing the person taking the penalty.

If necessary the first as well as the second half of the match will be prolonged for the taking of a penalty.

Note: The game can also be played outdoors on a larger pitch measuring 60m × 30m, where the lines are normally marked by means of tapes, and with minor technical changes in the Rules. A three-zone outdoor version also exists where 12-a-side teams play on a pitch 90m × 40m.

Reprinted by permission of the International Korfball Federation. Copies of the complete Rules of Korfball, including those for the above variations and explanations of the Rules, can be obtained from the British Korfball Association.

Men's Lacrosse

The Field of Play

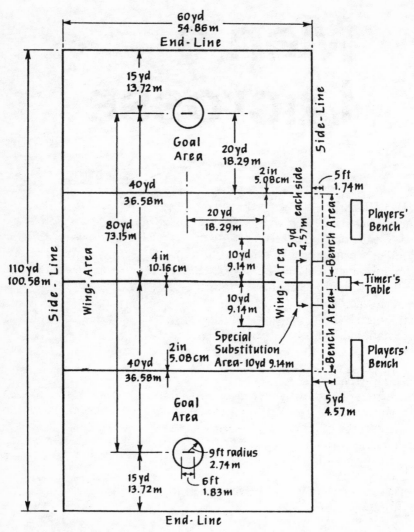

Note: Offside (centre) line - 4 in, 10.16 cm
      All other lines - 2 in, 5.08 cm

Men's Lacrosse

THE RULES

These rules have been approved by the English Lacrosse Union as the code for the playing of Men's Lacrosse in all games under its jurisdiction or under the auspices of affiliated Associations, Unions, Clubs or bodies after 1 September 1988. The ultimate interpretation of the Rules shall be the sole prerogative of the Referees and Rules Committee of the English Lacrosse Union. In order to assist players, coaches, Referees and others, those areas in which these rules differ from the new International Rules have been printed in Italics.

THE GAME

Lacrosse is played by two teams of 10 players each. The purpose of each team is to score by causing the ball to enter the goal of its opponents, and to prevent the other team from securing the ball and scoring. The ball is kept in play by being carried, thrown or batted with the crosse, rolled or kicked in any direction, subject to the restrictions laid down in the following Rules.

The ball may not be touched by the hand, except by a goalkeeper who is within his goal-crease.

1. THE PLAYING FIELD

1. Dimensions

1.1 The lacrosse playing field shall be, where possible, a rectangular field 110yd (100.58m) long and 60yd (54.86m) wide.

1.2 The boundaries of the field shall be marked with white lines. An extra heavy white line shall be marked through the centre of the field perpendicular to the side-lines; this line shall be designated the centre-line. The boundary lines on the long sides of the field shall be designated side-lines; those at each end shall be designated end-lines.

1.3 Flag markers or pylons shall be placed at the four corners of the field, at each end of the gate within the special substitution area, and at that end of the half-way line which is opposite the bench area. If flag markers are used, they must be made of flexible material so that they will bend a minimum of 90 degrees without breaking. If pylons are used, they must be made of plastic or rubber.

2. The Goals

2.1 Each goal shall consist of two vertical posts joined by a rigid cross-bar. These posts shall be 6ft (1.83m) apart and the top cross-bar shall be 6ft (1.83m) from the ground (all inside measurements). The goal-posts and cross-bar shall be collectively designated the pipes.

2.2 The goal-posts shall be centred and shall be placed 80yd (73.15m) apart and 15yd (13.72m) from each end-line.

2.3 The pipes shall be made of *wood or an approved metal or alloy and each shall be of not more than 3in (7.6cm) square or equivalent circular cross section. The material used and the shape shall be such as to prevent injury resulting from collision with them.* The pipes shall be painted orange *or white* and secured to the ground.

A line shall be drawn between the goal-posts to indicate the plane of the goal, and it shall be designated the goal-line.

2.4 Where ground-pipes are used, there must be a board measuring 1in by 3in by 18in (2.54cm by 7.62cm by 0.46m) securely fastened to each ground-pipe directly behind the vertical post at an angle of 45 degrees.

3. The Goal-Crease

3.1 Around each goal there shall be plainly marked a circle known as the goal-crease. This circle shall be marked by using the mid-point of the goal-line as the centre and drawing a circle around that point with a radius of 9ft (2.74m).

3.2 The goal-crease area is the circular ground territory about each goal within and including the goal-crease.

4. The Goal-Nets

4.1 Each goal must be fitted with a pyramidal-shaped cord netting which shall be fastened to the goal-posts, the cross-bar and the ground so as to prevent the passage of the ball. The mesh of the net shall not exceed 1.5in (3.81cm). The centre of the goal-net shall be fastened to the ground at a point 7ft (2.13m) behind the centre of the goal-line. The pipes and the goal-net shall be collectively designated the cage.

4.2 The goal-nets must be adjusted so that the ball may pass completely through the imaginary plane of the goal at any point.

4.3 Goal-nets may be any solid colour.

5. The Goal-Areas

5.1 At each end of the field a line shall be marked from side-line to side-line 20yd (18.29m) from the centre-line. These lines shall be designated goal-area lines.

5.2 The areas between the goal-area lines and the end-lines (but excluding the lines themselves) at each end of the field shall be designated the goal-areas.

6. The Wing-Areas

6.1 Lines parallel to the side-lines shall be marked on each side of the field 20yd (18.29m) from an imaginary line joining the centres of the goal-lines; the lines shall extend 10 yd (9.14m) on each side of the centre-line. These lines shall be designated the wing-area lines.

6.2 The areas between the wing-area lines and the side-lines, and confined within the extremities of the wing-area lines, but excluding those lines, shall be designated the wing-areas.

7. The Centre of the Field

7.1 A point on the centre-line equidistant from each side-line shall be marked with an 'X' and shall be designated the centre.

8. The Special Substitution Area

8.1 The special substitution area shall be indicated by two lines marked on the side of the field *on the same side of the field as the benches*. These lines shall be 5ft (1.74m) in length and shall extend away from the field of play at right angles to the side-line from points on the side-line 5yd (4.57m) from the centre-line.

8.2 That part of the side-line between the special substitution-area lines shall thus be 10yd (9.14m) in length, and shall be designated the gate.

9. The Timer's Table and the Benches

9.1 *Where possible, a timer's table shall be used.* The timer's table shall be placed, *where possible*, at least 5yd (4.57m) from the side-line at the centre-line.

9.2 Benches for the competing teams shall be placed *in each bench area at least 10yd (9.14m) from the imaginary extension of the half-way line and, where possible*, at least 6 yd (5.47m) from the side-line, parallel to the side-line.

10. The Bench Areas

10.1 The bench areas are located off the playing field and are between the special substitution area lines *and their imaginary extensions* and the imaginary extensions of the goal-area lines.

11. The Coaches' Area

11.1 *Where possible*, a dotted restraining line shall be placed 5ft (1.74m) from the side-line. It shall be parallel to the side-line and extend the length of the bench area. The area bounded by the side-line, the dotted restraining line, the special substitution area line and the imaginary extension of the goal-area line shall be designated the coaches' area.

12. Lines

12.1 All lines referred to in this section (except the centre-line and the goal-lines) shall be 2in (5.08cm) in width. The centre-line shall be 4in (10.16cm) in width. The goal-lines shall be the same width as the pipes.

12.2 Where other lines appear on the field of play, the lines referred to in this section shall be all of one colour, and that colour shall contrast with the colour of the other lines.

13.1 The Penalty Box

13.1 The penalty box shall consist of two seats for each team *at the centre of the field on the bench side of the field. Where possible, the seats shall be at least 5 yd (4.57m) from the side-line.*

2. EQUIPMENT

14. The Ball

14.1 The ball shall be of white, *yellow*, or orange rubber and between 7.75in (19.69cm) and 8in (20.32cm) in circumference. It shall be between 5 and 5.25 ounces in weight, and, when dropped on to a hard wooden floor from a height of 72in (1.83m), shall bounce to a height of between 45in (114.3cm) and 49in (124.46cm).

14.2 Balls shall be supplied by the home team.

14.3 *Where possible*, the home team shall supply ball boys with extra balls at each side and each end of the field. The ball boys shall wear helmets, gloves and boxes.

15. The Crosse

15.1 The crosse shall be of an overall length of between 40in (101.6cm) and 72 in (182.88cm).

15.2 The head of the crosse shall measure between 4in (10.16cm) and 10in (25.4cm) inside measurement at its widest point.

15.3 The stick of the designated goalkeeper shall be an exception to Rules 15.1 and 15.2, above. There may be one stick up to 15in (38.1cm) inside measurement in use by each team at any one time, and it must be used by the designated goalkeeper. The goalkeeper's stick may be any desired length.

15.4 The head of the crosse shall be made of wood, laminated wood, plastic, or any other material approved by the *ELU*, and the shaft shall be made of wood, aluminium or any other material approved by the *ELU*. Where a handle is made of metal, it must have a plastic or wood plug on the end, or it must be adequately taped to prevent injury. The head of the crosse shall be approximately perpendicular to the handle.

15.5 The head of the crosse shall be constructed as follows:

Either both walls shall be of wood, laminated wood, plastic or other material approved by the *ELU*;

Or one wall shall be made of wood, laminated wood, plastic or other material approved by the *ELU*, and the other wall shall be made by weaving gut lacing from the tip of the head to the handle in such a manner that it prevents the tip from catching on an opponent's crosse.

15.6 The wooden or plastic walls of the crosse shall not be above 2in (5.08cm) in height; where a wall is made of gut, it may be any height.

15.7 The centre line of the handle shall cross the head approximately 2.5in (6.35cm) from the wall.

15.8 There shall be a guard stop at the throat of the crosse. The stop must be perpendicular to the handle of the crosse and wide enough to let the ball rest loosely on the stop. The guard stop shall be a minimum of 10in (25.4cm) from the outside edge of the head of the crosse. The stop shall be constructed so that no part of the ball can be under the stop.

15.9 The head and side(s) of the crosse shall have holes bored in them to facilitate the weaving of the stringing.

15.10 The net of the crosse shall be constructed of gut, rawhide, clock cord, linen or synthetic material and shall be roughly triangular in shape.

16. Prohibitions Relating to the Crosse

16.1 No player shall use a crosse in which the pocket has been permitted to sag to such a depth that the top surface of a lacrosse ball placed therein is below the bottom edge of the sidewalls when the crosse is held horizontal to the ground with the net to the bottom of the crosse. This prohibition shall not apply to the crosse of the designated goalkeeper.

16.2 No player shall use a crosse which is constructed or strung so as to be designed to withhold the ball from play.

16.3 No player shall use a crosse of trick construction or stringing which tends to retard the normal and free dislodgement of the ball by an opponent.

16.4 No stick may be tampered with in any way so as to give a player an advantage over his opponent.

16.5 Any strings which are not part of the stick as manufactured shall be limited to a hanging length of 2in (5.08cm).

16.6 The mesh of the net must be substantially all of one colour.

16.7 Adjustable length handles are illegal.

17. Personal Equipment

17.1 All players are required to wear protective gloves, suitable boots or shoes, and a protective helmet equipped with a face mask and a chinstrap which must be properly fastened on both sides.

All equipment, including helmets, gloves, shoulder pads, arm pads and kidney pads, shall be of the approved lacrosse pattern and style. It shall be manufactured by a recognised lacrosse manufacturer, and, in the opinion of the officials, it shall not endanger the wearer or any other player. Any equipment manufactured in the UK must be approved by the ELU before it is used.

The fingers may not be cut out of a player's gloves, and the entire finger must be encased within, and must be part of the glove. A player may not play with his fingers outside the glove. A player may cut the palms out of his gloves.

Boots or shoes shall be of non-metallic construction except for the studs and the eyelets. They shall have no sharp edges or points which may injure other players.

Play must be suspended immediately if a player loses any of the required equipment in a scrimmage area. Otherwise, the official shall delay the sounding of his whistle in the same manner as set forth in Rule 80, which deals with the slow whistle technique, *except that the signal flag is not thrown under these circumstances.*

17.2 *The normal dress shall be the team's registered jersey or shirt, shorts and socks.* Each player is required to wear a jersey with a block or Gothic number centred on the front and the back. The number on the front of the jersey shall be at least *6in (15.1cm)* high, and the number on the back shall be at least *8in (20.3cm)* high. The numbers on the front and back of a player's jersey shall be the same, and no duplicate numbers shall be permitted on the same team. *The colour of the numbers shall be contrasting with the colour of the jerseys.*

17.3 The visiting team shall notify the home team of the colour of the jerseys which they are going to wear in the game, and the home team must wear jerseys of a contrasting colour.

18. Prohibitions Relating to Personal Equipment

18.1 No player shall wear or carry equipment which, in the opinion of the officials, endangers himself or other players.

18.2 No player shall wear anything on the outside of his jersey which might obstruct the view of his numbers.

18.3 The special equipment worn by the goalkeeper shall not exceed standard equipment so far as shin guards, throat guards and chest protectors are concerned.

18.4 No player shall wear hockey goalkeeper gloves.

18.5 Track suit trousers may be worn by any player, but for a particular team they must be of the same colour, and it is recommended that they be of a different colour from those worn by the opponents.

3. THE TEAMS

19. Number of Players

19.1 Ten players shall constitute a full team. There shall be 1 goalkeeper, 3 defenders, 3 midfielders and 3 attackers.

Before the commencement of the game, each team must nominate to the Referee(s):

A defenceman to serve the goalkeeper's penalty time.

An attacker, known as the 'in-home', to serve penalty time for team offences.

19.2 If, because of injuries or men out of the game due to expulsion fouls, a team cannot keep 10 players in the game, then it may continue the game with fewer than 10 players, but no exceptions will be made to the regular rules for this situation.

20. Substitutes

20.1 A team may have up to *3* substitutes.

21. Captains

21.1 Each team shall designate a captain or co-captains, and they shall act as the representatives of their team on the field of play during the game. Where a team designates co-captains, one of them shall be designated the official representative of that team on the field.

21.2 The privilege of the captains to act as the representatives of the team on the field does not grant them the right to enter into argument with an official or to criticise any decision of an official.

21.3 Should the captain leave the field of play, either he or his coach should designate to the nearest Referee the name and number of the replacing captain. If a team is without a designated captain at any time during the play of the game, then one of the Referees may designate an acting-captain.

22. Coaches

22.1 A team may have any number of coaches but, *if more than one coach is to be used, then a* team shall designate one coach as its head coach. The head coach shall be responsible for making all decisions for his team which are not specifically delegated to his captain.

22.2 The head coach shall at all times conduct himself like a gentleman, and he shall endeavour in every way to have his players and substitutes also conduct themselves like gentleman. He shall also be in control of and responsible for the actions and conduct of all non-playing members of his squad and any and all persons officially connected with his team. He shall assist the officials to keep the game under control at all times. It shall be his duty, upon the request of an official, effectively to control any actions of spectators which are not in conformity with good sportsmanship.

22.3 It shall be the responsibility of the home head coach to see:

(i) That the playing field is in proper condition for play.

(ii) That the players and substitutes are properly equipped to play.

(iii) That the *chief bench official and any other bench officials* are on hand with all the equipment necessary for them to carry out their resective functions.

(iv) That balls and, *where possible*, ball boys are provided.

22.4 *Where a team does not have a coach, then the duties specified in this rule shall be carried out by the captain(s).*

4. CONTROL OF THE GAME

23. The Officials

23.1 The game of lacrosse shall be controlled by *up to* 3 Referees, one of whom shall be designated the Head Referee. Their duties shall be equal in all respects, except that, in the settlement of any dispute, the decision of the Head Referee shall be final. The Referees shall have authority over the play of the game, with control and jurisdiction over the *bench officials*, players, substitutes, coaches, anyone officially connected with the teams, and spectators.

23.2 The authority of the Referees shall begin with their *arrival at the ground*, and terminate *at a reasonable time after the end of the match*.

23.3 By the sounding of his whistle, any of the Referees may suspend the play of the game for any reason which he deems necessary for the proper enforcement of the Rules of the Game.

23.4 The Referees shall keep a record of the goals by each team, and the number of the player scoring the goal. *Where a scorer is available, the*

Referees shall check the score with the official scorer at the end of each period, but the Referees' score shall be the official score of the game. *Where no timekeeper is available, one of the Referees shall keep a record of the time played in each period. He shall endeavour to warn the teams 2 minutes before the end of each period, and 30 seconds before the end of each period.*

23.5 The Referees shall wear similar uniforms. This shall be vertical black and white striped shirt, white shorts, black and white socks and a black cap.

24. The Chief Bench Official

24.1 A chief bench official (CBO) shall be *provided by the home club*, and he shall be equipped with a horn. He shall supervise and hold complete jurisdiction over coaches, substitutes and any other officials within the bench areas, the special substitution area and the penalty box. *Where possible*, he shall wear the same uniform as the Referees, except that he shall also wear a suitably inscribed armband.

24.2 The CBO shall:

(i) Check the substitution of players going on to and off the field of play.

(ii) Check that each team has the correct number of players on the field of play.

(iii) *Where there is only one Referee on the field of play, check that each team obeys the Off-side Rule; where there is more than one Referee on the field of play*, assist the Referees in checking that each team obeys the Off-side Rule.

(iv) Check that no illegal stick exchange occurs.

(v) Check that no illegal actions are carried out by a coach or official member of either squad.

(vi) Check that no foul is committed by a player or substitute who is in the act of leaving the field of play or in the act of entering the field of play, or who is in the bench area, the special substitution area or the penalty box.

Where the CBO becomes aware of such an infringement, he shall sound a warning, and subsequently advise the nearest Referee of the nature of the foul. The CBO's horn itself does not stop the play of the game.

24.3 The CBO shall acknowledge receipt and understanding of the Referees' signals relating to penalties, penalty periods or any other matters relating to the play of the game, by repeating the signal. He shall then relay the decisions of the Referees to the *other bench officials*, as appropriate.

24.4 The CBO shall advise the coaches, if so requested, as to the decisions of the Referees.

24.5 *Where there is no timekeeper, the CBO shall keep a record of the time taken during team time-outs and of the time intermissions between playing periods.* The CBO shall notify each team 30 seconds before the restart of play during a team time-out, and 1 minute before the start of each period.

24.6 *Where there is no scorer, the CBO shall keep a record of the number of each player upon whom a personal penalty is inflicted.* The CBO shall notify the nearest Referee if any player has incurred 5 personal fouls.

24.7 The CBO shall sound his horn if a team asks him for a time-out.

24.8 *Where there is no penalty timekeeper, the CBO shall be equipped with a time-piece which can record time in seconds. He shall time the period of any penalty imposed by the Referees, and shall audibly count down the penalty time to the player concerned and to any substitute who may be about to go on to the field in place of the penalised player, as follows: 30 seconds, 15 seconds, 10, 9, 8 . . . 3, 2, 1, Release.*

24.9 *Where there is no scorer, the CBO shall keep an accurate record of the number of time-outs taken by each team, and he shall notify the nearest Referee immediately if a team exceeds the number allowed in a half or an overtime period.*

24.10 *The home team shall supply a competent CBO who is fully conversant with the rules of lacrosse. Should the home team fail to do so, then the head Referee shall instruct the coach or, where there is no coach, the captain(s) of the home team to select a player or substitute who is capable of undertaking the duties, to act as the CBO. The selected player shall take no further part in the playing of the game.*

25. The Timekeeper

25.1 A timekeeper *may* be appointed, and he must be equipped with a time-piece which is able to record time in seconds.

25.2 The timekeeper shall keep an accurate record of the time played in each period, and he shall go out on to the field of play for the last 30 seconds of play in each period to count down the remaining time to the closest Referee as follows; 30 seconds, 25 seconds, 20 seconds, 15 seconds, 14, 13 . . . 3, 2, 1, Time.

25.3 The timekeeper shall keep an accurate record of the time intermissions between playing periods, and he shall notify the chief bench official 1 minute prior to the start of each period of play.

25.4 The timekeeper shall keep an accurate record of the time taken during team time-outs, and he shall notify the chief bench official 30 seconds before the restart of play.

26. The Penalty Timekeepers

26.1 *One or* two penalty timekeepers *may* be appointed for each squad, and they shall be equipped with time-pieces which can record time in seconds. The penalty timekeepers shall be positioned at either side of the timer's table, behind the penalty box.

26.2 The penalty timekeepers shall time the period of any penalty imposed by the Referees, and shall audibly count down the penalty time to the player concerned and to any substitute who may be about to go on to the field in place of the penalised player, as follows: 30 seconds, 15 seconds, 10, 9, 8 . . . 3, 2, 1, Release.

27. The Scorers

27.1 Each team *may* provide a scorer and, unless otherwise designated by the Head Referee, the visiting scorer shall be the official scorer.

27.2 The scorers shall keep a record of the goals scored by each team, the name and number of the player scoring the goal, and the name and number of the player making an assist.

27.3 The scorers shall check with the Referees at the end of each period to ensure that they have the same score.

27.4 The scorers shall keep an accurate record of the number of time-outs taken by each team, and they shall notify the chief bench official immediately if a team exceeds the number allowed in a half or in an overtime period.

27.5 The scorers shall keep a record of the name and number of each player upon whom a penalty is inflicted, the type of foul, the duration of the penalty, and the game time of the penalty.

27.6 The scorers shall notify the chief bench official if any player should incur 5 personal fouls.

28. Mistakes by the Bench Officials

28.1 Where a chief bench official, timekeeper, penalty timekeeper, or scorer becomes aware that a mistake is being made which would result in a player or a team being penalised, the he shall promptly correct the mistake. If a goal is scored during the mistake and it is brought to the attention of the Referees before the next live ball, after the player in question has participated in the game, then the Referees shall allow or disallow the goal depending on the circumstances.

5. THE LENGTH OF THE GAME

29. Time of the Match

29.1 The match shall be divided into 4 periods of *20* minutes' duration each. 'Time-off' incurred in each quarter shall be added to the playing time of that quarter.

29.2 At the end of each quarter, the teams shall change ends. The interval between the first and second quarters shall be of 2 minutes' duration. At half-time, the interval shall be 10 minutes long. At three quarter-time, the interval shall be 3 minutes.

29.3 Between the first and second periods, and between the third and fourth periods, the players shall, on leaving the playing field, assemble in the bench area only; to go beyond this area, they must have the permission of the Referees.

At half-time, the teams may leave the playing field.

30. Uncompleted Match

30.1 *If less time than the regulation time has to be played either through failure of daylight or from any other cause, then the curtailment of playing time shall be at the discretion of the Referee who shall, if possible, arrange that all four quarters shall be of equal duration. If in any match it is not possible to play at least 60 minutes in all, then such a match shall not count in any competition and shall be replayed.*

31. Tied Game

31.1 In the event of the scores being tied at the end of regulation playing time, then, *subject to Rule 31.3 below*, 2 periods of overtime shall be played. The following procedure shall apply:

(i) There shall be an interval of 5 minutes, during which the teams shall change ends.

(ii) Both periods of overtime shall start with a face-off as at the start of each quarter, subject to the provisions of Rule 34.1 being followed.

(iii) The overtime periods shall be of 4 minutes' duration, and there shall be a 2-minute interval between them.

(iv) The teams shall change ends between the 2 overtime periods.

31.2 If the scores are still tied at the end of the 2 overtime periods, then the following 'sudden death' procedure will take place:

(i) The captains will toss a coin during a 1-minute intermission, with the winner selecting the goal which he wishes to defend.

(ii) Play will then resume with a face-off at the centre of the field, subject to the provisions of Rule 34.1 being followed, for 4-minute periods until a goal is scored.

(iii) At the end of each 4-minute period, the teams shall change ends, but the team in possession of the ball at the end of a period retain possession of the ball in the same relative position of the field as when the period ended, except that the ball shall not be put into play closer than 20yd (18.29m) from the cage, or with an opponent nearer to the player who has possession of the ball than 9ft (2.74m); play will then continue immediately.

If a sudden-death overtime period ends when the ball is loose, then the next period will start with a face-off in the same relative position as when play ended.

(iv) This procedure will continue until a goal is scored, thus deciding the winner.

31.3 *Where the governing body responsible for the organisation of a particular competition does not wish overtime to be played in matches in that competition, then it shall inform the clubs involved in that competition and the relevant Referees Association(s) of its decision. Where the scores in a game in such a competition are tied at the end of regulation playing time, then that match shall be declared a draw.*

32. Defaulted Game

32.1 *If any team fails to fulfil an engagement without, in the opinion of the relevant League Committee, giving adequate cause or reason, then that Committee shall either disqualify the defaulting team for that match and award its opponents a win, or it shall disqualify the team for the remainder of the competition, or it shall take any other action which it deems appropriate. In the first case, where relevant, the Committee may also deduct 1 point from the defaulting team's total points and, in the second case, where relevant, no points scored for or against the disqualified team shall count in the aggregates.*

6. THE PLAY OF THE GAME

33. Actions Prior to the Game

33.1 The Referee(s) and the CBO shall call together the captains of each team at the centre of the field approximately 5 minutes before the start of the game. The head Referee shall toss a coin to determine choice of goals; the visiting captain shall call the toss. At this time, any special ground rules shall be explained.

33.2 The Referees and the CBO shall then draw up the starting line-ups in lines facing each other at the centre of the field, with their left sides towards the goal they are defending. Equipment shall be inspected and any special ground rules explained.

34. Facing at the Centre

34.1 Play shall normally be started at the beginning of each period, and after each goal has been scored, by facing the ball at the centre of the field, subject to the following exceptions:

(i) In the event of an extra man situation at the conclusion of *any* period, then the next period shall be commenced by awarding the ball to the team which had possession at the conclusion of the prior period in the same relative position on the field. However, if the period ends with no team in possession, the ball shall be faced at the centre with all the usual restrictions.

(ii) Once a Referee has placed the ball between the sticks at a face-off, then the players are 'set', and any movement of a player's stick or gloves prior to the whistle will result in possession being awarded to the offended team. The player is allowed to move his feet or his body, provided that this movement is not transmitted to the gloves or stick.

34.2 The players facing shall stand on the same side of the centre-line as the goal each is defending, with their crosses resting on the ground along the centre-line and parallel to it. Each player must have both hands on the handle of his own crosse, not touching any strings, and both gloved hands must be on the ground. The feet shall not touch the crosse. No part of either crosse may touch, and the walls must be approximately 1 in (2.54cm) apart, with the backs of the crosses facing each other. Both hands and feet must be to the left of the throat of the crosse. Neither player may be in contact with his opponent's body by encroaching on his opponent's territory.

34.3 The Referee shall make certain that the heads of the crosses match evenly, and he then shall place the ball between and in the centre of the two crosses, resting on the lower wall of both crosses. The ball must not be touching the ground.

34.4 When the Referee sounds his whistle to start play, each player may attempt to direct the course of the ball by movement of his crosse in any manner he desires. Kicking or stepping on an opponent's crosse is illegal. A player may not 'kick through' his own crosse in order to move the crosse of his opponent.

34.5 Whilst the two players who are participating in the face-off are still down in the face-off position, and the ball is still between and in contact with their sticks, it shall be illegal for any other player to make contact with the body or crosse of either of those two players.

34.6 No player who is using a left-handed crosse shall take part in a face-off. A stick in which the net is woven to the head in such a manner that a lip or hook is formed which might ensnare the ball shall be illegal for use in face-offs.

34.7 At the time of a centre face-off, a team which has 10 players on the field of play (excluding the penalty box) shall confine the goalkeeper and 3 other players in its defence goal-area, 3 players in its attack goal-area, and 1 player in each of its wing-areas. When the whistle sounds to start play, the players in the wing-areas shall be released. All other players are confined to the specified goal-areas until possession of the ball is gained by any player, the ball touches or crosses a goal-area line, or the ball goes out-of-bounds.

34.8 In the above circumstances, when possession is gained by a player, the Referee shall rotate his right arm in full circular cranking motion and shout 'possession'. When the ball touches or crosses a goal-area line before possession has been called, the Referee shall rotate his right arm in full circular cranking motion and shout 'free ball'.

34.9 Where a team has 1 or more players out of the game on penalty, then that team shall be exempt from confining its players to the goal- and wing-areas to the extent of its players in the penalty box. Such a team shall have the right to choose the confining area(s) in which it shall exercise its exemption, but it must obey the off-side rule.

34.10 At a centre face-off, before 'possession' or 'free ball' have been called, if a Referee mistakenly blows his whistle, then the ball shall be re-faced at the centre of the field with the same restrictions as the original face-off.

34.11 If a foul is committed at a centre face-off before 'possession' or 'free ball' have been called, then confined players will not be released from the goal-area until until the whistle blows to resume play.

34.12 If the ball goes directly out-of-bounds from a face-off, then it shall be re-faced at the same place as the previous face, and subject to the same restrictions as the previous face.

35. Facing Other Than at the Centre

35.1 When a face-off occurs other than at the centre of the field, then the following rules shall apply:

(i) The crosses of the 2 players shall be placed at right angles to an imaginary line running from the ball to the centre of the nearest goal-line.

(ii) The defending player shall stand between his crosse and his own goal, so as to have his back to his own goal.

(iii) The attacking player shall face towards the goal he is attacking.

(iv) The conditions laid down in Rule 34 apply as to the method of facing.

(v) The ball shall not be faced closer to the cage than 20yd (18.29m) in any direction, and it shall be moved laterally to a point 20yd (18.29m) from the cage, if required.

(vi) The ball shall not be faced closer to a boundary line than 20ft (6.1m).

(vii) At the time the whistle sounds to start the face-off, no player shall be within 10yd (9.14m) of the players facing the ball.

36. Free Play

36.1 When a player has been awarded the ball for any reason, no opposing player may take a position closer to him than 9ft (2.74m).

36.2 A free play shall not take place closer to the cage than 20yd (18.29m) in any direction, and the ball shall be moved laterally to a point 20yd (18.29m) from the cage, if required.

36.3 A free play shall not take place within 3yd (2.74m) of the gate, and the ball shall be moved laterally into the field of play until it is 3 yd (2.74m) from the nearest part of the gate, if required.

37. Scoring

37.1 A goal counts 1 point, and is scored when a loose ball passes from the front completely through the imaginary plane formed by the rear edges of the goal-line as a base, the cross-bar as the top, and the goal-posts as the two sides. Should the ball be caused to pass through the plane of the goal by one of the defending players, it counts as a goal for the attacking team.

37.2 When the ball passes through the plane of the goal in the following circumstances, however, a goal does not count:

 (i) After a Referee's whistle has sounded to indicate the end of a period.

 (ii) After the period has ended, regardless of whether or not a Referee's whistle has sounded.

(iii) After a Referee's whistle has sounded for any reason, even though the sounding of the whistle was inadvertent.

(iv) When any part of the body of an attacking player is touching the goal-crease area.

 (v) When the attacking team has more than 10 men on the field of play (including the penalty box) at the time.

(vi) When the attacking team has more men than it should have on the actual field of play (excluding the penalty box) at the time.

(vii) When the attacking team or both teams are off-side at the time.

38. Possession of the Ball

38.1 A player shall be considered in possession of the ball when he has control of it and could perform any of the normal functions of play such as carrying, cradling, passing or shooting.

38.2 A team shall be considered in possession of the ball when a player on that team has possession of the ball.

38.3 A ball not in a player's possession or a team's possession is a loose ball.

39. Ball Out-of-Bounds

39.1 Play shall be suspended at any time when the ball is out-of-bounds.

39.2 When a player with the ball in his possession steps on or beyond a boundary line, or any part of his crosse or body touches the ground on or beyond the boundary line, then the ball is out of bounds, and the player shall lose possession of it. The ball shall be awarded to any player of the opposing team who is ready immediately to make the free play, at the point where the ball was declared out-of-bounds.

39.3 When a loose ball touches the boundary line or the ground outside of a boundary line, or when it touches anything on or outside of a boundary line, then it is out-of-bounds, and the following rules shall apply:

(i) Except on a shot or a deflected shot at the goal, the ball shall be awarded at the point where it was declared out-of bounds to any player on the opposing team to that player who last touched it who is ready immediately to make the free play.

(ii) When a loose ball goes out-of-bounds as a result of a shot or a deflected shot at goal, it shall be awarded to the team one of whose in-bound players was nearest to the ball when it became out-of-bounds. If two in-bound players of opposite teams are equidistant from the ball when it goes out-of-bounds, then it shall be faced.

(iii) A shot or deflected shot remains a shot until: The ball comes to rest on the field of play; or

A player gains possession of the ball; or

The ball goes out-of-bounds; or

A player deliberately causes the ball to go out-of-bounds.

39.4 If the ball goes directly out-of-bounds from a face-off, then it shall be faced again at the same place as the previous face-off, and subject to the same restrictions as the previous face-off.

39.5 If the ball is out-of-bounds within the confines of the gate, or within 3yd (2.74m) of any part of the gate, then it shall be moved laterally into the field of play until it is 3yd (2.74m) from the nearest part of the gate before play is resumed.

40. Body-checking: *The Take-out and Shoulder-charging*

40.1 Body-checking *and taking-out* an opponent is permitted in the game of lacrosse, provided the opponent is in possession of the ball or is within 9ft (2.74m of a loose ball. *A body-check is the placing of the body in the way of and facing an approaching opponent, so that the latter is simply impeded. A take-out is the hitting of an opponent with the shoulder.* See Rule 68 concerning illegal body-checking *and illegal take-outs*.

40.2 *A player may use a shoulder-to-shoulder charge against an opponent with whom he is engaged or is about to be engaged in a ground scuffle, providing that the opponent is within 9ft (2.74m) of a loose ball.*

41. Checking with the Crosse

41.1 A player may check an opponent's crosse with his own crosse, provided that the opponent has possession of the ball, the opponent is within 9ft (2.74m) of a loose ball, or the ball is in flight within 9ft (2.74m) of the opponent. For the purpose of all Rules except the Off-side Rules, the Centre Face-off Possession Rules, and the Crease Rules, the gloved hand holding the crosse is considered as part of the crosse. See Rules 69 and 70 concerning illegal checking.

42. The Pick

42.1 The use of the pick by an offensive player is permitted, provided that the offensive player is stationary and motionless at the time the contact is made. See Rule 52 concerning an illegal pick.

43. Time-outs

43.1 There are 2 types of time-outs, those called by the officials, and those called by the teams.

43.2 A Referee or the chief bench official may call an official time-out for any reason which he deems necessary for the proper enforcement of the Rules of the game.

43.3 When a player is injured and, in the opinion of an official, the injury is serious, then play shall be suspended immediately. Otherwise, the Referee shall delay the sounding of his whistle as follows:

If the attacking team is in possession of the ball in the attack half of the field and, in the opinion of the Referee, a scoring play is imminent, then the Referee shall delay the sounding of his whistle in the same manner as laid down under the 'slow whistle procedure', Rule 80, except that a signal flag is not dropped under these circumstances.

If the ball is loose, then the Referee shall delay the sounding of his whistle until possession is secured and, if a scoring play is imminent, the play is completed, in the same manner as laid down under the 'slow whistle procedure', Rule 80, except that the signal flag is not thrown under these circumstances.

43.4 A team request a time-out provided:

The ball is dead; or

The team requesting the time-out has possession of the ball in its attacking half of the field.

43.5 A time-out may be called by a coach, a captain, or the player who has possession of the ball. The request may be made to a Referee or to the chief bench official.

43.6 A team time-out shall be 90 seconds long. A team shall be limited to 1 time-out per half, and 1 time-out per 4-minute overtime period. No time-outs shall be allowed in a sudden-death overtime period. A time-out taken between periods is charged to the preceding period.

7. SUBSTITUTION

44. Substitution

44.1 Maximum substitution may take place at any time, subject to the following paragraphs.

44.2 The substituting player must wait in the substitution area for the player whom he is replacing to leave the field of play, and only then may he enter the field of play. Both players must go through the gate. Players may substitute on the fly, and they may do so on either side of the centre-line, provided that the Off-side Rule is observed.

44.3 If the player leaving the field of play is bound to the half of the field which he is in by the Off-side Rule, then the provisions of the Off-side Rule will be deemed to have been observed if the substitute steps out of the substitution area on to the field of play at the same time as the player leaving the field steps into the substitution area.

44.4 The following exceptions shall apply:

(i) On the scoring of a goal, at the end of a period, and during a time-out of any kind, substitution may be effected from any point on the side-line, and not necessarily through the gate. In such cases, it will not be necessary for the substituting player to remain on the side-line until his counterpart leaves the field of play, but his team must have the correct number of players on the field when play is restarted.

(ii) If an official time-out has been called because an injured player is unable to continue, then that player shall be removed from the field as soon as possible to the nearest boundary, and the substitute must report immediately.

8. GOAL-CREASE AND GOALKEEPER

45. The Designated Goalkeeper

45.1 Where a player on a team begins the game using a goalkeeper's stick, then that player shall be deemed to be the designated goalkeeper.

45.2 Where the designated goalkeeper is replaced by another player using a goalkeeper's stick, then that substitute shall be deemed to be the designated goalkeeper.

45.3 If the designated goalkeeper leaves the field of play and is not replaced by another player using a goalkeeper's stick, then the following rules shall apply:

(i) If the designated goalkeeper exchanges crosses with a team-mate prior to leaving the field, then that player shall be deemed to be the designated goalkeeper until such time as the crosses are re-exchanged.

(ii) If there is no goalkeeper's crosse in use by a team at any time, then the captain or coach of that team must nominate a player to act as the designated goalkeeper.

46. Privileges of the Designated Goalkeeper

46.1 While in his own goal-crease, the designated goalkeeper shall have the following privileges and protections:

(i) He may stop or block the ball in any manner with his crosse or body, and he may block the ball or bat it away with his hand, but he may not catch the ball with his hand: nor may he pick the ball up with his hand. He or any member of the defending team may receive a pass while in the crease area.

(ii) No opposing player may initiate contact with the goalkeeper or his crosse while the goalkeeper is within the goal-crease area whether the goalkeeper has the ball in his possession or not. An attacking player may reach into the goal-crease area to play a loose ball, so long as he does not initiate contact with the goalkeeper.

(iii) An exception to Rule 46.1(ii), above, is that the crosse of the goalkeeper, when extended outside the cylinder above the goal-crease area, except when the ball is in the crosse, is subject to being checked under the same circumstances as the crosse of any other player.

47. Prohibitions Relating to the Goal-Crease

47.1 An attacking player shall not be in his opponents' goal-crease area at any time while the ball is live in his opponents' half of the field.

47.2 A goalkeeper or defending player who is outside the goal-crease area and who has the ball in his possession may not enter the goal-crease area.

47.3 A player who is in his goal-crease area may not remain in the goal-crease area with the ball in his possession for longer than 4 seconds. This shall be *audibly* counted by the nearest Referee as 1001, 1002, 1003, 1004. If a player tries to circumvent the 4-second rule by deliberately dropping the ball and then picking it up, then he will be assessed a technical foul.

47.4 For the purpose of this *section*, a player is considered to be within the goal-crease area when any part of his body is touching the goal-crease area, and he is considered to be outside the goal-crease area when no part of his body is touching the goal-crease area, and part of his body is touching the ground outside the goal-crease area.

9. TECHNICAL FOULS

48. The Penalty for Technical Fouls

48.1 The penalty for a technical foul shall be as follows:

(i) If the offending team has possession of the ball, or if the ball is loose at the time a technical foul is committed, then possession shall be awarded to the opposing team at the point where the ball was when the foul occurred.

(ii) If the opponents of the offending team have possession of the ball at the time a technical foul is committed, then the penalty shall be suspension from the field of play for 30 seconds for the player committing the foul.

48.2 If a technical foul occurs prior to the start of the game, or after the scoring of a goal or the end of a period, then the offending player is suspended from the game for 30 seconds and the ball is faced, subject to the exception specified in Rule 34.1(ii). If the technical foul occurs at some other time during the course of the game, but while the play is suspended, then the general Rule rather than this exception shall apply.

49. The Nature of a Technical Foul

49.1 Technical fouls are those of a less serious kind. Any breach of the Rules of play as set forth in this section shall be a technical foul unless that breach is specifically listed as a personal or expulsion foul in Sections 10 or 11. Some of the technical fouls which require definition are listed below, but this section is not intended to be comprehensive and all-inclusive.

50. Interference

50.1 A player may not interfere in any manner with an opponent in an attempt to keep him from a loose ball except when both are within 9ft (2.74m) of such loose ball.

50.2 A player may not, by the use of his body or his crosse, interfere with a player who is in pursuit of an opponent who has possession of the ball.

50.3 A player may not guard an opponent so closely as to prevent the opponent's free movement when the opponent is not in possession of the ball.

50.4 Nothing in this rule is intended to prohibit a legal offensive pick.

51. Pushing

51.1 A player may not push an opponent with his crosse.

51.2 A player may not push an opponent *with any part of his body, except that the use of a shoulder-to-shoulder charge against an opponent with whom a player is engaged or is about to be engaged in a ground scuffle, provided that the opponent is within 9ft (2.74m) of a loose ball, is legal.*

Pushing is defined as exerting enough pressure to force an opponent to move in a direction other than that in which he intends to go or, if in the direction in which he intends to go, then at a greater speed than he intends.

52. Illegal Pick

52.1 No offensive player shall move into and make contact with a defensive player with the purpose of blocking that defensive player from the man he is marking. Before any contact is made by the defensive player, the offensive player must be stationary and motionless, and he must be standing in his normal stance.

52.2 No offensive player shall hold his crosse rigid or extend his crosse rigid to impede the normal movement of a defender.

53. Holding

53.1 A player shall not hold an opponent or an opponent's crosse except as hereinafter permitted:

(i) A player may hold off an opponent who is in possession of the ball or who is within 3 yd (2.74m) of a loose ball with either closed gloved hand on the handle of his crosse, or with either forearm. Both hands of the player who is doing the holding must be on his crosse. The holding off must merely be the exerting of equal pressure.

(ii) A player in possession of the ball may protect his crosse with his hand, arm, or other part of his body when an opponent makes a play to check his crosse. The hand, arm, or other part of his body may only be used to stop the stick check, and it must not be used to hold, push, or control the direction of the movement of the checker's crosse or body.

54. Kicking an Opponent's Crosse

54.1 A player may not deliberately step on or kick the crosse of an opponent.

55. Handling the Ball

55.1 A player shall not touch the ball with his hand(s) while it is in play, except the goalkeeper in his crease as defined in Rule 46.1(i).

56. Withholding the Ball from Play

56.1 A player shall not withhold the ball from play in any manner.

A player shall not lie on a loose ball on the ground.

A player shall not trap a loose ball on the ground with his stick longer than is necessary for him to control the ball and pick it up in one continuous motion.

56.2 A player with the ball in his possession shall not hold his crosse in close proximity to his body with the purpose of preventing an opponent from dislodging the ball.

56.3 A player with the ball in his possession may not grasp any portion of the head of the stick with his hand.

57. Illegal Actions with the Crosse

57.1 A player shall not throw his crosse under any circumstances.

57.2 A player shall not take part in the play of the game in any manner unless he is grasping his crosse with at least one hand. A broken crosse is considered no crosse.

57.3 During the play of the game, a player may not exchange his crosse for another except to replace a broken crosse, but players who are legally on the playing field may exchange crosses.

57.4 Should a player lose his crosse in any legal way so that repossession of his crosse would cause him to violate a rule, then the 'slow whistle technique' (Rule 80) shall be employed by the Referees, except that the signal flag is not thrown under these circumstances. Should the crosse be in the crease so as possibly to interfere with the goalkeeper's play of an attempted shot at goal, then play shall be suspended immediately.

58. Illegal Actions by Team Officials

58.1 A coach, trainer or other person officially connected with a team shall not:

(i) Enter the field of play without the permission of an official, except during a team time-out or between periods.

(ii) Use artificial aids to communicate with players on the field of play.

(iii) Leave the area on his bench's side of the field between the special substitution area line and the imaginary extension of the goal-area line.

58.2 This rule does not prohibit a coach from communicating, from his bench area, with a player who is on the field of play or in the penalty box.

59. Illegal Procedure

59.1 Any action by a player or a substitute of a technical nature which is not in conformity with the rules and regulations governing the play of the game shall be termed illegal procedure. The following paragraphs give examples of illegal procedure.

59.2 Leaving the penalty box before being authorised to do by the penalty time-keeper is a foul. The offending player shall be returned to the penalty box to serve out his unexpired time plus 30 seconds. If the ball is loose or in the possession of his own team, then it shall be awarded to the opposing team. If a goal is scored by the player's opponents, then any unexpired time on a technical foul shall be nullified, but he must still serve the 30 seconds for illegal entry into the game. During an authorised time-out or between periods, a player may leave the penalty box, but he must return at the commencement of play to complete his suspension.

59.3 Delaying the game is a foul. An individual player is guilty of delaying the game if, during a stoppage in play, he bats, kicks or throws the ball away. In such a case, if a time penalty is to be served, then the individual concerned must serve it himself. At the discretion of the Referees, such conduct may be construed as unsportsmanlike conduct.

A team is guilty of delaying the game when:

(i) It is not ready to start the game at the beginning of a period, or after a time-out.

(ii) It is not ready to start the game 30 seconds after a goal has been scored.

(iii) It is not ready to start the game when the Referees are ready to restart the game after a stoppage has occurred because of a foul or an out-of-bounds ball.

(iv) It is not ready to restart the game when the Referees are ready to restart the game after equipment has been adjusted.

When a team is guilty of delaying the game, and a time penalty is to be served, then it shall be served by the in-home.

59.4 Participation in the play of the game by an out-of-bounds player is a technical foul.

59.5 A team which does not have the required number of men in each designated area at the time the whistle is blown to start a centre face-off has committed a technical foul. See Rules 34.7 and 34.8.

59.6 Failure to be at least 10yd (9.14m) from a face-off at the time the whistle is blown is a technical foul.

59.7 Failure to be at least 9ft (2.74m) from an opponent having a free play is a technical foul.

59.8 Any breach of the rules relating to substitution as laid down in Rule 44 is a technical foul.

59.9 Any breach of the Rules relating to the goal-crease as laid down in Rule 47 is a technical foul.

59.10 Any breach of the Rules relating to time-outs as laid down in Rule 43 is a technical foul.

59.11 It is a technical foul for a team to have more than 10 men (including men in the penalty box) in the game at any time, *except after the scoring of a goal, at the end of a period, and during a time-out of any kind.*

59.12 It is a technical foul for a team to have more men than it should have on the actual field of play (excluding the penalty box) at any time, *except after the scoring of a goal, at the end of a period, and during a time-out of any kind.*

59.13 *Where a coaches' area is marked out*, only coaches are allowed in the coaches' area, and it is thus a technical offence for a player or substitute to enter this area.

60. Stalling

60.1 Any deliberate action on the part of a team in posession of the ball to maintain possession of the ball outside the attack goal-area by holding or passing the ball without reasonable effort to attack its opponents' goal is a technical foul known as 'stalling'.

60.2 A team playing with fewer players than its opponents due to penalties cannot be guilty of stalling.

60.3 A team which has possession of the ball in their attack goal area cannot be guilty of stalling.

60.4 Where a Referee feels that a team in possession of the ball outside the attack goal-area is not making a reasonable attempt to attack its opponents' goal, then he shall ask that team to 'get it in'; the team must then carry or pass the ball into the attack goal-area within a reasonable time. Once the ball is in the attack goal-area, then the team in possession shall keep it in the attack goal-area. If the ball subsequently leaves the stalling area (the attack goal-area) before the defending team has had possession of the ball, except as a result of a foul by the defending team or a deflection by the defending team or a shot, then the team which has been asked to 'get it in' shall lose possession to their opponents.

60.5 This Rule shall not prevent a team from employing a careful passing game for the purpose of manoeuvring the opposing team out of position.

61. Illegal Crosse

61.1 Should it come to the attention of a Referee that a player is using a crosse (other than trick stringing) which is illegal under the provisions of Rules 15 or 16, then the Referee shall demand that the player adjust the crosse to conform to specification, or exchange it for another. For a second violation against the same player, the Referee shall inflict a technical penalty and place the illegal crosse in the custody of the official scorer for the remainder of the game.

62. Illegal Equipment

62.1 Should it come to the attention of a Referee that a player is wearing equipment which is illegal under the provisions of Rules 17 or

18, then the Referee shall demand that the player conform to specification. Should the player fail to do so, then he shall be compelled to withdraw from the game until such time as he has complied with the regulations governing equipment, a substitute being allowed for him immediately. For a second violation by the same player, the Referee shall inflict a technical penalty, and he shall be compelled to withdraw from the game until such time as he has complied with the regulations.

63. Off-side

63.1 Except as provided for in Rule 63.4, a team is off-side, provided that the ball is in play, when:

(i) It has fewer than 3 men in its attack half of the field between the centre-line and the end-line; or

(ii) It has fewer than 4 men in its defensive half of the field between the centre-line and the end-line.

63.2 Except in cases where a goal is scored when one or both teams are off-side, the following rules shall apply:

(i) When only one team is off-side, a technical penalty shall be inflicted in accordance with Rule 48.

(ii) Where both teams are off-side, and one of the teams has possession of the ball, the teams shall be placed on-side, and play resumed with the team which had possession of the ball retaining possession.

(iii) Where both teams are off-side, and neither team has possession of the ball, the teams shall be placed on-side, and the ball shall be faced at the place where it was when the whistle went.

63.3 The following rules shall apply when one or both teams are off-side at the time a goal is scored:

(i) When only the defending team is off-side, then the goal shall stand, and no penalty shall be inflicted.

(ii) When only the attacking team is off-side, the goal shall not stand, and the ball shall be awarded to any member of the defensive team 20yd (18.29m) laterally from the cage.

(iii) When both teams are off-side, the goal shall not stand, and the ball shall be faced 20yd (18.29m) laterally from the cage.

63.4 The following exceptions shall apply to the foregoing rules concerning off-side.

(i) When 4 or more men from one team are in the penalty box at the same time, then that team is required to have 3 men in its attack half of the field and the remainder of its players is in its defensive half of the field at all times. Under these conditions, no penalty shall result from the failure of such a team to have 4 players in its defensive half.

(ii) If a player, seeing that he is going to go off-side before he can stop, runs out-of-bounds instead of off-side, then no penalty shall result from the failure of his team to have the required number of players in that half of the field.

64. Thrusting Crosse at Face of Opponent
64.1 A player shall not push, thrust or flick his crosse at the face of an opponent.

65. Avoidable Lateness
65.1 When a team fails to appear on the field ready to play at the appointed time for the start of a match, then that team has committed a technical foul. The penalty shall be served by the in-home.

10. PERSONAL FOULS

66. The Penalty for a Personal Foul
66.1 The penalty for a personal foul shall be suspension from the game for a period of 1 to 3 minutes, depending upon the Referees' diagnosis of the severity and intention of the foul. If the foul occurs prior to the start of the game, or after the scoring of a goal or the end of a period, then the ball shall be faced. Otherwise, the ball shall normally be given to the team which has been fouled.

67. The Nature of a Personal Foul
67.1 Personal fouls are those of a more serious kind. Any breach of the rules of play as set forth in this section shall be a personal foul.

68. Illegal Body-check *and Illegal Take-out*
68.1 *A body-check is the placing of the body in the way of and facing an approaching opponent, so that the latter is simply impeded. A take-out is the hitting of an opponent with the shoulder.* A body-check *or a take-out* of an opponent who is not in possession of the ball or within 9ft (2.74m) of a loose ball is illegal.

68.2 An avoidable body-check *or take-out* of an opponent after he has thrown the ball is illegal.

68.3 A *take-out* of an opponent in which initial contact is from the rear, *or below the hips*, or at or above the neck is illegal, unless the player *taken-out* turns his back or jumps or moves in such a manner as to make what started as a legal *take-out* appear illegal.

68.4 When a player uses his spread arm or arms in a body-check *or a take-out*, then they must be kept below the shoulders of the opponent throughout the entire body-check *or take-out*, and both hands must remain in contact with the crosse.

68.5 Blocking an opponent with the head, known as spearing, is illegal.

68.6 *Taking-out* an opponent who is lying on the ground, or who is down on one or both knees, is illegal.

68.7 *Unneccessary roughness must not be used during a body-check or a take-out.*

69. Slashing

69.1 Under no circumstances shall a player swing his crosse at an opponent's crosse with deliberate viciousness or reckless abandon, and a foul is committed in such circumstances whether or not the opponent's crosse or body is struck.

69.2 A strike by the crosse on the helmet or neck of an opponent is illegal, except when done by a player in the act of passing or shooting.

69.3 A player shall not strike any part of the body of an opponent, other than the gloved hand holding the stick, in an attempt to dislodge the ball from his opponent's crosse, but a check shall not be declared illegal if, in an attempt to protect his crosse, the player in possession uses some part of his body, other than his head or neck, to ward off the thrust of the defensive player's crosse and, as a result, the defensive player's crosse strikes some part of the attacking player's body other than his head or neck.

69.4 For the purpose of this Rule, mere contact is not a strike. The contact must be a definite blow, and not merely a brush.

70. Cross-check

70.1 A player may not check or hold an opponent with that part of the handle of his crosse which is between his hands, either by thrusting his crosse away from him or by holding it extended from his body.

71. Tripping

71.1 A player shall not intentionally trip an opponent with any part of his crosse or body.

72. Unnecessary Roughness

72.1 An excessively violent infraction of the rules against holding or pushing is a personal foul, designated unnecessary roughness.

72.2 A deliberate and excessively violent contact made by a defensive player against an offensive player who has legally established a screening position shall be designated unnecessary roughness.

72.3 Any avoidable act by a player which is deliberate and excessively violent shall be designated unnecessary roughness, whether it be with the body or the stick.

73. Unsportsmanlike *or Ungentlemanly Conduct*

73.1 No player, substitute, non-playing member of a squad, coach or anyone officially connected with a competing team shall:

(i) Enter into argument with an official as to any decision which he has made.

(ii) In any way attempt to influence the decision of an official.

(iii) Use threatening, profane or obscene language or gestures to an official or to any member of the opposing squad.

(iv) Commit any act considered unsportsmanlike *or ungentlemanly* by the Referees.

(v) Repeatedly commit the same technical foul.

73.2 Where an unsportsmanlike *or ungentlemanly* conduct penalty has been inflicted, and the penalised person continues to act in an unsportsmanlike *or ungentlemanly* manner, the Referees have the right to banish him from the bench area.

73.3 No player or substitute shall use a crosse with trick stringing which is designed to hold the ball and to retard the normal and free dislodgement of the ball by an opponent. A player using such a stick shall be given a 3-minute penalty, and the stick shall be placed in the custody of the official scorer for the remainder of the game.

73.4 A team which repeatedly abuses Rule 34 by breaking from a restricted zone at a centre face-off shall be guilty of unsportsmanlike *or ungentlemanly* conduct.

74. Player Committing 5 Personal Fouls

74.1 Any player committing 5 personal fouls shall be 'fouled out' of the game, and shall not be allowed to take any further part in it.

74.2 A substitute for such a player shall be allowed to enter the game at such a time as the fouled out player would have been permitted to re-enter the game had he not committed 5 personal fouls.

11. EXPULSION FOULS

75. The Penalty for an Expulsion Foul

75.1 The penalty for an expulsion foul shall be suspension for the remainder of the game.

75.2 In the case of an expulsion foul against a player or a substitute, a substitution may be made after a lapse of 3 minutes.

75.3 In the case of an expulsion foul against a coach, non-playing member of a squad, or someone officially connected with a team, the in-home of the offending team shall be suspended from the game for 3 minutes, and he must remain in the penalty box for the entire 3 minutes.

75.5 *Should a player, substitute, coach, non-playing member of a squad or someone officially connected with a team commit an expulsion foul, then he shall be referred to the Disciplinary Committee immediately. After the game, the Referee concerned shall, immediately and in writing, fully report the facts to the Secretary of the Referees' Committee of the Regional Association in whose area the game was played, and the Secretary shall immediately refer the case to the Disciplinary Committee of that Regional Association for attention.*

76. The Nature of an Expulsion Foul

76.1 The act of deliberately striking or attempting to strike an opponent, a non-playing member of the opponents' squad, a coach or anyone controlling the play of the game with the hand, crosse, ball or otherwise by a player, a substitute, non-playing member of a squad, a coach or anyone officially connected with a team may be an expulsion foul.

76.2 Refusal to accept the authority of the officials, or the use of foul or abusive language, *or unsportsmanlike or ungentlemanly conduct* may be an expulsion foul.

12. EXECUTION OF PENALTIES

77. Player Committing Foul

77.1 A player who has been sent out of the game by a Referee shall raise his stick at full arm's length above his head from the time he is sent off until the time he reaches the penalty box, and he shall report immediately to the *CBO*. He must remain in the penalty box, subject to the rules below, until released by the *CBO* or the penalty timekeeper.

77.2 In the case of a time penalty, the time refers to the time for which the player will be off the field and out of the game. The timing of a penalty will begin when the penalised player sits down on one of the seats in the penalty box, or when the whistle blows to restart play, whichever is the later. If there are no empty seats left in the relevant penalty box, then the penalised player should kneel on one knee beside the seats.

77.3 If a penalised player is going to re-enter the game himself when his penalty time has expired, then he may spend the last 5 seconds of his penalty time on one knee beside the gate on his own team's side of the centre-line. He must then re-enter the game through the gate.

77.4 If a substitute is to replace the penalised player when the penalty time has expired, then the penalised player should spend the whole of the penalty time on the seat. The substitute may then spend the last 5 seconds of the penalty time on one knee beside the gate on his own team's side of the centre-line, prior to entering the field through the gate. The penalised player should then return to the players' bench.

77.5 Penalty time will only be served during normal playing time. Stoppages in play for all time-outs will also temporarily interrupt penalty time. During an authorised time-out, or between periods, a penalised player may leave the penalty box, but he must return at the commencement of play to complete his suspension.

77.6 Penalty time will end when the time of the penalty has expired, except that the scoring of a goal against a team having one or more players serving penalty time for technical fouls shall release the player or players from serving the balance of their penalty time. This shall not apply in the case of personal fouls, where the designated penalty time shall be served regardless of whether or not a goal is scored.

77.7 *Should a goalkeeper commit a technical or personal foul of a non-violent and non-abusive nature, then the nominated defender will serve the penalty time incurred, in order to prevent a possible injury to an inadequately protected deputy. In such circumstances, a personal foul will be recorded against the goalkeeper (and not against the defender) for the purpose of 'fouling out' after five personal fouls.*

Should the goalkeeper commit a foul of a violent or abusive nature, then he must serve the penalty time himself.

Should the goalkeeper commit an expulsion foul, or should he commit a fifth personal foul, then he must leave the game immediately.

77.8 *If the goalkeeper has to leave the field because of injury, or because he has committed a violent or abusive foul, or because he has been 'fouled out' after 5 personal fouls, or because he has committed an expulsion foul, then the Referees shall call an official time-out so that a deputy can don the goalkeeper's protective equipment. If the goalkeeper subsequently returns to the game then, at the next dead ball, the Referees shall call an official time-out so that the original goalkeeper can replace the deputy, and don his protective equipment.*

78. Restarting Play After a Penalty

78.1 When a penalty occurs in the offended team's defensive half of the field and penalty time is to be served, the ball shall be awarded to any player of the offended team on the offensive side of the centre-line. In all other cases, the ball shall be awarded to any player of the offended team at the point where the ball was when play was suspended, the exceptions being as follows:

(i) Where the ball is within 20yd (18.29m) of the cage. In this case the ball shall be moved to a position laterally across the field 20yd (18.29m) from the cage and awarded to any player of the offended team.

(ii) In the event of the goalkeeper or a defending player offending against the crease rules, the ball shall be awarded to any player of the attacking team 20yd (18.29m) laterally from the cage.

(iii) In the event of a crease offence by an attacking player which does not involve a time penalty, the ball shall be awarded to a member of the defending team 20yd (18.29m) laterally from the cage.

78.2 If a goal is scored during a slow whistle play for a technical foul, then no penalty is given. If a goal is not scored during a slow whistle play, then a time penalty is given, and the ball is awarded to the attacking team at the place where it was when play was suspended, subject to Rule 78.1(i) being followed.

79. Simultaneous Fouls

79.1 When a member of a team commits a foul, and then a member of the opposing team commits a foul, then the fouls shall be considered simultaneous fouls, provided that the fouls are not separated by a whistle which has restarted play, or by the scoring of a goal.

79.2 When simultaneous fouls have been committed, the following rules shall apply:

(i) All fouls being technical, the fouls cancel, and the team in possession retains possession where the ball was when the whistle sounded. If not team is in possession, the ball is faced where it was when the whistle sounded.

(ii) If at least one of the fouls is a personal foul, then penalty time shall be served for all the fouls, and the following rules shall apply:

If one team incurs more total penalty time than the other, then the team with the lesser total penalty time shall be awarded the ball. If the ball is awarded in that team's defensive half of the field, then the free play shall be taken from the offensive side of the centre-line.

If the total penalty times are equal, then the team in possession of the ball shall retain possession of it. If the ball is awarded in that team's defensive half of the field, then the free play shall be taken from the offensive side of the centre-line.

If the total penalty times are equal, and neither team has possession of the ball, then the ball shall be faced where it was when the whistle blew.

(iii) For the purpose of totalling penalty time in the case of simultaneous fouls, an expulsion foul shall count as a 3-minute penalty.

80. Slow Whistle Technique

80.1 If a defending player commits a foul, and the attacking team has possession of the ball in its attack half of the field at the time that the foul occurs, and, in the opinion of the Referees, a scoring play is imminent, and the act of fouling does not cause the attacking player who is in possession to lose the ball, then the Referee must drop a signal flag and withhold his whistle until such time as the scoring play has been completed.

80.2 The scoring play shall be considered to have been completed when:

  (i) The attacking team has lost control of the ball.

  (ii) The attacking team has clearly lost the opportunity of scoring a goal on the original play.

  (iii) The attacking team has taken a shot.

  (iv) In the case of the flag being dropped when the ball is in front of the defending team's goal, the attacking team, having caused the ball to go behind the goal, and having then brought it to the front of the goal, cause it to go behind their opponents' goal again.

  (v) In the case of the flag being dropped when the ball is behind the defending team's goal, the attacking team, having brought the ball to the front of the goal, cause it to go behind the goal again.

80.3 The slow whistle technique shall be employed whether or not the foul is committed against the man in possession of the ball.

80.4 A pass is a movement of the ball caused by a player in control throwing or bouncing the ball to a team-mate.

80.5 During a slow whistle situation, a shot remains a shot until:

  (i) It is clearly obvious that a goal will not be scored.

  (ii) Added impetus is given to the ball by any member of the attacking team.

  (iii) Possession is gained by a member of the defending team.

  (iv) After hitting the goalkeeper and/or the pipe(s), the ball touches any player of either team other than the defending goalkeeper; at such time the ball shall be declared dead immediately.

80.6 Where a flag is thrown mistakenly then, when the whistle subsequently blows to stop the play, the ball shall be awarded to the team which has possession. If neither team has possession, then the ball shall be faced.

80.7 Where the CBO sounds his horn to indicate that a foul has been committed in circumstances where a slow whistle should be employed, then the procedures outlined above should be followed, except that the Referee shall drop his hat to acknowledge the horn.

13. SPECIAL SITUATIONS

81. Special Situations

81.1 Where an official is called upon to inflict a penalty against a team where no definite player is involved, or where the penalty is against someone other than a player in the game, then he shall inflict the suspension upon the in-home. If multiple fouls of this type occur, then the penalties shall be inflicted against additional attack players.

81.2 Where the person committing the foul is a substitute, then the foul shall be assessed against him so far as the record is concerned, and he may only re-enter the game subject to the same restrictions as though he were a player at the time the foul was committed.

81.3 If the ball becomes caught in a player's crosse, then a Referee shall audibly count 1001, 1002, 1003, 1004. If, at the end of those 4 seconds, the ball has not been dislodged, then play shall be stopped and the ball shall be faced.

81.4 If the ball becomes caught in a player's uniform or equipment, other than his crosse, then play shall be suspended immediately, and the ball shall be faced.

81.5 Rules 81.3 and 81.4 shall not apply to the designated goalkeeper when he is within his goal-crease. If, in such circumstances, the ball becomes caught in the stick, clothing or equipment of the designated goalkeeper, then the defensive team shall be awarded the ball 20yd (18.29m) laterally from the cage.

81.6 Should the ball become mired in the mud *either* within the crease-area or *outside the crease*, time shall be suspended by the Referees and the ball shall be faced.

81.7 Should the ball become ensnared in the goal netting, time shall be suspended by the Referees and the ball shall be awarded to the defensive team 20yd (18.29m) laterally from the cage.

Reprinted by permission of the English Lacrosse Union. For reasons of space, the Additional Rulings (which have the same authority as the Rules) have been omitted. Copies of the complete Rules and Additional Rules of Men's Lacrosse can be obtained from the Union.

Women's Lacrosse

Women's Lacrosse

1. THE CROSSE

A. Construction

(1) Basic materials: aluminium (handle only), fibreglass, gut, leather, nylon, plastic, rubber or wood. (Recessed metal screws may be used to affix the head to the handle).

(2) The head of the crosse shall be triangular in concept and shall be affixed to the handle in such a way that it shall basically be in the same plane as the handle.

(3) The pocket of the crosse shall be strung traditionally, i.e. 4 or 5 thongs with 8–12 stitches of cross lacing (no mesh).

(4) The crosse shall be free of all sharp or protruding parts or edges and shall, in every way, provide for the safety of all players.

B. Dimensions

(1) Overall length: 0.9m (36in) minimum, 1.1m (44in) maximum. NB. For a young or small player a crosse shorter than 0.9m (36in) will be permitted in order for it to fit comfortably along the full length of her arm.

(2) Head: All width measurements as measured on a line perpendicular to the extension of the handle.

(*a*) Width overall: 18cm (7in) minimum 23cm (9in) maximum

(*b*) Width when measured: 2.5cm (1in) above the bridge in a wooden crosse shall be 6.7–7.6cm (2⅝–3in) inside and 7.6–10.1cm (3–4in) outside.

(*c*) Length as measured from the centre of the stop or bridge to the top of the head shall be 25.4cm (10in) minimum 30.5cm (12in) maximum.

(*d*) Depth: The combined measurements of the pocket containing the ball with either a wood or plastic wall shall not exceed 6.3cm (2.5in) the diameter of the ball.

(3) Walls: Wood or moulded crosse, 3.2–4.5cm (1¼in–1¾in) measured at the highest point of the wall. Guard: Soft or woven 3.2cm (1¼in) to 7.0cm (2¾in) measured at the highest point of the wall.

(4) Weight: 567g (20oz) maximum.

Note: Metric measurements are actual IFWLA measurements, and imperial measurements are a guide.

C. A crosse is legal if:

(1) It complies with the criteria in Rule 1A and 1B.

(2) The top of the ball, when dropped into the pocket of a crosse held horizontally, remains even with or above the top of the wooden or plastic walls.

(3) The ball moves freely within all parts of the pocket, i.e. the ball cannot become wedged between the wood, guard and bridge of a wooden crosse or the stop of a moulded crosse.

(4) It meets the manufacturer's specifications.

D. All the equipment, including the crosses, that is to be used in the game must be checked and approved by the Umpire prior to the game. At any time during the game the Umpire may, at discretion, call time-out and re-check the equipment in use.

(1) Should the equipment be found to be legal, the game shall be restarted by the ball being given to the player who was in possession of the ball or the nearest to the ball when time-out was called.

(2) Should the equipment be found to be illegal, it shall be removed from the game and placed at the scorer's table for the remainder of that half. The player may continue to play with legal equipment. Any illegal equipment may be legalised and re-checked at half-time or before any overtime period by the Umpire for use in the second half or overtime period.

(3) After the removal of illegal equipment, the game shall be restarted with a free position to the opponent nearest the ball when play was stopped. In the event that a goal was scored, the goal does not count and play resumes with a free position goalkeeper. All players must stand, unless directed by the Umpire to move. Only the captain(s) may request a crosse check for legality.

E. Goalkeeper crosse:

Crosse width of head 30.5cm, length 1.22m (48in), width inside measurement 30cm, outside measurement 32.5cm, head length 40cm, depth of side wall at highest point 7cm, depth of pocket unlimited mesh or thongs. Weight 26oz. Handle may be graphite. (*Trial 1990–91*.)

2. THE BALL

The ball is rubber of any solid colour, not less than 20cm (7¾in) nor more than 20.3cm (8in) in circumference. It must weigh not less than 142g (5oz) nor more than 149g (5¼oz). It must have a bounce of not less than 1.1m (44in) nor more than 1.3m (51in) when dropped from 1.8m (72in) on to concrete at a temperature of approximately 18°–23°C (65°–75°F). The ball must meet manufacturer's specifications.

3. THE PLAYING AREA

A. The playing area has no measured boundaries. An area of 110 × 60m (120 × 70yd) is desirable (see diagram on page 625). The goals are 92m (100yd) apart measured from goal-line to goal-line. There must be at least 9m (10yd) playing space behind each goal-line running the width of the field. The minimum distance from goal-line to goal-line is 82m (90yd). There is a circle radius 9m (10yd) in the centre of the field and through the centre of this a line 3m (3.3yd) in length, parallel to the goal-lines. Five marks 31cm (1ft) in length should be marked 11m (12.1yd) from the goal-line at 90° angles in front, 45° angles in front, 45° angles diagonally on a line from each goal-post and to the goal-circle line. The distance from goal for free space shall be marked by a full semi-circle, 15m from the goal-line, around the front of the goal, designating the maximum distance for free space to goal. All lines are 5cm (2in) wide.

B. Directions for 11m area/marking area. (*Trial 1990–91*) (see diagram on page 624). The 2 side-lines are made first. Run string from point A at back of goal-circle that is perpendicular to the goal-line at its centre to the points on goal-circle B where, if the goal-line were extended, it would intersect the circle. Extend and mark these lines (45°degree angle) from the goal-line (B) 9.08m to point C. To mark the curve of the arc, measure from the centre of the goal-line D 11m (12.1yd) to G connecting the side-lines. 15m fan: inscribe a semicircle E from the centre of the goal-line D 15m (49.2ft).

C. The playing area must be flat and free of glass, stones, and any protruding objects. The boundaries must be decided before the match by the captains and the Umpires – See Rule 7(c). The lines marking the centre and goal-circles are part of these areas. No marks may be added to or removed from the field.

4. THE GOALS

Each goal consists of two perpendicular posts or pipes, constructed of wood or metal, 1.83m (6ft) high and 1.83m (6ft) apart, joined at the top

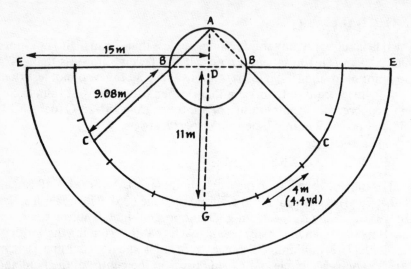

by a cross-bar 1.83m (6ft) from the ground (inside measurements). The goal-posts (pipes) must not extend upwards beyond the goal-posts nor the cross-bar sideways beyond the goal-posts. The posts and cross-bar should be white and be 5cm (2in) square or 5cm (2in) in diameter. Pipe goals painted orange are acceptable. A line called the goal-line must be drawn between the two posts, continuous with them and of the same width. The netting, not more than 4cm (1.5in) mesh, must be attached to the posts and cross-bar and to a point on the ground 1.83m (6ft) behind the centre of the goal-line; it must be firmly pegged down. NB. Goals with ground poles are legal but not recommended. If the side and bottom supports of the goal are exposed, they must be padded.

5. THE GOAL-CIRCLE

The goal-circle is a circle radius 2.6m (8.5ft) measured from the centre of the goal-line to the outer edge of the goal-line. The goal-circle line shall be 5cm (2in) wide.

6. THE TEAMS

Sixteen players constitute a full team. No more than 12 players per team shall take the field at one time; one team member acts as captain.

7. THE CAPTAINS

The captain's responsibilities are:
    (a) To toss for choice of ends with the Umpire.
    (b) To agree on the playing time with the Umpire.
    (c) To agree on the boundaries with the Umpire.

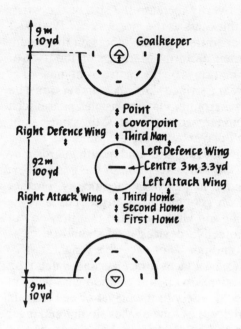

9m
10yd   Goalkeeper

Right Defence Wing

Point
Coverpoint
Third Man

Left Defence Wing
Centre 3m,3.3yd
Left Attack Wing

92m
100yd

Right Attack Wing   Third Home
Second Home
First Home

9m
10yd

9m   3m
10yd   3.2yd

9m, 10yd

92m
100yd

3m
3.3yd

3m
3.3yd

9m
10yd

The Teams   *The Playing Area*

(*d*) To indicate a substitute for an injured player.

(*e*) To designate an acting-captain if the captain leaves the field.

(*f*) To confer with the Umpires if the weather conditions make the continuation of play questionable, but the Umpire's decision is final.

(*g*) The captain and/or coach may approach the Umpire at half-time or after the game if a clarification of rules is needed – See Rule 21-A-5.

(*h*) Only the captain(s) may request a crosse check for legality.

Note: Where co-captains (2 or more) are nominated (for all level of matches) one co-captain must be deemed the captain for that match and be so named on the scoresheet.

(*i*) The captain shall wear a visible armband of contrasting uniform colour. (*Trial 1990–91.*)

8. UNIFORM

A. Players must wear composition or rubber soled boots or shoes. No spikes are allowed. Plastic, leather or rubber cleats-studs may be worn.

B. The goalkeeper may use a body pad, a face mask and/or helmet, gloves and a throat protector. Gloves may be padded to maximum specification of Brine L35, L20 or equivalent glove provided that the cuffs are tied firmly and do not overtly increase the size of the wrist. Body padding may be the same thickness as the glove. (*Trial 1990–91.*)

C. All players must wear numbers differing from others on their team shirts on the front and back of their uniform. Markings on the back of the shirt must be at least 8in tall: markings on the centre front must be at least 4in tall. If a team elects to wear a striped shirt, the numbers must be superimposed on a solid block background. Players' visible apparel such as tights, socks, undershirts and undergarments must be the same colour as either the kilt or shirt, with all players wearing the same.

D. Close-fitting gloves, noseguards, eye guards and mouth guards may be worn by all players. Players, with the exception of the goalkeeper, are not allowed to wear protective headgear or face masks. Further protective devices necessitated on genuine medical grounds may be used, providing that both captains and Umpires agree that they do not endanger other players. All protective devices used should be close fitting, padded where necessary and not be of excessive weight.

E. Players may not wear earrings, necklaces, bracelets and watches on the field of play. Medical jewellery with information visible, soft jewellery and rings must be taped securely to the player or be removed entirely. Barrettes/hair slides are legal as long as they do not endanger other players. The Umpire has the power to rule any decoration as dangerous and to remove it from the field of play.

F. The goalkeeper's colours must be the same corresponding colours as her team-mates'. The top must be the same colour; the bottom must be in agreement with the predominant colour. Goalkeepers may wear their team shirt either inside or outside the body pad. (*Trial 1990–91.*)

G. No equipment, including protective devices, may be used unless it complies with the rules or manufacturer's specifications and is deemed not dangerous to the other players by the Umpires.

9. DURATION OF PLAY

A. The maximum regulation playing time is 50 minutes, or such time agreed by the captains – See Rule 7(*b*). At half-time, which may not exceed 10 minutes, the players must change ends. Time-out, which may not exceed 2 minutes per incident for a field player, 5 minutes for a goalkeeper, is taken for a stoppage that occurs due to accident or injury – See Rule 10-C.

B. In all games the clock is to be stopped on the Umpire's whistle and arm signal after each goal during the entire game, and on every whistle in the last 2 minutes of each half. NB: This rule is recommended for representative matches and is open to consultation at other levels of play.

C. Play should be continuous, but at the discretion of the Umpire time-out is taken for unusual circumstances, e.g. a broken crosse, animal on the field, lost ball, a ball that had gone too far out-of bounds, spectator interference, delay of game, to check a crosse, or to give warnings or suspensions.

D. If weather conditions make play dangerous, the Umpire is authorised to suspend the game after consultation with the captains. The Umpire's decision is final. A game is considered legal and complete if 80% of playing time has elapsed. If an interrupted game (one in which less than 80% of playing time has elapsed) is replayed, it must be played from the beginning.

E. The whistle is used only to stop play. Play is restarted verbally. The Umpire will also give a visual arm signal by raising her arm above her head and moving it down to her side as she gives the verbal 'play'. The only exception to this is in the case of 'throw' where the arm signal to restart the clock is on the actual arm movement forward on the toss of the ball as she says the word 'play'.

10. SUBSTITUTION

A. Limited to 2 players per team at any one time, on a dead ball. Time-out taken for substitution. Unlimited substitutions allowed during the game. Player(s) must advise the timekeeper/scorer of the impending substitution(s) before the Umpire's whistle. The timekeeper/scorer will sound a hooter thus advising the Umpire of the substitution(s), the Umpire will beckon substitute on. The substituting player(s) may take the field before the player they are substituting for has left the field. Umpires to ensure that proper field position is taken by substituting player.

B. Substitution can be made for a suspended player but a suspended player may not re-enter the game under any circumstances. The substitute for a suspended player may not enter the game until 3 minutes' playing time has elapsed after the suspension.

C. If a field player is incapacitated for longer than 2 minutes the game is restarted without her. If no substitute has taken her place, she may return with the Umpire's permission while the game is in progress. A maximum recovery time of 5 minutes is allowed for the goalkeeper.

D. Substitution procedure

(1) Before a substitute enters the game, she must report to the scorer's table and indicate the name and number of the player she is replacing.

(2) If substitution is being made other than at half-time, the timer will sound a horn at the first stoppage of play to notify the Umpire of the substitution.

(3) Only those players who have been checked in at the scorer's table prior to the sounding of the horn may enter the game at that time. Anyone else coming to the table after the sounding of the horn must wait until the next stoppage of play.

(4) Time out is taken for substitution and must be made without delay.

(5) The substitute must assume the same location as the person she is replacing, except when it occurs after a goal.

E. For an illegal substitution the Umpire will call time out and remove the illegal player. A free position will be given to the opponent nearest the ball. If an illegal player is discovered on the attacking team after a goal is scored and before the next draw, the goal will not count, the illegal player will be removed and a free position will be awarded to the opposing goalkeeper. (An extra player is considered an illegal substitute.)

11. START OF THE GAME

The game is started and restarted after every goal and after every half-time by a draw on the centre line. All other players' feet must be outside the centre circle until after the words 'ready draw'.

The Draw

The opponents each stand with one foot toeing the centre line. The crosses are held in the air, above hip level, wood/plastic to wood/plastic, angle to collar, parallel to and above the centre line and back to back, so that the players' crosses are between the ball and the goal they are defending. The ball is placed between the crosses by the Umpire. On the words 'ready draw' from the Umpire, the two opponents must immediately draw their crosses up and away from one another. The flight of the ball must attain a height higher than the heads of the players taking the draw. After one caution per game for an illegal draw by a specific player, the opponent is awarded a free position. A throw is awarded after one caution if both players draw illegally. For the free position the offending centre is placed 4m (4.4yd) away at an angle of 45° to the centre line towards the goal she is defending.

12. SCORING

A. The team scoring the greater number of goals is the winner. In the event of the scores being equal, the result is a draw/tie. A goal is scored by the whole ball passing completely over the goal-line, between the posts, and under the cross-bar from in front, having been propelled by the crosse of an attacking player, or the crosse or person of a defending player.

B. A goal is not scored when:

(1) The ball is put through the goal by a non-player.

(2) The ball comes off the person of an attacking player.

(3) The ball enters the goal after the whistle has been blown or the horn has been sounded.

(4) The player shooting has followed through over the circle with any part of herself or her crosse, or any other attacking player had entered the circle.

(5) The goalkeeper, while within the circle, is interfered with in any way by an attacking player.

(6) The Umpire has ruled that the shot is dangerous – Rule 19-A-7.

(7) The ball enters the goal while the attacking team has an illegal player(s) on the field.

(8) The ball enters the goal from a crosse that does not meet specifications.

(9) If the player who shot the goal adjusts her crosse after an Umpire's request for a crosse inspection, the goal will not count, and the crosse will be removed from that half. Play is restarted by the goalkeeper.

C. *Playing off a tie game where required:*

(1) When the score is tied at the end of regular playing time, both teams will have a 5-minute rest and toss a coin for choice of ends.

(2) Six minutes of stop-clock overtime will be played. The clock will be stopped after 3 minutes of play in order for teams to change ends with no delay for coaching. The game will be restarted by a centre draw. The team who is ahead at the end of 6 minutes wins the game.

(3) If the teams are still tied after 6 minutes have elapsed, the teams will have a 3-minute rest and change ends.

(4) The winner will then be decided on a 'sudden victory' stop-clock overtime of not more than 6 minutes in length with the teams changing ends after 3 minutes. The game will be restarted by a centre draw. The team scoring the first goal wins the game.

(5) Play will continue with 'sudden victory' stop-clock overtime periods of 6 minutes in length with 3 minutes in between the change of ends until a winning goal is scored.

13. STAND

The ball is 'dead' when the Umpire blows her whistle and no player except the goalkeeper within her goal circle or her deputy may move, unless directed by the Umpire, until the game has been restarted. The Umpire directs any player who moves to return to her original position.

14. OUT-OF-BOUNDS

When the ball goes out-of-bounds, the Umpire blows her whistle and the players must stand.

A. When one player is nearest the ball, she takes the ball in her crosse from the place where the ball went out-of-bounds, stands 4m (4.4yd) inside the agreed boundary and on the signal and word 'play' the game proceeds.

B. The players involved maintain their same relationship relative to the other players at the time the whistle was blown except the player with the ball must be given 1m of clear space by the opponent or opponents.

C. When two opposing players are equally near the ball, a throw is taken – See Rule 15(*b*).

D. Play must not be resumed within 8m (8.8yd) of the goal-circle.

15. THE THROW

The two players must stand with feet and crosse at least 1m (1yd) apart and each is nearer the goal she is defending and facing in towards the game. The Umpire stands between 4m and 8m (4.4 and 8.8yd) from the players, and on the word 'play', throws the ball with a short high throw so that the players take it as they move in towards the game. No player may be within 4m (4.4yd) of the players taking the throw. If the throw is inaccurate or is not touched by either player, the throw is taken again.

A throw is taken when:

(*a*) The ball goes into the goal off a non-player – See Rule 12-B-1 – with the throw being taken to the side of the goal by two opposing field players nearest the goal.

(*b*) The ball goes out of bounds and two opposing players are equally near the ball – See Rule 14-C.

(*c*) There is an incident unrelated to the ball and players are equidistant from the ball – See Rule 16-A-2.

(*d*) A ball lodges in the clothing of a field player or Umpire – See Rule 17-A – or cannot be dislodged from the crosse of a field player – See Rule 17-B.

(*e*) Two players commit minor or major fouls simultaneously – See Rule 19-A-13.

(*f*) The game is restarted after an incident related to the ball when neither team had possession and two opposing players are equally near the ball unless the accident has been caused by a foul – See Rule 16-A-2.

(*g*) The game is stopped for any reason not specified in the rules.

16. ACCIDENT, INTERFERENCE OR ANY OTHER INCIDENT

A. If the game has to be stopped due to an accident, injury, illness, interference or an incident either related or unrelated to the ball at the time the whistle is blown, the game is restarted in one of the following ways:

(1) If a foul has occurred, a free position is awarded on a spot determined by the Umpire – See Rule 20.

(2) If no foul is involved in the stoppage of play, the ball is given to the player who was in possession, or nearest to it, at the time play was stopped. If two players are equidistant from the ball, a throw is taken.

B. Time-out is called at the discretion of the Umpire. No one from the side-line may come on to the field without the permission of the Umpire and no side-line personnel may come on to the field for the purpose of coaching. No player may leave her area of the field for the purpose of being coached. If a field player is incapacitated for longer than 2 minutes the game is restarted without her. If no substitute has taken her place she may return with the Umpire's permission while the game is in progress. A maximum recovery time of 5 minutes is allowed for the goalkeeper – See Rule 10-B.

17. BALL LODGED IN CLOTHING OR CROSSE

When the ball lodges:

A. In the clothing of a player or Umpire, a throw is taken with the nearest opponent.

B. In the crosse, the crosse must be struck on the ground and the ball dislodged immediately, otherwise a throw is taken where the player caught the ball – Rule 15(*d*).

C. In the goal netting or in the clothing or pads of the goalkeeper while she is within the goal-circle, she removes the ball, places it in her crosse and proceeds with the game – Rule 17-B-3.

18. GOAL-CIRCLE RULES

A. Only one player, either the goalkeeper or the person deputising for her, is allowed in the goal-circle at any one time. No other player is allowed to enter or have any part of her body or crosse on or over the goal-circle line at any time. A ball resting on the goal-circle line is the goalkeeper's.

B. The goalkeeper or anyone deputising for her while within the goal-circle:

(1) Must clear the ball within 10 seconds after it has entered the goal-circle.

(2) May stop the ball with either hand and/or body as well as her crosse. If she catches the ball with her hand she must put it in her crosse and proceed with the game.

(3) Must remove a ball lodged in her clothing or pads, place it in her crosse, and proceed with the game – See Rule 17-C.

(4) May reach out her crosse and bring the ball back into the goal-circle provided no part of her body is grounded outside the goal-circle.
C. When the goalkeeper or anyone deputising for her is outside the goal-circle:

(1) She loses all her goalkeeping privileges.

(2) She may only re-enter the goal-circle without the ball.

(3) She may propel the ball into the goal-circle and then follow it in.

(4) She must return to the goal-circle to play the ball if it is inside the circle.

D. The penalty for violation of Rule 18 is a free position no closer than 11m (12.1yd) out to either side level with the goal-line.

19. FOULS

A. Major Field Fouls
A player must not:

(1) Roughly or recklessly check/tackle another player's crosse. A crosse may be checked in a direction towards the body as long as the check/tackle is controlled. No player's crosse may hit or cause her opponent's crosse to hit her body. (*Note*: The attack player has a responsibility not to run her crosse into the defender's crosse. NB: A crosse or ball within a crosse width of a player's head or neck is deemed potentially dangerous.

(2) Hold her crosse within a crosse width around the face or throat of an opponent when she is level with or behind her.

(3) A player must not hold her crosse so close in front of her face or body, or another team-mate's face or body, with or without cradling, making a legal, safe check impossible.

(4) Reach around and across the body of an opponent to check the handle of her crosse with her feet behind her opponent.

(5) Charge, block, barge, shoulder or back into an opponent, or push with the hand. Move into the path of an opponent without giving the player a chance to stop or change her direction. When a player is running to receive the ball a 'blind side' defence player must give her enough time or space to change her direction.

Block/Charge: A player must not extend her body sideways by limb or crosse thereby impeding the progress of an opponent. If any contact occurs the player must give way, or this position is illegal and is penalised as a major foul for detaining. (*Trial 1990–91*.)

The player may use her crosse to extend her space to include the area in front of her body to the width of her shoulders and to the length of her outstretched arms. In establishing her space in this way, the whole crosse should be held within the width of the shoulders and not extend forwards beyond the reach of her outstretched arms.

If an opponent uses her body to push on to or interfere with any part of the legally held crosse then this is charging.

(6) Propel the ball or follow through with her crosse in a dangerous or uncontrolled manner at any time.

Before making a pass or shot, players must look immediately prior to playing the ball to ensure there is no danger to any other players. (*Trial 1990–91.*)

(7) Shoot dangerously or without control.

(*a*) A dangerous shot is judged on the basis of the combination of distance, force and placement.

(*b*) A shot may not be directed at the goalkeeper's body, especially her head or neck. This would not apply if she moves into the path of the ball.

(*c*) A shot may be uncontrolled even if it misses the goal.

(8) With any part of her body guard the goal outside the goal-circle so as to obstruct the free space to goal between the ball and the goal-circle which denies the attack the opportunity to shoot safely and encourages shooting at an unprotected player.

(*a*) This positioning applies only if initiated by the defender and not if she is drawn into the free space to goal by an attacking player.

(*b*) The positioning applies to a defender not intentionally playing the player with the ball.

Note: Refer to Rule 22 for definition.

(9) Detain an opponent at any time by holding, tagging, pressing, or pushing against her body, clothing or crosse with an arm, leg, body or crosse. Hold the crosse of an opponent after a check to the extent that her balance or movement is impeded.

(10) Trip an opponent deliberately or otherwise.

(11) A player must not screen or set a moving or stationary pick out of the visual field of an opponent. A pick is a technique in which a player without the ball, by her positioning, forces the opponent to take another route.

(12) *Swiping*. When swiping occurs in the field of play, the whistle is blown immediately. A card must be given. When swiping occurs in the critical scoring area, a held whistle is in effect; however, when the scoring play is over, a card must be given. Swiping is the swinging of a crosse at an opponent's crosse or body with deliberate viciousness or recklessness, whether or not the opponent's crosse or body is struck.

Automatic yellow card will be given for a swipe, repeated fouls after a verbal caution, check to head, dangerous propelling of ball into a player.

(13) In a simultaneous Major/Minor Foul the Major Foul takes precedence over Minor Foul.

(14) Marking area: 11m in front of goal. When defending within the

11m area the defender cannot remain in that area for more than 3 seconds unless marking an opponent within a stick and arm's length (2m). No more than one defender may mark the same non-ball player in this area in order to be exempt from the 3-second and/or Obstruction of the Free Space to Goal Rules. (*Trial 1990–91.*)

The defence is not exempt from the 3-second and/or Obstruction of the Free Space to Goal Rules by virtue of double teaming a non-ball attack player in this area. The 3-second count will continue against the original non-marking defence player within this area until there is again only one defender on the non-ball attack player.

A defender who is marking an unmarked opponent who is standing directly behind the goal-circle cannot be penalised for the 3-second Rule when drawn into a double or multiple team by the attacking non-ball player(s). The 3-second Rule is in effect when the team in possession of the ball crosses the ball over the centre line into their attacking half of the field.

B. Minor Field Fouls

A player must not:

(1) Guard a ground ball with her foot or crosse or push an opponent off a ground ball.

(2) Guard the crosse with an arm:

(*a*) If one hand is removed from the crosse, the free hand may not be used to ward off an opponent deliberately or otherwise with or without contact.

(*b*) Elbows may not be used so as to protect the crosse.

(3) Touch the ball with her hand, except as in Rules 17-C and 18-B.

(4) Allow any part of her body, deliberately or otherwise, to impede, accelerate or change the direction of the ball to her team's distinct advantage. *Note*: Ball contact from an unexpected deflection should not be penalised. However, if the goalkeeper blatantly attempts to stop a shot on goal by playing the ball off her body while outside the goal-circle it shall be called a Major Foul.

(5) Check/tackle an opponent's crosse when she is trying to get possession of the ball. This applies only if the opponent could have received the ball.

(6) Hold the crosse of opponent for a short time after a check.

(7) Throw her crosse in any circumtances.

(8) Take part in the game if she is not holding her crosse.

(9) Draw illegally after one 'caution'. Illegal draws occur when:

(*a*) One player draws too soon.

(*b*) No attempt is made to draw up and away.

(*c*) The ball does not go above the heads of both centres.

(10) Intentionally delay the game.

(11) On a centre draw, step into the centre circle before the word 'draw'.

(12) Play with an illegal crosse.

(13) Substitute illegally.

(14) Deliberately cause the ball to go out of bounds. NB: Verbal caution will be given to keep the ball in play. The foul will be called when a team after having been cautioned intentionally runs or passes the ball out of bounds.

(15) Request for a second time the inspection of any crosse meeting specifications.

(16) Adjust the strings/thongs of her crosse after an official inspection of her crosse has been requested during the game. The crosse must be removed.

Note: Any player who repeatedly commits the same Minor Foul will be penalised as a Major Foul. Repeatedly means 3 times. Repeated fouls may be treated as misconduct.

(17) The goalkeeper is restricted from going 15m in front of the goal. (*Trial 1990–91.*)

C. Goal-Circle Fouls

(1) A field player must not enter or have any part of her body or crosse in the goal-circle at any time, unless she is deputising for the goalkeeper – See Rule 18-A.

(2) The goalkeeper or her deputy must not:

(*a*) When inside the goal-circle, continue to hold the ball in her crosse, but must pass within 10 seconds – See Rule 18-B.

(*b*) When inside the goal-circle, reach beyond the goal-circle to play the ball in the air or on the ground with her hand.

(*c*) When any part of her is grounded outside the goal-circle, draw the ball into her goal-circle.

(*d*) When outside the goal-circle with the ball, step back into the goal-circle until she no longer has the ball.

(*e*) The goalkeeper, when outside the goal-circle, throw away part of her equipment to her deputy.

D. Team Offences

(1) **Delay of game** – failure to stand where directed by an Umpire;
– deliberately cause the ball to go out of bounds.

(*a*) *Verbal caution* (see Guideline on page 636): Time-out called. Green card to offender, stating, 'This is your verbal caution for delay of game'. Players are directed to their proper positions and play is restarted. The green card cautions the entire team that a similar offence may be penalised.

(*b*) *Captain's caution* (for further offence): Time-out. Green card to captain stating, 'This is a second caution for delay of game'. Minor Foul free position. Further similar offence may be penalised as a Major Foul with yellow card (warning) to offender.

(*c*) *Next Offence*: Time-out. Yellow card to offender stating, 'This is a warning for delay of game'. Major Foul free position. Further similar offence may be penalised as a Major Foul with a red card (suspension) to offender.

(*d*) *Further offences*: Time-out. Red card to offender stating, 'This is a suspension for delay of game'. Major Foul free position.

(2) **Persistent Minor Fouls** (see Guideline below)

(*a*) *Team caution*: Time-out. Green card to captain stating, 'This is your team's caution for . . . (state reason)'. Minor Foul free position. Further similar offence may be penalised as a Major Foul with yellow card (warning) to offender.

(*b*) *Next Offence*: Time-out. Yellow card to offender stating, 'This is a warning for . . . (state reason)'. Major Foul free position. Further similar offence may be penalised as a Major Foul with a red card (suspension) to offender.

(*c*) *Further Offences*: Time-out. Red card to offender stating, 'This is a suspension for . . . (state reason)'. Major Foul free position.

Guideline: The Umpire may notice fouls occurring persistently due either to lack of skill, recklessness or an attempt to gain an unfair advantage. The penalty is awarded as appropriate to the offence, and a time-out is taken. A verbal caution is given to indicate that repetition of that foul by any members of that team may be more severely penalised. A green card is shown to the captain, ensuring that this caution has been acknowledged. Repetition of this foul may be penalised by awarding the penalty next in the order of severity shown, each successive foul incurring one increase in the penalty.

E. Misconduct and Suspensions

(1) A player must not:

(*a*) Conduct herself in a rough, dangerous or unsportsmanlike manner.

(*b*) Persistently cause infringement of the Rules.

(*c*) Deliberately endanger the safety of an opposing player.

(*d*) Exhibit any type of behaviour which in the Umpire's opinion amounts to misconduct.

(2) The penalty for violation of the Misconduct and Suspension Rule shall be the same as for all Major Fouls. The Umpire has the power to suspend from further participation in the game, and/or send from the field without any previous warning, a player, coach, or bench personnel

guilty of flagrant or repeated violation of the Rules, dissent, misconduct, or abusive language.

(3) (*a*) In addition to awarding a free position, the Umpire may give any number of verbal cautions. She may warn the offending player by showing a yellow card to the player and to the scorer. She will then, on further offence, suspend the player from further participation in that game. The suspension of a player will be noted by showing a red card.

(*b*) A suspended player may be replaced by a substitute but no player may enter the game except as provided in Rule 10-A-C.

(*c*) Time-out must be called to administer warnings and suspensions.

(*d*) In the event that a coach or team personnel is warned or suspended, the game is restarted within 30 seconds with a free position to the opponent nearest the ball when the play was stopped.

(*e*) If the coach or team personnel does not leave the field after the request by the Umpire, their team must forfeit the game. If that team is behind, the score stands, and if that team is ahead the score shall be 1–0.

(4) The coach and team personnel must remain outside the agreed boundary of the field. A coach or team personnel must not stand by or pass in front of the opponent's bench.

20. PENALTY FOR FOULS

The penalty for a foul is a free position. In the event of two players fouling simultaneously a throw is taken. For a Minor Field Foul the offending player is placed no closer than 4m (4.4yd) from the player taking the free position, in the direction from which she approached before committing the foul. For a Major Field Foul the offender will be placed 4m (4.4yd) behind the player taking the free position.

Free position placement of players

A. All players must stand. The Umpire indicates where the player taking the free position is to stand, and where the offending player is to stand.

(1) No player or her crosse is allowed within 4m (4.4yd) of the player taking the free position; if anyone is within this distance she must move to a position indicated by the Umpire.

(2) A free position must not be taken within 11m of the goal-line. The free position will be taken on a line which passes from the centre of the goal-line through the point where the foul occurred. No player or her crosse is allowed within 4m (4.4yd) of the player taking the free position; if anyone is within this distance she must move to a position indicated by the Umpire. The goalkeeper's free position is taken from within the goal-circle unless she has been fouled outside the circle. For a Minor

Foul within the 15m area by the defending team, a free position will be awarded to the attacking player at the 15m line with the offending player moved to 4m of free position.

(3) *Penalty lane* is a path to goal defined by parallel lines that extend the width of the goal-circle to the ball carrier. All players must clear the penalty lane of crosses and any parts of the body when a Major Foul is awarded within 11m of goal.

(4) The penalty for a dangerous shot shall be taken by the goalkeeper within the goal-circle.

(5) If the foul prevented an almost certain goal, the Umpire can order any player or players from between such free positions and the goal.

(6) If any defence players are in the free space to goal with the implementation of a foul they should not be penalised unless, after the word 'play', they make no effort to remove themselves to a legal position.

Note: This rule applies on a free position between 15m and 8m of the goal-circle for a Major Foul and for Minor Fouls in the critical scoring area.

B. Resumption of Play

(1) The player awarded the free position then takes the ball in her crosse and on the arm signal and the word 'play' from the Umpire, the game is restarted and player may run, pass or shoot.

C. Advantage Flag

(1) Advantage is a held whistle for a Major Foul within 15m of goal with a yellow signal flag thrown when an attack player is in a scoring play. The Umpire will call verbally 'flag'. If the scoring play is unsuccessful, the foul is then penalised (also in effect when an attack player in the 15m area is on a scoring play and a Major Foul is committed against an attack team-mate without the ball). The Umpire may, at any time following the foul, blow the whistle to halt potentially dangerous play.

Scoring play is a continuous effort by the attacking team to move the ball toward the goal and to complete a shot on goal.

The scoring play is over when:

(*a*) A shot is taken and the attacking team loses possession.

(*b*) The attacking team loses possession.

(*c*) The attacking team passes or carries the ball behind the level of the goal-line a second time.

(*d*) The attacking team stops the continuous attempt to score, or the player with the ball is forced by the defence to lose her forward momentum.

(*e*) The attacking team commits a Major Foul. A throw is taken when this occurs.

Penalty: If the scoring play is unsuccessful, the free position is taken where the foul occurred if between 11–15m of goal. If the foul occurred within the 11m area the free position will be taken at the closest hash mark on the 11m line and the penalty lane cleared. The free position is taken by the closest attack player, Major Foul against the closest defender.

21. UMPIRES, SCORERS AND TIMERS

A. The Umpire will:

(1) Prior to the game inspect the grounds, goals, balls, crosses, clothing, boots/shoes, jewellery and protective equipment and see that they are in accord with the Rules.

(2) See that the timers and scorers understand their responsibilities.

(3) Determine which Umpire will be in charge of the game. The Charge Umpire will effect the toss for choice of ends and discuss ball colour with the captains.

(4) Report goals to the scorer.

(5) Be available for questions from captains or coaches during half time – See Rule 7(*g*).

(6) Make the final decision, after consultation with captains, on whether to continue a game due to weather conditions or any other extenuating circumstances – See Rules 7(*f*) and 9-D.

(7) Make the game official by signing the scorebook.

(8) Umpire the game in accordance with the recommended procedures put forth by the IFWLA.

(9) Umpire, at the same goal, both halves of the game.

Note: The Umpire's decision is final and without appeal.

B. Held Whistle

An Umpire may refrain from enforcing any rule when it would penalise the non-offending team. If a player retains possession of the ball even though she has been fouled the Umpire should indicate that she has seen the foul by an arm signal and by saying 'Advantage —'.

C. The scorer will:

(1) Record the line-ups of both teams and substitutes prior to the game.

(2) Keep an accurate record of the goals scored and the time each was scored.

(3) Record the name and number of a substitute.

D. The timer will:

(1) Check with the Umpires prior to the beginning of the game to see what the length of the halves will be.

(2) Stop the clock at the whistle and arm signal after each goal – See Rule 9-B.

(3) Start the clock on the arm signal and verbal 'ready draw' at each draw.

(4) During the last 2 minutes of each half of the game, stop the clock on every whistle, then restart the clock on the Umpire's verbal and arm signals – See Rule 9-B-E.

(5) Indicate to the nearest Umpire when there are 30 seconds remaining in each half.

(6) Count out loud to the Umpire the last 10 seconds of each half, sounding the horn when the time is up.

(7) Stop the clock for any other circumstances only upon the time-out signal and whistle from the Umpire.

(8) Notify the Umpire when there are 2 minutes remaining in each half of the game.

(9) Let the Umpire know when 5 and 10 minutes have elapsed between halves.

Arm Signals for Umpires

Blocking: Place open hands on the hips and move them to touch hips with in and out motion.

Charging: Place right hand behind head.

Empty crosse check: Use the right hand with clapping motion on the left hand. Clap and hold for a held crosse.

Free position or possession of ball on out-of-bounds: Indicates the direction with one arm raised horizontally towards the goal of the team in possession.

Goal: Arms are raised above the head and then turn and point both arms horizontally toward the centre of the field.

Goal-circle foul: Point to goal-circle and then indicate direction of free position.

Head whistle: Arm raised horizontally shoulder level in the direction of the offended player's goal.

Illegal ball off the body: Indicate by pointing to the body part that touched the ball.

Illegal check on the body: Make a chopping motion with one hand on body part where contact was made.

No goal: With the arms extended toward the ground, swing them out and in so that they cross each other.

Obstruction of free space to goal: Arms held in front of the body with palms toward face, with one hand closer to the face, hands up, palms in a line about 6in toward the face.

Pushing or body contact: Make a pushing motion with two arms out in front of the body.

Re-draw: Place arms fully extended horizontally in front of the body – begin with hands together and extend them up and out with a quick motion.

Rough-check: Use the arm to make a large chop motion against the wrist of the opposite arm.

Substitution: Making a beckoning motion with one arm to entering player.

Ten-second count for substitution and ball in goal-circle: Make a small chop motion with one arm for each second counted.

Time-in: Hand open above the head with arm fully extended; then drop the arm in a chopping motion to start the clock.

Time-out: Turn towards the timer and cross fully extended arms at the wrist above the head.

22. DEFINITIONS

(1) Clear space indicates the space between players which is free of crosses or any parts of the body.

(2) Creeping is movement by a field player when she is to stand after a whistle is blown to indicate a stoppage of play for any reason.

(3) Free space to goal is a path to goal as defined by two lines extending from the ball to the outside of the goal circle. *Proviso*: No defence player will be penalised if positioned behind the extension of the goal-line.

(4) A player may be said to be actively marking an opponent if she is within a stick and arm length extended (or approximately 2m) of her opponent.

(5) Pick is a technique in which a player without the ball, who by her positioning forces the opponent to take another route.

(6) Swiping is the swinging of a crosse at an opponent's crosse or body is struck.

(7) Penalty lane is a path to goal defined by parallel lines that extend the width of the goal-circle to the ball carrier.

Reprinted by permission of the All-England Women's Lacrosse Association. Manufacturer's specifications for the crosse, ball, goals and nets, as well as Special Recommendations, are given in full in the IFWLA International Lacrosse Rules, which can be obtained from the All-England Women's Lacrosse Association.

Netball

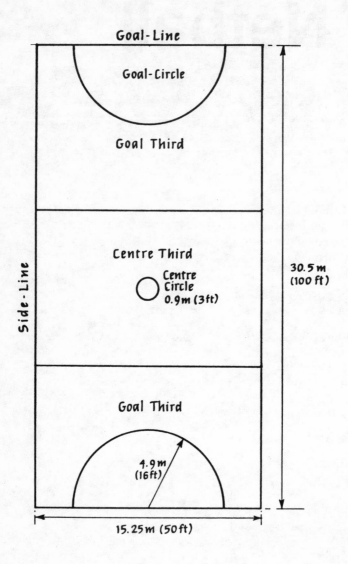

The Court

Goal-Line

Goal-Circle

Goal Third

Centre Third

Centre
Circle
0.9m (3ft)

30.5 m
(100 ft)

Side-Line

Goal Third

4.9m
(16ft)

15.25 m (50 ft)

Netball

THE GAME
Netball is an International Sport. It is played by two teams of 7 players and is based on throwing and catching. Goals are scored within a defined area by throwing the ball into a ring attached to a 3.05m (10ft) high post.

I. ORGANISATION OF THE GAME

1. Equipment
1.1 *Court*
1.1.1 The court shall have a firm surface and shall be 30.5m (100ft) long and 15.25m (50ft) wide. The longer sides shall be called side-lines and the shorter sides goal-lines.

1.1.2 The court shall be divided into three equal parts – a centre third and two goal thirds – by two transverse lines drawn parallel to the goal-lines.

1.1.3 A semicircle with a radius of 4.9m (16ft) and with its centre at the mid-point of the goal-line, shall be drawn in each goal third. This shall be called the goal circle.

1.1.4 A circle, 0.9m (3ft) in diameter shall mark the centre of the court. This shall be called the centre circle.

1.1.5 All lines are part of the court, and shall be not more than 50mm (2in) wide.

1.2 *Goalposts*
1.2.1 A goalpost 3.05m (10ft) high shall be placed at the mid-point of each goal-line. A metal ring 380mm (15in) in diameter shall project horizontally 150mm (6in) from the top of the post, the attachment to allow 150mm (6in) between the post and the near side of the ring. The

ring shall be of steel rod 15mm ($\frac{5}{8}$in) in diameter, fitted with a net clearly visible and open at both ends. Both rings and net are considered to be part of the goalpost. If padding is used on the goalpost it shall not be more than 25mm (1in) thick.

1.2.2 The post, which shall be 65mm (2.5in)–100mm (4in) in diameter or up to 100mm (4in) square, may be inserted in a socket in the ground or may be supported by a metal base which shall not project on the court.

1.3 *Ball*

The ball shall be a netball or an association football size 5, and shall measure between 690mm (27in) and 710mm (28in) in circumference and weigh between 400g (14oz) and 450g (16oz). The ball may be of leather, rubber or similar material.

1.4 *Players*

1.4.1 Shoes or boots may be worn. They shall be of lightweight material. Spiked soles are not allowed.

1.4.2 Registered playing uniforms, which shall include initials of playing positions, shall be worn at all times. Playing initials shall be worn both front and back above the waist and shall be 200mm (8in) high.

1.4.3 No sharp adornment or item of jewellery, except a wedding ring, shall be worn. If a wedding ring is worn, it shall be taped.

1.4.4 Fingernails shall be cut short.

2. Duration of Game

2.1 The game shall consist of four quarters of 15 minutes each, with an interval of 3 minutes between the first-second and third-fourth quarters and with a maximum of 10 minutes at half-time. The mean average time as requested by the respective teams shall determine the length of the interval at half time. An interval may be extended by the Umpires to deal with any emergency. Teams shall change ends each quarter.

2.2 Where any one team plays two or more matches in one day, or where time is limited, the game shall consist of two halves of 20 minutes each with a maximum of 5 minutes' interval at half-time. The mean average time as requested by the respective teams shall determine the length of the interval at half-time. Teams shall change ends at half-time.

2.3 Playing time lost for an accident or any other cause must be noted and added to that quarter or half of the game. In no case shall extra time be allowed except to take a penalty shot.

NETBALL   647

2.4 In certain climatic conditions the duration of the game shall be predetermined by the countries concerned.

3. Officials

The Officials are: umpires, scorers, timekeepers. The Team Officials are: coach, manager, captain. All umpires, official scorers and official timekeepers at international matches shall be women.

3.1 *Umpires*

3.1.1 There shall be two Umpires who shall have control of the game and give decisions. They shall umpire according to the rules and decide on any matter not covered by the rules. The decision of the Umpire shall be final and shall be given without appeal.

3.1.2 The Umpire's whistle shall start and stop the game. Starting or restarting the game after an interval shall be controlled by the Umpire into whose half the play is to be directed.

3.1.3 After the players have taken their positions on the court, the Umpires shall toss for goal-end. The Umpire winning the toss shall control that half of the court designated the northern half.

3.1.4 Umpires shall wear clothes distinct from those of the players and preferably white or cream in colour. Suitable shoes shall be worn.

3.1.5 Each Umpire shall:

(i) Control and give decisions only in one half of the court unless appealed to by the other Umpire for a decision in the other half and be ready for such an appeal at all times. For this purpose the length of the court is divided in half across the centre from side-line to side-line.

(ii) Umpire in the same half of the court throughout the game.

(iii) Re-start the game after all goals scored in the half being controlled.

(iv) Give decisions for the throw-in for one goal-line and for the whole of one side-line and shall call 'play' when all other players are on the court. The Umpire responsible for the side-line is responsible for making decisions related to infringements by the player throwing in and the defending opponents.

(v) Keep outside the court except when it is necessary to enter it to secure a clear view of play, or to indicate the point from which a penalty must be taken, or to take a toss-up. If the ball strikes the Umpire during play, or if an Umpire interferes with the movements of the players, play does not cease unless one team has been unduly penalised, in which case a free pass shall be awarded to that team.

(vi) When a toss-up has been awarded, appeal where necessary to the other Umpire to take the toss-up and that Umpire shall control points listed in section IV – Rule 18.4 (Toss-up 18.4.2–18.4.6).

(vii) Move along the side-line and behind the goal-line to see play and make decisions.

(viii) Refrain from blowing the whistle to penalise an infringement when by so doing the non-offending team would be placed at a disadvantage. An Umpire *may* call 'advantage' to indicate an infringement has been observed and not penalised. Having blown the whistle for an infringement the penalty must be taken.

(ix) Not criticise or coach any team while a match is in progress.

(x) Check that during a stoppage for injury or illness, other players remain on court. During this stoppage coaching is not permitted.

(xi) State the infringement and penalty and *may* use hand signals to clarify decisions.

3.2 *Scorers*
3.2.1 There shall be two scorers who shall:

(i) Keep a written record of the score together with a record of the centre pass.

(ii) Record each goal as it is scored unless notified to the contrary by the Umpire. This constitutes the official score of the game.

(iii) Keep a record of all unsuccessful shots.

(iv) Call the centre pass if appealed to by the Umpire, and inform the Umpire immediately if the incorrect centre pass is indicated.

3.2.2 If the Umpires disagree with the scorers they call for time to be taken while both Umpires and scorers consult the scoresheet.

3.3 *Timekeepers*
3.3.1 There shall be a timekeeper who shall:

(i) Take time when the game is started by the Umpire's whistle and shall signal the end of each quarter or half to the Umpire.

(ii) Take time when instructed by the Umpire who shall blow the whistle to stop play. To restart play the Umpire shall signal to the timekeeper and blow the whistle for play to be resumed.

(iii) Ensure that when instructed by the Umpire time lost for a stoppage is played in the quarter or half in which this occurs.

3.4 *Captains*
3.4.1 The Captains shall:

(i) Toss for choice of goal or first centre pass and notify the Umpires of the results.

(ii) During an interval or after stoppage for injury or illness notify the Umpires and the opposing captain that they have changed the position of players whether or not a substitute is involved.

3.4.2 They have the right to approach an Umpire during an interval or after the game for clarification of any Rule.

3.4.3 During an interval appeal to the Umpire for extra time to deal with an emergency affecting a member of the team and if the appeal is granted notify the opposing captain of the amount of time that is to be added to the interval.

Penalty for 3.4.1(ii): A free pass shall be awarded the first time a player enters an area which was off-side in relation to that player's previous playing area.

This pass shall be taken:
(i) From the place in the off-side area where the infringement occurred:
(ii) By a player allowed in that area;
(iii) After time has been allowed for the captain of the other team to rearrange playing positions if so wished.

The player concerned shall be permitted to remain in the position now being played.

4. The Team

4.1 The game is designed for single-sex competition.

4.2 A team shall consist of 7 players whose playing positions shall be:
Goal Shooter (GS)
Goal Attack (GA)
Wing Attack (WA)
Centre (C)
Wing Defence (WD)
Goal Defence (GD)
Goalkeeper (GK)

4.3 Three substitutes only are permitted in any one game. These may be used to replace players on court in the event of injury, illness, or during an interval.

4.4 No team may take the court with fewer than 5 players.

5. Late Arrivals

5.1 No player arriving after play has started is allowed to replace a player who has filled the position of the late-comer.

5.2 Late arrivals may not enter the game while play is in progress, but after notifying the Umpires may take the court:
(i) After a goal has been scored. In this case the player must play in a position left vacant in the team.

(ii) Immediately following an interval.

(iii) After a stoppage for injury or illness.

Penalty for 5.2(i) and 5.2(ii): A free pass to the opposing team where the infringer was standing, and the infringer shall leave the court until the next goal is scored or until after the next interval.

6. Substitution

6.1 Substitution on court is allowed for up to 3 players in any one game in the event of injury, illness, or during an interval. At the time a substitution is made playing positions may be changed.

6.2 It is the responsibility of the team captain to notify the Umpire and the opposing captain if substitutions and/or changes in playing positions are made.

6.3 Sufficient time shall be allowed for the opposing team to make substitutions and/or changes in playing positions if desired.

6.4 If a substitute is played the original player may take no further part in the game.

Penalty for 6.2: A free pass shall be awarded the first time a player enters an area which was off-side in relation to that player's previous playing area.

This pass shall be taken:

(i) From the place in the off-side area where the infringement occurred:

(ii) By a player allowed in that area:

(iii) after time has been allowed for the captain of the other team to rearrange playing positions if so wished.

The player concerned shall be permitted to remain in the position now being played.

7. Stoppages

7.1 Play may be stopped for injury or illness. When a player is injured or ill a stoppage of up to 5 minutes is allowed from when time is called to decide whether the injured or ill player is fit to continue play. The decision shall be left to the team's officials.

7.2 Play may be stopped by an Umpire for any emergency relating to:

(i) The equipment, court, weather or interference by outside agencies.

(i) A player's person or clothing.

(iii) Officials officiating for the match.

7.3 To stop play the Umpire shall blow the whistle and instruct the timekeeper to take time. The Umpire shall decide the length of time for the stoppage and shall ensure that play is restarted as soon as possible.

7.4 To restart play the Umpire shall signal to the timekeeper and blow the whistle for play to be resumed.

7.5 The game is continued from the spot where the ball was when play stopped other than when:
  (i) The ball is out of court, in which case a throw-in is taken.
  (ii) The Umpire is unable to say who was in possession of the ball or the ball was on the ground when play was stopped, in which case a toss-up is taken between any two opposing players allowed in that area, as near as possible to the spot where the ball was when play ceased.
(iii) The stoppage is due to obstruction or contact, in which case the infringement is penalised where it occurred and play continues.

7.6 During a stoppage for injury or illness, other players remain on court. During this stoppage coaching is not permitted.

7.7 After injury or illness when no substitution is made for a player unable to resume play, the injured or sick player may return to the vacant position after notifying an Umpire of her intention to return to the game.

II. AREAS OF PLAY

8. Players' Areas
8.1 The playing area for each player is as follows and as shown in the diagram on page 652:

Goal Shooter – 1, 2
Goal Attack – 1, 2, 3
Wing Attack –   2, 3
Centre –   2, 3, 4
Wing Defence –   3, 4
Goal Defence –   3, 4, 5
Goalkeeper –   4, 5

Lines bounding each area are included as part of that area.

8.2 Positions of players may be changed only:
  (i) During an interval.
  (ii) After stoppage caused by an injury or illness

Playing Areas

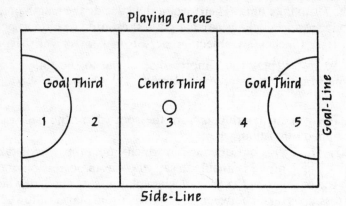

Side-Line

Penalty: See Penalty for 3.4.1(ii).

9. Off-side
9.1 *One Player Off-side*
9.1.1 A player with or without the ball shall be off-side if any area other than the playing area for that designated position is entered.

9.1.2 A player may reach over and take the ball from an off-side area or may lean on the ball provided no body contact is made with the ground.

Penalty: A free-pass to the opposing team where the infringement occurred.

9.2 *Simultaneous Off-side*
When any two opposing players go off-side at the same moment:

(i) If neither makes any contact with the ball, they are not penalised and play continues.

(ii) If one of them is in possession of the ball or touches it, a toss-up is taken between those two players in their own area of play except as provided for under 9.2(iv).

(iii) If both of them are in possession of the ball or touch it, a toss-up is taken between those two players in their own area of play except as provided for under 9.2(iv);

(iv) If one player who is allowed only in the goal third goes off-side into the centre third, and an opposing player simultaneously goes off-side into the goal third, one or both in contact with the ball, a toss-up is taken in the centre third between any two opposing players allowed in that area.

10. Out of Court

10.1 *The ball* is out of court when:
  (i) It touches the ground outside the court.
  (ii) It touches an object or person in contact with the ground outside court.
  (iii) It is held by a player in contact with the ground, an object or a person outside the court.
Penalty for 10.1: A throw-in to the team opposing the one who last had contact with the ball, to be taken where the ball crossed the line.

10.2 A *ball* which hits any part of the goalpost and rebounds into play is not out of court.

10.3 *A player in contact with the ball* is out of court when:
  (i) The ground outside the court is touched.
  (ii) Any object or person outside the court is touched.

10.4 *A player having no contact with the ball* may stand or move out of court, but before playing the ball the player must re-enter the court and no longer have contact with the ground out of court.
Penalty for 10.3 and 10.4: A throw-in to the opposing team where the ball crossed the line.

10.5 Defending actions may only be attempted by players standing on court or jumping from court.
Penalty for 10.5: Penalty pass or penalty pass or shot opposite the spot where the infringer attempted to defend.

10.6 If the ball is caught simultaneously by two opposing players one of whom lands out of court, a toss-up is taken on court between those two players opposite to the point where the player was out of court.

10.7 A player who has left the court to retrieve a ball or to take a throw-in must be permitted to re-enter the court directly.
Penalty for 10.7: Penalty pass or penalty pass or shot to the opposing team where the infringement occurred.

III. CONDUCT OF THE GAME

11. Positioning of Players for Start of Play

11.1 The Centre in possession of the ball shall stand with both feet within the centre circle. The line is considered part of the centre circle.

11.2 The opposing centre shall be in the centre third and free to move.

11.3 All other players shall be in the goal third which is part of their playing area and free to move. It is the responsibility of the Umpire to check the players' positions before blowing the whistle.

11.4 No other player is allowed in the centre third until the whistle has been blown to start the game.

Penalty

1. If one player enters the centre third before the whistle is blown, a free pass to the opposing team where the infringement occurred.

2. When any two opposing players simultaneously enter the centre third before the whistle has been blown:

(i) If neither makes contact with the ball, they are not penalised and play continues.

(ii) If one of them touches or catches the ball, a toss-up is taken between those two players near to where the infringement occurred.

12. Start of Play

12.1 *Organisation of the Start of Play*

12.1.1 The Umpire shall blow the whistle to start and restart play.

12.1.2 The pass made by a Centre in response to the Umpire's whistle at the start and restart of play shall be designated a centre pass.

12.1.3 Play shall be started and restarted, after every goal scored and after each interval, by a centre pass taken alternately by the two Centres throughout the game.

12.1.4 If, at a centre pass, the ball is still in the Centre's hands when the Umpire's whistle is blown to signal the end of a quarter or half, that team will take the pass after the interval.

12.2 *Controlling the Centre Pass*

12.2.1 When the whistle is blown the Centre in possession of the ball shall throw it within 3 seconds and shall obey the Footwork Rule.

12.2.2 The centre pass shall be caught or touched by a member of the attacking team who is standing or who lands within the centre third. A player who lands with the first foot, or on both feet simultaneously, wholly within the centre third, is judged to have received the ball in that third. That player's subsequent throw shall be considered to have been made from the centre third. A player who lands on both feet simulta-neously, with one foot wholly within the centre third and the other wholly within the goal third, is judged to have received the ball in the goal third.

12.2.3 If a member of the team taking the centre pass catches the ball in the goal third without having touched it in the centre third, a free pass shall be awarded to the opposing team, to be taken in the goal third close to the point where the ball crossed the line.

12.2.4 If a member of the opposing team touches or catches the centre pass in the centre third, or in the goal third, or with feet astride the transverse line, the Advantage Rule shall apply.

12.2.5 If the ball from the centre pass goes untouched over the side-line bounding the centre third, a throw-in is awarded to the opposing team where the ball crossed the line.

13. Playing the Ball

13.1 A player may:

(i) Catch the ball with one or both hands.

(ii) Gain or regain control of the ball if it rebounds from the goalpost.

(iii) Bat or bounce the ball to another player without first having possession of it.

(iv) Tip the ball in an uncontrolled manner once or more than once and then.

(*a*) Catch the ball; or

(*b*) Direct the ball to another player.

(v) Having batted the ball once, either catch the ball or direct the ball to another player.

(vi) Having bounced the ball once, either catch the ball or direct the ball to another player.

(vii) Roll the ball to herself to gain possession.

(viii) Fall while holding the ball but must regain footing and throw within 3 seconds of receiving the ball.

(ix) Lean on the ball to prevent going off-side.

(x) Lean on the ball on court to gain balance.

(xi) Jump from a position in contact with the court and play the ball outside the court, provided that neither the player nor the ball makes contact with the ground, or any object or person outside the court while the ball is being played.

13.2 A player may not:

(i) Deliberately kick the ball (if a ball which is thrown accidentally hits the leg of a player it is not a kick).

(ii) Strike the ball with a fist.

(iii) Deliberately fall on the ball to get it.

(iv) Attempt to gain possession of the ball while lying, sitting or kneeling on the ground.

(v) Throw the ball while lying, sitting or kneeling on the ground.

(vi) Use the goalpost as a support in recovering the ball going out of court.

(vii) Use the goalpost as a means of regaining balance, or in any other way for any other purpose.

Penalty: Free pass to the opposing team where the infringement occurred.

13.3 A player who has caught or held the ball shall play it or shoot for goal within 3 seconds. To play the ball a player may:

(i) Throw it in any manner and in any direction to another player;

(ii) Bounce it with one or both hands in any direction to another player.

13.4 A player who has caught or held the ball may not:

(i) Roll the ball to another player.

(ii) Throw the ball and play it before it has been touched by another player.

(iii) Toss the ball into the air and replay it.

(iv) Drop the ball and replay it.

(v) Bounce the ball and replay it.

(vi) Replay the ball after an unsuccessful shot at goal unless it has touched some part of the goalpost.

Penalty: Free pass to the opposing team where the infringement occurred.

13.5 *Passing Distances*
13.5.1 *Short Pass*

(i) On the court: At the moment the ball is passed there must be room for a third player to move between *the hands* of the thrower and those of the receiver.

(ii) At the throw-in: At the moment the ball is passed there must be room on the Court between *the hands* of the thrower and those of the receiver for a third player to attempt an interception.

Penalty: Free pass to the opposing team where the ball was caught.

13.5.2 *Over a Third*

(i) The ball may not be thrown over a complete third without being touched or caught by a player who, at the time of touching or catching the ball, is wholly within that third or who landed in that third.

(ii) The player who lands with the first foot wholly within the correct third is judged to have received the ball in that third. The subsequent throw shall be considered to have been made from the third in which the player first landed.

(iii) The player who lands on both feet simultaneously with one foot wholly within the correct third and the other in the incorrect third shall be penalised.

Penalty: Free pass to the opposing team taken just beyond the second line that the ball has crossed, except where the ball thrown from the centre third passes out of court over the goal-line, when a throw-in shall be taken.

14. Footwork

14.1 A player may receive the ball with one foot grounded or jump to catch and land on one foot and then:

(i) Step with the other foot in any direction, lift the landing foot and throw or shoot before this foot is regrounded.

(ii) Step with the other foot in any direction any number of times, pivoting on the landing foot. The pivoting foot may be lifted but the player must throw or shoot before regrounding it.

(iii) Jump from the landing foot on to the other foot and jump again, but must throw the ball or shoot before regrounding either foot.

(iv) Step with the other foot and jump, but must throw the ball or shoot before regrounding either foot.

14.2 A player may receive the ball while both feet are grounded, or jump to catch and land on both feet simultaneously and then:

(i) Step with either foot in any direction, lift the other foot and throw or shoot before this foot is regrounded;

(ii) Step with either foot in any direction any number of times pivoting on the other. The pivoting foot may be lifted but the player must throw or shoot before regrounding it.

(iii) Jump from both feet on to either foot, but must throw or shoot before regrounding the other foot.

(iv) Step with either foot and jump but must throw the ball or shoot before regrounding either foot.

14.3 A player in possession of the ball may not:

(i) Drag or slide the landing foot.

(ii) Hop on either foot.

(iii) Jump from both feet and land on both feet unless the ball has been released before landing.

Penalty: A free pass to the opposing team where the infringement occurred.

15. Scoring a Goal

15.1 A goal is scored when the ball is thrown or batted over and completely through the ring by Goal Shooter or Goal Attack from any point within the goal circle including the lines bounding the goal circle:

(i) If another player throws the ball through the ring no goal is scored and play continues.

(ii) If a defending player deflects a shot for goal and the ball then passes over and completely through the ring a goal is scored.

(iii) Goal Shooter or Goal Attack may shoot for goal or pass if the ball is won at a toss-up in the goal circle.

(iv) If the whistle for an interval or 'time' is blown before the ball has passed completely through the ring, no goal is scored.

(v) If the whistle for an interval or 'time' is blown *after* a penalty pass or shot has been awarded to Goal Shooter or Goal Attack in the goal circle, a penalty shot shall be completed.

15.2 In taking a shot for goal a player shall:

(i) Have no contact with the ground outside the goal circle either during the catching of the ball or whilst holding it. It is not contact with the ground to lean on the ball, but if this happens behind the goal-line the ball is considered to be out of court.

(ii) Shoot within 3 seconds of catching or holding the ball;

(iii) Obey the Footwork Rule.

Penalty: A free-pass to the opposing team in the goal circle where the infringement occurred.

15.3 A defending player may not cause the goalpost to move so as to interfere with the shot at goal.

Penalty: Penalty pass or shot to the opposing team to be taken:

(i) From where the infringer was standing unless this places the non-offending team at a disadvantage.

(ii) If the infringer was out of court, on court near where the infringer was standing.

16. Obstruction

16.1 An attempt to intercept or defend the ball *may* be made by a defending player if the distance on the ground is not less than 0.9m (3ft) from a player in possession of the ball. When the ball is received, this distance is measured as follows:

(i) If the player's landing, grounded or pivoting foot remains on the ground, the distance is measured from that foot to the nearer foot of the defending player.

(ii) If the player's landing, grounded or pivoting foot is lifted, the distance is measured from the spot on the ground from which the foot was lifted, to the nearer foot of the defending player.

(iii) If the player is standing or lands on both feet simultaneously and remains grounded on both feet, the distance is measured from whichever is the nearer foot of that player to the nearer foot of the defending player;

(iv) If the player is standing or lands on both feet simultaneously and either foot is lifted, the other foot is considered to be the grounded foot from which the 0.9m (3ft) distance is measured.

16.2 From the correct distance, a defending player *may* attempt to intercept or defend the ball:

(i) By jumping towards the player with the ball, but if the landing is within 0.9m (3ft) of that player and interferes with the throwing or shooting motion, obstruction occurs.

(ii) If the player with the ball steps forward to lessen the distance of 0.9m (3ft) between them.

16.3 A player *may* be within 0.9m (3ft) of an opponent in possession of the ball providing no effort is made to defend and there is no interference with that opponent's throwing or shooting action.

16.4 From the correct distance, a defending player *may not* attempt to intercept or defend the ball by stepping towards an opponent with the ball.

16.5 *Obstruction of a player not in possession of the ball*

16.5.1 A player is obstructing if within a distance of 0.9m (3ft) (measured on the ground) from an opponent without the ball, any movements are employed by that player (whether attacking or defending) which take the arms away from the body, other than those involved in natural body balance. Within this distance a player is not obstructing if the arms are outstretched:

(i) To catch, deflect or intercept a pass or feint pass.

(ii) To obtain a rebound from an unsuccessful shot at goal.

(iii) Momentarily to signal for a pass, or to indicate the intended direction of movement.

16.6. *Obstruction by intimidation*

When a player with or without the ball intimidates an opponent it is obstruction.

Penalty for 16.1 to 16.6: Penalty pass or penalty pass or shot where the infringer is standing except where this places the non-offending team at a disadvantage, when the penalty shall be taken where the obstructed player was standing.

16.7 *Defending a player who is out of court*
16.7.1 A player may defend an opponent who has chosen to go out of court provided that the defending player does not leave the court or own playing area in order to defend.
Penalty: A penalty pass or penalty pass or shot from the point where the infringing player leaves the court.
16.7.2 A player who goes out of court to collect a ball, to take a throw-in, or for any other valid reason, must be allowed back into the area of play near to the point at which the player left the court or took the throw-in. Any opponent attempting to defend is penalised.
Penalty: A penalty pass or penalty pass or shot on court immediately opposite the point where the obstruction occurred.

16.8 *Obstruction by a player from out of court*
16.8.1 A player who is standing out of court may not attempt to defend a player who is on the court.
Penalty: A penalty pass or penalty pass or shot on the court opposite the point where the defending player is standing.

17. Contact
17.1 *Personal Contact*
17.1.1 No player shall come into personal contact with an opponent in such a manner as to interfere with the opponent's play either accidentally or deliberately.
17.1.2 In an effort to get free a player:
   (i) Shall not push an opponent in any way.
   (ii) Trip or knock an opponent in any way.
17.1.3 In an effort to contact the ball a player shall not bump or rush into an opponent.
17.1.4 In an effort to defend, a player shall not:
   (i) Keep an elbow against an opponent.
   (ii) Hold an opponent; this includes feeling to keep near an opponent.
   (iii) Push an opponent.
   (iv) Charge an opponent; that is, when jumping bump against a player.
17.1.5 Whether attempting to get free, or to defend, a player is responsible for any personal contact.
   (i) If taking up a position so near an opponent that contact is inevitable.

(ii) If moving so quickly into the path of a moving player that contact cannot be avoided.

17.1.6 A player shall not contact another on any other occasion or in any other way in such a manner as to interfere with the opponent's play.

17.2 *Contact with the ball*

17.2.1 A player, while holding the ball, shall not touch or push an opposing player with it in such a manner as to interfere with that opponent's play.

17.2.2 A player shall not, either accidentally or deliberately, place a hand or hands on, or remove from an opponent's possession, a ball held by an opposing player.

17.2.3 Where 17.2.1 and 17.2.2 occur simultaneously a toss-up is taken between those two players.

Penalty for 17.1 to 17.2.2: Penalty pass or penalty pass or shot where the infringer is standing except where this places the non-offending team at a disadvantage, when the penalty shall be taken where the contacted player was standing.

IV. CONDUCTING PENALTIES

The penalties awarded for the breaking of the Rules are:

Free Pass
Penalty Pass or Shot
Throw-in
Toss-up

18. General Rules

for the taking of penalties are:

(i) A penalty for an infringement on court is taken where the infringement occurred except:

(*a*) Where the Advantage Rule applies, i.e. the Umpire shall refrain from blowing the whistle to penalise an infringement when by so doing the non-offending team would be placed at a disadvantage.

(*b*) As provided for under Penalty for Rules 16 and 17, Obstruction and Contact.

(ii) The Umpire indicates the correct place.

(iii) The penalties, with the exception of the toss-up, are awarded to a team. Any member of the opposing team may take the penalty if allowed in the area where the penalty is awarded.

(iv) The player taking the penalty must throw the ball within 3 seconds after taking up a position at the correct place and being in possession of the ball.

(v) In the taking of a free pass, penalty pass or shot or throw-in, the Footwork Rule applies as though the foot placed at the point indicated were equivalent to the landing foot in a one-foot landing or to receiving the ball with one foot grounded.

(vi) If the player taking a free pass, or penalty pass or shot, infringes the rules set out in (iv) and (v) above, a free pass is awarded to the opposing team.

(vii) If a player taking a throw-in infringes (iii) to (v) above, a throw-in is awarded to the opposing team.

18.1 *Free Pass*

18.1.1 A free pass is awarded for infringements of the Rules on the court with the exception of the Rules of Obstruction, Contact, simultaneous offences by two opposing players and interference with the goalpost.

18.1.2 When a free pass is awarded, the ball may be thrown by any player in the opposing team allowed in that area, but the ball may not be thrown over a complete third of the court without being touched or caught by a player.

18.2 *Penalty Pass or Shot*

18.2.1 A penalty pass or a penalty pass or shot is awarded for infringement of the Rules of Obstruction and Contact.

18.2.2 A player penalised for Obstruction and Contact must stand beside and away from the thrower taking the penalty and must make no attempt to take part in the play until the ball has left the thrower's hands. If the infringer moves before the ball has left the thrower's hands the penalty shall be retaken unless the pass or shot is successful.

18.2.3 The penalty shall be taken from where the infringer was standing except where this puts the non-offending team at a disadvantage, when the penalty shall be taken where the obstructed or contacted player was standing.

18.2.4 Any player allowed in the area may take the penalty.

18.2.5 (i) An attempt to intercept the penalty pass or shot may be made by any opposing player other than the offender.

(ii) If an opponent obstructs or contacts the thrower during the taking of the penalty pass or shot, a penalty pass or shot shall be awarded at the spot where the second infringer was standing unless this places the non-offending team at a disadvantage.

(iii) Both the original and second offenders must stand beside and away from the thrower taking the penalty and make no attempt to take part in the play until the ball has left the thrower's hands.

18.2.6 When two members of a team simultaneously obstruct or contact a member of the opposing team, each offender shall stand beside and away from the thrower taking the penalty. They must make no attempt to take part in the play until the ball has left the thrower's hands.

18.2.7 A Goal Shooter or Goal Attack taking a penalty pass in the goal circle, may either pass or shoot for goal.

18.3 *Throw-in*

18.3.1 When the ball goes out of court, it shall be put into play by a member of the team opposing either:

(i) The player on court who last had contact with the ball.

(ii) The player who received the ball with any part of her touching the ground outside the court.

18.3.2 The player throwing the ball in shall:

(i) Stand outside the court and place one foot up to but not on the line at the point where the Umpire indicates that the ball has crossed the line.

(ii) Wait for the Umpire to say 'play' when all other players are on the Court.

(iii) Throw within 3 seconds of the Umpire calling 'play'.

(iv) Not enter the court until the ball has been thrown.

(v) Throw into the nearest third of the court from behind a goal-line, or the nearest or adjacent third from behind a side-line.

(vi) Throw only from behind a line bounding her own playing area. If using the Footwork Rule the player must remain behind this area until she has released the ball.

(vii) Apply the Footwork Rule as in Section IV: Conducting Penalties – Rule 18: General Rules (v).

Penalties for infringement occurring at the throw-in:

1. By the thrower – a throw-in is awarded to the opposing team at the spot where the infringement occurred except under (v) above when the penalty for breaking the 'over a third' Rule applies.

2. When a player obstructs or contacts during a throw-in, a penalty pass or penalty pass or shot is awarded on court.

3. If the ball fails to enter the court the penalty throw-in shall be taken by the opposing team from the original throw-in point.

4. When the ball from a throw-in goes out of court without being touched, a throw-in shall be taken by the opposing team from behind the point where the ball last went out.

5. If the ball is sent out of court simultaneously by two players in opposing teams or the Umpire cannot decide who touched the ball last, there shall be a toss-up opposite the point where the ball went out – refer Rule 18.4.7(ii).

18.4 *Toss-up*

18.4.1 A Toss-up puts the ball into play when:

(i) Opposing players gain simultaneous possession of the ball with either or both hands.

(ii) Opposing players simultaneously knock the ball out of court.

(iii) Opposing players are involved and the Umpire is unable to determine the last player to touch the ball before it goes out of court.

(iv) Opposing players are simultaneously off-side one in possession of or touching the ball.

(v) Opposing players make simultaneous contact which interferes with play.

(vi) After an accident the Umpires unable to say who had the ball, or the ball was on the ground when play stopped.

18.4.2 The toss-up is taken on court between the two opposing players concerned as near as possible to the place where the incident occurred.

18.4.3 The two players shall stand facing each other and their own goal-ends with arms straight and hands to sides, but feet in any position. There shall be a distance of 0.9m (3ft) between the nearer foot of one player and that of her opponent. They shall not move from that position until the whistle is blown. If one player moves too soon, a free pass is awarded to the opposing team.

18.4.4 The Umpire shall release the ball midway between the two players from just below the shoulder level of the shorter player's normal standing position. Momentarily, the Umpire shall be stationary and shall hold the ball in the palm of one hand and shall flick it vertically not more than 600mm (2ft) in the air as the whistle is blown.

18.4.5 The ball may be caught, or it may be batted in any direction except directly at the opposing player. All other players may stand or move anywhere within their playing area as long as they do not interfere with the toss-up.

18.4.6 Goal Shooter or Goal Attack may shoot for goal or pass if the ball is won at a toss-up in the goal circle.

18.4.7 When the toss-up cannot be taken where the incident occurred because of the boundaries involved, the following applies:

(i) Where the incident involves two opposing players across a line dividing areas one of which is common to both players, the toss-up is taken between those two players in the common area.

(ii) Where the incident involves two opposing players from adjoining playing areas across a transverse line and no area is common to both, the toss-up is taken in the centre third between any two opposing players allowed in that area.

(iii) When two opposing players simultaneously knock the ball out of court over a line bounding an area which is not common to both, the toss-up is taken between any two opposing players allowed in that area, on court opposite the point where the the ball crossed the line.

V. DISCIPLINE

1. The breaking of Rules and/or the employment of any action nnot covered by the wording of the Rules, in a manner contrary to the spirit of the game, is not permitted. This includes:

(i) The breaking of rules:

(*a*) Between the scoring of a goal and the restart of play.

(*b*) Between a ball going out of court and the throw-in.

(*c*) Between the awarding and taking of any penalty on court.

Penalty for (i): Immediately the play restarts, the Umpire shall penalise the infringement unless the non-offending team is placed at a disadvantage.

(ii) The deliberate delaying of play.

Penalty for (ii): Free pass unless the non-offending team is placed at a disadvantage.

(iii) Deliberate action to prevent a player from re-entering the Court after throwing in or retrieving a ball.

Penalty for (iii): Penalty pass or penalty pass or shot where the infringer was standing.

An Umpire may:

(i) Order a player to leave the court, but only when sure that the ordinary penalty is sufficient and, except in extreme cases, only after a warning.

(ii) Stand a player off the court for a specified part of the game, e.g. until the next goal is scored, until the next interval or for the rest of the game.

When a player is suspended, that player may not be replaced.

In the event of a Centre being suspended, that team may move only *one* player to allow play to continue.

That player shall continue to play as Centre until the next interval. At the end of the suspension period the suspended player must return to the vacant position.

2. During playing time an Umpire has the right to warn against any coaching from the side-lines and if coaching persists, after due warning may penalise the team which may benefit.

Reprinted by permission of the All-England Netball Association. For reasons of space, two Appendixes (dealing with Hand Signals and AENA Recommendations) have been omitted. A copy of the complete Rules of Netball, with these Appendixes, may be obtained from the Association.

THE LAWS OF

Rackets

The Laws of Rackets

The Singles Game

1. The game is 15 up, that is, the player who first wins 15 points wins the game, except when:

(*a*) The score reaches 13-all for the first time in any game when hand-out – the receiver – may, before the next point has been started, set the game to 5, or to 3, i.e. the first player winning 5 or 3 points wins the game.

(*b*) Similarly at 14-all for the first time in any game hand-out may set the game to 3 (this cannot occur if set has been declared at 13-all).

(*c*) In both the above examples, i.e. at 13-all or 14-all, hand-out may choose no set. This means the first player winning 2 points at 13-all or 1 point at 14-all wins the game.

2. When a player fails to serve or to return the ball in accordance with the Laws of the Game, his opponent wins the rally. A rally won by hand-in – the server – scores a point. A rally won by hand-out – the receiver – makes him hand-in.

3. The ball after being served, whether the service is good or not – unless it is called a double fault by the marker – is in play until it has bounced twice, or until after being properly returned it has failed to hit the front wall above the board, or until it has touched a player, or until it has gone out of court.

4. The right to serve first in a match shall be decided by the spin of a racket.

5. At the beginning of each game and of each hand the server may serve from either box, but must thereafter alternate as long as he remains hand-in, or until the end of the game. If the server serves from the wrong box by mistake and if this is not immediately noticed by the Marker and/or Referee, there shall be no penalty and the service shall

count as good except that hand-out may, if he does not attempt to take the service, ask that it be served from the correct box.

6. Hand-in serves his hand-out and loses the right to serve:

(*a*) If the ball is served on to or below the board, or out of court, or against any part of the court before it strikes the front wall.

(*b*) If he fails to strike the ball, or strikes the ball more than once.

(*c*) If he serves two consecutive faults, i.e. a double-fault.

NB The ball is out of court when it touches the front, sides or back of the court above the area prepared for play, or when it touches, or passes over, any cross bars or other parts of the roof or electric light fittings of the court.

7. A service is a fault (except as provided by Law 6):

(*a*) If at the moment of striking the ball the server fails to have one foot at least on the floor within, and not touching, the line surrounding the service box. This is a foot fault.

(*b*) If the ball is served on to, or below, the service or cut line on the front wall.

(*c*) If the ball served first bounces on or before the short line (called short by the Marker).

(*d*) If the ball served, first bounces in the wrong receiving half of the court, i.e. left of the court from the left-hand box and right from the right-hand box.

8. Hand-out may take a fault unless it has already been called a double fault by the Marker. If he attempts to do so the service becomes a valid start to the rally, fault or not.

9. A player wins a rally:

(*a*) Under Law 6.

(*b*) If his opponent fails to make a legitimate return of the ball in play.

(*c*) If the ball in play touches his opponent, or anything he wears or carries (other than his racket when in the act of striking), except:

(i) As is otherwise provided by Laws 11, 12 and 14.

(ii) In the case of a fault which hand-out does not attempt to take.

10. A return is good if the striker returns the ball above the board without it previously touching the floor, or the back wall, or any part of the striker's body or clothing, before it has bounced twice and if he does not hit the ball twice or hit it out of court. *No player may attempt to return the ball by boasting it off the back wall.*

11. If the ball, after being struck and before reaching the front wall, hits the striker's opponent, or his opponent's racket or anything he wears or carries, a let shall be allowed providing the return would have been good. If the return would not have been good the striker shall lose the rally.

NB Play shall cease even if the ball goes up.

12. Notwithstanding anything contained in these Laws, a let may be allowed, on appeal by either player, in the following circumstances:

(*a*) If the player is prevented from obtaining a fair view of the ball, or from reaching the ball, or from striking at the ball.

(*b*) If, owing to the position of the striker, his opponent is unable to avoid being touched by the ball.

(*c*) If the ball in play touches any other ball in the court.

(*d*) If the player refrains from hitting the ball owing to a reasonable fear of injuring his opponent.

(*e*) If the player in the act of striking the ball touches his opponent or his racket.

NB No let shall be allowed:

(i) In respect of any stroke which a player attempts to make, unless in making the stroke, he or his racket touches an opponent.

(ii) Unless the striker could have made a good return.

13. An appeal to the Referee may be made against any decision of the Marker provided that with regard to service the following Laws shall apply:

(*a*) A let shall be allowed if the receiver is not ready and does not in any way attempt to take the service.

(*b*) If the receiver attempts to take a first service no appeal may be made, but when he does not attempt to take it:

(i) If he appeals against the Marker's call of play and the Referee allows the appeal, the service becomes a fault.

(ii) If the server appeal to the Referee against a call or fault the marker's decision is reversed, a let shall be allowed.

(*c*) When the Marker calls fault to a second service, the receiver shall not attempt to take it. If the Marker's decision is reversed on appeal to the Referee a let shall be allowed.

(*d*) When the Marker calls play and therefore deems good a second service, the receiver may appeal to the Referee even if he has taken the service. If the appeal is upheld the receiver is awarded the rally and immediately becomes the server or hand-in.

NB No appeal shall be made by the server (or receiver if he has taken that particular service) against foot faults called by the Marker or Referee.

14. If the player strikes at and misses a ball, he may make further attempts to return it but the following provisions shall apply:

If the ball accidentally touches his opponent or his racket, the player shall lose the rally unless he could have made a good return in which case a let may be allowed by the Referee. In all other respects the Laws shall apply as if the player had not struck at the ball.

15. If in the course of play the Marker calls 'not up' or 'out of court' or

'time' or if any player appeal for a let, the rally shall cease immediately. If the Marker's call of 'not up' or 'out of court' is reversed on appeal to the Referee, a let shall be allowed.

16.   If a let is allowed, the service or rally shall be void and the server must serve again from the same side. A let does not annul a previous fault.

17.   After the first service is delivered, play shall be continuous, so far as is practical. During a game players must consult with the Referee before they leave the court except between games when 1 minute shall be allowed. The Referee may suspend play for bad light or unsuitable court conditions or for other reasons at his discretion. In the event of play being suspended for the day the match shall restart from the point at which it was suspended.

18.   After the delivery of a service (i.e. after the start of a rally), no appeal shall be made for anything that occurred before the service was delivered except by appeal to the Referee to adjust the score if this is incorrectly called by the Marker.

19.   A new ball may only be requested by the receiver, i.e. when he is hand-out but not between the first and second service or after a let has been given. The server may appeal to the Referee who may change the ball if he considers it unfit for play.

20.   There must be a new ball to begin each game.

21.   If the Referee is unable to decide an appeal he must allow a let to be played, except on service line or short line appeals. (See also Duties of the Referee No. 10.)

22.   The Referee is responsible for calling foot faults; he may also nominate one or two Umpires specifically to watch for these, to help him keep the score and from which side the service is to be delivered.

23.   Each player must get out of the way, after making a stroke, as much and as quickly as possible. He must do all he can to:

(*a*)   Give his opponent a good view of the ball.

(*b*)   Avoid interfering with him in getting to, and striking at, the ball.

(*c*)   Leave him, as far as the striker's position allows, free to play the ball to any part of the court, i.e. directly to the front wall or side walls.

When a player fails to do any of these things, the Referee may on appeal, or without waiting for an appeal, award a let, or award the rally to his opponent, if in his opinion this is fair under the circumstances and taking into account what would have taken place had there been no such interference.

24.   In the case of consistent interference by one player with another and/or in the case of negligent or dangerous play the Referee may halt play irrespective of any appeal being made and award the rally against the offending player.

25.   The Referee has the power to order:

(*a*) A player, who has left the court, or who is wasting time during a game whilst on court, to play on immediately.

(*b*) A player to leave the court for any reason whatsoever and may award the match to his opponent if he feels this is appropriate.

26. There shall be a Marker and, whenever possible, a Referee for all matches. In the absence of a Referee the Marker shall also act as Referee. The Referee shall give no decision unless an appeal is made, except for correcting an incorrect score (see Law 18) or to call a foot fault or as specifically noted in Law 24.

27. The Referee or, in his absence, the Marker has the power at his absolute discretion to award a rally to the opponent of a player, after due warning of the penalty to come, continues to:

(*a*) Dispute the Referee's decision.

(*b*) Make provocative or derogatory remarks to the Referee or Marker.

(*c*) Cause unnecessary delay between rallies (Law 25*a*) or to the resumption of play after a decision has been made by the Referee.

In the event of persistent offence by a player following warning and the award of a rally, the Referee may award the match to the opponent. (See also Law 25*b* and Duties of the Referee No. 11.)

The Four-handed or Doubles Game

1. The Laws of singles shall apply to doubles and wherever the words server, hand-out, striker, opponent or player are used in the Laws of singles, such words (wherever applicable) shall be taken to include his partner in doubles.

2. Only one of a pair shall serve in the first hand of a game.

3. The order of serving may be changed at the beginning of any game. The player, however, who is serving when a game is won must continue to serve in the following game, but need not serve first thereafter in that game.

4. If the player, who should serve second, serves first by mistake, hand-out – either player in that pair – may object provided that he does so before a point has been scored or an attempt has been made to take the first service. If no such objection is made, the server may complete his hand and his partner shall then serve, but in subsequent hands if the error has been noted by any player on court, or by the Marker and/or the Referee, the pair must revert to their original order.

5. If in any hand a player serves again, after he has ceased to be hand-in, in other words if he serves a second time accidentally having been put out, that point shall not count provided the mistake is discovered before either of his opponents has served subsequently.

6. If a player does not serve when he should do so and one of his opponents serves instead, the player loses his right of service, unless it is

claimed before he, or his partner, has attempted to take a service, or before a point has been scored.

7. In each pair one player shall receive service from the left and one player shall receive service from the right. This order of receiving service may only be changed at the start of each game but before the first rally has begun.

8. Appeals against service faults may be made by the striker receiving service as in Law 13 (Singles) and his right of appeal shall also apply to his partner when he himself is not receiving.

9. Hand-in scores a point if the player in the right-hand court returns or attempts to return a service which has been served to the left-hand court, and vice versa.

10. While the service is being delivered, the player who is receiving that service may stand where he pleases. His partner must stand behind the server, in such a position that the server has an unimpeded swing. The server's partner, at the moment of service, must stand near the back wall and in the court into which the service is not being delivered.

Note: In these Laws of singles and doubles the expression:

Court means the whole building in which the game of rackets is played. The back of the court is divided by a *half court line* into two halves, called the right (or forehand) court, and the left (or backhand) court.

Cut Line or Service Line means the line drawn on the front wall.

Half Court Line means the line on the floor, drawn from the short line to the back wall.

Hand-in means the player who serves.

Hand-out means the player who receives the service.

A Rally means the ensuing play after a serve.

To Serve means to start the ball in play by striking at it with a racket.

Service Board means: The board across the lower part of the front wall.

Service Box means the small squares on each side of the court from which the service alternately is delivered.

Short Line means the line drawn across the floor parallel to the front wall.

Striker means the player whose turn it is to play and strike the ball after it has hit the front wall.

Reprinted by permission of the Tennis and Rackets Association. Copies of the complete Laws of Rackets, including Duties of the Referee, Guidance for Referees and Guidance for Markers, may be obtained from the Association. The Laws were drawn up by Major Spens in 1890. Revised by the Tennis, Rackets and Fives Association in 1911. Revised by the Tennis and Rackets Association in 1923, 1950, 1966 and 1985.

Real Tennis

The Court

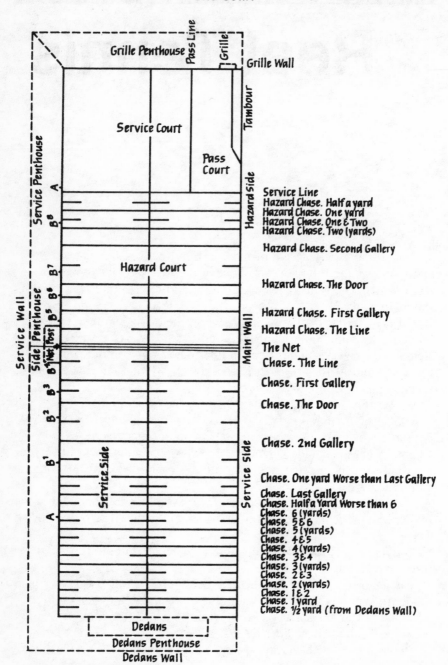

A, A Points where Galleries begin
B¹ to B³ Gallery Posts

The Laws of Real Tennis

1. Definitions (see diagram of the court on the opposite page).

In these laws the following words have the following meanings:

Back Walls. The walls between the floor and the penthouses adjoining the main wall.

Bandeau. The strip of wall immediately below a penthouse, usually made of the same material as the penthouse.

Better. One chase is better than another if it is made on the same side of the court and further from the net (Law 8). In marking chases, better means that the ball makes a chase:

(*a*) Further from the net than the line mentioned; and

(*b*) Nearer to that line than to any other yard or gallery line (Law 8*b*).

Bisque. One stroke in a set conceded to an opponent (Law 22).

Chase. A chase is made whenever the ball falls in the hazard court, or anywhere on the service side, or enters a gallery, except the winning gallery (Law 8).

. . . *attacking a* – When a chase is being played for, the opponent of the player who made the chase is said to be attacking the chase (Laws 10 and 11).

. . . *calling a* – The Marker calls a chase when he states the chase that is to be played for.

. . . *defending a* – When a chase is being played for, the player who made the chase is said to be defending the chase (Laws 10 and 11).

. . . *lines* – The lines marked on the floor to enable the Marker to mark chases are called chase lines or chases (Law 7).

. . . *marking a* – The Marker marks a chase when that chase is made.

. . . *off* – See Law 11(*b*).

. . . *the line* – See Line, Chase the.

Court. The enclosure in which the game is played. The court is divided into two sides, the service side and the hazard side (q.v.).

Dead. A ball is said to be dead when it ceases to be in play.

Dedans. The opening at the back of the service side.

Double. If the ball falls before it is struck it is a double.

Double Hit. A double hit shall not be called if the player has made one continuous stroke at the ball unless:

(*a*) During the course of such stroke the ball has struck another surface of the court between one contact with the racquet and another; or

(*b*) The ball remains in contact with the racquet for so long a time as to constitute a throw.

Drop. A ball is said to drop when, after passing the net, it first touches the floor, or enters an opening, without having previously touched the floor.

Enter a Gallery or an Opening. See Opening, Entering an.

Fall. A ball is said to fall when, after having dropped, it touches the floor again, or enters an opening.

Fault Line. The line on the floor nearest the grille and extending from the service line to the grille wall.

Gallery. An opening below the penthouse opposite to the main wall.

The starting galleries are named as follows, starting from the net:

(*a*) On the service side, the line, the first gallery, the door, the second gallery, the last gallery;

(*b*) On the hazard side, the line, the first gallery, the door, the second gallery, the winning gallery.

Gallery Post. The post between two galleries is considered to be part of the gallery nearer the net.

The part of the gallery net that surrounds a gallery post is part of that post.

Good Return. See Return.

Grille. The opening in the grille wall.

Grille Wall. The back on the hazard side.

Half-Court Line. The line that bisects the floor, between the main wall and the side wall.

Hazard Chase or Hazard Side Chase. A chase made on the hazard side of the court.

Hazard Court. The floor on the hazard side from the net up to, but not including, the service line.

Hazard Side. The side of the court on the left of the net when facing the main wall.

In Play. A ball served is in play until:

(*a*) The service becomes a fault; or

(*b*) Either player fails to make a good return.

Ledge. The horizontal surface of a wall that forms an opening.

Line, Chase the, is chase at the line of the net. On the floor it is the area between the net and the first gallery line. The line gallery is that between the net post and the post next to it.

Main Wall. The wall that has no penthouse.

Net Post. The post supporting the net under the penthouse.

Nick. The junction of the wall and the floor, or a return when the ball, as it drops or falls, touches the wall and the floor simultaneously.

Opening. Any gallery or winning opening.

Opening, Entering an. A ball enters an opening when a good return or service:

(*a*) Touches the post (see Gallery Post), net, or tray of that opening; or

(*b*) Touches anything lying in that opening (if an article is lying in an opening any part of it, even outside, is considered to be in that opening); or

(*c*) Comes to rest in or on the ledge of that opening; or

(*d*) In the case of the grille, touches the woodwork at the back of the framing of the grille.

Out of Court. A ball is out of court if it touches any part of:

(*a*) The walls above the area prepared for play; or

(*b*) The roof or roof beams or girders (in some courts a ball is out of court if it passes over a beam or girder); or

(*c*) The lighting equipment.

Passing the Net. The ball passes the net when it crosses it between the net post and the main wall, or when it crosses the line bisecting the side penthouse.

Rest. A stroke or series of strokes, commencing when the ball is served and terminating when the ball is dead.

Return, or Return of the Ball in Play. The return of the ball is good if;

(*a*) It is struck before it falls; and

(*b*) It is struck so that it passes the net without having previously touched the floor or anything lying on the floor, or the net post, or without having entered an opening; and

(*c*) It has not touched the player or anything he wears or carries except his racket in the act of striking the ball; and

(*d*) It does not go out of court; and

(*e*) It is struck definitely and is not a double hit; and

(*f*) It is not on the side of the net opposed to the player when he strikes it; and

(*g*) In courts where there is a wing net between the net post and the net, it does not touch the wing net before crossing the net.

Except that such a return is not good if:

(*h*) The player touches the net before striking the ball; or (*i*) The player touches the net after the ball and before the ball is dead; or

(*j*) The ball, after passing the net, rebounds and drops on the side from which it was played (even if it touches the net before so dropping the return is not good).

Service. The method of starting a rest.

Service Court. The part of the floor on the hazard side that lies between the side wall, the grille wall, the fault line and the service line (including those two lines).

Service Line or Winning Gallery Line. The line which is nearest and parallel to the grille wall.

Service Penthouse. That part of the side penthouse which is on the hazard side of the court including the line that bisects the side penthouse.

Service Side. The side of the court on the right of the net when facing the main wall.

Service Wall. The wall above the side penthouse.

Side Penthouse. The penthouse above the galleries, up to its junction with the other penthouses.

Side Wall. The wall below the side penthouse.

Striker. The player who last struck the ball.

Striker-out. The player who is to take the service.

Tray. The inner part of the bottom of an opening behind the ledge, usually made of wood.

Uneven Odds. When points given and/or received are not the same in each game, and/or when one or more bisques or half-bisques are given.

Winning Gallery. The last gallery on the hazard side.

Winning Openings. The dedans, the grille, and the winning gallery.

Worse. One chase is worse than another if it is made on the same side of the court and nearer to the net (Law 8).

In marking chases, worse means that the ball makes a chase:

(*a*) Nearer to the net than the line mentioned; and

(*b*) Nearer to that line than to any other yard or gallery line (Law 8*b*).

2. Net

The height of the net above the level of the floor shall be:

(*a*) At the centre, 3ft; and

(*b*) At the main wall and below and edge of the penthouse, 5ft.

3. Balls

The balls shall be not less than $2\frac{7}{16}$in and not more than $2\frac{9}{16}$in in diameter. They shall not be less than $2\frac{1}{2}$oz and not more than $2\frac{3}{4}$oz in weight.

4. Rackets
Racket frames must be made of wood and designed for tennis unless, exceptionally, the Association approves another specification.

5. Sides
(*a*) The choice of sides at the beginning of a match is decided by spin of a racket.

(*b*) Subsequently the players change sides only when two chases have been scored or when one player is at 40 or advantage and one chase has been scored.

(*c*) If the players change sides before they should have done so, or do not change sides when they should, any strokes so played on the wrong side shall be scored and play shall continue as if no mistake had been made; except that any chase scored (Law 9) in excess of the proper number shall be annulled if the mistake is discovered before that chase has been played for (Law 10).

6. Service
The service is always given by the player who is on the service side.

A service is good if it is not a fault.

A service is a fault:

(*a*) If the server, while serving, does not stand on the floor further from the net than the second gallery line; or

(*b*) If the server misses the ball or does not definitely strike it or strikes it more than once; or

(*c*) If the ball served, before touching the side penthouse, touches any part of the court except the service wall (if the ball touches the edge of the penthouse before touching anything else it is a fault); or

(*d*) If the ball served leaves the penthouse or service wall without touching the service penthouse (if the ball, after striking the service wall or side penthouse in dropping touches the edge of the service penthouse it is a good service); or

(*e*) If the ball served goes out of court; or

(*f*) If the ball served strikes the main wall before dropping; or

(*g*) If the ball served drops anywhere except in the service court or in the winning gallery.

A service that has become a fault may not be returned, but one that would otherwise become a fault may be volleyed provided that if the striker-out volleys a service before the ball has touched some part of the court he loses that point.

If striker-out is not ready for a service and does not attempt to take it, a let (Law 16) shall be allowed.

7. Chase Lines, How Marked

Chase lines are marked on the floor as follows; and see also the diagram on page 676:

Service Side:
  Half-a-yard,
  One yard,
  One and two,
  Two,
and so on up to six, then:
  Half-a-yard worse than six.
  The last gallery,
  Half-a-yard worse than the last gallery,
  A yard worse then the last gallery,
  The second gallery,
  The door, and
  The first gallery.

Hazard Side: The same as on the service side, except that all chases between two and the second gallery are omitted and the last or winning gallery line is called the service line.

8. Chases, How Made

(*a*) When the ball enters a gallery (except the winning gallery) or falls on the floor (unless it falls on or further from the net than the service line) it makes a chase at the gallery it enters or at the line on which it falls.

(*b*) When it falls between two lines it makes a chase better or worse than the yard line or the gallery line nearest to the spot where it fell, except that:

(1) It makes chase better than half a yard when it so falls; and

(2) When it falls better or worse than the line 'a yard worse than the last gallery' the chase is called 'nearly a yard worse than the last gallery' or 'more than a yard worse than the last gallery'; and

(3) When it falls nearer to the net than to the first gallery line it makes chase the line; and

(4) When it drops or falls in the net on the side opposed to the striker or drops on the side opposed to the striker and then falls on the side from which it was struck, it makes chase the line on the side opposed to the striker; and

(5) When it drops or falls on another ball on the floor it makes a chase as if it had fallen where that other ball was lying.

9. Chase, How and When Scored

(*a*) When no chase is being played for, a chase is scored when made in accordance with Law 8.

(*b*) When a chase is scored, the score in strokes is unaltered.

10. Chases, When Played For

When two chases have been scored, or when one player is at 40 or advantage and one chase has been scored, the players change sides and the chase or chases in the order in which they were made are immediately played for.

A chase is played for once only, unless there is a let (Law 16).

11. Chases, How Won or Lost

When a chase is being played for:

(*a*) The player attacking the chase loses it if:

(1) He serves two consecutive faults; or

(2) He does not make a good return; or

(3) He makes a chase worse than the one being played for;

(*b*) It is a chase off when the player attacking the chase makes a chase equal to the one being played for (when it is chase off the chase is annulled and the score is unaltered);

(*c*) The player attacking the chase wins it if:

(1) His opponent serves two consecutive faults; or

(2) His opponent does not make a good return (unless the player attacking the chase makes a chase worse than or equal to the one being played for), in which case paragraph (*a*) or (*b*) of this rule applies; or

(3) He makes a chase better than the one being played for.

12. Errors Regarding Chases

(*a*) If the chase to be played for is wrongly called by the Marker, the server may appeal before delivering the service, and the striker-out before attempting to take it. If there is no such appeal, the chase played for shall be that called by the Marker immediately before the service is delivered, notwithstanding that this may be different from that marked when the chase was scored.

(*b*) If there has been any misunderstanding as to what chase the Marker called, the rest as played shall stand or a let (Law 16) may be allowed, whichever the Marker considers equitable in view of all the circumstances.

(*c*) If, through any mistake, at the end of the game there is a chase that has been scored and not played for, that chase is annulled.

(*d*) If the players change sides when too few or too many chases have been made, see Law 5.

13. Strokes, How Won

A player wins a stroke:

(*a*) If he wins a chase (Law 11*c*); or

(*b*) If his opponent loses a chase (Law 11*a*); or

(*c*) If a return or a good service played by him enters a winning opening, or falls on the service line or between the service line and grille wall; or

(*d*) If when no chase is being played for and provided that no chase is made his opponent does not make a good return; or

(*e*) If his opponent serves two consecutive faults (Law 6).

14. Strokes and Games, How Scored

In each game, when either player wins his first stroke his score is called 15; when he wins his second stroke, 30; when he wins his third stroke, 40; and when he wins his fourth stroke, he wins the game, except as below.

When both players have won three strokes, the score is called deuce, and it is called advantage to the player who then wins the next stroke.

If the player who is at advantage wins the next stroke, he wins the game; if he loses it, the score is again called deuce, and so on until the player who is at advantage wins a stroke and the game.

15. Sets, How Won

The player who first wins 6 games in a set wins it unless, extraordinarily, a different number of games is stipulated.

16. Let

In the case of a let:

(*a*) The rest to which it refers counts for nothing; and

(*b*) If a chase was being played for, it is then played for again; and

(*c*) If there was a previous fault, it is not annulled.

17. Continuous Play

(*a*) After the first service has been delivered, play shall be continuous and, having regard to all the circumstances, reasonably expeditious unless the Referee (or, if none, the Marker) decides otherwise.

(*b*) No player may leave the court without the express permission of the Referee (or, if none, the Marker) and then only for a good reason and for the shortest possible time.

(*c*) The Referee (or, if none, the Marker) has the power:

(i) To order any player who has left the court, with or without permission under (*b*) above, to return and play on; and

(ii) To order any player to leave the court or (as the case may be) to remain off the court; and

(iii) To order any player to resume or to expedite play; and

(iv) To give warnings and to award the match, as he, in his absolute discretion taking account of all the circumstances, thinks fit, to any player, and in the case of such an award, whether or not he has previously given a warning to the player in question under this paragraph (iv).

18. Referee

A Referee shall be appointed, if possible, before the start of a match if requested by the event organisers, the Marker or a player. If the match has commenced without a Referee, one may still be appointed at the request of the event organisers or the Marker.

If so requested the Referee shall:

(a) Call faults on the penthouse;

(b) Keep a written record of the score;

(c) Watch for cases in case the Marker is unsighted and asks for the Referee's opinion; and

(d) Correct errors in the calling of the score and of previously scored chases.

The Referee shall also:

(a) Ensure that spectators in the dedans do not disturb the players;

(b) Be well versed in the *Laws of Tennis*;

(c) Ensure that Law 17 is complied with; and

(d) Be responsible for the conduct of the match. If, in his opinion, the behaviour of a player is thwarting his opponent(s) unfairly, or is bringing the game of tennis into disrepute, he shall warn the offending player that further offensive behaviour would result in forfeiture of the match. Should that player continue to offend, the Referee shall award the match to his opponent(s) forthwith.

19. Marker

Save for the provisions of Laws 17 and 18 the Marker has overall control of the match and his decisions are final. Although players are not allowed to appeal, either to the Marker or the Referee, on marking decisions, they may check the accuracy of the score and the calling of a previously scored chase. In the absence of a Referee the Marker shall assume all the duties and responsibilities of the Referee.

20. Three- or Four-handed Games (also called Doubles)

(a) Before commencing each set the players on the service side select the partner who is to serve. He is then the server and striker-out for his side throughout the game, and for alternate games throughout the set, his partner serving and striking-out in the other games. Similarly the players on the hazard side then decide who is to be striker-out and server.

(*b*) A return of service is not good if made by striker-out's partner, unless the ball served has dropped in the service court between the half-court line and the fault line (including those two lines).

(*c*) Apart from the above, the Laws for Singles apply to Doubles and a player and his partner are in all cases subject to the same laws as a player in Singles.

(*d*) If the wrong player serves, whether or not the correct player returns, the service, the marker shall call a let, but if the error goes unnoticed, all completed sets shall stand as if correctly scored.

HANDICAPS

21. Half Odds
When half odds handicaps are played, the position taken in the first game of each set is always that most favourable to the player conceding the handicap. If a handicap involves half odds received and owed, full odds when received will alternate with, rather than coincide with, full odds owed and vice versa (e.g. receive $\frac{1}{2}$15 owe $\frac{1}{2}$30 is played love owe 30 in the first game, receive 15 owe 15 in the second and so on).

22. Bisque
The player receiving the bisque may take it to win one stroke in each set at any time subject to the following:
(*a*) He may not take it during a rest; and
(*b*) If server, he may not take it after serving one fault; and
(*c*) If he takes it to win or to defend a chase, he may not do so before the time comes to change sides. Then, if there is only one chase, he may take it and need not change sides, or he may take it after changing sides but, after he has passed the net, he may not go back again.

If there are two chases the player must change sides before he takes it to win or to defend either of them.

23. Half-bisque
The player receiving a half-bisque may take it:
(*a*) To call chase off and so annul a chase about to be played for; or
(*b*) To annul a fault served by him; or
(*c*) To add a second fault to one served by his opponent; or
(*d*) The handicapper may give a half-bisque as being one bisque in

every alternate set, in which case the bisque must be taken in the odds set.

Apart from (*b*) the conditions regarding taking a bisque (Law 22) apply equally to a half-bisque.

24. Cramped Odds

Unless specifically stated the limiting conditions of cramped odds do not apply to service. Cramped odds may be such as are fixed by the handicapper but the more usual forms are as follows.

(*a*) *Bar the Openings*. The giver of the odds loses a stroke whenever a ball returned by him enters an opening.

(*b*) *Bar the Winning Openings*. The giver of the odds loses a stroke whenever a ball returned by him enters the dedans, the grille, or the winning gallery.

(*c*) *Chase*. When a player gives a specified chase this applies only to a chase on the service side. Any chase made by the giver of the odds worse than the one specified loses him a stroke. Any chase made by the receiver of the odds worse than the one specified is considered equal to the one specified.

(*d*) *Half-court*. The players shall agree or the handicapper decide to which half-court, on each side of the net, the giver of the odds shall play. He loses a stroke if a ball returned by him drops in the other half-court or in an opening or in half the dedans in the other half-court.

A ball that drops on the half-court line does not lose him a stroke.

After the ball has dropped the ordinary rules apply.

(*e*) *Round Services*. The striker-out may refuse to take any service that does not touch the grille penthouse. If he attempts to take such a service that service becomes good, if not otherwise a fault.

(*f*) *Touch no Side Walls*. The giver of the odds loses a stroke if the ball in play returned by him touches the side wall, the service wall, or the main wall, or enters a gallery.

(*g*) *Touch No Walls*. The giver of the odds loses a stroke whenever a ball in play returned by him touches any wall, or enters an opening.

A ball that falls in a nick is not considered to have touched the wall.

A penthouse is not a wall.

A bandeau is part of a wall.

The above odds are also given in the form that the ball must drop before touching a wall, etc., but after dropping it may touch them without penalty. In this form it is usually called 'Touch no walls full pitch'.

25. Warm Up

In matches sanctioned by the Association, the players shall be permitted a warm-up period ending 5 minutes following:

 (i) The scheduled start of play or; if later

(ii) The arrival of the last player on court.

DIRECTIONS TO THE MARKER
It is the duty of the Marker:

To see that the net is at the correct height and that it remains correct.

To call faults.

To call the strokes when won or when asked to do so.

To mark the chases when scored.

To direct the players to change sides.

To call the chase or chases as the players change sides and to call each chase before it is played for, but not otherwise to repeat the chases.

To remove balls lying on the floor.

To keep the ball troughs replenished.

GLOSSARY OF TENNIS TERMS
(*See also the definitions contained in Law 1*)

Advantage. See Law 14.

All the Walls, also called Touch no Walls, see Law 24(*g*).

Attack. See Law 1: Chase, attacking a—.

Back Wall. See Law 1.

Bandeau. See Law 1.

Bar the Opening. See Law 24(*a*).

Bar the Winning Openings. See Law 24(*b*).

Batteries. The portions of wall between the openings and the floor.

Better. See Laws 1 and 8.

Bisque. See Laws 1 and 22.

Boast. A return that is struck against a wall on the same side of the net as the striker (presumably derived from *Bosse*).

Boasted Force. A boast that drops in a winning opening. The term is usually employed only for a force to the dedans.

Bobble Service. A slow service that bounces frequently on the service penthouse and that should drop near the grille wall.

Boomerang Service. A service that touches the service penthouse, the grille penthouse, the high back wall and then returns to the service penthouse before dropping close to and moving parallel with the grille wall.

Chase. See Law 1.

Coup de Brèche. A straight force that drops in the dedans near to one of its outer edges.

Coup de Cabasse. A return that drops in the dedans after first striking the wall between the last gallery and the dedans wall (called after a French professional of that name who played this difficult stroke).

Coups de Chandelle. A lofted return that drops or (more usually) falls in the dedans.

Coup d'Orléans. A return that is struck against the service wall and drops in the dedans direct (called after Philippe Egalité, Duc d'Orleans, who invented or practised this stroke).

Coup de Temps. The stroke usually attempted off the back wall when the ball is too near to the wall and floor for an ordinary return to be made. The stroke is commenced before the ball reaches the wall so that immediately it leaves it the stroke can be completed with the minimum amount of further movement and acceleration of the racket.

Court. See Law 1.

Cramped Odds. Handicaps that prohibit certain strokes or services. See Law 24.

Dead. See Law 1.

Dedans. See Law 1.

Defend. See Law 1:Chase, defending a—.

Deuce. See Law 14.

Door. See Law 1 (Gallery) and 7.

Double. See Law 1.

Doubles. See Law 20.

Drop. See Law 1.

Drop Service. A high service, delivered from near the main wall, that should drop near to the grille wall.

Du Tout. The score of a player who requires one stroke to win the set. See Law 14 (Game-ball).

Enter a Gallery or an Opening. See Law 1.

Fall. See Law 1.

Fault. See Law 6.

Fifteen. See Law 15.

First Gallery. See Laws 1 (Gallery) and 7.

First Stroke. The return of the service.

Fly Net. Not used in modern courts. In some old courts there was a fly net high up in each of the four corners. A ball striking the fly net was not out of court.

Force. A stroke that drops into an opening, usually a winning opening. The term is not used for a slow lofted return.

Forty. See Law 15. Originally this score was 45, but was subsequently called 40 for the sake of brevity.

Four-handed Game. See Law 20.

Gallery. See Law 1.

Gallery Lines. Chase lines that correspond to galleries (see Laws 7 and 8*a*).

Gallery Net. The net attached to a gallery post to separate a gallery from the one next to it.

Gallery Post. See Law 1.

Game. See Law 14.

Giraffe Service. A high underhand service delivered from near the side penthouse. (After dropping on the service penthouse the ball should drop on the floor near the fault line and to the grille wall.)

Good Return. See Law 1 (Return).

Good Service. See Law 6.

Grille. See Law 1.

Grille Penthouse. The Penthouse above the grille wall.

Grille Wall. See Law 1.

Half a yard. See Law 7.

Half-bisque. See Law 23.

Half-Court. See Law 1.

Half Odds. See Law 21.

Hazard Chase. See Law 1.

Hazard Court. See Law 1.

Hazard Side. See Law 1.

Joues. The inner vertical walls of the dedans, grille, winning gallery and last gallery. A ball in touching a joue is not thereby deemed to have entered an opening (see Law 1).

Last Gallery. See Laws 1 (Gallery) and 7.

Ledge. See Law 1.

Let. See Law 16.

Line. The cord that supports the net.

Line, Chase the. See Law 1.

Love. The score of a player who has not yet won a stroke in the game or a game in the set in question.

Love Game. A game won by a player in which his opponent does not score a stroke.

Love Set. A set won by a player in which his opponent does not score a game.

Lune. A winning opening that was found in some old courts. There was no standard size, shape or position for lunes, but they were usually placed above the dedans and grille penthouses.

Net Post. See Law 1.

Nick. See Law 1.

Odds. Any form of handicap is called odds. See Laws 21 to 24.

Opening. Entering an. See Law 1.

Out of Court. See Law 1.

Passing the Net. See Law 1.

Penthouse. The sloping roof of the dedans, galleries and grille, extending along three sides of the court.

Piqué Service. The server stands near to the main wall and to the second gallery line. He serves overhead on to the service penthouse and as near as possible to the service line. After striking the service wall the ball should drop near to the grille wall and the fault line.

Play Line. The line painted on the walls to mark the upper limits of the area prepared for play (see Law 1, Out of Court).

Post. See Net Post and Gallery Post, Law 1.

Railroad Service. An overhead service usually delivered by the server standing near the side wall between the last gallery and the dedans wall. (The ball may touch the penthouse once or more times. On leaving the penthouse the ball, unless volleyed, should strike the grille wall with a twist on it that brings it back towards the side wall. A less common form of railroad service has the opposite twist on the ball so that it tends to go in the direction of the tambour after dropping.)

Referee. See Law 18.

Rest. See Law 1.

Rough. The side of the racket on which the knots are.

Second Gallery. See Laws 1 (Gallery) and 7.

Service. See Law 1.

Service Court. See Law 1.

Service Line. See Law 1.

Service Penthouse. See Law 1.

Service Side. See Law 1.

Service Wall. See Law 1.

Set. See Law 15. A match is won by the player who first wins an agreed number of sets. Each set is a separate unit and no game won in one set has any effect on another set. The method of scoring by sets appears to have been adopted in the 16th century. Prior to that games only were scored. At first 2 games won a set. At later periods, 3, 4, 6 and 8 game sets were usual.

Side Penthouse. See Law 1.

Side Wall. See Law 1.

Side Wall Service. Delivered from near the side penthouse. The ball usually touches the service wall before the service penthouse but need not do so. The twist on it should be such that it clings to the grille wall after dropping.

Smooth. The side of the racket on which there are no knots.

Striker. See Law 1.

Striker-Out. See Law 1.

Stroke. See Laws 13 and 14.

Tambour. The projection on the main wall near the grille. The whole of the projection should be called the tambour though the term is more commonly applied only to that part of it that is at an angle to the main wall.

Thirty. See Law 14.

Three-handed Game. See Law 20.

Touch No Walls. See Law 24(*g*).
Touch No Side Walls. See Law 24 (*f*).
Twist Service. An underhand service delivered from near the side penthouse. The ball does not usually touch the service wall. The twist on it should be that, after striking the grille wall, it comes back towards the side wall.
Tray. See Law 1.
Uneven Odds. See Law 1.
Wing Net. A net put up in some courts for the protection of the marker in front of the net or post and attached to the underside of the service penthouse.
Winning Gallery. See Law 1.
Winning Openings. See Law 1.
Worse. See Law 1.
Yard. See Law 7.

Reprinted by permission of the Tennis and Rackets Association. Revised by the Tennis and Rackets Association in 1966, 1975 and 1982 (incorporating amendments of 1980) and amendments made in 1984, 1985 and 1991.

THE RULES OF

Rounders

Rounders

THE PITCH

(*a*) *Running Track*
The running track shall be the area used by the batsman when running, as shown in the diagram on page 696, and will extend 2m beyond 4th post.

(*b*) *Bowling Square*
The bowling area shall be 2.5m square. All lines shall be considered as part of the square.

(*c*) *Batting Square*
The batting area shall be 2m square. The front line shall be parallel with and 7.5m away from the front line of the bowling square. All lines shall be considered as part of the square. There shall be a solid line extending from the front right-hand corner of the batting square to the position of the 1st post.

(*d*) *Forward Area and Backward Area*
 (i) The front line of the batting square shall be extended in both directions by solid lines measuring at least 12m in length.
 (ii) This line and the area in front of it, and the imaginary continuation of it, shall be called the forward area.
(iii) The area behind this line, and the imaginary continuation of it, shall be called the backward area.
(iv) At least 10m behind the backward/forward area line, and 15m either side of the front right-hand corner of the batting square, lines shall be drawn to mark the positions for waiting batsmen and batsmen out.
 (v) There shall be a 2m line from 4th post, extending into the backward area, at right angles to the backward/forward line.

2. EQUIPMENT

All equipment should be manufactured for the purpose and approved by the National Rounders Association.

(*a*) *Posts*

Each of the four posts shall be vertical and 1.2m above the ground. The four posts shall be supported in a base and not fixed in the ground.

(*b*) *The Ball*

The ball shall be leather, as approved by the NRA. It shall weigh a minimum of 70g and a maximum of 85g it shall measure a minimum of 17cm and a maximum of 19cm in circumference. Only NRA 'white' licensed balls shall be used in matches.

(*c*) *The Bat*

The bat shall be round, and shall not measure more than 17cm round the thickest part, nor than 46cm in length.

(*d*) *Clothing*

Spiked footwear is prohibited. Studs are allowed provided they measure more than 30mm in circumference at the base and are not longer than 12mm in length.

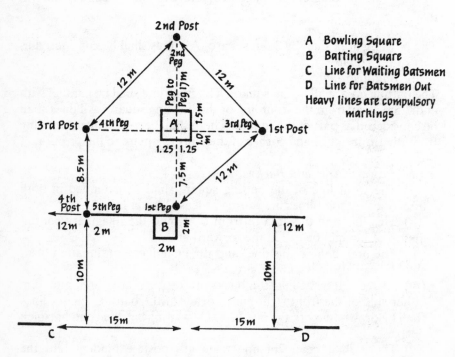

Heavy lines are compulsory markings

(e) The Base

Any corners of the base shall be to a minimum radius of 30mm. There shall be no sharp projections, points or surfaces. The collar of the base (where applicable), in which the post is fitted should be no higher than 50mm. The base should be sufficiently weighted to be capable of supporting its post during inclement weather conditions. *NB* For the purpose of rule interpretation, the base and post will be deemed as the same; however, when separated, then only the base will count.

3. TEAMS

(a) The Game

The game shall be played between two teams each consisting of a maximum of 9 players or a minimum of 6 players. In the case of teams of mixed sexes, a maximum of 5 males only is allowed.

(b) Substitutes

Two substitutes nominated prior to the start of the game may be used at any dead ball situation, after first informing the Umpires and the other team. In a mixed team a maximum of 5 males may be on the field of play at any one time.

(c) Numbers

All players, substitues included, shall be clearly numbered. The number shall be clearly visible to the umpires at all times.

4. INNINGS

(a) An innings shall start at the time the first ball is bowled, after the Umpire has called 'play', and terminate when all the batsmen shall be declared out.

(b) The captains shall toss a coin for the choice of innings.

(c) The Batsman's Umpire shall call by name or number the next player to bat. If a player receives a delivery before being called a void ball will be declared. A team shall keep the same batting order throughout an innings.
Penalty: Out. As for Batsmen Out – See Rule 10(a) (vi).

(d) A match shall consist of two innings.

(e) A team leading by 5 or more rounders in the first innings shall have the option of requiring the other team to follow on. A team enforcing this option will forfeit their second innings unless their opponents level or lead the first-innings score, and the game shall be deemed to have finished.

(f) A player put out in an innings shall not take the place of a missing batsman.

5. BATTING

A batsman:

(*a*) While waiting for his turn to bat shall be in the backward area, well away from 4th post and batting square. His required position is shown on the diagram on page 696.

(*b*) Shall have only one good ball bowled to him and shall also be deemed to have hit the ball if he strikes the ball with the bat or the hand holding the bat.

(*c*) Shall stand with both feet within the batting square and shall not cross the front or back line of the square during hitting, or in the course of attempting to hit a good ball, or until the ball has passed him.

(*d*) May, at his own discretion, take a no-ball and score in the usual way: he shall be considered to have taken the ball if he has come within reach of, made contact with or passed 1st post.

(*e*) Must run to the 1st post after having hit, attempted to hit, or let pass the first good ball delivered by the bowler.

(*f*) Who hits a ball so that it pitches in the backward area shall have made a backward hit. (This does not refer to balls that drop in the forward area and afterwards go behind).

(*g*) Shall be entitled, if he is the man left in on entering the square:

 (i) To have the option of 3 good balls but shall forfeit the right to any remaining balls if he is caught or takes the ball. (He shall be considered to have taken the ball if he has come within reach of, made contact with or passed 1st post). He can then be put out in any of the usual ways or when the ball has been thrown full pitch or placed in the batting square.

(ii) To a rest of 1 minute after each rounder he may score.

6. PROCEDURE OF GAME

Whilst waiting at a post a member of the batting team shall have the advantage of running on if a no-ball is bowled and not taken by the batsman. He can, at his discretion, continue to run round the track in the normal way. Similarly a runner need not run on for every ball bowled unless the next batsman immediately behind him is obliged to run. More than one batsman may be put out between the delivery of consecutive balls.

A bowler may leave his square to field the ball. A bowler can be changed only after delivering a good ball or at the Umpires' discretion. In the event of a bowler being unable to continue bowling after being injured, or after being sent off by an Umpire after having bowled a no-ball, the Umpire shall allow a substitute bowler to continue, upon the request of the fielding captain. Any no-balls bowled by the previous bowler shall be accredited to the substitute bowler. During the change the ball shall be deemed dead.

A dummy throw or bowl is not allowed. The ball must be delivered in the direction of the batting square. A player losing contact through this dummy ball will be allowed to return to his original position.

7. RUNNING ROUND THE TRACK

A batsman:

(a) Shall run round the track carrying his bat to reach 4th post, having passed outside or halted at the previous posts in the order 1st, 2nd and 3rd. On reaching 4th post he shall rejoin the waiting batsmen.

Penalty. The Umpire shall declare the player out if he runs deliberately inside a post or deliberately drops or throws his bat. (When trying to make contact with a post, a batsman who goes inside the post owing to obstruction by a fielder is not out.)

(b) Shall not wait between posts.

Penalty. The Umpire shall order him to continue to the next post.

(c) Stopping (even temporarily) within reach of a post shall make and maintain contact with it using his hand or bat, except that he may run on whenever the bowler is not in possession of the ball and in his square.

Penalty. (1) If he does not make contact the Umpire shall order him to do so, and if he does not the Umpire shall declare him out.

(2) If he loses contact or runs at any time when the bowler has the ball and is in his square (except an overrun – See Rule 7(d) – or unless ordered to do so by the Umpire – See Rule 7(e) or during the bowler's action but before he releases the ball) the umpire shall declare him out.

(d) Shall *continue* his run to the next post if he is between posts when the bowler becomes in possession of the ball and is in his square, but may not run past the post.

Penalty. The Umpire shall order the player back to the post he passed.

(e) May not remain at the same post as another batsman.

Penalty. The Umpire shall order the player who batted first to run on and he may be put out in the usual ways.

(f) When completing the track, shall not overtake any batsman who is running ahead.

Penalty. The Umpire shall declare the batsman who overtakes to be out.

(g) Shall not run beyond the first post after a backward hit until the ball returns or has been returned to the forward area.

Penalty. The Umpire shall order him back to 1st post.

(h) Must touch 4th post with his hand or bat.

Penalty. The Umpire shall declare him out if 4th post is touched with the ball by the fielding side provided that another ball has not been bowled.

(*i*) Shall not return to a post unless he is ordered to do so by the Umpire, or unless in the Umpire's opinion he has over-run a post.

Penalty. The Umpire shall order him on to the next post and he may be put out in the usual ways. A batsman may return to 4th post to make contact before the next ball is bowled.

8. OBSTRUCTION

Fielding side
A fielder shall be considered to have obstructed if he impedes, in any way, a batsman during his hitting action or when he is on the running track, or is attempting to make contact with the post, whether or not the fielder is holding the ball. He shall also be considered to have obstructed if he verbally misleads the other team.

Penalty. The Umpire shall award half a rounder to the batting team and the batsman shall be allowed to maker contact with the post to which he is running.

Batting side
(*a*) While waiting to bat, or after being given out, shall stand behind the marked line in the backward area out of the way of the backstop and 4th post fielders.

Penalty. The Umpire shall award half a rounder to the fielding side, in the event of obstruction.

(*b*) A batsman shall be considered to have obstructed if he:

(i) Impedes the player who is fielding the ball by deviating from the running track.

(ii) Intentionally deflects the course of the ball.

(iii) Verbally misleads the other team.

Penalty. The Umpire shall declare the batsman out and any rounder scored due to that obstruction shall be declared void.

(*c*) Whilst running round the track within the Rules, a batsman shall have right of way.

(*d*) A non-striking batsman causing obstruction and a rounder being scored by the striking batsman on this ball, the rounder would be declared void, but the striking batsman would remain in. (The obstructing batsman would be declared out.)

9. SCORING

The Winning Team
The team scoring the greater number of rounders shall win the game.

If a batsman stops within reach of a post, the fielders may prevent him from scoring by touching the next post with the ball or the hand holding the ball – See Rule 9(*b*) (iii). This does not prevent the batsman from continuing his run.

One Rounder

(*a*) One rounder only may be scored from any one hit. In the case of a no-ball which is hit and caught, the batsman may still score in the usual way.

(*b*) One rounder shall be scored if, after having hit the ball, the batsman succeeds in running round the track and touches the 4th post, or from 1st post when the ball returns or has been returned by a fielder to the forward area after a backward hit, provided that:

(i) He has not overtaken any other batsman – See Rule 7(*f*).

(ii) The bowler has not delivered another ball:

(iii) If he stopped at a post, the post *immediately ahead* has not been touched by a fielder with the ball or the hand holding the ball.

Half a Rounder

Half a rounder shall be scored by the batsman if he completes the track fulfilling the same conditions as for one rounder but without hitting the ball.

A Penalty Half Rounder

A penalty half rounder shall be awarded to the batting team when:

(*a*) The bowler delivers two consecutive no-balls to the same batsman. After a penalty half rounder for two consecutive no-balls is awarded, the previous no-balls are cancelled and the count starts again; or

(*b*) A fielder obstructs a batsman. See Rule 8, Obstruction. A penalty half rounder shall be awarded to the fielding team when waiting batsmen obstruct the fielders. See Rule 8, Obstruction.

One Rounder and Penalty Half Rounders

It should be noted that the rounder may be scored with the addition of the award:

(*a*) One penalty half rounder if the ball that is the second consecutive no-ball to that batsman.

(*b*) One penalty half rounder if the batsman is obstructed.

(*c*) Two penalty half rounders if the ball that is bowled if the second consecutive no-ball to that batsman and the batsman is obstructed.

10. BATSMEN OUT

(*a*) *A batsman* shall be declared out:

(i) If the ball is caught from bat or hand holding the bat, except on a no-ball.

(ii) If his foot projects over the front or back line of the batting square before he has hit the ball or it has passed him, except on a no-ball.

(iii) If he runs to the inside of a post, unless prevented from reaching it by an obstructing fielder.

(iv) If a fielder touched the post immediately ahead with the ball or with the hand holding the ball, while the batsman is running to that post and before the batsman has touched the post, excepting 1st post in the case of a no-ball. *NB* If the post is separated from the base, the base is touched.

(v) If he obstructs a fielder or intentionally deflects the course of the ball – See Rule 8, Obstruction.

(vi) If he overtakes another batsman.

(vii) If he loses contact or runs at any time when the bowler has the ball and is in his square (except an overrun – See Rule 7(*d*) – or unless ordered to do so by an Umpire See Rule 7(*e*).

(viii) During the bowler's action but before he releases the ball.

(ix) If after having been ordered to make contact with a post a batsman has not done so.

(x) If he drops or throws his bat deliberately.

(*b*) *Side out.* Where there is no batsman awaiting his turn to bat, all the batsmen on the running track can be put out simultaneously, by the ball being thrown full pitch or placed by any fielder into the batting square before any one of them has reached 4th post.

11. NO-BALL

(*a*) Decisions on height are based on the actual height of the batsman. Decisions on direction are based on the position of the batsman when the bowler releases the ball.

(*b*) A no-ball is one that:

(i) Is not delivered with a continuous and smooth underarm action (this does not prevent spin).

(ii) Is bowled when the bowler fails to keep both feet within the square until the ball is released (the lines of the square are considered to be part of the square and the bowler should be penalised *only* when any part of his foot projects over the line).

(iii) Is wide on the non-hitting side of the batsman.

(iv) Is higher than the top of the head or lower than the knee when it reaches the batsman – See Rule 11(*a*).

(v) Would hit the batsman – See Rule 11(*a*).

(vi) Hits the ground on the way to the batsman.

UMPIRES

There shall be two Umpires, the Batsman's Umpire, who shall stand on a level with the batsman in the batting square and in a position to see the

1st post without turning his head, and the Bowler's Umpire, who shall stand in such a position that he can see all the infringements of Rules for which he is responsible. This may necessitate a change of position to facilitate his view of a left-handed batsman.

The Umpires' decisions on any aspect of the game shall be final but they should appeal to each other on any point that is doubtful.

The Umpires should both keep a record of the score.

The Umpires should exchange positions after the first innings of both sides have been completed.

Captains may appeal.

The Umpire has the right to order a player off the pitch for unsportsmanlike conduct, with no substitution being possible.

Duties of Batsman's Umpire

(i) Call 'Rounder' or 'Half Rounder' and give the score of both sides, after a rounder or half rounder is scored or awarded.

(ii) Call 'No-ball' for balls that are not delivered with a continuous and smooth underarm action or for any balls that are too high or too low.

(iii) Call 'No-ball' if the bowler puts his foot over the front line of the bowling square – See Rule 11(*b*) (ii).

(iv) Give decisions concerning the batting square, 1st and 4th posts, backwards hits and all catches, and call 'Backward hit'.

(v) Call by name or number the next player to bat.

Duties of Bowler's Umpire

(i) Call 'Play' at beginning of each innings.

(ii) Call 'No-ball' for wides, for balls straight at or on the non-hitting side of the batsman.

(iii) Give decisions concerning 2nd and 3rd posts.

(iv) Call 'No-ball' if the bowler projects his foot over the back or side lines of the bowling square – See Rule 11(*b*).

A SIMPLE METHOD OF MARKING A ROUNDERS PITCH

The Pitch

The simplest way of marking the pitch is by using lengths of string. Put a peg into the ground where the right-hand front corner of the batting square is to be, and directly opposite that another peg at a distance of 17m. This gives the position of the 2nd post.

Take a length of string measuring 24m and tie a knot in the centre (each half 12m). Tie one end of the string to each peg and carry the centre knot out to the right until the string is taut. At the knot put in another peg. This gives the position of the 1st post. Then carry the centre knot to the left, pull the string taut, put in a peg. This gives the position of the 3rd post.

Take a length of string 17m long with a centre knot (each half 8.5m) and tie one end to the peg at 3rd post and the other to the peg first put in at the corner of the batting square. Carry the knot to the left. This gives the position of the 4th post.

The Bowling Square (2.5m by 2.5m)

To locate the centre of the front line of the square, stretch the 17m string from the first peg to the second post, then measure a distance of 7.5m along the string. The front line of the bowling square can then be marked, 1.25m either side of the string and parallel to the front line of the batting square. The other three sides of the square can then be marked. It will be found that if the string is stretched between the 1st and 3rd posts it cuts the side lines of the square 1m from the front line.

The Batting Square (2m by 2m)

The front line is made by marking a line extending 2m from the first peg towards and in a direct line with the 4th post and parallel to the front line of the bowling square. The remaining three sides of the square can then be marked.

The front line of the batting square is extended in both directions for at least 12m by solid lines.

Lines

Mark the line from the right-hand front corner of the batting square to 1st post; lines for waiting batsmen and batsmen out; and 2m line from 4th post into backward area.

Reprinted by permission of the National Rounders Association.

Rugby League Football

The Field of Play

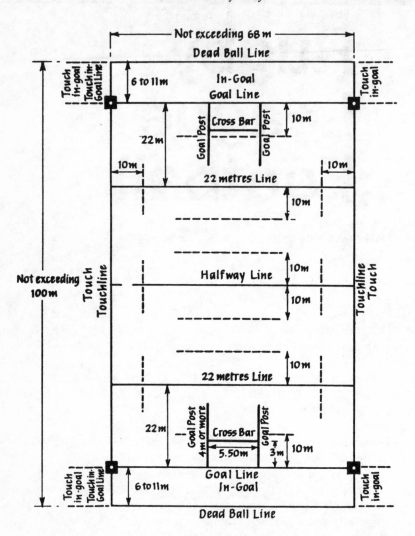

Rugby League Football

1. THE PLAYING FIELD

The plan of the playing field on the opposite page with the markings thereon and the Notes relating thereto are part of these Laws.

NOTES:
1. The touch-lines are in touch, the touch-in-goal lines are touch-in-goal, the goal-lines are in the in-goal area and the dead-ball line is beyond in-goal.
2. ⊡ Indicates a corner-post (see Glossary) placed at the intersection of each goal-line and touch-line. A corner-post is in touch-in-goal. Touch-judges should at all times ensure that corner-posts are correctly positioned.
3. The goal-posts are considered to extend indefinitely upwards. It is recommended that the bottom 2m of each upright be padded.
    ⴄ shaped goal-posts are permissible provided the relevant dimensions are observed and the rear stanchion lies outside the field of play.
4. For adult games the dimensions should be as near maximum as possible. Minimum permissible dimensions should be laid down in the rules of the competition in which a match is played.
5. The broken lines in the plan shall consist of marks or dots on the ground not more than 2m apart. It is of advantage for transverse broken lines to be marked across the full width of the field but if restricted as shown in the Plan then each shall be not less than 15m long.

2. GLOSSARY

The terms set out below shall have the meanings assigned to them:
Advantage. Allowing the advantage means allowing play to proceed if it

is to the advantage of the side which has not committed an offence or infringement.

Attacking team is the team which at the time has a territorial advantage. If a scrum is to be formed on the half-way line the team which last touched the ball before it went out of play is the attacking team.

Back as applied to a player means one who is not taking part in the scrum.

Ball back means to form a scrum where the ball was kicked from after it has entered touch on the full.

Behind when applied to a player means, unless otherwise stated, that both feet are behind the position in question. Similarly in front implies with both feet. When applied to a position on the field-of-play, behind means nearer to one's own goal-line than the point in question. Similarly in front of means nearer to one's opponents' goal-line.

Blind-side means the side of the scrum or of the play-the-ball nearer to touch (cf. open side).

Charging-down is blocking the path of the ball with hands, arm or body as it rises from an opponent's kick.

Converting a try is the act of kicking a goal following the scoring of a try.

Corner post is a post surmounted by a flag placed at the intersection of each touch-line and goal-line. The post shall be of non-rigid material and shall be not less than 1.25m high. The corner-posts are in touch-in-goal.

Dead ball means that the ball is out of play.

Defending team is the team opposing the attacking team (See above).

Differential penalty differs in one respect from a penalty kick in that a goal cannot be scored from it.

Drop goal, sometimes referred to as a field goal, is a goal scored by propelling the ball on the full, over the cross-bar by drop-kicking it.

Drop kick is a kick whereby the ball is dropped from the hands (or hand) and is kicked immediately it rebounds from the ground.

Drop-out means a drop-kick from between the posts or from the centre of the 22m line when bringing the ball back into play.

Dummy is the pretence of passing or otherwise releasing the ball while still retaining possession of it.

Field-of-play is the area bounded by, but not including, the touch-lines and goal-lines.

Forward means in a direction towards the opponents' dead-ball line. As applied to a player it means one who is at the time packing down in the scrum.

Forward pass is a throw towards the opponents' dead-ball line (See Section 10).

Foul play refers to the types of misconduct specified in Section 15, Law 1(*a*) (*b*) (*c*) and (*d*).

Free kick is the kick awarded to a team which kicks into touch from a penalty kick. The kick is taken 10m in from touch opposite the point of entry into touch and the ball may be kicked in any manner in any direction but a goal cannot be scored from it, nor can ground be gained by kicking into touch on the full.

General play refers to all aspects of play after a match has been started or restarted by a place kick, drop-out, penalty kick, free kick or scrum.

Full time means the end of the game. Also referred to as no-side.

Goal. See Section 6.

Grounding the Ball means:

(*a*) Placing the ball on the ground with hand or hands; or

(*b*) Exerting a downward pressure on the ball with hand or arm, the ball itself being on the ground; or

(*c*) Dropping on the ball and covering it with the part of the body above the waist and below the neck, the ball itself being on the ground.

Half-time means the end of the first half of the game.

Handover is the surrendering of the ball to the opposition after a team has been tackled the statutory number of successive times (Section 11, paragraph 7).

Heel is when a player propels the ball behind him with the sole or heel of his foot.

Hook is the act of the hooker when he strikes with a foot for the ball in the scrum.

In-goal. See the diagram on page 706.

In possession means to be holding or carrying the ball.

Kick means imparting motion to the ball with any part of the leg (except the heel) from knee to toe inclusive.

Kick-off. See Section 8.

Knock-on means to knock the ball towards the opponents' dead-ball line with hand or arm.

Loose arm is an offence by the hooker if he packs with one arm loose in the scrum.

Loose ball is when during play the ball is not held by a player and is not being scrummaged.

Loose head refers to the front-row forward in the scrum who is nearest to the Referee.

Mark is the point at which a penalty kick or free kick is awarded or a scrum is formed.

Obstruction is the illegal act of impeding an opponent who does not have the ball.

Off-side, as applied to a player, means that he is temporarily out of play and may be penalised if he joins in the game (See Section 14).

On-side means that a player is not off-side.

Open-side means the side of the scrum or the play-the-ball further from touch (cf. blind side).

On the full means the ball is kicked over a given line without first bouncing.

Pack refers collectively to the forwards of any one team. To pack down means to form a scrum.

Pass is a throw of the ball from one player to another.

Penalise is to award a penalty kick against an offending player.

Penalty Kick. See Section 13.

Place Kick is to kick the ball after it has been placed on the ground for that purpose.

Playing Area is the area enclosed by the fence, or other such line of demarcation, which prevents the encroachment of spectators.

Playing field is the area bounded by, but not including, the touch-lines and dead-ball lines.

Play-the-ball is the act of bringing the ball into play after a tackle (See Section 11).

Prop is the front-row forward in each team nearest to the scrum-half who is putting the ball into the scrum.

Punt is a kick whereby the ball is dropped from the hand or hands and is kicked before it touches the ground.

Put-in, also known as feeding the scrum, is the rolling of the ball into the scrum.

Scrum or scrummage or scrimmage (See Section 12). Where a team loses the advantages of the loose head and put-in the scrum is said to be awarded against that team.

Strike, as applied to the foot, means to attempt to secure possession of the ball, usually by heeling it, in a scrum or at a play-the-ball.

Tackle. See Section 11.

Touch-down is the grounding of the ball by a defending player in his own in-goal.

Touch-in-goal. See Section 9.

Try. See Section 6.

Upright tackle is where the player in possession is effectively tackled without being brought to the ground (See Section 11).

Voluntary tackle is where the player in possession voluntarily stops play when not effectively tackled (See Section 11).

3. THE BALL

1. The game shall be played with an oval air-inflated ball, the out casing of which shall be of leather or other material approved by the

International Board, and nothing shall be used in its construction which might prove dangerous to the players.

2. The dimensions of the ball shall be:

	Desired Dimensions	*Permissible Min.*	*Permissible Max.*
Length	28cm	27cm	29cm
Longest circumference	74cm	73cm	75cm
Widest circumference	59cm	58cm	61cm
Weight (clean and dry)	410g	380g	440g

3. The Referee shall blow his whistle immediately he notices that the size and shape of the ball no longer comply with the Laws of the Game.

4. THE PLAYER AND PLAYERS' EQUIPMENT

The game shall be played by two teams each consisting of not more than 13 players.

2. Each team shall inform the Referee, prior to the commencement of the game, the names of up to 4 substitutes and may at any time during the course of the game replace up to two players from among those substitutes. A player once replaced shall take no further part in the game. A replacement must be sanctioned by the Referee and can only be effected when the ball is out of play or play is stopped because of injury.

3. For ease of identification it is permissible for players' clothing to bear numbers (1 to 13 with additional numbers for the substitutes), the numbers normally relating to the positions of the players in their respective teams, these positions being referred to be name as set out hereunder.

Backs:
1. Full-back
2. Right wing threequarter
3. Right centre threequarter
4. Left centre threequarter
5. Left wing threequarter
6. Stand-off half or five-eighth
7. Scrum half

Forwards:
8. Prop
9. Hooker
10. Front-row forward

11. Second-row forward
12. Second-row forward
13. Loose forward

4. (*a*) A player shall not wear anything that might prove dangerous to other players.

(*b*) A player's normal gear shall consist of a jersey of distinctive colour and/or pattern (preferably numbered), a pair of shorts, stockings of distinctive colour and/or pattern and studded boots or shoes.

(*c*) Protective clothing may be worn provided it contains nothing of a rigid nature.

(*d*) The Referee shall order a player to remove any part of his equipment which might be considered dangerous and shall not allow the player to take any further part in the game until the order is obeyed. The player shall retire from the playing field to remove the offending item if the start or restart of the game would otherwise be delayed.

(*e*) The colours of the jerseys worn by competing teams shall be easily distinguishable and, if, in the opinion of the Referee similarity between the jerseys might affect the proper conduct of the game he may, at his discretion, order either team to change jerseys in accordance with the Rules governing the competition in which the game is played.

(*f*) Studs on boots or shoes shall be no less than 8mm diameter at the apex and, if made of metal, shall have rounded edges.

5 MODE OF PLAY

1. The object of the game shall be to ground the ball in the opponents' in-goal to score tries (See Section 6) and to kick the ball over the opponents' cross-bar to score goals (See Section 6).

2. The captains of the two teams shall toss for choice of ends in the presence of the Referee. The team of the captain losing the toss shall kick-off to start the game.

3. Once play has started any player who is on-side or not out of play can run with the ball, kick it in any direction and throw or knock it in any direction other than towards his opponents' dead-ball line (See Section 10 for Knock-on and Forward Pass).

4. A player who during play is holding the ball may be tackled by an opposing player or players in order to prevent him from running with the ball or from kicking or passing it to one of his own team (See Section 11 for Tackle).

5. A player who is not holding the ball shall not be tackled or obstructed (See Section 15).

6. SCORING – TRIES AND GOALS

1. A try shall count 4 points. A conversion goal or a penalty goal shall count 2 points. A drop goal during play shall count 1 point.

2. The game shall be won by the side scoring the greater number of points. If both sides score an equal number of points, or if both sides fail to score, then the game shall be drawn.

3. A try is scored when:

(a) A player first grounds the ball in his opponents' in-goal, provided that he is not in touch or touch-in-goal or on or over the dead-ball line.

(b) Opposing players simultaneously ground the ball in the in-goal area provided that the attacking player is not in touch or touch-in-goal or on or over the dead-ball line.

(c) A tackled player's momentum carries him into the opponents' in-goal where he grounds the ball even if the ball has first touched the ground in the field-of-play but provided that when the ball crosses the goal-line the player is not in touch or touch-in goal or on or over the dead-ball line.

(d) The Referee awards a penalty try which he may do if, in his opinion, a try would have been scored but for the unfair play of the defending team. A penalty try is awarded between the goal-posts irrespective of where the offence occurred.

(e) An attacking player carrying the ball comes into contact with the Referee or a Touch-Judge or an encroaching spectator in the opponents' in-goal and play is thereby irregularly affected.

4. The try is awarded:

(a) Where grounded if scored as in 3(a) and 3(b) above.

(b) Where it first crosses the goal-line if scored as in 3(c) above.

(c) Between the posts if a penalty try.

(d) Where contact took place if scored as in 3(e) above.

5. Only the Referee may award a try but he may take into consideration advice given by the Touch-Judges before arriving at his decision. He shall signal that a try has been scored by pointing to where the try has been awarded but should only do so after looking at the two Touch-Judges to ensure they are not reporting a prior incident.

6. A goal is scored if the whole of the ball at any time during its flight passes over the opponents' cross-bar towards the dead-ball line after being kicked on the full by a player (and not being touched in flight by any other player) in any of these circumstances:

(a) By a place-kick after a try has been scored and counts 2 points.

(b) By a place-kick or a drop-kick when a penalty kick as been awarded and counts 2 points.

(c) By a drop-kick during play from any position in the field-of-play and counts one point.

7. A kick at goal after a try may be taken from any point on an imaginary line drawn parallel to the touch-line in the field-of-play and through the point where the try was awarded. A kick at goal from a penalty kick may be taken from the mark or from any point on an imaginary line drawn from the mark towards the kicker's own goal-line and parallel to the touch-line.

8. When a kick at goal is being taken following a try, the opposing players shall stand outside the field-of-play. Players of the kicker's team must be behind the ball.

When a kick at goal is being taken from a penalty kick, the opponents shall retire to their goal-line or not less than 10m from the mark (See Section 13).

It is illegal to attempt to distract the attention of a player who is kicking at goal.

9. For the purpose of judging a kick at goal, the goal-posts are assumed to extend indefinitely upwards.

10. When a kick at goal is being taken, the Referee shall assign one Touch-Judge to each post. If a Touch-Judge is of the opinion that a goal has been scored he shall raise his flag above his head. If the kick is unsuccessful he shall wave his flag in front of him and below the waist. If there is no disagreement between the Touch-Judges their decision shall be accepted. In the event of disagreement, the Referee shall decide.

7. TIME-KEEPING

1. The game shall normally be of 80 minutes' duration. At half-time there shall be an interval of 5 minutes, but this may be extended or reduced by the Referee.

2. A team shall defend one in-goal for the first half of the game and then change ends for the second half.

3. If time expires in either half when the ball is out of play or a player in possession is tackled and has not risen to his feet, the Referee shall immediately blow his whistle to terminate play. If the ball is in play when time expires, the Referee shall terminate play when next the ball goes out of play or a player in possession is tackled but time shall be extended to allow a penalty kick or a kick at goal to be taken, in which case the half is terminated when next the ball goes out of play or a tackle is effected, unless a further penalty is awarded, in which case time is again extended for the kick to be taken.

4. Extra time shall be added to each half to compensate for time wasted or lost from any cause. The Referee shall be the sole judge of extra time. He shall inform the respective captains how much extra time is to be played and shall keep a written record of same except where these duties have been delegated to a timekeeper.

5. If the continuance of play endangers an injured player the Referee may stop the game. If, when the game is stopped, a player is in possession of the ball the game shall be recommenced by that player playing-the-ball. Otherwise play shall be restarted with a scrum at the point where the ball was when play was stopped the team then in possession or last in possession having the loose head and the put-in.

8. THE KICK-OFF AND DROP-OUT

1. The kick-off is a place-kick from the centre of the half-way line. The team which loses the toss for choice of ends kicks-off to start the first half of the game and their opponents kick-off to start the second half.

When points have been scored, the team against which the points have been scored shall kick-off to restart the game.

2. The game is restarted with a place kick from the centre of the 22m line if:

(*a*) An attacking player last touches the ball before it goes out of play over the dead-ball line, or into touch-in-goal except from a penalty kick (see 3 below) or from a kick-off from the centre of the half-way line (See 4*g* and 5*b* below).

(*b*) An attacking player infringes in the in-goal area. In the event of a deliberate breach by an attacking player a penalty kick is awarded 5m in the field-of-play in line with where the breach was committed (See Section 13).

(*c*) A defending player, in his in-goal, takes a kick in general play from an opponent on the full.

The ball may be kicked in any direction and is immediately in play. Opposing players shall retire 10m from the 22m line and shall not advance until the ball has been kicked. Defending players shall not advance in front of the ball before it is kicked. Any deliberate offence by either team shall incur a penalty to be awarded at the centre of the 22m line.

3. If the ball goes dead in-goal from a penalty kick (not necessarily a kick at goal) the game is restarted with a drop-out by a defending player from the centre of the 22m line.

4. The game is restarted with drop-out by a defending player from the centre of his goal-line if:

(*a*) A defending player last touches the ball before it goes over the dead-ball line or into touch-in-goal.

(*b*) A defending player accidentally infringes in the in-goal area.

(*c*) A defending player touches down in the in-goal area.

(*d*) A defending player in possession is tackled in the in goal area.

(*e*) A defending player kicks the ball into touch on the full from his own in-goal.

(*f*) The ball or a defending player carrying the ball touches the Referee, a Touch-Judge, or an encroaching spectator in the in-goal area and play is thereby irregularly affected.

(*g*) The ball goes over the dead-ball line or into touch-in-goal other than on the full from a kick-off from the centre of the half-way line without being touched by or touching a defending player.

5. See Law 2 of this Section re ball caught on the full before being made dead in-goal.

6. A player who kicks-off or drops-out shall be penalised if he:

(*a*)   Advances in front of the appropriate line before kicking the ball.

(*b*)   Kicks the ball on the full over the touch-line, touch-in goal line, or over the dead-ball line.

(*c*)   Kicks the ball so that it fails to travel at least 10m forward in the field-of-play.

(*d*)   Kicks the ball other than in the prescribed manner.

7. Any other player shall be penalised if he:

(*a*)   Wilfully touches the ball from a kick-off or drop-out before it has travelled 10m forward in the field-of play.

(*b*)   Runs in front of one of his own team who is kicking-off or dropping-out.

(*c*)   Approaches nearer than 10m to the line from which the kick is being taken when an opponent is kicking-off or dropping-out.

8. A penalty kick resulting from any offence at the kick-off shall be taken from the centre of the half-way line.

Any penalty kick resulting from the restarting of play from the 22m line shall be taken from the centre of that line.

A penalty kick resulting from any offence at the drop-out from between the posts shall be taken from the centre of the line drawn parallel to and 10m from the goal-line.

9. TOUCH AND TOUCH-IN-GOAL

1. The ball is in touch when it or a player in contact with it touches the touch-line or the ground beyond the touch-line or any object on or outside the touch-line except when a player, tackled in the field-of-play, steps into touch as he regains his feet, in which case he shall play-the-ball in the field-of-play.

The ball is in touch if a player jumps from touch and while off the ground touches the ball. The ball is not in touch if during flight it crosses the touch-line but is knocked back by a player who is off the ground after jumping from the field-of-play.

2. The ball is in touch-in-goal when it or a player in contact with it touches the touch-in-goal line, or any object on or outside the touch-in-goal lines.

3. When a ball has entered touch or touch-in-goal, the point of entry shall be taken as the point at which the ball first crossed the touch or touch-in-goal line.

4. If the ball is kicked by or bounces off a player in a forward direction – except from in-goal, Section 8, Paragraph 4(*e*) – and it goes into touch on the full, a scrum is formed where contact with the ball was made (but not nearer than 10m to the touch-line or 5m to the goal-line) – See Section 12.

5. If the ball is kicked into touch from a penalty kick the game is restarted by placing the ball on the ground 10m infield opposite the point of entry into touch – see Section 13.

6. Other than as outlined in Paragraphs 4 and 5 above, the game is restarted after the ball has gone into touch by forming a scrum 10m in-field opposite the point of entry into touch but not nearer than 5m to the goal-line – See Section 12.

10. KNOCK-ON AND FORWARD PASS

1. A player shall be penalised if he deliberately knocks-on or passes forward.

2. If, after knocking-on accidentally, the player knocking-on regains or kicks the ball before it touches the ground, a goal-post, a cross-bar or an opponent, then play shall be allowed to proceed. Otherwise play shall stop and a scrum shall be formed.

3. To charge-down a kick is permissible and is not a knock-on.

11. THE TACKLE AND PLAY-THE-BALL

1. A player in possession may be tackled by an opposing player or players. It is illegal to tackle or obstruct a player who is not in possession.

2. A player in possession is tackled:

(*a*) When he is held by one or more opposing players and the ball or the hand or arm holding the ball comes into contact with the ground.

(*b*) When he is held by one or more opposing players in such a manner that he can make no further progress and cannot part with the ball.

(*c*) When, being held by an opponent, the tackled player makes it evident that he has succumbed to the tackle and wishes to be released in order to play-the-ball.

(*d*) When he is lying on the ground and an opponent places a hand on him.

3. Once a player in possession has been tackled it is illegal for any player to move or try to move him from the point where the tackle is effected.

4. A player in possession shall not deliberately and unnecessarily allow himself to be tackled by voluntarily falling to the ground when not held by an opponent. If a player drops on a loose ball, he shall not remain on the ground waiting to be tackled if he has time to regain his feet and continue play.

5. If a tackled player, because of his momentum, slides along the ground, the tackle is deemed to have been effected where his slide ends – See Section 6, Paragraph 3(*c*).

6. If any doubt arises as to a tackle, the Referee should give a verbal instruction to 'play on' or shout 'held' as the case may be.

7. A team in possession shall be allowed 5 successive 'play-the-balls'; but if tackled a 6th time, or there is an infringement by that team after the 5th play-the-ball, which in other circumstances would result in a scrum (other than a scrum following a ball being kicked into touch after landing in the field-of-play), the ball not having been touched by an opponent during the sequence of tackles, the ball shall be brought into play by an opposing player playing-the-ball at the point of tackle or infringement. The play-the-ball for this purpose shall not be counted for the purposes of the tackle count and shall operate as provided for in Paragraph 10 of this Section.

8. A tackled player shall not intentionally part with the ball other than by bringing it into play in the prescribed manner. If, after being tackled, he accidentally loses possession, a scrum shall be formed.

9. Once a tackle has been completed, no player shall take or attempt to take the ball from the tackled player.

10. The play-the-ball shall operate as follows:

(*a*) The tackled player shall be immediately released and shall not be touched until the ball is in play.

(*b*) The tackled player shall without delay regain his feet where he was tackled, lift the ball clear of the ground, face his opponents' goal-line and drop or place the ball on the ground in front of his foremost foot.

(*c*) One opponent may take up position immediately opposite the tackled player.

(*d*) Neither the tackled player nor the player marking him shall raise a foot from the ground before the ball has been released.

(*e*) When the ball touches the ground if may be kicked or heeled in any direction by the foot of either the tackled player or the player marking him. The ball is in play when it has come clear of the two players in the play-the-ball movement, i.e. the tackled player and the player marking him.

(*f*) A player of each side, to be known as the acting half-back, may stand immediately and directly behind his own player taking part in the play-the-ball and must remain in this position until the ball has come clear of the two players in the play-the-ball movement.

(*g*) Players, other than the two taking part in the play-the-ball and the two acting half-backs, are out of play if they fail to retire 5m or more behind their own player taking part in the play-the-ball or to their own goal-line. Having retired 5m they may not advance until the ball has come clear of the two players in the play-the-ball movement. A player who is out of play may again take part in the game when the advantage gained by not retiring has been lost.

11. The play-the-ball must be performed as quickly as possible. Any player who intentionally delays the bringing of the ball into play shall be penalised.

12. If part of the tackled player is on or over the goal-line but the ball is in the field of play and tackled player shall play the ball where it lies. If a player is tackled in an upright position bestriding the goal-line, he is deemed to be tackled in the in-goal area.

12. THE SCRUM

1. A scrum is formed to restart play whenever play is not being restarted with a kick-off, a drop-out (Section 8), a penalty kick (Section 13) or a play-the-ball (Section 11).

2. To form a scrum not more than 3 forwards of either side shall interlock arms and heads and create a clear tunnel at right angles to the touch-line. The forward in the centre of a front-row (i.e. the hooker) shall bind with his arms over the shoulders of the 2 supporting forwards. Not more than 2 second-row forwards on each team shall pack behind their respective front rows by interlocking arms and placing their heads in the two spaces between the hooker and his front-row forwards. The loose forward of each side shall pack behind his second-row forwards by placing his head in the space between them. All forwards must pack with their bodies and legs at right angles to the tunnel and the upper parts of their bodies horizontal. Once the ball has been put in the scrum no other play can lend his weight to it.

3. No more than 6 players on each team shall assist in the formation of a scrum and when the ball is in the scrum no more than 7 players of each side shall act as backs.

4. It is permissible for the forwards to push once the scrum has been correctly formed, but if it moves an appreciable distance to the disadvantage of any one team before the ball is put in, then the Referee shall order the scrum to re-form in its original position.

5. (*a*) At the scrum the non-offending team shall have the loose head and the put-in.

(*b*) In the case of a mutual infringement, the attacking team shall have the loose head and the put-in.

6. (*a*) The ball shall be put into the scrum from the Referee's side by holding it in a horizontal position with a point in each hand and rolling it along the ground. It must be put into the centre of the tunnel formed by opposing front-row forwards.

(*b*) The ball shall not be put in before the scrum has been correctly formed.

(*c*) There shall be no undue delay in putting the ball into the scrum.

(*d*) The player putting it in shall not hesitate or dummy and after putting it in he shall immediately retire behind his own pack of forwards.

7. The scrum half of the team not having the put-in shall retire behind his last row of forwards. All other players outside the scrum (other than the scrum half putting the ball in) shall retire 5m or more behind the last row of forwards in their respective teams in the scrum and shall remain so until the ball has emerged correctly from the scrum.

8. When the ball is in the scrum it can only be played with the foot.

The front-row forwards shall not advance their feet into the tunnel or have one foot raised before the ball is put in or strike for the ball before the hookers.

A hooker may strike for the ball with either foot once it has contacted the ground in the centre of the tunnel.

After the hookers have struck for the ball the other forwards in the scrum may kick or heel the ball.

No player shall wilfully collapse a scrum or wilfully have any part of him other than his feet in contact with the ground.

A player shall not wilfully delay the correct formation of a scrum.

9. To be in play, the ball must emerge from between and behind the inner feet of the second-row forwards.

If the ball does not emerge correctly and the fault cannot be attributed to any one team then it should be put into the scrum once again.

10. If a scrum is ordered it shall normally be formed where the breach of Laws occurs. If such breach is within 10m of a touch-line or 5m of a goal-line the scrum shall be brought in 10m from the touch-line and 5m from the goal-line.

11. If a penalty kick is awarded relating to a scrum offence and the scrum has wandered from its original position, the mark is where the scrum was first formed.

12. If the ball emerges correctly from the scrum it is in play even though the scrum has wheeled. Any forward can detach himself from the scrum to gather or kick the ball. Any back can similarly play it provided he remained behind the scrum until the ball emerged.

13. PENALTY KICK

1. A penalty kick shall be awarded against any player who is guilty of misconduct (Section 15) provided that this is not to the disadvantage of the non-offending side. Unless otherwise stated, the mark is where the offence occurs. If misconduct occurs in touch, the mark shall be 5m from the touch-line in the field-of-play and opposite where the offence occurred or, *in the case of obstruction, where the ball next bounces or is caught in the field-of-play, or 5m opposite the point of entry if the ball enters touch on the full, or 5m from the goal-line if the ball crosses the goal-line on the full, whichever is to the greater advantage of the non-offending side.* If the offence is committed by a defender in his own in-goal or an attacker in his opponents' in-goal, the mark is taken 5m into the field-of-play opposite where the offence occurred. In the event of further misconduct by the offending side, the Referee shall advance the mark once only 10m towards the offending team's goal-line.

2. A player may take a penalty kick by punting, drop-kicking, or place-kicking the ball from any point on or behind the mark and equidistant from the touch-line. Other than when kicking for goal the ball may be kicked in any direction, after which it is in play.

3. Players of the kicker's side must be behind the ball when it is kicked.

   Players of the team opposing the kicker shall retire to their own goal-line or 10m or more from the mark towards their own goal-line and shall not make any attempt to interfere with or distract the attention of the kicker. They may advance after the ball has been kicked.

4. If the ball is kicked into touch without touching any other player the kicking team shall restart play with a free kick. Opposing players shall retire 10m from the point of entry into touch or to their own goal-line.

5. No player shall deliberately take any action which is likely to delay the taking of a penalty kick.

6. If the kick is not taken as stated or if a player of the kicker's team infringes, a scrum shall be formed at the mark.

7. When the Referee penalises a player he must explain the nature of the offence.

8. If a penalty is awarded for an offence by the attacking team in the opponents' in-goal area the mark shall be 5m in the field-of-play opposite where the offence occurred. For an offence in-goal by the defending team which incurs a penalty, the mark is in the field-of-play 5m from the goal-line and opposite where the offence occurred, except for foul play against a try scorer (See Paragraph 9 below).

9. If a player fouls an opponent who is touching down for a try, a penalty kick at goal shall be taken from in front of the goal-posts after the attempt to convert the try. After this kick has been taken the ball shall be deemed dead and play shall be restarted from the half-way line. This Law applies to the period during which the ball is touched down for a try and not to any subsequent period.

10. (*a*) If a player fouls an opponent who is attempting a drop goal, a penalty kick shall be awarded in front of the goal-posts.

(*b*) If the attempt at drop goal is successful, a kick at goal must be taken from the penalty kick and play restarted from the centre of the half-way line irrespective of the outcome of that kick.

(*c*) If the attempt at drop goal is unsuccessful, the penalty kick can be taken in any manner provided for in the Laws and play restarted according to the outcome of that kick.

14. OFF-SIDE

1. A player is off-side except when he is in his own in-goal if the ball is kicked, touched or held by one of his own team behind him.

2. An off-side player shall not take any part in the game or attempt in any way to influence the course of the game. He shall not encroach within 10m of an opponent who is waiting for the ball and shall immediately retire 10m from any opponent who first secures possession of the ball.

3. An off-side player is placed on-side if:

(*a*) An opponent moves 10m or more with the ball.

(*b*) An opponent touches the ball without retaining it.

(*c*) One of his own side in possession of the ball runs in front of him.

(*d*) One of his own side kicks or knocks the ball forward and takes up a position in front of him in the field-of-play.

(*e*) He retires behind the point where the ball was last touched by one of his own team.

15. PLAYER'S MISCONDUCT

1. A player is guilty of misconduct if he:

(*a*) Deliberately trips, kicks or strikes another player.

(*b*) Attacks the head of an opponent when effecting a tackle.

(*c*) Drops knees first on to an opponent who is on the ground.

(*d*) Uses any dangerous throw when affecting a tackle.

(*e*) Deliberately breaks the Laws of the Game.

(*f*) Uses foul or obscene language.

(*g*) Disputes a decision of the Referee or Touch-Judge.

(*h*) Re-enters the field-of-play without the permission of the Referee or a Touch-Judge having previously temporarily retired from the game.

(*i*) Behaves in any way contrary to the true spirit of the game.

(*j*) Deliberately obstructs an opponent who is not in possession.

16. DUTIES OF REFEREE AND TOUCH-JUDGES

1. In all matches a Referee and two Touch-Judges shall be appointed or mutually agreed upon by the contesting teams.

2. The Referee shall enforce the Laws of the Game and may impose penalties for any deliberate breach of the Laws. He shall be the sole judge on matters of fact except those relating to touch and touch-in-goal (See Paragraph 11 below).

3. He shall record the tries and goals scored during the match.

4. He shall be the sole timekeeper except where this duty has been delegated to another person (See Section 7).

5. He may, at his discretion, temporarily suspend or prematurely terminate a match because of adverse weather, undue interference by spectators, misbehaviour by players, or any other cause which, in his opinion, interferes with his control of the game.

6. He shall not allow anyone apart from the players on to the playing area without permission.

7. In the event of misconduct by a player, the Referee shall, at his discretion, caution, temporarily suspend for 10 minutes, or dismiss the offender.

8. The players are under the control of the Referee from the time they enter the playing area until they leave it.

9. The Referee must carry a whistle which he shall blow to commence and terminate each half of the game. Except for these occasions the blowing of the whistle shall temporarily stop the play. The Referee shall blow the whistle:

(*a*) When a try or a goal has been scored.

(*b*) When the ball has gone out of play.

(*c*) When he detects a breach of the Laws of the Game, except when to stop the play would be to the disadvantage of the non-offending team.

(*d*) When play is irregularly affected by the ball or the player carrying the ball coming into contact with the Referee, a Touch-Judge, or with any person not taking part in the match or with any object which should not normally be on the playing field.

(*e*) When any irregularity, not provided for in these Laws, occurs and one team unjustifiably gains an advantage.

(*f*) When a stoppage is necessary in order to enforce the Laws or for any other reason.

10. If the Referee judges on a matter of fact, he shall not subsequently alter that judgement but he may cancel any decision made if prior foul play of which he had no knowledge is reported to him by a Touch-Judge.

11. The Referee shall accept the decision of a neutral Touch-Judge relating to touch and touch-in-goal play and to kicks at goal.

12. Each Touch-Judge shall remain in touch, one on each side of, and near to, the playing field except:

(*a*) When judging kicks at goal (See Section 6); and

(*b*) When reporting a player's misconduct which has escaped the notice of the Referee.

13. Each Touch-Judge must carry a flag, triangular in shape, the longest sides being equal and not less than 30cm and the short side being not less than 23cm. The flag must be attached by the short side to a stick, the length of which shall be not less than 45cm.

14. A Touch-Judge shall indicate when and where the ball goes into touch by raising his flag and standing opposite the point of entry into touch except in the case of ball back (See Section 9, Paragraph 4) when the Touch-Judge must indicate that no ground has been gained by waving his flag above his head accentuating the movements in the direction of the kicker's goal-line.

15. If the ball enters touch-in-goal the Touch-Judge shall wave his flag above his head and then point it towards the goal-posts if the ball last touched a defending player, or towards the 22m line if it was last touched by an attacking player.

16. Touch-Judges shall assist the Referee in judging kicks at goal (See Section 6, Paragraph 10).

17. When a penalty kick is being taken, the nearer Touch-Judge shall take up a position near the touch-line 10m beyond the mark to act as a marker for the team which is required to retire. He shall wave his flag horizontally in front of him if any player fails to retire 10m.

18. In cases where circumstances in connection with the match are likely to be made the subject of official investigation, the Referee and Touch-Judges shall report to the investigating authority only and shall refrain from expressing criticism or comment through other channels.

Reprinted by permission of the Rugby Football League. Full notes and interpretations of these Laws, and the Referee's signals, can be found in the official Rugby Football League's International Laws of the Game and Notes on the Laws, obtainable from the Rugby Football League.

Rugby Union Football

The Field of Play

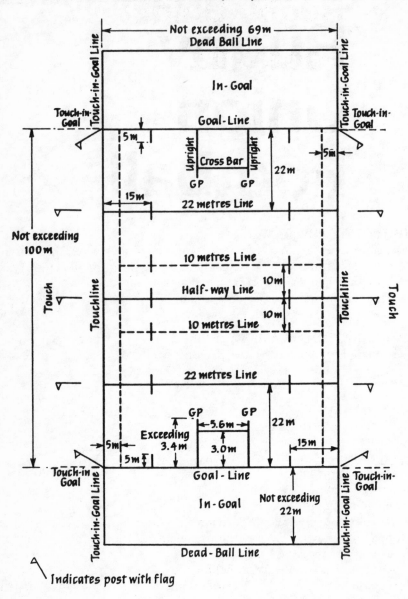

Rugby Union Football

OBJECT OF THE GAME

The object of the game is that two teams of 15 players each, observing fair play according to the Laws and a sporting spirit, should by carrying, passing, and kicking the ball score as many points as possible, the team scoring the greater number of points to be the winner of the match.

DECLARATION OF AMATEURISM

The game is an amateur game. No one is allowed to seek or to receive payment or other material reward for taking part in the game.

DEFINITIONS

The following terms have the meaning assigned to them:

Beyond or **behind** or **in front** of any position implies 'with both feet', except when unsuited to the context.

Dead means that the ball is for the time being out of play. This occurs when the Referee blows his whistle to indicate a stoppage of play or when an attempt to convert a try is unsuccessful.

Defending team means the team in whose half of the ground the stoppage to play occurs and the opponents of the defending team are referred to as **the attacking team**.

Kick. A kick is made by propelling the ball with part of the leg or foot (except the heel), from knee to toe inclusive. If the player is holding the ball, he must propel it out of his hands, or if it is on the ground, he must propel it a visible distance.

Drop kick. A drop kick is made by letting the ball fall from the hand (or hands) to the ground and kicking it at the first rebound as it rises.

Place kick. A place kick is made by kicking the ball after it has been placed on the ground for that purpose.

Punt. A punt is made by letting the ball fall from the hand (or hands) and kicking it before it touches the ground.

Mark. The mark is the place at which a free kick or penalty kick is awarded.

Line through the mark (or place). Except where specifically stated otherwise, the words 'a line through the mark' or 'a line through the place' always means a line parallel to the touch line.

Union means the controlling body under whose jurisdiction the match is played and in the case of an International Match it means the International Rugby Football Board or a Committee thereof.

Other definitions are included in and have effect as part of the Laws.

LAWS

1. Ground
The field-of-play is the area shown on the plan on page 726, bounded by, but not including, the goal-lines and touch-lines. The playing area is the field-of-play and in-goal. The playing enclosure is the playing area and a reasonable area surrounding it.

The plan, including all words and figures thereon, is to take effect as part of these Laws.

The terms appearing on the plan are to bear their apparent meaning and to be deemed part of the definitions as if separately included.

(1) All lines shown on the plan must be suitably marked out. The touch-lines are in touch. The goal-lines are in-goal. The dead-ball line is *not* in-goal. The touch-in-goal lines and corner posts are in touch-in-goal. The goal-posts are to be erected in the goal-lines. The 22m lines are in the 22m areas.

(2) The game must be played on a ground of the area (maximum) shown on the plan and marked in accordance with the plan. The surface must be grass-covered or, where this is not available, clay or sand, provided the surface is not of dangerous hardness.

(3) Any objection by the visiting team about the ground or the way it is marked out must be made to the Referee before the first kick-off.

2. Ball
(1) The ball when new shall be oval in shape, of four panels, and of the following dimensions:

Length in line	280 to 300mm
Circumference (end on)	760 to 790mm
Circumference (in width)	580 to 620mm
Weight	400 to 440g

(2) The dimensions of the ball may be reduced only for younger schoolboys.

(3) Balls may be specially treated to make them resistant to mud and easier to grip. The casings need not be of leather.

3. Number of Players

(1) A match shall be played by not more than 15 players in each team.

(2) When a Union authorises matches to be played with fewer than 15 players, the Laws of the Game shall apply except that there shall be no fewer than 3 players in a scrummage at all times.

(3) Replacement of players shall be allowed in recognised trial matches as determined by the Unions having jurisdiction over the match.

(4) In all other matches, a player may be replaced only on account of injury and subject to the following conditions.

(*a*) Not more than 2 players in each team may be replaced.

Exceptions: Up to 6 players may be replaced:

　(i) In matches between teams of schoolboys or teams where all players are under age 21, the age limitation being applied from the commencement of the official season of the visited Union.

　(ii) In domestic matches as determined by the Union having jurisdiction over the match.

(*b*) A player who has been replaced must *not* resume playing in the match.

(5) (*a*) In matches in which a national representative team is playing, a player may be replaced *only* when, in the opinion of a medical practitioner, the player is so injured that he should not continue playing in the match.

(*b*) For such competitions and other domestic matches as a Union gives express permission, an injured player may be replaced on the advice of a medically trained person, or if a medically trained person is not present, with the approval of the Referee.

(6) If the Referee is advised by a doctor or other medically trained person or for any other reason considers that a player is so injured that it would be harmful for him to continue playing, the Referee shall require the player to leave the playing area.

For this purpose the Referee may also require a player to leave the field to be examined medically.

(7) Any objection by either team as regards the number of players in a team may be made to the Referee at any time but the objection shall not affect any score previously obtained.

4. Players' Dress

(1) A player must not wear dangerous projections such as buckles or rings.

(2) Shoulder pads of the 'harness' type must not be worn. If the Referee is satisfied that a player requires protection following an injury to a shoulder, the wearing of a pad of cottonwool, sponge rubber or similar soft material may be permitted provided the pad is attached to the body or sewn on to the jersey.

(3) Studs of a player's boots must conform to the British Standard BS 6366: 1983. They must be circular, securely fastened to the boots and of the following dimensions:

Maximum length (measured from sole)   18mm
Minimum diameter at base   13mm
Minimum diameter at top   10mm
Minimum diameter of integral washer   20mm

The wearing of a single stud at the toe of a boot is prohibited.

(4) The Referee has power to decide before or during the match that any part of a player's dress is dangerous. He must then order the player to remove the dangerous part and permit him to resume playing only after it has been removed.

5. Toss, Time
No-side is the end of a match.

(1) Before a match begins the captains shall toss for the right to kick-off, or the choice of ends.

(2) The duration of play in a match shall be such time not exceeding 80 minutes as shall be directed by the Union or, in the absence of such direction, as agreed upon by the teams or, if not agreed, as fixed by the Referee. In International matches two periods of 40 minutes each shall be played.

(3) Play shall be divided into two halves. At half-time the teams shall change ends and there shall be an interval of not more than 5 minutes.

(4) A period not exceeding 1 minute shall be allowed for treatment of an injury to a player or for any other permitted delay. A longer period may be allowed only if the additional time is required for the removal of an injured player from the playing area.

Playing time lost as a result of any such permitted delay or of delay in taking a kick at goal shall be made up in that half of the match in which the delay occurred, subject to the power vested in the Referee to declare no-side before time has expired.

6. Referee and Touch-Judges

A. Referee
(1) There shall be a Referee for every match. He shall be appointed

by or under the authority of the Union or, in case no such authorised Referee has been appointed, a Referee may be mutually agreed upon between the teams or, failing such agreement, he shall be appointed by the home team.

(2) If the Referee is unable to officiate for the whole period of a match a replacement shall be appointed either in such manner as may be directed by the Union, or in the absence of such direction, by the Referee or, if he is unable to do so, by the home team.

(3) The Referee shall keep the time and the score, and he must in every match apply fairly the Laws of the Game without any variation or omission, except only when the Union has authorised the application of an experimental Law approved by the International Board.

(4) He must not give any instruction or advice to either team prior to the match. During the match he must not consult with anyone except only:

(a) Either or both Touch-Judges on a point of fact relevant to their functions, or on matters relating to Law 26(3); or

(b) In regard to time.

(5) The Referee is the sole judge of fact and of Law. All his decisions are binding on the players. He cannot alter a decision except when given before he observes that a Touch-Judge's flag is raised or before he has received a report related to Law 26(3) from a Touch-Judge.

(6) The Referee must carry a whistle and must blow it:

(a) To indicate the beginning of the match, half-time, resumption of play after half-time, no-side, a score or a touch-down; and

(b) To stop play because of infringement or otherwise as required by the Laws.

(7) During a match no person other than the players, the Referee and the Touch-Judges may be within the playing enclosure or the playing area unless with the permission of the Referee which shall be given only for a special and temporary purpose.

Play may continue during minor injuries with a medically trained person being permitted to come on to the playing area to attend the player or the player going to the touch-line. Continuation of play during minor injuries is subject to the Referee's permission and to his authority to stop play at any time.

(8) (a) All players must respect the authority of the Referee and they must not dispute his decisions. They must (except in the case of a kick-off) stop playing at once when the Referee has blown his whistle.

(b) A player must when so requested, whether before or during the match, allow the Referee to inspect his dress.

(c) A player must not leave the playing enclosure without the Referee's permission. If a player retires during a match because of injury or otherwise, he must not resume playing in that match until the Referee has give him permission.

Penalty. Infringement by a player is subject to penalty as misconduct.

B. Touch-Judges

(1) There shall be two Touch-Judges for every match. Unless Touch-Judges have been appointed by or under the authority of the Union, it shall be the responsibility of each team to provide a Touch-Judge.

(2) A Touch-Judge is under the control of the Referee who may instruct him as to his duties and may overule any of his decisions. The Referee may request that an unsatisfactory Touch-Judge be replaced and he has power to order off and report to the Union a Touch-Judge who in his opinion is guilty of misconduct.

(3) Each Touch-Judge shall carry a flag (or other suitable object) to signal his decisions. There shall be one Touch-Judge on each side of the ground and he shall remain in touch except when judging a kick at goal.

(4) He must hold up his flag when the ball or a player carrying it has gone into touch and must indicate the place of throw-in and which team is entitled to do so. He must also signal to the Referee when the ball or a player carrying it has gone into touch-in-goal.

(5) The Touch-Judge shall lower his flag when the ball has been thrown in except on the following occasions when he must keep it raised;

(*a*) When the player throwing in the ball puts any part of either foot in the field-of-play;

(*b*) When the ball has not been thrown in by the team entitled to do so;

(*c*) When, at a quick throw-in, the ball that went into touch is replaced by another or is handled by anyone other than the players.

It is for the Referee to decide whether or not the ball has been thrown-in from the correct place.

(6) In matches in which a national representative team is playing and in such domestic matches for which a Union gives express permission, and where Referees recognised by the Union are appointed as Touch-Judges, the Touch-Judges shall report incidents of foul play and misconduct under Law 26(3) to the Referee for the match.

A Touch-Judge may signal such an incident to the Referee by raising his flag to a horizontal position pointing directly across the field at a right angle to the touch-line. The Touch-Judge must remain in touch and continue to carry out his other functions until the next stoppage in play when the Referee shall consult him regarding the incident. The Referee may then take whatever action he deems appropriate and any consequent penalties shall be in accordance with Law 26(3).

(7) When a kick at goal from a try, free kick or penalty kick is being taken both Touch-Judges must assist the Referee by signalling the result

of the kick. One Touch-Judge shall stand at or behind each of the goal-posts and shall raise his flag if the ball goes over the cross-bar.

7. Mode of Play

A match is started by a kick-off, after which any player who is on-side may at any time:

Catch or pick up the ball and run with it;

Pass, throw or knock the ball to another player;

Kick or otherwise propel the ball;

Tackle, push or shoulder an opponent holding the ball;

Fall on the ball;

Take part in scrummage, ruck, maul or line-out;

provided he does so in accordance with these Laws.

8. Advantage

The Referee shall not whistle for an infringement during play which is followed by an advantage gained by the non-offending team. An advantage must be either territorial or such possession of the ball as constitutes an obvious tactical advantage. A mere opportunity to gain advantage is not sufficient.

9. Ball or Player Touching Referee

(1) If the ball or a player carrying it touches the Referee in the field-of-play, play shall continue unless the Referee considers either team has gained an advantage in which case he shall order a scrummage. The team which last played the ball shall put it in.

(2) (*a*) If the ball in a player's possession or a player carrying it touches the Referee in that player's in-goal, a touch-down shall be awarded.

(*b*) If a player carrying the ball in his opponents' in-goal touches the Referee before grounding the ball, a try shall be awarded at that place.

10. Kick-off

Kick-off is (a) a place kick taken from the centre of the half-way line by the team which has the right to start the match or by the opposing team on the resumption of play after the half-time interval or by the defending team after a goal has been scored, or (b) a drop kick taken at or from behind the centre of the half-way line by the defending team after an unconverted try.

(1) The ball must be kicked from the correct place; otherwise it shall be kicked off again.

(2) The ball must reach the opponents' 10m line, unless first played by an opponent; otherwise it shall be kicked off again, or a scrummage

formed at the centre, at the opponents' option. If it reaches the 10m line
and is then blown back, play shall continue.

(3) If the ball pitches directly into touch, touch-in-goal or over or on
the dead-ball line, the opposing team may accept the kick, have the ball
kicked off again, or have a scrummage formed at the centre.

(4) The *kicker's team* must be behind the ball when kicked; otherwise
a scrummage shall be formed at the centre.

(5) The *opposing team* must stand on or behind the 10m line. If they
are in front of that line or if they charge before the ball has been kicked,
it shall be kicked off again.

11. Method of Scoring
Try. A try is scored by first grounding the ball in the opponent's in-goal.

A try shall be awarded if one would probably have been scored but for
foul play by the opposing team.
Goal. A goal is scored by kicking the ball over the opponents' cross-bar
and between the goal-posts from the field-of-play by any place kick or
drop kick, except a kick-off, drop-out or free kick, without touching the
ground or any player of the kicker's team.

A goal is scored if the ball has crossed the bar, even though it may
have been blown backwards afterwards and whether it has touched the
cross-bar or either goal-post or not.

A goal is scored if the ball has crossed the bar notwithstanding a prior
offence of the opposing team.

A goal may be awarded if the ball is illegally touched by any player of
the opposing team and if the Referee considers that a goal would
otherwise probably have been scored.

The scoring values are as follows:

A try	4 points
A goal scored after a try	2 points
A goal from a penalty kick	3 points
A dropped goal otherwise obtained	3 points

12. Try and Touch-down
Grounding the ball is the act of a player who:

(*a*) *While holding the ball in his hand (or hands) or arm (or arms)
brings the ball in contact with ground; or*

(*b*) *While the ball is on the ground either places his hand (or hands) or
arm (or arms) on it with downward pressure, or falls upon it and the ball
is anywhere under the front of his body from waist to neck inclusive.*

Picking up the ball from the ground is not grounding it.

A. Try
(1) A player who is on-side scores a try when he carries the ball into

his opponents' in-goal, or the ball is in his opponents' in-goal (and he first grounds it there).

(2) The scoring of a try includes the following cases:

(a) If a player carries, passes, knocks or kicks the ball into his in-goal and an opponent first grounds it.

(b) If, at a scrummage or ruck, a team is pushed over its goal-line and before the ball has emerged it is first grounded in in-goal by an attacking player.

(c) If the momentum of a player, when tackled, carries him into his opponents' in-goal and he first there grounds the ball.

(d) If a player first grounds the ball on his opponents' goal-line or if the ball is in contact with the ground and a goal-post.

(e) If a tackle occurs in such a position that the tackled player whilst complying with the Law is able to place the ball on or over the goal-line.

(3) If a player grounds the ball in his opponents' in-goal and picks it up again, a try is scored where it was first grounded.

(4) A try may be scored by a player who is in touch or in touch-in-goal provided he is not carrying the ball.

B. Penalty try

A penalty try shall be awarded between the posts if but for foul play by the defending team a try would probably have been scored, or it would probably have been scored in a more favourable position than that where the ball was grounded.

C. Touch-down

(1) A touch-down occurs when a player first grounds the ball in his in-goal.

(2) After a touch-down, play shall be restarted either by a drop-out or a scrummage, as provided in Law 14.

D. Scrummage after grounding in case of doubt

Where there is doubt as to which team first grounded the ball in in-goal, a scrummage shall be formed 5m from the goal-line opposite the place where the ball was grounded. The attacking team shall put in the ball.

13. Kick at Goal after a Try

(1) After a try has been scored, the scoring team has the right to take a place kick or drop kick at goal, on a line through the place where the try was scored.

If the scoring team does not take the kick, play shall be restarted by a drop kick from the centre, unless time has expired.

(2) If a kick is taken:

(*a*) It must be taken without undue delay.

(*b*) Any player including the kicker may place the ball.

(*c*) The *kicker's team*, except a placer, must be behind the ball when kicked.

(*d*) If the kicker kicks the ball from a placer's hands without the ball being on the ground, the kick is void.

(*e*) The *opposing team* must be behind the goal-line until the kicker begins his run or offers to kick when they may charge or jump with a view to preventing a goal.

(3) Neither the kicker nor a placer shall wilfully do anything which may lead the opposing team to charge prematurely. If either does so, the charge shall not be disallowed.

Penalty. For an infringement by the *kicker's team* – the kick shall be disallowed.

For an infringement by the *opposing team* – the charge shall be disallowed. If, however, the kick has been taken successfully, the goal shall stand. If it was unsuccessful, the kicker may take another kick under the original conditions without the charge and may change the type of kick.

14. In-goal

In-goal is the area bounded by a goal-line, touch-in-goal lines and dead-ball line. It includes the goal-lines and goal-posts but excludes touch-in-goal lines and dead-ball line.

Touch-in-goal occurs when the ball, or a player carrying it, touches a corner post, a touch-in-goal line or the ground or a person or object on or beyond it. The flag is not part of the corner post.

5m Scrummage

(1) If a player carrying the ball in in-goal is so held that he cannot ground the ball, a scrummage shall be formed 5m from the goal-line opposite the place where he was held.

The attacking team shall put in the ball.

(2) (*a*) If a defending player heels, kicks, carries, passes or knocks the ball over his goal-line and it there becomes dead except where a try is scored, or he wilfully knocks or throws the ball from the field-of-play into touch-in-goal or over his dead-ball line, or

(*b*) If a defending player in in-goal has his kick charged down by an attacking player are he carried the ball back from the field-of-play, or a defending player put it into in-goal and the ball is then touched down or goes into touch-in-goal or over the dead-ball line; or

(*c*) If a defending player carrying the ball in the field-of-play is forced into his in-goal and he then touches down, or

(*d*) If, at a scrummage or ruck, a defending team with the ball in its possession is pushed over its goal-line and before the ball has emerged first grounds it in in-goal;

a scrummage shall be formed 5m from the goal-line opposite the place where the ball or a player carrying it crossed the goal-line. The attacking team shall put in the ball.

Drop-out
(3) Except where the ball is knocked on or thrown forward in the field-of-play or in in-goal, if an attacking player kicks, carries, or passes the ball and it travels into his opponents' in-goal either directly or after having touched a defender who does not wilfully attempt to stop, catch or kick it, and it is there grounded by a player of *either team*, or goes into touch-in-goal or over the dead-ball line a drop-out shall be awarded.

Penalties. (*a*) A penalty try shall be awarded when by foul play in in-goal the defending team has prevented a try which otherwise would *probably* have been scored.

(*b*) A try shall be disallowed and a penalty kick awarded, if a try would *probably not* have been gained but for foul play by the attacking team.

(*c*) For foul play in in-goal while the ball is out of play the penalty kick shall be awarded at the place where play would otherwise have restarted and, in addition, the player shall either be ordered off or cautioned that he will be sent off if he repeats the offence.

(*d*) For wilfully charging or obstructing in in-goal a player who has just kicked the ball the penalty shall be either a penalty kick in the field-of-play 5m from the goal-line opposite the place of infringement, at the option of the non-offending team, a penalty kick where the ball alights as provided for an infringement of Law 26(3) Penalty (ii)(*b*).

(*e*) For other infringements in in-goal, the penalty shall be the same as for a similar infringement in the field-of-play except that the mark for a penalty kick or free kick shall be in the field-of-play 5m from the goal-line opposite the place of infringement and the place of any scrummage shall be 5m from the goal-line opposite the place of infringement but not within 5m of the touch-line.

15. Drop-out
A drop-out is a drop kick awarded to the defending team.

(1) The drop kick must be taken from anywhere on or behind the 22m line; otherwise the ball shall be dropped out again.

(2) The ball must cross the 22m line; otherwise the opposing team may have it dropped out again, or have a scrummage formed at the centre of the 22m line. If it crosses the 22m line and is then blown back, play shall continue.

(3) If the ball pitches directly into touch, the opposing team may accept the kick, have the ball dropped out again, or have a scrummage formed at the centre of the 22m line.

(4) The *kicker's team* must be behind the ball when kicked; otherwise a scrummage shall be formed at the centre of the 22m line.

(5) The *opposing team* must not charge over the 22m line; otherwise the ball shall be dropped out again.

16. Fair-catch (Mark)

(*a*) *A player makes a fair-catch when being stationary with both feet on the ground in his 22 m area or in his in-goal he cleanly catches the ball direct from a kick, knock-on or throw-forward by one of his opponents and, at the same time, he exclaims 'Mark!'*

A fair-catch may be obtained even though the ball on its way touches a goal-post or cross-bar and can be made in in-goal.

(*b*) *A free kick is awarded for a fair-catch.*

(1) The kick shall be taken by the player making the fair-catch, unless he is injured in doing so. If he is unable to take the kick within 1 minute a scrummage shall be formed at the mark. His team shall put in the ball.

(2) If the mark is in in-goal, any resultant scrummage shall be 5m from the goal-line on a line through the mark.

17. Knock-on or Throw-forward

A knock-on occurs when the ball travels forward towards the direction of the opponents' dead-ball line after a player loses possession of it, or a player propels or strikes it with his hand or arm, or it strikes a player's hand or arm.

A throw-forward occurs when a player carrying the ball throws or passes it in the direction of his opponents' dead-ball line. A throw-in from touch is not a throw-forward. If the ball is not thrown or passed forward but it bounces forward after hitting a player or the ground, it is not a throw-forward.

(1) The knock-on or throw-forward must not be *intentional*.

Penalty. Penalty kick at the place of infringement or in accord with Law 14, Penalty (*e*).

(2) If the knock-on or throw-forward is *unintentional*, a scrummage shall be formed either at the place of infringement or, if it occurs at a line-out, 15m from the touch-line along the line-of-touch unless:

(*a*) A fair catch has been allowed; or

(*b*) The ball is knocked on by a player who is in the act of charging down the kick of an opponent but is not attempting to catch the ball; or

(*c*) The ball is knocked on one or more times by a player who is in the act of catching or picking it up or losing possession of it and is recovered by that player before it has touched the ground or another player.

18. Tackle

A tackle occurs when a player carrying the ball in the field-of-play is held by one or more opponents so that while he is so held he is brought to the ground or the ball comes into contact with the ground. If the ball carrier is on one knee, or both knees, or is sitting on the ground or is on top of another player who is on the ground, the ball carrier is deemed to have been brought to the ground.

(1) (*a*) A tackled player must immediately pass the ball, or release the ball and get up or move away from the ball.

(*b*) A player who goes to the ground and gathers the ball or with the ball in his possession but who is not tackled must immediately get up on his feet with the ball, or pass the ball, or release the ball and get up or move away from the ball.

(*c*) Any other player must be on his feet before he can play.

(2) It is illegal for any player:

(*a*) To prevent a tackled player from passing or releasing the ball, or getting up or moving away after he has passed or released it.

(*b*) To pull the ball from a tackled player's possession or attempt to pick up the ball before the tackled player has released it.

(*c*) While lying on the ground after a tackle to play or interfere with the ball in any way or to tackle or attempt to tackle an opponent carrying the ball.

(*d*) To wilfully fall on or over a player lying on the ground with the ball in his possession.

(*e*) To wilfully fall on or over players lying on the ground with the ball between them, or in close proximity.

(*f*) While lying on the ground in close proximity to the ball to prevent an opponent from gaining possession of it.

(3) A player must not fall on or over the ball emerging from a scrummage or ruch.

Penalty: Penalty kick at the place of infringement.

(4) A try may be scored if the momentum of a player carries him into his opponents' in-goal even though he is tackled.

19. Lying with, on or Near the Ball

The requirements of this Law are now incorporated into Law 18.

20. Scrummage

A scrummage, which can take place only in the field-of-play, is formed by players from each team closing up in readiness to allow the ball to be put on the ground between them but is not formed within 5m of the touch-line. If the ball in a scrummage is on or over the goal-line the scrummage is ended.

The middle player in each front row is the hooker, and the player on either side of him are the props.

The middle line means an imaginary line on the ground directly beneath the line formed by the junction of the shoulders of the two front rows.

Forming a scrummage

(1) A team must not wilfully delay the forming of a scrummage.

(2) Every scrummage shall be formed at the place of infringement or as near thereto as is practicable within the field-of-play. It must be stationary with the middle line parallel to the goal-lines until the ball has been put in.

Before commencing engagement each front row must be in a crouched position with heads and shoulders no lower than their hips and so that they are no more than one arm's length from their opponents' shoulders.

In the interest of safety each front row should touch on the upper arms and then pause prior to engagement in the sequence: crouch – touch – pause – engage.

(3) It is dangerous play for a front row to form down some distance from its opponents and rush against them.

(4) A minimum of 5 players from each team shall be required to form a scrummage. While the scrummage is in progress a minimum of 5 players shall remain bound on the scrummage until it ends. Each front row shall have 3 players in it *at all times*. The head of a player in the front row shall not be next to the head of a player of the same team.

(5) (*a*) While a scrummage is forming and is taking place, the shoulders of each player in the front row must not be lower than his hips; all players in each front row must adopt a normal stance; both feet must be on the ground and not be crossed; the hookers must be in a hooking position; a hooker's foot must not be in front of the forward feet of his props.

(*b*) While the scrummage is taking place, players in each front row must have their weight firmly on at least one foot and be in a position for an effective forward shove and the shoulders of each player must not be lower than his hips.

(*c*) When 5 players of a team form the scrummage the 2 players in the second row must remain bound to each other until the scrummage ends.

Binding of players

(6) (*a*) The players of each front row shall bind firmly and continuously while the scrummage is forming, while the ball is being put in and while it is in the scrummage.

(*b*) The hooker may bind either over or under the arms of his props but, in either case, he must bind firmly around their bodies at or below the level of the armpits. The props must bind the hooker similarly. The hooker must not be supported so that he is not carrying any weight on either foot.

(*c*) The outside (loose head) prop *must* either bind his opposing (tight head) prop with his left arm inside the right arm of his opponent, or place his left hand or forearm on his left thigh. The tight head prop *must* bind with his right arm outside the left upper arm of his opposing loose head prop. He may grip the jersey of his opposing loose head prop with his right hand but only to keep himself and the scrummage steady and he must not exert a downward pull.

(*d*) All players in a scrummage, other than those in a front row, must bind with at least one arm and hand around the body of another player of the same team.

(*e*) No outside player other than a prop may hold an opponent with his outer arm.

Putting the ball into the scrummage

(7) When an infringement occurs the team not responsible shall put in the ball. In all other circumstances, unless otherwise provided, the ball shall be put in by the team which was moving forward prior to the stoppage or, if neither team was moving forward, by the attacking team.

(8) The ball shall be put in without delay as soon as the two front rows have closed together. A team must put in the ball when ordered to do so and on the side first chosen.

(9) The player putting in the ball shall:

(*a*) Stand *1m* from the scrummage and midway between the two front rows.

(*b*) Hold the ball with both hands midway between the two front rows at a level midway between his knee and ankle.

(*c*) From that position put in the ball without any delay or without feint or backward movement, i.e. with a single forward movement, and at a quick speed straight along the middle line so that it first touches the ground immediately beyond the width of the nearer prop's shoulders.

(10) Play in the scrummage begins when the ball leaves the hands of the player putting it in.

(11) If the ball is put in and it comes out at either end of the tunnel, it shall be put in again, unless a free kick or penalty kick has been awarded. If the ball comes out otherwise than at either end of the tunnel and if a penalty kick has not been awarded play shall proceed.

Restrictions on front row players

(12) All front row players must place their feet so as to allow a clear

tunnel. A player must not prevent the ball from being put into the scrummage, or from touching the ground at the required place.

(13) No front row player may raise or advance a foot until the ball has touched the ground.

(14) When the ball has touched the ground, any foot of any player in either front row may be used in an attempt to gain possession of the ball, subject to the following:

Players in the front rows must not *at any time* during the scrummage:

(*a*) Raise both feet off the ground at the same time; or

(*b*) Wilfully adopt any position or wilfully take any action, by twisting or lowering the body or by pulling on an opponent's dress, which is likely to cause the scrummage to collapse; or

(*c*) Wilfully kick the ball out of the tunnel in the direction from which it is put in.

Restrictions on players

(15) Any player who is not in either front row must not play the ball while it is in the tunnel.

(16) A player must not:

(*a*) Return the ball into the scrummage; or

(*b*) Handle the ball in the scrummage except in the act of obtaining a 'push over' try or touch-down; or

(*c*) Pick up the ball in the scrummage by hand or legs; or

(*d*) Wilfully collapse the scrummage; or

(*e*) Wilfully fall or kneel in the scrummage; or

(*f*) Attempt to gain possession of the ball in the scrummage with any part of the body except the foot or lower leg.

(17) The player putting in the ball and his immediate opponent must not kick the ball while it is in the scrummage.

(18) A scrummage must not be wheeled beyond a position where the middle line becomes parallel to the touch-line. The scrummage will be reformed at the site of the stoppage, the ball to be put in by the side that has gained possession or otherwise by the same team.

Penalty. (*a*) For an infringement of paragraphs 2, 4, 5, 6*d*, 6*e*, 8, 9, 12, 13, 14, 15, 16*a* and 17, a free kick at the place of infringement;

(*b*) For an infringement of paragraphs 1, 3, 6*a*, 6*b*, 6*c*, 14*a*, 14*b* and 16*b*, 16*c*, 16*d*, 16*e*, 16*f*, a penalty kick at the place of infringement.

For Off-side at Scrummage see Law 24B.

21. Ruck

A ruck, which can take place only in the field-of-play, is formed when the ball is on the ground and one or more players from each team are on their feet and in physical contact, closing around the ball between them. If the ball in a ruck is on or over the goal-line the ruck is ended.

(1) A player joining a ruck must have his head and shoulders no lower than his hips. He must bind with at least one arm around the body of a player of his team in the ruck.

(2) A player must not:

(*a*) Return the ball into the ruck.

Penalty. Free kick at the place of infringement.

(*b*) Handle the ball in the ruck except in the act of securing a try or touch-down.

(*c*) Pick up the ball in the ruck by hand or legs.

(*d*) Wilfully collapse the ruck.

(*e*) Jump on top of other players in the ruck.

(*f*) Wilfully fall or kneel in the ruck.

(*g*) While lying on the ground interfere in any way with the ball in or emerging from the ruck. He must do his best to roll away from it.

Penalty. Penalty kick at the place of infringement.

For Off-side at Ruck see Law 24C.

22. Maul

A maul, which can take place only in the field-of play, is formed by one or more players from each team on their feet and in physical contact closing round a player who is carrying the ball.

A maul ends when the ball is on the ground or the ball or a player carrying it emerges from the maul or when a scrummage is ordered.

(1) A player joining a maul must have his head and shoulders no lower than his hips.

Penalty. Free kick at the place of infringement.

(2) A player is not in physical contact unless he is caught in or bound to the maul and not merely alongside it.

(3) A player must not:

(*a*) Jump on top of other players in a maul.

(*b*) Wilfully collapse a maul.

(*c*) Attempt to drag another player out of the maul.

Penalty. Penalty kick at the place of infringement.

(4) When the ball in a maul becomes unplayable a scrummage shall be ordered and the team which was moving forward immediately prior to the stoppage shall put in the ball, or if neither team was moving forward, the attacking team shall put it in.

23. Touch and Line-out

A. Touch

(1) The ball is in touch when it is not being carried by a player and it touches a touch-line or the ground or a person or object beyond it, or

when it is carried by a player and it or the player carrying it touches a touch-line or the ground beyond it.

(2) If the ball is not in touch and has not crossed the plane of the touch-line, a player who is in touch may kick the ball or propel it with his hand but not hold it.

B. Line-out

The line-of-touch is an imaginary line in the field-of-play at right angles to the touchline through the place where the ball is to be thrown in.

Formation of line-out

(1) A line-out is formed by at least 2 players from each team lining up in single lines parallel to the line-of-touch in readiness for the ball to be thrown in between them. The team throwing in the ball shall determine the maximum number of players from either team who so line up. Such players are those 'in the line-out', unless excluded below.

(2) Until the ball is thrown in each player in the line-out must stand at least 1m from the next player of his team in the line-out and avoid physical contact with any other player.

(3) The line-out stretches from 5m from the touch-line from which the ball is being thrown in to a position 15m from that touch-line.

(4) Any player of either team who is further than 15m from the touch-line when the line-out begins is not in the line-out.

(5) A clear space of 500mm must be left between the two lines of players.

Throwing in the ball

(6) When the ball is in touch the place at which it must be thrown in is as follows:

(*a*) When the ball goes into touch from a penalty kick, free kick, or from a kick within 22m of the kicker's goal-line, at the place where it touched or crossed the touch-line.

(*b*) When the ball pitches directly into touch after having been kicked otherwise than as stated above, opposite the place from which the ball was kicked or at the place where it touched or crossed the touch-line if that place be nearer to the kicker's goal-line.

(*c*) On all other occasions when the ball is in touch, at the place where it touched or crossed the touch-line.

In each instance the place is where the ball last crossed the touch-line before being in touch.

(7) The ball must be thrown in at the line-out by an opponent of the player whom it last touched, or by whom it was carried, before being in touch. In the event of doubt as to which team should throw in the ball, the attacking team shall do so.

(8) The ball must be thrown in without delay and without feint.

(9) A *quick throw-in* from touch without waiting for the players to form a line-out is permissible provided the ball that went into touch is used, it has been handled only by the players and it is thrown in correctly.

(10) The ball may be brought into play by a quick throw-in or at a formed line-out. In either event the player must throw in the ball at the place indicated, and so that it first touches the ground or touches or is touched by a player at least 5m from the touch-line along the line-of-touch, and while throwing in the ball, he must not put any part of either foot in the field-of-play.

If any of the foregoing is infringed, the opposing team shall have the right, at its option, to throw in the ball or to take a scrummage.

If on the second occasion the ball is not thrown in correctly a scrummage shall be formed and the ball shall be put in by the team which threw it in on the first occasion.

Beginning and end of line-out

(11) The line-out begins when the ball leaves the hands of the player throwing it in.

(12) The line-out ends when:

(*a*) A ruck or maul is taking place and all feet of players in the ruck or maul have moved beyond the line-of-touch; or

(*b*) A player carrying the ball leaves the line-out; or

(*c*) The ball has been passed, knocked back or kicked from the line-out; or

(*d*) The ball is thrown beyond a position 15m from the touch-line; or

(*e*) The ball becomes unplayable.

Peeling off

Peeling off occurs when a player (or players) moves from his position in the line-out for the purpose of catching the ball when it has been passed or knocked back by another of his team in the line-out.

(13) When the ball is in touch players who approach the line-of-touch must *always* be presumed to do so for the purpose of forming a line-out. Except in the peeling off movement such players must not leave the line-of-touch, or the line-out when formed, until the line-out has ended. A player must not begin to peel off until the ball has left the hands of the player throwing it in.

Exception. At a quick throw-in, when a player may come to the line-of-touch and retire from that position without penalty.

(14) In a peeling off movement a player must move parallel and close to the line-out. He must keep moving until a ruck or maul is formed and he joins it or the line-out ends.

Restrictions on players in line-out

(15) *Before* the ball has been thrown in and has touched the ground or has touched or been touched by a player, any player in the line-out must not:

(*a*) Be off-side; or

(*b*) Push, charge, shoulder or bind with or in any way hold another player of *either* team; or

(*c*) Use any other player as a support to enable him to jump for the ball; or

(*d*) Stand within 5m of the touch-line or prevent the ball from being thrown 5m.

(16) *After* the ball has touched the ground or touched or been touched by a player, any player in the line-out must not:

(*a*) Be off-side; or

(*b*) Hold, push, shoulder or obstruct an opponent not holding the ball; or

(*c*) Charge an opponent except in an attempt to tackle him or to play the ball.

(17) Except when jumping for the ball or peeling off, each player in the line-out must remain at least 1m from the next player of his team until the ball has touched or has been touched by a player or has touched the ground.

(18) Except when jumping for the ball or peeling off, a clear space of 500mm must be left between the two lines of players until the ball has touched or has been touched by a player or has touched the ground.

(19) A player in the line-out may move into the space between the touch-line and the 5m mark only when the ball has been thrown beyond him and, if he does so he must not move towards his goal-line before the line-out ends, except in a peeling off movement.

(20) Until the line-out ends, no player may move beyond a position 15m from the touch-line except as allowed when the ball is thrown beyond that position in accordance with the *Exception* following Law 24D(1)(*d*).

Restrictions on players not in line-out

(21) Players of either team who are not in the line-out may not advance from behind the line-out and take the ball from the throw-in except only a player at a quick throw-in, or a player advancing at a long throw-in, or a player participating in the line-out (as defined in Section D of Law 24), who may run into a gap in the line-out and take the ball provided he does not charge or obstruct any player in the line-out.

Penalty. (*a*) for an infringement of paragraphs 1, 2, 3, 4, 5, 8, 13, 14, 15*d*, 17, 18 or 19, a free kick 15m from the touch-line along the line-of-touch.

(*b*) For an infringement of paragraphs 15*a*, 15*b*, 15*c*, 16 or 20, a penalty kick 15m from the touch-line along the line-of-touch.

(*c*) For an infringement of paragraph 21 a penalty kick on the offending team's off-side line (as defined in Law 24D) opposite the place of infringement, but not less than 15m from the touch-line.

Place of Scrummage. Any scrummage taken or ordered under this Law or as the result of any infringement in a line-out shall be formed 15m from the touch-line along the line-of-touch. *For Off-side at Line-out see Law 24D*.

24. Off-Side

Off-side means that a player is in a position in which he is out of the game and is liable to penalty. In general play *the player is in an off-side position because he is in front of the ball when it has been last played by another player of his team. In play at* scrummage, ruck, maul *or* line-out *the player is off-side because he remains or advances in front of the line or placed stated in, or otherwise infringes, the relevant sections of this Law*.

A. Off-side in general play

(1) A player is in an off-side position if the ball has been kicked, or touched, or is being carried by one of his team behind him.

(2) There is no penalty for being in an off-side position unless:

(*a*) The player plays the ball or obstructs a opponent; or

(*b*) He approaches or remains within 10m of an opponent waiting to play the ball or the place where the ball pitches. Where no opponent is waiting to play the ball but one arrives as the ball pitches, a player in an off-side position must not obstruct or interfere with him.

Exceptions.

(i) When an off-side player cannot avoid being touched by the ball or by a player carrying it, he is 'accidentally off-side'. Play should be allowed to continue unless the infringing team obtains an advantage, in which case a scrummage should be formed at that place.

(ii) A player who receives an unintentional throw-forward is not off-side.

(iii) If, because of the speed of the game, an off-side player finds himself unavoidably within 10m of an opponent waiting to play the ball or the place where the ball pitches, he shall not be penalised provided he retires without delay and without interfering with the opponent.

Penalty. Penalty kick at the place of infringement, or, at the option of the non-offending team, a scrummage at the place where the ball was last played by the offending team. If the latter place is in-goal the penalty kick shall be taken or the scrummage shall be formed 5m from the goal-line on a line through the place.

B. Off-side at scrummage
The term off-side line means a line parallel to the goal-lines through the hindmost foot of the player's team in the scrummage.

While a scrummage is forming or is taking place:

(1) A player is off-side if:

(*a*) He joins it from his opponents' side; or

(*b*) He, not being in the scrummage nor the player of either team who puts the ball in the scrummage, fails to retire behind the off-side line or to his goal-line, whichever is the nearer, or places either foot in front of the off-side line while the ball is in the scrummage.

A player may leave a scrummage provided he retires immediately behind the off-side line. If he wishes to rejoin the scrummage, he must do so behind the ball. He may not play the ball as it emerges between the feet of his front row if he is in front of the off-side line.

Exception. The restrictions on leaving the scrummage in front of the off-side line do not apply to a player taking part in wheeling a scrummage providing he immediately plays the ball.

(2) A player is off-side if he, being the player on either team who puts the ball in the scrummage, remains, or places either foot, in front of the ball while it is in the scrummage.

(3) A player is off-side if he, being the immediate opponent of the player putting in the ball, takes up a position on or moves to the opposite side of the scrummage in front of the off-side line.

Penalty. Penalty kick at the place of infringement.

C. Off-side at ruck or maul
The term off-side line means a line parallel to the goal-lines through the hindmost foot of the player's team in the ruck or maul.

(1) *Ruck or maul otherwise than at line-out*

While a ruck or maul is taking place (including a ruck or maul which continues after a line-out has ended), a player is off-side if he:

(*a*) Joins it from his opponents' side; or

(*b*) Joins it in front of the ball; or

(*c*) Does not join the ruck or maul but fails to retire behind the off-side line *without delay*; or

(*d*) Unbinds from the ruck or leaves the maul and does not *immediately* either rejoin it behind the ball or retire behind the off-side line; or

(*e*) Advances beyond the off-side line with either foot and does not join the ruck or maul.

Penalty. Penalty kick at the place of infringement.

(2) *Ruck or maul at line-out*

The team 'participating in the line-out' has the same meaning as in Section D of this Law. A player participating in the line-out is not obliged to join or remain in the ruck or maul and if he is not in the ruck or maul he continues to participate in the line-out until it has ended. While a line-out is in progress and a ruck or maul takes place, a player is off-side if he:

(a) Joins the ruck or maul from his opponents' side; or

(b) Joins it in front of the ball; or

(c) Being a player who is participating in the line-out and is not in the ruck or maul, does not retire to and remain at the off-side line defined in this section (*Penalty*. Penalty kick 15m from the touch-line along the line-of-touch); or

(d) Being a player who is not participating in the line-out, remains or advances with either foot in front of the off-side line defined in Section D of this Law.

Penalty. Penalty kick on the offending team's off-side line (as defined in Section D of this Law) opposite the place of infringement, but not less than 15m from the touch-line.

D. Off-side at line-out

The term participating in the line-out refers exclusively to the following players: those players who are in the line-out, the player who throws in the ball, his immediate opponent who may have the option of throwing in the ball, and one other player of either team who takes up position to receive the ball if it passed or knocked back from the line-out.

All other players are not participating in the line-out.

The term 'off-side line' means a line 10m behind the line-of-touch and parallel to the goal-lines or, if the goal-line be nearer than 10m to the line-of-touch, the 'off-side line' is the goal-line.

Off-side while participating in line-out

(1) A participating player is off-side if:

(a) *Before* the ball has touched a player or the ground he wilfully remains or advances with either foot in front of the line-of-touch, unless he advances solely in the act of jumping for the ball.

(b) *After* the ball has touched a player or the ground, if he is not carrying the ball, he advances with either foot in front of the ball, unless he is lawfully tackling or attempting to tackle an opponent who is participating in the line-out. Such tackle or attempt to tackle must, however, start from his side of the ball.

(c) In a peeling off movement he fails to keep moving close to the line-out until a ruck or maul is formed and he joins it or the line-out ends.

(d) Before the line-out ends he moves beyond a position 15m from the touch-line.

Exception: Players of the team throwing in the ball may move beyond a position of 15m from the touch-line for a long throw-in to them. They may do so only when the ball leaves the hand of the player throwing it in and if they do so their opponents participating in the line-out may follow them. If players so move and the ball is not thrown to or beyond them they must be penalised for off-side.

Penalty. Penalty kick 15m from the touch-line along the line-of-touch.

(2) The player throwing in the ball and his immediate opponent must:

(*a*) Remain within 5m of the touch-line; or

(*b*) Retire to the off-side line; or

(*c*) Join the line-out after the ball has been thrown in 5m; or

(*d*) Move into position to receive the ball if it is passed or knocked back from the line-out provided no other player is occupying that position at that line-out.

Off-side while not participating in line-out

(3) A player who is not participating is off-side if before the line-out has ended he advances or remains with either foot in front of the off-side line.

Exception. Players of the team throwing in the ball who are not participating in the line-out may advance for a long throw-in to them beyond the line-out. They may do so only when the ball leaves the hand of the player throwing in the ball and, if they do, their opponents may advance to meet them. If players so advance for a long throw-in to them and the ball is not thrown to them they must be penalised for off-side.

Players returning to on-side position

(4) A player is not obliged, before throwing in the ball, to wait until players of his team have returned to or behind the line-out but such players are off-side unless they return to an on-side position *without delay*.

Penalty. Penalty kick on the offending team's off-side line opposite the place of infringement, but not less than 15m from the touch-line.

25. On-side

On-side means that a player is in the Game and not liable to penalty for off-side.

Player made on-side by action of his team

(1) Any player who is off-side in general play, *including* an off-side player who is within 10m of an opponent waiting to play the ball or where the ball pitches and is retiring as required, becomes on-side as a result of any of the following actions of his team:

(*a*) When the off-side player has retired behind the player of his team who last kicked, touched or carried the ball; or (*b*) When one of his team carrying the ball has run in front of him; or

(*c*) When one of his team has run in front of him after coming from the place or from behind the place where the ball was kicked. In order to put the off-side player on-side, this other player must be in the playing area. But he is not debarred from following up in touch or touch-in-goal.

Player made on-side by action of opposing team

(2) Any player who is off-side in general play, *except* an off-side player within 10m of an opponent waiting to play the ball or where the ball pitches, becomes on-side as a result of any of the following actions: when an opponent carrying the ball has run 5m or when an opponent kicks or passes the ball, or when an opponent *intentionally* touches the ball and does not catch or gather it.

An off-side player within 10m of an opponent waiting to play the ball or where the ball pitches *cannot* be put on-side by *any* action of his opponents. Any *other* off-side player in general play is *always* put on-side when an opponent plays the ball.

Player retiring at scrummage, ruck, maul or line-out

(3) A player who is in an off-side position when a scrummage, ruck, maul or line-out if forming or taking place and is retiring as required by Law 24 (Off-side) becomes on-side when an opponent carrying the ball has run 5m, or when an opponent has kicked the ball.

An off-side player in this situation is *not* put on-side when an opponent passes the ball.

26. Foul Play

Foul Play is any action by a player which is contrary to the letter and spirit of the Game and includes obstruction, unfair play, misconduct, dangerous play, unsporting behaviour, retaliation and repeated infringements.

Obstruction

(1) It is illegal for any player:

(*a*) Who is running for the ball to charge or push an opponent also running for the ball, except shoulder to shoulder.

(*b*) Who is in an off-side position wilfully to run or stand in front of another player of his team who is carrying the ball thereby preventing an opponent from reaching the latter player.

(*c*) Who is carrying the ball after it has come out of a scrummage, ruck, maul or line-out, to attempt to force his way through the players of his team in front of him.

(*d*) Who is an outside player in a scrummage or ruck to prevent an opponent from advancing round the scrummage or ruck.

Penalty. Penalty kick at the place of infringement. A penalty try may be awarded.

Unfair play, repeated infringements

(2) It is illegal for any player:

(*a*) Deliberately to play unfairly or wilfully infringe any Law of the Game.

(*b*) Wilfully to waste time.

(*c*) Wilfully to knock or throw the ball from the playing area into touch, touch-in-goal or over the dead-ball line.

(*d*) To infringe repeatedly any Law of the Game.

Penalty. Penalty kick at the place of infringement. A penalty try may be awarded. For offences under 2c occurring in in-goal, Law 14 penalty *e* applies. For offences under 2d a player may be cautioned and, if he repeats the offence, must be ordered off.

Misconduct, dangerous play

(3) It is illegal for any player:

(*a*) To strike an opponent.

(*b*) Wilfully to hack or kick an opponent or trip him with the foot, or to trample on an opponent lying on the ground.

(*c*) To tackle early, or late or dangerously, including the action known as a stiff arm tackle.

(*d*) Who is not running for the ball wilfully to charge or obstruct an opponent who has just kicked the ball.

(*e*) To hold, push, charge, obstruct or grasp an opponent not holding the ball, except in a scrummage, ruck or maul. (*Except in a scrummage or ruck, the dragging away of a player lying close to the ball is permitted. Otherwise pulling any part of the clothing of an opponent is holding.*)

(*f*) In the front row of a scrummage to form down some distance from the opponents and rush against them.

(*g*) Wilfully to cause a scrummage or ruck or maul to collapse.

(*h*) While the ball is out of play to molest, obstruct or in any way interfere with an opponent or be guilty of any form of misconduct.

(*i*) To commit any misconduct on the playing area which is prejudicial to the spirit of good sportsmanship.

Penalty. A player guilty of misconduct and dangerous play shall either be ordered off or else cautioned that he will be ordered off if he repeats the offence. For a similar offence after caution the player must be ordered off.

In addition to a caution or ordering off a penalty try or a penalty kick shall be awarded as follows:

(i) If the offence prevents a try which would otherwise *probably* have been scored, a penalty try shall be awarded.

(ii) The place for a penalty kick shall be:

(*a*) For offences other than (*d*) and (*h*), at the place of infringement.

(*b*) For an infringement of (*d*) the non-offending team shall have the option of taking the kick at the place of infringement or where the ball alights, and if the ball alights:

in touch, the mark is 15m from the touch-line on a line parallel to the goal-lines through the place where it went into touch; or

within 15m from the touch-line, it is 15m from the touch-line on a line parallel to the goal-lines through the place where it alighted;

in-goal, touch-in-goal, or over or on the dead-ball line, it is 5m from the goal-line on a line parallel to the touch-line through the place where it crossed the goal-line or 15m from the touch-line, whichever is the greater.

When the offence takes place in touch the 'place of infringement' in the optional penalty award is 15m from the touch-line opposite to where the offence took place.

If the offence takes place in touch-in-goal (Law 14), the 'place of infringement', in the optional penalty award, is in the field-of-play 5m from the goal-line and 15m from the touch-line.

(*c*) In the case of an offence against (*h*) at any place where the ball would next have been brought into play if the offence had not occurred, or, if that place is on or beyond the touch-line, 15m from the place, on a line parallel to the goal-lines.

(iii) For an infringement in in-goal, a penalty kick is to be awarded as provided for offences under Law 14 Penalties.

(iv) For an offence under Law 26(3)(*h*), the penalty kick is to be taken at whichever is the place where play would restart, i.e. at the 22m line (at any point the non-offending team may select), or at the centre of the halfway line, or, if a scrummage 5m from the goal line would otherwise have been awarded, at that place or 15m from the touch-line on a line 5m from the parallel to the goal-line, whichever is the greater.

(v) For an offence which occurs outside the playing area while the ball is *still in play* and which is not otherwise covered in the foregoing, the penalty kick shall be awarded in the playing area 15m from the touch-line and opposite to where the offence took place.

(vi) For an offence reported by a Touch-Judge under Law 6B(6) a penalty kick may be awarded where the offence occurred or at the place where play would restart.

Player ordered off

A player who is ordered off shall take no further part in the match. When a player is ordered off, the Referee shall, as soon as possible after the match, send to the Union, or other disciplinary body having jurisdiction over the match, a report naming the player and describing the circumstances which necessitated the ordering off. The Union or other disciplinary body having jurisdiction over the match shall consider such report and any other evidence they deem appropriate. They shall then take such action and impose such punishment as they see fit.

27. Penalty kick

A penalty kick is a kick awarded to the non-offending team as stated in the Laws. It may be taken by any player of the non-offending team and by any form of kick provided that the kicker, if holding the ball, must propel it out of his hands or, if the ball is on the ground, he must propel it a visible distance from the mark. He may keep his hands on the ball while kicking it.

(1) The non-offending team has the option of taking a scrummage at the mark and shall put in the ball.

(2) When a penalty kick is taken the following shall apply:

(*a*) The kick must be taken without undue delay.

(*b*) The kick must be taken at or behind the mark on a line through the mark, and the kicker may place the ball for a place kick. If the place prescribed by the Laws for the award of a penalty kick is within 5m of the opponents' goal-line, the mark for the penalty kick or a scrummage taken instead of it shall be 5m from the goal-line on a line through that place.

(*c*) The kicker may kick the ball in any direction and he may play the ball again, without any restriction except that if he has indicated to the Referee that he intends to attempt a kick at goal, or has taken any action indicating such intention, he must not kick the ball in any other way. A player kicking for touch may only punt or drop kick the ball. Any indication of intention is irrevocable.

(*d*) The *kicker's team*, except the placer for a place kick, must be behind the ball until it has been kicked.

(*e*) The *opposing team* must run without delay (and continue to do so while the kick is being taken and while the ball is being played by the kicker's team) to or behind a line parallel to the goal-lines and 10m from the mark, or to their own goal-line if nearer to the mark, if a kick at goal is taken they must remain there motionless with their hands by their sides until the kick has been taken. Retiring players will not be penalised if their failure to retire 10m is due to the rapidity with which the kick has been taken, but they must not stop retiring and enter the game until an opponent carrying the ball has run 5m.

(*f*) The *opposing team* must not prevent the kick or interfere with the kicker in any way. This applies to actions such as wilfully carrying, throwing or kicking the ball away out of reach of the kicker.

Penalty. For an infringement by the *kicker's team* – a scrummage at the mark. For an infringement by the *opposing team* – a penalty kick 10m in front of the mark or 5m from the goal-line, whichever is the nearer, on a line through the mark. Any player of the non-offending team may take the kick.

28. Free Kick

A free kick is a kick awarded for a fair-catch, or to the non-offending team as stated in the Laws.

A goal shall not be scored by the kicker from a free kick unless the ball has first been played by another player.

For an infringement it may be taken by any player of the non-offending team.

It may be taken by any form of kick provided that the kicker, if holding the ball, must propel it out of his hands or, if the ball is on the ground, he must propel it a visible distance from the mark. He may keep his hand on the ball while kicking it.

(1) The team awarded a free-kick has the option of taking a scrimmage at the mark and shall put in the ball.

(2) When a kick is taken, it must be taken without undue delay.

(3) The kick must be taken at or behind the mark on a line through the mark and the kicker may place the ball for a place kick.

(4) If the place prescribed by the Laws for the award of a free kick is within 5m of the opponents' goal-line, the mark for the free kick, or the scrummage taken in place of it, shall be 5m from the goal-line on a line through that place.

(5) The kicker may kick the ball in any direction and he may play the ball again without restriction.

(6) The *kicker's team*, except a placer for a place kick, must be behind the ball until it has been kicked.

(7) The *opposing team* must not wilfully resort to any action which may delay the taking of a free-kick. This includes actions such as wilfully carrying, throwing or kicking the ball away out of reach of the kicker.

(8) The *opposing team* must retire without delay to or behind a line parallel to the goal-lines and 10m from the mark or to their own goal-line if nearer to the mark, or 5m from their opponents' goal-line if the mark is in-goal. Having so retired, players of the opposing team may charge with a view to preventing the kick, as soon as the ball has been placed on the ground or the kicker begins his run or offers to kick. Retiring players will not be penalised if their failure to retire 10m is due to the rapidity with which the kick has been taken, but they may not stop retiring and enter the game until an opponent carrying the ball has run 5m.

(9) If having charged fairly, players of the opposing team prevent the kick from being taken, and do not gain advantage, the kick is void.

(10) Neither the kicker nor the placer shall wilfully do anything which

may lead the opposing team to charge prematurely. If either does so, the charge shall not be disallowed.

Penalty. For an infringement by the *kicker's team* or for a void kick – a scrummage at the mark and the *opposing team* shall put in the ball. If the mark is in in-goal, the scrummage shall be awarded 5m from the goal-line on a line through the mark. For an infringement by the *opposing team* – a free kick 10m in front of the mark or 5m from the goal-line whichever is nearer, on a line through the mark. Any player of the non-offending team may take the kick.

Reprinted by permission of the International Rugby Football Board. Full notes and interpretation of these Laws, with IRFB Directives, RFU Rulings, Referee's Signals and a Mini-Rugby Directive can be found in The Laws of the Game of Rugby Football, obtainable from the Rugby Football Union.

Softball

Softball

*Softball may be played as a Fast Pitch (FP) game or as a
Slow Pitch (SP). The Pitching Regulations for the two
alternatives are set out in Rule 6 on page 773. Other
variations between the two games are marked (FP) or (SP)
in the Rules.*

1. DEFINITIONS

1. Altered Bat. A bat is altered when the physical structure of a legal bat
has been changed. Replacing the grip with another legal grip is not
considered altering the bat. A 'flare or cone' grip attached to the bat is
an altered bat.

2. Appeal Play. A live or dead ball appeal play is a play upon which an
umpire cannot make a decision until requested by a manager, coach or
player of the defensive team. The appeal must be made before the next
pitch, legal or illegal. If the appeal is made at the end of an inning or at
the end of a game, said appeal will not be accepted if all the players of
the defensive team have abandoned fair territory.

3. Base on Balls. A base on balls permits a batter to gain first base
without liability to be put out and is awarded to a batter by the umpire
when four pitches are judged to be balls.

4. Base Path. A base path is an imaginary line 1.0m (3ft) to either side of
a direct line between the bases.

5. Baserunner. A baserunner is a player of the team at bat who has
finished his/her turn at bat, reached first base, and has not yet been put
out.

6. Batted Ball. A batted ball is any ball that hits the bat or is hit by the
bat and which lands either in fair or foul territory. No intention to hit the
ball is necessary.

7. Batter's Box. The batter's box is the area to which the batter is
restricted while in position with the intention of helping his/her team to
obtain runs. The lines are considered inside the batter's box. Prior to the
pitch the batter must have both feet entirely within the lines of the
batter's box.

8. Batter-baserunner. A batter-baserunner is a player who has finished
his/her turn at bat but has not yet been put out or touched first base.

9. Batting Order. The batting order is the official listing of offensive players in the order in which members of that team must come to bat. When the line-up card is submitted, it shall also include the players' positions.

10. Blocked Ball. A blocked ball is a batted or thrown ball that is touched, stopped, or handled by a person not engaged in the game, or which touches any object which is not part of the official equipment or official playing area.

Effect: The ball is dead. For offensive equipment causing a blocked ball (and creating interference), the player being played on is out. If no apparent play is obvious, no runner will be called out, but all runners will return to the last base touched at the time of the dead ball declaration.

11. Bunt. A bunt is a legally tapped ball not swung at, but intentionally met with the bat and tapped slowly within the infield.

12. Catch. A catch is a legally caught ball which occurs when the fielder catches a batted or thrown ball with his/her hands or glove. If the ball is merely held in the fielder's arms or prevented from dropping to the ground by some part of the fielder's body or clothing, the catch is not completed until the ball is in the grasp of the fielder's hands or glove. It is not a catch if a fielder, immediately after he/she contacts the ball, collides with another player or wall or falls to the ground, and drops the ball as a result of the collision or falling to the ground. In establishing a valid catch, the fielder shall hold the ball long enough to prove he/she has complete control of the ball and that his/her release of the ball is voluntary and intentional. If a player drops the ball while in the act of throwing it, it is a valid catch.

13. Catcher's Box. The catcher's box is that area within which the catcher must stand while and until the pitched ball is released. The lines are to be considered within the catcher's box.

14. Charged Conference. A charged conference takes place when:

(*a*) (*Defensive Conference*) The defensive team requests a suspension of play for any reason and a representative (not in field) of the defensive team enters the playing field and gives the umpire cause to believe that he/she has delivered a message (by any means) to the pitcher. When the representative from the dugout enters the field and removes the pitcher from the pitching position, it is not a charged conference for the new pitcher, but is a charged conference for the pitcher removed from the pitching position. It is not a charged conference for the defence if they confer during a charged offensive conference, as long as they are made to play ball when the offence is ready.

(*b*) (*Offensive Conference*) The offensive team requests a suspension of play to allow the manager or other team representatives to confer with the batter or baserunner. It is not a charged conference when a pitcher is putting on a warm-up jacket while on base, or if the offence confers while the defensive team is in conference, as long as the offence is ready to play when the defence is ready. Refer to Rule 5, Section 9.

15. Chopped Ball. (SP only) A chopped hit ball is one at which the batter strikes downward with a chopping motion of the bat so that the ball bounces high into the air.

16. Coach. A coach is a member of the team at bat who takes his/her place within the coach's lines on the field to direct the players of his/her team in running the bases. Two coaches are allowed. One coach can have in his/her possession in the coach's box, a scorebook, pen or pencil, and an indicator, which shall be used for scorekeeping or record keeping purposes only.

17. Dead Ball. The ball is not in play and is not considered in play again until the pitcher has the ball in his/her possession and is within 2.5m (8ft) of the pitcher's plate and the plate umpire has called 'Play ball'.

18. Defensive Team. The defensive team is the team in the field.

19. Dislodged Base. A dislodged base is a base dislodged from its proper position.

20. Double Play. A double play is a play by the defence in which two offensive players are legally put out as a result of continuous action.

21. Fair Ball. A fair ball is a batted ball that:

(*a*) Settles or is touched on fair territory between home and first base or between home and third base.

(*b*) Bounds past first or third base on or over fair territory.

(*c*) Touches first, second or third base.

(*d*) While on or over fair territory touches the person or clothing of an umpire or player.

(*e*) First falls on fair territory beyond first and third base.

(*f*) While over fair territory, passes out of the playing field beyond the outfield fence.

Note: A fair fly shall be judged according to the relative position of the ball and the foul line, including the foul pole, and not as to whether the fielder is on fair or foul territory at the time he/she touches the ball. It does not matter whether the ball first touches fair or foul territory, as long as it does not touch anything foreign to the natural ground in foul territory and complies with all other aspects of a fair ball.

22. Fair Territory. Fair territory is that part of the playing field within and including the first and third base foul lines from home base to the bottom of the extreme playing field fence and perpendicularly upwards.

23. Fielder. A fielder is any player of the team in the field.

24. Fly Ball. A fly ball is any ball batted into the air.

25. Force-out. A force-out is an out which can be made only when a baserunner loses the right to the base which he/she is occupying because the batter becomes a baserunner, and before the batter or a succeeding baserunner has been put out.

26. Foul Ball. A foul ball is a batted ball that:

(*a*) Settles on foul territory between home and first base, or between home a third base.

(*b*) Bounds past first or third base on or over foul territory.

(*c*) First touches on foul territory beyond first or third base..

(*d*) While on or over foul territory, touches the person or clothing of an umpire or player, or any object foreign to the nature ground.

(*e*) Touches batter or bat in batter's hand while within the batter's box.

Note: A foul fly shall be judged according to the relative position of the ball and the foul line, including the foul pole, and not as to whether the fielder is on foul or fair territory at the time he/she touches the ball.

27. Foul Tip. A foul tip is a batted ball which:

(*a*) Goes directly from the bat to the catcher's hands;

(*b*) Goes no higher than the batter's head; and

(*c*) Is legally caught by the catcher.

Note: It is not a foul tip unless caught, and any foul tip that is caught is a strike. In Fast Pitch the ball is in play. In Slow Pitch the ball is dead. It is not a catch if it is a rebound, unless the ball first touched the catcher's hand or glove.

28. Helmet.

(*a*) A helmet may or may not have ear flaps and shall be the type which has safety features equal to or greater than those provided by the full plastic cap with padding on the inside. A liner covering the ears only does not meet the Rule specifications.

(*b*) A helmet worn by a catcher may be the skull type without the ear flaps.

29. Home Team. The home team is the team on whose grounds the game is played, or if the game is played on neutral ground, the home team shall be designated by mutual agreement or by a flip of a coin.

30. Illegal Bat. An illegal bat is one that does not meet the requirements of Rule 3. Section 1.

31. Illegally Batted Ball. An illegally batted ball occurs when:

(*a*) A batter hits a ball fair or foul while his/her entire foot is completely out of the box, on the ground, when he/she hits the ball.

(*b*) Any part of the batter's foot is touching home plate when he/she hits the ball.

(*c*) The batter hits the ball with an illegal bat.

32. Illegally Caught Ball. An illegally caught ball occurs when a fielder catches a batted or thrown ball with his/her cap, mask, glove, or any part of his/her uniform while it is detached from its proper place.

33. In Flight. In flight describes any batted, thrown, or pitched ball which has not yet touched the ground or some object other than a fielder.

34. In Jeopardy. In jeopardy is a term indicating that the ball is in play and an offensive player may be put out.

35. Infield. The infield is that portion of the field in fair territory which includes areas normally covered by infielders.

36. Infield Fly. An infield fly is a fair fly ball (not including a line drive or an attempted bunt) which can be caught by an infielder with ordinary effort, when first and second, or first, second and third based are occupied, before two are out. The pitcher, catcher and any outfielder who positions himself/herself in the infield on the play shall be considered infielders for the purpose of this rule.

Note: When it seems apparent that a batted ball will be an infield fly, the umpire shall immediately declare 'infield fly, if fair – the batter is out' for the benefit of the runners. The ball is alive and runners may advance at the risk of the ball being caught, or retouch and advance after the ball is touched, the same as on any fly ball. If the hit becomes a foul ball, it is treated the same as any foul.

If a declared infield fly is allowed to fall untouched to the ground, and bounces foul before passing first or third base, it is a foul ball. If a declared infield fly falls untouched to the ground outside the baseline, and bounces fair before passing first or third base, it is an infield fly.

37. Inning. An inning is that portion of a game within which the teams alternate on offence and defence and in which there are three outs for each team. A new inning begins immediately after the final out of the previous inning.

38. Interference. Interference is the act of an offensive player or team member which impedes, hinders or confuses a defensive player attempting to execute a play.

39. Legal Touch. A legal touch occurs when a runner or batter-baserunner who is not touching a base is touched by the ball while it is securely held in the fielder's hand. The ball is not considered as having been securely held if it is juggled or dropped by the infielder after having touched the runner, unless the runner deliberately knocks the ball from the hand of the fielder. It is sufficient for the runner to be touched with the hand or glove in which the ball is held.

40. Legally Caught Ball. A legally caught ball occurs when a fielder catches a batted or thrown ball, provided it is not caught in the fielder's hat, cap, mask, protector, pocket, or other part of his/her uniform. It must be caught and firmly held with hand or hands.

41. Line Drive. A line drive is a fly ball that is batted sharply and directly into the playing field.

42. Obstruction. Obstruction is the act of:

(*a*) A defensive player or team member which hinders or prevents a batter from striking or hitting a pitched ball.

(*b*) A fielder, while not in possession of the ball, or not in the act of fielding a batted ball, which impedes the progress of a baserunner who is legally running bases.

43. Offensive Team. The offensive team is the team at bat.

44. Outfield. The outfield is that portion of the field which is outside the diamond formed by the baselines or the area not normally covered by an infielder and within the foul lines beyond first and third bases, and boundaries of the grounds.

45. Overslide. An overslide is the act of an offensive player when as a baserunner he overslides a base he/she is attempting to reach. It is usually caused when his/her momentum causes him/her to lose contact with the base which then causes him/her to be in jeopardy. The batter-runner may overslide first base without being in jeopardy if he/she immediately returns to that base.

46. Overthrow. An overthrow is a play in which a ball is thrown from one fielder to another to retire a runner who has not reached or is off base, and which goes into foul territory beyond the boundary lines of the playing field.

47. Passed Ball. (FP only) A passed ball is a legally delivered ball that should have been held or controlled by the catcher with ordinary effort.

48. Pitch. The act performed by the pitcher in throwing the ball to the batter. *Note*: If the pitch becomes or goes out of play, one base is awarded all runners.

49. Pitcher's Circle. (FP only) The pitcher's circle is the area within 2.5m (8ft) of the pitcher's plate. The lines are considered within the circle.

50. Pivot Foot. The pivot foot is that foot with which the pitcher pushes off the pitcher's plate.

51. 'Play Ball'. 'Play ball' is the term used by the plate umpire to indicate that play shall begin or be resumed when the pitcher has the ball in his/her possession and is within 2.5m (8ft) of the pitcher's plate. All defensive players, except the catcher, who must be in the catcher's box, must be in fair territory to put the ball in play.

52. Quick Return Pitch. A quick return pitch is one made by the pitcher with the obvious attempt to catch the batter off balance. This would be before the batter takes his/her desired position in the batter's box or while he/she is still off balance as a result of the previous pitch.

53. Runner. The term runner means batter-baserunner or baserunner.

54. Starting Players. The players listed on the official line-up given to the umpire-in-chief and/or the plate umpire.

55. Stealing. Stealing is the act of a baserunner attempting to advance during a pitch to the batter. Stealing is not allowed in Slow Pitch.

56. Strike Zone.

(*a*) (FP only) The strike zone is that space over any part of home plate which is between the batter's armpits and the top of his/her knees when the batter assumes his/her natural batting stance.

(*b*) (SP only) The strike zone is that space over any part of home plate which is between the batter's highest shoulder and his/her knees when the batter assumes his/her natural batting stance.

57. Throw. The act performed by a fielder when throwing the ball to another fielder.

Note: If the throw becomes blocked or goes out of play, two bases are awarded all runners from the last base touched at the time of the throw.

58. Time Out. Time out is the term used by the umpire to order the suspension of play.

59. Triple Play. A triple play is a continuous action play by the defence in which three offensive players are put out.

60. Turn at Bat. A turn at bat begins when a player first enters the batter's box and continues until he/she is put out or becomes a baserunner.

61. Wild Pitch. (FP only) A wild pitch is a legally delivered ball so high, so low, or so wide of the plate that the catcher cannot or does not stop and control it with ordinary effort.

2. THE PLAYING FIELD

1. The playing field is the area shown on the plan on page 766, within which the ball may be legally played and fielded. The playing field shall have a clear and unobstructed area within the minimum radius of 60.0m (200ft) for Female Fast Pitch and 70.0m (225ft) for Male Fast Pitch; 75.0m (250ft) for Female Slow Pitch and 85.0m (275ft) for Male Slow Pitch from home plate between the foul lines. Outside the foul lines and between home plate and the backstop there shall be an unobstructed area of not less than 8.0m (25ft) nor more than 9.0m (30ft) in width.

Sections 2, 3, and 4, concerning Special Rules and Obstructions, Baselines and Layout of the Diamond are given in full in the International Softball Federation Official Guide and Rule Book.

3. EQUIPMENT

1. The Official Bat.
2. Warm-up Bats.
3. The Official Softball.

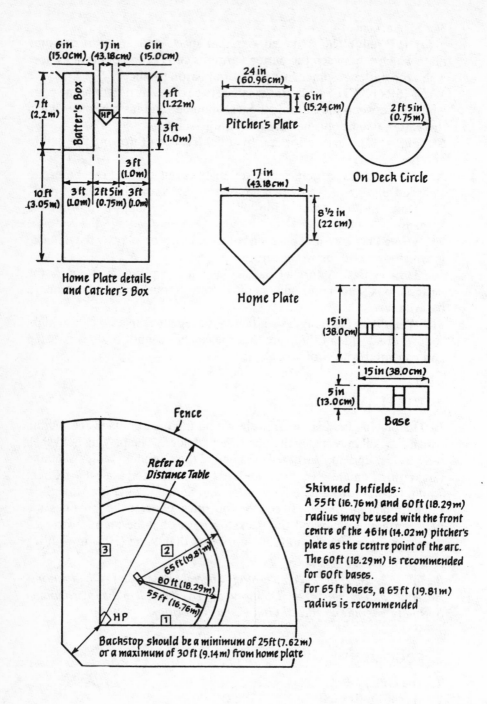

6 in
(15.0 cm)   17 in   6 in
(43.18 cm) (15.0 cm)

7 ft
(2.2 m)

Batter's Box

HP

4 ft
(1.22 m)

3 ft
(1.0 m)

3 ft
(1.0 m)

10 ft
(3.05 m)   3 ft   2 ft 5 in   3 ft
(1.0 m) (0.75 m) (1.0 m)

Home Plate details
and Catcher's Box

24 in
(60.96 cm)

6 in
(15.24 cm)

Pitcher's Plate

2 ft 5 in
(0.75 m)

On Deck Circle

17 in
(43.18 cm)

8½ in
(22 cm)

Home Plate

15 in
(38.0 cm)

15 in (38.0 cm)

5 in
(13.0 cm)

Base

Fence

Refer to
Distance Table

3

2

1

HP

65 ft (19.81 m)

80 ft (18.29 m)

55 ft (16.76 m)

Skinned Infields:
A 55 ft (16.76 m) and 60 ft (18.29 m)
radius may be used with the front
centre of the 46 in (14.02 m) pitcher's
plate as the centre point of the arc.
The 60 ft (18.29 m) is recommended
for 60 ft bases.
For 65 ft bases, a 65 ft (19.81 m)
radius is recommended

Backstop should be a minimum of 25 ft (7.62 m)
or a maximum of 30 ft (9.14 m) from home plate

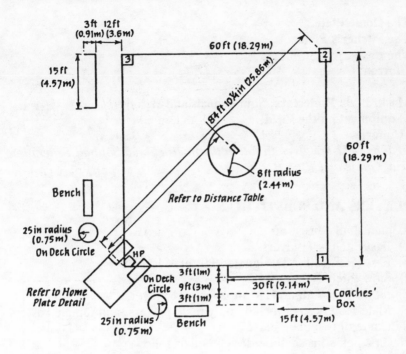

3ft 12ft
(0.91m) (3.6m)

60ft (18.29m)

15ft
(4.57m)

3

2

84ft 10¼in (25.86m)

8ft radius
(2.44m)

60ft
(18.29m)

Refer to Distance Table

Bench

25in radius
(0.75m)
On Deck Circle

HP

Refer to Home
Plate Detail

On Deck
Circle

25in radius
(0.75m)

Bench

1

3ft (1m)
9ft (3m)
3ft (1m)

30ft (9.14m)

Coaches'
Box

15ft (4.57m)

ADULT	DISTANCE TABLE			
GAME	DIVISION	BASES	PITCHING	FENCES
Fast Pitch	Female	60' (18 29m)	40 (12 2m)	200' (60 96m)
	Male	60 (18 29m)	46 (14 0m)	225 (68 58m) min
				250 (76 20m) max
Modified	Female	60 (18 29m)	40 (12 2m)	200' (60 96m)
	Male	60 (18 29m)	46 (14 0m)	265 (80 80m)
Slow Pitch	Female	65' (19 81m)	46 (14 0m)	250' (76 20m)
	Male	65' (19 81m)	46 (14 0m)	275 (83 82m)
	Co-Ed	65' (19 81m)	46 (14 0m)	275 (83 82m)
	Super	65 (19 81m)	46 (14 0m)	300' (91 44m)

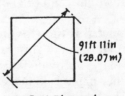

77ft 9¼in
(23.70m)

55 Foot Diamond

YOUTH				FENCES	
GAME	DIVISION	BASES	PITCHING	Minimum	Maximum
Slow Pitch	Girls 10-under	55' (16 76m)	35 (10 67m)	150' (45 72m)	175 (53 34m)
	Boys 10-under	55 (16 76m)	35 (10 67m)	150' (45 72m)	175 (53 34m)
	Girls 12-under	60 (18 29m)	40 (12 2m)	175 (53 34m)	200' (60 96m)
	Boys 12-under	60 (18 29m)	40 (12 2m)	175 (53 34m)	200' (60 96m)
	Girls 15-under	65 (19 81m)	46 (14 0m)	225 (68 58m)	250 (76 20m)
	Boys 15-under	60 (18 29m)	46 (14 0m)	250' (76 20m)	275 (83 82m)
	Girls 19-under	65 (19 81m)	46 (14 0m)	225 (68 58m)	250 (76 20m)
	Boys 19-under	65 (19 81m)	46 (14 0m)	275 (83 82m)	300 (91 44m)
Fast Pitch	Girls 10-under	55 (16 76m)	35 (10 67m)	150' (45 72m)	175' (53 34m)
	Boys 10-under	55 (16 76m)	35 (10 67m)	150' (45 72m)	175 (53 34m)
	Girls 12-under	60 (18 29m)	35 (10 67m)	175 (53 34m)	200' (60 96m)
	Boys 12-under	60 (18 29m)	40 (12 2m)	175 (53 34m)	200' (60 96m)
	Girls 15-under	60 (18 29m)	40 (12 2m)	175 (53 34m)	200' (60 96m)
	Boys 15-under	60 (18 29m)	46 (14 0m)	175 (53 34m)	200' (60 96m)
	Girls 19-under	60 (18 29m)	40 (12 2m)	200' (60 96m)	225' (68 58m)
	Boys 19-under	60 (18 29m)	46 (14 0m)	200 (60 96m)	225' (68 58m)

91ft 11in
(28.07m)

65 Foot Diamond

4. **The Home Plate.**
5. **The Pitcher's Plate.**
6. **The Bases.**
7. **Gloves.**
8. **Shoes.**
9. **Mask, Body Protectors, Shin Guards and Helmets.**
10. **Equipment on the Field.**
11. **Uniform.**

Sections 1–11 are given in full in the International Softball Federation Official Guide and Rule Book.

4. PLAYERS AND SUBSTITUTES

1. A team shall consist of:

(*a*) Fast Pitch – 9 players.

(*b*) Fast Pitch with a Designated Hitter – 10 players.

(*c*) Slow Pitch – 10 players.

(*d*) Slow Pitch with an Extra Player – 11 players.

(*e*) Male rosters shall include only male players, and female rosters shall include only female players.

2. Players' positions shall be designated as follows:

(*a*) Fast Pitch: pitcher, catcher, first baseman, second baseman, third baseman, shortstop, left fielder, centerfielder and right fielder.

(*b*) Fast Pitch with a Designated Hitter: same as Fast Pitch in paragraph (*a*) above plus a Designated Hitter.

(*c*) Slow Pitch: same as Fast Pitch in paragraph (*a*) above plus a short fielder.

(*d*) Slow Pitch with an extra player: same as Slow Pitch in paragraph (*c*) above, plus an Extra Player who bats.

Note: Players of the team in the field may be stationed anywhere on fair territory, except the catcher, who must be in the catcher's box, and the pitcher, who must be in a legal pitching position at the start of each pitch, or within 2.5m (8ft) of the pitcher's plate when putting the ball in play.

3. Designated Hitter (FP only)

(*a*) A Designated Hitter, referred to as a DH (FP only), may be used for any player, provided it is made known prior to the start of the game and his/her name is indicated on the line-up sheet.

(*b*) The DH must remain in the same position in the batting order for the entire game.

(*c*) The DH may be substituted for at any time either by a pinch-hitter or a pinch-runner who then becomes the DH. The substitute must be a player who has not yet been in the game.

(*d*) The DH may not enter the game on defence.

(*e*) The DH replaced by a pinch-hitter or pinch-runner may not return to the game.

(*f*) The defensive player for whom the DH is batting cannot play offence at any time during the game.

(*g*) The player for whom the DH is batting must appear in the last place (No. 10) in the batting order given to the umpire-in-chief and/or the plate umpire.

4. Extra Player (SP only)

(*a*) An Extra Player, referred to as an EP, is optional, but if one is used, it must be made known prior to the start of the game, and be listed in the scoring sheet in the regular batting order. If the EP is used, he/she must be used the entire game. Failure to complete the game with the EP results in forfeiture of the game – Rule 4, Section 6(*d*).

(*b*) The EP must remain in the same position in the batting order for the entire game.

(*c*) If an EP is used, all must bat and any can play defence. Defensive position can be changed, but the batting order must remain the same.

(*d*) The EP may be substituted for at any time, either by a pinch-runner or pinch-hitter, who then becomes the EP. The substitute must be a player who has not yet been in the game. The starting EP can re-enter one time.

5. Any of the starting players, except the DH (FP only) or the EP (SP only), may be withdrawn and re-enter once, provided such player occupies the same batting position whenever he/she is in the line-up. *Note*: The original player and the substitute(s) cannot be in the line-up at the same time.

Effect – Sections 3–5:

(*a*) The penalty for an illegal DH, EP, or re-entry entering the game offensively is as follows:

(1) If the illegal player is discovered while at bat, he/she is ejected. Any advance of baserunners while the illegal batter is at bat, is legal.

(2) If the illegal player is discovered after completing his/her turn at bat and prior to the next pitch, the illegal player is ejected and any advance of baserunners as a result of a walk or base hit by the illegal batter, is nullified.

(3) If the illegal player is discovered after completing his/her turn at bat and after the next pitch, the illegal player is ejected and any advance by baserunners while the illegal batter was at bat, is legal.

(*b*) The penalty for an illegal DH, EP, or re-entry entering the game defensively is as follows:

(1) If the illegal player is discovered after he/she makes a play and prior to the next pitch, the offensive team has the option of taking the result of the play, or have the last batter go back to bat, assuming balls and strikes prior to the discovery of the illegal player and having all

baserunners return to the base they were prior to the play. The illegal player is ejected.

(2) If the illegal player is detected after a pitch to the next batter, the illegal player is ejected and all plays stand.

(*c*) The penalty for an illegal re-entry is the ejection of both the manager/coach (whose name appears on the line-up card) and the player in violation.

6. A team must have the required number of players present to start or continue a game. No player's name shall be on the starting line-up unless the player is available in the team area in uniform. Requirements are:

(*a*) Fast Pitch – 9 players.

(*b*) Fast Pitch with a Designated Hitter – 10 players.

(*c*) Slow Pitch – 10 players.

(*d*) Slow Pitch with an Extra Player – 11 players.

7. A player shall be officially in the game when his/her name has been entered on the official scoresheet or has been announced. A substitute may take the place of a player whose name is in his/her team's batting order. The following regulations govern the substitution of players:

(*a*) The manager or team representative of the team making the substitution shall immediately notify the plate umpire at the time a substitute enters. Failure to do so would create an illegal substitution with the penalty, immediate ejection from the game when the infraction is discovered, and shall not participate again as a player or coach. All play while the illegal substitute is in the game shall stand.

(*b*) Substitute players will be considered in the game when announced to the plate umpire. A player will not violate the substitution rule until one pitch has been thrown.

Note: *The use of an illegal substitute is handled as a protest by the offended team. If the team manager or player in violation informs the umpire prior to the opposing team's protest, there is no violation regardless how long the player(s) was illegally in the game.*

(*c*) Any player may be removed from the game at any time.

(*d*) A player removed from the game shall not participate in the game again except as a coach. *Exception*: The starting line-up may re-enter one time (See Rule 4, Section 5).

Effect – Section 7(*d*): The penalty for an illegal re-entry of any player shall be ejection of the player in violation and the manager/coach listed on the line-up card.

(*e*) Multiple substitutions can be made for the player listed on the starting line-up, but no substitute can return to the game after being removed. The starting player who re-enters, and is substituted for a second time, would not be allowed to participate in the game any more. The player who re-enters can play any position on defence, and must remain in the same batting order as listed as a starter. *Exception*: If a pitcher who has been removed from the pitching position after 2 defensive conferences in the same inning, this starting pitcher can re-enter, but not as a pitcher (Rule 6, Section 11).

5. THE GAME

1. The choice of the first or last bat in the inning shall be decided by a toss of a coin, unless otherwise stated in the rules of the organisation under which the schedule of games is being played.

2. The fitness of the ground for a game shall be decided solely by the plate umpire.

3. A regulation game shall consist of seven innings.

(*a*) A full seven innings need not be played if the team second at bat scores more runs in six innings or before the third out in the last of the seventh inning.

(*b*) A game that is tied at the end of seven innings shall be continued by playing additional innings, or until one side has scored more runs than the other at the end of a complete inning, or until the team second at bat has scored more runs in their half of the inning before the third out is made.

(*c*) A game called by the umpire shall be regulation if five or more complete innings have been played or if the team second at bat has scored more runs than the other team has scored in five or more innings. The umpire is empowered to call a game at any time because of darkness, rain, fire, panic, or other cause which puts the patrons or players in peril.

(*d*) A regulation tie game shall be declared if the score is equal when the game is called at the end of five or more completed innings, or if the team second at bat has equalled the score of the first team at bat in the incomplete inning.

(*e*) These provisions do not apply to any acts on the part of players or spectators which might call for forfeiture of the game. The umpire may forfeit the game if attacked physically by any team member or spectator.

(*f*) A forfeited game shall be declared by the umpire in favour of the team not at fault in the following cases:

(1) If a team fails to appear on the field, or being on the field, refuses to begin a game for which it is scheduled or assigned at the time scheduled or within a time set for forfeitures by the organisation in which the team is playing.

(2) If, after the game has begun, one side refuses to continue to play, unless the game has been suspended or terminated by the umpire.

(3) If, after play has been suspended by the umpire, one side fails to resume playing within 2 minutes after the umpire has called 'Play ball'.

(4) If a team employs tactics palpably designed to delay or to hasten the game.

(5) If, after a warning by the umpire, any one of the Rules of the game is wilfully violated.

(6) If the order for the removal of a player is not obeyed within 1 minute.

(7) If, because of the removal of the players from the game by the Umpire or for any cause, there are less than 9 (Fast Pitch), 10 (Fast Pitch with DH) or 10 (Slow Pitch) players on either team.

(g) Games that are not considered regulation, or regulation tie games, shall be replayed from the beginning. Original line-ups may be changed when the game is replayed. *Exception*: When a World Championship or Continental game is suspended by the chief umpire, it shall be resumed at the exact point where the game was suspended.

4. The winner of the game shall be the team that scores the most runs in a regulation game.

(a) The score of a called regulation game shall be the score at the end of the last complete inning unless the team second at bat has scored more runs than the first team at bat in the incomplete inning. In this case, the score shall be that of the incomplete inning.

(b) The score of a regulation tie game shall be the tie score when the game was terminated. A regulation tie game shall be replayed from the beginning.

(c) The score of a forfeited game shall be 7–0 in favour of the team not at fault.

5. Tiebreaker. Starting with the top of the tenth inning, and each half inning thereafter, the offensive team shall begin its turn at bat, with the player who is scheduled to bat ninth in that respective half-inning being placed on second base. The player who is running can be substituted in accordance with the substitution rules.

6. One run shall be scored each time a baserunner legally touches first, second, third bases and home plate before the third out of the inning.

7. A run shall *not* be scored if the third out of the inning is a result of:

(a) The batter being put out before legally touching first base.

(b) A baserunner being forced out due to the batter becoming a baserunner.

(c) (FP only) A baserunner leaving base before the pitcher releases the ball to the batter. (SP only) A baserunner leaving base before the pitched ball reached home plate or before the pitched ball is batted.

8. No succeeding runner shall score a run when a preceding runner has been declared the third out of an inning.

9. There shall be only two charged conference between the manager or other team representative and the batter or baserunner in an inning.

Umpires shall not permit any such conference in excess of two in an inning.

Penalty: Ejection of the manager or coach insisting on another charged conference.

6. PITCHING REGULATIONS

Fast Pitch

1. The pitcher shall take a position with both feet firmly on the ground and in contact with, but not off the side of, the pitcher's plate.

(*a*) The pitcher, while standing on the pitcher's plate, must take the signal from the catcher or look at the catcher. If a signal is taken, it must be taken while pitcher has both feet in contact with the pitcher's plate. The ball must be held in *one* hand (bare or gloved) and the hands must be separated.

(*b*) Preliminary to pitching, the pitcher must bring his *whole* body to a full and complete stop facing the batter with his/her shoulders in line with first and third base and with the ball held in both hands in front of the body. This full and complete stop position must be maintained for a minimum of 1 second and not more than 10 seconds before starting the pitch.

(*c*) The pitcher shall not be considered in the pitching position unless the catcher is in position to receive the pitch.

(*d*) The pitcher may not take the pitching position on or near the pitcher's plate without having the ball in his/her possession.

2. The pitch starts when one hand is taken off the ball or the pitcher makes any motion that is part of his/her windup. In the act of delivering the ball, the pitcher shall not take more than one step which must be forward, toward the batter, and simultaneous with the delivery of the ball to the batter. 'Toward the batter' is interpreted as within the 60.0cm (24in) width of the pitcher's plate. The pivot foot may remain in contact or may push off and drag away from the pitching plate prior to the front foot touching the ground, as long as the pivot foot remains in contact with the ground. Pushing off with the pivot foot from a place other than the pitcher's plate is illegal.

Note: It is not a step if the pitcher slides his/her foot across the pitcher's plate, provided contact is maintained with the pitcher's plate.

3. A legal delivery shall be a ball which is delivered to the batter with an underhanded motion.

(*a*) The release of the ball and the follow through of the hand and wrist must be forward, past the straight line of the body.

(*b*) The hand shall be below the hip and the wrist not farther from the body than the elbow.

(*c*) The pitch is completed with a step toward the batter.

(*d*) The catcher must be within the outside lines of the catcher's box when the pitch is released.

(*e*) The catcher shall return the ball directly to the pitcher after each pitch, except after a strikeout or put out made by the catcher.

Exception: Section 3(*e*) does not apply when (*a*) a batter becomes a baserunner, (*b*) there are runners on base, or (*c*) a foul ball is fielded close to the foul line by the catcher who throws to first base for a possible out.

Effect – Section 3(*e*): an additional 'ball' is awarded to the batter.

(*f*) The pitcher has 20 seconds to release the next pitch.

4. The pitcher may use any windup desired, providing:

(*a*) He/she does not make any motion to pitch without immediately delivering the ball to the batter.

(*b*) He/she does not use a rocker action in which, after having the ball in both hands in pitching position, he/she removes one hand from the ball, takes a backward and forward swing and returns the ball to both hands in front of the body.

(*c*) He/she does not use a windup in which there is a stop or reversal of the forward motion.

(*d*) He/she does not make more than one revolution of the arm in the windmill pitch. A pitcher may drop his/her arm to the side and to the rear before starting the windmill motion.

(*e*) He/she does not continue to windup after taking the forward step which is simultaneous with the release of the ball.

5. The pitcher shall not deliberately drop, roll, or bounce the ball while in the pitching position in order to prevent the batter from striking it.

6. The pitcher shall not, at any time during the game, be allowed to use tape or other substances on his pitching hand or fingers, nor shall a pitcher use a ball that has a foreign substance on it. Under the supervision and control of the umpire, powdered resin may be used to dry the hands. The pitcher shall not wear a sweatband, bracelet, or similar type item on the wrist or forearm of the pitching arm.

7. No player shall take a position in the batter's line of vision or, with deliberate unsportsmanlike intent, act in a manner to distract the batter.

Effect – Section 7: The offender shall be ejected from the game and an illegal pitch shall be declared, even though a pitch may not be released.

Effect – Sections 1–7: Any infraction of Sections 1 to 7 is an illegal pitch with the exception of Section 3(*e*) which is covered separately. The ball is dead. A ball is called on the batter. Baserunners are entitled to advance one base without liability to be put out.

Exception: If the pitcher completes the delivery of the ball to the batter and the batter hits the ball and reaches first base safely and all baserunners advance at least one base then the play stands and the illegal pitch is nullified. A delayed dead ball will be signified by the umpire by extending his/her left arm horizontally.

Exception: If there are no baserunners on base and an illegal pitch hits the batter, the batter is awarded first base.

Note: An illegal pitch shall be called immediately when it becomes illegal. If called by the plate umpire, it shall be called in a voice so that the catcher and the batter will hear it. The plate umpire will also give the delayed dead ball signal. If called by the base umpire, it shall be called so that the nearest fielder shall hear it. The base umpire shall also give the delayed dead ball signal. Failure of players to hear the call shall not void the call.

8. At the beginning of each half inning, or when a pitcher relieves another, no more than 1 minute may be used to deliver no more than 5 pitches to the catcher or other team-mate. Play shall be suspended during this time. Foe excessive warm-up pitches a pitcher shall be penalised by awarding a ball to the batter for each pitch in excess of 5.

9. The pitcher shall not throw to a base while his/her foot is in contact with the pitcher's plate after he/she has taken the pitching position.

Effect – Section 9: Illegal pitch, the ball is dead, a ball is called on the batter and all runners advance one base. If the throw from the pitcher's plate is during an appeal play, the appeal is cancelled.

Note: The pitcher can remove himself/herself from the pitching position by stepping backwards off the pitcher's plate. Stepping forward or sideways constitutes an illegal pitch.

10. No pitch shall be declared when:

(*a*) The pitcher pitches during the suspension of play.

(*b*) The pitcher attempts a quick return of the ball before the batter has taken position or is off balance as a result of a previous pitch.

(*c*) The runner is called out for leaving the base too soon.

(*d*) The pitcher pitches before a baserunner has retouched his/her base after a foul ball has been declared and the ball is dead.

Effect – Section 10(*a*)–(*d*): The ball is dead and all subsequent action on that pitch is cancelled.

(*e*) No player, manager or coach shall call 'time' or employ any other word or pose of trying to make the pitcher commit an illegal pitch.

Effect – Section 10(*e*): No pitch shall be declared and a warning issued to the offending team. A repeat of this type of act by the team warned shall result in the offender being ejected from the game.

11. There shall be only one charged conference between the manager or other team representative from the dugout with each and every pitcher in an inning. The second charged conference shall result in the removal of the pitcher from the pitching position for the remainder of the game.

12. If the ball slips from the pitcher's hand during his/her windup or during the backswing, a ball is declared on the batter, the ball will remain in play, and the runners may advance at their own risk.

Modified Fast Pitch

All fast pitch pitching rules are in effect except:

(*a*) The pitcher must release the ball on the first forward swing of the pitching arm past the hip.

(*b*) The pitcher may not use a windmill or slingshot-type pitch, nor may he make a complete revolution in the delivery. *Note*: A slingshot-type pitch is defined as turning the body toward first or third base and bending the arm at the elbow during the backswing.

(*c*) The pitcher may take the ball behind his back on the backswing.

(*d*) The pitcher may drop his arm to the side and to the rear, but the ball may not be seen in the open palm at the top of the backswing, nor may it be outside the pitcher's wrist at any time on the forward swing.

(*e*) The pitcher may not have a stop or reversal of the forward motion of the pitching arm, and he must have a smooth follow-through of the pitching arm on the delivery.

(*f*) There is no penalty for touching the hip on the forward swing.

(*g*) The pitcher's palm may be facing up or down on the release of the ball.

(*h*) The pitcher may not continue to wind-up after releasing the ball, nor may he make any motion to pitch without immediately delivering the ball to the batter.

Slow Pitch

1. The pitcher shall take a position with one or both feet firmly on the ground and with one or both feet in contact with, but not off the side of, the pitcher's plate. At the time of delivery, both the pivot and the non-pivot foot must be within the width 60.0cm (24in) of the pitcher's plate.

(*a*) Preliminary to pitching, the pitcher must come to a full and complete stop, with the ball held in one or both hands in front of the body. The front of the body must face the batter.

(*b*) This position must be maintained at least 1 second and not more than 10 seconds before starting the delivery.

(*c*) The pitcher shall not be considered in pitching position unless the catcher is in position to receive the pitch.

2. The pitch starts when the pitcher makes any motion that is part of his/her windup after the required pause. Prior to the required pause, any windup may be used. The pivot foot must remain in contact with the pitcher's plate until the pitched ball leaves the hand. It is not necessary to take a step, but if one is taken, it may be forward or backward, provided the foot is in contact with the pitching plate when the ball is released and the stop is within the width 60.0cm (24in) of the pitching plate.

3. A legal delivery shall be a ball which is delivered to the batter with an underhanded motion.

(*a*) The pitch shall be released at a moderate speed. The speed is left entirely up to the umpire. The umpire shall warn the pitcher who delivers a pitch with excessive speed. If the pitcher repeats such an act after being warned, he/she shall be removed from the pitcher's position for the remainder of the game.

(*b*) The hand shall be below the hip.

(*c*) The ball must be delivered with a perceptible arc of at least 2.0m (6ft) from the ground. The pitched ball shall not reach a height of more than 3.5m (12ft) at its highest point from the ground.

(*d*) The catcher must be within the outside lines of the catcher's box until the pitched ball is batted or reaches home plate.

(*e*) The catcher shall return the ball directly to the pitcher after each pitch, except after a strikeout or putout made by the catcher. The pitcher has 20 seconds to release the next pitch.

Effect – Section 3(*e*): An additional ball is awarded to the batter.

4. The pitcher may use any windup desired, providing:

(*a*) He/she does not make any motion to pitch without immediately delivering the ball to the batter.

(*b*) His/her windup is a continuous motion.

(*c*) He/she does not use a windup in which there is a stop or reversal of the forward motion.

(*d*) He/she delivers the ball toward home plate on the first forward swing of the pitching arm past the hip.

(*e*) He/she does not continue to windup after he/she releases the ball.

5. The pitcher shall not, at any time during the game, be allowed to use any foreign substances upon the ball, the pitching hand or the fingers.

6. At the beginning of each half inning or when a pitcher relieves another, no more than 1 minute may be used to deliver no more than *3 pitches* to the catcher or other team-mate. Play shall be suspended during this time. For excessive warm-up pitches, a pitcher shall be penalised by awarding a ball to the batter for each pitch in excess of 3.

7. The pitcher shall not throw to a base during a live ball while his/her foot is in contact with the pitcher's plate after he/she has taken the pitching position.

Note: The pitcher can remove himself/herself from the pitching position by stepping backwards off the pitcher's plate. Stepping forward or sideways constitutes an illegal pitch. It is an illegal pitch if a fielder takes up a position in the batter's line of vision, or with deliberate unsportsmanlike intent, acts in a manner to distract the batter.

Note: A pitch does not have to be released.

Effect – Section 1–7: Any infraction of Sections 1 to 7 is an illegal pitch. The ball is dead. A ball shall be called on the batter. Baserunners do not advance.

Exception: If a batter strikes at any illegal pitch, it shall be a strike, and there shall be no penalty for such an illegal pitch. The ball shall remain in play if hit by the batter. If an illegal pitch is called during an appeal play, the appeal is cancelled.

Note: An illegal pitch shall be called immediately when it becomes illegal. If called by the plate umpire, it shall be called in a voice so that the catcher and the batter will hear it. The plate umpire will also give the delayed dead ball signal. If called by the base umpire, it shall be called so that the nearest fielder shall hear it. The base umpire shall also give the delayed dead ball signal. Failure of players to hear the call shall not void the call.

8. No pitch shall be declared when:

(*a*) The pitcher pitches during the suspension of play.

(*b*) The pitcher attempts a quick return of the ball before the batter has taken his/her position or is off balance as a result of a previous pitch.

(*c*) The runner is called out for leaving the base too soon.

(*d*) The pitcher pitches before the baserunner has retouched his/her base after a foul ball has been declared, and the ball is dead.

(*e*) The ball slips from the pitcher's hand during his/her windup or during the backswing.

Effect – Section 8(*a*)–(*e*): The ball is dead and all subsequent action on that pitch is cancelled.

(*f*) No player, manager or coach shall call 'time' or employ any other word or phrase or commit any act while the ball is alive and in play for the obvious purpose of trying to make the pitcher commit an illegal pitch.

Effect – Section 8(*f*): No pitch shall be declared and a warning issued to the offending team. A repeat of this type act by the team warned shall result in the offender being removed from the game.

9. There shall be only one charged conference between the manager, or other team representative from the dugout, with each and every pitcher in an inning. The second charged conference shall result in the removal of the pitcher from the pitching position for the remainder of the game.

7. BATTING

1. The batter shall take his/her position within the lines of the batter's box.

(*a*) The batter shall not have his/her entire foot touching the ground completely outside the lines of the batter's box or touching home plate when the ball is hit.

(*b*) The batter shall not step directly across in front of the catcher to the other batter's box while the pitcher is in position ready to pitch.

(*c*) The batter shall not enter the batter's box with an illegal bat.

Effect – Section 1(*a*)–(*c*): The ball is dead, the batter is out, baserunners may *not* advance.

(*d*) The batter shall not enter the batter's box with an altered bat.

Effect – Section 1(*d*): The ball is dead, the batter is out, and without warning, the batter is ejected from the game, and baserunners may not advance.

(*e*) The batter must take his/her position within 20 seconds after the umpire has called 'Play ball'.

Effect – Section 1(*e*): The ball is dead. The batter is out.

2. Each player of the side at bat shall become a batter in the order in which his/her name appears on the scoresheet.

(*a*) The batting order of each team must be on the scoresheet and must be delivered before the game by the manager or captain to the plate umpire. He/she shall submit it to the inspection of the manager or captain of the opposing team.

(*b*) The batting order delivered to the umpire must be followed throughout the game unless a player is substituted for another. When this occurs, the substitute must take the place of the removed player in the batting order.

(*c*) The first batter in each inning shall be the batter whose name follows that of the last player who completed a turn at bat in the preceding inning.

Effect – Section 2(*b*)–(*c*): Batting out of order is an appeal play which may be made by the manager, coach, or player of the defensive team only.

(1) If the error is discovered while the incorrect batter is at bat, the correct batter may take his/her place, assume any balls and strikes, and any runs scored or bases run while the incorrect batter was at bat shall be legal.

(2) If the error is discovered after the incorrect batter has completed his/her turn at bat and before there has been a pitch to another batter, the player who should have batted is out. Any advance or score made because of a ball batted by the improper batter or because of the improper batter's advance to first base on a hit, an error, a base on balls, or a hit batter shall be nullified. The next batter is the player whose name follows that of the player called out for failing to bat. If the batter declared out under these circumstances is the third out, the correct batter in the next inning shall be the player who would have come to bat had the player been put out by ordinary play.

(3) If the error is discovered after the first pitch to the next batter, the turn at bat of the incorrect batter is legal, all runs scored and bases run

are legal, and the next batter in order shall be the one whose name follows that of the incorrect batter. No one is called out for failure to bat. Players who have not batted and who have not been called out have lost their turn at bat until reached again in the regular order.

(4) No baserunner shall be removed from the base he/she is occupying to bat in his/her proper place. He/she merely misses his/her turn at bat with no penalty. The batter following him/her in the batting order becomes the legal batter.

(*d*) When the third out in an inning is made before the batter has completed his/her turn at bat, he/she shall be the first batter in the next inning, and the ball and strike count on him/her shall be cancelled.

3. The batter shall not hinder the catcher from fielding or throwing the ball by stepping out of the batter's box, or intentionally hinder the catcher while standing within the batter's box.

Effect – Section 3: The ball is dead and base runners must return to the last base that, in the judgement of the umpire, was touched at the time of the interference. The batter is out.

4. Members of the team at bat shall not interfere with a player attempting to field a foul fly ball.

Effect – Section 4: The ball is dead and the batter is out, and baserunners must return to the base legally held at the time of the pitch.

5. The batter shall not hit a fair ball with the bat a second time in fair territory.

Note: If the batter drops the bat and the ball rolls against the bat in fair territory and, in the umpire's judgement, there was no intention to interfere with the course of the ball, the batter is not out and the ball is alive and in play.

Effect – Section 5: The ball is dead, the batter is out, and baserunners may not advance.

6. A strike is called by the umpire:

(*a*) (FP only) When any part of a legally pitched ball enters the strike zone before touching the ground and at which the batter does not swing.

Effect – Section 6(*a*): (FP) The ball is in play and the baserunners may advance with liability to be put out.

(SP only) For each legally pitched ball entering the strike zone before touching the ground and at which the batter does not swing. It is not a strike if the pitched ball touches home plate and is not swung at. Any pitched ball that hits the ground or plate cannot be legally swung at by the batter. *Note*: If the batter swings and misses the pitch prior to the ball hitting the ground or plate, it is a strike.

Effect – Section 6(*a*): (SP) The ball is dead.

(*b*) (FP only) For each legally pitched ball struck at and missed by the batter.

Effect – Section 6(*b*): The ball is in play and the baserunners may advance with liability to be put out.

(SP only) For each pitched ball struck at and missed by the batter. Any pitched ball that hits the ground or plate cannot be legally swung at by the batter. *Note*: If the batter swings and misses the pitch prior to the ball hitting the ground or plate, it is a strike.

Effect – Section 6(*b*): (SP) The ball is dead.

   (*c*) For each foul tip held by the catcher.

Effect – Section 6(*c*) (FP) The ball is in play and baserunners may advance with liability to be put out. The batter is out if it is the third strike. (SP) The batter is out if it is the third strike. The ball is dead on any strike.

   (*d*) For each foul ball not legally caught on the fly when the batter has less than two strikes.

   (*e*) For each pitched ball struck and missed which touches any part of the batter.

   (*f*) When any part of the batter's person is hit with his/her own batted ball when he/she is in the batter's box and he/she has less than two strikes.

   (*g*) When a delivered ball by the pitcher hits the batter while the ball is in the strike zone.

Effect – Section 6(*d*)–(*g*): The ball is dead and baserunners must return to their bases without liability to be put out.

7. A ball is called by the umpire:

   (*a*) For each pitched ball which does not enter the strike zone or touches the ground before reaching home plate or touches home plate and which is not struck at by the batter.

Effect – Section 7(*a*): (FP) The ball is in play and baserunners are entitled to advance with liability to be put out. (SP) The ball is dead. Baserunners may not advance.

   (*b*) For each illegally pitched ball.

Effect – Section 7(*b*): (FP) The ball is dead and baserunners are entitled to advance one base without liability to be put out. (SP) The ball is dead. Baserunners may not advance.

   (*c*) (SP only) When a delivered ball by the pitcher hits the batsman outside of strike zone.

   (*d*) When the catcher fails to return the ball directly to the pitcher as required in Rule 6, Section 3(*e*).

   (*e*) When the pitcher fails to pitch the ball within 20 seconds.

   (*f*) For each excessive warm-up pitch.

Effect – Section 7(*c*)–(*f*): (SP only) The ball is dead. Baserunners may not advance. (FP only) The ball is in play.

8. A fair ball is a legally batted ball which:

(*a*) Settles or is touched on fair territory between home and first base or between home and third base.

(*b*) Bounds past first or third base on or over fair territory.

(*c*) Touches first, second, or third base.

(*d*) While on or over fair territory touches the person or clothing of an umpire or player.

(*e*) First falls on fair territory beyond first or third base.

(*f*) While over fair territory passes out of the playing field beyond the outfield fence.

Effect – Section 8(*a*)–(*f*): The ball is in play and baserunners are entitled to advance any number of bases with liability to be put out. The batter becomes a baserunner unless the infield fly rule applies.

(*g*) While on or over fair ground, lands behind a fence or into a stand a distance of more than 60.0m (200ft) Female Fast Pitch, 70.0m (225ft) Male Fast Pitch, 75.0m (250ft) Female Slow Pitch, or 85.0m (275ft) Male Slow Pitch from home plate. This is considered a home run. If the distance is less than these distances, it is a two-base hit.

(*h*) Hits a foul line pole on the fly. If the ball hits the pole above the fence level, it shall be a home run.

9. A foul ball is a legally batted ball which:

(*a*) Settles on foul territory between home and first base or between home and third base.

(*b*) Bounds past first or third base on or over foul territory.

(*c*) First touches on foul territory beyond first or third base.

(*d*) While on or over foul territory touches the person or clothing of an umpire, or player, or any object foreign to the natural ground.

(*e*) Touches batter or bat in batter's hand while within the batter's box.

Effect – Section 9(*a*)–(*d*): (1) The ball is dead unless it is a legally caught foul fly. If a foul fly is caught, the batter is out. (2) A strike is called on the batter unless he already had two strikes. (3) Baserunners must return to their bases without liability to be put out unless a foul fly is caught. In this case, the baserunner may advance with liability to be put out after the ball has been touched.

10. A foul tip is a batted ball which goes directly from the bat, not higher than the batter's head, to catcher's hands and is legally caught by the catcher.

Note: It is not a foul tip unless caught, and any foul tip that is caught is a strike. In Fast Pitch, the ball is in play; in Slow Pitch, the ball is dead.

Effect – Section 10: (FP) a strike is called, the ball remains in play and baserunners may advance with liability to be put out. (SP) A strike is called, the ball is dead.

11. The batter is out under the following circumstances:

(*a*) When the third strike is struck at and missed and touches any part of the batter's person.

(*b*) When a batter appears in the batter's box with, or is discovered using, an altered bat. *Note*: The batter is also ejected from the game.

(*c*) When the batter enters the batter's box with an illegal bat or is discovered using an illegal bat.

(*d*) When a fly ball is legally caught.

(*e*) Immediately when he hits an infield fly with baserunners on first and second, or on first, second and third with less than two outs. This is called the infield fly rule.

(*f*) The batter is out if a fielder intentionally drops a fair fly ball (including a line drive) (FP or SP) or a bunt (FP only) which can be caught by an infielder, with ordinary effort, with first, first and second, first and third, or first, second and third base occupied with less than two outs.

Note: A trapped ball shall not be considered as having been intentionally dropped.

Effect – Section 11(*f*): The ball is dead, and baserunners must return to last base touched at the time of the pitch.

(*g*) The batter-baserunner is out if a preceding runner who is not yet out, and in the umpire's judgement, intentionally interferes with a fielder who is attempting to catch a thrown ball or to throw a ball in an attempt to complete the play.

(*h*) (FP only) When the third strike is caught by the catcher.

(*i*) (FP only) When he/she has three strikes if there are less than two outs and first base is occupied.

(*j*) (FP only) When he/she bunts foul after the second strike. If the ball is caught in the air, it remains alive and in play.

(*k*) (SP only) When a third strike is called, including an uncaught foul ball that is hit after two strikes.

(*l*) (SP only) When he/she bunts or chops the ball downward.

12. The batter or baserunner is not out if a fielder making a play on him/her uses an illegal glove. The manager of the offended team has the option of having the batter bat over and assuming the ball and strike count he/she had prior to the pitch he/she hit, or taking the result of the play.

13. On-deck batter.

(*a*) The on-deck batter is the offensive player whose name follows the name of the batter in the batting order.

(*b*) The on-deck batter shall take a position within the lines of the on-deck circle nearest his/her bench.

(*c*) The on-deck batter may leave the on-deck circle:

(1) When he/she becomes the batter.

(2) To direct baserunners advancing from third to home plate.

(*d*) When the on-deck better interferes with the defensive player's opportunity to make a play on a runner, the runner closest to home plate at the time of the interference shall be declared out.

(*e*) The provision of Rule 7, Section 4, shall apply to the on-deck batter.

8. BASERUNNING

1. The baserunners must touch bases in legal order (i.e. first, second, third and home plate).

(*a*) When a baserunner must return while the ball is in play, he/she must touch the bases in reverse order.

Effect – Section 1(*a*): The ball is in play and baserunners must return with liability to be put out.

(*b*) When a baserunner acquires the right to a base by touching it before being put out, he/she is entitled to hold the base until he/she has legally touched the next base in order or is forced to vacate it for a succeeding baserunner.

(*c*) When a baserunner dislodges a base from its proper position neither he/she nor succeeding runners in the same series of plays are compelled to follow a base unreasonably out of position.

Effect – Section 1(*b*)–(*c*): The ball is in play and baserunners may advance with liability to be put out.

(*d*) A baserunner shall not run bases in reverse order either to confuse the fielders or to make a travesty of the game.

Effect – Section 1(*d*): The ball is dead and the baserunner is out.

(*e*) Two baserunners may not occupy the same base simultaneously.

Effect – Section 1(*e*): The runner who first legally occupied the base shall be entitled to it; the other baserunner may be put out by being touched with the ball.

(*f*) Failure of a *preceding* runner to touch a base, or to leave a base legally on a caught fly ball and who is declared out does not affect the status of a succeeding baserunner who touches bases in proper order. However, if the failure to touch a base in regular order or to leave a base legally on a caught fly ball, is the third out of the inning, *no* succeeding runner may score a run.

(*g*) No runner may return to touch a missed base or one he/she had left illegally, after a following runner has scored.

(*h*) After the ball becomes dead, no runner may return to touch a missed base, a base he/she has left after advancing to and touching a base beyond the missed base, or a base he/she left illegally, even after the ball becomes alive.

(*i*) No runner may return to touch a missed base or one he/she had left illegally, once he enters his/her team dugout or bench area.

(*j*) When a walk is issued, all runners must touch all bases in legal order.

(*k*) Bases left too soon on a caught fly ball must be retouched while *en route* to awarded bases.

(*l*) Awarded bases must also be touched and in proper order.

2. The batter becomes a baserunner:

(*a*) As soon as he/she hits a fair ball.

(*b*) (FP only) When the catcher fails to catch the third strike before the ball touches the ground when there are less than two outs and first base is unoccupied, or anytime there are two outs. This is called the third strike rule.

(*c*) When a fair ball strikes the person or clothing of an umpire on foul ground.

Effect – Section 2(*a*)–(*c*) The ball is in play and the batter becomes a batter-baserunner with liability to be put out.

(*d*) When four balls have been called by the umpire.

Effect – Section 2(*d*): (FP) The ball is in play unless it has been blocked. The batter is entitled to one base without liability to be put out. (SP) The ball is dead. Baserunners may not advance unless forced. If the pitcher desires to walk a batter intentionally, he/she may do so by notifying the plate umpire, who shall award the batter first base. If two batters are to be walked intentionally, the second cannot be administered until the first reaches first base. *Note*: The awards must be made in order, not two at one time.

(*e*) When the catcher or any other fielder obstructs or prevents the batter from striking at a pitched ball.

Effect – Section 2(*e*): The ball is dead. The batter is awarded first base. Baserunners may not advance unless forced.

(1) The procedure to follow: The umpire shall give a delayed dead ball signal.

(2) The manager of the batting team has the option of taking the award for 'catcher obstruction' as described above, or he/she may take the result of the play.

(3) If the batter hits the ball and reaches first base safely, and if all other runners have advanced at least one base on the batted ball, catcher obstruction is cancelled. All actions as a result of the batted ball stand. No option is given.

(*f*) When a fair ball strikes the person or clothing of the umpire or a baserunner on fair ground. If the baserunner is hit with a fair ball while touching a base, he is not out.

Effect – Section 2(*f*): If the ball hits an umpire or baserunner (*a*) after touching a fielder (including the pitcher), the ball is in play; (*b*) after passing a fielder other than the pitcher, the ball is in play; or (*c*) before passing a fielder without being touched, the ball is dead. In (*c*) if the baserunner is hit by the ball, he is out, and the batter is entitled to first base without liability to be put out, unless in the umpire's judgement, no infielder had a chance to play the ball. Any baserunner not forced by the batter-baserunner must return to the base he had reached prior to the interference. When a ball touches a baserunner who is in contact with a base, the ball becomes dead or remains live depending on the position of the fielder closest to the base.

(g) (FP only) When a pitched ball not struck at, or not called a strike, touches any part of the batter's person or clothing while he/she is in the batter's box. It does not matter if the ball strikes the ground before hitting him/her. The batter's hands are not to be considered as part of the bat.

Effect: Section 2(g): The ball is dead and the batter is entitled to one base without liability to be put out unless he/she made no effort to avoid being hit. In this case, the plate umpire calls either a ball or a strike.

(h) (FP only) When a called illegally pitched ball, not struck at, touches any part of the batter's person or clothing while he/she is in the batter's box, *and there are no runners on base*. It does not matter if the ball strikes the ground before hitting him/her. The batter's hands are not to be considered part of the bat.

Effect – Section 2(h): The ball is dead and the batter is entitled to one base without liability to be put out unless he/she made no effort to avoid being hit. With runners on base, refer to Rule 6. Effect Section 1–7: Illegal Pitch.

3. Baserunners are entitled to advance with liability to be put out under the following circumstances:

(a) (FP only) When a ball leaves the pitcher's hand on a pitch.

(b) When the ball is overthrown into fair or foul territory and is not blocked.

(c) When the ball is batted into fair territory and is not blocked.

(d) When a legally caught fly ball is first touched.

(e) If a fair ball strikes the umpire or a baserunner after having passed an infielder other than the pitcher or having been touched by an infielder including the pitcher, the ball shall be considered in play. Also, if a fair ball strikes an umpire on foul ground, the ball shall be in play.

Effect – Section 3(a)–(e): The ball is alive and in play.

4. A player forfeits his/her exemption from liability to be put out:

(a) If while the ball is in play he fails to touch the base to which he/she was entitled before attempting to make the next base. If the runner put out is the batter-baserunner at first base or any other baserunner forced to advance because the batter became a baserunner, this out is a force-out.

(b) If after over-running first base, the batter-baserunner tries to continue to second base.

(*c*) If after dislodging the base, the batter-baserunner tries to continue to the next base.

5. Baserunners are entitled to advance without liability to be put out:

(*a*) When forced to vacate a base because the batter was awarded a base on balls.

Effect – Section 5(*a*): (FP) The ball remains in play unless it is blocked. Baserunner affected is entitled to one base and may advance further at his/her own risk if the ball is in play. (SP) The ball is dead.

(*b*) When a fielder obstructs the baserunner from making a base, unless the fielder is trying to field a batted ball, has the ball ready to touch the baserunner, or is about to receive the thrown ball.

Note: 'About to receive the thrown ball' means the ball must be between the advancing baserunner and the defensive player about to catch the ball. If the ball is outside this area, 'obstruction' should be called.

Effect – Section 5(*b*): When any obstruction occurs (including a rundown), the umpire will signal a delayed dead ball. The ball will remain alive.

(1) If the obstructed runner is put out prior to reaching the base he would have reached had there not been obstruction, a dead ball is called, and the obstructed runner (and each other runner affected by the obstruction) will always be awarded the base or bases he would have reached, in the umpire's judgement, had there not been obstruction.

(2) If the obstructed runner is put out after passing the base he would have reached had there not been obstruction, the obstructed runner will be called out. The ball remains alive.

(3) When a runner, while advancing or returning to a base, is obstructed by a fielder who neither has the ball nor is attempting to field a batted or thrown ball, or a fielder who fakes a tag without the ball, the obstructed runner (and each other runner affected by the obstruction) will always be awarded the base or bases he would have reached, in the umpire's judgement, had there been no obstruction. If the umpire feels there is justification, a defensive player making a fake tag could be removed from the game.

Note: Obstructed baserunners are still required to touch all bases in proper order, or they could be called out on a proper appeal by the defensive team. In the case of a fake tag, a warning should be given to both teams. The next fake tag should result in the ejection of said player. A player may be ejected without warning if the umpire feels there is justification.

(4) Catcher obstruction is covered under Rule 8, Section 2(*e*).

Effect – Section 5(*b*)(3): The play shall proceed until no further action is possible. The umpire shall then call 'Time' and impose such penalties, if any, as in his/her judgement will nullify the act of obstruction.

(*c*) (FP only) When a wild pitch or passed ball goes under, over, through or lodges in the backstop.

Effect – Section 5(*c*): The ball is dead. All baserunners are awarded one base only. The batter is awarded first base only on the fourth ball.

(*d*) When forced to vacate a base because the batter was awarded a base.

(1) (FP only) For being hit by a pitched ball.

(2) For being obstructed by the catcher when striking at a pitched ball.

Effect – Section 5(*d*)(1)–(2): The ball is dead and baserunners may not advance farther than the base to which they are entitled.

(3) (FP only) If, with a runner on third base and trying to score by means of a squeeze play or a steal, the catcher or any other fielder steps on, or in front of home plate without possession of the ball, or touches the batter or his/her bat, the pitcher shall be charged with an illegal pitch, the batter shall be awarded first base on the obstruction, and the ball is dead.

(*e*) (FP only) When a pitcher makes an illegal pitch.

Effect – Section 5(*e*): The ball is dead and baserunners may advance to the base to which they are entitled without liability to be put out.

(*f*) When a fielder contacts or catches a fair batted or thrown ball and his/her cap, mask, glove or any part of his/her uniform while it is detached from its proper place on his/her person.

Effect – Section 5(*f*): The baserunners shall be entitled to three bases if a batted ball, or two bases if a thrown ball, and in either case the baserunners may advance further at their own risk. If the illegal catch or touch is made on a fair hit ball, which in the opinion of the umpire would have cleared the outfield fence in flight, the runner shall be awarded a home run.

(*g*) When the ball is in play and is overthrown (beyond the boundary lines) or is blocked.

Effect – Section 5(*g*): All runners will be awarded two bases, and the award will be governed by the position of the runners when the ball left the fielder's hand.

(1) When a fielder loses possession of the ball such as on an attempted tag, and the ball then enters the dead ball area or becomes blocked, all runners are awarded one base from the last base touched at the time the ball entered the dead ball area or became blocked. If a runner touches the next base and returns to his original base, the original base he left is considered the last base touched for purposes of an overthrow award.

(*h*) When a fair-batted ball goes over the fence or into the stands, it shall entitle the batter to a home run unless it passes out of the grounds or into a distance less than 60.0m (200ft) Female Fast Pitch, 70.0m

(225ft) Male Fast Pitch, 75.0m (250ft) Female Slow Pitch or 85.0m (275ft) Male Slow Pitch from home plate, in which case the batter shall be entitled to two bases only. The batter must touch the bases in regular order. The point at which the fence or stand is less than 60.0m (200ft) Female Fast Pitch, 70.0m (225ft) Male Fast Pitch, 75.0m (250ft) Female Slow Pitch or 85.0m (275ft) Male Slow Pitch from home plate shall be plainly indicated for the umpire's guidance.

(*i*) When a fair ball bounds or rolls into a stand, over, under or through a fence; bounds out of play unintentionally off a defensive player; or leaves the boundaries of the playing field after touching the ground in fair territory.

Effect – Section 5(*i*): The ball is dead and all baserunners are awarded two bases from time of pitch.

(*j*) (1) When a live ball is unintentionally carried by a fielder from playable territory into dead ball territory, the ball becomes dead. All baserunners are awarded one base from the last base touched at the time he/she enters dead ball territory.

Note: A fielder carrying a live ball into the dugout or team area to tag a player is considered to have unintentionally carried it there.

(2) If, in the judgement of the umpire, a fielder intentionally carries a live ball from playable territory into dead ball territory, the ball becomes dead and all baserunners are awarded two bases from the last base touched at the time he/she entered dead ball territory.

Note: A dead ball line is considered in play.

6. A baserunner must return to his/her base under the following circumstances:

(*a*) When a foul ball is illegally caught and is so declared by the umpire.

(*b*) When an illegally batted ball is declared by the umpire.

(*c*) When a batter or baserunner is called out for interference. Other baserunners shall return to the last base which was, in the judgement of the umpire, legally touched by him/her at the time of the interference.

(*d*) (FP only) When there is interference by the plate umpire or his/her clothing with the catcher's attempt to throw.

(*e*) When any part of the batter's person is touched by a pitched ball swung at and missed.

(*f*) When a batter is hit by a pitched ball, unless forced.

(*g*) When a foul ball is not caught.

Effect – Section 6(*a*)–(*g*): (1) The ball is dead. (2) The baserunners must return to base without liability to be put out except when forced to go to the next base because the batter became a baserunner. (3) No runs shall score unless all bases are occupied. (4) Baserunners need not touch the intervening bases in returning to base but must return promptly. (5) However, they must be allowed sufficient time to return.

(*h*) (SP only) Base Stealing. Under no conditions is a runner permitted to steal a base when a pitched ball is not batted. The runner must return to his/her base.

Effect – Section 6(*h*): Baserunners may leave their base when a pitched ball is batted or reaches home plate, but must return to that base immediately after each pitch not hit by the batter.

(*i*)   When a caught fair fly ball (including a line drive) (FP or SP) or bunt (FP only) which can be caught by an infielder with ordinary effort is intentionally dropped with less than two outs, with a runner on first base, first and second, first and third, or first, second and third base.

7. Batter-baserunners are out under the following circumstances:

(*a*)   (FP only) When the catcher drops the third strike and he/she is legally touched with the ball by a fielder before touching first base.

(*b*)   (FP only) When the catcher drops the third strike and the ball is held on first base before the batter-runner reaches first base.

(*c*)   When after a fair ball is hit, he/she is legally touched with the ball before he/she touches first base.

(*d*)   When after a fair ball is hit, the ball is held by a fielder touching first base with any part of his/her person before the batter-baserunner touches first base.

(*e*)   When after a fly ball is hit, the ball is caught by a fielder before it touches the ground or any object other than a fielder.

(*f*)   When after a fair ball is hit or a base on balls is issued, or when the batter may legally advance to first base on a dropped third strike (FP only) he/she fails to advance to first base and instead enters his/her team area.

Effect – Section 7(*a*)–(*f*): The ball is in play and the batter-baserunner is out.

(*g*)   When he/she runs outside the 1.0m (3ft) line and in the opinion of the umpire interferes with the fielder taking the throw at first base. However, he/she may run outside the 1.0m (3ft) line to avoid a fielder attempting to field a batted ball.

(*h*)   When he/she interferes with a fielder attempting to field a batted ball or intentionally interferes with a thrown ball. If this interference, in the judgement of the umpire, is an obvious attempt to prevent a double play, the baserunner closest to home plate shall also be called out.

(*i*)   When a batter-baserunner interferes with a play at home plate in an attempt to prevent an obvious out at the plate. The runner is also out.

(*j*)   When he/she touches a batted ball over fair ground a second time while his/her bat or any part of his/her body is out of the batter's box in fair territory.

(*k*)   When he/she moves back toward home plate to avoid or delay a tag by a fielder.

Effect – Section 7(*g*)–(*k*): The ball is dead and the batter-baserunner is out. Other baserunners must return to the last base legally touched at the time of or before the illegal action. *Note*: In the case of an altered bat, the player is also ejected from the game.

8. The baserunner is out:

(*a*) When in running to any base, he/she runs more than 1.0m (3ft) from a direct line between a base and the next one in regular or reverse order to avoid being touched by the ball in the hand of a fielder.

(*b*) When, while the ball is in play, he/she is legally touched with the ball in the hand of the fielder while not in contact with a base.

(*c*) When, on a force-out, a fielder tags him/her with the ball or holds the ball on the base to which the baserunner is forced to advance the runner reaches the base.

(*d*) When the baserunner fails to return to touch the base he/she previously occupied when play is resumed after suspension of play.

(*e*) When a baserunner physically passes a preceding baserunner before that runner has been put out.

Effect – Section 8(*a*)(*e*): The ball is in play and the baserunner is out.

(*f*) When the baserunner leaves his/her base to advance to another base before a caught fly ball has touched a fielder, provided the ball is returned to a fielder and legally held on that base or a fielder legally touches the baserunner before the baserunner returns to his/her base. *Note*: The dead ball appeal procedure can be used (See Rule 8, Section 8, Effect 4).

(*g*) When the baserunner fails to touch the intervening base or bases in regular or reverse order and the ball is in play and legally held on that base, or the baserunner is legally touched while off the base he/she missed. *Note*: The dead ball appeal procedure can be used (See Rule 8, Section 8, Effect 4).

(*h*) When the batter-baserunner legally overruns first base, attempts to run to second base and is legally touched while off base.

(*i*) In running or sliding for home plate, he/she fails to touch home plate, and makes no attempt to return to the plate, when a fielder holds the ball in his/her hand while touching home plate, and appeal to the umpire for the decision.

Effect – Section 8 (*f*)–(*i*):

(1) These are appeal plays and the defensive team loses the privilege of putting the baserunner out if the appeal is not made before the next legal or illegal pitch.

(2) Appeal plays may be made while the ball is in play, or during a dead ball, and the baserunner is out.

Note: On appeal plays, the appeal must be made before the next legal or illegal pitch, or before the defensive team has left the field. The defensive team has left the field when all players have clearly left their normal fielding positions and have left fair territory on their way to the bench or dugout area.

(3) (FP only) Baserunners may leave their base during live ball appeal plays when the ball leaves the 2.5m (8ft) radius around the pitcher's plate; or when the ball leaves the pitcher's possession; or when the pitcher makes a throwing motion indicating a play or fake throw.

(4) *Dead ball appeal.* Once the ball has been returned to the infield and 'Time' has been called by the umpire (or the ball becomes dead), any defensive player with or without possession of the ball, may make a verbal appeal on a runner missing a base or leaving a base too soon. The administering umpire should acknowledge the appeal, and then make a decision on the play. Baserunners cannot leave their base during this period, as the ball remains dead until the next pitch.

(*j*)   When a baserunner is struck with a fair batted ball while off base and before it passes an infielder excluding the pitcher, unless in the umpire's judgement, no infielder had a chance to play the ball.

(*k*)   When a runner intentionally kicks a ball which an infielder has missed.

Effect – Section 8(*j*)–(*k*): The ball is dead and the baserunner is out. No bases may be run unless necessitated by the batter becoming a baserunner.

(*l*)   When the baserunner interferes with a fielder attempting to field a batted ball or intentionally interferes with a thrown ball. If this interference, in the judgement of the umpire, is an obvious attempt to prevent a double play, the immediate succeeding runner shall also be called out.

(*m*) When with a baserunner on third base, the batter interferes with a play being made at home plate with less than two outs.

(*n*)   When anyone, other than another baserunner, physically assists a baserunner while the ball is in play.

(*o*)   When the coach near third base runs in the direction of home plate on or near the base line while a fielder is attempting to make a play on a batted or thrown ball and thereby draws a throw to home plate. The baserunner nearest to third base shall be declared out.

(*p*)   When one or more members of the offensive team stand or collect at or around a base to which a baserunner is advancing, thereby confusing the fielders and adding to the difficulty of making the play.

Note: Members of a team includes bat boy or any other person authorised to sit on team's bench.

(*q*)   When the baserunner runs the bases in reverse order to confuse the defensive team or to make a farce out of the game. This includes the batter-baserunner moving back toward home plate to avoid or delay a tag by a fielder.

(*r*) If a coach intentionally interferes with a thrown ball.

(*s*) When a runner, after being declared out or after scoring, interferes with a defensive player's opportunity to make a play on another runner, the runner closest to home plate at the time of the interference, shall be declared out.

Effect – Section 8(*l*)–(*s*): The ball is dead and the baserunner is out. Other baserunners must return to the last base legally touched at the time of or before the illegal action.

(*t*) When a defensive player has the ball and is waiting for the runner and the runner remains on his/her feet and deliberately, with great force, crashes into the defensive player, the runner is to be declared out.

Effect – Section 8(*t*): The runner is out, the ball is dead and all other runners must return to the last base touched at the time of the collision. *Note*: If the act is determined to be flagrant, the offender shall be ejected.

(*u*) (FP only) When the baserunner fails to keep contact with the base to which he/she is entitled until a legally pitched ball has been released. When a baserunner is legitimately off his/her base after a pitch or the result of a batter completing his/her turn at bat, while the pitcher has the ball within the 2.5m (8ft) radius of the pitcher's plate, he/she must immediately attempt to advance to the next base or immediately return to his/her base.

(1) Failure to immediately proceed to the next base or return to his/her base, once the pitcher has the ball within the 2.5m (8ft) radius of the pitcher's plate, shall result in the baserunner being declared out.

(2) Once the runner returns to a base for any reason he/she shall be declared out if he/she leaves said base unless a play is made on him/her or another runner (a fake throw is considered a play); or the pitcher no longer has possession of the ball within the 2.5m (8ft) radius; or the pitcher releases the ball by a pitch to the batter.

Note: A base on balls or dropped third strike in which the runner is entitled to run is treated the same as a batted ball. The batter-runner may continue past first base, and is entitled to run toward second base, as long as he/she does not stop at first base. If he/she stops after he/she rounds first base, he/she then must comply with Section 8(*u*)(1).

(*v*) (SP only) When the baserunner fails to keep contact with the base to which he is entitled, until a legally pitched ball has reached home plate.

Effect – Section 8(*u*)–(*v*): The ball is dead. No pitch is declared and the baserunner is out.

(*w*) When he/she abandons a base, does not attempt to advance to the next base, and enters the team area or leaves the field of play. The baserunner shall be declared out immediately when he/she enters the team area or leaves the field of play.

9. Baserunners are not out under the following circumstances:

(*a*) When a baserunner runs behind the fielder and outside the baseline in order to avoid interfering with a fielder attempting to field the ball in the base path.

(*b*) When a baserunner does not run in a direct line to the base providing the fielder in the direct line does not have the ball in his/her possession.

(*c*) When more than one fielder attempts to field a batted ball and the baserunner comes in contact with the one who, in the umpire's judgement, was not entitled to field the ball.

(*d*) When a baserunner is hit with a fair batted ball that has passed through an infielder, excluding the pitcher, and in the umpire's judgement, no other infielder had a chance to make an out.

(*e*) When a baserunner is touched with a ball not securely held by a fielder.

(*f*) When the defensive team does not request the umpire's decision on an appeal play until after the next pitch.

(*g*) When a batter-baserunner passes first base after touching it and returns directly to the base.

(*h*) When the baserunner is not given sufficient time to return to a base, he/she shall not be called out for being off base before the pitcher releases the ball. He/she may advance as though he/she had left the base legally.

(*i*) A runner who has legally started to advance cannot be stopped by the pitcher receiving the ball while on the pitching plate nor by stepping on the plate with the ball in his/her possession.

(*j*) When a baserunner holds his/her base until a fly ball touches a fielder and then attempts to advance.

(*k*) When hit by a batted ball when touching their base, unless they intentionally interfere with the ball or a fielder making a play.

(*l*) When a baserunner slides into a base and dislodges it from its proper position, the base is considered to have followed the runner.
Effect – Section 9(*l*): A baserunner having made such a base safely shall not be out for being off that base. He/she may return to that base without liability to be put out when the base has been replaced. A runner forfeits this exemption if he/she attempts to advance beyond the dislodged base before it is again in proper position.

(*m*) When a fielder makes a play on a runner while using an illegal glove. The manager of the offended team has the option of having the entire play, including the batter's turn at bat, nullified, with the batter batting over, assuming the ball and strike count he/she had before he/she hit the ball and the runners returned to the original bases which they held prior to the batted ball or taking the result of the play.

(*n*) When the baserunner is hit by a fair batted ball, after it is touched by or touches any fielder, including the pitcher.

9. DEAD BALL – BALL IN PLAY

1. The ball is dead and not in play in the following circumstances:

(*a*) When the ball is batted illegally.

(*b*) When the batter steps from one box to another when the pitcher is ready to pitch.

(*c*) When a ball is pitched illegally.

Exception – Section 1(*c*): (FP) If the pitcher completes the delivery of the ball to the batter and the batter hits the ball, reaches first base safely and all baserunners advance at least one base, then the play stands and the pitch is no longer illegal. (SP) If the batter swings at an illegal pitch, the play stands and the pitch is no longer illegal.

(*d*) When 'No pitch' is declared.

(*e*) When a pitched ball touches any part of the batter's person or clothing whether the ball is struck at or not.

(*f*) When a foul ball is not caught.

(*g*) When a baserunner is called out for leaving the base too soon on a pitched ball.

(*h*) When the offensive team causes the interference:

(1) When a batter intentionally strikes the ball a second time, strikes it with a thrown bat, or deflects its course in any way while running to first base.

(2) When a thrown ball is intentionally touched by a coach.

(3) When a fair ball strikes a baserunner or umpire before touching an infielder including the pitcher or before passing an infielder other than the pitcher. (*Exception*: If no infielder had a chance to make a play, Rule 8, Section 8).

(4) When the batter interferes with the catcher.

(5) When a member of the offensive team interferes intentionally with a live ball.

(6) When a runner intentionally kicks a ball which a fielder has missed.

(7) (FP only) When, with a baserunner on third base, the batter interferes with the play being made at home plate with less than two outs.

(*i*) When the ball is outside the established playing limits of the playing area. A ball is considered 'outside the playing field' when it touches the ground, person on the ground or object outside the playing area.

(*j*) If an accident to a runner is such as to prevent him/her from proceeding to a base to which he/she is awarded, a substitute runner shall be permitted for the injured player.

(*k*) In case of interference and batter or fielder.

(*l*) (SP only) When the batter bunts or chops the pitched ball.

(*m*) (FP only) when a wild pitch or passed ball goes under, over or through the backstop.

(*n*) When time is called by the umpire.

(*o*) When any part of the batter's person is hit with his/her own batted ball when he/she is in the batter's box.

(*p*) When a baserunner runs bases in reverse order either to confuse the fielders or to make a travesty of the game.

(*q*) When the batter is hit by a pitched ball.

(*r*) When, in the judgement of the umpire, the coach touches or helps the runner physically to assist him/her to return or to leave a base or when the coach near third base runs in the direction of home plate on or near the baseline while the fielder is attempting to make a play on a batted or thrown ball and thereby draws a throw to home plate.

(*s*) (FP only) When there is interference by the plate umpire or his/her clothing with the catcher's attempt to throw.

(*t*)   When one or more members of the offensive team stand or collect at or around a base to which a baserunner is advancing, thereby confusing the fielders and adding to the difficulty of making a play.

(*u*) (FP only) When the baserunner fails to keep contact with the base to which he/she is entitled until a legally pitched ball has been released.

(*v*) (SP only) When a baserunner fails to keep contact with the base to which he/she is entitled until a legally pitched ball has reached home plate.

(*w*) (SP only) After each strike or ball.

(*x*) When the catcher obstructs the batter's attempt to hit a pitch.

Exception – Section 1(*x*): The ball remains alive if the batter reaches first base safely and all other runners have advanced at least one base.

(*z*) When a blocked ball is declared.

(*aa*)When a batter enters the batter's box with or uses an altered bat.

(*ab*)When a batter enters the batter's box with, or uses an illegal bat.

(*ac*)When a caught fair fly ball (including a line drive) (FP and SP) or bunt (FP) which can be handled by an infielder with ordinary effort is intentionally dropped with less than two outs and a runner on first base, first and second, first and third, or first, second and third base.

(*ad*)When a fielder intentionally carries a live ball into dead ball territory.

(*ae*)When time has been called and an appeal is being made by a defensive player.

Effect – Section 1(*a*)–(*ae*): Baserunners cannot advance on a deadball, unless forced to do so by reason of the batter having reached first base as entitled to or they are awarded a base or bases.

2. The ball is in play in the following circumstances:

(*a*) At the start of the game and each half inning when the pitcher has the ball while standing in his/her pitching position and the plate umpire has called 'Play ball'.

(*b*) When the infield fly rule is enforced.

(*c*) When a thrown ball goes past a fielder and remains in playable territory.

(*d*) When a fair ball strikes an umpire or baserunner on fair ground after passing or touching an infielder.

(*e*) When a fair ball strikes an umpire on foul ground.

(*f*) When the baserunners have reached the bases to which they are entitled when the fielder illegally fields a batted or thrown ball.

(*g*) When a baserunner is a called out for passing a preceding runner.

(*h*) When no play is being made on an obstructed runner, the ball shall remain alive until the play is over.

(*i*) When a fair ball is legally batted.

(*j*) When a baserunner must return in reverse order while the ball is in play.

(*k*) When a baserunner acquires the right to a base by touching it before being put out.

(*l*) When a base is dislodged while baserunners are progressing around the bases.

(*m*) When a baserunner runs more than 1.0m (3ft) from a direct line between a base and the next one in regular or reverse order to avoid being touched by the ball in the hand of a fielder.

(*n*) When a baserunner is tagged or forced out.

(*o*) When the umpire calls the base runner out for failure to return and touch the base when play is resumed after a suspension of play.

(*p*) When an appeal play is legally being made. *Exception*: After time out has been called and a dead ball appeal is being made.

(*q*) When the batter hits the ball.

(*r*) When a live ball strikes a photographer, groundskeeper, policeman, etc. assigned to the game.

(*s*) When a fly ball has been legally caught.

(*t*) When a thrown ball strikes an offensive player.

(*u*) If the batter drops the bat and the ball rolls against the bat in fair territory and, in the umpire's judgement, there was no intention to interfere with the course of the ball, the batter is not out and the ball is alive and in play.

(*v*) When a thrown ball strikes an umpire.

(*w*) Whenever the ball is not dead as provided in Section 1 of this Rule.

(*x*) When a thrown ball strikes a coach.

(*y*) (FP only) When a ball has been called on the batter and when four balls have been called but the batter may not be put out before he/she reaches first base.

(*z*) (FP only) When a strike has been called on the batter and when three strikes have been called on the batter.

(*aa*)(FP only) When a foul tip has been legally caught.

(*ab*)(SP only) As long as there is a play as a result of the hit by the batter. This includes a subsequent appeal play.

(*ac*)(FP only) If the ball slips from a pitcher's hand during his/her windup or during the back swing.

3. (SP only) The ball remains alive until the umpire calls 'Time' which should be done when the ball is held by a player in the infield area and in the opinion of the umpire, all play has ceased.

10. UMPIRES

1. Power and duties. The umpires are the representatives of the league or organisation by which they have been assigned to a particular game, and as such are authorised and required to enforce each section of these Rules. They have the power to order a player, coach, captain or manager to do or omit to do any act which in their judgement is necessary to give force and effect to one or all of these Rules and to inflict penalties as herein prescribed. The plate umpire shall have the authority to make decisions on any situations not specifically covered in the rules.

2. The Plate Umpire

3. The Base Umpire

4. Responsibilities of a Single Umpire

5. Change of Umpires

6. Umpire's Judgement

7. Signals

8. Suspension of Play

9. Violations and Penalty

11. PROTESTS

General information for Umpires, Sections 2–9 and Rule 11 are given in full in the International Softball Federation Official Guide and Rule Book.

12. SCORING

1. The official scorer shall keep records of each game as outlined in the following rules. He/she shall have the sole authority to make all decisions involving judgement. For example, it is the scorer's responsibility to determine whether a batter's advance to first base is the result of a hit or an error. However a scorer shall not make a decision which conficts with the Official Playing Rules or with an umpire's decision.

2. The Box Score

(*a*) Each player's name and the position or positions he/she has played shall be listed in the order in which he/she batted or would have batted unless he/she is removed or the game ends before his/her turn at bat.

(1) (FP only) The Designated Hitter (DH) is optional, but if one is used, it must be made known prior to the start of the game, and be listed on the scoresheet in the regular batting order. Ten names will be listed, with the tenth name being the player playing defence only. This tenth player listed may never bat.

(2) (SP only) The Extra Player (EP) is optional, but if one is used, it must be made known prior to the start of the game, and be listed on the scoresheet in the regular batting order. Eleven names will be on the official batting order, and all will bat.

Note: If a DH is used, he/she must be used the entire game. Failure to complete the game with a DH results in forfeiture of the game. The DH may never enter the game on defence. If he/she does, Rule 4, Section 4 covers the penalty.

(*b*) Each player's batting and fielding record must be tabulated.

(1) The first column shall show the number of times at bat by each player, but a time at bat shall not be charged against the player when:

    a. He/she hits a sacrifice fly that scores a runner.

    b. He/she is awarded a base on balls.

    c. He/she is awarded first base because of interference or obstruction.

    d. (FP only) He/she hits a sacrifice bunt.

    e. (FP only) He/she is hit by a pitched ball.

(2) The second column shall show the number of runs made by each player.

(3) The third column shall show the number of base hits made by each player. A base hit is a batted ball that permits the batter to reach the base safely.

    a. When a batter reaches first base or any succeeding base safely on a fair ball which settles on the ground, clears the fence or strikes the fence before being touched by a fielder.

    b. When a batter reaches first base safely on a fair ball which is hit with such force or such slowness or which takes an unnatural bounce, making it impossible to field with ordinary effort in time to retire the runner.

    c. When a fair ball which has not been touched by a fielder becomes dead because of touching the person or clothing of a runner or umpire.

d. When the fielder unsuccessfully attempts to retire a preceding runner and in the scorer's judgement, the batter-baserunner would not have been retired at first base by perfect fielding.

(4) The fourth column shall show the number of opponents put out by each player.

a. A putout is credited to a fielder each time he/she:

(1) Catches a fly ball or line drive.

(2) Catches a thrown ball which retires a batter or baserunner.

(3) Touches a baserunner with ball when the baserunner is off the base to which he/she is entitled.

(4) Is nearest the ball when a runner is declared out for being struck by a fair ball or interference with the fielder.

b. A putout is credited to the catcher.

(1) When a third strike is called.

(2) When the batter bunts or chops the ball downward (SP only)

(3) When the batter fails to bat in correct order.

(4) When the batter interferes with the catcher.

(5) The fifth column shall show the number of assists made by each player. An assist shall be credited:

a. To each player who handles the ball in any series of plays which results in the putout of the baserunner. Only one assist and no more shall be given to any player who handles the ball in any putout. A player who has aided in a rundown or other play of the kind shall be credited with both an assist and a putout.

b. To each player who handles or throws the ball in such a manner that a putout would have resulted except for an error of a team-mate.

c. To each player who, by deflecting a batted ball, aids in a putout.

d. To each player who handles the ball in a play which results in a baserunner being called out for interference or for running out of base line.

(6) The sixth column shall show the number of errors made by each player. Errors are recorded in the following situations:

a. For each player who commits a misplay which prolongs the turn at bat of the batter or life of the present runner.

b. For the fielder who fails to touch the base after receiving the ball to retire the runner on a force-out or when a baserunner is compelled to return to base.

c. For the catcher if a batter is awarded first base for interference.

d. For the fielder who fails to complete a double play because of dropping the ball.

e. For the fielder, if a baserunner advances a base, because of his failure to stop or try to stop, a ball accurately thrown to a base providing there was occasion for the throw. When more than one player could receive the throw, the scorer must determine which player gets the error.

3. A base hit shall not be scored in the following cases:

(*a*) When a runner is forced out by a batted ball or would have been forced out, except for a fielding error.

(*b*) When a player fielding a batted ball retires a preceding runner with ordinary effort.

(*c*) When a fielder fails in an attempt to retire a preceding runner and in the scorer's judgement, the batter-baserunner could have been retired at first base.

4. A sacrifice fly is scored when, with less than two outs, the batter scores a runner with a fly ball which is caught: or, the ball or the line drive handled by an outfielder (or an infielder running in the outfield) which is dropped and a runner scores, and if in the scorer's judgement, the runner could have scored after the catch, had the fly ball been caught.

5. A run batted in is a run scored because of one of the following reasons:

(*a*) A safe hit.

(*b*) A sacrifice bunt (FP) or sacrifice (FP and SP).

(*c*) A foul fly caught.

(*d*) An infield putout or fielder's choice.

(*e*) A baserunner forced home because of interference, the batter being hit with a pitched ball or being given a base on balls.

(*f*) A home run and all runs scored as a result.

6. A pitcher shall be credited with a win in the following situations:

(*a*) When he/she is the starting pitcher and has pitched at least four innings and his/her team was not only in the lead when he/she is replaced but remains in the lead for the remainder of the game.

(*b*) When a game is ended after five innings of play and the starting pitcher has pitched at least three innings and his/her team scores more runs than the other team when the game is terminated.

7. A pitcher shall be charged with a loss regardless of the number of innings he/she has pitched if he/she is replaced when his/her team is behind in the score and his/her team thereafter fails to tie the score or gain the lead.

8. The summary shall list the following items in this order:

(*a*) The score by innings and the final score.

(*b*) The runs batted-in and by whom hit.

(*c*) Two-base hits and by whom hit.

(*d*) Three-base hits and by whom hit.

(*e*) Home runs and by whom hit.

(*f*) Sacrifice flies and by whom hit.

(*g*) Double plays and players participating in them.

(*h*) Triple plays and players participating in them.
(*i*) Number of bases on balls given by each pitcher.
(*j*) Number of batters struck out by each pitcher.
(*k*) Number of hits and runs allowed by each pitcher.
(*l*) The name of the winning pitcher.
(*m*) The name of the losing pitcher.
(*n*) The time of the game.
(*o*) The names of the umpires and scorers.
(*p*) (FP only) Stolen bases and by whom.
(*q*) (FP only) Sacrifice bunts.
(*r*) (FP only) The names of batters hit by a pitched ball and the name of the pitcher who hit them.
(*s*) (FP only) The number of wild pitches made by each pitcher.
(*t*) (FP only) The number of passed balls made by each catcher.
9. (FP only) Stolen bases are credited to a baserunner whenever he/she advances one base unaided by a hit, a putout, an error, a force-out, a fielder's choice, a passed ball, a wild pitch or an illegal pitch.
10. All records of a forfeited game shall be included in the official records except that of a pitcher's won-lost record.

Reprinted by permission of the International Softball Federation. Some of the Rules given here, concerning Equipment, Pitches and Umpires, have been abbreviated for reasons of space. Copies of the complete Official Rules of Softball may be obtained from the Great Britain Softball Association.

Squash Rackets

Squash Court Dimensions
(All dimensions are in millimetres)

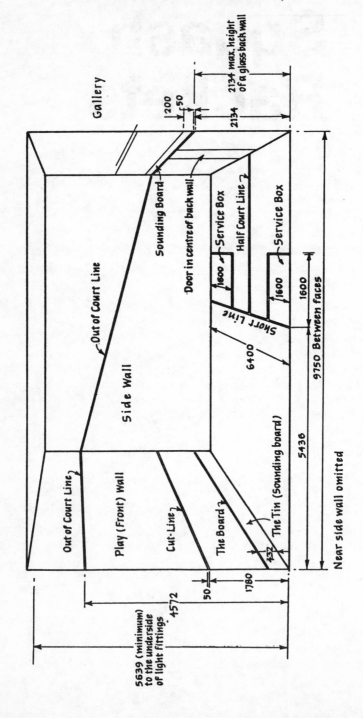

Squash Rackets

1. The Game

The game of squash rackets is played between two players, each using a standard racket, with a standard ball and in a court constructed to ISRF standard dimensions.

2. The Score

A match shall consist of the best of 3 or 5 games at the option of the organisers of the competition. Each game is to 9 points, in that the player who scores 9 points wins the game except that, on the score being called 8-all for the first time, the receiver shall choose, before the next service is delivered, to continue that game either to 9 points (known as 'no set') or to 10 points (known as 'set two'), in which latter case the player who scores 2 more points wins the game. The receiver shall in either case clearly indicate his choice to the Marker, Referee and his opponent.

The Marker shall call either 'no set' or 'set two' as applicable before play continues.

3. Points

Points can be scored only by the server. When the server wins a stroke, he scores a point; when the receiver wins a stroke, he becomes the server.

4. The Service

4.1 The right to serve first is decided by the spin of a racket. Thereafter the server continues to serve until he loses a stroke, whereupon his opponent becomes the server, and this procedure continues throughout the match. At the commencement of the second and each subsequent game, the winner of the previous game serves first.

4.2 At the beginning of each game and each hand, the server has the choice of either box and thereafter shall serve from alternate boxes while remaining the server. However, if a rally ends in a let he shall serve again from the same box.

4.3 For a service to be good, there must be no foot fault and the ball, before being struck, shall be dropped or thrown in the air and shall not hit the walls, floor, ceiling or any objects suspended from the walls or ceiling; it shall be served directly on to the front wall between the cut-line and the out-line so that on its return, unless volleyed, it reaches the floor within the back quarter of the court opposite to the server's box. Should a player, having dropped or thrown the ball in the air, make no attempt to strike it, the ball shall be dropped or thrown again for that service. A player with the use of only one arm may utilise his racket to propel the ball into the air before striking it.

4.4 A service is good when it does not result in the server serving his hand out (Rule 4.6).

4.5 A service is a fault:

4.5.1 If at the time of striking the ball the server fails to have part of one foot in contact with the floor within the service box and no part of that foot touching the service line (called a foot fault). Part of the foot may project over this line provided that it does not touch the line.

4.5.2 If the ball is served on to or below the cut-line but above the board.

4.5.3 If the first bounce of the ball, unless volleyed, is on the floor on or outside the short or half-court lines of the back quarter of the court opposite to the server's box.

Any combination of types of faults in the one service counts as only one fault.

4.6 The server serves his hand out and loses the stroke:

4.6.1 If he serves a fault.

4.6.2 If the ball, after being dropped or thrown for service, touches the walls, floor, ceiling or any object(s) suspended from the walls or ceiling before being served.

4.6.3 If the server makes an attempt but fails to strike the ball.

4.6.4 If, in the opinion of the Referee, the ball is not struck correctly.

4.6.5 If the ball is served on to or below the board, or out, or against any part of the court before the front wall.

4.6.6 If the ball, after being served and before it has bounced more than once on the floor, or before it has been struck at by the receiver, touches the server or anything he wears or carries.

4.7 The server shall not serve until the Marker has completed calling the score.

5. The Play

After a good service has been delivered the players return the ball alternately until one fails to make a good return, the ball otherwise ceases to be in play in accordance with the Rules, or on a call by the Marker or Referee.

6. Good Return

6.1 A return is good if the ball, before it has bounced more than once upon the floor, is returned correctly by the striker on to the front wall above the board, without first touching the floor or any part of the striker's body or clothing, or the opponent's racket, body or clothing, provided the ball is not hit out.

6.2 It shall not be considered a good return if the ball touches the board before or after it hits the front wall and before it bounces on the floor, or if the racket is not in the player's hand at the time the ball is struck.

7. Let

A let is an undecided stroke. The rally in respect of which a let is allowed shall not count and the server shall serve again from the same box.

A let shall not cancel a previous fault.

8. Strokes

A player wins a stroke:

8.1 Under Rule 4.6 when the player is the receiver.

8.2 If the opponent fails to make a good return of the ball, unless a let is allowed or a stroke is awarded to the opponent.

8.3 If the ball touches his opponent or anything he wears or carries when his opponent is the non-striker, except as is otherwise provided by Rules 9, 10 and 13.1.1.

8.4 If a stroke is awarded to him by the Referee as provided for in the Rules.

9. Hitting an Opponent with the Ball

If the ball, before reaching the front wall, hits the striker's opponent or his racket, or anything he wears or carries, the ball shall cease to be in play and:

9.1 Unless Rule 9.2 applies, the striker shall win the stroke if the ball would have made a good return and would have struck the front wall without first touching any other wall.

9.2 If the ball would have made a good return but the striker has either followed the ball round and turned or allowed it to pass around him – in either case by striking the ball to the right of his body after the ball had passed to his left (or vice versa) then a let shall be allowed in all cases.

9.3 If the ball either had struck or would have struck any other wall and would have made a good return, a let shall be allowed unless, in the opinion of the Referee, a winning stroke has been intercepted, in which case the striker shall win the stroke.

9.4 If the ball would not have made a good return, the striker shall lose the stroke.

10. Further Attempts to Hit the Ball

If the striker strikes at and misses the ball, he may make further attempts to strike it. If, after being missed, the ball touches his opponent or his racket, or anything he wears or carries, then if, in the Referee's opinion:

10.1 The striker could otherwise have made a good return, a let shall be allowed; or

10.2 The striker could not have made a good return, he loses the stroke.

If any such further attempt is successful, resulting in a good return being prevented from reaching the front wall by hitting the striker's opponent or anything he wears or carries, a let shall be allowed in all circumstances. If any such further attempt would not have made a good return, then the striker shall lose the strike.

11. Appeals

An appeal may be made against any decision of the Marker. Appeals to the Referee under Rule 11 should be prefaced with the words 'Appeal please'. Play shall then cease until the Referee has given his decision. If an appeal under rule 11 is disallowed the Marker's decision shall stand. If the Referee is uncertain he shall allow a let, except where provided for in the Notes to Referees after Rules 11.2.1 and 11.2.2. Appeals upheld or Referee intervention under Rule 20.4 are dealt with in each specific situation below.

11.1 *Appeals on service.*

11.1.1 If the Marker calls 'fault', 'foot fault', 'not up', 'down' or 'out' to the service the server may appeal. If the appeal is upheld a let shall be allowed.

11.1.2 If the Marker fails to call 'fault', 'foot fault', 'not up', 'down' or 'out' to the service the receiver may appeal, either immediately or at the end of the rally if he has played or attempted to play the ball. If, in the opinion of the Referee, the service was not good he shall stop play immediately and award the strokes to the receiver.

11.2 *Appeals on play other than service*

11.2.1 If the Marker calls 'not up', 'down' or 'out' following a player's return, the player may appeal. If the appeal is upheld the Referee shall allow a let except that if, in the opinion of the Referee:

– The Marker's call has interrupted that player's winning return he shall award the stroke to the player.

– The Marker's call has interrupted or prevented a winning return by the opponent, he shall award the stroke to the opponent.

11.2.2 If the Marker fails to call 'not up', 'down' or 'out' following a player's return the opponent may appeal either immediately, or at the end of the rally if he has played or attempted to play the ball. If, in the opinion of the Referee, the return was not good he shall stop play immediately and award the stroke to the opponent.

12. Interference

12.1 After playing a ball, a player must make every effort to get out of his opponent's way. That is:

12.1.1 A player must make every effort to give his opponent a fair view of the ball.

12.1.2 A player must make every effort not to obstruct the opponent in the latter's direct movement to the ball. At the same time the opponent must make every effort to get to, and where possible play the ball.

12.1.3 A player must make every effort to allow his opponent freedom to play the ball.

12.1.4 A player must make every effort to allow his opponent freedom to play the ball directly to the front wall.

If a player fails to fulfil one of the requirements of Rule 12.1 (1 to 4) above, whether or not he has made every effort to do so, then interference will have occurred.

12.2 If any such form of interference has occurred, and, in the opinion of the Referee, the player has not made every effort to avoid causing it, the Referee shall not appeal, or on stopping play without waiting for an appeal, award the stroke to his opponent, provided the opponent was in a position to make a good return.

12.3 However, if interference has occurred but in the opinion of the Referee the player has made every effort to avoid causing it, and the opponent could have made a good return, the Referee shall on appeal, or on stopping play without waiting for an appeal, allow a let, except that if his opponent is prevented from making a winning return by such interference from the player, the Referee shall award the stroke to the opponent.

12.4 When, in the opinion of the Referee, a player refrains from playing the ball which, if played, would clearly have won the rally under the terms of Rule 9.1 or 9.3, he shall be awarded the stroke. However, if his playing of the ball would have been a further attempt a let shall be allowed.

12.5 If either player makes unnecessary physical contact with his opponent, the Referee may stop play, if it has not already stopped, and apply the appropriate penalty.

13. Lets

13.1 In addition to lets allowed under other Rules, lets may or shall be allowed in certain other cases:

13.1.1 If, owing to the position of the striker, the opponent is unable to avoid being touched by the ball before the return is made.

13.1.2 If the ball in play touches any articles lying on the floor.

13.1.3 If the striker refrains from hitting the ball owing to a reasonable fear of injuring his opponent.

13.1.4 If, in the opinion of the Referee, either player is distracted by an occurrence on or off the court.

13.1.5 If, in the opinion of the Referee, a change in court conditions has affected the result of the rally.

13.2 A let shall be allowed:

13.2.1 If the receiver is not ready and does not attempt to return the service.

13.2.2 If the ball breaks during play.

13.2.3 If the Referee is asked to decide an appeal and is unable to do so.

13.2.4 If an otherwise good return has been made, but the ball goes out of court on its first bounce.

13.3 If the striker appeals for a let under Rules 13.1 (2 to 5) above, in order for a let to be allowed he must have been able to make a good return. For a non-striker appeal under Rules 13.1.2, 13.1.4 and 13.1.5 this is not a requirement.

13.4 No let shall be allowed under Rules 13.1.3 and 13.2.1 if the striker attempts to play the ball but may be allowed under Rules 13.1.2, 13.1.4, 13.1.5, 13.2.2, 13.2.3 and 13.2.4.

13.5

13.5.1 An appeal by the player is necessary for a let to be allowed under Rules 13.1.3 (striker only), 13.1.4, 13.2.1 (striker only) and 13.2.3.

13.5.2 An appeal by the player or Referee intervention without appeal is applicable to Rules 13.1.2, 13.1.5, 13.2.2 and 13.2.4.

13.5.3 Where a player is struck by the ball as described in Rule 13.1.1 the Referee shall decide without appeal whether a let is to be allowed or the stroke awarded to the striker.

14. The Ball

14.1 At any time, when the ball is not in actual play, another ball may be substituted by mutual consent of the players or, on appeal by either player, at the discretion of the Referee.

14.2 If the ball breaks during play, it shall be replaced promptly by another ball.

14.3 If a ball has broken but this has not been established during play, a let for the rally in which the ball broke shall be allowed if the server appeals prior to the next service, or if the receiver appeals prior to attempting to return that service.

14.4 The provisions of Rule 14.3 do not apply to the final rally of a game. Appeal in this case must be immediately after the rally.

14.5 If a player stops play during a rally to appeal that the ball is broken only to find subsequently that the ball is not broken, then that player shall lose the stroke.

15. Warm-up

15.1 Immediately preceding the start of play, the Referee shall allow on the court of play a period of 5 minutes to the two players together for the purpose of warming up the ball to be used for the match.

After $2\frac{1}{2}$ minutes of the warm-up, the Referee shall call 'half-time' and ensure that the players change sides unless they mutually agree otherwise. The Referee shall also advise when the warm-up period is complete with the call of 'Time'.

15.2 Where a ball has been substituted under Rule 14 or when the match is being resumed after considerable delay, the Referee shall allow the ball to be warmed up to playing condition. Play shall resume on the direction of the Referee, or upon mutual consent of the players, whichever is the earlier.

15.3 The ball may be warmed up by either player between games, unless there is an objection by one of the players. In the case of an infringement the Referee shall apply Rule 17.

16. Continuity of Play

After the first service is delivered, play shall be continuous so far as is practical, provided that:

16.1 At any time play may be suspended, owing to bad light or other circumstances beyond the control of the players, for such period as the Referee shall decide. The score shall stand.

If another court is available when the court originally in use remains unsuitable, the match may be transferred to it if both players agree, or as directed by the Referee.

In the event of play being suspended for the day, the score shall stand unless both players agree to start the match again.

16.2 An interval of 90 seconds shall be permitted between all games. Players may leave the court during such intervals but shall be ready to resume play by the end of the stated time. When 15 seconds of the interval permitted between games are left, the Referee shall call '15 seconds' to advise the players to be ready to resume play. At the end of the interval the Referee shall call 'Time'.

By mutual consent of the players, play may commence prior to the expiry of the 90-second time interval.

It is the responsibility of the players to be within earshot of the court to hear the calls of '15 seconds' and 'Time'.

16.3 If a player satisfies the Referee that a change of equipment, clothing or footwear is necessary, the player may leave the court. He is required to effect the change as quickly as possible and the Referee shall allow him a period not exceeding 2 minutes for this purpose. If the player fails to return within the allotted time the Referee shall apply the provisions of Rule 17.

16.4 In the event of an injury to a player, the Referee shall decide if it was:

16.4.1 Self-inflicted.

16.4.2 Accidentally contributed to or accidentally caused by his opponent.

16.4.3 Caused by the opponent's deliberate or dangerous play or action.

16.5 The Referee shall apply the provisions of Rule 17 to a player, who, in his opinion, delays play unreasonably. Such delay may be caused by:

16.5.1 Unduly slow preparation to serve or to receive service.

16.5.2 Prolonged discussion with the Referee.

16.5.3 Delay in returning to the court, having left under the terms of Rules 16.2 and 16.3.

17. Conduct on Court

If the Referee considers that the behaviour of a player on court could be intimidating or offensive to an opponent, official or spectator, or could in any other way bring the game into disrepute the player shall be penalised.

Where a player commits any of the offences listed in the Rules 12.5, 15.2, 15.3, 16.2, 16.3 or the ISRF Code of Conduct (Appendix 6.1), one of the following penalty provisions may be applied:

Warning by the Referee (called a Conduct Warning).

Stroke awarded to opponent (called a Conduct Stroke).

Game awarded to opponent (called a Conduct Game).

Match awarded to opponent (called a Conduct Match).

18. Control of a Match

A match is normally controlled by a Referee, assisted by a Marker. One person may be appointed to carry out the functions of both Referee and Marker. When a decision has been made by the Referee, he shall announce it to the players and the Marker shall repeat it with the subsequent score.

19. Duties of a Marker

19.1 The Marker calls the play followed by the score, with the server's score called first. He shall call 'fault', 'foot fault', 'out', 'not up', or 'down' as appropriate, and shall repeat the Referee's decisions.

19.2 If the Marker makes a call, the rally shall cease.

19.3 If play ceases, and the Marker is unsighted or uncertain, he shall advise the players and shall call on the Referee to make the relevant decision; if the Referee is unable to do so, a let shall be allowed.

19.4 The Marker calls 'Hand Out' to indicate a change of server.

20. Duties of a Referee

20.1 The Referee shall allow or disallow appeals for lets, and award strokes; make decisions where called for by the Rules, including when a player is struck by the ball and for injuries; and shall decide all appeals, including those against the Marker's calls or lack of calls. The decision of the Referee shall be final.

20.2 The Referee shall exercise control:

20.2.1 Upon appeal by one of the players.

20.2.2 As provided for in Rules 4, 9, 10, 11, 12, 13, 14, 15, 16, 17, 18 and 19.

20.3 The Referee shall not intervene in the Marker's calling of the score unless, in the opinion of the Referee, the score has been called incorrectly in which case he shall have the Marker call the correct score.

20.4 The Referee shall not intervene in the Marker's calling of the play unless, in the opinion of the Referee, the Marker has made an error in stopping play or allowing play to continue, in which case the Referee shall immediately rule accordingly.

20.5 The Referee is responsible for ensuring that all rules relating to time are strictly enforced.

20.6 The Referee is responsible for ensuring that court conditions are appropriate for play.

20.7 The Referee may award a match to a player whose opponent fails to be present on court, ready to play, within 10 minutes of the advertised time of play.

APPENDIX

DEFINITIONS

Adjudicator. A person responsible for the conduct of players and officials throughout the tournament.

Appeal. A player's request to the Referee to consider an on or off court situation. 'Appeal' is used throughout the Rules in two contexts:

(1) Where the player requests the Referee to consider varying a Marker's decision; and

(2) Where the player requests the Referee to allow a let. The correct form of appeal by a player is 'Appeal please' or 'Let please'.

Attempt. The Referee shall decide what is an attempt to play the ball. An attempt is made when, in the opinion the Referee, the striker has moved his racket towards the ball from his backswing position with the intention of making a good return.

The Board is the lower horizontal line marking on the front wall, with the tin beneath it for the full width of the court.

Box (Service). A square delineated area in each quarter court, bounded by part of the short line, part of the side wall and by two other lines and from within which the server serves.

Competition. A championship, tournament, league or other competitive match.

Correctly. The ball being hit by the racket (held in the hand) not more than once nor with prolonged contact on the racket.

Cut-line. A line upon the front wall, the top edge of which is 1.83m (6ft) above the floor and extending the full width of the court.

Down. The expression used to indicate that an otherwise good return has struck the board or tin or has failed to reach the front wall. ('Down' is also used as a Marker's call.)

Game. Part of a match, commencing with a service and concluding when one player has scored or been awarded 9 or 10 points (in accordance with the Rules).

Game Ball. The state of the score when the server requires 1 point to win the game in progress. ('Game ball' is also used as a Marker's call.)

Half-Court Line. A line set upon the floor parallel to the side walls, dividing the back of the court into 2 equal parts, meeting the short line at its midpoint, forming the 'T'.

Half-time. The midpoint of the warm-up (also used as a Referee's call).

Hand. The period from the time a player becomes server until he becomes receiver.

Hand-out. Condition when a change of server occurs. ('Hand-out' is also used as a Marker's call to indicate that a change of hand has occurred.)

Match. The complete contest between two players commencing with the warm-up and concluding when both players have left the court at the end of the final rally (covers broken ball rule).

Match Ball. The state of the score when the server requires 1 point to win the match. ('Match ball' is also used as a Marker's call.)

Not Up. The expression used to indicate that a ball has not been struck in accordance with the Rules. 'Not up' covers all services or returns which are not good and are neither down nor out – with the exception of faults and foot faults. ('Not up' is also used as a Marker's call.)

Out. The expression used to indicate that a ball has struck the out line or a wall above such line or the roof, or has passed over any part of the roof (e.g. cross-bars). ('Out' is also used as a Marker's call.)

Out Line. A continuous line comprising the front-wall line, both side-wall lines and the back-wall line and marking the top boundaries of the court.

Note: When a court is constructed without provision of such a line, i.e. the walls comprise only the area used for play, or without the provision of part of such a line (e.g. a glass back wall), and the ball in play strikes part of the horizontal top surface of such a wall and deflects back into court, such a ball is out. Because of the difficulty in ascertaining just where the ball strikes the wall, the decision as to whether such a ball is out should be made by observing the deflection back into court – an abnormal deflection indicating that the ball is out. This decision should be made in the normal manner by the Marker, subject to appeal to the Referee.

Point. A unit of the scoring system. One point is added to a player's score when he is server and wins a stroke.

Quarter (Court). One half of the back part of the court which has been divided into two equal parts by the half-court line.

Rally. Series of returns of the ball, comprising one or more such returns. A rally commences with a service and concludes when the ball ceases to be in play.

Reasonable Backswing. The initial action used by a player in moving his racket away from his body as preparation prior to racket movement forward towards the ball for contact. A backswing is reasonable if it is not excessive. An excessive backswing is one in which the player's racket arm is extended towards a straight arm position and/or the racket is extended with the shaft approximately horizontal. The Referee's decision on what constitutes a reasonable as distinct from excessive backswing is final.

Reasonable Follow-through. The action used by a player in continuing the movement of his racket after it has contacted the ball. A follow-through is reasonable if it is not excessive. An excessive follow-through is one in which the player's racket arm is extended towards a straight arm position with the racket also extended with the shaft horizontal –

particularly when the extended position is maintained for other than a momentary period of time. An excessive swing is also one in which the arm extended towards a straight position takes a wider arc than the continued line of flight of the ball, even though the racket shaft is in the correct vertical position. The Referee's decision on what constitutes a reasonable as distinct from excessive follow-through is final.

Service. The method by which the ball is put into play by the server to commence a rally.

Short Line. A line set out upon the floor parallel to and 5.49m (18ft) from the front wall and extending the full width of the court.

Standard. The description given to balls, rackets and courts that meet existing ISRF specifications.

Striker. The player whose turn it is to hit the ball after it has rebounded from the front wall, or who is in the process of hitting the ball, or who – up to the point of his return reaching the front wall – has just hit the ball.

Stroke. The gain achieved by the player who wins a rally, either in the normal course of play or on award by the Referee, and which results in either the scoring of a point or a change of hand.

The Tin is situated between the board and the floor for the full width of the court and shall be constructed in such a manner as to make a distinctive noise when struck by the ball.

The **Tournament Referee** is given overall responsibility for all marking and refereeing matters throughout the tournament, including appointment and replacement of officials to matches.

General Note

The use of the word 'shall' in the Rules indicates compulsion and the lack of any alternative. The word 'must' indicates a required course of action with considerations to be taken into account if the action is not carried out. The word 'may' indicates the option of carrying out or not carrying out the action. When the words 'he', 'him' and 'his' are used in the Rules, they shall be taken to mean 'she', 'her' and 'hers' as appropriate.

Reprinted by permission of the Squash Rackets Association. For reasons of space, the following items have been omitted: Notes to Officials and Appendixes concerning Markers' and Referees' Calls, Dimensions of a Squash Court and a Racket, Specification for Squash Racket Balls, Colour of Players' Clothing, Code of Conduct and Guidelines for National Federations, their Affiliated Associations and Tournament Organiser, Copies of the complete Rules of Squash can be obtained from the Association.

THE LAWS OF

Table Tennis

Table Tennis

The masculine gender is used throughout but may refer to men or women.

3.1 The Table

3.1.1 The upper surface of the table, known as the playing surface, shall be rectangular, 2.74m long and 1.525m wide, and shall lie in a horizontal plane 76cm above the floor.

3.1.2 The playing surface shall include the top edges of the table but not the sides of the table top below the edges.

3.1.3 The playing surface may be of any material and shall yield a uniform bounce of about 23cm when a standard ball is dropped on to it from a height of 30cm.

3.1.4 The playing surface shall be uniformly dark coloured and matt, but with a white side-line, 2cm wide along each 2.74m edge and a white end-line, 2cm wide, along each 1.525m edge.

3.1.5 The playing surface shall be divided into two equal courts by a vertical net running parallel with the end-lines, and shall be continuous over the whole area of each court.

3.1.6 For doubles, each court shall be divided into two equal half-courts by a white centre-line, 3mm wide, running parallel with the side-lines; the centre-line shall be regarded as part of each right half-court.

3.2 The Net Assembly

3.2.1 The net assembly shall consist of the net, its suspension and the supporting posts.

3.2.2 The net shall be suspended by a cord attached at each end to an upright post 15.25cm high, the outside limits of the post being 15.25cm outside the side-line.

3.2.3 The top of the net, along its whole length, shall be 15.25cm above the playing surface.

3.2.4 The bottom of the net, along its whole length, shall be as close as possible to the playing surface and the ends of the net shall be as close as possible to the supporting posts.

3.3 The Ball
3.3.1 The ball shall be spherical, with a diameter of 38mm.
3.3.2 The ball shall weigh 2.5g.
3.3.3 The ball shall be made of celluloid or similar plastics material and shall be white or yellow, and matt.

3.4 The Racket
3.4.1 The rackets may be of any size, shape or weight but the blade shall be flat and rigid.
3.4.2 At least 85% of the blade by thickness shall be of natural wood; an adhesive layer within the blade may be reinforced with fibrous material such as carbon fibre, glass fibre or compressed paper, but shall not be thicker than 7.5% of the total thickness or 0.35mm, whichever is the smaller.
3.4.3 A side of the blade used for striking the ball shall be covered with either ordinary pimpled rubber with pimples outwards having a total thickness including adhesive of not more than 2mm, or sandwich rubber with pimples inwards or outwards having a total thickness including adhesive of not more than 4mm.
3.4.3.1 'Ordinary pimpled rubber' is a single layer of non-cellular rubber, natural or synthetic, with pimples evenly distributed over its surface at a density of not less than 10 per sq cm and not more than 50 per sq cm.
3.4.3.2 'Sandwich rubber' is a single layer of cellular rubber covered with a single outer layer of ordinary pimpled rubber, the thickness of the pimpled rubber not being more than 2mm.
3.4.4 The covering material shall extend up to but not beyond the limits of the blade, except that the part nearest the handle and gripped by the fingers may be left uncovered or covered with any material.
3.4.5 The blade, any layer within the blade and any layer of covering material or adhesive shall be continuous and of even thickness.
3.4.6 The surface of the covering material on a side of the blade, or of a side of the blade if it is left uncovered, shall be uniformly dark-coloured and matt; any trimming round the edge of the blade shall be matt and no part of it shall be white.
3.4.7 Slight deviations from continuity of surface or uniformity of colour due to accidental damage, wear or fading may be allowed provided that they do not significantly change the characteristics of the surface.

3.4.8 At the start of a match and whenever he changes his racket during a match a player shall show his opponent and the Umpire the racket he is about to use and shall allow them to examine it.

3.5 Definitions

3.5.1 A **rally** is the period during which the ball is in play.

3.5.2 A **let** is a rally of which the result is not scored.

3.5.3 A **point** is a rally of which the result is scored.

3.5.4 The **racket-hand** is the hand carrying the racket.

3.5.5 The **free hand** is the hand not carrying the racket.

3.5.6 A player **strikes** the ball if he touches it with his racket, held in the hand, or with his racket-hand below the wrist.

3.5.7 A player **volleys** the ball if he strikes it in play when it has not touched his court since last being struck by his opponent.

3.5.8 A player **obstructs** the ball if he, or anything he wears or carries, touches it in play when it has not passed over the playing surface or his end-line, not having touched his court since last being struck by his opponent.

3.5.9 The **server** is the player due to strike the ball first in a rally.

3.5.10 The **receiver** is the player due to strike the ball second in a rally.

3.5.11 The **Umpire** is the person appointed to control the match.

3.5.12 The **Assistant Umpire** is the person appointed to assist the Umpire with certain duties.

3.5.13 Anything that a player **wears or carries** includes anything that he was wearing or carrying at the start of the rally.

3.5.14 The ball shall be regarded as passing **over** or **around** the net if it passes under or outside the projection of the net assembly outside the table or if, in a return, it is struck after it has bounced back over the net.

3.5.15 The **end-line** shall be regarded as extending indefinitely in both directions.

3.6 A Good Service

3.6.1 Service shall begin with the ball resting on the palm of the free hand, which shall be stationary, open and flat, with the fingers together and the thumb free.

3.6.2 The free hand, while in contact with the ball, shall at all times be above the level of the playing surface and behind the server's end-line.

3.6.3 The whole of the racket shall be above the level of the playing surface from the last moment at which the ball is stationary on the palm of the free hand until the ball is struck.

3.6.4 The server shall then project the ball near vertically upwards, by hand only and without imparting spin, so that it rises at least 16cm after leaving the palm of the free hand.

3.6.5 As the ball is falling from the highest point of its trajectory the server shall strike it so that:

3.6.5.1 In singles, it touches first his court and then, passing directly over or around the net assembly, touches the receiver's court.

3.6.5.2 In doubles, it touches first his right half-court and then, passing directly over or around the net assembly, touches the receiver's right half-court.

3.6.6 When the ball is struck, it shall be behind the server's end-line but not farther back than the part of the server's body, other than his arm, head or leg, which is farthest from the net.

3.6.7 It is the responsibility of the player to serve so that the Umpire or Assistant Umpire can see that he complies with the requirements for a good service.

3.6.7.1 Except when an Assistant Umpire has been appointed, the Umpire may, on the first occasion in a match at which he has a doubt about the correctness of a player's service, interrupt play and warn the server without awarding a point.

3.6.7.2 On any subsequent occasion in the same match at which the same player's service action is of doubtful correctness, for the same or for any other reason, the player shall not be given the benefit of the doubt and shall lose a point.

3.6.7.3 Whenever there is a clear failure by the server to comply with the requirements for a good service no warning shall be given and he shall lose a point, on the first as on any other occasion.

3.6.8 Exceptionally, strict observance of any particular requirement for a good service may be waived where the Umpire is notified, before play begins, that compliance with that requirement is prevented by physical disability.

3.7 A Good Return

3.7.1 The ball, having been served or returned, shall be struck so that it passes over or around the net assembly and touches the opponent's court, either directly or after touching the net assembly.

3.8 The Order of Play

3.8.1 In singles, the server shall first make a good service, the receiver shall then make a good return and thereafter server and receiver alternately shall each make a good return.

3.8.2 In doubles the server shall first make a good service, the receiver shall then make a good return, the partner of the server shall then make a good return, the partner of the receiver shall then make a good return and thereafter each player in turn in that sequence shall make a good return.

3.9 In Play
3.9.1 The ball shall be in play from the last moment at which it is stationary before being projected in service until:
3.9.1.1 It touches anything other than the playing surface, the net assembly, the racket held in the hand or the racket hand below the wrist; or
3.9.1.2 The rally is otherwise decided as a let or a point.

3.10 A Let
3.10.1 The rally shall be a let:
3.10.1.1 If in service the ball, in passing over or around the net assembly, touches it, provided the service is otherwise good or the ball is volleyed or obstructed by the receiver or his partner.
3.10.1.2 If the service is delivered when the receiving player or pair is not ready, provided that neither the receiver nor his partner attempts to strike the ball.
3.10.1.3 If failure to make a good service or a good return or otherwise to comply with the Laws is due to a disturbance outside the control of the player.
3.10.1.4 If play is interrupted by the Umpire or Assistant Umpire.
3.10.2 Play may be interrupted:
3.10.2.1 To correct an error in the order of serving, receiving or ends.
3.10.2.2 To introduce the expedite system.
3.10.2.3 To warn or penalise a player.
3.10.2.4 Because the conditions of play are disturbed in a way which could affect the outcome of the rally.

3.11 A Point
3.11.1 Unless the rally is a let, a player shall lose a point:
3.11.1.1 If he fails to make a good service.
3.11.1.2 If he fails to make a good return.
3.11.1.3 If he volleys or obstructs the ball, except as provided in Law 3.10.1.1.
3.11.1.4 If he strikes the ball twice successively.
3.11.1.5 If the ball touches his court twice successively.
3.11.1.6 If he strikes the ball with a side of the racket blade whose surface does not comply with the requirements of 3.4.3.
3.11.1.7 If he, or anything he wears or carries, moves the playing surface.
3.11.1.8 If his free hand touches the playing surface.
3.11.1.9 If he, or anything he wears or carries, touches the net assembly.
3.11.1.10 If, as he serves, he or his partner stamps his foot.

3.11.1.11 If, in doubles, except in serving or receiving, he strikes the ball out of proper sequence.

3.11.1.12 If, under the expedite system, he serves and the receiving player or pair makes 13 successive good returns.

3.12 A Game

3.12.1 A game shall be won by the player or pair first scoring 21 points unless both players or pairs score 20 points, when the game shall be won by the player or pair first scoring subsequently 2 points more than the opposing player or pair.

3.13 A Match

3.13.1 A match shall consist of the best of 3 games or the best of 5 games.

3.13.2 Play shall be continuous throughout a match except that any player shall be entitled to claim an interval of not more than 2 minutes between successive games.

3.14 The Choice of Serving, Receiving and Ends

3.14.1 The right to make first choice shall be decided by lot.

3.14.2 The player or pair winning this right may:

3.14.2.1 Choose to serve or to receive first, when the loser shall have the choice of ends.

3.14.2.2 Choose an end, when the loser shall have the choice of serving or receiving first.

3.14.2.3 Require the loser to make the first choice, when the winner shall have whichever choice is not made by the loser.

3.14.3 In doubles the pair having the right to serve first in each game shall decide which of them will do so, and

3.14.3.1 In the first game of a match, the opposing pair shall then decide which of them will receive first.

3.14.3.2 In subsequent games of the match, the first receiver will be determined by the choice of server, as provided in 3.15.5.

3.15 The Order of Serving, Receiving and Ends

3.15.1 After 5 points have been scored the receiving player or pair shall become the serving player or pair and so on until the end of the game, or until each player or pair has scored 20 points or until the introduction of the expedite system.

3.15.2 In doubles:

3.15.2.1 The first server shall be the selected player of the pair having the right to serve first and the first receiver shall be the appropriate player of the opposing pair.

3.15.2.2 The second server shall be the player who was the first receiver and the second receiver shall be the partner of the first server.

3.15.2.3 The third server shall be the partner of the first server and the third receiver shall be the partner of the first receiver.

3.15.2.4 The fourth server shall be the partner of the first receiver and the fourth receiver shall be the first server.

3.15.2.5 The fifth server shall be the player who was the first server and the players shall thereafter serve in the same sequence until the end of the game.

3.15.3 If both players or pairs have scored 20 points or if the expedite system is in operation the sequence of serving and receiving shall be the same but each player shall serve for only 1 point in turn until the end of the game.

3.15.4 The player or pair who served first in a game shall receive first in the immediate subsequent game of the match.

3.15.5 In each game of a doubles match after the first, the first server having been chosen, the first receiver shall be the player who served to him in the immediately preceding game.

3.15.6 In the last possible game of a doubles match the pair due next to receive shall change the order of receiving when first either pair scores 10 points.

3.15.7 The player or pair starting at one end in a game shall start at the other end in the immediately subsequent game of the match.

3.15.8 In the last possible game of a match the players shall change ends when first either player or pair scores 10 points.

3.16 Out of Order of Serving, Receiving and Ends

3.16.1 If a player serves or receives out of turn, play shall be interrupted by the Umpire as soon as the error is discovered and shall resume with those players serving and receiving who should be server and receiver respectively at the score that has been reached, according to the sequence established at the beginning of the match, and, in doubles, to the order of serving chosen by the pair having the right to serve first in the game during which the error is discovered.

3.16.2 If the players have not changed ends when they should have done so, play shall be interrupted by the Umpire as soon as the error is discovered and shall resume with the players at the ends at which they should be at the score that has been reached, according to the sequence established at the beginning of the match.

3.16.3 In any circumstances, all points scored before the discovery of an error shall be reckoned.

3.17 The Expedite System

3.17.1 The expedite system shall come into operation if a game is

826 TABLE TENNIS

unfinished after 15 minutes' play, or at any earlier time at the request of both players or pairs.

3.17.1.1 If the ball is in play when the time limit is reached, play shall be interrupted by the Umpire and shall resume with service by the player who served in the rally that was interrupted.

3.17.1.2 If the ball is not in play when the time limit is reached, play shall resume with the service by the player who received in the immediately preceding rally of the game.

3.17.2 Thereafter, each player shall serve for 1 point in turn until the end of the game, and if the receiving player or pair makes 13 good returns the server shall lose a point.

3.17.3 Once introduced, the expedite system shall remain in operation for the remainder of the match.

These Rules have been adopted by the International Table Tennis Federation, are approved by the English Table Tennis Association and have been reprinted with their permission. For reasons of space some of the Rules have been abbreviated. Copies of the Rules of Table Tennis, including Disciplinary Regulations and Regulations for International Competitions, may be obtained from the Federation.

THE RULES OF

Tennis

The Tennis Court

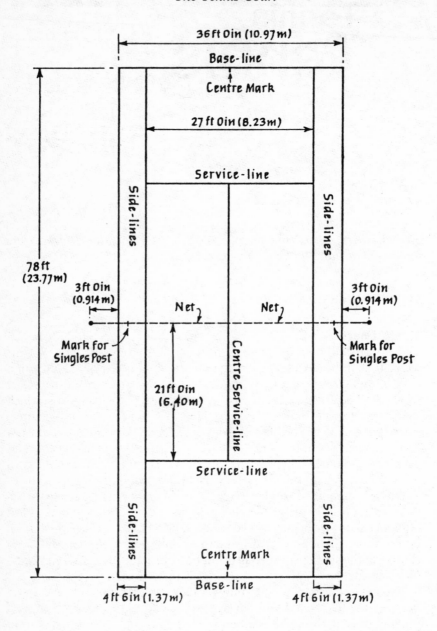

Tennis

Except where otherwise stated, every reference in these Rules to the masculine includes the feminine gender.

THE SINGLES GAME

1. The Court

The Court shall be a rectangular, 78ft (23.77m) long and 27ft (8.23m) wide. It shall be divided across the middle by a net suspended from a cord or metal cable of a maximum diameter of ⅓in (0.8cm), the ends of which shall be attached to, or pass over, the tops of the two posts, which shall be not more than 6in (15cm) square or 6in (15cm) in diameter. These posts shall not be higher than 1in (2.5cm) above the top of the net cord. The centres of the posts shall be 3ft (0.914m) outside the court on each side and the height of the posts shall be such that the top of the cord or metal cable shall be 3ft 6in (1.07m) above the ground.

When a combined doubles (see Rule 34) and singles court with a doubles net is used for singles, the net must be supported to a height of 3ft 6in (1.07m) by means of two posts, called singles sticks, which shall be not more than 3in (7.5cm) square or 3in (7.5cm) in diameter. The centres of the singles sticks shall be 3ft (0.914m) outside the singles court on each side.

The net shall be extended fully so that it fills completely the space between the two posts and shall be of sufficiently small mesh to prevent the ball passing through. The height of the net shall be 3ft (0.914m) at the centre, where it shall be held down taut by a strap not more than 2in (5cm) wide and completely white in colour. There shall be a band covering the cord or metal cable and the top of the net of not less than 2in (5cm) nor more than 2½in (6.3cm) in depth on each side and completely white in colour. There shall be no advertisement on the net, strap band or singles sticks.

The lines bounding the ends and sides of the court shall respectively be called the base-lines and the side-lines. On each side of the net, at a distance of 21ft (6.40m) from it and parallel with it, shall be drawn the service-lines. The space on each side of the net between the service-line and the side-lines shall be divided into two equal parts called the service-courts by the centre service-line, which must be 2in (5cm) in width, drawn half-way between, and parallel with, the side-line. Each base-line shall be bisected by an imaginary continuation of the centre service-line to a line 4in (10cm) in length and 2in (5cm) in width called the centre mark, drawn inside the court, at right angles to and in contact with such base-lines. All other lines shall not be less than 1in (2.5cm) nor more than 2in (5cm) in width, except the base-line, which may be 4in (10cm) in width, and all measurements shall be made to the outside of the lines. All lines shall be of uniform colour. If advertising or any other material is placed at the back of the court, it may not contain white or yellow. A light colour may only be used if this does not interfere with the vision of the players.

If advertisements are placed on the chairs of the linesmen sitting at the back of the Court, they may not contain white or yellow. A light colour may only be used if this does not interfere with the vision of the players.

Note: In the case of the Davis Cup or other Official Championships of the International Tennis Federation, there shall be a space behind each base-line of not less than 21ft (6.40m), and at the sides of not less than 12ft (3.66m). The chairs of linesmen may be placed at the back of a court within the 21ft (6.4m) or at the side of the court within the 12ft (3.66m), provided they do not protrude into that area more than 3ft (0.914m).

2. Permanent Fixtures

The permanent fixtures of the court shall include not only the net, posts, singles sticks, cord or metal cable, strap and band, but also, where there are any such, the back and side stops, the stands, fixed or movable seats and chairs round the court, and their occupants, all other fixtures around and above the court, and the Umpire, Net-cord Judge, Foot-fault Judge, Linesmen and Ball Boys when in their respective places.

Note: For the purpose of this Rule, the word Umpire comprehends the Umpire, the persons entitled to a seat on the court, and all those persons designated to assist the Umpire in the conduct of a match.

3. The Ball

The ball shall have a uniform outer surface and shall be white or yellow in colour. If there are any seams they shall be stitchless. The ball shall be more than 2½in (6.35cm) and less than 2⅝in (6.67cm) in diameter, and more than 2oz (56.7g) and less than 2⅟₁₆oz (58.5g) in weight.

The ball shall have a bound of more than 53in (135cm) and less than 58in (147cm) when dropped 100in (254cm) upon a concrete base. The ball shall have a forward deformation of more than 0.220in (0.56cm) and less than 0.290in (0.74cm) and a return deformation of more than 0.350in (0.89cm) and less than 0.425in (1.08cm) at 18lb (8.165kg) load. The two deformation figures shall be the averages of three individual readings along three axes of the ball and no two individual readings shall differ by more than 0.030in (0.08cm) in each case.

For play above 4,000ft (1219m) in altitude above sea level, two additional types of ball may be used. The first type is identical to those described above except that the bound shall be more than 48in (121.93cm) and less than 53in (135cm) and shall have an internal pressure that is greater than the external pressure. This type of tennis ball is commonly known as a pressurised ball. The second type is identical to those described above except that they shall have a bound of more than 53in (135cm) and less than 58in (147cm) and shall have an internal pressure that is approximately equal to the external pressure and have been acclimatised for 60 days or more at the altitude of the specific tournament. This type of tennis ball is commonly known as a zero-pressure or non-pressurised ball.

4. Racket

Rackets failing to comply with the following specifications are not approved for play under the Rules of Tennis:

(*a*) The hitting surface of the racket shall be flat and consist of a pattern of crossed strings connected to a frame and alternately inter-laced or bonded where they cross; and the stringing pattern shall be generally uniform, and in particular not less dense in the centre than in any other area. The strings shall be free of attached objects and protrusions other than those utilised solely and specifically to limit or prevent wear and tear or vibration, and which are reasonable in size and placement for such purposes.

(*b*) The frame of the racket shall not exceed 32in (81.28cm) in overall length, including the handle and 12½in (31.75cm) in overall width. The strung surface shall not exceed 15½in (39.37cm) in overall length, and 11½in (29.21cm) in overall width.

(*c*) The frame, including the handle, shall be free of attached objects and devices other than those utilised solely and specifically to limit or prevent wear and tear or vibration, or to distribute weight. Any objects and devices must be reasonable in size and placement for such purposes.

(*d*) The frame, including the handle, and the strings, shall be free of any device which makes it possible to change materially the shape of the racket, or to change the weight distribution, during the playing of a point.

The International Tennis Federation shall rule on the question of whether any racket or prototype complies with the above specifications or is otherwise approved, or not approved, for play. Such ruling may be undertaken on its own initiative, or upon application by any party with a bona fide interest therein, including any player, equipment manufacturer or National Association or members thereof. Such rulings and applications shall be made in accordance with the applicable Review and Hearing Procedures of the ITF, copies of which may be obtained from the office of the Secretary.

5. Server and Receiver
The players shall stand on opposite sides of the net; the player who first delivers the ball shall be called the server, and the other the receiver.

6. Choice of Ends and Service
The choice of ends and the right to be server or receiver in the first game shall be decided by toss. The player winning the toss may choose or require his opponent to choose:

(a) The right to be server or receiver, in which case the other player shall choose the end; or

(b) The end, in which case the other player shall choose the right to be server or receiver.

7. The Service
The service shall be delivered in the following manner. Immediately before commencing to serve, the server shall stand with both feet at rest behind (i.e. further from the net than) the base-line, and within the imaginary continuations of the centre-mark and side-line. The server shall then project the ball by hand into the air in any direction and before it hits the ground strike it with his racket, and the delivery shall be deemed to have been completed at the moment of the impact of the racket and the ball. A player with the use of only one arm may utilise his racket for the projection.

8. Foot-fault
(a) The server shall throughout the delivery of the service:

(i) Not change his position by walking or running. The server shall not, by slight movements of the feet which do not materially affect the location originally taken up by him, be deemed 'to change his position by walking or running'.

(ii) Not touch, with either foot, any area other than that behind the base-line within the imaginary extension of the centre-mark and side-lines.

(*b*) The word 'foot' means the extremity of the leg below the ankle.

9. Delivery of Service

(*a*) In delivering the service, the server shall stand alternately behind the right and left courts beginning from the right in every game. If service from a wrong half of the court occurs and is undetected, all play resulting from such wrong service or services shall stand, but the inaccuracy of station shall be corrected immediately it is discovered.

(*b*) The ball served shall pass over the net and hit the ground within the service court which is diagonally opposite, or upon any line bounding such court, before the receiver returns it.

10. Service Fault

The service is a fault:

(*a*) If the server commits any breach of Rules 7, 8 or 9(*b*).

(*b*) If he misses the ball in attempting to strike it.

(*c*) If the ball served touches a permanent fixture (other than the net, strap or band) before it hits the ground.

11. Second Service

After a fault (if it is the first fault) the server shall serve again from behind the same half of the court from which he served that fault, unless the service was from the wrong half, when, in accordance with Rule 9, the server shall be entitled to one service only from behind the other half.

12. When to Serve

The server shall not serve until the receiver is ready. If the latter attempts to return the service, he shall be deemed ready. If, however, the receiver signifies that he is not ready, he may not claim a fault because the ball does not hit the ground within the limits fixed for the service.

13. The Let

In all cases where a let has to be called under the Rules, or to provide for an interruption to play, it shall have the following interpretations:

(*a*) When called solely in respect of a service that one service only shall be replayed.

(*b*) When called under any other circumstance, the point shall be replayed.

14. The Let in Service
The service is a let:

(*a*) If the ball served touches the net, strap or band, and is otherwise good, or, after touching the net, strap or band, touches the receiver or anything which he wears or carries before hitting the ground.

(*b*) If a service or a fault is delivered when the receiver is not ready (See Rule 12).

In case of a let, that particular service shall not count, and the server shall serve again, but a service let does not annul a previous fault.

15. Order of Service
At the end of the first game the receiver shall become server, and the server receiver; and so on alternately in all the subsequent games of a match. If a player serves out of turn, the player who ought to have served shall serve as soon as the mistake is discovered, but all points scored before such discovery shall be reckoned. A fault served before such discovery shall not be reckoned. If a game shall have been completed before such discovery, the order of service remains as altered.

16. When Players Change Ends
The players shall change ends at the end of the first, third and every subsequent alternate game of each set, and at the end of each set unless the total number of games in such set is even, in which case the change is not made until the end of the first game of the next set. If a mistake is made and the correct sequence is not followed, the players must take up their correct station as soon as the discovery is made and follow their original sequence.

17. The Ball in Play
A ball is in play from the moment at which it is delivered in service. Unless a fault or a let is called it remains in play until the point is decided.

18. Server Wins Point
The server wins the point:

(*a*) If the ball served, not being a let under Rule 14, touches the receiver or anything which he wears or carries, before it hits the ground.

(*b*) If the receiver otherwise loses the point as provided by Rule 20.

19. Receiver Wins Point
The Receiver wins the point:

(*a*) If the server serves two consecutive faults.

(*b*) If the server otherwise loses the point as provided by Rule 20.

20. Player Loses Point
A player loses the point if:

(*a*) He fails, before the ball in play has hit the ground twice consecutively, to return it directly over the net, except as provided in rule 24(*a*) or (*c*).

(*b*) He returns the ball in play so that it hits the ground, a permanent fixture, or other object, outside any of the lines which bound his opponent's court, except as provided in Rule 24(*a*) or (*c*).

(*c*) He volleys the ball and fails to make a good return even when standing outside the court.

(*d*) In playing the ball he deliberately carries or catches it on his racket or deliberately touches it with his racket more than once.

(*e*) He or his racket (in his hand or otherwise) or anything which he wears or carries touches the net, posts, singles sticks, cord or metal cable, strap or band, or the ground within his opponent's court at any time while the ball is in play.

(*f*) He volleys the ball before it has passed the net.

(*g*) The ball in play touches him or anything that he wears or carries, except his racket in his hand or hands.

(*h*) He throws his racket at and hits the ball.

(*i*) He deliberately and materially changes the shape of his racket during the playing of the point.

21. Player Hinders Opponent
If a player commits any act which hinders his opponent in making a stroke, then, if this is deliberate, he shall lose the point or if involuntary, the point shall be replayed.

22. Ball Falls on Line
A ball falling on a line is regarded as falling in the court bounded by that line.

23. Ball Touches Permanent Fixture
If the ball in play touches a permanent fixture (other than the net, posts, singles sticks, cord or metal cable, strap or band) after it has hit the ground, the player who struck it wins the point; if before it hits the ground, his opponent wins the point.

24. A Good Return
It is a good return:

(*a*) If the ball touches the net, posts, singles sticks, cord or metal cable, strap or band, provided that it passes over any of them and hits the ground within the court.

(*b*) If the ball, served or returned, hits the ground within the proper court and rebounds or is blown back over the net, and the player whose turn it is to strike reaches over the net and plays the ball, provided that neither he nor any part of his clothes or racket touches the net, posts, singles sticks, cord or metal cable, strap or band or the ground within his opponent's court, and that the stroke be otherwise good.

(*c*) If the ball is returned outside the posts, or singles sticks, either above or below the level of the top to the net, even though it touches the posts or singles sticks, provided that it hits the ground within the proper court.

(*d*) If a player's racket passes over the net after he has returned the ball, provided the ball passes the net before being played and is properly returned.

(*e*) If a player succeeds in returning the ball, served or in play, which strikes a ball lying in the court.

Note: In a singles match, if, for the sake of convenience, a doubles court is equipped with singles sticks for the purpose of a singles game, then the doubles posts and those portions of the net, cord or metal cable and the band outside such singles sticks shall at all times be permanent fixtures, and are not regarded as posts or parts of the net of a singles game.

A return that passes under the net cord between the singles stick and adjacent doubles posts without touching either net cord, net or doubles post, and falls within the court, is a good return.

25. Hindrance of a Player
In case a player is hindered in making a stroke by anything not within his control, except a permanent fixture of the court, or except as provided for in Rule 21, a let shall be called.

26. Score in a Game
If a player wins his first point, the score is called 15 for that player; on winning his second point, the score is called 30 for that player; on winning his third point, the score is called 40 for that player, and the fourth point won by a player is scored game for that player except as below:

If both players have won 3 points, the score is called deuce: and the next point won by a player is scored advantage for that player. If the same player wins the next point, he wins the game: if the other player wins the next point the score is again called deuce; and so on, until a player wins the 2 points immediately following the score at deuce, when the game is scored for that player.

27. Score in a Set

(*a*) A player (or players) who first wins 6 games wins a set; except that he must win by a margin of 2 games over his opponent and where necessary a set shall be extended until this margin is achieved.

(*b*) The tie-break system of scoring may be adopted as an alternative to the advantage set system in paragraph (*a*) of this Rule, provided the decision is announced in advance of the match.

In this case, the following Rules shall be effective:

The tie-break shall operate when the score reaches 6 games all in any set, except in the third or fifth set of a three-set or five-set match respectively when an ordinary advantage set shall be played, unless otherwise decided and announced in advance of the match.

The following system shall be used in a tie-break game.

Singles

(i) A player who first wins 7 points shall win the game and the set, provided he leads by a margin of 2 points. If the score reaches 6 points all the game shall be extended until this margin has been achieved. Numerical scoring shall be used throughout the tie-break game.

(ii) The player whose turn it is to serve shall be the server for the first point. His opponent shall be the server for the second and third points and thereafter each player shall serve alternately for 2 consecutive points until the winner of the game and set has been decided.

(iii) From the first point, each service shall be delivered alternately from the right and left courts, beginning from the right court. If service from a wrong half of the court occurs and is undetected, all play resulting from such wrong service or services shall stand, but the inaccuracy of station shall be corrected immediately is is discovered.

(iv) Players shall change ends after every 6 points and at the conclusion of the tie-break game.

(v) The tie-break game shall count as one game for the ball change, except that, if the balls are due to be changed at the beginning of the tie-break, the change shall be delayed until the second game of the following set.

Doubles

In doubles the procedure for singles shall apply. The player whose turn it is to serve shall be the server for the first point. Thereafter each player shall serve in rotation for 2 points, in the same order as previously in that set, until the winners of the game and set have been decided.

Rotation of Service

The player (or pair in the case of doubles) who served first in the tie-break game shall receive service in the first game of the following set.

28. Maximum Number of Sets

The maximum number of sets in a match shall be five, or, where women take part, three.

29. Role of Court Officials

In matches where an Umpire is appointed, his decision shall be final; but where a Referee is appointed, an appeal shall lie to him from the decision of an Umpire on a question of Law, and in all such cases the decision of the Referee shall be final.

In matches where assistants to the Umpire are appointed (Linesmen, Net-cord Judges, Foot-fault Judges) their decisions shall be final on questions of fact, except that if in the opinion of an Umpire a clear mistake has been made he shall have the right to change the decision of an assistant or order a let to be played. When such an assistant is unable to give a decision, he shall indicate this immediately to the Umpire who shall give a decision. When an Umpire is unable to give a decision on a question of fact he shall order a let to be played.

In Davis Cup matches or other team competitions where a Referee is on court, any decision can be changed by the Referee, who may also instruct an Umpire to order a let to be played. The Referee, in his discretion, may at any time postpone a match on account of darkness or the condition of the ground or the weather. In any case of postponement the previous score and previous occupancy of courts shall hold good, unless the Referee and the players unanimously agree otherwise.

30. Continuous Play and Rest Periods

Play shall be continuous from the first service until the match is concluded, in accordance with the following provisions.

(a) If the first service is a fault, the second service must be struck by the server without delay. The receiver must play to the reasonable pace of the server and must be ready to receive when the server is ready to serve.

When changing ends a maximum of 1 minute 30 seconds shall elapse from the moment the ball goes out of play at the end of the game to the time the ball is struck for the first point of the next game.

The Umpire shall use his discretion when there is interference which makes it impractical for play to be continuous. The organisers of international circuits and team events recognised by the ITF may determine the time allowed between points, which shall not at any time exceed 30 seconds.

(b) Play shall never be suspended, delayed or interfered with for the purpose of enabling a player to recover his strength, breath, or physical condition. However, in the case of accidental injury, the Umpire may allow a one-time 3-minutes suspension for that injury. The organisers of international circuits and team events recognised by the ITF may extend the one-time suspension period from 3 minutes to 5 minutes.

(*c*) If, through circumstances outside the control of the player, his clothing footwear or equipment (excluding racket) becomes out of adjustment in such a way that it is impossible or undesirable for him to play on, the Umpire may suspend play while the maladjustment is rectified.

(*d*) The Umpire may suspend or delay play at any time as may be necessary and appropriate.

(*e*) After the third set, or when women take part the second set, either player is entitled to a rest, which shall not exceed 10 minutes, or in countries situated between latitude 15 degrees north and latitude 15 degrees south, 45 minutes, and furthermore, when necessitated by circumstances not within the control of the players, the Umpire may suspend play for such a period as he may consider necessary. If play is suspended and is not resumed until a later day, the rest may be taken only after the third set (or when women take part the second set) of play on such a later day, completion of an unfinished set being counted as one set.

If play is suspended and is not resumed until 10 minutes have elapsed in the same day, the rest may be taken only after three consecutive sets have been played without interruption (or when women take part two sets), completion of an unfinished set being counted as one set.

Any nation and/or committee organising a tournament, match or competition, other than the international Tennis Championships (Davis Cup and Federation Cup), is at liberty to modify this provision or omit it from its regulations, provided this is announced before the event commences.

(*f*) A tournament committee has the discretion to decide the time allowed for a warm-up period prior to a match but this may not exceed 5 minutes and must be announced before the event commences.

(*g*) When approved point penalty and non-accumulative point penalty systems are in operation, the Umpire shall make his decisions within the terms of those systems.

(*h*) Upon violation of the principle that play shall be continuous, the Umpire may, after giving due warning, disqualify the offender.

31. Coaching

During the playing of a match in a team competition, a player may receive coaching from a captain who is sitting on the court only when he changes ends at the end of a game, but not when he changes ends during a tie-break game. A player may not receive coaching during the playing of any other match. The provisions of this rule must be strictly construed.

After due warning an offending player may be disqualified. When an approved point penalty system is in operation, the Umpire shall impose penalties according to that system.

Note: The word 'coaching' includes any advice or instruction.

32. Changing Balls
In cases where balls are to be changed after a specified number of games, if the balls are not changed in the correct sequence, the mistake shall be corrected when the player, or pair in the case of doubles, who should have served with new balls is next due to serve. Thereafter the balls shall be changed so that the number of games between changes shall be that originally agreed.

THE DOUBLES GAME

33. The Doubles Game
The above Rules shall apply to the doubles game except as below.

34. The Doubles Court
For the doubles game, the court shall be 36ft (10.97m) in width, i.e. 4½ft (1.37m) wider on each side than the court for the singles game, and those portions of the singles side-lines which lie between the two service-lines shall be called the service side-lines. In other respects, the court shall be similar to that described in Rule 1, but the portions of the singles side-lines between the base-line and service-line on each side of the net may be omitted if desired.

35. Order of Service in Doubles
The order of serving shall be decided at the beginning of each set as follows:

The pair who have to serve in the first game of each set shall decide which partner shall do so and the opposing pair shall decide similarly for the second game. The partner of the player who served in the first game shall serve in the third; the partner of the player who served in the second game shall serve in the fourth, and so on in the same order in all the subsequent games of a set.

36. Order of Receiving in Doubles
The order of receiving the service shall be decided at the beginning of each set as follows:

The pair who have to receive the service in the first game shall decide which partner shall receive the first service, and that partner shall continue to receive the first service in every odd game throughout that set. The opposing pair shall likewise decide which partner shall receive the first service in the second game and that partner shall continue to receive the first service in every even game throughout that set. Partners shall receive the service alternately throughout each game.

37. Service Out of Turn in Doubles
If a partner serves out of his turn, the partner who ought to have served shall serve as soon as the mistake is discovered, but all points scored, and any faults served before such discovery, shall be reckoned. If a game shall have been completed before such discovery, the order of service remains as altered.

38. Error in Order of Receiving in Doubles
If during a game the order of receiving the service is changed by the receivers, it shall remain as altered until the end of the game in which the mistake is discovered, but the partners shall resume their original order of receiving in the next game of that set in which they are receivers of the service.

39. Service Fault in Doubles
The service is a fault as provided for by Rule 10, or if the ball touches the server's partner or anything which he wears or carries; but if the ball served touches the partner of the receiver, or anything which he wears or carries, not being a let under Rule 14(*a*) before it hits the ground, the server wins the point.

40. Playing the Ball in Doubles
The ball shall be struck alternately by one or other player of the opposing pairs, and if a player touches the ball in play with his racket in contravention of this Rule, his opponents win the point.

Reprinted by permission of the International Tennis Federation. Copies of the complete Rules of Tennis, including additional Notes, Regulations for Making Tests and the Rules of Wheelchair Tennis, may be obtained from the Federation.

THE RULES OF

Volleyball

The Playing Area

The Playing Court

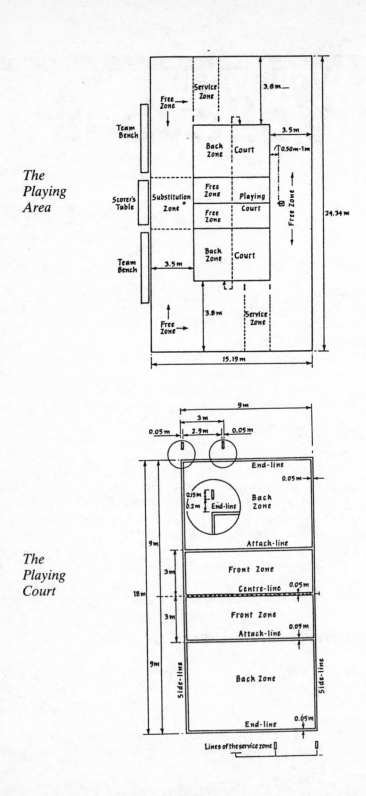

Volleyball

THE GAME

Volleyball is a team sport played by two teams of 6 players on a playing court divided by a net. The ball is played by hitting it with hands and arms. The object of the game is for each team to send the ball regularly over the net to ground it on the opponent's court, and to prevent the ball from being grounded on its own court.

The ball is put into play by the right back-row player, who serves, hitting the ball over the net to the opponent's court. A team is entitled to hit the ball three times (in addition to the block contact) to return it to the opponent's court. A player is not allowed to hit the ball twice consecutively (except when blocking). The rally continues until the ball touches the ground, goes out or a team fails to return it properly.

In volleyball, only the serving team may score a point (except in the deciding set). When the receiving team wins a rally, it gains the right to serve (also scoring a point in the deciding set) and its players rotate one position clockwise. Rotation ensures that players play both at the net and on the back court.

The team wins a set by scoring 15 points with a 2-point lead and wins the match by winning 3 sets. In the event of a 16-16 tie, the team scoring the 17th point wins the set with only a 1-point lead.

1. FACILITIES AND EQUIPMENT

1. PLAYING AREA

The playing area includes the playing court and the free zone.

1.1 Dimensions

1.1.1 The playing court is a rectangle measuring 18m × 9m, surrounded by a free zone a minimum of 3m wide and with a space free from any obstructions up to a height of a minimum of 7m from the playing surface.

1.1.2 For official international competitions, the free zone shall measure a minimum of 5m from the side-lines and of 8m from the end-lines. The free space shall measure a minimum of 12.5m in height from the playing surface.

1.2 Playing Surface

1.2.1 The surface must be flat, horizontal and uniform.

1.2.2 For official international competitions, only a wooden or synthetic surface is allowed. Any surface must be previously approved by the FIVB.

1.2.3 The playing surface must not present any danger of injury to the players. It is forbidden to play on rough or slippery surfaces.

1.2.4 On indoor courts the surface of the playing court must be of a light colour. For official international competitions, white colours for the lines, and other colours for the playing court and the free zone are required.

1.2.5 On outdoor courts, a slope of 5mm per metre is allowed for drainage.

Court lines made of solid materials are forbidden.

1.3 Lines on the Court

1.3.1 All lines are 5cm wide. They must be of a light and different colour from the floor and any other lines.

1.3.2 *Boundary lines.* Two side-lines and two end-lines mark the playing court. Both side-lines and end-lines are drawn inside the dimensions of the playing court.

1.3.3 *Centre Line.* The axis of the centre-line divides the playing court into two equal courts measuring 9m × 9m each. This line extends beneath the net from side-line to side-line.

1.4 Zones of the Playing Court

1.4.1 *Front Zone.* On each court the front zone is limited by the axis of the centre-line and the attack-line drawn 3m back from that axis (its width included). The front zone is considered to extend indefinitely beyond the side-lines.

1.4.2 *Service Zone.* The service zone is a 3m-wide area behind the end-line. It is laterally delimited by two short lines, each 15cm long drawn 20cm behind the end-line and perpendicularly to it, one as the extension of the right side-line and the other 3m to its left. Both are included in the width of the zone. In depth, the service zone extends to the edge of the free zone.

1.4.3 *Substitution zone.* The substitution zone is limited by the imaginary extension of both attack-lines up to the scorer's table.

1.5 Temperature
The minimum temperature shall not be below 10°C (50°F). For official international indoor competitions, the maximum temperature shall not be higher than 25°C (77°F) and the minimum not lower than 16°C (61°F).

1.6 Lighting
For official international indoor competitions, the lighting on the playing area should be 1000 to 1500 lux, measured at 1m above the playing surface.

2. NET AND POSTS

2.1 Net
The net is 1m in depth and 9.5m long, placed vertically over the axis of the centre-line. It is made of 10cm square black mesh. At its top there is a horizontal band, 5cm wide, made of two-fold white canvas and sewn along its full length. Each extreme end of the band has a hole through which passes a cord fastening the band to the posts to keep the top of the net taut. Within the band there is a flexible cable for fastening the net to the posts and keeping its top taut. At the bottom of the net (with no horizontal band) there is a rope, threaded through the meshes for fastening it to the posts and keeping the lower part of the net taut.

2.2 Side Bands
Two white bands, 5cm wide and 1m long, are fastened vertically to the net and placed above each side-line. They are considered as part of the net.

2.3 Antennae
An antenna is a flexible rod, 1.8m long and 10mm in diameter. It is made of fibre glass or similar material. Two antennae are fastened at the outer edge of each side band and placed on the opposite sides of the net. The top 80 cm of each antenna extend above the net and are marked with 10cm stripes of contrasting colours, preferable red and white. The antennae are considered as part of the net and laterally delimit the crossing space.

2.4 Height of the Net
2.4.1 The height of the net shall be 2.43m for men and 2.24m for women.
2.4.2 It is measured from the centre of the playing court with a

measuring rod. The two ends of the net (over the side-lines) must both be at the same height from the playing surface and may not exceed the official height by more than 2cm.

2.5 Posts

2.5.1 The posts supporting the net must be rounded and smooth, with a height of 2.55m, preferably adjustable.

2.5.2 They must be fixed to the ground at a distance of 0.50m–1m from each side-line. Fixing the posts to the ground by means of wires is forbidden. All dangerous or obstructing devices must be eliminated.

2.6 Additional Equipment

All additional equipment is determined by FIVB regulations.

3. THE BALL

3.1 Characteristics

The ball shall be spherical, made of a flexible leather case with a bladder inside made of rubber or a similar material.
- Colour: uniform and light.
- Circumference: 65–67cm.
- Weight: 260–280g.
- Inside pressure: 0.40–0.45kg/cm^2

3.2 Uniformity of Balls

All balls used in a match must have the same characteristics regarding circumference, weight, pressure, type etc. Official international competitions must be played with FIVB approved balls.

3.3 Three-ball System

For official international competitions 3 balls shall be used. In this case, 6 ball retrievers are stationed, one at each corner of the free zone and one behind each Referee.

2. PARTICIPANTS

4. TEAMS

4.1 Composition and registration

4.1.1 A team may consist of a maximum of 12 players, one coach, one assistant coach, one trainer and one medical doctor. For official international competitions, the medical doctor must be accredited beforehand by the FIVB.

4.1.2 Only the players recorded on the scoresheet may participate in the match.

4.1.3 Once the team captain and the coach have signed the score-sheet, the recorded players cannot be changed.

4.2 Captain
4.2.1 The team captain shall be indicated on the scoresheet.
4.2.2 The team captain is identified with a stripe of 8cm × 2cm, of a different colour to the shirt, underlining the number on his chest.
4.2.3 When the team captain is not on the court, the coach or the team captain himself will designate another player to act as the game captain.

5. PLAYERS' EQUIPMENT

5.1 Equipment
5.1.1 A player's equipment consists of a shirt, shorts and shoes.
5.1.2 Shirt and shorts must be uniform, clean and of the same colour.
5.1.3 Shoes must be light and pliable with rubber or leather soles without heels.
5.1.4 (*a*) Player's shirts must be numbered from 1 to 15 (preferably 1 to 12).
(*b*) The numbers must be placed in the centre of the front and back.
5.1.5 The numbers must be of a contrasting colour to the shirts and a minimum of 10cm in height on the chest and of 15cm on the back. The stripe forming the numbers shall be a minimum of 2cm wide.

5.2 Authorised Changes
5.2.1 If both teams arrive at a match dressed in shirts of the same colour, the home team must change. On a neutral site, the team listed first on the scoresheet shall change.
5.2.2 The First Referee may authorise one or more players:
– To play barefoot.
– To change wet shirts between sets or after substitution, provided that the colour, design and number of the new shirt(s) is (are) the same.
5.2.3 In cold weather, the First Referee may authorise the teams to play in training suits, provided that they are of the same colour and design for the whole team and properly numbered (Rule 5.1.4).

5.3 Forbidden Objects and Uniforms
5.3.1 It is forbidden to wear any object that may cause an injury to a player, such as jewellery, pins, bracelets, casts, etc.
5.3.2 Players may wear glasses at their own risk.
5.3.3 It is forbidden to wear uniforms without official numbers (Rules 5.1.4 and 5.1.5), or of a different colour from other players.

6. RIGHTS AND RESPONSIBILITIES OF THE PARTICIPANTS

6.1 Basic Responsibilities

6.1.1 Participants must know the Rules of the Game and abide by them.

6.1.2 Participants must accept Referees' decisions with sportsmanlike conduct, without disputing them. In case of doubt, clarification may be requested through the game captain and only through him.

6.1.3 Participants must behave respectfully and courteously in the spirit of *fair play*, not only towards the Referees, but also towards other officials, the opponents, team-mates and spectators.

6.1.4 Participants must refrain from actions or attitudes aimed at influencing the decisions of the Referees or covering up faults committed by their team.

6.1.5 Participants must refrain from actions aimed at delaying the game.

6.1.6 Both the team captain and the coach are responsible for the conduct and discipline of their team members.

6.1.7 Communication between team members during the match is permitted (Rule 6.3.4).

6.2 Captain

6.2.1 Prior to the match the team captain:

(*a*) Signs the scoresheet.

(*b*) Represents the team at the toss.

6.2.2 During the match the team captain functions as the game captain while on the court. The game captain is authorised to speak to the Referees while the ball is out of play (Rule 6.1.2):

(*a*) To ask for an explanation on the application or interpretation of the Rules. He also submits to the Referee involved the requests or questions of his team-mates. If the explanation does not satisfy him, he must immediately indicate to the Referee that he reserves the right to record his disagreement on the scoresheet as an official protest at the end of the match (Rule 26.2.4).

(*b*) To ask authorisation:

 – To change uniforms or equipment.

 – To verify the positions of the teams.

 – To check the floor, the net, the ball, etc.

(*c*) To request regular game interruptions (Rule 20.1).

6.2.3 At the end of the match, the team captain:

(*a*) Thanks the Referees and signs the scoresheet to ratify the outcome.

(*b*) If he previously expressed a disagreement to the First Referee, he may confirm it as a protest, recording it on the scoresheet (Rule 6.2.2*a*).

6.3 Coach

6.3.1 Prior to the match, the coach records or checks the names and numbers of his players on the scoresheet and then signs it.

6.3.2 Prior to each set, he gives the scorer or the Second Referee the line-up sheet duly filled in and signed.

6.3.3 During the match he must sit on the team bench nearest to the scorer (Rule 6.5.2).

6.3.4 During the match, the coach, as well as other members of the team, may give instructions to the players on the court but only while sitting on the bench or within the warm-up area, without disturbing or delaying the match.

6.4 Assistant Coach

6.4.1 The assistant coach sits on the team bench, but has no right to intervene in the match.

6.4.2 Should the coach have to leave his team, the assistant coach may assume his function, at the request of the game captain and with the authorisation of the First Referee.

6.5 Location of Participants

6.5.1 The team benches are located beside the scorer's table, outside the free zone.

6.5.2 The players not in play should sit on the team bench or stand in the warm-up area on their side of the court. The coach and other team members should sit on the bench.

6.5.3 Only team members are permitted to sit on the bench during the match and to participate in the warm-up session (Rule 4.1.1).

6.5.4 The players not in play may warm up without balls in the areas assigned to this purpose. The warm-up areas, sized approximately 3m × 3m, are located in the bench-side corners of the playing area, outside the free zone.

6.5.5 During the set intervals, balls may be used by the players in the free zone.

3. POINT, SET AND MATCH WINNER

7. SCORING SYSTEM

7.1 To Win a Match

7.1.1 A match is won by the team that wins 3 sets.

7.1.2 In the case of a 2-2 tie, the deciding (5th) set is played as a tie-break with the rally-point system (Rule 7.4).

7.2 To Win a Set

7.2.1 A set is won by the team that first scores 15 points with a minimum lead of 2 points. In the case of a 14-14 tie, the play is continued until a 2-point lead is reached (16-14, 17-15).

7.2.2 However, a point limit is reached at 17, i.e. after a 16-16 tie the team scoring the 17th point wins the set with only a point lead.

7.3 To Win a Rally

Whenever a team fails to serve or return the ball, or commits any other fault, the opposing team wins the rally, with one of the following consequences:

7.3.1 If the opposing team served, it scores a point and continues to serve.

7.3.2 If the opposing team received the service, it gains the right to serve without scoring a point (side-out).

7.4 To Win a Rally in the Deciding (5th) Set

In the deciding set, a point is scored when a team wins a rally, with one of the following consequences:

7.4.1 The serving team scores a point and continues to serve.

7.4.2 The receiving team gains the right to serve and scores a point.

7.5 Default and Incomplete Team

7.5.1 If a team refuses to play after being summoned to do so, it is declared in default and forfeits the match with the result 0–3 for the match and 0–15 for each set.

7.5.2 A team that, without justifiable reason, does not appear on the playing court on time is declared in default with the same result as in Rule 7.5.1.

7.5.3 A team declared *incomplete* for the set or for the match (Rules 9.3 and 11.4) loses the set or the match. The opposing team is given the points or, the points and the sets needed to win the set or the match. The incomplete team keeps its points and sets.

4. PREPARATION OF THE MATCH: STRUCTURE OF PLAY

8. PREPARATION OF THE MATCH

8.1 Toss

8.1.1 Before the warm-up, the First Referee carries out a toss in the presence of the two team captains.

The winner of the toss chooses:

– Either the right to serve or receive the service;

– Or the side of the court.

The loser takes the remaining alternative.

8.1.2 If a deciding (5th) set is to be played, the First Referee will carry out another toss.

8.2 Warm-up Session

8.2.1 Prior to the match, if the teams have previously had another playing court at their disposal, each team will have a 3-minute warm-up period at the net; if not, they may have 5 minutes each.

8.2.2 If both captains agree to warm up at the net together, the teams may do so for 6 to 10 minutes, according to Rule 8.2.1.

8.2.3 In the case of consecutive warm-ups, the team that has the first service takes the first turn at the net.

9. TEAM LINE-UP

9.1 Before the start of each set, the coach has to present the starting line-up of his team on a line-up sheet. This sheet is submitted, duly signed, to the Second Referee or the scorer (Rule 10.1.2). The players who are not in the starting line-up of a set are the substitutes for that set.

9.2 Rotation order as determined by the starting line-up has to be maintained throughout the set.

9.3 There must always be 6 players per team in play.

9.4 Once the line-up sheet has been delivered, no change in line-up is authorised.

9.5 If there is a discrepancy between the line-up sheet and actual positions of players, the players must move to the positions indicated on the line-up sheet before the start of the set. There will be no penalty. If one or more players on the court are not registered on the line-up sheet, the players on the court must be changed according to the line-up sheet, without penalty. However, if the coach wishes to keep such non-registered players(s) on the court, he has to request regular substitutions(s) which will then be recorded on the scoresheet.

10. PLAYERS' POSITIONS AND ROTATION

10.1 Positions

10.1.1 At the moment the ball is hit by the server, each team must be within its own court (except the server) in 2 rows of 3 players. These rows may be broken.

10.1.2 The 3 players along the net are front-row players and occupy positions 4 (left), 3 (centre) and 2 (right). The other 3 are back-row players occupying positions 5 (left), 6 (centre) and 1 (right). Each back-row player must be positioned further back from the net than the corresponding front-row player.

10.1.3 The positions of players are determined and controlled according to the positions of their feet contacting the ground as follows:

(*a*) Each front-row player must have at least a part of one foot closer to the net than the feet of the corresponding back-row player.

(*b*) Each right (left) side player must have at least a part of one foot closer to the right (left) side-line than the feet of the centre player of his row.

10.1.4 Once the ball has been served, the players may move around and occupy any position on their own court and in the free zone.

10.2 Rotation

When the receiving team has gained the right to serve, its players must rotate one position clockwise (player in position 2 rotates to position 1 to serve, player in 1 rotates to 6, etc.).

10.3 Positional Faults

10.3.1 The players of a team commit a fault if they are not in their correct positions at the moment the ball is hit by the server (Rule 10.1.1).

10.3.2 If the server commits a serving fault (Rule 17.8) at the moment of hitting the ball, his fault prevails over a positional fault and is thus penalised. If, after the ball has been hit, the service becomes a fault (Rule 17.9), it is a positional fault that will be penalised.

10.3.3 A positional fault leads to the following consequences:

– The fault is penalised with the loss of a rally (Rule 13.2.1);

– The players are returned to their correct positions.

10.4 Rotation Faults

10.4.1 A rotation fault is committed when the service is not made according to the rotation order (Rule 9.1). This corresponds to a positional fault; the error must be corrected and the team at fault penalised according to Rule 10.3.3.

10.4.2 The scorer should determine the exact moment the fault was committed. All points scored subsequently by the team at fault must be cancelled. The opponent's points remain valid. If the points scored while the player was out of position or out of service order cannot be determined, a penalty is the only sanction.

11. SUBSTITUTION OF PLAYERS

11.1 Definitions

A substitution is the act by which the Referees authorise a player to leave the court and another player to occupy his position.

11.2 Limitations of Substitutions

11.2.1 Six substitutions is the maximum permitted per team per set. One or more players may be substituted at the same time.

11.2.2 A player of the starting line-up may leave the game and re-enter, but only once in a set, and only to his previous position in the line-up.

11.2.3 A substitute player may enter the game only once per set, in place of a player of the starting line-up, and he can only be replaced by the same player.

11.3 Exceptional Substitution

An injured player who cannot continue playing should be legally substituted. If this is not possible, the team is entitled to make an *exceptional* substitution, beyond the limits of Rule 11.2.

11.4 Substitution for Expulsion

An *expelled* or *disqualified* player (Rule 24.2.3-4) must be replaced through a legal substitution. If that is not possible, the team is declared *incomplete* (Rule 7.5.3).

11.5 Illegal Substitution

11.5.1 A substitution is illegal if it exceeds the limitations indicated in Rule 11.2.

11.5.2 When a team makes an illegal substitution and the play is resumed (Rule 12.1), the following procedure shall apply:
– The fault is penalised with the loss of a rally;
– The substitution is rectified;
– The points scored by the team at fault after the fault was committed are cancelled. The opponent's points remain valid.

5. PLAYING ACTIONS

12. STATES OF PLAY

12.1 Ball in Play

The rally begins with the Referee's whistle. However, the ball is 'in play' from the service hit.

12.2 Ball Out of Play

The rally ends with the Referee's whistle. However, if the whistle is due to a fault made in play, the ball is 'out of play' the moment the fault was committed (Rule 13.2).

12.3 Ball 'In'

The ball is 'in' when it touches the floor of the playing court including the boundary lines (Rule 1.3.2).

12.4 Ball 'Out'

The ball is 'out' when it:

(*a*) Falls on the floor completely outside the boundary lines.

(*b*) Touches an object outside the court, the ceiling or a person out of play.

(*c*) Touches the antennae, ropes, posts or the net itself outside the antannae/sidebands.

(*d*) Crosses completely the vertical plane of the net, totally or even partly outside the crossing space (Rules 15.1.2 and 15.1.3).

13. PLAYING FAULTS

13.1 Definition

13.1.1 Any playing action contrary to the Rules is a playing fault.

13.1.2 The Referees judge the faults and determine the penalties according to these Rules.

13.2 Consequences of a Fault

13.2.1 There is always a penalty for a fault; the opponent of the team committing the fault wins the rally according to Rule 7.3, or Rule 7.4 in the deciding set.

13.2.2 If two or more faults are committed successively, only the first one is counted.

13.2.3 If two or more faults are committed by opponents simultaneously, a *double fault* is counted and the rally is replayed.

14. PLAYING THE BALL

14.1 Team Hits

14.1.1 The team is entitled to a maximum of three hits (in addition to blocking, Rule 19.2.1) for returning the ball over the net.

14.1.2 The hits of the team include not only intentional hits by the player, but also unintentional contacts with the ball.

14.1.3 A player may not hit the ball two times consecutively (except Rule 19.2.2).

14.2 Simultaneous Contacts

14.2.1 Two or three players may touch the ball at the same moment.

14.2.2 When two (three) team-mates touch the ball simultaneously, it is counted as two (three) hits (except at blocking). If two (three) team-mates reach for the ball but only one player touches it, one hit is counted. If players collide, no fault is committed.

14.2.3 If there are simultaneous contacts by opponents over the net and the ball remains in play, the team receiving the ball is entitled to another three hits. If such a ball goes 'out', it is the fault of the team on the opposite side. If simultaneous contacts by opponents lead to a 'held ball' it is a *double fault* (Rule 13.2.3) and the rally is replayed.

14.3 Assisted Hit

A player is not permitted to take support from a team-mate or any structure/object in order to reach the ball. However, the player who is about to commit a fault (touch the net to cross the centre-line etc.) may be stopped or held back by a team-mate.

14.4 Characteristics of the Hit

14.4.1 The ball may be touched with any part of the body above and including the waist.

14.4.2 The ball must be hit cleanly and not held (including lifted, pushed, carried or thrown). It can rebound in any direction.

14.4.3 The ball may touch various parts of the body, provided that the contacts take place simultaneously.

Exceptions:

(*a*) At blocking, consecutive contacts may occur with one or more blocker(s) provided that the contacts occur during one action.

(*b*) At the first hit of the team (19.2), unless it is played over-hand using fingers, the ball may contact various parts of the body consecutively, provided that the contacts occur during one action.

14.5 Faults in Playing the Ball

(*a*) *Four hits*: A team hits the ball four times before returning it (Rule 14.1.1).

(*b*) *Irregular hit*: The ball touches a player below his waist (Rule 14.4.1).

(*c*) *Assisted hit*: A player takes support from a team-mate or any structure/object in order to reach the ball (Rule 14.3).

(*d*) *Held ball*: A player does not hit the ball cleanly (Rule 14.4.2).

(*e*) *Double contact*: A player hits the ball twice in succession or the ball contacts various parts of his body successively (Rules 14.1.3 and 14.4.3).

15. BALL AT THE NET

15.1 Ball Crossing the Net

15.1.1 The ball sent to the opponent's court must go over the net within the crossing space. The crossing space is the part of the vertical plane of the net limited as follows:

– Below, by the top of the net;

– At the sides, by the antennae and their imaginary extension; and
– Above, by the ceiling.

15.1.2 A ball heading towards the opponent's side outside the crossing space may be played back, provided that it has not completely crossed the vertical plane of the net at the moment of contact.

15.1.3 The ball is 'out' when it crosses completely the lower space under the net.

15.2 Ball Touching the Net
While crossing the net (Rule 15.1.1), the ball may touch it except during the service.

15.3 Ball in the Net (other than the service ball)
15.3.1 A ball driven into the net may be recovered within the limits of the three team hits.

15.3.2 If the ball rips the mesh of the net or tears it down, the rally is cancelled and replayed.

16. PLAYER AT THE NET
Each team must play within its own court and playing space.

16.1 Reaching Over the Net
16.1.1 In blocking, a blocker may touch the ball beyond the net, provided that he does not interfere with the opponent's play before or during the latter's action (Rule 19.3).

16.1.2 A player is permitted to pass his hand beyond the net after his attack-hit, provided that his contact has been made within his own playing space.

16.2 Penetration Under the Net
16.2.1 It is permitted to penetrate into the opponent's space under the net, provided that this does not interfere with the opponent's play.

16.2.2 Penetration into the opponent's court:

(*a*) To touch the opponent's court beyond the centre-line with a foot or feet is permitted, provided that some part of the penetrating foot/feet remains either in contact with or directly above the centre-line.

(*b*) To contact the opponent's court with any other part of the body is forbidden.

16.2.3 A player may enter the opponent's court after the ball is out of play (Rule 12.2). A player may penetrate into the opponent's free zone, provided that he does not interfere with the opponent's play.

16.3 Contact With the Net
16.3.1 It is forbidden to touch any part of the net or the antenna.

16.3.2 Once the player has hit the ball, he may touch the posts, ropes or any other object outside the total length of the net provided that it does not interfere with play.

16.3.3 When the ball is driven into the net and causes it to touch an opponent, no fault is committed.

16.4 Player's Faults at the Net
It is a fault if:

(*a*) A player touches the ball in the opponent's space before or during the opponent's attack-hit (Rule 16.1.1).

(*b*) A player penetrates into the opponent's space under the net interfering with the latter's play (Rule 16.2.1).

(*c*) A player penetrates into the opponent's court (Rule 16.2.2).

(*d*) A player touches the net.

17. SERVICE

17.1 Definition
The service is the act of putting the ball into play by the right back-row player, placed in the service zone, who hits the ball with one hand or arm.

17.2 First Service in a Set
17.2.1 The first service of sets 1 and 5 is executed by the team that has obtained the right to serve at the toss (Rule 8.1).

17.2.2 The other sets will be started with the service of the team that did not serve first in the previous set.

17.3 Service Order
17.3.1 The players must follow the service order recorded on the line-up sheet (Rule 9.2).

17.3.2 After the first service in a set, the player to serve is determined as follows:

(*a*) When the serving team wins the rally, the player who served before, serves again.

(*b*) When the receiving team wins the rally, it gains the right to serve and rotates (Rule 10.2). The player who moves from the right front-row position to the right back-row position will serve.

17.4 Authorisation of the Service
The First Referee authorises the service after having checked that the server is in possession of the ball in the service zone and that the teams are ready to play.

17.5 Execution of the Service

17.5.1 The server may move freely within the service zone. At the moment of the service hit or take-off for a jump service, the server must not touch the court (the end-line included) or the ground outside the zone. After his hit, he may step or land outside the zone, or inside the court.

17.5.2 The server must hit the ball within 5 seconds after the First Referee whistles for service.

17.5.3 A service executed before the Referee's whistle is cancelled and repeated.

17.5.4 The ball shall be hit with one hand or any part of the arm after being tossed or released and before it touches the playing surface.

17.6 Service Attempt

17.6.1 If the ball, after having been tossed or released by the server, lands without touching him, it is considered a service attempt.

17.6.2 After a service attempt, the Referee must authorise the service again and the server must execute it within the next 5 seconds.

17.6.3 No further service attempt will be permitted.

17.7 Screening

The players of the serving team must not prevent their opponents, through screening, from seeing the server and the path of the ball.

17.7.1 A player of the serving team makes an individual screen if he waves his arms, jumps or moves sideways etc. when the service is being executed, and the ball is served over him.

17.7.2 A team makes a collective screen when the server is hidden behind a group of two or more team-mates, and the ball is served over them.

17.8 Serving Faults

The following faults lead to a change of service, even if the opponent is out of position.
The server:

(*a*) Violates the service order (Rule 17.3).

(*b*) Does not execute the service properly (Rule 17.5).

(*c*) Violates the rule of service attempt (Rule 17.6).

17.9 Serving Faults After Hitting the Ball

After the ball has been correctly hit, the service becomes a fault (unless a player is out of position) if the ball:

(*a*) Touches a player of the serving team or fails to cross the vertical plane of the net.

(*b*) Touches the net (Rule 15.2).

(*c*) Goes 'out' (Rule 12.4).
(*d*) Passes over an individual or collective screen (Rule 17.7).

18. ATTACK-HIT

18.1 Definition
18.1.1 All actions to direct the ball towards the opponent, except service and block, are considered to be attack-hits.
18.1.2 An attack-hit is completed the moment the ball completely crosses the vertical plane of the net or is touched by the blocker.

18.2 Front-Row Player's Attack-hit
The front-row player may carry out an attack-hit at any height provided that his contact with the ball has been made within his own playing space (except Rule 18.4*d*).

18.3 Restrictions to a Back-Row Player's Attack-hit
18.3.1 A back-row player may carry out an attack-hit at any height from behind the front zone. At his take-off his foot (feet) must neither have touched nor crossed over the attack line. After his hit he may land within the front zone (Rule 1.4.1).
18.3.2 A back-row player may also carry out an attack-hit from the front zone, if at the moment of contact any part of the ball is below the top of the net.

18.4 Attack-hit Faults
A player commits an attack-hit fault when:
(*a*) He hits the ball within the playing space of the opposing team.
(*b*) He hits the ball 'out' (Rule 12.4).
(*c*) As a back-row player, he completes an attack-hit from the front zone, if at the moment of the hit the ball is entirely above the top of the net (Rules 18.1.2 and 18.3.2).
(*d*) He completes an attack-hit on the opponent's service, when the ball is in the front zone and entirely above the top of the net.

19. BLOCK

19.1 Definition
Blocking is the action of players close to the net to intercept the ball coming from the opponents by reaching higher than the top of the net.
19.1.1 *Block attempt.* A block attempt is the action of blocking without touching the ball.
19.1.2 *Completed block.* A block is completed whenever the ball is

touched by a blocker. Only front-row players are permitted to complete a block.

19.1.3 *Collective block.* A collective block is executed by 2 or 3 players close to each other and is completed when one of them touches the ball.

19.2 Block and Team Hits

A block contact is not counted as a team hit (Rule 14.1.1).

19.2.1 After a block contact, a team is entitled to 3 hits to return the ball.

19.2.2 The first hit after the block may be executed by any player, including the one who has touched the ball at the block.

19.3 Blocking within the Opponents' Space

In blocking the player may place his hands and arms beyond the net, provided that his action does not interfere with the opponents' play. Thus, it is not permitted to touch the ball beyond the net until the opponent has executed an attack-hit.

19.4 Blocking Contact

19.4.1 Consecutive (quick and continuous) contacts may occur with one or more blockers provided that the contacts are made during one action.

19.4.2 These contacts may occur with any part of the body, above and including the waist.

19.5 Blocking Faults

(*a*) The blocker touches the ball in the opponent's space either before or simultaneously with the opponent's action (Rule 19.3).

(*b*) The ball touches the blocker below the waist (Rule 19.4.2).

(*c*) As a back-row player, he completes a block or participates in a completed one (Rules 19.1.2 and 19.1.3).

(*d*) He blocks the ball in the opponent's space from outside the antenna.

(*e*) He blocks the opponent's service.

(*f*) The ball is sent 'out' off the block.

6. INTERRUPTIONS AND DELAYS

20. REGULAR GAME INTERRUPTIONS

20.1 Categories

Regular game interruptions are for *time-outs* and *player substitutions*.

20.2 Number of Regular Interruptions
Each team is entitled to a maximum of 2 time-outs and 6 player substitutions per set.

20.3 Request for Regular Interruptions
Interruptions may be requested only by the coach or the game captain, when the ball is out of play and before the whistle for service, by showing the corresponding hand-signal.

20.4 Sequence of Interruptions
One or two time-outs and one request for player substitution by either team may follow one another, with no need to resume the game. A team is not authorised to request consecutive interruptions for player substitutions unless the game has been resumed. However, 2 or more players may be substituted during the same interruption (Rule 20.6.2).

20.5 Time-out
20.5.1 A time-out lasts for 30 seconds.

20.5.2 During a time-out, the players in play must go to the free zone near their bench.

20.6 Player Substitution
20.6.1 A substitution shall last only the time needed for recording the substitution on the scoresheet, and allowing the entry and exit of players.

20.6.2 If the coach intends to make more than one substitution, he must signal the number at the time of his request. In this case, substitutions must be made in succession, one pair of players after another.

20.6.3 At the moment of the request, the player(s) must be ready to enter, standing close to the coach (Rule 6.3.3). If that is not the case, the substitution is not granted and the team is sanctioned for a delay (Rule 21.2).

20.6.4 Substitutions must be carried out in the substitution zone (Rule 1.4.3).

20.7 Improper Requests
Among others, it is improper to request an interruption:

(*a*) During a rally or at the moment of, or after, the whistle to serve (Rule 20.3).

(*b*) By a non-authorised team-member (Rule 20.3).

(*c*) For player substitution before the game has been resumed from a previous substitution by the same team (Rule 20.4).

(*d*) After having exhausted the authorised number of time-outs and player substitutions (Rule 20.2).

Any improper request that does not delay the game shall be rejected without any sanction unless repeated in the same set (Rule 21.1*d*).

21. DELAYS TO THE GAME

21.1 Type of Delay
An improper action of a team that defers resumption of the game is a delay and includes:
(*a*) Delaying substitution.
(*b*) Prolonging other interruptions, after having been instructed to resume the game.
(*c*) Requesting an illegal substitution (Rule 11.2).
(*d*) Repeating an improper request in the same set (Rule 20.7).
(*e*) Delaying the game by a player in play.

21.2 Sanctions for Delays
21.2.1 The first delay by a team in a set is sanctioned with a *delay warning*.
21.2.2 The second and following delays of any type by the same team in the same set constitute a fault and are sanctioned with a *delay penalty*: loss of a rally.

22. EXCEPTIONAL GAME INTERRUPTIONS

22.1 Injury
22.1.1 Should a serious accident occur while the ball is in play, the Referee must stop the game immediately. The rally is then replayed.
22.1.2 If an injured player cannot be substituted, legally or exceptionally (Rule 11.3), the player is given a 3-minute recovery time, but not more than once for the same player in the match. If he does not recover, his team is declared incomplete (Rules 9.3 and 7.5.3).

22.2 External Interference
If there is any external interference during the game, play has to be stopped and the rally is replayed.

22.3 Prolonged Interruptions
If unforeseen circumstances interrupt the match, the First Referee, the organiser and the control committee, if there is one, shall decide the measures to be taken to re-establish normal conditions.
22.3.1 Should one or several interruptions occur, not exceeding 4 hours in total, then:
(*a*) If the match is resumed on the same playing court, the interrupted set shall continue normally with the same score, players and positions. The sets already played will keep their scores.

(*b*) If the match is resumed on another court, the interrupted set is cancelled and replayed with the same starting line-ups. The sets already played will keep their scores.

22.3.2 Should one or several interruptions occur, exceeding 4 hours in total, the whole match shall be replayed.

23. INTERVALS AND CHANGE OF COURTS

23.1 Intervals
The interval between all sets lasts 3 minutes. During this period of time, the change of courts and line-up registration of the teams on the scoresheet are made.

23.2 Change of Courts
23.2.1 After each set, the teams change courts, with the exception of the deciding set (Rule 8.1.2). Other team members change benches.

23.2.2 In the deciding set once a team reaches 8 points, the teams change courts without delay and the player positions remain the same. If the change is not made at the proper time, it will take place as soon as the error is noticed. The score at the time that the change is made remains the same.

7. MISCONDUCT

24. MISCONDUCT
Incorrect conduct by a team member towards officials, opponents, team-mates or spectators is classified in four categories according to the degree of the offence.

24.1 Categories
24.1.1 Unsportmanlike conduct: arguing, intimidation etc.

24.1.2 Rude conduct: acting contrary to good manners or moral principles, expressing contempt.

24.1.3 Offensive conduct: defamatory or insulting words or gestures.

24.1.4 Aggression: physical attack or intended aggression.

24.2 Sanctions
Depending on the degree of the incorrect conduct, according to the judgement of the First Referee, the sanctions to be applied are:

24.2.1 *Misconduct warning*: For unsportsmanlike conduct, no penalty is given but the team member concerned is warned against repetition in the same set. The warning is recorded on the scoresheet.

24.2.2 *Misconduct penalty*: For rude conduct, the team is penalised with the loss of a rally which is recorded on the scoresheet.

24.2.3 *Expulsion*: Repeated rude conduct is sanctioned by expulsion. The player must leave the playing court and is not permitted to play (or in the case of another team member, not allowed to carry out his function) for the rest of the set.

24.2.4 *Disqualification*: For offensive conduct and aggression, the player (or any other team member) must leave the playing area and the team bench for the rest of the match.

24.3 Sanction Scale

The repetition of misconduct by the same person in the same set is sanctioned progressively as shown in the sanction scale below. Disqualification due to offensive conduct or aggression does not call for a previous sanction.

Degree of Misconduct	Number of times	Sanction	Cards shown	Consequence
1. Unsportmanlike Conduct	First	Warning	Yellow	Warning: no penalty
	Second	Penalty	Red	Loss of a rally
	Third	Expulsion	Both jointly	Leave the playing court for the set
2. Rude Conduct	First	Penalty	Red	Loss of a rally
	Second	Expulsion	Both jointly	Leave the playing court for the set
3. Offensive conduct 4. Aggression	First	Disqualification	Both separately	Leave the playing court and the team bench for the match

24.4 Misconduct Before and Between Sets

Any misconduct occurring before or between sets is sanctioned according to Rule 24.2 and sanctions apply in the following set.

Reprinted by permission of the British Volleyball Federation. For reasons of space, Section II, concerning Referees and other officials, has been omitted. Copies of the complete Volleyball International Rules may be obtained from the English Volleyball Association.

THE RULES OF

Water Polo

Water Polo

1. Field of Play and Equipment

1.1 The promoting club or organisation shall be responsible for the correct measurements and markings of the field of play and shall provide all stipulated fixtures and equipment.

1.2 For dimensions and markings, see the diagram on page 885.

2. Goals

See Rule 9.3 on page 886.

3. The Ball

3.1 The balls for men's and women's water polo are to be round and fully inflated and with an air chamber with self-closing valve.

3.2 The balls are to be waterproofed without external strapping and without a covering of grease or similar substance.

3.3 For men's water polo, the pressure in the ball shall be 200kPa (kiloPascals; 13-14 psi atmospheric). The circumference must not be less than 0.68m nor more than 0.71m. The weight of the ball must not be less than 400g nor more than 450g.

3.4 For women's water polo, the pressure in the ball shall be 180kPa. The circumference must not be less than 0.65m nor more than 0.67m. The weight of the ball shall be the same as in men's water polo.

4. Flags

4.1 The Referees must be provided with a stick 0.70m long, fitted with a white flag on one end and a blue one on the other, each flag to be 0.35m × 0.20m.

4.2 Each Goal Judge must be provided with a red flag and a white one, each measuring 0.35m x 0.20m, mounted upon separate sticks which shall be 0.50m long. One of the Secretaries must be provided with a white flag and a blue one to signal re-entrance of excluded players, and the other one with a red flag with which to signal third personal fouls (Rule 25). These flags also shall be of the dimension prescribed above.

5. Caps

5.1 One team must wear dark blue and the other white caps, except goalkeepers, who must wear red caps. Caps must be tied with tapes under the chin. If a player loses his cap, it must be replaced at the next stoppage of the game. For Olympic Games, World Championships, and other FINA events caps must be fitted with malleable ear protectors, and it is recommended that they be used for all other competitions. The malleable ear protectors of the goalkeepers must be of the same colour as those of the team's field players' caps. The caps of the players may have in front the international three-letter country code and small national flag of minimum 0.04m of height each.

5.2 Caps must be numbered on both sides, numbers being 0.10m in height.

5.3 The goalkeeper shall wear cap No.1 and the other caps shall be numbered 2 to 13. A substitute goalkeeper shall wear the goalkeeper's cap. No player is allowed to change his cap number without the Referee's permission.

6. Teams

6.1 Each team shall consist of 7 players, one of whom will be the goalkeeper and wear the goalkeeper's cap, and no more than 6 reserves, who may be used as substitutes. Prior to taking part in a match the players must discard all articles likely to cause injury. The Referee shall satisfy himself that the players observe this condition. A player failing to comply must be dismissed from the game. Players must wear trunks with separate drawers or slips underneath. *Note*: When a player is dismissed from the game in accordance with WP 6.1, a substitute may immediately take his place.

6.2 Players shall not be allowed to have grease, oil, or any similiar composition of the body. If the Referee discovers before starting the game that such substance has been used, he must order the offending substance to be removed immediately. Should this offence be detected after the game has started, the player concerned must be ordered from the water for the whole game, and a substitute may enter immediately within 2m from the corner of the field of play at his own goal-line at the point nearest the Goal Judge (or on the side opposite the Timekeeper if there are no Goal Judges).

6.3 The captains must be playing members and be responsible for the good conduct and discipline of their respective teams.

6.4 Prior to the commencement of the game the captains must, in the presence of the Referee, toss for choice of ends or colours, the winner to have the choice of ends or colours.

6.5 While within the 4m area the goalkeeper is exempt from the following clauses of Rule 21:

Standing and walking (Rule 21.4).

Striking at the ball with clenched fist (Rule 21.6).

Jumping from the floor (Rule 21.8).

Touching the ball with both hands at the same time (Rule 21.10).

6.6 The goalkeeper must not go or touch the ball beyond the half-distance line. The penalty for his doing so is a free throw to the nearest opponent to be taken from where the offence occurred.

6.7 The goalkeeper may shoot at his opponents' goal as long as he is still within his half of the field of play (Rule 15.2).

6.8 When a goalkeeper is penalised for holding or pushing off from the bar, rail or trough at the end of the pool, a free throw must be taken from the 2m line opposite the point at which the foul occurred.

6.9 If a goalkeeper taking a free throw or goal throw releases the ball and before any other player has touched it regains possession and allows it to pass through his own goal, a corner throw must be awarded. If in the same circumstances, he releases the ball and after another player has touched it regains possession and allows it to pass through his own goal, a goal must be awarded.

7. Substitutes

7.1 A substitute shall not be allowed for a player who has been ordered from the water according to Rule 22.10 and Rule 22.1.6.2.

7.2 A substitute must be ready to replace a player without delay; if he is not ready the Referee may restart the game without him. In which case he may not take part in the match until the next stoppage.

7.3 In case of accident, illness, or injury a substitute takes his position in the water where the accident occurred and will take the free throw or corner throw which may have been awarded the injured player, but should there be no substitute, another player shall take the throw.

7.4 Should a goalkeeper retire from a game through accident, illness, or injury, Rule 26.2 shall apply. A goalkeeper who has been replaced by a substitute may, if he returns to the game, play anywhere.

7.5 The captain, coach, or team manager must notify the Referee of substitutions.

8. Officials

8.1 For Olympic Games and World Championships, the officials shall consist of two Referees, two Goal Judges, Timekeepers and Secretaries.

8.2 For all other competitions there must be at least a Secretary, a Timekeeper and either (*a*) two Referees, or (*b*) one Referee, and two Goal Judges. However, it is recommended that two Referees be used for all competitions. Each Timekeeper and Secretary may have assistants as needed.

8.3 The officials shall have powers and duties as specified below except that if a competition is held with two Referees and without Goal Judges, the Referees shall assume the duties specified for Goal Judges in Rule 10, except that it shall not be necessary for them to make any of the flag signals specified in those Rules.

9. Referees

9.1 The Referees are in absolute control of the game. Their authority over the players is effective during the whole of the time that they and the players are within the precincts of the pool.

9.2 Each must be provided with a shrill whistle with which to start and restart the game and to declare goals, goal throws, corner throws (whether signalled by the Goal Judge or not) and infringements of the Rules.

9.3 All decisions of the Referees on questions of fact are final and their interpretation of the rules must be obeyed during the game.

9.4 A Referee may refrain from declaring a foul if, in his opinion, such declaration would be an advantage to the offender's team. *Note*: it is important that the Referee shall apply this principle to the full extent; for example, to declare a foul in favour of a player who is in possession of the ball and making progress towards his opponent's goal, or whose team is in possession of the ball, is considered to give an advantage to the offender's team.

9.5 He may alter his decision providing he does so before the ball is again in play.

9.6 He has power to order any other player from the water in accordance with the appropriate Rules, and should a player refuse to leave the water when so ordered the game must be stopped. The Referee may order any player, official or spectator from the pool precincts if his behaviour prevents the Referee from carrying out his duties in a proper and impartial manner.

9.7 He may stop the game at any time if, in his opinion, the behaviour of the players or spectators or other circumstances prevent it being brought to a proper conclusion.

9.8 If the game has to be stopped, the Referee must report his actions to the competent authority.

10. Goal Judges

10.1 The Goal Judges must take up position opposite a Referee and they must mutually agree upon ends. They must stand directly level with the goal-line and stay there for the whole game.

10.2 Their duties are to signal with the white flag for a goal throw (Rule 17), with a red flag for a corner throw (Rule 18), with both flags for a goal (Rule 15) and with a red flag for an improper re-entry of an excluded player (See Rule 22.1.6 and Rule 22.4). Their further duty is to throw in a new ball when the original ball goes outside the field of play. Goal Judges shall each have a supply of balls. When the original ball goes out of the field of play in a manner resulting in a goal throw or corner throw, the Goal Judge shall give a new ball immediately to the goalkeeper for each goal throw or to the nearest member of the attacking team for each corner throw.

10.3 Goal Judges shall be responsible to the Referee for the correct score of each team at their respective ends.

10.4 Goal Judges should exhibit the red flag to indicate to the Referee that players are correctly positioned on their respective goal-lines, according to Rule 14, but the Referee's whistle to start or restart the game takes immediate effect.

11. Timekeepers

11.1 The Timekeepers must be fully acquainted with the Rules of Water Polo and each must be provided with a water polo stop-watch and a shrill whistle.

11.2 The duties of the Timekeepers shall be (a) to record on the watch the exact periods of actual play and the intervals between periods as provided by these Rules, (b) to record the respective periods of exclusion of any player or players who may be ordered from the water in accordance with these Rules and (c) to record the periods of continuous possession of the ball by each team (Rule 21.13).

11.3 The Timekeeper recording the 35 seconds shall reset the clock when the ball leaves the hand of the player shooting at the goal. He shall again recommence the time when a team gains possession of the ball; or if it goes out of the field of play, when the ball is put into play.

11.4 All signals to stop must be by whistle. Play is resumed when the ball leaves the hand of the player taking a free throw, goal throw, corner throw or penalty throw or when one player touches the ball after a neutral throw.

11.5 A Timekeeper must signal the end of each period, independently of the Referee. His signal takes immediate effect with the exceptions stated in Rule 21.13.5 and Rule 24.11. The last minute of any game and of any extra time shall be audibly announced.

11.6 The Timekeepers must be near a Referee.

12. Secretaries

The duties of Secretaries shall be:

12.1 To maintain a record of all players, the score, all exclusion and penalty fouls (time, colour and cap number), and to signal the award of a third personal foul (Rule 25) to any player, with a red flag and a whistle.

12.2 To control the periods of exclusion of players and to signal permission for re-entry upon expiration of their respective periods of exclusion by raising the flag corresponding with the colour of the player's cap.

12.3 To signal any improper entry (including after a flag signal by a Goal Judge of an improper re-entry), which signal stops play immediately

13. Duration of the Game

13.1 The duration of the game shall be 4 periods of 7 minutes each actual play. The teams shall change ends before commencing a new period. There shall be a 2 minute interval between periods. Time starts when a player touches the ball at the start of any period of the game. At all signals for stoppages the recording watch must be stopped until play is resumed.

13.2 Should there be level scores at full time in any game for which a definite result is required, any continuation into extra time must be after an interval of 5 minutes. There shall then be played 2 periods of 3 minutes each actual play, with an interval of 1 minute for changing ends.

13.3 After the first 2 periods of extra time, if there is still not a result, the subsequent period of time between each set of extra quarters will be 3 minutes with an interval of 1 minute for changing ends. This system of extra time shall be continued until a decision has been reached.

13.4 A player who has been ordered from the water by the Referee – but not for the rest of the game – shall resume with his team during extra time only when his penalty time has expired, a goal has been scored, or the defending team regains possession of the ball and put it into play, whichever time is the shortest.

14. The Start of Play

14.1 At the commencement of each period of play, the players must take up positions on their respective goal-lines, about 1m apart and at least 1m from either goal-post. More than two players are not allowed between the goal-posts.

14.2 When he has ascertained that the teams are ready, the Referee shall give the starting signal by a blast of his whistle and immediately afterwards release or throw the ball into the centre of the field of play.

15. Method of Scoring

15.1 A goal is scored by the ball passing fully over the goal-line, between the goal-posts and subject to the following conditions:

15.2 A goal may be scored by any part of the body, except the clenched fist, provided that at the start or restart of the game the ball has been played by 2 or more players. The team to which they belong or the place in the field of play from where the goal is scored is immaterial. The ball is played by 2 players if the ball is passed by 1 player at the start or restart of the game towards another player who then scores a goal.

15.3 Any attempt by the goalkeeper to stop the ball before it has been played in this way does not constitute 'playing' and should the ball cross the goal-line or hit the goal-post or goalkeeper, the goalkeeper must be awarded a goal throw.

15.4 Dribbling the ball through the goal posts is permissible.

15.5 Should a foul occur before the foregoing conditions have been complied with, Rules 20 to 25 operate.

16. Restarting after a Goal

16.1. After a goal has been scored, players must take up positions on their respective halves of the field of play, behind the half-distance line, when a player of the team not having scored shall restart the game from the centre of the field of play. Upon the Referee signalling by one blast of the whistle, the ball must be put into play, promptly, by passing it to another player of his team who must be behind the half-distance line when he receives it.

16.2 Actual play is resumed when the ball leaves the hand of the player making the restart.

16.3 A restart made improperly must be retaken.

16.4 When the start or restart is from the goal-line, no portion of a player's body, at water level, may be beyond the goal-line. When the restart is from the centre, no part of a player's body may be beyond the half-distance line.

17. Goal Throws

17.1 When the entire ball passes over the goal-line, excluding that portion between the goal-posts, having last been touched by one of the attacking team, a goal throw is awarded to the defending goalkeeper, to be taken from any place within the 2m area. See also Rules 20.8 and 21.14.

17.2 The Referee must signal a goal throw by whistle immediately upon the ball crossing the goal-line.

17.3 In the event of a goalkeeper's being out of the water, another player must take the throw from the place within the 2m area.

17.4 A goal throw taken improperly must be retaken, except as provided by Rule 21.16.

18. Corner Throws

18.1 When the entire ball passes over the goal-line, excluding that portion between the goal-posts, having last been touched by one of the defending team, a corner throw is awarded to the oppossing team, to be taken at the 2m mark on the side where the ball goes out.

18.2 Should the ball go out of the field of play between the goal-line and the 2m line, a corner throw must be taken from the 2m mark on the side where the ball went out.

18.3 The Referee must signal a corner throw by whistle immediately upon the ball crossing the goal-line.

18.4 A corner throw is taken from the 2m mark.

18.5 When a corner throw is taken, no attacking player may be within the 2m line.

18.6 Should a defending goalkeeper be out of the water when a corner throw is awarded, another player of his team may take up a position on the goal-line, but without the limitations and privileges of a goalkeeper.

18.7 If a goalkeeper taking a free throw or goal throw releases the ball and before any other player has touched it regains possession and allows it to pass through his own goal, a corner throw must be awarded.

18.8 A corner throw taken improperly must be retaken.

18.9 If a corner throw is taken before the attacking players have left the 2m area, the throw must be retaken.

18.10 If a player taking a free throw passes the ball towards his own goalkeeper and before any other player has touched it, the ball crosses the goal-line or enters the net, a corner throw must be awarded. An attempt by the goalkeeper to stop the ball is not regarded as 'touching' for the purposes of this Rule.

19. Neutral Throws

19.1 When one or more players of each team commit a foul at the same moment which makes it impossible for the Referee to distinguish which player offended first, he must take the ball and throw it into the water in such a manner that the players of both teams have an equal opportunity to reach the ball after it has touched the water. Rules 20.7 and 20.8 must be applied.

19.2 All neutral throws awarded within the 2m area are to be taken on the 2m line opposite the point at which the incident took place.

19.3 If from a neutral throw a Referee is of the opinion that the ball has fallen in a position to the advantage of one team, he must take the throw again.

19.4 Should the ball strike or lodge in an overhead obstruction, it must be considered out of play, and the Referee must stop the game and conduct a neutral throw. In that case, the ball may not be played until it has touched the water. Should the ball rebound from the goal-posts or cross-bar or from the side of the field of play at water level, it remains in play except as provided by Rules 15.3 and 20.8. If the ball rebounds from the side of the field of play above water level, it is considered to be out of play.

20. Free Throws

20.1 The Referee must blow his whistle to declare fouls and exhibit the flag corresponding in colour to the caps worn by the team to which the free throw is awarded.

20.2 A free throw awarded for a foul committed within the 2m area by a defending player must be taken from the 2m line opposite the point at which the foul occurred. With this exception, and the exception in Rule 18.2, free throws are to be taken from the point at which the foul occurred. Should the game be stopped through illness, or accident, or other unforeseen reason, the team in possession of the ball at the time is awarded a free throw at that point when time is resumed.

20.3 The responsibility for returning the ball to the player who is to take the free throw is primarily that of the side to which the free throw is awarded. The opponents have no duty to do this but no player may deliberately throw the ball away to prevent the normal progress of the game. See also Rule 22.1.5.

20.4 A goalkeeper awarded a free throw must take the throw himself, and the throw is subject to the limitation and privileges of a goalkeeper.

20.5 A free throw must be made to enable other players to observe the ball leaving the hand of the thrower. It is permitted to dribble the ball before passing to another player.

20.6 As soon as the ball leaves the hand of a player taking a free throw it is in play. In the meantime all players are allowed to change position.

20.7 Except as provided by Rule 6.9 in all cases of a free throw, corner throw or neutral throw at least 2 players (excluding the defending goalkeeper) must play or touch the ball before a goal can be scored. *Ruling*: To touch the ball means to touch intentionally.

20.8 Except as provided by Rule 6.9, an attempt by the goalkeeper to stop the ball from an attacking player before it has been touched or played by a second player is not regarded as touching, and should the ball cross the goal-line or hit the goal-posts or the goalkeeper, the goalkeeper must be awarded a goal throw.

20.9 A free throw taken improperly must be retaken, except as provided by Rule 21.16.

20.10 Should a player send the ball out of the field of play at either side, a free throw is awarded to the opposing team, to be taken at the point where the ball left the field of play, except when Rule 18.2 applies.

21. Ordinary Fouls

Except as provided by Rules 6.8 or 20.2, the punishment for an ordinary foul shall be a free throw to the opposing team to be taken by any one of its players. The following shall be ordinary fouls, except for goalkeepers (See Rule 6.5):

21.1 To advance beyond the goal-line at the start or restart of the game, before the Referee has given the signal.

21.2 To assist a player at the start or restart or during a game.

21.3 To hold on to, or push off from the goal-posts or their fixtures. To hold on to the rails, except at start or restart, to hold on to, or push off from, the sides or ends during actual play.

21.4 To take any active part in the game when standing on the floor of the pool; to walk when play is in progress.

21.5 To take or hold the ball under water when tackled.

21.6 To strike at the ball with clenched fist.

21.7 To touch the ball before it reaches the water when thrown in by the Referee.

21.8 To jump from the floor of the pool to play the ball or tackle an opponent.

21.9 To deliberately impede or prevent the free movement of an opponent unless he is holding the ball. Swimming on the shoulders, back or legs of an opponent constitutes impeding. 'Holding' is lifting, carrying or touching the ball. Dribbling the ball is not considered to be holding.

21.10 To touch the ball with both hands at the same time.

21.11 To push, or push off from an opponent.

21.12 To be within 2m of the opponents' goal-line or to remain there except when behind the line of the ball. *Ruling*: It is not an offence if the player taking the ball into the 2m area passes the ball to his associate who is behind the line of the ball and who shoots at goal immediately before the first player can leave the 2m area.

21.13 To waste time.

21.13.1 For a team to retain possession of the ball for more than 35 seconds without shooting at their opponents' goal is deemed to be wasting time, and a free throw shall be awarded against the player last having touched the ball before this foul is signalled.

21.13.2 Should a team shoot at goal as above and regain possession upon the ball rebounding or being in any other manner kept in play, the measurement of 35 seconds shall immediately recommence from 35.

21.13.3 Time recommences from 35 when the ball comes into the possession of the opposing team, or immediately the ball is put into play after an exclusion foul. *Ruling*: The ball does not leave the possession of the holding team merely by being touched in flight by an opponent player, provided that it is not deflected into the possession of the opposing team.

21.13.4 Time recommences when the ball comes into the possession of a team as the result of a neutral throw.

21.13.5 If at the expiration of the 35 seconds or at the end of the periods, the ball is in flight and crosses the goal-line between the goal-posts, the resultant goal shall be allowed.

21.13.6 At expiration of the 35 seconds the free throw shall be taken by the opposing player nearest the point at which the game is stopped and undue delay by any member of the penalised team shall be punished as an exclusion foul.

21.13.7 It is always permissible for the Referee to penalise a foul under Rule 21.13 before the period of 35 seconds has expired.

21.13.8 There should be at least two 35-second clocks placed at diagonal corners of the field of play. They shall be at the corners beside the Goal Judges.

21.14 For the goalkeeper to go or touch the ball outside his own half of the field of play.

21.15 To take a penalty throw otherwise than in the prescribed manner.

21.16 To delay unduly when taking a free throw, a goal throw, or a corner throw. The time allowed for a player to take such a throw is left to the discretion of the Referee. It must be reasonable and without undue delay but does not have to be immediate.

22. Exclusion Fouls

22.1 It is an exclusion foul for a player:

22.1.1 To hold, sink or pull back an opponent not holding the ball.

22.1.2 To kick or strike an opponent or make disproportionate movements with that intent.

22.1.3 To splash in the face of an opponent intentionally.

22.1.4 To be guilty of misconduct. Misconduct is violence, the use of foul language, persistent foul play etc. (This is deemed to be an offence against Rule 22.9.)

22.1.4.1 A player must not leave the water or sit or stand on the steps or side of the pool during a game except:

(*a*) During an interval;

(*b*) In case of illness or accident; or

(*c*) By permission of the Referee.

22.1.4.2 A player infringing Rule 22.1.4.1 must be deemed guilty of misconduct. A player having left the water legitimately may re-enter at his own goal-line at the point nearest the Goal Judge by permission of the Referee.

22.1.5 To interfere with the taking of a free throw, goal throw, corner throw, or penalty throw. Interference includes:

(*a*) Deliberately throwing away the ball to prevent the normal progress of the game.

(*b*) Any attempt to play the ball before it leaves the hand of the thrower.

22.1.6 For an excluded player to re-enter or a substitute to enter the water improperly.

22.1.6.1 Improper entry is to enter or re-enter:

(*a*) Without permission of the secretary at the expiration of the 20-seconds expulsion time.

(*b*) Without being waved in by the defensive Referee in accordance with the provisions of Rule 22.3.

(*c*) By jumping or pushing off from the side or wall of the pool or field of play.

(*d*) From any place other than prescribed by Rule 22.4.

22.1.6.2 When this offence occurs during the last minute of the final quarter of any game, or during the last minute of any of the 2 periods of extra time (Rule 13.2) the offender shall be excluded for the remainder of the game without substitution and a penalty throw shall be awarded to the opposing team.

22.1.6.3 Entry at any time of a player not entitled under the Rules to participate at that time (except for a player awaiting the passage of 20-second exclusion period to be entitled to participate) shall cause such player to be excluded from the remainder of the game with immediate substitution when appropriate, and one penalty throw will be awarded to the opposing team.

22.1.6.4 At any time when a player awaiting the passage of an expulsion period enters illegally with the object of preventing a goal, it is deemed to constitute a violation of Rule 23, and after the player has left the water to complete the original exclusion period, a penalty throw shall be awarded to the opposing team. This penalty takes precedence over the penalty otherwise provided under Rule 22.1.6 (exclusion or penalty throw). If the attacking team will be able to shoot at goal, the Referee should wait to see if a goal is scored before awarding the penalty and excluding the player. If the goal is scored, no penalty is awarded but the offending player is to be awarded with a personal fault (except in the circumstances of Rule 22.1.6.2). Play shall recommence in the normal fashion.

22.2 Except as otherwise expressly provided in these Rules, the punishment for an exclusion foul is exclusion from the field of play. The offender shall be excluded from the field of play until the earliest occurrence of the following:

(*a*) After expiration of 20 seconds actual play;

(*b*) When a goal is scored; or

(*c*) When the defending team retakes possession of the ball or restarts play after a stoppage of play.

22.3 A free throw is to be taken by a player of the opposing team after the excluded player has commenced to leave the field of play and the Referee has signalled the free throw to be taken. The penalty period will start upon the taking of the free throw. If the player leaving the field of play intentionally interferes with the play, it shall constitute a penalty foul and a penalty throw shall be awarded. Upon a change of possession, referred to above, all players excluded for 20 seconds re-enter immediately upon the signal of the defensive Referee. A change of possession does not occur merely because of the end of a period. This depends on the result of the start of the next period.

22.4 After expiration of time the excluded player himself or a member of his team may re-enter within 2m from the corner of the field of play on the side of the Goal Judge (or where the Goal Judge ought to be) under his goal-line and without affecting the alignment of the goals. This Rule takes priority over all others in regard to the re-entry of excluded players.

22.5 In the case of simultaneous exclusion fouls by members of both teams, the offending players shall be excluded and a neutral throw be taken. Both excluded players will return at the earliest occurrence of the following:

(*a*) After expiration of 20 seconds actual play;

(*b*) When a goal is scored; or

(*c*) When the defending team retakes possession of the ball or restarts play after a stoppage of play.

22.6 If before a free throw, corner throw, goal throw, neutral throw or penalty throw is taken, an offence against Rules 21.9, 21.11, or 22 is committed by a member of the team not in possession of the ball, the offender shall be ordered from the water for a period of 20 seconds actual play, until a goal is scored, or until the attacking team loses possession of the ball, whichever period is shortest and the original throw maintained. If a member of the team in possession of the ball commits an offence described in Rule 22.6, a free throw shall be awarded to the opposing team (except where a penalty throw had been awarded it shall be maintained).

22.7 If in the circumstances of Rule 22.6 simultaneous exclusion fouls are committed by players from opposing teams, both players shall be excluded from the water for a period of 20 seconds actual play, until a goal is scored, or until the attacking team loses possession of the ball, whichever period is the shortest, and the original free throw shall be maintained.

22.8 In the special circumstances described in Rule 22.7, an offence committed by a player of either team against Rules 21.9 or 21.11 shall be deemed to be an exclusion foul and a personal foul shall be recorded against the player having committed the offence.

22.9 To refuse obedience to, or show disrespect for the officials. The offender shall be excluded from the remainder of the game and a substitute may enter the game at his own goal-line at the point nearest the Goal Judge at the earliest occurrence of the following:

(*a*) After expiration of 20 seconds actual play;

(*b*) When a goal is scored; or

(*c*) When the defending team retakes possession of the ball or restarts play after a stoppage of play.

It shall be deemed to be disobedience if a player excluded under Rule 22.2 (who is to re-enter in accordance with Rule 22.2) removes himself from the water (unless in accordance with Rule 26.1). The Referee may punish a goalkeeper by exclusion for the time provided in Rule 22.2 if he disobeys his instruction to comply with Rule 24.7.

22.10 To commit an act of brutality against another player or an official. A free throw *must* be awarded to the opponent team and the offending player *must* be excluded from the remainder of the game and *must not be substituted*. Brutality includes deliberately striking or kicking or deliberately attempting to strike or kick.

23. Penalty Fouls

It shall be a penalty foul to commit any foul within the 4m area, but for which a goal would probably have resulted.

23.1 In addition to other offences, it is an exclusion foul to pull down the goal, or to play the ball with clenched fist or with both hands in the 4m area with the object of preventing a goal from being scored. A penalty throw must be awarded.

23.2 When the goalkeeper or any other player pulls over the goal completely with the object of preventing a goal, the player has shown disrespect and must be excluded from the remainder of the game (Rule 22.9). A substitute may enter the game within 2m from the corner of the field of play on the side of the Goal Judge (or on the side opposite the

Timekeeper if there are not Goal Judges), under his goal-line after the expiration of 20 seconds of actual play, when a goal has been scored, or when the attacking team loses possession of the ball, whichever period is the shortest. The exclusion of this offending player is in addition to awarding the penalty throw.

24. Penalty Throws

24.1 Should a player be fouled within his opponent's 4m area according to Rules 22.1.2 or 22.10 or commit a foul according to Rules 23, 22.1.6.2 or 22.3, a penalty throw *must* be awarded against the offender's team. The Referee must announce the offender's number to the Secretary.

24.2 When a penalty throw is awarded the offending player shall be ordered from the water only if the offence is so serious as to justify ordering from the water for the remainder of the game (See Rules 22.10, 22.1.6.2 and 25.1).

24.3 A penalty throw may be executed by any player of the team to which it is awarded, except the goalkeeper, and the player taking the throw may elect to do so from any point on his opponent's 4m line.

24.4 The player taking a penalty throw must await the signal of the Referee which shall be given by whistle and by simultaneously lowering the respective flag from a vertical to a horizontal position. The player must have possession of the ball and immediately throw it with an uninterrupted movement directly at the goal (see Rule 21.15). Should the ball rebound from the goal-posts or cross-bar it remains in play and it is not necessary for the ball to be played by any other player before a goal can be scored.

24.5 A penalty throw may commence by lifting the ball from the water or with the ball held in the raised hand. It is permissible for the ball to be taken backwards from the direction of the goal in preparation for the forward throw at the goal, but the throw shall commence immediately upon the signal, and continuity of the movement shall not be broken before the ball leaves the thrower's hand.

24.6 All players except the defending goalkeeper, or the other player according to Rule 24.8, must leave the 4m area until a penalty throw is taken, and no player may be within 2m of the player taking the throw.

24.7 The goalkeeper must taken a position anywhere on the goal-line and the Referee will withhold the signal to throw until satisfied on this point. *Ruling*: No portion of the goalkeeper's body, at water level, may be beyond the goal-line.

24.8 Should the defending goalkeeper be ordered from the water before or after the award of a penalty throw, another player of his team may take a position on the goal-line before the throw is taken, but without the privileges and limitations of a goalkeeper.

24.9 A player must take a penalty throw as described. The penalty for not complying shall be a free throw to the player's nearest opponent.

24.10 If the taking of a penalty throw is interfered with or Rules 24.6 and 24.7 are not complied with, the offenders must be punished in accordance with Rule 22.9 and the throw must be retaken.

24.11 If, at precisely the same time as the Referee awards a penalty throw or before a penalty throw is completed, the timekeeper whistles for an interval, or full time, the shot at goal must be allowed and should the ball rebound into the field of play from the goal-post, cross-bar or goalkeeper, it is dead. (*Note*: When a penalty throw is to be taken in accordance with this Rule 24.11, all players except the defending goalkeeper and the player taking the penalty throw shall leave the water.)

25. Personal Fouls

25.1 A player committing an exclusion foul anywhere in the field of play shall be awarded a personal foul, and upon being awarded a third such personal foul in any one game he shall be excluded from the remainder of the game, and a substitute may enter at his own goal-line at the point nearest to the Goal Judge after expiration of the exclusion time under the Rules.

25.2 If such a third personal foul results from a foul requiring the award of a penalty throw, the entry of the substitute shall be immediate and before the penalty throw is taken.

26. Accident, Injury and Illness

26.1 In the case of accident or illness, the Referee may, at his discretion, suspend the game for not more than 3 minutes. It shall be the duty of the Referee to instruct the Timekeeper when any 3-minute stoppage for injury shall commence.

26.2 In the event of a player retiring from the game through any medical reason, the Referee may permit his immediate substitution by a reserve. The player so retiring shall not be allowed at any time to re-enter the game. Otherwise a player may be substituted only:

(1) in accordance with provisions of Rules 6.1, 6.2, 22.9, or 25;

(2) During the interval between periods of play;

(3) After a goal has been scored; or

(4) Prior to the commencement of extra time.

During extra time the provisions of (1), (2), and (3) above shall apply.

AGE GROUP RULES

1 All age group competitors remain qualified from 1 January to the following 31 December at their age at close of day (12 midnight) on 31 December of the year of competition.

2   Age groupings for water polo are as follows:

15 years of age and under.

16 and 17 years of age.

18, 19 and 20 years of age.

The age for Junior World Championships is 20 years and under.

FACILITIES

1. Field-of-play for men: the distance between the respective goal-

Pools for Water Polo

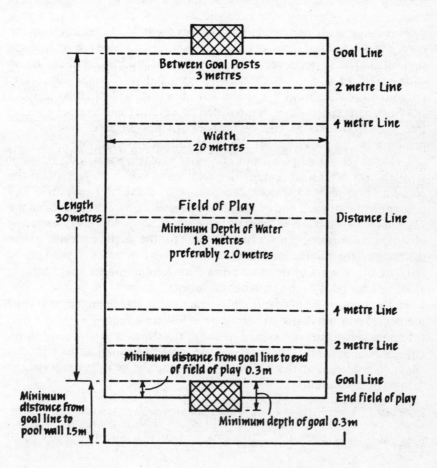

lines shall be 30m. The width of the field-of-play shall be 20m. The depth of the water nowhere shall be less than 1.8m, preferably 2m.

2. Field-of-play for women: for matches played by women the measurements shall be 25m by 17m. The depth of the water shall nowhere be less than 1.8m, preferably 2m.

3. The water temperatures shall not be less than 26° ±1°C.

4. The light intensity shall not be less than 600 lux.

5. Exceptions from 1 and 2 may be allowed on the discretion of the federation controlling the match.

Equipment for Water Polo Pools

1 Distinctive marks shall be provided on both sides of the field of play to denote the goal lines, lines 2m and 4m from that line, and half distance between the goal-lines. These markings shall be clearly visible throughout the game. As uniform colours the following are recommended for these markings: goal-line and half-distance line – white; 2m from goal-line – red; 4m from goal-line – yellow. A red or other visible coloured sign shall be placed on the end of the field of play 2m from the corner of the field of play on the side of the Goal Judge (or on the side opposite to the Timekeeper if there are no Goal Judges). The boundary of the field of play at both ends is 0.3m behind the goal-line. The minimum distance from the goal-line to the pool wall shall be 1.5m.

2 Sufficient space shall be provided to enable the Referees to have free way from end to end of the field of play. Space shall also be provided at the goal-lines for the Goal Judges.

3 Goals: The goal-posts and cross-bar must be of wood, metal or synthetic (plastic) with rectangular sections of 0.075m square with the goal-line and painted white. The goal-posts must be fixed, rigid and perpendicular at each end of the playing space, equal distances from the sides and at least 0.3m in front of the ends of the field of play or of any obstruction. Any standing or resting place for the goalkeeper other than the floor of the pool is not permitted.

4 The inner sides of the goal-posts must be 3m apart.

5 The underside of the crossbar must be 0.9m above the water surface when the water is 1.5m or more in depth, and 2.4m above the bottom of the pool when the depth of the water is less than 1.5m.

6 Limp nets must be attached to the goal fixtures to enclose the entire goal space, securely fastened to the goal-posts and cross-bar and allowing not less than 0.3m clear space behind the goal-line everywhere within the goal area.